mylabschool

From watching actual classroom video footage of teachers and students interacting to building standards-based lessons and web-based portfolios . . . from a robust resource library of the "What Every Teacher Should Know About" series to complete instruction on writing an effective research paper . . . **MyLabSchool** brings together an amazing collection of resources for future teachers. This website gives you a wealth of videos, print and simulated cases, career advice, and much more.

Use **MyLabSchool** with this Allyn and Bacon Education text, and you will have everything you need to succeed in your course. Assignment IDs have also been incorporated into many Allyn and Bacon Education texts to link to the online material in **MyLabSchool** . . . connecting the teachers of tomorrow to the information they need today.

PEARSON AB

VISIT www.mylabschool.com to learn more about this invaluable resource and Take a Tour!

Here's what you'll find in mylabschool

Where the classroom comes to life!

VideoLab ►

Access hundreds of video clips of actual classroom situations from a variety of grade levels and school settings. These 3- to 5-minute closed-captioned video clips illustrate real teacher–student interaction, and are organized both topically *and* by discipline. Students can test their knowledge of classroom concepts with integrated observation questions.

Becoming a Teacher

First year teacher Penny Brandenburg talks about why she became a teacher. Her philosophy of teaching is to encourage the students to take ownership of their learning.

00:22/4:53 sec

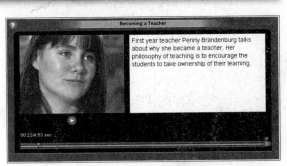

◄ Lesson & Portfolio Builder

This feature enables students to create, maintain, update, and share online portfolios and standards-based lesson plans. The Lesson Planner walks students, step-by-step, through the process of creating a complete lesson plan, including verifiable objectives, assessments, and related state standards. Upon completion, the lesson plan can be printed, saved, e-mailed, or uploaded to a website.

Here's what you'll find in (mylabschool™

Where the classroom comes to life!

Simulations ►

This area of MyLabSchool contains interactive tools designed to better prepare future teachers to provide an appropriate education to students with special needs. To achieve this goal, the IRIS (IDEA and Research for Inclusive Settings) Center at Vanderbilt University has created course enhancement materials. These resources include online interactive modules, case study units, information briefs, student activities, an online dictionary, and a searchable directory of disability-related web sites.

◄ Resource Library

MyLabSchool includes a collection of PDF files on crucial and timely topics within education. Each topic is applicable to any education class, and these documents are ideal resources to prepare students for the challenges they will face in the classroom. This resource can be used to reinforce a central topic of the course, or to enhance coverage of a topic you need to explore in more depth.

Research Navigator ►

This comprehensive research tool gives users access to four exclusive databases of authoritative and reliable source material. It offers a comprehensive, step-by-step walk-through of the research process. In addition, students can view sample research papers and consult guidelines on how to prepare endnotes and bibliographies. The latest release also features a new bibliography-maker program—AutoCite.

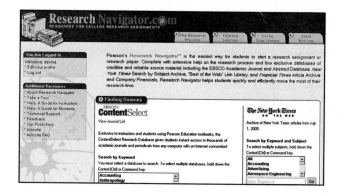

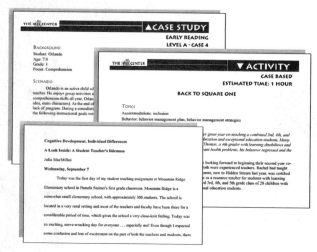

◄ Case Archive

This collection of print and simulated cases can be easily accessed by topic and subject area, and can be integrated into your course. The cases are drawn from Allyn & Bacon's best-selling books, and represent the complete range of disciplines and student ages. It's an ideal way to consider and react to real classroom scenarios. The possibilities for using these high-quality cases within the course are endless.

TENTH EDITION

Looking in Classrooms

Thomas L. Good
University of Arizona

Jere E. Brophy
Michigan State University

PEARSON

Boston   New York   San Francisco
Mexico City   Montreal   Toronto   London   Madrid   Munich   Paris
Hong Kong   Singapore   Tokyo   Cape Town   Sydney

Executive Editor and Publisher: *Stephen D. Dragin*
Editorial Assistant: *Katie Heimsoth*
Marketing Manager: *Weslie Sellinger*
Editorial Production Service: *Omegatype Typography, Inc.*
Composition Buyer: *Linda Cox*
Manufacturing Buyer: *Linda Morris*
Electronic Composition: *Omegatype Typography, Inc.*
Interior Design: *Omegatype Typography, Inc.*
Photo Researcher: *Omegatype Typography, Inc.*
Cover Administrator: *Linda Knowles*

For related titles and support materials, visit our online catalog at www.ablongman.com.

Between the time website information is gathered and then published, it is not unusual for some sites to have closed. Also, the transcription of URLs can result in typographical errors. The publisher would appreciate notification where these errors occur so that they may be corrected in subsequent editions.

ISBN-10: 0-205-49678-4   ISBN-13: 978-0-205-49678-5

Library of Congress Cataloging-in-Publication Data

Good, Thomas L.
   Looking in classrooms / Thomas L. Good, Jere E. Brophy. — 10th ed.
     p. cm.
   Includes bibliographical references and index.
   ISBN-13: 978-0-205-49678-5 (pbk.)
   ISBN-10: 0-205-49678-4 (pbk.)
  1. Teaching. 2. Classroom management. 3. Observation (Educational method) I. Brophy, Jere E. II. Title.
   LB1025.3.G66 2008
   371.102—dc22

                  2007009463

Printed in the United States of America

10 9 8 7 6 5 4 3   11 10 09 08

Photo Credits: p. 1, Bill Aron/PhotoEdit; p. 47 (top), Will Hart/PhotoEdit; p. 47 (bottom), David Frazier/PhotoEdit; p. 71 (top), David Young-Wolff/PhotoEdit; p. 71 (bottom), Frank Siteman; p. 98, Frank Siteman; p. 143, Jeff Greenberg/PhotoEdit; p. 181, Frank Siteman; p. 216, T. Lindfors/Lindfors Photography; p. 247, Michael Newman/PhotoEdit; p. 275, Michael Newman/PhotoEdit; p. 301, Bill Aron/PhotoEdit; p. 335, Frank Siteman; p. 364, T. Lindfors/Lindfors Photography; p. 401, Bill Aron/PhotoEdit; p. 424, Frank Siteman

Thomas L. Good is professor and head of the Department of Educational Psychology at the University of Arizona. His long term interests include the improvement of teaching and classroom learning. This work has been supported by many agencies including the National Institute of Health, the National Science Foundation, the National Institute of Education, the Carnegie Foundation, the Spencer Foundation, and the U.S. Department of Education. He also has broad interests in policy issues such as effective schooling and proactive youth development. His recent work has argued the need to view American youth as an investment, not as a problem as do many policy makers.

Jere Brophy is University Distinguished Professor of Teacher Education and Educational Psychology at Michigan State University. A clinical and developmental psychologist by training, Brophy has conducted research on teachers' achievement expectations and related self-fulfilling prophecy effects; teachers' attitudes toward individual students and the dynamics of teacher–student relationships; students' personal characteristics and their effects on teachers, relationships between classroom processes, and student achievement; teachers' strategies for managing classrooms and coping with problem students; and teachers' strategies for motivating students to learn. Most recently, he has focused on curricular content and instructional method issues involved in teaching social studies for understanding, appreciation, and life application.

BRIEF CONTENTS

CONTENTS

CHAPTER *2*

Teacher Expectations 47

CHAPTER *3*

Management I: Preventing Problems   71

CHAPTER 4

Management II: Coping with Problems Effectively   98

CHAPTER 5

Motivation 143

CHAPTER

Students' Interactions with One Another   181

CHAPTER *7*

Addressing Heterogeneity in Learning Ability and Achievement Progress

216

CHAPTER 10

Active Teaching   301

CHAPTER *11*

Helping Students to Construct Usable Knowledge   335

CHAPTER *12*

Assessing Students' Learning   364

CHAPTER *13*

Technology and Classroom Teaching   401

CHAPTER *14*

Growing as a Teacher   424

PREFACE

We are pleased to publish the tenth edition of *Looking in Classrooms,* which has enjoyed over three decades of continuous publication. The book was recently honored at a presidential session of the American Educational Research Association, where it was recognized as a major impetus for the movement to use classroom observational research to improve classroom practice. Although we take pride in being recognized among the pioneers in classroom observational research, we do not want this to overshadow the fact that this edition of *Looking in Classrooms* provides a comprehensive, contemporary analysis of teaching and learning in classrooms. This new edition provides a major review and updating of the book as well as brand new chapters that expand our classroom analysis into new areas.

As with previous editions, this edition of *Looking in Classrooms* is designed to help teachers, student teachers, principals, and supervisors to effectively observe classrooms. Our second goal is to describe classroom observational research that provides powerful insights for understanding and improving classroom learning. Classroom research is translated and presented in terms of useful instructional activities that can enhance students' learning and social development.

Looking in Classrooms is written for all educators interested in classroom learning. However, it is uniquely valuable for students preparing to be teachers, beginning teachers, those in the first few years of teaching, and those working to enhance the professional development of new teachers. Unlike some texts, we discuss the very real and complex problems that teachers face in the classroom.

Helping teachers to be successful in the classroom must begin by pinpointing factors that reduce teachers' satisfaction and their effectiveness, and information and strategies for reflecting on and resolving their professional concerns. Research on beginning teachers' acute concerns is one primary source for identifying important content that teachers need. For some time, the field has known that beginning teachers find classroom management exceedingly difficult, and this edition of *Looking in Classrooms* provides detailed conceptual understanding of student socialization and practical strategies for dealing with the day-to-day issues of classroom management.

However, in the last decade, beginning teachers' concerns have taken a new shape. Although classroom management issues are still moderately important to new teachers, they are no longer the dominant concern. This change may reflect the fact that teacher education programs have had some success in preparing teachers for the realities of classroom management. New concerns focus on dealing with the increasing diversity of students' instructional needs. New teachers express the clear need for insight and practical strategies to successfully address the diverse learning needs of their students. Not surprisingly, they also want more information about how best to communicate with the parents of their students. Parents often come from cultures that differ from that of the teacher, and teachers often need to interact with parents who speak languages other than English.

As noted, new to this edition is a thorough updating of all chapters to highlight new research. By integrating new research with past understandings, we hope to provide the best possible research evidence and to clarify its relationship to effective practice. We have also prepared four new chapters for this edition. Two new chapters address student diversity—one from the standpoint of understanding and appreciating it, and one on how to use this knowledge to effectively plan instruction for a diverse student population. A third new chapter deals with technology and its role in the classroom. We develop a disposition toward the use of technology that recognizes that it is not a panacea, but can be tremendously useful if linked to important instructional goals. Finally, we have added a valuable chapter on measuring and assessing student performance.

A Brief Description of Each Chapter

This revision provides comprehensive coverage of research on teaching as it applies to classroom learning and instruction. Chapter 1 provides information about how teachers and observers can collect information in classrooms to enhance teaching. Case studies, whole-class observation, and other procedures are discussed.

Chapter 2 provides useful information about how teachers form expectations about students and the potential effects these expectations can have on students' performance. The chapter addresses how teachers can develop and communicate appropriate expectations to encourage student performance.

Chapter 3 addresses a major concern of new teachers—how to create classrooms that are warm and friendly, and also how to set the conditions for productive learning. Chapter 3 provides detailed information about establishing classroom activities and routines to prevent misbehavior and to encourage active student involvement.

Chapter 4 discusses ways to handle misbehavior when it occurs. It also offers advice about how to deal with different types of students and specific types of problems.

Chapter 5 discusses student motivation from different theoretical perspectives. It presents information and strategies designed not only to encourage student involvement in work but also to value subject matter knowledge, to strive to understand it, and to apply it to everyday life.

Chapter 6 examines student–student communication and community. Various structures of students working with other students are discussed, including small-group teams, peer tutoring, and long-term project work. In this chapter, we also stress when and how to successfully use peer learning formats.

Chapters 7 and 8 collectively address what appear to be new teachers' primary concerns—dealing with diverse learning and instructional needs and communication with parents. Chapter 7 emphasizes ways to address heterogeneity in students' learning ability and achievement progress. Chapter 8 discusses the need for understanding, valuing, and affirming students' culture, both as an important goal in itself and as a way to improve communication with students and parents.

Chapter 9 deals with the complex issue of curriculum planning. As the knowledge explosion continues, teachers must increasingly decide what knowledge is worth teaching and how to build it continuously throughout the school year. This planning task has recently become more complex because of state and federal demands for certain types of content and knowledge to be included in the curriculum.

Chapters 10 and 11 examine how content can best be taught. As a group, educators are becoming more enlightened about when multiple strategies are called for, ranging from situations in which teachers provide rich, explicit teaching (here, good teachers do not simply transmit knowledge, they explain and help students to understand it), to situations in which students actively construct knowledge using the teacher and peers as resources. Chapter 10 focuses on explicit, active learning and Chapter 11 on building communities of learners and allowing students both opportunities and responsibility for individual and social learning. The strengths and weaknesses of each model are thoroughly discussed.

Chapter 12 provides the knowledge and skills for assessing student progress in both the active teaching perspective and the social constructivist perspective of active learning.

Chapter 13 is a new chapter that discusses the role of technology in classroom learning and instruction. Technology has considerable potential, but this potential frequently goes unrealized because technology is used poorly. We present a way of deciding when to use technology, and provide examples of effective usage.

Chapter 14 ends the book with a frank discussion of the fact that many teachers do not stay in teaching for long. Many teachers leave the field after the first year and as many as 50 percent quit teaching within five years. Importantly, this edition of *Looking in Classrooms* offers ways to address these problems and ways to grow as a teacher so that teaching is satisfying and successful.

Supplements to This Text

Supplements further enhance and strengthen the tenth edition of *Looking in Classrooms*.

The newly revised **Instructor's Manual with Test Bank** includes test questions and answers and additional exercises and activities for each chapter.

mylabschool is a collection of online tools for your success in this course, on your licensure exams, and in your teaching career.

Visit www.mylabschool.com to access the following:

- Video footage of real-life classrooms, with opportunities for you to reflect on the videos and offer your own thoughts and suggestions for applying theory to practice
- An extensive archive of text and multimedia cases that provide valuable perspectives on real classrooms and real teaching challenges
- Allyn & Bacon's Lesson and Portfolio Builder application, which includes an integrated state standards correlation tool
- Research paper assistance using Research Navigator™, which provides access to three exclusive databases of credible and reliable source material: EBSCO's ContentSelect Academic Journal Database, *The New York Times* Search-by-Subject Archive, and "Best of the Web" Link Library

- Career Center with resources for Praxis exams and licensure preparation, professional portfolio development, and job search and interview techniques

*A*cknowledgments

The continuing success of this book is in large measure due to the important contributions of others too numerous to thank individually. We do thank the many faculty, students, and anonymous reviewers over the years who provided constructive feedback allowing us to revise editions to capture emerging ideas representing helpful conceptions of teaching practice. We have had many editors over the years, all of whom helped to frame and reframe *Looking in Classrooms* to keep it a fresh, contemporary perspective of classroom learning and teaching. We do name three of our editors who were (and are) uniquely helpful to us and our book. Lane Akers was the young field editor who originally signed the book and convinced his publishing house to take a chance on two young, unknown authors. Chris Jennison was there for us in the middle years when conceptions of good practice were rapidly changing (often without good research to support the new visions), and helped us as we resisted demands to report on popular but untested ideas. Finally, we acknowledge our current editor, Steve Dragin, whose support and belief in this revision has led us to put more effort into this edition than any since the first edition. We hope readers will be as satisfied with our efforts as we are.

We also wish to thank the following reviewers of the tenth edition: Susan C. Scott, University of Central Oklahoma; Janet Stivers, Marist College; and Maria Yon, University of North Carolina, Charlotte.

Writing a text demands considerable support, and the authors want to acknowledge the help of several individuals who assisted with typing, editing, and so forth: Alyson Lavigne, Amy Peebles, Janie Rentieria, and Toni Sollars. We especially wish to thank two people, Amanda Rabidue Bozack and June Benson, who helped to type, proof, and improve the manuscript in countless ways.

CHAPTER

[handwritten: observe: why how]

[handwritten: collect data analyze change behavior]

Classroom Life

*[handwritten: This Book:
① Describe classrooms
② make suggestions
③ current edu. research]*

This book has three major purposes. First, to help teachers and prospective teachers develop ways to <u>describe</u> what goes on in classrooms. Second, to suggest how you can <u>positively influence</u> the learning and social development of your students. Third, to help you <u>understand current</u> educational research, use related theories and concepts appropriately, and combine knowledge of research with knowledge of your own classroom in order to improve teaching.

Teachers are sometimes unaware of what they do or why they engage in a classroom practice. This lack of perception can result in unproductive behavior. Our intent is to show you how to observe and describe classroom behavior. If you can become aware of what happens in the classroom and monitor both your own intentions and behaviors and those of your students, you can enhance communication and performance.

Historically, those who wrote for teachers seldom visited classrooms or studied them systematically. <u>Philip Jackson</u> reversed this trend in 1968 with the publication of

Life in Classrooms, and the paucity of research on classrooms has been addressed fully over the past forty years (Darling-Hammond & Bransford, 2005). Jackson's classic work debunked many myths about teaching and provided evidence to show that teaching is difficult. He noted that teachers and students must deal with crowds, complexity, and power. Jackson's work demonstrated that classroom decision making is not easy, in part because classrooms are complex environments in which teachers make quick decisions with incomplete information.

Building on Jackson's framework, Doyle (1986, 2006) presented four dimensions that frame classroom teaching and learning:

1. *Multidimensionality.* Records and schedules must be kept, and work must be monitored, collected, and evaluated. A single event can have multiple consequences. Waiting a few seconds for one student to answer a question may increase that student's motivation but negatively influence the interest of another student who would like to respond. *more than one thing at a time*
2. *Simultaneity.* Many things happen at the same time. During a discussion, a teacher not only listens and responds to students' ideas but also monitors unresponsive students for signs of comprehension and tries to keep the lesson moving at a good pace.
3. *Immediacy.* Teachers must respond to many events that happen rapidly.
4. *Unpredictable and public classroom climate.* Things often happen in ways that are unanticipated. Furthermore, much of what happens to a student is also seen by other students. Students make inferences about how the teacher feels toward certain students by the way the teacher interacts in spontaneous situations.

*A*ction-System Knowledge

Leinhardt et al. (1991) distinguish between subject-matter knowledge and action-system knowledge. *Subject-matter knowledge* is the information needed to present content. *Action-system knowledge* refers to skills for planning lessons, making pacing decisions, explaining material clearly, responding to individual differences, and helping students to construct knowledge.

In this book we deal with action-system knowledge, and we help you to learn common language for discussing classroom events. Systematic study of such knowledge will help you learn how to manage classrooms; present information, concepts, and assignments effectively; and design engaging learning environments that allow students to be active learners and to develop the capacity for self-regulated learning. This information complements the subject-matter knowledge you gain in other courses.

Even with both kinds of knowledge, however, some teachers may not reach their full potential because they do not know how to apply the knowledge they possess.

Lacking an integrated set of theories and belief systems to provide a framework for informed decision making, they may not have <u>effective strategies for organizing information gleaned</u> from monitoring and interpreting the rapid succession of classroom events.

We provide information to help you develop an integrated approach that reflects your teaching style. In addition to knowledge, however, much teaching involves hypothesis testing. For example, you might assume that a student who has been out of his or her seat creating behavior problems needs more structure (e.g., more explicit directions, self-checking devices) to work alone productively. However, other factors, such as boredom, may be producing the misbehavior. If the problem is not improved by the correction strategies suggested by the first hypothesis, other strategies will be needed. Teachers who have a rich fund of action-system knowledge can develop better hypotheses and more appropriately <u>adapt their behavior to students' needs</u>.

Teaching presents enduring problems. Teachers must teach a class or group much of the time but still try to respond to the needs of individuals. Students differ not only in how much knowledge they have about a subject but also in how they view adults and how they cope with ambiguity. Previous experiences and home cultures have important consequences for their beliefs about schooling (McCaslin & Murdock, 1991; Moll, 1992). Teachers do more than manage learners. They also deal with students as social beings, and students learn more than subject matter in school (McCaslin & Good, 1996). Teachers have to recognize students' differences in learning and adjust instruction accordingly. Ladson-Billings (1994) illustrated the need for differentiated instruction this way:

> In a classroom of thirty children, a teacher has one student who is visually impaired, one who is wheelchair-bound, one who has limited English proficiency, and one who is intellectually gifted. If the teacher presents identical work in identical ways to all of the students, is she acting equitably or inequitably? The visually impaired student cannot read the small print on an assignment, the wheelchair-bound student cannot do push-ups in gym, the foreign-language student cannot give an oral report in English, and the intellectually gifted student learns nothing by spelling words she mastered several years ago. (p. 33)

Differentiated instruction

Unless we carefully consider a particular manifestation of teaching practice, we may interpret it in terms of our own histories as children and students (for better or worse). For example, many of us have been socialized not to appreciate loud, spontaneous behavior. This may make us more likely to interpret such behavior as aggressive than would someone who was socialized differently. Similarly, many of us have learned to expect that genuine interest in something is accompanied by verbal animation ("Isn't this exciting?" "Look how important this is!"), and we may not realize that others express interest differently. Our view of appropriate behavior in a third-grade class is likely to depend heavily on our own experiences in intermediate elementary grades unless we attempt to benefit from research, scholarship, and the experience of others.

study others' interpretations because mine is not the only way.

An Elementary School Example

As you read the following example, try to identify teaching behaviors or attitudes that you believe are effective or ineffective—and consider why you feel that way. What would you have done differently if you had been the teacher? Jot down your ideas as you read.

Sally Turner is a sixth-grade teacher at Maplewood Elementary School, which is located in a moderate-sized midwestern community. She has twenty-four students, who come primarily from lower-middle-class and working-class homes. The majority are white (thirteen students), three are African American, five are Hispanic, and three are Asian. Sally has taught at Maplewood since graduating from college three years ago.

The following scene takes place in October. The students have been reading about Columbus in their text and on the Internet. The scene begins as Sally passes out copies of a map showing the sea routes that Columbus followed on his four trips to the New World.

Billy: *(Almost shouting)* I didn't get no map.

Teacher: *(Calmly and deliberately)* Billy, share Rosie's map. Tim, you can look with either Margaret or Damian.

Tim: Can I look with Jill?

Teacher: *(Slightly agitated)* Okay, but don't play around. You and Jill always get into trouble. *(Most of the students turn to look at Jill and Tim.)* I don't want you two fooling around today *(smiling but stated with some irritation)*. Okay, does everybody have a map? I wanted to pass out these maps before we start. You can see that the route of each voyage is traced on the map. There were four trips with different routes. Pay special attention during the discussion because you'll need to know the information for tomorrow's quiz. If the discussion goes well, I have a special treat for you—a video clip on Columbus's voyage and one on astronauts.

Class: *(In a spontaneous, exuberant roar)* Yea!

Teacher: Who can tell me something about Columbus's background?

Emily: *(Calling out)* He was born in 1451 in Italy.

Teacher: Good answer, Emily. I can tell you've been reading. Now, can anyone tell me who influenced Columbus's urge to explore unknown seas? *(She looks around and calls on Roberto, one of several students who have raised their hands.)*

Roberto: He'd read about Marco Polo's voyage to Cathay and about the bunch of expensive stuff he found.

Teacher: Okay. Jan, when did Columbus first land in America?

Jan: In 1492.

Teacher: Terrific! I know you've been reading. Good girl! Where did Columbus stop for supplies?

Manuel: *(Laughingly)* But Ms. Turner, the date was on the map you passed out.

Teacher: *(With irritation)* Manuel, don't call out without raising your hand!

Billy: *(Calling out)* The Canary Islands.

Teacher: Okay, Billy. Now, what were the names of the three ships? *(She looks around the room and calls on Tyler, who has his hand up.)* Tyler, you tell us. *(Tyler's face turns red and he stares at the floor.)* Tyler Taylor! Don't raise your hand unless you know the answer. Okay, class, who can tell me the names of the three ships? *(She calls on Brandon, who has his hand up.)*

Brandon: *(Hesitantly)* The *Santa Maria,* the *Nina,* and the . . .

Teacher: *(Supplying the answer)* Pinta. Nancy, how long did this first voyage to the New World take?

Nancy: *(Shrugging her shoulders)* I don't know.

Teacher: Think about it. It took a long time, Nancy. Was it less or more than 100 days? *(Silence)* The answer was on the first page of the reading material. Class, can anyone tell me how long the first voyage took? *(No hands are raised.)* Well, you better learn that because it will be on the exam! Now, who can tell me why Columbus came to the New World? *(Maria and two other students raise their hands.)* Maria?

Maria: *(Firmly and loudly)* Because they wanted to discover new riches, like the explorers going to the Far East.

Teacher: *(She pauses and looks at Max and Helen, who are talking, and at Manuel, who is headed for the pencil sharpener. Max and Helen immediately cease their conversation.)* Manuel, sit down this minute. *(Manuel heads for his seat.)* What were you doing, anyway?

Manuel: *(Smiling sheepishly)* Jan wanted me to sharpen her pencil.

Jan: *(Red-faced and alarmed)* Ms. Turner, that's not true! *(Class laughs.)*

Teacher: Quiet, both of you. You don't need a sharp pencil. Sit down. *(Resuming discussion)* Good answer, Maria. You were really alert. Why else, Maria? Can you think of any other reason?

Nancy: *(Calling out)* Because they wanted to find a shortcut to the treasures of the Far East. The only other way was over land, and it was thousands of miles over deserts and mountains.

Teacher: *(Proudly)* Good, Nancy! Now, who were "they"? Who wanted the riches?

Billy: *(Calling out)* Queen Isabella and King Ferdinand. She paid for the trip because she thought Columbus would make her rich.

Teacher: Okay, Billy, but remember to raise your hand before speaking. Why do you think Columbus was interested in making the trip? Just to find money?

Class: *(Calling out)* No!

Teacher: Well, what problems did the sailors have? *(She looks around and calls on Manuel, who has his hand up.)*

Manuel: Well, they were away from home and couldn't write. Sort of like when I go to summer camp. I don't write. I was lonely the first few days, but . . .

Teacher: *(Somewhat confused and irritated)* Well, that's not exactly what I had in mind. Did they get sick a lot? Class, does anyone know? *(She looks around the room and sees Claire with a raised hand.)*

Claire: I don't remember reading about sailors getting sick with Columbus, but I know that sailors then got sick with scurvy and they had to be careful. *(Hank approaches the teacher with great embarrassment and asks in hushed tones if he can go to the bathroom; permission is granted.)*

Teacher: Yes. Good answer, Claire. Claire, did they try to prevent scurvy?

Claire: They carried lots of fruit. . . . You know, like lemons.

Teacher: Okay, Claire, but what special kind of fruit was important to eat? *(Claire blushes and Ms. Turner silently forms the soft "c" sound with her mouth.)*

Claire: Citrus.

Teacher: Very good! What other problems did the sailors have? *(She calls on Matt, who has his hand up.)*

Matt: Well, they didn't have any maps and they didn't know much about the wind or anything, so they were afraid of the unknown and scared of sailing off the earth. *(Laughter)*

Teacher: *(Noticing that many students are gazing at the floor or looking out the window, she begins to speak louder and more quickly.)* No, educated people knew that the earth was round. You should read more carefully.

Alice: *(Calling out)* But even though a few educated people believed the earth was round, Columbus's sailors didn't believe it. They called the Atlantic Ocean the "Sea of Darkness," and Columbus had to keep two diaries. He showed the sailors the log with the fewest miles so they wouldn't get scared. But the men threatened mutiny anyway.

Teacher: *(With elation)* Excellent answer, Alice. Yes, the men were afraid of the unknown; however, I think most of them knew that the earth was round. Okay, Matt, you made me drift away from my question: Why did Columbus want to go? What were reasons for his trip other than money? James, what do you think? *(James shrugs his shoulders.)* Well, when you read your lesson, class, look for that answer. It's important and I might test you on it. *(With exasperation)* Tim! Jill! Stop pushing each other this instant! I told you two not to play around. Why didn't you listen to me?

Tim: *(With anger)* Jill threw the map in her desk. I wanted to use it so I could trace my own map.

Jill: But it's my map and . . .

Teacher: *(Firmly)* That's enough! I don't want to hear any more. Give me the map and the three of us will discuss it during recess.

Principal: *(Talking over the PA system)* Teachers, I'm sorry to break in on your classes, but I have an important announcement to make. The high school band will not be with us this afternoon. So 2:00 to 2:30 classes will not be canceled. Since I have interrupted your class, I would also like to remind you that tonight is PTA. Teachers, be sure that the students remind . . . *(During the announcement many pupils begin private conversations with their neighbors.)*

Teacher: *(Without much emotion or enthusiasm)* It's not recess time yet. Listen, we still have work to do. Tell you what we're going to do now. I've got two video clips: One describes the United States astronauts' first trip to the moon; the other describes Columbus's first trip to the New World. Watch these videos closely because after we see them, I'm going to ask you to tell me the similarities between the two trips. Ralph, turn off the lights.

Hank: *(Returning from his trip to the restroom)* Hey, Mrs. Turner, why are the lights out? It's spooky in here!

Alice: *(Impishly)* It's the Sea of Darkness! *(Class breaks out in a spontaneous roar)*

Teacher: Quiet down, class! It's time to see the video clip—a long, dangerous, and exciting trip is about to begin.

Juan: *(Speaking audibly but not loudly)* If I had been there, I'd have said "Buena suerte y buen viaje, Señor Columbus." *(Classmates clap and acknowledge their interest.)*

Teacher and class watch 20-minute videotape of the voyage.

Hank: *(Calling out as soon as the program finishes)* My sister told me that Columbus was a mean man!

Teacher: Hank, what do you mean when you say "mean"?

Hank: My sister told me she had read that Columbus lied to his men to get here, that he brought slaves, and that he brutally killed the Native Americans.

Teacher: During the next two days we'll spend time discussing the voyage and its importance. We'll talk about what happened on the trip and what happened once they reached North America. Hank is right: some cruel things happened, and we will talk about "means and ends" issues as we did last week when we discussed the environment and jobs. We need to discuss various aspects of history—history from everybody's point of view, what we want, and how we get there.

Juan: *(Playfully)* My brother, Ramon, told me that Indians are called Indians only because Columbus was so confused that he thought he was in India.

Yevette: *(With evident concern)* Juan, don't be so stupid. The problem is not just Columbus. My mother told me about the policy of Manifest Destiny. That stupid thinking made it OK for us Americans to kill Native Americans because they were in the way. We murdered Native Americans because we wanted their land.

James: *(Calling out almost belligerently)* Yeah, but Native Americans killed people from other tribes and white settlers. Don't knock Columbus. Look at what's been happening in the Middle East the past few years.

Teacher: James, don't blurt out without permission. Yevette, don't personalize your argument with Juan. Remember what we were talking about this morning. A classroom community is built on mutual respect. Now back to our discussion of Columbus.

Maria: *(With interest)* Last night I was surfing the Web and looking for information, one report called Columbus an immigrant. Is that true?

Our example illustrates many points, such as teachers are busy, teaching is complex, and the pace of classroom life is hurried. Sally had a constant stream of student behavior to react to, and she had to make a number of decisions instantaneously. This example illustrates that teaching problems are by no means simple to conceptualize or resolve.

What were the teacher's *strengths* and *weaknesses?* If you were to discuss this classroom dialogue with the teacher, what would you ask or tell her? You may want to repeat this exercise when you finish reading the book in order to assess the information you have gained or any changes in your perspective that may occur between now and then. Complete the exercise now; then read our analysis in the following section.

Analysis of the Class Discussion

Like most teachers, Sally Turner has strengths and weaknesses. Our comments are organized around four topics basic to most teaching situations: motivation, management, instruction, and expectations. These topics are discussed at length in separate chapters: the discussion here provides an introduction.

Motivation

Sally's attempt to breathe life into history by linking Columbus's explorations to a more recent event is notable. In her efforts to help students identify personally with content, she has gone to the trouble to order video clips both of Columbus's voyage (a simulation description) and of the astronauts' trip to the moon. However, even the latter trip occurred before these students were born. It might have been more effective if Sally had attempted to stimulate students' thoughts about the unknown with events that were more personal (e.g., first trip to a camp) or more immediate (soldiers keeping peace and fighting in Iraq).

Introducing the Lesson.   Some of what Sally communicates to students is likely to harm their motivation. Perhaps most striking is her tendency to emphasize that the discussion is important because it will prepare students to take a test. She does not suggest that learning is enjoyable or important for its own sake. Note especially Sally's poor introduction to the lesson. She stresses that students will be tested but provides little additional rationale for the discussion of Columbus's voyage. Her introduction should have focused more on positive learning goals and less on tomorrow's quiz. Although it is probably useful to tell students once that material is important and will be on a quiz, Sally comments several times that listening is important because of future testing. Such behavior may convince students that learning is done only to please adults or to receive high grades. Sally's attempt to make the history associated with Columbus's discovery of America more personal and meaningful to students is good. Nevertheless, the lesson itself is dry, and students' role in the discussion is relatively passive, she never asks students to think about and examine their own "text-to-self," "text-to-text," or "text-to-world" connections.

Feedback.   Sally does a fair job of giving feedback to students about the correctness of their responses. You may be surprised to learn that teachers frequently fail to provide students with this information when they should do so (i.e., whenever they are not *deliberately* withholding comments in order to encourage brainstorming or to allow students to discover and correct misconceptions on their own). They do not respond to students' answers, or they respond in a way that makes it difficult for some students to know whether their responses are correct. An example of such ambiguous teacher feedback is, "So, you think it's 1492?" Many students, especially low achievers, will not know whether a response is right or wrong unless the teacher specifically tells them. If students are to learn basic facts and concepts, they must know whether their statements are adequate.

let students know if they are right / wrong

Classroom Management

In terms of classroom management (e.g., creating a learning environment, maintaining student involvement), Sally appears to be an average teacher. Her students are generally attentive, and there are few interruptions to the discussion. Although students do not seem enthusiastically engaged, Sally has established at least minimal conditions of classroom rapport and management structure. Her efforts to remind students of the need to respect other students are constructive. Sally could improve in several areas. First, she did not have enough maps for all students. Equipment and material shortages inevitably lead to trouble, especially when students are to keep the material. A careful count of the maps might have prevented both the minor delay at the beginning of the discussion and the major disruption (students fighting over a map) that occurred later. On discovering the shortage and after hearing Tim's request to sit with Jill, Sally might have responded, "Okay, that's fine. Sit with Jill, because I know that you and Jill can share cooperatively. Billy and Tim, I'm sorry you didn't get maps. I didn't make enough copies, but I'll make each of you a copy this afternoon." This action would have assured Billy and Tim that they would get maps and made it less likely that they would "take the law into their own hands." Also it would have encouraged more appropriate expectations, and perhaps better cooperation, from Jill and Tim. The teacher's original remark ("You and Jill always get into trouble") placed Jill and Tim in the spotlight by implying that misbehavior was "expected" from them. By subtly condoning misbehavior, the teacher actually made it more likely.

← self fuil-fullng prophecy

Credibility.   Sally has developed the bad habit of not following up on what she says. During the discussion, she says on several occasions. "Don't call out answers, raise your hand." However, she repeatedly accepts answers that are called out. Recall this instance:

Teacher: (*With irritation*) Manuel, don't call out without raising your hand!

Billy: (*Calling out*) The Canary Islands.

Teacher: Okay, Billy . . .

Such discrepant behaviors may lead to countless discipline problems if they convince students that Sally does not mean what she says or is not aware of much that happens in the classroom.

✷ **Rhetorical Questions.**   In two situations involving off-task behavior, Sally uses rhetorical questions that cause needless difficulty. For example, Manuel has already started back to his seat when she needlessly asks, "What were you doing, anyway?" Similarly, in her exchange with Jill and Tim, Sally pointlessly queries, "Why don't you listen to me?" This lull allows the lesson to deteriorate and the whole class is distracted. Rhetorical questions often communicate negative expectations that typically lead to clowning or other disruptive student behavior. Consider how you feel when someone says to you, "Why don't you listen?" or "Can't you do anything right?"

Instruction

The instructional guidance in the lesson is limited and unsatisfactory. It is difficult to understand what Sally wants students to learn and how this lesson fits into the overall unit (how students will use the information later). Effective teaching requires that teachers plan sequences of lessons, not just isolated lessons.

Teacher Questions.   The instruction in the lesson resides in the teacher's questions. For the most part, these appear to be rather mechanical—time-filling rather than thought-provoking. Table 1.1 presents the first eleven questions Sally asks. Most of them are factual, and the questions seem more like an oral quiz than an attempt to initiate a meaningful discussion.

Assessment of students' factual knowledge is important. But if it is overemphasized in discussion, students may believe that the teacher is interested only in finding out who knows the answers. Discussion then becomes a fragmented ritual rather than a meaningful process.   *←*

Sally Turner's students might have been more interested in the discussion if they had been involved more directly through questions of value and opinion, such as: How would you feel if you were isolated from your parents and friends for several days? How would you feel being in a five-by-seven-foot room and unable to leave it? Would you like to be a sailor working on a ship week after week, not knowing where you were going or what you would see? Would you volunteer for such a voyage? Why? Was the discovery of the New World important? Why? Would it be important to explore a new planet like Venus? Why?

Table 1.1   Partial List of Content Questions Sally Asked

1. Who can tell me something about Columbus's background?
2. Who influenced Columbus's voyage to explore unknown seas?
3. When did Columbus first land in America?
4. Where did Columbus stop for supplies?
5. What were the names of the three ships?
6. How long did this first voyage to the New World take?
7. Was it less or more than 100 days?
8. Why did Columbus come to the New World?
9. Can you think of any other reason?
10. Who wanted the riches?
11. Why do you think Columbus was interested in making the trip? Just to find money?

Some of these questions (e.g., "Why was the discovery of the New World important?") could be considered factual if the book gives answers to them. How students react to such questions depends on the teacher. Too often teachers' questions implicitly say, "Tell me what the book said." Students should be encouraged to process and respond to what they read, not just memorize it. For example, Sally might ask, "The book states two reasons why the Spaniards sponsored voyages of discovery. What were these reasons, and what beliefs and values underlay them?" Similarly, she might ask, "Why was the trip not made before 1492?"

Sally also could ask students to evaluate the social consequences of the events discussed. Was it worth the time and money to send astronauts to the moon? What did we learn (e.g., technological or medical information) as a result of the space program? Alternatively, she could initiate discussion of the risks of explorations, perhaps by noting the numerous ships that have been lost at sea or tragedies in space exploration (e.g., the explosion of the space shuttle *Challenger*). Or, she could comment on the expanding role of women astronauts, pilots, and scientists.

Teacher Questions after Student Responses.   Sally seldom encourages students to evaluate their own thinking (e.g., "Well, that's one way; what are some other ways that Columbus could have boosted his crew's morale?" "That's an accurate statement of how the crew members felt, but what about Columbus? Do you think he was fearful?"). Nor does she ask questions to help students evaluate their classmates' answers (e.g., "Juan gave his opinion about sailing with Columbus. Billy, do you agree with him? How do you feel?" "What are some other reasons in addition to the good ones that Tim gave?"). Opportunities to explore a question in depth help teachers and students to determine whether they *really* understand the material.

To reiterate, Sally does a good job of giving students feedback about the correctness of answers, and on occasion she does probe for additional information. That is, she seeks an additional response from a student after the first response, for clarification (e.g., "What do you mean?") or elaboration (e.g., "Why do you think that is so?" "How does this relate to . . . ?").

Appropriate probing helps students to consider thoughtfully the implications of what they think about the material. Probing techniques should be gentle ways to focus students' attention and to help them think. For example, an automatic response to "When did Columbus discover America?" is an unthinking "1492." However, the question "Why not 1400?" forces consideration of what the world was like in 1400, and more generally extends understanding and appreciation of Columbus's voyage.

Calling on Students.   Sally calls on only one student who does not volunteer. Otherwise, students call out the answer or Sally calls on a student who has a hand up. It is often useful for teachers to call on students who seldom raise their hands, such as shy students or low achievers. Students who avoid public-response situations need to be given opportunities to learn that they can participate successfully. If students learn that their teacher calls only on those who raise their hands, they may become inattentive.

call on those who don't participate

Some teachers unconsciously call on students who are likely to know the answer as a strategy to provide self-reinforcement. Teachers need to recognize that no matter how well they plan, students often fail to understand ideas and require reteaching using different procedures and examples. To make good decisions about whether students understand material, they need to get feedback from a representative sample of students, including timid students and low achievers (Mulryan, 1995; Rohrkemper & Corno, 1988).

Student Questions.   Sally does not encourage students to ask questions or to evaluate classmates' responses. She could have encouraged students in this way: "Today I have several questions that I want to find answers for, and you probably have some questions that weren't answered in the reading material. Maybe the class and I can help you answer these questions. Any questions that we can't answer we'll look up on the Web or in the school library. Why did Queen Isabella pick Columbus to head the voyage and not some other sailor? I think that's an interesting question! Now let's have *your* questions. I'll list them on the board and we'll see if we can answer them by the end of the discussion."

Although it is not necessary to solicit questions for every discussion period, it is wise to do so frequently, to show students that the purpose of discussion is to satisfy their needs and interests as well as the teacher's. Furthermore, in asking for questions the teacher communicates clear messages to students:

1. I have important questions, and I want your viewpoint.
2. You certainly must have important questions too.
3. We'll have an interesting discussion as we address one another's questions.
4. If you need more information, we'll get it.

If used consistently, such an approach will, in time, teach students that discussion is not a quiz but a profitable and enjoyable process of sharing information and developing understanding.

You should communicate enthusiasm and respect for students who ask questions. Some teachers call for student questions but then react to them in ways that discourage students from asking about issues that interest them. Comments such as "That was answered in the book" may convince a student that the teacher doesn't really want questions or that the student is the only one in class who does not know the answer.

Teacher Expectations

Teachers hold expectations about individual students, about groups, and about whole classes (more on this in Chapter 2). Furthermore, they communicate these expectations in their classroom behavior and assignments. The communication of expectations has both positive and negative consequences. Much research has focused on teachers' interactions with high and low achievers. Since we do not identify students' achievement levels in the example, it is not possible for you to determine whether Sally acts differently toward students she believes to be high or low performers. However, we can assess her behavior toward boys and girls and comment on her gender expectations.

Teacher Behavior toward Male and Female Students.   Sally does not praise boys but frequently praises girls. It is not possible to say that she always favors girls, but during this class discussion, she is more responsive and supportive to female students. Also, though Sally makes few attempts to improve poor responses by any of the students, she more often does so with girls than with boys. When a boy gives a poor response, she accepts it and either provides the answer herself or calls on another student. However, on two occasions she prompts a girl who is having difficulty responding. When Nancy fails to answer the question "How long did the voyage take?" Sally first provides a clue ("It took a long time") and then reduces the complexity of the question ("Was it less or more than a hundred days?"). Similarly, when Claire cannot remember the word *citrus,* Sally provides a nonverbal clue.

Teacher Sensitivity to Cultural Diversity.   When the teacher announces the start of the video, Juan, with evident interest, wishes Columbus "good luck and a pleasant trip" in Spanish, and the class appears to appreciate his good humor. It's not possible for you to determine Sally's overall sensitivity to students from different cultural and socioeconomic backgrounds (because we did not provide this information), but in this instance she did not take advantage of Juan's heritage and possible personal interest by discussing Spanish culture or even Spain's role in the world at that time. Connections with students' cultures are an important aspect of teaching (J. A. Banks, 2006; Neito, 2004). After the video, however, Sally is willing (and perhaps had planned) to discuss the controversial issues that surround the voyage. When teachers discuss history, it's appropriate to include multiple perspectives (in this case, the perspectives of the Native Americans as well as the Spaniards). Sally's awareness of cultural issues is evident in her willingness to engage in this type of analysis in the classroom.

Reaction to Students' Spontaneous Comments.   Sally fails to discuss even directly relevant topics that students introduce spontaneously. Seemingly, part of her plan is to get students to appreciate both the sense of adventure and the apprehension that explorers face. When two students mention parallel anxieties, however, Sally fails to respond. Manuel talks about his loneliness during the first few days of summer camp. Sally could have asked, "Why did you feel this way during the first few days of camp?" "How did you feel on your first day at school?" After such a discussion, the students would likely better appreciate the newness of the situation the explorers faced and their related stress and excitement. Good teachers help students to make text-to-self connections.

A similar opportunity arises when Hank alludes to the spookiness of the room, and Alice cleverly labels it the "Sea of Darkness." Sally could have profitably paused to point out that Alice's remark was a good one, and perhaps to add in a quiet voice, "Okay, now listen. For one minute, no one will make a noise. Let's pretend that we are on the *Pinta*. We have been at sea for two months. It is now completely dark, and the only noise is the roar of the sea and the creaking of the boat. We are all scared because no one has ever sailed this sea! What will we run into in the darkness?" Teachers often stimulate good discussions when they capitalize on spontaneous student comments or questions. If they do not react positively to students' self-initiated questions and concerns, the students will stop asking.

In response to the comments by Yevette and James, Sally might have reminded the class (especially Yevette and James) of the need for classroom community. Given that Yevette had brought a relevant and major concept (Manifest Destiny) to the discussion (and James drew connection to a current topic) it would seem useful to continue the conversation with Yevette, or possibly to draw other students into the conversation. Consider the following response: "Yevette, I know you have strong feelings about this topic, but remember that we are all working hard to build a community of mutual respect, and the word 'stupid' is not to be used. Now, tell me more about how the policy of Manifest Destiny relates to Columbus and the problem of genocide. Was the systematic practice of genocide toward Native Americans true in all parts of the country, or only in certain geographical areas? What do the rest of you think about Yevette's assertion?" Following this, Sally might have continued along these lines: "James suggests that Native Americans were as ruthless as white settlers. Are there any data to support or refute his position? What Web site and book resources might be helpful?

Preplanning.   Teachers can help themselves and students to be better prepared for readings and discussions by posing questions in advance. "Next week, we will be discussing Columbus's discovery of the New World. This event is an important part of our history, but it is also a story that has many parts. Why did this voyage take place and how did the sailors making the trip feel? Were they excited or afraid? How would you have felt? How do you think the Native Americans felt when they saw strange sails appearing on the horizon?"

Learning to Analyze Classrooms

Our brief analysis of Sally's teaching yields some inferences about her classroom behavior and beliefs. Admittedly, one example is enough information on which to base only the most speculative conclusions. However, it should encourage an observer to look for more information to confirm or negate tentative hypotheses (e.g., that Sally does not want students to respond unless they know the answer). Some teachers, especially beginners, unwittingly discourage students from responding unless they know the answer perfectly. They find that silence or incorrect answers are difficult to respond to and are often embarrassing or threatening.

A Secondary School Example*

As you read the following classroom dialogue (Ms. Chavez's class), make notes about effective and ineffective teaching techniques and why you identify them that way. We do not analyze this dialogue because we want you to form your own impressions and complete your own analysis, and then to discuss it with your peers.

Ms. Chavez has rolled the math department computer into her class for the morning and has connected it to her LCD viewer. Her twenty-eight first-year algebra students, seated at round tables in groups of threes and fours, are working on a warm-up problem. The day before they had had a test on functions. For the warm-up to today's class, Ms. Chavez has asked students to set up a table of values and graph the function $y = |x|$.

She has chosen this problem as a way to introduce some ideas for a new unit on linear, absolute-value, and quadratic functions. During the warm-up, students can be heard talking quietly to one another about the problem: "Does your graph look like a V-shape?" "Did you get two intersecting lines?" Walking around the room. Ms. Chavez listens to these conversations while she takes attendance. After about five minutes, she signals that it is time to begin the whole-group discussion.

A girl volunteers and carefully draws her graph on a large dry-erase board at the front of the room. As she does this, most students are watching closely, glancing down at their own graphs, checking for correspondence. A few students are seen helping others who had some difficulties producing the graph.

Another student suggests that they enter the function into the computer and watch it produce the graph. Several other students chime in, "Yeah!" The first girl does this, and the class watches as the graph appears on the overhead screen. It matches the graph she sketched, and the class cheers, "Way to go, Elena!"

Ms. Chavez then asks the class to sketch the graphs of $y = |x| + 1$, $y = |x| + 2$, and $y = |x| - 3$ on the same set of axes and write a paragraph that compares and contrasts the results with the graph of $y = |x|$. "Feel free to work alone or with the others in your group," she tells them. After a few minutes, two students exclaim, "All the graphs have the same shape!" A few other students look up. Another student observes, "They're like angles with different vertex points." "Then they're really congruent angles," adds his partner.

Ms. Chavez circulates through the class, listening to the students' discussions, asking questions, and offering suggestions. She notices one group has produced only one branch of the graphs. "Why don't you choose a few negative values for x and see what happens?" Another group asks, "What would happen if we tried $|x| - 3$?" "Try it!" urges Ms. Chavez. The students continue working, and the conversation is lowered to murmurs once again. Then the members of one group call out, "Hey, we've got something! All these graphs are just translations of $y = |x|$, just like we learned in the unit on geometry." "That's an interesting conjecture you have," remarks Ms. Chavez. She looks expectantly at the other students. "Do the rest of you agree?" They are still, many looking hard at their graphs. One student says, slowly, "I'm not sure I get it." A boy in the group that made the conjecture about translations explains, "Like $y = |x| + 2$ is like $y = |x|$

---

*Reprinted with permission from *Professional Standards for Teaching Mathematics*, copyright 1991 by the National Council of Teachers of Mathematics. All rights reserved.

Math Journals!

moved up two spaces and $y = |x| - 3$ is moved down three spaces. It's like what Louella said about them being like angles with different vertex points."

Ms. Chavez decides to provoke the class to pursue this. She asks if anyone thinks they can graph $y = |x| + 4$ without first setting up a table of values. Hands shoot up. "Ooooh!" Scanning the class, Ms. Chavez notices Lionel, who does not volunteer often has his hand up. He looks pleased when she invites him to give it a try. Lionel sketches his graph on the dry-erase board. Elena again enters the equation of the graph into the computer and the class watches as the graph is produced. The computer-generated graph verifies Lionel's attempt. Again there are cheers. Lionel gives a sweeping bow and sits down.

Ms. Chavez asks the students to write in their journals, focusing on what they think they understand and what they feel unsure about from today's lesson. They lean over their notebooks, writing. A few stare into space before beginning. She gives them about ten minutes before she begins to return the tests. She will read the journals before tomorrow's class. At the end of the period, she distributes the homework that she has prepared. The worksheet includes additional practice on the concept of $y = |x| \pm c$ as well as something new to provoke the next day's discussion: $y = |x \pm c|$.

Over the next couple of weeks, students explore linear, quadratic, and absolute-value functions. Nearing the end of this unit, Ms. Chavez decides to engage students in reflecting on and assessing how far they have come. As she assigns homework for that evening, she announces, "I'd like each of you to write two questions that you think are fair and would demonstrate that you understand the major concepts of this unit. I'll use several of your ideas to create the test. And here's a challenge for the last part of your assignment: You just drew the graph of $f(x) = x\sim - 2x$ as a part of the review. Think about everything we've done so far this semester, and see if you can remember any ideas that will help you draw the graph of $f(x)$."

Effective Teaching

Would you prefer to be in Ms. Turner's or Ms. Chavez's class? Do you think you would learn more in one class than the other? Do you think you would enjoy one more than the other? Why might other students disagree with you? As we think about "effective teaching," we need to become sensitive to the types of "effects" that are considered most desirable. Classrooms are not only about learning subject matter but also involve learning to become self-reliant and self-evaluative and to work productively with others. Classrooms can help us to sharpen our sense of identity and understanding of culture, and explore and internalize the issues of fairness and morality (Jackson, Boostrom, & Hansen, 1995). Thus, what constitutes effective teaching is partly dependent on the context of the school and its collective values (Is the development of the capacity for self-management seen as important as, or less important than, subject-matter achievement?). American citizens have various ideas about the most critical outcomes of schooling and hence effective teaching has various definitions (Nichols & Good, 2004; Rothstein, 2000).

Consider the exchange between an African American teacher and a student in an all African American classroom as presented in Table 1.2. How would you analyze this

Table 1.2   Language Diversity and Power

Teacher: What do you think about the book?

Joey: I think it's nice.

Teacher: Why?

Joey: I don't know. It just told about a black family, that's all.

Teacher: Was it difficult to read?

Joey: No.

Teacher: Was the text different from what you have seen in other books?

Joey: Yeah. The writing was.

Teacher: How?

Joey: It used more of a Southern-like accent in this book.

Teacher: Uhm-hmm. Do you think that's good or bad?

Joey: Well, uh, I don't think it's good for people down this-a-way, cause that's the way they grow up talking anyway. They ought to get the right way to talk.

Teacher: Oh. So you think it's wrong to talk like that?

Joey: Well . . . *(Laughs)*

Teacher: Hard question, huh?

Joey: Uhm-hmm, that's a hard question. But I think they shouldn't make books like that.

Teacher: Why?

Joey: Because they are not using the right way to talk and in school they take off for that, and lil' chirren grow up talking like that and reading like that so they might think that's right, and all the time they are getting bad grades in school talking like that and writing like that.

Teacher: Do you think they should be getting bad grades for talking like that?

Joey: *(Pauses, answers very slowly)* No . . . no.

Teacher: So you don't think that it matters whether you talk one way or another?

Joey: No, not long as you understood.

Teacher: Uhm-hmm. Well, that's a hard question for me to answer, too. It's, ah, that's a question that's come up in a lot of schools now as to whether they should correct children who speak the way we speak all the time. Cause when we're talking to each other we talk like that even though we might not talk like that when we get into other situations, and who's to say whether it's—

Joey: *(Interrupting)* Right or wrong.

Teacher: Yeah.

Joey: Maybe they ought to come up with another kind of . . . maybe Black English or something. A course in Black English. Maybe black folks would be good in that cause people talk, I mean black people talk like that, so . . . but I guess there's a right way and wrong way to talk, you know, not regarding what race. I don't know.

Teacher: But who decided what's right or wrong?

Joey: Well that's true . . . I guess white people did. *(Laughter. End of tape.)*

Source: Lisa L. Delpit, "The Silenced Dialogue: Power and Pedagogy in Educating Other People's Children." *Harvard Educational Review,* Volume 58:3 (August 1988), 280–298. Copyright © 1988 by the President and Fellows of Harvard College. All rights reserved. For more information please visit www.harvardeducationalreview.org.

teaching? How does your analysis compare with those of your classmates? To what extent does this example relate to the issue in Ms. Turner's classroom (history/literature being considered from multiple perspectives)?

*I*ncreasing Teacher Awareness through Classroom Observation

We have had the opportunity to review Sally's teaching from different perspectives, and you have developed ideas about how Sally could improve her practice. Let's think about Sally for a moment. At the end of the day, how much of this lesson will she remember? Will she have any basis for improving her practice? Based on our work with teachers we suspect that Sally will not remember much about the quality of her interactions with students, and will not have many ideas for improvement. Engaging twenty plus students in a common task and adjusting to the needs of individual students is absorbing, so unless you make special efforts to monitor and reflect on your teaching as you teach, you will have little basis for improvement at the end of the day. The first step is to recognize that classrooms are complex. You can see only certain aspects because events unfold so quickly and many things happen at the same time.

Classrooms Are Complex

In a single day, an elementary teacher may engage in more than a thousand interpersonal exchanges with students. Teachers in secondary schools may have interactions with 150 different students a day. Yet teachers must interpret and respond to student behavior on the spot. It is not surprising that most teachers are hard pressed to keep track of the number and substance of the contacts they have with individual students. It may not be important to remember all such contacts; however, they must recall certain information (the ten students who did not get a chance to present their class reports, the student who had trouble with vowel sounds during reading, etc.). Those who study teachers often comment on how busy teachers are. For example, according to Maeroff (1991):

> Being a schoolteacher is having so much to do and so little time to do it that keeping up with the growth in knowledge is a luxury. Even the most dedicated teacher finds that trying to stay abreast of subject matter is like paddling upstream on a fast-moving river. For the typical high school teacher, meeting with 125 to 175 students a day, marking many of the papers at night, and preparing for the next day's classes—not to mention maintaining a family life and possibly a part-time job—it is a task without beginning or ending. (p. 36)

Teachers' Awareness of Their Classroom Behavior

A study we conducted (Good & Brophy, 1972) provided clear evidence that teachers are unaware of some of their behavior. We found that teachers differed widely in the extent to which they stayed with students in failure situations (repeated or rephrased a question,

#'s of daily interactions

interesting question to ask teachers?

asked a new question) or gave up on them (gave the answer or called on someone else). Interviews with teachers showed that they were largely unaware of the extent to which they generally gave up on or stayed with students, let alone of their behavior toward specific students.

Monitoring even seemingly simple aspects of teacher–student interaction can be challenging in a fast-moving, complicated social setting such as a classroom (Erikson, 2006). Many teachers cannot accurately recall the extent to which they call on boys versus girls, the frequency with which students approach them, the number of private contacts they initiate with students, or the amount of class time they spend on procedural matters. This lack of awareness is one reason why, in too many classrooms, student gender, race, ethnicity, or culture predict the quality of students' learning opportunities (Delpit, 1995; Sadker & Sadker, 1994).

Benefits of Classroom Observation

A conceptual system allows teachers to classify what they do as they do it, making it possible for them to monitor their behavior and to remember it later. The terms *conceptual* and *observational tools* refer to a descriptive vocabulary. Every social organization, game, or system has a language of its own. For example, bridge has a unique descriptive vocabulary, as does football. Persons who do not understand such terms as *three no-trump* or *first down* cannot fully understand the game. Language for describing classrooms is more complex, but learnable.

Most school districts have video equipment so that teachers can see themselves in action. At first glance, videotaping seems like a useful learning aid—what better way for teachers to improve than to see themselves as others do? Unfortunately, studies report that after teachers have viewed videotapes, the changes in their teaching behavior are not impressive.

Seeing a video of oneself teaching is like sitting in a classroom watching another teacher. The behavior is rapid and complex. If you do not know what to look for, you will not see much. However, if you have conceptual frameworks, or when you view videotapes with a consultant who can provide specific feedback or with materials describing what to look for, positive changes can occur. Videotapes are likely to help teachers improve their classroom behavior only if specific teaching behaviors are highlighted and analyzed, or if teachers possess a set of conceptual tools that they can use to analyze their own teaching. Further, there is evidence that when teachers are given suggestions (as opposed to directives) about ways to think about teaching, teacher conferences are more likely to be productive.

Sherin (2004) notes that videos of teaching have played an important role in teacher education since at least the mid-1960s. Even though conceptions of what constitutes "good teaching" have changed considerably over time, videotapes (and their modern form—Hypermedia—which are available on CDs) remain a viable part of teacher education programs because videos allow for analysis, debate, and reflection about teaching.

A potentially powerful use of video and CDs exists in professional development work in schools. This technology may help teachers gain much insight to the analysis and improvement of teaching. Although video has some limitations, such as it focuses on only part of what of takes place in a classroom, it has three important features:

1. Videos provide a record.
2. Videos can be collected and edited.
3. Video collections can include a diverse set of practices.

That videos provide a permanent record yields many advantages. For instance, teachers may "see" the differences in their perceptions of a lesson captured on videotape, peer teachers can also discuss the lesson from multiple perceptions, and teachers can look at improvements with the class or individual students (Lewis, Perry, & Murata, 2006). Once it became possible to digitalize video, it could be used more flexibly. For example, an in-service group can watch four minutes of a lesson to see if predicted events are realized. A ten-minute segment might include how different classes react to the same five-minute introduction or how a lesson evolves over a week (Sherin, 2004).

Bliss and Reynolds (2004) note that the study of teachers' performance that waned in the 1990s has regained its important status. The study of teacher performance—how teachers teach—is supported by such groups as the National Council for Accreditation of Teacher Education and the National Board for Professional Teaching Standards. Indeed, many states will require you to perform at an acceptable level on a measure of teaching before you receive a teaching credential. (For more information about specific programs and the use of video analysis and teaching standards, see Brophy, 2004; Foster, Walker, & Song, 2007.)

We believe that providing you with concepts to describe classroom processes will help you to monitor more of your behavior and thus improve how you conceptualize and plan for teaching. For example, knowledge of variables such as *wait time* can help you increase the time you wait for students to respond when it is appropriate to do so. Similarly, awareness of a tendency to *give up* on low achievers can help you to remember to ask new questions, provide clues, rephrase questions, or otherwise seek to improve the performance of these students when they cannot respond to a question. Use of this knowledge will help you learn to ask questions that elicit the information you really want to know from students instead of answers that regurgitate low-level responses.

Teachers who are trying to understand their behavior can apply observational techniques such as those presented here. Consider the "Sea of Darkness" example earlier in this chapter. If Sally Turner had videotaped the lesson, most of the dimensions discussed in our analysis might have become evident to her—high rates of factual questions, lack of a clear pattern to the questions, different reactions toward boys and girls, and so forth. Teachers who videotape (or even tape-record) their lessons occasionally (e.g., once every two weeks) can derive many of the same benefits as having an observer in the classroom. Video costs have dropped sharply in recent years and high-quality video equipment and products are now very affordable (Horn, 2001; Brophy, 2004).

However, neither teachers nor observers are likely to acquire many new insights unless they know how to collect information, know what behaviors to look for, and have a conceptual framework to guide their analyses. This is perhaps why many teachers report that they often learn little after principals and supervisors visit their classrooms. Currently, there is considerable interest in developing teacher capacity for observing and learning from live observations of teaching. One notable application of teacher observation called Lesson Study originated in Japan (Lewis, Perry, & Murata, 2006). Here teachers watch a peer teach a live lesson with the intent of helping the teacher to analyze the lesson in order to generate suggestions for improvement. This can be useful, especially if teachers have a common language for discussing classroom events. The observation of live teaching has unique advantages but most advantages can be achieved with videotapes (without the cost of teachers leaving their own classroom). In Chapter 14 we will provide extended information about how teachers can learn from one another.

*O*bservational Records

Teachers can strengthen their awareness of classroom life by asking peers or supervisors to observe them, or by engaging in self-study. However, such work is hard to do well, partly because teachers and observers can and do *misinterpret* classroom behavior. Not only is our ability to perceive behavior in the classroom reduced by a fast pace and not knowing what to look for, but on occasion what we think we see is not congruent with "reality." Our beliefs, past experiences, and prejudices can lead us to incorrectly interpret what we see.

Personal Biases

Didactic
v.
Discovery

Supporters of various theories of teaching may interpret what they see in classrooms differently (Jackson, Boostrom, & Hansen, 1995; Posner, 1985). Those who hold a didactic view believe that teaching is primarily transmitting knowledge and providing clear demonstrations to show how the knowledge operates. A discovery view focuses on student experimentation and opportunity to learn inductively from inquiry activities, with a minimum of teacher structure and explanation. An observer who prefers a didactic approach might find it difficult to assess fairly a teacher who uses a discovery approach, and vice versa.

To observe accurately we must identify and examine our biases. An observer who is irritated by assertive, highly verbal teachers may see such teachers as punitive and rigid; whereas, another observer may view them as well organized and articulate. Similarly, a teacher may see two students exhibit the same behavior yet interpret the behavior differently. For example, Mr. Nowicki, who teaches tenth-grade American history, is talking when Derek Jackson calls out, "Why are we talking about this?" Knowing Derek to be a troublemaker and class clown, Mr. Nowicki assumes Derek wants to waste time or provoke an argument, so he responds aggressively, "If you would pay attention, you'd know what we're doing. Pay attention!" Compare this response with Mr. Nowicki's reply to Jim Braden, who calls out in the same tone, "Why are we talking about this?" Because Mr. Nowicki "knows" that Jim is a good, dependable student, he views Jim's words not as a provocation but as a serious question. He reasons that if Jim does not understand the purpose of the discussion, nobody does. He responds, "Jim, I probably haven't made this clear. Last Friday we discussed. . . ."

Teachers react according to their interpretations of what students say, so their past experiences with a student often influence their response. We do not suggest that you should not interpret students' comments, but we argue that you should be *aware* when you do so. Some teachers fall into the trap of expecting a student to behave in a certain way and then systematically coloring their interpretations of the student's behavior, so that the behavior fulfills the teacher's expectation. The distinction between observed behavior and the teacher's interpretation of that behavior is often lost.

Delpit (1995) asserted that differences in class backgrounds and cultures can inter-fere with teacher–student communication and how teachers are rated by supervisors. She notes:

class/culture

> A further complication is that teachers from some cultures do not expect to have to show competence by talking about what they do. They expect that anyone wanting to know what they do in a classroom will watch them teach and then make judgments about their com-petence. From the perspective of many Native American teachers, the doing of a task should be evidence of competence, whereas Western academic culture views competence as being evidenced only in talking about what one has done. Teachers from some cultural groups will likely be reluctant in an interview setting to talk about what they may be very good at doing—and the assessor may assume, then, that the candidate is incapable of doing what he or she can't explain. (p. 148)

talking about own strengths

Dangers of Interpretation

note: "data" is plural

The value of interpreting behavior only after data are collected cannot be overstated. Quantitative and qualitative theorists agree on this important point (Butler, 2006; Evertson & Green, 1986; Green, Camilli, & Elmore, 2006). Quantitative researchers ask questions before they observe (Is instruction meaningful or rote?) and develop coding systems that are specifically designed to answer their questions. In contrast, qualitative researchers ask questions after collecting considerable observational data. As Erickson (1986) notes, however, the stereotype of a classroom observer (field worker) arriving with a tabula rasa (carrying only a toothbrush and hunting knife), first to find and then to study a question, is romantic and extreme.

Quantitative:
① question first
② collect data

Qualitative:
① observe
② ask questions

Erickson (2006) suggests that the observer's task is to become aware of possible frames of interpretation used by those observed (i.e., how did teachers and students view the behavior) and to subject observed behaviors to multiple interpretations. Ob-servers' decisions about whom to talk to and what to observe next are determined as data are collected and analyzed. Thus, whether observers are using coding categories or recording field notes, they must be nonjudgmental during data collection. Knowing the question in advance is not likely to prejudice the outcome of research if the question calls for collection of descriptive facts rather than ratings or value judgments, and the observer concentrates on collecting these facts before exploring their implications for classroom participants.

The teaching incident involving Mr. Nowicki illustrates that *inferences* should be withheld until after observers have collected and examined descriptive information. As we have noted, observers' backgrounds, particularly their experiences as students and their views of good teaching, can lead them to draw erroneous conclusions (Goodson, 1997).

Case Study Techniques

One useful way for students preparing to be teachers or for teachers to improve their observational skills is to conduct case studies that focus on one or a few students. Case studies that involve reporting observed behaviors are particularly helpful. They facilitate an ability to observe and describe behavior accurately, and these skills are necessary to the generation of effective, concrete plans for dealing with students. Traditional case studies are excellent analytical tools for expanding our ability to see and to interpret student behavior (for additional information, see Erickson, 1986; Miles & Huberman, 1994; & Yin, 2006).

Discovering Bias

Observers and teachers often misinterpret behavior because of their backgrounds and biases or because they try to prematurely interpret their findings. When we become aware of our attitudes, we can often better control our behavior. For example, the teacher who unhesitatingly says, "I am a fair grader. I am never influenced by the student as a person, and I grade only the paper," may be an unfair grader. Knowing who wrote a paper does influence most graders. With high achievers, teachers tend to read more into an answer than is there. They may demand more proof from other students (e.g., although the first paragraph in an essay is excellent, the teacher still suspects that the student does not really know the material).

Once teachers realize that they can hold biases that interfere with grading fairly, they can take steps to reduce the effects of those biases. For example, teachers can mask the identity of the student who wrote the paper before grading it, grade all papers on the first question before going to the next question, and score only content and not handwriting.

This advice also applies to student teachers. Goodwin (2001) stressed that student teachers must first understand their own beliefs, assumptions, and biases if they are to understand students. She argued the importance of helping teacher candidates to realize that they have had relatively privileged, or at least positive, school experiences. Hence, many have developed faulty conceptions of students' classroom motivations and needs. "These conceptions need to be problematized and examined so that students do not unconsciously and uniformly use them to define and respond to the children with whom they work" (p. 6).

[handwritten margin note: i am used to being treated as a high achiever]

[handwritten margin note: ways to prevent grading Bias ⟹]

Teachers should treat students in equally fair and facilitating ways. This does not mean identical behavior toward all students, however, because some students need more teacher contact, while others need more opportunity to work on their own. Ladson-Billings (1994) contends that many teachers <u>confuse equality and sameness</u>:

> The notion of equity as sameness only makes sense when all students *are* exactly the same. But even within the nuclear family children born from the same parents are not exactly the same. Different children have different needs and addressing those different needs is the best way to deal with them equitably. The same is true in the classroom. <u>If teachers pretend not to see students' racial and ethnic differences, they really do not see the students at all and are limited in their ability to meet their educational needs.</u> (p. 34)

Doing a case study is one way to come to know the student as both a learner and a social being. Enhanced knowledge of students helps teachers to further differentiate equality from sameness.

Using Case Study for Self-Study

The case study assignment described in this section gives you an opportunity to study your values, preferences, and attitudes. It allows you to <u>consider the types of students whom you find fun and exciting to work with and those who annoy or bore you.</u>

From the following list, select two contrast groups for study—any two except pairs 1 and 4. If you are not in an observation course or involved in student teaching, select peers who are in your class or select two college instructors and analyze their behavior. Better yet, arrange to observe in a class similar to the one you teach or will be teaching.

1. Select the two students with whom you would most enjoy working; that is, as a teacher, which two students would you choose first to be in your own room? (positive feelings)
2. Select the two students whom you dislike the most. (negative feelings)
3. Select two students for whom you have no strong feeling whatsoever. Use the class roster here so that you do not forget about anyone. (apathy, indifference, not noticing when they are absent)
4. Select two students (one boy, one girl) who best represent the child you would want your son or daughter to be like at this age. (identification)
5. Select two students who come from a cultural background that differs from your own. (need for new knowledge or understanding)

After selecting the four students, observe them closely. If you choose to take notes during class, be sure to obtain the teacher's permission. Some notes will have to be made after class. This is especially the case for teachers. The notes are for your own use, so their form is completely open. Bear in mind that any information you record in classrooms is confidential: Students should never be identified by name. Even notes that you take in class should include no actual student names (notes are often lost). For this case study, it is not necessary to collect data from the school files, which might influence the

Observation guidelines:

observation anyway. Normal classroom behavior is sufficient. If you are doing a study, you should be sure that your data collection is in line with university human subject guidelines. Teachers doing their own case studies should comply with their district's procedures.

Analyze the similarities and differences among the four students to get clues regarding the types of student behavior that are likely to elicit positive or negative responses in you. Consider the following questions when you compare and contrast the students:

1. What are they like physically? Do they have nice clothes? Are they attractive? Clean? Large or small for their age? Male or female?
2. What are their favorite subjects? What lessons bore them? What are their strong and weak points as students? As persons?
3. What are their most prominent behavioral characteristics? Do they smile a lot? Thank you for your attention? Seek you out in the classroom more or less than the average student? Do they raise their hands to answer often? Can they be depended on to do their own work? How mature are they? Are they awkward or clumsy?
4. What are their social characteristics? What socioeconomic level do they come from? What is their ethnic background?
5. What aspects of classroom life seem most satisfying to them? What is least enjoyable or threatening?

Conducting Case Studies

Case studies help teachers overcome the tendency to see students only within the student role. Attention is focused on students as unique individuals, and an attempt is made to empathize with them. Try to see the classroom as students see it and to understand what students are trying to accomplish.

First, who are the students? What are their background characteristics (age, gender, family background)? What are their orientations toward school? toward you or the teacher? toward classmates? What are their hobbies and interests? What are their strengths and weaknesses as individuals? as students? Thinking about such questions and jotting down tentative answers can help you develop an open mind toward students and learn to look at them in new ways. These steps may improve your knowledge of a certain student before you spend any time observing that student. For example, if you cannot name several strengths and weaknesses, your view of the student is probably biased. In our desire for simplicity and consistency in our perceptions, we tend to emphasize characteristics that fit together and reinforce our biases, and to slight those that do not.

No special preparation or equipment is required to systemically observe a student. An ordinary notebook and pen or pencil will do, or laptop computer. You should be near enough to see and hear the student, but not so close as to be inhibiting. Ideally, the student should not know you are observing him or her. If possible, observe the student outside class as well (during recess, at lunch, and between classes).

If the student presents a behavioral problem, try to formulate it as specifically as you can, using terms that translate into observable behavior. Include any relevant information about the contexts in which behavior occurs (subject matter, size of group, time of day, type of situation). Patterns in the student's behavior may increase your understanding of it. You also might notice important differences between situations in which the student is and is not a problem (interest in a topic, structure in an activity, active versus quiet activity, type of antecedent experience, presence of peers or other distracters).

Keep a running log of the students' behavior during observation periods. Observations should be dated and clearly separated from one another in the continuous log, and subdivided into natural units according to what was going on at the time (class periods and breaks between periods, different activities and settings within classes). The log should contain narrative descriptions of behavior along with interpretations about its possible meanings. It is important to keep objective descriptions of behavior separate from subjective interpretations concerning meaning, because interpretations may change as more information is collected. Probably the easiest way to do this is to use only the left half of the page for keeping the log of behavior. Interpretations can be written on the right half of the page later, when you review your notes and think about what you have observed.

If you interview students, you may find that their beliefs about school subjects and other topics differ from what you had concluded on the basis of your observation. Students can be excellent sources if information about how classrooms work. Interview techniques are beyond the scope of this book, but excellent suggestions about the use of the student interviews as well as how to conduct them can be found elsewhere (Brenner, 2006; McCaslin & Good, 1996; Rohrkemper, 1981, 1985; Spradly, 1979). Further background readings on ethnography (e.g., Anderson-Levitt, 2006) may be valuable preparation for doing case study work.

Fact versus Interpretation

When recording data for a case study, include as much pertinent and interpretable information as possible but stick with facts and avoid unsupported and perhaps incorrect interpretations. This objective is not difficult to achieve, but it may take some practice to learn to separate vague information from interpretable facts, and interpretable facts from interpretations themselves.

An Example.   Suppose an observer were watching Ron, a white student, when he became involved in an incident with Ralph, an African American student, and recorded: "Ralph taps Ron, points, and speaks. Ron replies, shaking head. Ralph gestures, speaks, Ron strikes Ralph, and a fight starts." This information is factual but it is too vague to be much good. Even if the words of the boys are not heard, their gestures and the general nature of their interaction can be described much more clearly. Let's look at another example.

> Ron is working quietly until bothered by Ralph. He listens, then refuses. Ralph becomes angry and abusive. Ron becomes aggressive, triggering a major racial incident.

Assuming that the observer could not hear what was said, this example is not so much an observation as an interpretation. Ron may or may not have "refused" whatever

Ralph wanted, Ralph may or may not have "provoked" Ron, and the incident may or may not be "racial." These are interpretations. They fit the facts and may be true, but this can also be said of many other possible interpretations. A competent observer would have recorded the facts as follows:

> Ralph taps Ron on the shoulder, shows his assignment, points to something, speaks. Ron looks, shakes head no, says something. Ralph replies with a disgusted look, downward gesture of arm. Turns away when finished speaking. Ron says something to Ralph from behind, then slaps Ralph's head. Ralph responds as if attacked, fight begins.

This description contains about as much useful information as could be recorded without becoming interpretive. About all that is missing is a description of Ron's facial expression and general manner when slapping Ralph. This information would be helpful in judging whether the head slap really was meant as an attack (if so, it would be an unusual behavior).

The interpretation of this information would raise questions about its meaning. Who actually started the trouble, and what started it? Is it accurate to call this a racial incident, or is the fact that one boy is African American and the other white irrelevant?

Ordinarily, the observer would get answers to these and related questions, because interactions as intense as fights usually involve loud talk, which is easy to hear. However, without more information, the interpretation of these facts would have to be confined to speculation. The first fact is that Ralph interrupted Ron by tapping his shoulder, pointing to the assignment, and saying something. The shoulder tap apparently did not bother Ron because he did not show any reaction to it. In fact, he did not appear angry until later. The fact that Ralph showed the assignment and pointed to something suggests that he was seeking help or information about it or was expressing an opinion. However, it is possible that what he had to say to Ron had nothing to do with the assignment. If so, he could have made a provocative statement, but not necessarily.

Ron responded by shaking his head no and saying something. This response could have been a refusal to listen, a refusal of a request, or an answer to Ralph's question, among other things. If Ralph had expressed an opinion, this could have been a disagreement by Ron. In any case, it is clear that Ron responded negatively to whatever Ralph asked or said.

Ralph's gesture and facial expression in his reply suggest disgust and/or anger, although it is not at all clear whether he provoked Ron in some way. He might have, but he might also have been giving an opinion. For example, he might have originally pointed out what he considered to be a stupid question and asked Ron if he understood it. Ron might have said that he didn't understand it either, and Ralph might have responded with a gesture and look of disgust while saying something like, "Why do they ask us stuff like this?"

Just as Ralph's behavior may or may not have involved provocation, Ron's behavior may or may not have involved aggression. It could have been an attack on Ralph, perhaps in retaliation for something Ralph said, but it also could have been horseplay. Boys frequently poke or slap one another as a way of teasing (but not attacking), and that could be what happened.

Ambiguous situations are common when classroom observations are collected in case studies, which is why it is important to physically separate facts about observations from interpretations of these observations. The factual record will remain constant even when interpretations change in the light of new evidence.

Avoiding Bias.   Recording and interpreting behavior are two distinct issues. You must determine what behavior to record and how to record it, and then interpret the behavior. You may have to experiment in order to find the appropriate degree of generality to use in describing behavior. You should not try to record literally everything that you see. Even if this were possible, you would be recording a great deal of information about trivial behaviors and expressions that have no interpretive importance. In contrast, in the interest of objectivity, it is important that you record observable behaviors. Thus, it would be appropriate to note that the student smiled or even smiled at the teacher, but it would be an interpretation to say that the student showed friendly warmth (as opposed to self-satisfaction, for example). Similarly, it would be appropriate to state that the student spent time apparently absorbed in thinking and problem solving, but it would be an interpretation to say that the student *was* thinking and problem solving. Perhaps the student has learned to give this appearance while daydreaming.

You want to highlight information relevant to your concerns about the student, but your record should keep everything in perspective. For example, if you are watching a student who gets into trouble with peers, you should have detailed descriptions of what happened on the two occasions when the student became involved in arguments. It should be clear, however, that these two occasions involved only a few minutes, and the record should provide a running account of what the student was doing during the rest of the period. What does the student do when not misbehaving? This question will cue your attention to positive behavior that the teacher should learn about and build on in future interactions with the student. Just as outstanding students have weaknesses, problem students have strengths.

Behavioral records should be reviewed and checked for completeness and accuracy at the first opportunity. At this time, you can also make initial interpretations, add clarification, and edit your notes. You may or may not be able to interpret everything you see, but your notes should be complete and unambiguous concerning what actually happened. In addition to a description of what transpired, there should be information about the qualitative aspects of the student's behavior (Was it random or purposeful? Was there anything unusual or noteworthy about it?) and explanations for the behavior (What stimulated it? What was its purpose?).

In reviewing behavioral comments, look for correlations and contradictions. Try to identify repeated patterns. Are they well known, or do they suggest new insights? Look for instances when a particular pattern might have been expected but did not occur. These could provide keys for developing ideas about how to get the student to change. If your notes suggest certain hypotheses but do not contain enough information to allow you to evaluate them, try to identify what information you need. Perhaps you can identify specific situations you could observe in the near future. For example, suppose the student challenged the teacher on two occasions when asked to read aloud. This could be a defense mechanism used in an attempt to avoid reading, perhaps because the student cannot read. You cannot tell from only two instances, but you could watch for this behavior in the future whenever the class is involved in oral reading, and you could check the student's reading achievement. Such supplementary information then can be added to the log at appropriate places to assist you in interpreting the student's behavior.

Teacher candidates can benefit in important ways from conducting case studies. For example, in interviews with her students, Goodwin (2001) has found that the process of conducting the case study helped future teachers to see how easy it is to blame or mislabel students because of the complexity of classroom settings. She reported that over time student teachers came to see students in more complex ways and also became more willing to assume greater personal responsibility for helping their students to learn.

The purpose of conducting a case study is to understand a student, not to "fix" the student. Although a case study suggests instructional implications, it must first develop an authentic understanding of the student. Developing a case "forces" student teachers to notice "key moments" that they might miss otherwise because of the rapid pace of classrooms. Goodwin (2001) contended:

> What is significant about key moments or turning points is that student teachers not only learn to see their case study child differently, but they shift responsibility for learning from the child to themselves as teachers; they stop blaming children for their failures, and start examining what they need to do to make learning happen for children. (p. 16)

Others also have noted the value of using case studies to help preservice teachers understand the complexity of adolescents. Roeser (2002) showed that the case study experience helped students to apply theoretical knowledge in more effective ways in understanding secondary students.

Simplifying the Observational Task

Case studies can yield in-depth information about one or two students. Sometimes, however, one might wish to study how teachers interact with different students under similar circumstances. The sheer physical complexity of classrooms makes this a very difficult task. While the teacher instructs a reading group, four students may be at the science table, three listening to tapes at the listening post, four reading at their desks, and three working individually on computers. No observer can monitor everything that takes place. Even relatively simple tasks may be impossible to code simultaneously. For instance, if an observer wants to code the number of hands raised when a teacher asks a question and note whether the student called on by the teacher has a hand up, the observer may still be counting hands when the teacher calls on the student and will thus be unable to determine whether the student had a hand up. One excellent way to overcome this complexity, especially when you begin observing in classrooms, is to study the behavior of a few students. You can study these students intensively, and their behavior will probably mirror what is taking place in the entire classroom. Focus on a few students (perhaps two high, two middle, and two low achievers—one female and one male at each level) or on a particular group of students (low achievers); then record certain things these students do. You might record the following information about high, middle, and low achievers:

1. How often do they raise their hands?
2. Do all students approach the teacher to receive help, or do some seldom approach the teacher?
3. How long does each reading group last?
4. Are the students involved in their work? How long do they work independently at their desks?
5. How often are students in different groups praised?
6. What do students do when they finish their experiment, while other students are still completing their lab assignment?

Another useful strategy is to limit the number of behaviors you observe at one time, perhaps restricting attention initially to five to ten behaviors. When we attempt to monitor too many things, we become confused and cannot record objectively. It is better to concentrate on a few behaviors for a while and then to code a new set.

Reliability of Observations

You should assess your ability to code classroom behavior accurately by comparing your observations with those of others. This is perhaps the easiest way to determine whether you are observing what happens and not allowing your personal biases to interfere with your observations.

In general, the observation forms we present in Appendix 1 at the end of this chapter and those that follow at the end of other chapters can be used reliably with some practice. If observers are watching a videotape and coding the number of academic questions a teacher asks, one observer may tally sixteen academic questions, whereas another tallies only ten. Agreement between the two observers can be estimated by using this simple formula suggested by Emmer and Millett (1970):

$$\text{Agreement} = 1 - \frac{A - B}{A + B}$$

The formula tells us to subtract the difference between the two observers' counts and to divide by the sum of their counts. The *A* term is always the larger number. Thus, agreement in this example would be:

$$1 - \frac{16 - 10}{16 + 10} = 1 - \frac{6}{26} = 1 - .23 = .77$$

General Plan for Observing in Classrooms

What you observe in a classroom will vary from situation to situation and from individual to individual. Some observers will be able to focus on six behaviors; others may be able to code ten. Some may be in the classroom eight hours a week, some only four. Some may see two or three different teachers; others will remain in the same room. Despite such situational differences, some general principles will apply when observing in classrooms. First, observers often try to reduce the complexity of classroom coding by focusing exclusively on the teacher. This is particularly true for teachers in training, who are still trying to determine what teachers do, but it is misplaced emphasis. The key to thorough classroom observation is *student response.*

Teachers who want to receive relevant feedback about their behavior and that of their students and observers who want to see what life in a classroom is like must be careful not to disturb the natural behavior in the classroom. By *natural* we mean the behavior that would take place if the observer were not present. Students, especially young ones, adjust quickly to the presence of an observer if teachers prepare them properly and if the observer behaves appropriately. The teacher should explain the observer's presence briefly, so students do not have to wonder about the observer or question to find out for themselves. For example, a second-grade class might be told, "Mr. Ramon will be with us today and the rest of the week. He is learning about being a teacher. Mr. Ramon will not disturb us because we have many things we want to finish and he knows how busy we are. Please do not disturb him because he, too, is busy and has his own work to do."

The observer can help by avoiding eye contact with the students and by refusing to be drawn into long conversations with them or to aid them in their seatwork, unless the observer is also a participant in classroom life. (Some university courses call for students to serve as teacher aides before they do their student teaching.)

Observers should not initiate contact with students or do anything to draw special attention to themselves (e.g., loudly ripping pages out of a notebook). It is especially important when two observers are in the same room that they not talk with each other, exchange notes, and so forth. Such behavior bothers both the teacher and the students and causes attention to be focused on the observers, so that natural behavior is disturbed.

Before coming into a classroom, observers should talk with the teacher about where they will sit, how they should be introduced to the students, and how they should respond when a student approaches them. The teacher and observers should agree on how to deal with students who are intent on making themselves known to the observer. At such meetings, observers can obtain curriculum materials and information about the students (seating chart, achievement ranking). Such information is necessary if the observer plans to conduct an intensive study of only a few students at different achievement levels. The information needed to use the coding forms at the end of subsequent chapters is presented in this chapter. If you wish detailed information about more advanced coding systems, consult Appendix 1 at the end of this chapter.

*U*sing Research and Observational Feedback

Research findings and concepts provide a way to think about classroom instruction, but they must be used as <u>tools, not rules</u>. Consider Adams and Biddle's (1970) discussion of the action zone, describing their finding that students who sat in the front row and in seats extending directly up the middle aisle received more opportunities to talk than other students. The action zone is a useful concept for identifying *possible* problems in the classroom; it suggests that students in some areas of a classroom may receive more response opportunities than students in other areas. If interpreted too literally, however, the concept could be taken to mean that action zones are always located in the front row and the middle of the class. A study by Alhajri (1981) showed that only one of thirty-two classrooms had an action zone like the one described by Adams and Biddle, although some kind of action zone was present in many classrooms. This research reaffirmed the value of the action zone concept as a tool for analyzing classroom instruction, even though it showed that action zones can take many forms. If observers or teachers monitor classes for only one type of action zone, they may not notice zones that take a different form.

example of "action zones" existing, but not always in same area

Duke (2000) found that classroom print environments differ between high- and low-SES classrooms, with students in high-SES classes generally receiving more stimulating exposure to literacy. However, good literacy environments were provided in some low-SES classrooms. Hence, these data do not suggest a need to change all low-SES first-grade classrooms; however, they do provide a conceptual tool to keep in mind when examining such classrooms. Further, these results do not specify what should occur even in classrooms that have less desirable print environments. Some degree of difference might be appropriate in some cases. Again, research cannot directly yield policy answers or prescriptions for teaching.

SES:

Considering the complexity of and variation among learning settings, research findings—no matter how clear the relevant theory or how robust the findings—must be interpreted in relation to individual teachers and schools. Effective use of any concept taken from research on teaching can take many forms, and a teaching behavior may be appropriate in some contexts but not in others.

*T*eachers as Decision Makers

Teachers need to be decision makers who understand that knowledge has to be applied to their particular setting. Teachers must *continuously* reflect on their classroom experiences and adapt their teaching to students. Teachers also need to obtain new information from research about ideas they can use to analyze their teaching or improve curriculum and instruction for students.

Fenstermacher (1983) distinguished the <u>structural elaboration</u> from the <u>personal</u> <u>elaboration</u> of research. Structural elaboration involves using research findings as

structural
elaboration:
uses research
as answer

personal elab:

answers or prescriptions. If, for example, researchers found that ten minutes of home-work was effective in a particular program, structural elaboration would advocate that all teachers use ten minutes of homework. In contrast, when research is used for per-sonal elaboration, the decision about how to apply research resides with the individual teacher, who thinks about the needs of his or her students. Teachers must have access to recent research-based knowledge—knowledge derived from observation of classrooms, but it is important that teachers reflect and form their own ideas about the value of the knowledge and its relevance to their contexts.

SUMMARY

Teachers are not aware of everything that goes on in the classroom, and this lack of awareness may interfere with their effectiveness. This problem exists for at least two rea-sons. First, classrooms are busy places, and teachers (and students as well) are so busy responding that they have little time to think about what they are doing. Many factors contribute to classroom complexity. Second, teachers are seldom observed systemati-cally, so they rarely receive valuable information about ways to increase their effective-ness. When they are observed, it is typically for purposes of evaluation. Fortunately, this situation is changing in some schools.

Teachers need to be aware of their own formative learning experiences (e.g., how discussions were handled in their family, instructional and management strategies used by their cooperating teacher, preferences of their initial principal, etc.) because these ex-periences may affect their classroom decision making and instruction in subtle but im-portant ways. To become active decision makers and to develop their own personal styles, teachers need to understand the knowledge base that supports teaching, includ-ing information not only about instructional strategies but also about student devel-opment, learning, and motivation. Teachers must be reflective (e.g., analyze classroom processes, discuss curriculum and instruction with peers) and sensitive to the context in which they teach and the instructional goals that are most important to them. Those who are aware of their own development, who are knowledgeable about research on classroom instruction and student learning, and who frequently reflect on their teach-ing, will be the most active decision makers. And, active decision making leads to effec-tive teaching.

Steps to
Reduce
Bias
in observations

Objective recording of behavior provides a way to guard against our biases and gain the most benefit from classroom observations. Personal bias in observing can be re-duced by (1) becoming aware of our biases; (2) observing specific behaviors, to allevi-ate the complexity of the classroom; and (3) checking our observational data against the observations of others. Exercises were suggested to help you observe objectively. We also discussed procedures for minimizing the observer's effect on the classroom, by observ-ing unobtrusively.

Finally, we suggested that although research and, particularly, observational data about classrooms are important, they should not dictate practice. Teachers must inte-grate rich data with their own beliefs, values, and purposes regarding instruction. Effective classroom teachers function as active decision makers.

SUGGESTED ACTIVITIES AND QUESTIONS

1. Consider the grade you teach (or plan to teach) and identify the ten most important skills, attitudes, or behaviors a teacher must possess in order to instruct effectively at this level. Keep this list so you can compare it with your thoughts after you have read the entire book.

2. If you could talk with Sally Turner about her lesson, what questions would you ask? Why? How might additional information change your opinion of her teaching?

3. Reread the example of Sally Turner's class and identify four instances in which she could have probed for improved student responses. Write the questions you would have asked.

4. We evaluated Sally's teaching. What teaching strengths or weaknesses did you identify that we did not mention? Explain why these behaviors are important.

5. We criticized Sally's introduction to the lesson. Improve the introduction by writing your own. What steps should a good introduction include? Why?

6. Reread the questions that Sally asks her class. How could you improve them? Write several questions of your own. Why are your questions better than hers?

7. If Sally's classroom were composed entirely of inner-city or suburban students, how would you assess her instruction? Does teaching have to be adjusted to the characteristics of students? Explain.

8. How would you describe Ms. Chavez's relative strengths and weaknesses?

9. Sometimes problems are in the eye of the beholder. What one person views as appropriate curiosity or initiative, another may believe is unwarranted intrusion or aggression. To explore more fully the ambiguity of behavior (and the need to interpret it), consider what selected behaviors (e.g., cooperation, initiative, leadership) mean to you in a particular instructional context. What student behaviors would imply appropriate initiative in a first-grade versus a seventh-grade classroom?

10. Initially, most of us find it difficult to monitor our teaching behavior, but improve with practice. When you teach try to monitor aspects of your behavior (e.g., the ratio of factual to thought questions) and see how your mental record compares with a record taken by a coder or with what you hear when you play back your tape-recorded lesson.

11. Why is it important that an observer have a conceptual system for describing classroom behavior and for noticing significant occurrences?

12. Visit a classroom or watch a videotape of a discussion and tally the number of times that the teacher: (a) asks a question, (b) responds to a student's answer, and (c) praises a student. Compare your tallies with another observer's by calculating the percentage of agreement between your observations.

APPENDIX 1.1

Observational Methods

There has been rapid growth in the use of observation systems in training and research, and the types of systems used to code classroom behavior have become more varied (Brophy, 2006; Erikson, 2006; Evertson & Green, 1986; Green, Camilli, & Elmore 2006). Here we provide four types of observational approaches. The first example we present in this appendix was prepared by Phyllis Blumenfeld and Samuel Miller for their students at the University of Michigan. It is an effective device for describing different means of collecting narrative and frequency-count information. We follow with the Brophy-Good Dyadic System, which allows coders to describe the types of interactions individual students share with the teachers. The Emmer system follows. It represents a way to code how a teacher treats the class as a whole or how the class reacts to the teacher. Finally, we present a brief description of ethnographic work conducted by Neil Duke at Michigan State University.

Coding Vocabulary: Blumenfeld and Miller

Narrative Strategies

collect narrative
+
frequency count info

Anecdotal Record

Characteristics:
a. Provides a brief sketch or illustration of a student's behavioral pattern or learning style (e.g., several brief anecdotes might be used to illustrate how a student reacts to a particular situation).

b. Indicates that students have mastered or applied concepts (e.g., brief anecdotes might be used to illustrate that students used knowledge from a subtraction lesson to solve a problem in another subject or outside of class).

Procedure:
1. Write down the incident as soon after it occurs as possible.
2. Identify the basic action of the key person and what was said.
3. Include a statement that identifies the setting, time of day, and basic activity.
4. In describing the central character's actions or verbalizations, include the responses or reactions of other people in the situation.
5. Whenever possible note exact words used, to preserve the precise nature of the conversation.
6. Preserve the sequence of the episode.
7. Be objective, accurate, and complete (i.e., do not interpret).

Running Record

Characteristics:
a. Running records are used to record the situation in a manner that lets someone else read the description later and visualize the scene or event as it occurred.

b. As opposed to anecdotal records, which provide a brief illustrative episode on a student, running records provide a detailed, continuous, or sequential descriptive account of the behavior and its immediate environmental context (eyewitness account par excellence).

c. Running records can be used to help locate the source of the problem or pattern of behavior. (If you wanted to know whether the teacher used effective questioning strategies, you could collect running records of lessons and later go to the records to pinpoint instances of the teacher using effective and ineffective questions.)

Procedure:
1. Describe the scene as it is when the observer begins the description.
2. Focus on the subject's behavior and whatever in the situation affects this behavior.
3. Be as accurate and complete as you can about what the subject says, does, and responds to within the situation.
4. Put brackets around all interpretive material generated by the observer so that the description stands out clearly and completely.
5. Include the "how" for whatever the subject does (e.g., teacher said to be quiet in a high voice while pointing her right hand at the students versus the teacher said to be quiet).
6. Give the "how" for everything done by anyone interacting with the subject (i.e., emphasis on the details, not on inferences).
7. For every action, report all the main steps in their proper order.
8. Describe behavior positively, rather than in terms of what was not done.
9. Use observational tools whenever possible (tape recorders, cameras, or videotape).

Comparison of Anecdotal and Running Records

Comparison Is Related to the Following Points:

a. *Length of observation.* Anecdotal records require shorter periods of time and are normally completed after the event has occurred, whereas running records are recorded as events occur and usually continue for extended periods of time.
b. *Amount of detail.* Running records demand a greater number of details than anecdotal records. Additionally, compared to anecdotal records, running records place little emphasis on impressions or interpretations (whenever they occur they are set off by brackets).
c. *Breadth of focus.* While both records are targeted on a particular student(s) or event(s), the running record includes much more information on the environmental context than does the anecdotal record. Anecdotal records are less sophisticated than running records—they are similar to a diary, whereas the running record is similar to a verbatim report.
d. *Systematicness.* Anecdotal records do not provide generally systematic evidence. They are brief illustrative sketches of incidents rather than evidence collected across situations and at different times.

Frequency Counts

We present two frequency count approaches—time sampling and event sampling. Read the characteristics and procedures for conducting each in order to understand the similarities and differences between the two approaches.

Time Sampling

Characteristics:

a. In time sampling, behaviors are observed over repeated intervals for different periods of time (e.g., three recordings of a behavior per 10 minutes for four 1-hour periods).

b. Time sampling is appropriate only for behaviors that occur fairly frequently, at least once every fifteen minutes on average.

c. This behavior is then looked on as a "sample" of the person's usual behavior(s).

Procedure:

1. Identify behaviors that occur regularly and define the behaviors so that others will agree with what the focus of the observation will be (e.g., on-task behavior that may be defined as (1) on-task, engrossed; (2) on-task, at work but not engrossed; (3) off-task, quietly disengaged; or (4) off-task, disruptive).

2. Decide how long the observation period will be and how many observations are needed within this period (e.g., three 1-hour observation periods during math where the observer codes on-task behavior of five children for 3 minutes, waits 7 minutes, records behavior during another 3-minute period, waits 7 minutes, and so on). If the behavior occurs during an observer wait period, it is not recorded.

Event Sampling

Characteristics:

a. In event sampling, the observer waits for the selected behavior to occur and records it (i.e., all selected behaviors that occur are recorded).

Procedure:

1. Clearly identify the kind of behavior you want to study (e.g., how students get the teacher's attention during seatwork).

2. Determine what kind of information you want to record (e.g., call the teacher's name, hold an object in front of his or her face, stand in front of teacher, ask teacher for assistance, cause a disruption).

3. Decide how many times you will observe and how long you will observe during each time (e.g., ten 40-minute seatwork classes).

Comparison of Time Sampling and Event Sampling

a. Both event and time sampling are useful for determining the frequency of behaviors or events, and both allow the collection of a large number of observations in a relatively short time.

b. Time sampling is limited to frequently or regularly occurring behaviors and counts only those behaviors that occur during a recording interval. Event sampling counts all instances of the behavior's occurrence, and the behavior does not have to occur frequently.

c. With both approaches the observer must determine what behaviors are to be observed, when they are to be observed, and for how long they are to be observed to obtain a sample set of behaviors typical of the student(s) in question.

Increasing Teacher Awareness through Classroom Observation

Method	Focus	Advantages/Disadvantages
Case study narratives	Single student	+ Provides a rich, detailed account of an individual's actions + Allows an in-depth examination of a single problem − Descriptions may be affected by the observer's biases − Conclusions may not apply to the same student in other classes or to other students
Frequency counts	Single student Small groups	+ Gives actual number of behaviors per unit of time, which allows comparisons among students or across classes + Allows teacher to receive immediate information on a problem without having to receive extensive training − Actual behaviors recorded may not explain all facets of the problem − Apart from the behavior in question, the teacher will not know what students are doing during the observation time
Classroom observation scale (COS)	Single student Small groups Whole class	+ Gives actual number of behaviors per unit of time, which allows comparisons among students or across classes − Usually involves more observer training than do other methods − Apart from the behavior in question, the teacher will not know what students are doing during the observation time
Questionnaire	Single student Small groups Whole class	+ Allows the collection of information on a variety of topics in a relatively short time + Since students respond to the same set of questions, questionnaires allow comparisons among individuals or across classes − Question construction is more difficult than it may appear (e.g., responses may be affected by how questions are worded) − Responses may not truly represent what students will do in actual situation (validity) − Responses may differ if questionnaire is given at another time (reliability)
Interview	Small groups Whole class	+ Yields more student information than do other methods + Allows greater flexibility to probe a student's response more deeply − Since students give more information, comparisons among students may be difficult − Responses given may be affected by student biases − Usually will take longer to conduct than other methods

(*continued*)

Increasing Teacher Awareness through Classroom Observation (*Continued*)

Method	Focus	Advantages/Disadvantages
Ethnography	Whole class	+ Relative to other methods it provides more information on the social context of the classroom − Since the purpose is to interpret behaviors, the analysis may be affected by observer bias − Since the focus is not on a particular set of behaviors for all students, comparisons among students or across classes are difficult − The purpose is not to answer specific questions but to describe the norms governing interactions in social settings—therefore, the information collected may not be appropriate for answering specific questions

Brophy-Good Dyadic Interaction System

Types of interactions individual students have w/teachers

There are many observational systems we can use to code classroom behavior. All systems are selective and code certain behaviors while ignoring other aspects of the classroom. Hence, the usefulness of a particular observation system depends on your goal. We present one observation system, the Brophy-Good dyadic interaction system, briefly.

In this particular system, the goal is to determine whether individual students receive more or less of certain behaviors than other students (e.g., Are high-achieving female students treated differently from low-achieving male students?). After you read the definitions and examine the coding sheets that follow, go back to Chapter 1 and examine the long classroom scene. Does the teacher provide equal opportunity for all students? Coding systems like the Brophy-Good system help us to be more systematic in our observations.

Brief Definitions of Variables Coded in Brophy-Good Dyadic Interaction System

The coding sheet (see Figure 1.1) uses the following definitions (presented in the order that they appear on the coding sheet). For an extended discussion of these definitions and coding examples, see Brophy and Good (1970).

Student-initiated question. A student asks the teacher a question in a public setting.

Reading or recitation. Student is called on to read aloud, go through an arithmetic table, and so on.

Discipline question. The discipline question is a unique type of direct question in which the teacher uses the question as a control technique, calling on the student

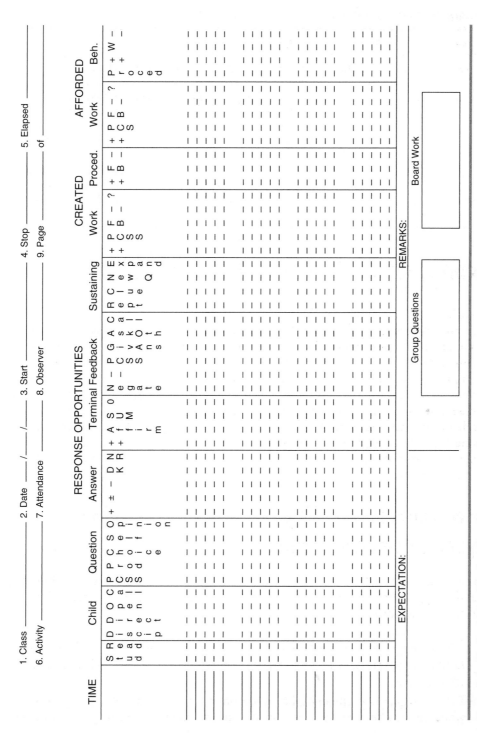

Figure 1.1 The Brophy-Good Dyadic Coding Sheet

39

to force him or her to pay better attention rather than merely providing a response opportunity in the usual sense.

Direct question. Teacher calls on a student who is not seeking a response opportunity.

Open question. The teacher creates the response opportunity by asking a public question and also indicates who is to respond by calling on an individual student, but the teacher chooses one of the students who has indicated a desire to respond by raising a hand.

Call-outs. Response opportunities created by students who call out answers to teachers' questions without waiting for permission to respond.

Process question. Requires students to explain something in a way that requires them to integrate facts or to show knowledge of their interrelationships. It most frequently is a "why?" or "how?" question.

Product question. Product questions seek to elicit a single correct answer that can be expressed in one word or a short phrase. Product questions usually begin with "who," "what," "when," "where," "how much," and "how many."

Choice question. In the choice question, the student does not have to produce a substantive response but may instead simply choose one of two or more implied or expressed alternatives.

Self-reference question. Asks the student to make some nonacademic contribution to classroom discussion ("show-and-tell"; questions about personal experiences, preferences, or feelings; requests for opinions or predictions, etc.).

Opinion question. Much like a self-reference question (i.e., there is no single correct answer) except that it elicits a student opinion on an academic topic ("Is it worth putting a person on the moon?").

Correct answer. If the student answers the teacher's question in a way that satisfies the teacher, the answer is coded as correct.

Part-correct answer. A part-correct answer is one that is correct but incomplete as far as it goes, or correct from one point of view but not what the teacher is looking for.

Incorrect answer. A response that is treated as simply wrong by the teacher.

Don't know. Student verbally says "I don't know" (or its equivalent) or nonverbally indicates that he or she doesn't know (shakes head).

No response. Student makes no response (verbally or nonverbally) to teacher question.

Praise. Praise refers to the teacher's evaluative reactions that go beyond the level of simple affirmation or positive feedback by verbally complimenting the student.

Affirmation of correct answers. Affirmation is coded when the teacher indicates that the student's response is correct or acceptable.

Summary. Teacher summarizes the student's answer (generally as part of the affirmation process).

No feedback reaction. If the teacher makes no verbal or nonverbal response whatever following the student's answer to the question, the teacher is coded for no feedback reaction.

Negation of incorrect answer. Simple provision of impersonal feedback regarding the incorrectness of the response, without going farther than this by communicating a negative personal reaction to the student. As with affirmation, negation can be communicated both verbally ("No," "That's not right," "Hmm-mm") and nonverbally (shaking the head horizontally).

Criticism. Evaluative reactions that go beyond the level of simple negation by expressing anger or personal criticism of the student in addition to indicating the incorrectness of the response.

Process feedback. Coded when the teacher goes beyond merely providing the right answer and discusses the cognitive or behavioral processes that are to be gone through in arriving at the answer.

Gives answer. This category is used when the teacher gives the student the answer to the question but does not elaborate sufficiently to be coded for process feedback.

Asks other. Whenever the student does not answer a teacher question and the teacher moves to another student in order to get the answer to that same question, the teacher's feedback reaction is coded for asks other.

Call-out. The call-out category is used when another student calls out the answer to the question before the teacher has a chance to call on someone.

Repeats question. Teacher asks a question, waits some time without getting the correct answer, and then repeats the question to the same student.

Rephrase or clue. In this feedback reaction, the teacher sustains the response opportunity by rephrasing the question or giving the student a clue as to how to respond to it.

New question. When the first question is not answered or is answered incorrectly, the teacher asks a new question that is different from the original, although it may be closely related. A question requiring a new answer is coded as a new question.

Expansion. Teacher responses to vague or incomplete statements that ask the student to provide more information ("I think I understand, but tell me . . .").

Dyadic Teacher–Student Contacts

The preceding material has dealt primarily with the coding of response opportunities and reading and recitation turns. Dyadic teacher–student contacts differ from response opportunities and reading and recitation turns in that the teacher is dealing privately with one student about matters idiosyncratic to him or her rather than publicly about material meant for the group or class as a whole.

Dyadic teacher–student contacts are divided into work-related contacts, procedural contacts, and behavioral or disciplinary contacts. They are also separately coded according to whether they are initiated by the teacher (teacher-afforded) or by the student (student-created). The coding also reflects certain aspects of the teacher's behavior in such contacts.

Work-Related Contacts

Work-related contacts include those teacher–student contacts that have to do with the student's completion of seatwork or homework assignments. They include clarification of the directions, soliciting or giving help concerning how to do the work, or soliciting or giving feedback about work already done. Work-related interactions are considered student-created if the student brings his or her work up to the teacher to talk about it, raises a hand, or otherwise indicates a desire to discuss it with the teacher. Work-related interactions are coded as teacher-afforded if the teacher gives feedback about work when the student has not solicited it (the teacher either calls the student to come up to his or her desk or goes around the room making individual comments to the students). Created contacts are not planned by the teacher and occur solely because the student has sought out the teacher; afforded contacts are not planned by the student and occur solely because the teacher initiates them. Separate space is provided for coding created and afforded work-related interactions on the coding sheets, and the coder indicates the nature of an individual dyadic contact by where the interaction is coded.

In addition to noting the interaction as a work interaction and as an interaction that is student-created or teacher-afforded, the coder also indicates the nature of the teacher's feedback to the student during the interactions. He or she indicates this by using one or more of the five columns provided for coding teachers' feedback in work-related interaction: praise ($+ +$), process feedback (pcss), product feedback (fb), criticism ($-$), or "don't know" (?). The first four of these categories have the same meaning as they have in other coding of teacher feedback. The additional "don't know" category is added for this coding because frequently the individual teacher–student interaction that occurs in a dyadic contact is carried on in hushed tones or across the room from the coder, where it is not possible to hear the content of the interaction. In such cases, the coder notes the occurrence of the work-related interaction and the fact that it was either teacher-afforded or student-created but enters the student's identification number in the "don't know" column (identified by the question mark on top).

Procedural Contacts

The category of procedural contacts includes all dyadic teacher–student interactions that are not coded as work-related contacts or as behavioral contacts. Thus it includes a wide range of types of contacts, most of which are initiated on the basis of the immediate needs of the teacher or student involved. Procedural contacts are created by the student for such purposes as seeking permission to do something, requesting needed supplies or equipment, reporting some information to the teacher (tattling on other students, calling attention to a broken desk or pencil, etc.), getting permission or information about how to take care of idiosyncratic needs (turning in lunch money, delivering a note from the parent to the principal, etc.), as well as a variety of other contacts. In general, any dyadic interaction initiated by the student that does not fit the definition of work-related contacts is coded as a procedural contact.

Behavioral Contacts

Behavioral contacts are coded whenever the teacher makes some comment on the student's classroom behavior. They are subdivided into praise, warnings, and criticism. The coder notes the information by entering the student's identification number under the appropriate column. Behavioral evaluation contacts are considered to be teacher-afforded, although they usually occur as reactions to the student's immediately preceding behavior. Nevertheless, they are teacher-afforded in the sense that the student usually does not want and does not expect the interaction and that the teacher chooses to single the student out for comment.

Emmer Observation System

How teacher treats class as a whole

The Brophy-Good dyadic interaction system allows us to code teachers' individual interactions with students. However, teachers do more than interact with individual students, and we need ways to classify and think about these aspects of classroom interaction as well.

One interesting and useful observational system has been prepared by Ed Emmer at the University of Texas (Emmer, 1971). We can present only a small part of this system here; if you are interested in more of the observational scales included in the manual and in details of training and reliability, consult Emmer at the University of Texas.

Emmer recommends that the scales be used approximately every fifteen minutes, because longer periods may reduce reliability by placing too much reliance on the observer's memory, and shorter intervals may fail to provide sufficient information to use the scale. He also suggests that the observer should sit where he or she can observe the teacher and students and be in a position to see the faces of as many students as possible.

What follows are examples of two of the twelve scales that appear in the Emmer system. Attention as defined for this scale refers to pupil orientation toward the teacher, the task at hand, or whatever classroom activities are appropriate. If pupils are attending to inappropriate activities or are engaged in self-directed behavior when they are supposed to be engaged in a class activity, this behavior is not considered attentive. Therefore, you should look for behavior that is focused on or engaged in whatever activity is appropriate, whether individual seatwork, group discussion, or listening to the presentation of information. Useful cues in recognizing attentive behavior include eye contact, body orientation, response to questions or other eliciting cues, and participation in class activity. Useful cues in recognizing inattentiveness include inappropriate social interaction, repetitive body movement, visual wandering, and engagement in behavior other than the sanctioned class activity. At times, it will be difficult to determine whether a student is attentive, such as when the teacher presents information and the student sits facing the teacher, with no observable behaviors indicating inattention. In such instances, the pupils are considered attentive until they behave otherwise.

To code behavior on this scale, scan the class on several occasions during each fifteen-minute observation period. Note how many pupils appear attentive or inattentive at a given time. After some practice you will find it easier to keep in mind your estimate of the number of inattentive students. Average your estimates of attention and record this average using the following scale.

1. Fewer than half of the students are attentive most of the time.
2. One-half to three-fourths of the students appear attentive most of the time; the remainder are attentive only some of the time.
3. Most of the students are attentive, but several (four to six) are attentive only some of the time.
4. Nearly all students are attentive, but a few (one, two, or three) are attentive only some of the time.
5. All of the students are attentive most of the time.

Note—the phrase "most of the time" means at least 75 percent of the time the observer checks the pupils for attentiveness.
Some examples follow from which inattention or attention may be inferred.

Inattention

Moving around the room at an inappropriate time

Reading a book during class discussion

Two students whispering

Sitting with elbows on desk, fingers holding eyelids open

Doodling with a pencil

Laying head on desk

Asking a question unrelated to the activity of the class

Staring fixedly at an object not related to class activity

Attention

Raising hand to volunteer a response

Maintaining eye contact, following teacher's movements

Turning to watch another student who is contributing to the class activity

Working on assigned activity

If a free-activity period, pupils engaged in some task

Teacher Presentation

The teacher presentation scale measures only one type of behavior. The observer's task is to estimate the relative amount of class time occupied by teacher presentation of substantive information. Teacher presentation means substantive (content-oriented) verbal or nonverbal behavior that provides information and does not imply or require pupil response or evaluate pupil behavior. Thus teacher questions, procedural directions, praise, and criticism are not instances of teacher presentation. Lecturing, reading to the class, answering pupil questions, and any other activity in which the teacher gives information are all instances of teacher presentation.

To use this scale, observe the teacher's behavior and note the amount of teacher presentation as compared to the total of all teacher behavior, pupil behavior, and periods of seatwork or other activities in which there is no verbal interaction.

1. Teacher presentation occurs 0–20 percent of the period.
2. Teacher presentation occurs 21–40 percent of the period.
3. Teacher presentation occurs 41–60 percent of the period.
4. Teacher presentation occurs 61–80 percent of the period.
5. Teacher presentation occurs 81–100 percent of the period.

Note that in order for a 5 to be scored, the observation period must be taken up almost entirely by teacher information-giving. Even a small amount of discussion or other activity is likely to cause the rating to be a 4 or less. On the other hand, a score of 1 occurs only when there is a very small amount of teacher information giving (less than 20 percent of the time).

Teacher presentation should not be confused with teacher talk, since the former may be only a small part of the latter. Although a question-and-answer session might contain 70 percent teacher talk, much of it may be teacher questions and evaluation rather than presentation. Be sure to distinguish teacher presentation from other teacher behaviors.

A Qualitative Study Conducted by Nell K. Duke

example of ethnographic work

As mentioned in the body of this chapter, Duke (2000) studied twenty classrooms during first-grade reading instruction in order to determine if, and how, literacy environments differed in high- and low-SES classrooms. During each classroom visit, she took descriptive notes and made preliminary codings of print on classroom walls, other surfaces, and classroom activities that use print in any way. She reported information about text or other uses of print that were (a) directed at students, (b) semipermanent in nature, and (c) displayed in some way, and she coded each text in terms of its level and origin, "text-level codes were letter-digraph, word, phrasal-sentential, and extended. Texts were coded for the highest level at which the majority of the text made meaning" (p. 451). Text origin refers to whether the teacher, student, or parent prepared the text, and in data presented in her research, codes referring to students' involvement in contributing to the text are very important. In her distinctions, she included cases in which a text was authored solely by one or more students, by student(s) and the teacher, by student(s) and a commercial producer, or by student(s), a commercial producer, and/or the teacher. She also coded the extent to which classroom environmental print was actually used and references to the environmental print that anyone in the room mentioned.

Some of her findings are presented in Table 1.3, which shows that high-SES classrooms typically presented students with higher and richer literacy experiences than did low-SES classrooms.

Table 1.3   Summary of Results: In High-SES Classrooms

Feature or Aspect of High-SES Classrooms	Statistical Significance
More books and magazines available on Visit 1	*
More books and magazines newly available on Visits 2–4	**
More books and magazines per student on Visit 1	**
More books and magazines available per student on Visits 2–4	*
More books and magazines displayed on Visit 1	*
More newly available books and magazines displayed on Visits 2–4	**
More uses for the classroom library	***
More classroom environmental print on Visit 1	
More new classroom environmental print on Visits 2–4	
More references to classroom environment print	**
Less class time spent on written language activities	**
A smaller proportion of class time with written language activities	****
A smaller proportion of school time with written language activities	
A greater proportion of time in activities in which print was more central	
A greater amount of time in activities in which print was only moderately central	**
A greater proportion of time with print in domains other than literacy (i.e., across the curriculum)	
A greater amount of time with print in most domains other than literacy	***
More extended texts among classroom environmental print	
A greater proportion of extended texts among classroom environmental print	
More extended texts among written language activities	
A greater proportion of extended texts among written language activities	**
A greater proportion of written language activity time devoted to activities in which students choose their reading material	**
A greater proportion of written language activities time devoted to activities in which students have a high degree of authorship	**
A greater proportion of classroom environmental print text authored at least partly by some students	
A greater proportion of written language activity time with text authored at least partly by students	
A greater proportion of written language activity time reading and writing for audiences beyond the teacher alone.	***

* $p < .10$
** $p < .05$
*** $p < .01$
**** Including time in which some students

Reprinted from Duke, N. (2000, Summer). For the rich it's richer: Print experiences and environments offered to children in very low- and very high-socioeconomic status first-grade classrooms. *American Educational Research Journal, 37*(2), 441–478.

CHAPTER

Teacher Expectations

MIDDLETON HEIGHTS ELEMENTARY

Actual experiments prove: This mysterious force can heighten your intelligence, your competitive ability, and your will to succeed. The secret: Just make a prediction! Read how it works.

The "mysterious force" featured in this blurb from the *Reader's Digest* is the potential of prophecies to become self-fulfilling. The blurb illustrates the wave of hype and enthusiasm that followed publication of a study that appeared to document the power of this "mysterious force" in, of all settings, elementary classrooms.

The Oak School experiment had been conducted by Robert Rosenthal and Lenore Jacobson (1968), who presented its findings in a book entitled *Pygmalion in the Classroom*. These researchers led elementary teachers to believe that certain students in their classes would "bloom" intellectually during the upcoming school year, and as a result, would make stronger achievement gains than would be expected based on their previous records. These predictions supposedly were based on results from a test administered early in the school year. It was a nonverbal intelligence test, but it was described to the teachers as designed to identify students who were about to bloom intellectually. A few students in each class were identified to their teachers as "bloomers." They actually had been selected randomly rather than on the basis of their test scores, yet they did show greater gains than their classmates on achievement tests given at the end of the year (although primarily in the first two grades). Rosenthal and Jacobson interpreted these results as evidence of the self-fulfilling prophecy effects of teachers' expectations. They reasoned that the expectations they created had caused the teachers to treat the "bloomers" differently, in ways that helped them to achieve more that year.

The Oak School findings were widely publicized, and in the process, often exaggerated (as the blurb from the *Reader's Digest* indicates). Knowledgeable researchers, however, were more skeptical. They noted that design and analysis problems suggested the need for caution in interpreting the study's results, and a replication attempt failed to produce the same findings. Even as debate over the original study continued, other researchers began studying teacher expectation effects and related topics, developing a growing literature that included many different kinds of studies (Brophy & Good, 1974). Eventually, this work produced a consensus that teachers' expectations can and sometimes do affect teacher–student interaction and student outcomes, but the processes involved are much more complex than originally believed (Good & Nichols, 2001; Jussim & Harber, 2005; Weinstein, Gregory, & Strambler, 2004).

Evidence of the potential causal effects of teachers' expectations came from experiments like the Oak School study, in which the teachers' expectations were induced by providing them with false information. Some of these experiments used the Oak School model and induced expectations concerning selected students within a single class. Other experiments induced expectations for entire classes (compared to other sections of the same course or previous classes taught by the same teachers). Sometimes these experimental studies failed to produce positive results, apparently because the teachers did not acquire the expectations that the experimenters were trying to induce. Much of the time, however, they were successful in showing that if teachers were led to hold high expectations for certain randomly selected students, these students made stronger achievement gains than their peers. In summary, experiments showed that induced teacher expectations can have causal effects on student achievement gains, although this result is not automatic and in most cases the achievement benefits are relatively modest.

These experiments demonstrated that teachers' expectations could have causal effects on student outcomes, but they did not show how the process plays out in the classroom. This required studies linking teachers' naturally formed expectations of their students with information about their classroom interactions with those students. In this type of study, teachers' expectations are assessed early in the school year before the teachers have had a chance to obtain much firsthand information about their students. For example, Palardy (1969) identified 10 first-grade teachers who believed that the boys in their classes would make as much progress in reading as the girls, and another 14 who expected the girls to do better. He selected five teachers from each group for further study. All taught in middle-class schools, used the same basal reading series, and worked with three reading groups in self-contained classrooms.

The boys and girls did not differ on reading readiness tests given in September. However, on reading achievement tests given in March, boys whose teachers believed that they could achieve as well as girls averaged 96.5, but boys whose teachers did not believe they could perform as well as girls averaged only 89.2. The girls in these classes averaged 96.2 and 96.7, respectively. Thus, boys did achieve less when taught by teachers who did not think that they could progress as rapidly as girls (the girls in these classes did not achieve any more than the girls in the other classes).

Palardy's study illustrated the downside of self-fulfilling prophecy effects of teachers' expectations. Whereas the Oak School study indicated that high expectations can lead to increased achievement, Palardy's study indicated that low expectations can lead to reduced achievement.

Two Types of Teacher Expectation Effects

The teachers in Palardy's study held expectations about the early reading achievement of boys versus girls based on their prior experiences, not on information about the boys and girls in their particular classes that year. However, other studies have collected information about teachers' expectations concerning particular students in their classes after they have had time to learn something about those students, then looked for differential patterns of teacher–student interaction or evidence of effects on student outcomes. These studies have led to a distinction between two major types of teacher expectation effects (Cooper & Good, 1983).

The first is the *self-fulfilling prophecy effect*, in which an originally unfounded expectation nevertheless leads to behavior that causes the expectation to become true. As an example, consider a sixth-grade band teacher who decides that Juanita Hernandez will be one of her best flute players because last year Juanita's older sister Rosa was the best flute player in the city. In fact, Juanita has only average music potential, but inflated expectations based on the family connection lead the teacher to warm up to her right away, express confidence that she will be a good musician, encourage her frequently in practice, and arrange for her to practice at home with Rosa. Chances are that this treatment will make Juanita a top performer before long, even though this probably would not have happened if the teacher had not treated her specially. Juanita's rapid progress can be seen as a self-fulfilling prophecy effect of her teacher's positive expectations and related instructional decisions.

The second type of expectation effect is the *sustaining expectation effect.* Here, the expectations are better founded, in that teachers expect students to sustain previously demonstrated patterns. However, the teachers take these patterns for granted to the point that they fail to see and capitalize on change in students' potential. For example, a second-grade teacher may assign students to the same high, middle, and low reading groups as their first-grade teacher did. However, some students may have improved their reading during the summer, to the point that they ought to be in a higher group.

Sustaining their first-grade group placement reduces the likelihood that the second-grade teacher will notice their improvement, and increases the likelihood that these students will show less reading achievement progress in second grade than they would have if they had been placed in higher groups.

Self-fulfilling prophecy effects are more powerful than sustaining expectation effects because they introduce significant change in student behavior instead of merely minimizing such change by sustaining established patterns. However, subtle sustaining expectation effects occur more frequently than powerful self-fulfilling prophecy effects. This chapter emphasizes self-fulfilling prophecies, but both types of expectation effects are important concepts for examining classrooms.

$\mathscr{H}$ow Expectations Become Self-Fulfilling

Teacher expectation effects in classrooms are simply special cases of the more general principle that any expectation can become self-fulfilling. Sometimes, our expectations about people cause us to treat them in ways that make them respond just as we expected.

For example, look ahead (or back) to your first teaching assignment. Most new teachers want to find out about the school principal with whom they will work. Suppose you spoke to a teacher at the school who said, "Ms. Garcia is wonderful. You'll love working for her. She's warm and pleasant, and she really takes an interest in you. Feel free to come to her with your problems; she's always glad to help." If you heard this about Ms. Garcia, how would you respond to her when you met her? Chances are, you would approach Ms. Garcia with confidence and tell her that you had heard good things about her and were looking forward to working with her.

In contrast, suppose the teacher had said, "Ms. Garcia? Well, she's hard to describe. I guess she's all right, but I don't feel comfortable around her; she makes me nervous. I get the feeling that she doesn't want to talk to me, that I'm irritating her or wasting her time." How might you act when meeting Ms. Garcia after hearing this description? You probably would not look forward to the meeting, and you might be nervous, inhibited, or overly concerned about making a good impression. You might approach her with hesitation, wearing a serious expression or a forced smile, and speak formally.

Now, consider how Ms. Garcia might respond to these two disparate approaches. Chances are, she would respond positively to the first approach. Faced with warmth and genuine-sounding compliments, she likely would respond in kind. Your behavior would put her at ease and cause her to see you as likeable.

But what if you took the nervous, formal approach? Again, Ms. Garcia probably would respond in kind. Your self-presentation likely would make her nervous and formal, if she were not already. She would respond in an equally bland and formal manner, and this probably would be followed by an awkward silence making you both increasingly nervous.

Brophy and Good's Model

The example shows that it is not just the expectation that causes self-fulfillment; it is the behavior that the expectation produces. This behavior then affects other people, making them more likely to act in expected ways. In our early research (Brophy & Good, 1970), we suggested a model to explain teacher expectation effects:

1. Early in the year, the teacher forms differential expectations for student behavior and achievement.
2. Consistent with these differential expectations, the teacher behaves differently toward different students.
3. This treatment tells students something about how they are expected to behave in the classroom and perform on academic tasks.
4. If the teacher's treatment is consistent over time, and if students do not actively resist or change it, it likely will affect their self-concepts, achievement motivation, levels of aspiration, classroom conduct, and interactions with the teacher.
5. These effects will complement and reinforce the teacher's expectations, so that students will come to confirm to those expectations more than they might have otherwise.
6. Ultimately, this will affect achievement and other student outcomes. High-expectation students will be led to achieve at or near their potential, but low-expectation students will not gain as much as they could have gained if taught differently.

Self-fulfilling prophecy effects of teachers' expectations occur only when *all* elements in the model are present. Often, one or more elements is missing. A teacher may not have clear-cut expectations about every student, or those expectations may change continually. Even when expectations are consistent, the teacher may not necessarily communicate them through consistent behavior. In this case, the expectations would not be self-fulfilling even if they turned out to be correct. Finally, students might prevent expectations from becoming self-fulfilling by counteracting their effects or resisting them in a way that makes the teacher change them.

Practice Examples

You can use the following practice examples to improve your understanding of the self-fulfilling prophecy concept. Read each example and determine whether you think a self-fulfilling prophecy is involved. If so, you should be able to identify: (1) the original expectation; (2) behaviors that consistently communicate this expectation in ways that make it more likely to be fulfilled, and (3) evidence that the original expectation has been confirmed. If the example does not contain all three elements, it does not illustrate a self-fulfilling prophecy.

1. Coach Winn knows that Sarah Brown is the daughter of a former professional tennis player. Although he has never seen Sarah play, she predicts, "Sarah will help our team in her sophomore year." In practice sessions, Sarah is treated like all the other team members. She plays the same number of matches and does the same drills, and the coach praises her only when her performance merits it. Sarah is the top-ranked player on the team in her sophomore year and is named to the league's all-star team.

NO
(2 missing)

2. Rick Wilson, a tenth-grade social studies teacher, believes that Antonio Navarro and Julia Suarez can be better students. Although they have earned only average grades, he has seen flashes of insight in them that suggest higher potential. Furthermore, their aptitude test scores are higher than their achievement profiles. However, both students have poor work habits. Neither spends much time working on seatwork assignments, and it is not uncommon for Antonio and Julia to fail to hand in homework two or three times a week. Mr. Wilson believes that both students can do better if he can motivate them to work harder, so he begins to call on them more often and to provide more detailed feedback on their seatwork and homework papers. By December, he has seen no progress. Nevertheless, he continues his efforts, and by May, Antonio is performing at a much higher level, but Julia's classroom behavior and test scores have not improved.

yes for An
no for J (-3)

3. Jean Rogers is giving directions to John Greene, a second-grader who is frequently in trouble. She has no confidence in John's sense of responsibility, so she gives him detailed instructions. "John, take this note to Ms. Turner's room. Remember: Don't make noise in the hall, don't stop to look in other classrooms, and above all, don't go outside." John responds with an obviously pained look, "Ms. Rogers, don't you trust me?"

NO 3

4. As the school year begins, Tom Bloom is assigned to Mary Ruiz, the best counselor in the school. The counselor knows that Tom will probably flunk out. He has low grades and poor writing skills. He is also shy, making it unlikely that he will get to know his instructors well or receive much help from them. Mary tells Tom that he is at risk for academic difficulty and urges him to enroll in the after-school study skills clinic and to devote extra time on weekends to his studies. In addition, she has Tom report to her office once a week. Tom realizes that Mary expects him to have trouble unless he works hard, so he works as hard as he can, ultimately earning two Bs and three Cs.

communicates her expec. in a way which makes it less likely to be true -

5. Bob Graney knows that Beth Blanton will be a problem. He had her older sister the year before and she was uncontrollable. Trying to keep Beth out of trouble, Bob seats her at a table away from the other third-graders in the room. Before long, though, Beth begins to throw things at her peers to attract their attention.

Yes

6. Tim Santoro teaches a consumer business course at Mill Tour High School. He believes that students need and want to perform enjoyable drill activities in class but are not interested in tasks that require higher-order thinking. Therefore, in his taxation unit he emphasizes how to fill out tax forms and quick ways to check for computation errors. His other units also emphasize practical exercises involving much drill and practice but comparatively little analysis (Why are taxes collected? How legitimate is the present system? What alternative taxation plans would yield the same revenue but distribute the burden differently?).

7. Judy Jones, a seventh-grade mathematics teacher, uses tests emphasizing speed rather than ability to group students for instruction. At the beginning of the year she teaches new material to her high group (students who did well on the speed test) but requires her low group to review sixth-grade material in order to build up their speed. However, the slower students work only a few of the review problems because they know how to do them and because they want to listen to the teacher work with the high group so that they will be ready to do the work. Their failure to complete the review problems during class strengthens the teacher's belief that the slower students need still more re-medial work, but these students start to do even fewer problems. Eventually, they even lose interest in listening to the teacher work with the high group (they are beginning to think that they never will get to work on similar problems). By the end of the year, many slow-group students are engaging in disruptive behavior.

yes

8. Melba Robinson is concerned about the peer-group adjustment of Dick Ainge, one of her second-graders. Dick has participated all year long in the races and games conducted during recess, but he began to withdraw from the group in the spring, when she introduced baseball. Although Dick is coordinated well enough, he had not played much baseball and had difficulty hitting and catching the ball. As a result, he was usually one of the last children chosen when teams were selected. After this hap-pened a few times, Dick began to withdraw, claiming that he did not want to play be-cause he had a headache or a sore foot. Melba recognized that embarrassment was the real reason.

To help Dick compensate for his deficiencies and maintain peer status, Melba began allowing him to serve as the umpire for ball games. This gave him an important, active role that she reinforced by praising Dick and calling other children's attention to his umpiring. In private contacts, she reassured Dick that he should not feel bad because he was not playing, because there could not be a ball game without an umpire.

yes – she be haved to keep Dick from improving

9. Delpit (1995) reported the following actual event:

> One evening I receive a telephone call from Terrence's mother, who is near tears. A single parent, she has struggled to put her academically talented fourteen-year-old African Amer-ican son in a predominately white private school. As an involved parent, she has spoken to each of his teachers several times during the first few months of school, all of whom assured her that Terrence was doing "just fine." When the first quarter's report cards were issued, she observed with dismay a report filled with Cs and Ds. She immediately went to talk to his teachers. When asked how they could have said he was doing fine when his grades were so low, each of them gave her some version of the same answer. "Why are you so upset? For him, Cs are great. You shouldn't try to push him so much." (p. xiii)

yes – teachers assumed T. was not capable of more

Analysis of Examples

Let us see how well you were able to identify self-fulfilling prophecies. We'll share our reactions to the first four examples. Compare your responses with those of your class-mates for examples 5 to 9.

In Case 1, Coach Winn's original expectation about Sarah is fulfilled. However, there is no evidence that the coach caused this through special behavior toward Sarah.

Thus, the coach's prediction did not act as a self-fulfilling prophecy, even though it was accurate.

Case 2 is a self-fulfilling prophecy for Antonio but not for Julia, even though the teacher believed that both students could do better. Rick Wilson's determined teaching apparently was successful in changing Antonio's perceptions and beliefs ("I can do math," "I should do it," "I want to"), thus improving his effort and achievement. However, Mr. Wilson's behavior did not improve Julia's performance (perhaps she viewed his increased questioning as nagging or as a lack of confidence in her ability).

In Case 3, the teacher gives John explicit instructions because she fears that he will misbehave. She subconsciously communicates this expectation through her behavior, and he picks it up. However, there is no evidence that his behavior changes accordingly, so this is not an example of a self-fulfilling prophecy. If Jean Rogers were to continue to treat John this way, though, he might begin to behave as she expects. At this point, her expectation would become self-fulfilling.

Case 4 is especially instructive. The counselor fears that Tom will flunk, and she communicates this expectation. Tom gets the message, but he reacts by working hard to prove himself. He ends up doing well, despite Mary's original expectation. This occurs because Mary communicates serious concern but follows up with attempts to deal with the problem (referring Tom to the study skills clinic, calling for extra study time, scheduling regular counseling appointments). In effect, the counselor works against her own expectation by engaging in compensation strategies designed to prevent the feared outcome. If, instead, she had communicated hopelessness and had done nothing to change the situation, her expectation probably would have been fulfilled.

Goldenberg (1992) presented two case studies that relate to the story of our fictional Tom Bloom. One was remarkably parallel, describing a student whose teacher feared failure from her but prevented it by working hard with her and enlisting special help at home. The other case was the opposite of the first. Here, the teacher had confidence that the student was bright and well-motivated, so she didn't get concerned when the student began to skip assignments and perform less capably. As a result, this student's achievement level kept slipping as the year progressed. By the time the teacher realized what was happening, it was too late to do much about it.

Don't assume bright students don't need attention →

*H*ow Teachers Form Expectations

Although research has focused on many topics including societal expectations for youth and their achievement (Nichols & Good, 2004), most research has focused on teachers' expectations for their students' <u>achievement</u> rather than for other student outcomes (motivation, conduct, social adjustment), and most has focused on expectations about individual students rather than groups or whole classes. Therefore, we will begin with research on teachers' expectations for individual students' achievement, considered in terms of the steps in the Brophy and Good model.

The model begins by stating that teachers form differential achievement expectations at the beginning of the school year. Investigators have studied the nature of the information that teachers use to form these expectations and the degree to which they tend to be accurate. Some of these studies have been experiments in which subjects (not necessarily teachers) are given only carefully controlled information about fictional students and asked to make predictions. For example, they might be given cumulative records containing identical test scores, grades, and comments by previous teachers, but half of the records would be accompanied by a picture of a white child and the other half by a picture of a black child. Such experiments have shown that expectations can be affected significantly by information about race, socioeconomic status, ethnicity, gender, physical appearance, past achievement, track or group placement, classroom conduct, or other personal characteristics (Jones, 1990). These findings are not surprising, given the limited information that experimental subjects had available.

factors which affect initial expectations

However, studies focusing on actual teachers' expectations concerning actual students in their classes suggest a much more positive picture. First, teachers do not passively accept phony information if it is contradicted by other information they have from more credible sources or from their own tests, assignments, or interactions with their students. Furthermore, these studies usually do not reveal much evidence of grossly biased judgments. For example, most impressions that teachers form from interacting with their students are based primarily on the students' participation in academic activities and performance on tests and assignments, not on gender, race, or other status characteristics.

teachers' primary source of expectations

In summary, practicing teachers usually develop mostly accurate expectations about their students, and usually correct the inaccurate ones as more information becomes available. This limits the possibilities for significant self-fulfilling prophecy effects (which are based on false or unjustified expectations), but it still leaves a lot of room for sustaining expectation effects.

(1) Form expectations
(2) communicate expectations
(3) student percieves dif. treatment

How Teachers Communicate Expectations to Students

The next step in the Brophy and Good model postulates that teachers communicate differential expectations to students by treating them differently. For example, relative to their treatment of low-expectation students in parallel situations, teachers might provide more support for the achievement progress of high-expectation students by creating warmer social-emotional relationships with them, offering them richer and more challenging learning opportunities, or providing them with more opportunities to pursue their own learning interests or get high-quality feedback on their progress. In fact, observational studies have documented that teachers often treat high versus low achievers differently in these and other ways, some of them quite subtle:

- Waiting less time for low achievers to answer a question (before giving the answer or calling on someone else)
- Giving low achievers answers or calling on someone else rather than trying to improve their responses (by giving clues or repeating or rephrasing questions)

- Inappropriate reinforcement: rewarding inappropriate behavior or incorrect answers by low achievers
- Criticizing low achievers more often for failure
- Praising low achievers less often for success
- Failing to give feedback to the public responses of low achievers
- Calling on low achievers less often to respond to questions, or asking them only easier, nonanalytic questions
- Generally paying less attention to low achievers or interacting with them less frequently
- Seating low achievers farther away from the teacher
- Demanding less from low achievers (e.g., teaching less, gratuitous praise, excessive offers of help)
- Interacting with low achievers more privately than publicly, and monitoring and structuring their activities more closely
- Differential administration or grading of tests or assignments, in which high achievers but not low achievers are given the benefit of the doubt in borderline cases
- Less friendly interactions with low achievers, including less smiling and fewer other nonverbal indicators of support
- Briefer and less informative feedback to questions from low achievers
- Less eye contact and other nonverbal communication of attention and responsiveness (forward lean, positive head nodding) in interaction with low achievers
- Less use of effective but time-consuming instructional methods with low achievers when time is limited
- Less acceptance and use of low achievers' ideas
- Exposing low achievers to an impoverished curriculum (overly limited and repetitive content, emphasis on factual recitation rather than on lesson-extending discussion, emphasis on drill and practice tasks rather than application and higher-level thinking tasks).

Several points should be made about these forms of differential teacher treatment. First, they do not occur in all classrooms. Teachers vary considerably in how much they differentiate in their treatment of students toward whom they hold different expectations.

Second, even teachers who differentiate consistently may be unaware of their behavior, thinking that they provide comparable levels of support to all of their students.

Third, some of these differences in teacher–student interaction patterns are due mostly or even entirely to the students rather than the teacher (e.g., if some students' contributions to lessons are mostly of low quality, it is difficult for the teacher to use their ideas frequently).

Fourth, some forms of differential treatment may represent appropriate individualizing of instruction rather than inappropriate projection of negative expectations. Low achievers appear to require more structuring of their activities and closer monitoring of their work, for example, and it makes sense at times to interact with them more privately than publicly. Thus, one should not assume that the forms of differential treatment described above are never appropriate. They are danger signals, however, especially if the differentiation is significant and occurs on many dimensions rather than one or two. Such a pattern suggests that the teacher is merely going through the motions of instructing low-expectation students, without genuinely trying to encourage their achievement progress.

Further, some forms of differential treatment directly affect students' opportunity to learn. If low achievers get less content and less feedback, they are almost certain to make less progress than high achievers, regardless of whether they are aware of this differential treatment. In addition to these expectation effects that occur directly through differences in exposure to content, indirect effects may occur through teacher behavior that affects students' self-concepts, motivation, performance expectations, or attributions for success or failure. This brings us to Step 3 of the Brophy and Good model, which postulates that students perceive differential treatment and its implications about what is expected of them.

Students' Perceptions of Differential Teacher Treatment

Students usually are aware of their teachers' differential patterns of interaction with different students. Even elementary students report that they see their teachers projecting higher achievement expectations and offering more opportunity and choice to high achievers, while structuring the activities of low achievers more closely and providing them with both more help and more negative feedback about their academic work and classroom conduct. Weinstein and McKown (1998) found that students noted differences on eight dimensions:

students

Inputs to the educational environment. (1) The ways in which students are grouped for instruction ("and so you know they're smart cause they're in the highest group"); (2) the tasks and materials through which the curriculum is enacted ("they read more books like thick books"); (3) the motivational strategies that teachers use to engage students ("like today, the teacher gave me an award saying I was the second top in the class"); and (4) the role that students play in directing their own learning ("the teacher doesn't actually work with [the smart kids] because they know how to do their stuff").

Educational outputs and feedback. (5) How students are evaluated ("a very soft voices lets you know you're doing well"), which includes beliefs about ability, the response opportunities afforded (and hence the achievement products obtained), and the assessments provided.

Climate factors at multiple levels. (6) The quality of classroom relationships ("not-so-smart girls can't play with the smart girls because smart girls just act like they ignore 'em"); (7) the quality of parent–classroom relationships ("The mother and father don't teach them anything at home"); and (8) the quality of classroom-school relationships ("the way you know a person is smart, Ms. _____ always picks them to go different places").

Synthesizing findings from student interviews and classroom observation studies, Good and Weinstein (1986) produced the summary shown in Table 2.1. To the extent that such differential patterns of interaction with students who differ in expectation or achievement level exist in a teacher's classroom, expectation effects on students' achievement are likely to occur, both directly through opportunity to learn and indirectly through differential treatment that affects their self-concepts or motivation.

Table 2.1   General Dimensions of Teachers' Communication of Differential Expectations and Selected Examples

	Students believed to be MORE capable have:	Students believed to be LESS capable have:
Task Environment		
Curriculum, procedures, task definition, pacing, quality of environment	More opportunity to perform publicly on meaningful tasks	Less opportunity to perform publicly, especially on meaningful tasks (supplying alternate endings to a story versus learning to pronounce a word correctly)
	More opportunity to think	Less opportunity to think, analyze (since much work is aimed at practice)
Group practices	More assignments that deal with comprehension, understanding (in higher-ability groups)	Less choice on curriculum assignments—more work on drill-like assignments
Locus of responsibility	More autonomy (more choice in assignments, fewer interruptions)	Less autonomy (frequent teacher monitoring of work, frequent interruptions)
Feedback and evaluation practices	More opportunity for self-evaluation	Less opportunity for self-evaluation
Motivational strategies	More honest/contingent feedback	Less honest/more gratuitous/less contingent feedback
Quality of teacher relationships	More respect for the learner as an individual with unique interests and needs	Less respect for the learner as an individual with unique interests and needs

Source: Goods, T., & Weinstein, R. (1986). Teacher expectations: A framework for exploring classrooms. In K.K. Zumwalt (Ed.), *Improving Teaching*. Reprinted by permission of the Association for Supervision and Curriculum Development.

*F*actors That Affect Expectation Communication

Context

School contexts vary in the opportunities they provide for differential teacher–student interaction, and thus for expectation effects to occur.

Grade Level.   Expectation effects are more likely in the early grades, before students' records of achievement and their academic self-concepts and attribution patterns become firmly established. In a review of experiments on induced teacher expectations, Raudenbush (1984) found that effects were stronger in grades 1 and 2 than in grades 3 through 6, then became strong again at grade 7, when students shifted to junior high school. In general, stronger effects might be expected whenever students are new to an institution and their instructors (Jussim & Harber, 2005).

[handwritten margin note: ✓ The effect a teacher's expectations has on student — elementary; new + 1 on 1]

Also, elementary students have the same teacher all day and frequently interact with that teacher individually, but secondary students see most teachers for an hour or less per day and do not spend much time interacting with them individually. Thus, there are more opportunities for expectations to be communicated, and in more different ways, in the elementary grades.

Time of Year.   Greater expectation effects on individual students are likely early in the year. As the year progresses, teachers begin to pay less attention to within-class differences between individuals and more attention to the progress of the class as a whole, adjusting the pace of instruction to suit its potential as they have come to perceive it (Cooper & Good, 1983).

[handwritten margin note: later in year teacher less concerned w/ differences w/in class]

Subject Matter.   Smith (1980) reported larger expectation effects on reading achievement than math achievement. This is probably because a greater variety of grouping and instructional practices is used in teaching reading than in teaching math, so there is more room for teachers to translate expectations into differential treatment of students.

[handwritten margin note: reading > math ...]

Nature of the Learning Environment.   The potential for expectation effects, especially the undesirable effects of low expectations, is greatest in classrooms that feature uniform rather than multiple goals, a narrow rather than a broad range of activity structures, norm-referenced achievement standards, and a competitive atmosphere (Good & Nichols, 2001; Perry & Weinstein, 1998; Weinstein, Gregory, & Strambler, 2004).

Teachers' Personal Characteristics

Some teachers are likely to show sizeable self-fulfilling prophecy effects, especially negative effects that reduce student achievement gains. In this regard, Brophy and Good (1974) identified three types of teachers.

Proactive teachers are guided by their own beliefs about what is appropriate in setting goals for the class as a whole and for individual students. If they set realistic goals

overreactive — reactive — proactive
limited by expectations \ *use expectations as a tool*

and have the needed skills, they are likely to help their students fulfill the expectations associated with these goals. Proactive teachers are the most likely to have positive expectation effects on their students.

At the other extreme are *overreactive* teachers who develop rigid, stereotyped perceptions of students based on students' prior records and on first impressions of their behavior. Overreactive teachers tend to treat students as stereotypes rather than as individuals, and they are the most likely to have negative expectation effects.

In between these extremes are *reactive* teachers who hold expectations lightly and adjust them in response to new feedback. Reactive teachers have minimal expectation effects on their students, tending to maintain existing differences between high and low achievers (although these differences will increase slightly because of different behaviors by students themselves that the teachers do not compensate for).

Babad (1985) found that expectation effects are more likely in classrooms taught by "high-bias" teachers who tend toward conventionalism, authoritarianism, or dogmatism. Related personal traits probably include: (1) a tendency to maintain expectations rigidly once they are formed; (2) a teacher role definition that minimizes the teacher's personal responsibility for ensuring students' learning; (3) viewing student ability as unitary and fixed rather than as multiple and open to improvement; (4) a tendency to notice and comment on the differences rather than similarities between students, and to take these into account when planning instruction; (5) a tendency to rationalize teaching failures rather than recognize and overcome them; and (6) poorly developed classroom management and instructional skills, which give the teacher more to be defensive about and thus more to rationalize.

These personal characteristics of teachers interact with their beliefs about appropriate curriculum and instruction to determine the nature and strength of expectation effects on the achievement of individual students in their classes. Teachers with all of the above-listed characteristics, for example, would tend to have powerful (and mostly negative) expectation effects, including self-fulfilling prophecy effects, on substantial numbers of their students if they were teaching in the primary grades using approaches that maximized the time that they spent with individuals and small groups but minimized the time spent with the class as a whole. In contrast, these same teachers might have only minor sustaining expectation effects if they were teaching mathematics to high school students and relying exclusively on a whole-class approach that provided the same instruction, tasks, and requirements to all students and minimized the time spent with individuals.

Students' Personal Characteristics

Individual differences among students also affect the size of teacher expectation effects. Some students are more sensitive than others to voice tones or other subtle communication cues, so they may infer teachers' expectations more often and accurately. Younger and more teacher-dependent students may also be more susceptible to teacher expectation effects.

Student motivation is treated comprehensively in Chapter 5, but we focus here on two special topics related to expectation effects: the struggles of persistently low achievers and the problems experienced by members of stereotyped groups.

The Struggles of Low Achievers.   Schooling presents special difficulties for students who consistently get low grades even when they apply themselves. Some will persist in trying hard to learn, remaining willing to ask questions, seek help, and put in extra work. However, accumulated frustration leads many others to begin to withdraw effort, copy or turn in incomplete work rather than seek help, and affect an air of apathy or disdain for schooling. This is especially likely if low achievers perceive that their teachers are just going through the motions with them, offering them an impoverished curriculum, and communicating low expectations in other ways. Many low achievers gradually become more and more passive in classrooms, a reaction that is understandable for two reasons (Good, 1981).

First, many teachers call on low achievers less often, wait less time for them to respond, give them answers rather than try to improve their poor responses, and praise fewer of their successes but criticize more of their failures. Given that low achievers are less likely to be able to answer correctly in the first place and that their mistakes occur in public, they must bear unusually high levels of ambiguity and risk when they participate actively in lessons. Under such circumstances, remaining passive is a good strategy for them.

Secondly, low achievers must adjust to more varied teacher treatment. Their teachers are likely to treat them inconsistently over the school year, trying one approach after another in an attempt to find a strategy that works. Also, they are more likely to have more than one teacher (if they are involved in compensatory or special education), which means exposure to more contrasting strategies. One teacher might call on them frequently in an attempt to get them to participate, while another mostly avoids them. One might rarely praise their successes, while another praises almost everything they do, even responses that are not correct. Faced with such conflicting treatment, low achievers may learn to avoid initiating and wait for the teacher to structure their behavior.

Stereotype Threat.   Students who belong to stereotyped groups may perform below their abilities on tasks that their group is expected to do poorly on, especially if they are reminded of their group membership before or during the task (Steele, Spencer, & Aronson, 2002). For example, African American students are usually aware that African Americans tend to score lower than European Americans on tests of intelligence or academic achievement, leading to stereotyped expectations that African American students will perform poorly on such tests (Brown, 1998). Even subtle reminders of this expectation can cause African American students to become concerned about confirming this stereotype when they take tests, and this concern can distract them from concentrating on meeting the test's demands. For example, Steele and Aronson (1995) showed that African American students did less well on a test if it was described as diagnostic of intellectual ability or if they were asked to identify their race immediately before taking the test.

Stereotype threat phenomena can occur with respect to members of any group who might be expected to perform poorly in a particular domain. For example, reductions in performance have been demonstrated for Latino students and students from lower socioeconomic status backgrounds on general achievement tests, for women relative to men on mathematics tests, for men relative to women on affective processing tasks, for

European American students relative to Asian American students on mathematics tests, and for white athletes relative to black athletes on an ostensible test of natural athletic ability (Steele, Spencer, & Aronson, 2002).

wise teachers:

In considering the implications of these findings, Cohen, Steele, and Ross (1999) suggested that wise teachers will create optimistic relationships with their students, focusing not on academic problems and failures but on encouraging students to feel a sense of belonging in the classroom and helping them to reach realistic achievement goals. When interacting with students, and especially when giving them feedback on their work, such teachers will combine articulation of high standards with expressions of confidence that the students can meet these standards if they apply themselves. Other authors who have written about effective teaching of minority and at-risk students similarly emphasize combining a warm and welcoming orientation toward these students and their families with persistent and determined efforts to help them achieve their potentials.

Several teams of investigators have successfully counteracted the power of stereotype threat to reduce students' performance on tests. Some addressed the problem directly by teaching vulnerable students about stereotype threat as a way to inoculate them against its effects (Johns, Schmader, & Martens, 2005). Others used less direct methods involving reminding students that they were capable learners in the domain being tested, emphasizing that ability in the domain is developed through learning efforts rather than being fixed, or leading them to attribute their anxiety about the testing situation to its novelty or some other external factor rather than their membership in the stereotyped group (Croizet et al., 2001).

Group, Class, and School Expectation Effects

So far, we have been discussing expectation effects on individual students in the same class. However, expectation effects can operate on groups, classes, or entire schools.

Group Effects

If teachers group by achievement level within class, placement into a high group is likely to accelerate a student's achievement, but placement into a low group is likely to retard it (Weinstein, 1976). Teachers tend to give their higher groups longer reading assignments, to provide more time for discussion of the story, to ask more higher-level comprehension questions, and to be generally more demanding with them than with low groups. They are quicker to interrupt low-group students when they make reading mistakes, and more likely to just give them the word or prompt them with phonetic cues rather than to offer semantic or syntactic cues that might help them intuit the word from its context. In general, low groups tend to get less interesting instruction, less emphasis on meaning, and more rote drill and practice (Allington, 1991; Good & Marshall, 1984; Ross et al., 1994).

Another factor is that low groups contain more immature, inattentive students who frequently disrupt lesson continuity. Compared with students in high groups, students in low groups spend more time off-task and are more likely to call out words or answers that are supposed to be supplied by other students (Eder, 1981).

Class Effects as Related to Teachers' Self-Efficacy Perceptions

People who enter achievement situations with self-efficacy perceptions believe that they can accomplish what the situation calls for, whereas people who lack these perceptions are unsure that they can or are even convinced that they cannot (Bandura, 1997). This generalization applies to teachers' perceptions of their chances of achieving goals such as managing their classrooms successfully, motivating their students to learn, and helping them to make strong achievement gains.

believe you can — it will help it be so!

Teachers who lack a healthy sense of efficacy tend to believe either that no teachers could succeed in their situation (because of their students' limited abilities, poor home cultures, antischool peer cultures, etc.) or that some teachers might be able to succeed but they personally cannot. In contrast, teachers with a sense of efficacy believe that they are capable of meeting their students' needs, even though it may be necessary to augment or even replace the typical instructional materials or teaching methods in order to do so. These teachers tend to be more confident and at ease, more positive (praising, smiling) and less negative (criticizing, punishing) in their interactions with their students, more successful in managing their classrooms, less defensive, more accepting of student disagreement or challenges, and more effective in stimulating student achievement gains (Ashton & Webb, 1986; Brophy & Evertson, 1976; Rimm-Kaufman & Sawyer, 2004; Ross, 1998).

Consequently, teachers' sense of efficacy, and the beliefs, expectations, and behaviors that accompany it, may exert expectation effects on entire classes of students. Some of these are connected to the teachers' subject-matter knowledge and preferences. For example, the time that teachers allocate to different subjects may be related to their attitudes toward those subjects. Schmidt and Buchmann (1983) found that teachers who enjoyed teaching reading more than writing gave more emphasis to reading in their language arts instruction, and teachers who enjoyed mathematics spent 50 percent more time on the subject each week than teachers who did not enjoy it.

Even if teachers spend similar time on a subject, they may differ in the learning opportunities they offer their students, depending on their beliefs about the students' aptitude, their instructional goals, and their subject-matter knowledge. Some may emphasize concept development, others may emphasize skills practice, and still others may focus on applications (Freeman & Porter, 1989). When teachers are knowledgeable about a subject, they tend to teach it with confidence, using a variety of instructional approaches and engaging in a lot of discussion with their students. When they are less familiar with the subject, they tend to lean on the textbook and use more worksheets and other lower level seatwork assignments (Carlsen, 1991).

positive effect of being knowledgeable about subject

Class-level expectation effects related to teachers' beliefs about students' aptitudes have been shown in studies of how teachers taught their high- and low-track classes. In low-track classes, the teachers were less clear about objectives, introduced content less clearly or completely, made fewer attempts to relate the content to students' interests or

Difference between high + low track classes

backgrounds, and were less reasonable in their work standards, less consistent in their discipline, less receptive to student input, and less likely to assign independent projects or introduce high-level and integrative concepts (Evertson, 1982; Oakes et al., 1993; Oakes, 2005). In general, the teachers tended to plan more thoroughly for the high-track classes than for the low-track classes.

Teachers who are assigned to low-track classes or who work in schools in which most students are relatively low achievers need to guard against slipping into impoverished patterns of curriculum and instruction. Good and Weinstein (1986) offered the following five suggestions for improving classrooms that feature low expectations and boring, unchallenging routines.

1. Broaden the goals of lessons and activities. Students need to practice and master basic content and skills, but they also need application opportunities. Something is wrong if students are usually working on phonics exercises but rarely reading, often practicing penmanship or copying spelling words but rarely writing, or regularly working on arithmetic computations but rarely trying to formulate or solve problems.

2. Pay attention to students' ideas and interests and encourage them to play a larger role in assessing their own performance. Students are often more passive and teacher-dependent in their learning than they need to be.

3. Increase opportunities for students to participate actively and use materials in meaningful ways. Teacher-led lessons should require more than just quiet listening, and follow-up assignments should require more than just working through highly structured practice exercises.

4. Besides asking factual questions, ask questions that require students to think, analyze, synthesize, or evaluate ideas. Include questions that can be answered at a variety of levels from a variety of points of view, so that a greater range of students can participate and experience success.

5. Focus on the positive aspects of learning. Encourage, reinforce, and note group progress toward learning goals. Minimize public comparisons of students with one another, criticism of the class as a whole, or suggestions that material to be learned is overly difficult or unrewarding.

School Effects

High expectations and commitment to bringing about student achievement are part of a pattern of attitudes, beliefs, and behaviors that characterize schools which are successful in maximizing students' learning gains. Teachers in effective schools not only hold higher expectations but act on them by setting goals expressed as minimally acceptable levels of achievement. They view student failure as a challenge and require students to redo failed work (with individualized help as needed) rather than writing them off or referring them to remedial classes (Good & Brophy, 1986; Teddlie & Stringfield, 1993).

Expectation Effects on Students' Personal and Social Development

This chapter is focused on teacher expectation effects on student achievement, but teachers' expectations also can shape students' personal and social development in the school setting. Students' beliefs, attitudes, expectations, and behavior can be socialized, both through deliberate actions and through other behaviors that communicate teachers' beliefs, attitudes, or expectations. Thus, the success of a teacher's classroom management efforts is determined in part by expectations communicated about student conduct; the classroom atmosphere depends in part on expectations communicated about student cooperation and interpersonal relationships; and student responsiveness to lessons and assignments is affected by expectations communicated about the meaningfulness, interestingness, or utility of school activities.

For example, when introducing classroom learning activities, teachers may say things that affect the ways in which their students perceive and respond to these activities. If the introductions imply that the activities are enjoyable, interesting, or otherwise worthwhile, students are likely to engage willingly. This is not true, however, for activities that teachers introduce in ways that suggest negative expectations (i.e., that they will be very difficult or unenjoyable) (Brophy et al., 1983).

Teachers who consistently communicate the expectation that "We're all in this together, learning and helping one another to learn," will tend to engender a positive, collaborative classroom atmosphere. In contrast, teachers who act more as critical evaluators than as supportive enablers of student learning are likely to end up with classrooms featuring passive alienation or destructive competitiveness.

Making Expectations Work for You

Expectations can be limiting and counterproductive, especially for the teachers we have described as overreactive. For proactive teachers, expectations can become tools for enhancing the effectiveness of their professional practice. So how can teachers avoid having negative expectation effects on their students and learn to make their expectations work for them?

You might think that you can avoid expectation problems by not forming any expectations at all. However, expectations cannot be suppressed or avoided. When events occur repeatedly, we come to expect them and see them as normal. Thus, teachers form expectations by interacting with their students, even if they try to avoid other sources of information, such as by refusing to read cumulative records. Where information about students comes from is not as important as whether the information is accurate and, especially, how it is used. Accurate information can be useful in planning to meet students' individual needs.

Should teachers have only highly positive expectations? This idea is appealing because confidence and determination are important teacher qualities, and a can-do attitude helps cut problems down to workable size. However, positive expectations should not be carried to the point of distorting reality. Large individual differences in learning abilities and interests cannot be eliminated through wishful thinking. Teachers will only frustrate themselves and their students if they set unrealistically high standards that students cannot reach.

Expectations should be *appropriate*, given students' current capabilities, and they should be accompanied by appropriate instructional behavior; that is, planned learning experiences that move students through a good curriculum at a pace that fosters continued success and improvement. Unfortunately, it can be difficult to determine what are appropriate expectations, either for the class as a whole or for individual students. We do know that expectations are often set too low, especially for students considered at risk for school failure. Interventions motivated by concerns about low expectations have achieved positive results through mechanisms such as reducing ability grouping or tracking, placing eighth-graders in pre-algebra classes rather than general mathematics classes (Mason et al., 1992), enabling students from inner-city schools to enroll in suburban schools (Kaufman & Rosenbaum, 1992), or working with teachers to provide a richer and more challenging curriculum for all students in their school but especially lower achievers (Mehan, 1997; Weinstein et al., 1991; Weinstein, Gregory, & Strambler, 2004).

Concerns about low expectations also have motivated recent state and federal initiatives featuring emphasis on standards and high-stakes tests, including the No Child Left Behind legislation. However, these initiatives appear to be doing more harm than good. Because the stakes attached to test scores are so high, schools have been mobilizing to boost their students' test scores, which is not the same thing as improving the quality of their education. Students are now getting a narrower curriculum in two respects. First, more time is being allocated to subjects included in the testing program (usually literacy and mathematics), which means that less time is being allocated to science, social studies, and other curriculum strands. Second, much of what occurs in literacy and mathematics classes is test preparation. The result is an impoverished, low-level, repetitive curriculum rather than an enriched one.

There also are reasons for concern that publication of test scores in newspapers, labeling of schools as failing, and an overall punitive approach, combined with unrealistically high success criteria, are creating expectation problems of their own. Teachers' sense of efficacy as professionals and students' sense of efficacy as learners are likely to suffer when their school is publicly labeled as failing. The increases in teacher morale problems, student dropout rates, and other "collateral damage" from the recent high-stakes testing emphasis underscore the fact that stating unrealistically high expectations and then trying to force people to meet them is not a solution to expectation problems (Thomas, 2005).

So what might teachers do to avoid both needlessly low expectations and inappropriately high ones? We think it is helpful to frame expectations within the context of establishing appropriate curricular goals and intended outcomes for a class as a whole, rather than within a context of grouping or labeling students according to their supposed ability levels or learning potentials. In short, try to determine what big ideas, skills, values, and dispositions are most important for students at the grade level to learn, then focus on ensuring that this learning is accomplished. Focusing on what they want their students to learn helps teachers to mobilize their resources and continue to move forward, whereas dwelling on students' supposed limitations leads to discouragement and reduced commitment. We also recommend paying attention to students' full range of abilities, keeping expectations flexible and current, and emphasizing the positive.

In Developing Expectations, Consider Students' Full Range of Abilities

Scores on intelligence and achievement tests provide only partial information about students' abilities. Students also possess other forms of intellectual aptitude that they can bring to bear as learning resources if the forms of curriculum and instruction in use in the classroom allow them to do so. For example, Gardner (1999) argued that people possess at least eight types of intellectual abilities in varying degrees:

1. *Linguistic.* Sensitivity to the meaning and order of words and ability to make varied use of language; exhibited by translators and poets
2. *Logical-mathematical.* Ability to handle chains of reasoning and recognize patterns; exhibited by mathematicians and scientists
3. *Spatial.* Ability to perceive the visual world accurately and re-create or transform it based on those perceptions; exhibited by sculptors and architects
4. *Musical.* Sensitivity to pitch, melody, rhythm, and tone; exhibited by composers and singers
5. *Bodily-kinesthetic.* Ability to use the body and handle objects skillfully; exhibited by athletes, dancers, and surgeons
6. *Interpersonal.* Ability to notice and make distinctions among other people; exhibited by politicians, salespeople, and religious leaders
7. *Intrapersonal.* Ability to understand one's own feelings and emotional life; exhibited by therapists and social workers
8. *Naturalists.* Ability to discriminate among living things and other aspects of the natural world

Gardner noted that the curricula and tests traditionally emphasized in schooling have focused on linguistic and logical-mathematical abilities to the relative neglect of the others. He advocated better-rounded curricula and more use of project learning methods that would allow students to develop their complete range of abilities and bring them to bear as learning resources. Others also have stressed the need for teachers to socialize beliefs that ability can be improved, to recognize different types of abilities as important, and to avoid relying only on math and reading as sources for making judgments about "good" students (Perry & Weinstein, 1998; Wanlass, 2000).

Keep Expectations Flexible and Current

Expectations based on recurring classroom events can be very compelling. If Susan regularly fails to do homework assignments, her teacher may gradually stop trying to change Susan's work habits and begin to accept her poor performance as "what is to be expected." To avoid falling into this rut, teachers need to keep their expectations flexible and bear in mind their role as instructors. If expectations are allowed to become too strong or too fixed, they can distort perception and behavior.

Once formed, expectations tend to be self-perpetuating because they guide both perceptions and behavior. When we expect to find something, we are much more likely to see it than when we are not looking for it. This is part of the reason why teachers often fail to notice the strengths of students who are frequent discipline problems. When expecting misbehavior, teachers may miss many of these students' academic accomplishments that someone else might have noticed and reinforced.

The fact that a student could not do something yesterday does not mean that he or she cannot do it today, but the teacher will not find out unless the student is given a chance. Expectations stress the stable, unchanging aspects of the world, but teachers are change agents trying to make students different from what they are today. Therefore, teachers must keep their expectations in perspective. To the extent that expectations are negative, they represent problems to be solved, not definitions of reality to which a teacher must adapt.

Emphasize the Positive

Teachers should form and project expectations that are as positive as they can be while still remaining realistic. Such expectations should represent genuine beliefs about what can be achieved and therefore should be taken seriously as goals toward which to work in instructing students. Students who are perceived as having less ability suffer from having a redundant curriculum in which the same topics are presented again and again. Bored by the sameness, they gradually invest less energy, which leads their teachers to think that they need even more structure and smaller steps.

Delpit (1995) makes a similar point, noting that because teachers assume deficits in some students, they teach less to those students instead of more:

> We say we believe that all children can learn, but few of us really believe it. Teacher education usually focuses on research that links failure and socioeconomic status, failure and cultural differences, and failure and single-parent households. It is hard to believe that these children can possibly be successful after their teachers have been so thoroughly exposed to so much negative indoctrination. When teachers receive that kind of education, there is a tendency to assume deficits in students rather than to locate and teach to strengths. To counter this tendency, educators must have knowledge of children's lives outside of school so as to recognize their strengths. (p. 172)

Steele (1992), who has written extensively on issues concerning the schooling of African American students, expresses the problem this way:

> The challenge and the promise of personal fulfillment, not remediation (under whatever guise), should guide the education of these students. Their present skills should be taken into account, and they should be moved along at a pace that is demanding but doesn't defeat them. Their ambition should never be scaled down, but should instead be guided to inspiring goals even when extraordinary dedication is called for. Frustration will be less crippling than alienation. Peer psychology is everything: remediation defeats, challenge strengthens—affirming their potential, crediting them with their achievements, inspiring them. (p. 78)

In conclusion, learn to think in terms of stretching students' minds by stimulating them and encouraging them to achieve as much as they can, not in terms of "protecting" them from failure or embarrassment. Help them to develop self-appraisal skills to understand their learning more fully, as well as learn to regulate their thinking, effort, and affect in order to stay more focused on the work and its "doability" rather than on extraneous factors such as the amount of time it will take or its level of difficulty (see Dembo & Eaton, 2000; Paris & Paris, 2001).

SUMMARY

In this chapter we have discussed the positive and negative effects that our expectations can have on student learning. Student expectations are important because low expectations can hinder their performance through the types of questions we ask and the types of assignments and responsibilities we provide. Similarly, high expectations can have useful effects on students' learning. We have emphasized that high or low expectations are not magically self-fulfilling—both because teachers may not communicate their expectations consistently, and because students may not accept them.

We have provided an explicit model for examining how teachers may communicate expectations to individuals, groups, and to whole classes of students. Detailed examples are provided to illustrate the diverse ways that expectation cues are communicated. Research has focused primarily on how teachers communicate differential expectations to individual students in whole class settings, although there is research on differential opportunities for students who are assigned to high- or low-ability groups. In general, students who are perceived to be higher in ability receive more challenge, scaffolding, and academic responsibility than those students who are believed to have less ability.

We have noted that there are individual differences in both teachers and students in terms of how expectations are expressed and perceived. Some teachers are more likely to communicate low expectations than are others, and some students are more susceptible to teacher influences than are other students. We end the chapter by noting that our expectations for student performance can be too high as well as too low. Finally, we provide advice as to how best communicate appropriately high expectations in your class.

SUGGESTED ACTIVITIES AND QUESTIONS

1. In this chapter, we talked primarily about how teachers communicate performance expectations to students in core academic subjects. How might expectations be communicated in art, music, or gym classes?
2. How do teachers determine at what pace to teach content and for what level of understanding to hold students accountable? How do teachers make such decisions if they work in a school that is very different from the school they attended? Try to interview two teachers from the level at which you intend to teach and determine how they developed expectations for class performance. If teachers are not available, arrange interviews with three or four classmates and discuss for a given academic subject.

3. Which student in your preservice teacher education courses (or teachers at your school) are the brightest? What information have you used to form your opinions? How accurate do you think your estimates are?

4. Do you think that teachers tend to underestimate or overestimate the learning potential of the following: loud, aggressive males; quiet, passive males; loud, aggressive females; quiet, passive females; students who are neat and follow directions carefully; students with speech impediments; and students who complain that schoolwork is uninteresting? Why?

5. What are ways in which teachers might inadvertently support stereotyping of students by projecting classroom messages like "Asian students always do well in math"? How might teachers communicate different expectations for female and male students?

6. Write an original example of a self-fulfilling prophecy based on something that happened to you, a relative, or a classmate.

7. Role-play the beginnings and endings of lessons. You be the teacher and let classmates play students at a specific grade level. Try to communicate appropriate expectations.

8. How might beginning teachers guard against indiscriminately accepting the expectations that other teachers hold for students?

9. How might teachers or principals communicate high and low performance expectations to new teachers?

Management I: Preventing Problems

lassroom management is important. New teachers often fear that students will not respect them. Experienced teachers usually cite establishing management as a major goal in the first few weeks of the year. Principals give low ratings to teachers who lack control of their classes (Torff & Sessions, 2005). Students want to be respected, but they also want their teachers to establish safe, orderly learning environments (Hoy & Weinstein, 2006).

Becoming an effective classroom manager is crucial to teachers' sense of well-being. Management difficulties are associated with teacher anxiety and stress. If prolonged, they can lead to depression and burnout (Brouwers & Tomic, 2000; Emmer & Gerwels, 2006; Friedman, 2006).

Teachers must make decisions about management on a daily basis. Consider the following four vignettes, and think about how you would respond in each situation.

Jan Thornton teaches physics at Riverside High School. She has become concerned that students are not reading the assignments intended to prepare them for laboratory work, so they often miss the point of the experiments. She decides to start giving pop quizzes over assigned readings. Is this a good idea?

Bill Novak, a sixth-grade teacher at Truman Middle School, gives students thirty-minute assignments each day. He expects students to work alone, while he grades papers. He believes that after a twenty-minute lecture-discussion, students should be able to work independently and that this practice builds self-reliance. Do you agree?

Celia Cruz teaches ninth-grade English at St. John High School. She writes the names of students on the board when they misbehave. When she does so, the "named" student settles down and other students seem less disturbed than when she speaks aloud to a misbehaving student. Students know that there will be consequences if their name goes on the board twice. What do you think about this strategy?

Jim Barlow, the art teacher at Bayside High School, doesn't believe in "school detention." However, if students accumulate enough classroom reprimands, he requires them to do service work (e.g., painting scenery for the theater group or painting over graffiti in the community on a weekend). Students and parents are told about this consequence at the start of the school year. Is this an effective technique?

*M*anagement Research

Advice to teachers about classroom management once was based mostly on untested theory or individual testimonials about "what works best for me." Much of it was contradictory and little was supported by solid evidence. However, research on classroom management has yielded a knowledge base that offers a coherent set of principles to guide decisions about how to manage classrooms (Evertson & Weinstein, 2006). The findings indicate that teachers who approach management as a process of establishing and maintaining an effective learning environment are more successful than teachers who emphasize their roles as disciplinarians. Teachers *are* authority figures and need to require students to follow certain rules and procedures. However, these are means for organizing the classroom to support teaching and learning, not ends in themselves. Classroom management should help students gain capacity for self-regulation.

*S*tudent Role

Expectations about appropriate student activities and behavior can be called the *student role*. Unfortunately, popular notions of the student role usually include restriction of movement, regimentation of activity, and subordination of individual desires to the authority of the teacher. Rules help provide for orderly group functioning, but at a price.

Much behavior that is considered natural and appropriate elsewhere, such as boisterous talk or play, is forbidden in the classroom, and certain forms of peer collaboration or helping are considered cheating.

These considerations suggest the value of a cost-benefit approach to classroom management, in which proposed techniques are assessed with attention to both their desired and their undesired effects. For example, overly restrictive practices such as requiring students to remain silent unless addressed by the teacher do not further any worthwhile goal. We recommend an approach that has been shown to be effective for establishing good learning environments in classrooms, while at the same time being the least costly to the classroom atmosphere.

[handwritten margin note: Over restrictive: Students remain silent | tight ship | bribery | ∨ chaos]

Classroom Examples

Consider four common types of classrooms:

1. This class is chaotic. The teacher continually struggles to establish control but never fully succeeds. Directions and even threats are often ignored, and punishment is not effective for long.
2. This class is also noisy, but the atmosphere is more positive. The teacher tries to make school fun by introducing lots of stories, videos, games, and enrichment activities, holding academic activities to a minimum, and making them as pleasant as possible. Even so, attention to lessons is spotty and assignments often are not done carefully.
3. This class is quiet and well disciplined because the teacher has established many rules and makes sure they are followed. Infractions are noted quickly and cut short with stern warnings or if necessary with punishment. The students usually obey, but the atmosphere is uneasy. Trouble is always brewing under the surface, and whenever the teacher leaves the room, the class "erupts."
4. This class seems to run by itself. The teacher spends most of the time teaching, not managing. When working independently, students follow instructions and complete assignments without close supervision. The noises they produce are the harmonious sounds of productive involvement in activities, not the shouts of boisterous play or disputes. When noise does become disruptive, a simple reminder from the teacher usually suffices. Observers sense warmth and "we-ness" in this class and are positively impressed.

The classroom learning environment develops gradually, in response to the teacher's communication of expectations, modeling of behavior, and approach to management. A class that is interested and attentive with one teacher can become bored or rebellious with another.

We have described four teacher prototypes. The first "can't cope," the second "bribes the students," the third "runs a tight ship," and the fourth "has cooperative students." Before reading on, take time to think about these four teachers. Assume that they began the year with roughly equivalent groups of students. List three attitudes or behaviors for each teacher that might help explain why their classrooms now differ. What might be their expectations about students?

Essential Teacher Attitudes

Establishing good personal relationships with students is fundamental to successful classroom management (Marzano & Marzano, 2003; Pianta, 2006). Therefore, display attitudes and personal qualities that make you a teacher whom students like and respect. Get to know your students and show that you value them. You need not be demonstrably affectionate; enjoyment of students and concern for their individual welfare will come through in how you treat them.

Students who like and respect their teachers will want to please them. They also will be more likely to imitate their teachers' behavior, adopt their attitudes, and sympathize when they are challenged (instead of allying with defiant students). At first, some students may doubt what a new teacher tells them because they have experienced discrepancies between what adults preach and what they practice. Consequently, you will need to establish credibility early in the school year and then maintain it. *Credibility* is established largely by making sure that words and actions coincide, pointing this out when necessary (e.g., "George, please understand that I try to give you and everyone in the class a fair deal, and in return I need you to respect and trust me. If I ever do anything to let you down, let me know right away so we can straighten it out.").

Credibility provides structure that students want and need. If they can depend on what teachers say, they will be less likely to test them and more able to accept responsibility for their own behavior. When teachers establish fair rules and enforce them consistently, rule breakers can get angry only at themselves. However, when teachers enforce rules inconsistently, those students who are punished will feel picked on.

Appropriate expectations provide a basis for establishing credibility. Students tend to conform not so much to what teachers say as to what they actually expect. If students learn that "No talking over there" really means "Keep the noise down to a tolerable level," they will respond to the second message, not the first. This would be all right, except that sometimes the teacher really means "No talking." At these times, the students will react in the usual way, and conflict may result. To avoid this, think through what you really expect from students and then ensure that your own behavior is consistent with those expectations.

[handwritten margin note: say what you mean — students are not mind readers.]

The Teacher as a Model

People in general and children in particular learn many things by observing models, including attitudes, values, problem-solving strategies, and social behavior. Teachers are important models for their students. However, modeling is not something that teachers can turn on or off at will: Modeling effects can occur at any time. Consequently, you will need to model the personal characteristics and classroom behavior that you are trying to develop in your students. If there is a discrepancy between preaching and practice, students will respond to what you do, not what you say.

[handwritten margin note: public nature of classroom]

What Can Be Learned from Observing Models

Exposure to a model can lead to either imitation or incidental learning. *Imitation* occurs when the learner observes the model's behavior and then copies it. For example, if you typically respond to student embarrassment with tact and sympathy, the class will tend to follow suit. However, if you typically react with sarcasm, students may begin to taunt a peer who makes a mistake.

Incidental learning occurs when observers "incidentally" make inferences about a model's beliefs, attitudes, and values. That is, they make inferences about what kind of person would behave as the model behaves. Consider teachers' responses to students' board work. When students make mistakes, one teacher might point out the mistake and ask them to try to correct it, whereas another might call on someone else to do the problem correctly.

handwritten: ① how teacher treats other students - infer they too will be treated this way.

The first teacher's students incidentally would learn "The teacher is supportive and helpful. It is safe to make a mistake." The second teacher's students would learn "I had better be ready to perform when I get called to the board. The teacher has little patience with anyone who can't do the problem correctly. I will raise my hand if I know the answer, but if I am not sure, I'd better try to escape the teacher's attention so I don't get embarrassed."

Factors That Affect What Is Learned from Observing Models

What is learned from observing models depends on several factors (Bandura, 1997). One is the familiarity of the situation and the behavior expected in it. Modeling effects are more likely when we are unclear about how to behave. Unsure of what to do, we observe and imitate the behavior of other people in the situation. Their behavior tells us what is normal.

In classrooms, modeling effects are strongest at the beginning of the year. Students make inferences about whether their new teachers mean what they say, invite or discourage questions and comments, are patient and helpful or frustrated and discouraged in dealing with slow learners, and so on. Teachers' behavior early in the year sets the tone for classroom climate dimensions such as supportive versus competitive, tension felt by students, and the degree to which students are responsible for their own behavior. Once the class has settled into predictable routines, established patterns tend to persist and established expectations tend to lead to self-fulfilling prophecy effects, for good or ill.

handwritten: Time of year

In addition to situational factors, modeling effects depend on the personality and behavior of the model. Teachers who form personal relations with their students and are individuals whom the students admire are more apt to be imitated than teachers who remain at a distance or stress the contrasts between themselves and their students. Students will imitate a warm, enthusiastic teacher whom they like, and probably adopt many of that teacher's attitudes and beliefs. Students are less likely to imitate teachers whom they dislike or do not respect, although they may acquire a great deal of undesirable incidental learning about such teachers from observing them (Fallona & Richardson, 2006; Lewis, 2006).

handwritten: teacher's personality... what would make students admire their teacher

Students' reactions to one another also are affected by modeling. When they observe a respected teacher praise a classmate for particular behavior, or when they discover through incidental learning that the teacher holds the classmate in high regard,

handwritten: how teachers behavior toward students effects how students treat ea. other

they are likely to imitate the classmate. If the teacher rejects or mistreats a classmate, they may follow suit.

Modeling as a Classroom Management Tool

You can instruct students in classroom routines through modeling—showing them how to use the pencil sharpener or operate audiovisual equipment, for example. Everyday modeling should include listening attentively when students answer questions, handling equipment carefully and replacing it properly, and remaining conspicuously quiet during times for concentrated thinking. Teacher modeling is important for developing self-regulation of behavior by acting on well-thought-out decisions rather than impulses; developing respect for others by treating them as worthwhile, valued people; developing a good group climate by avoiding hostile criticism, scapegoating, and playing favorites; and responding to problems with rational attempts to diagnose and solve them.

Explain the rationales underlying your decisions and rules to students. This kind of modeling helps students link causes to their consequences and see rules as a means of achieving larger goals. Also, students are more willing to accept and internalize rules that they understand. Explanations help them to see rules and decisions as thoughtful attempts to solve recognized problems. Consider a teacher who has just acquired a computer for use in the classroom:

Teacher: The computer will be kept back in the corner, and you can go there to edit your writing and to work on special projects. We need to work out ways to see that everyone gets a chance.

John: Why not let us sign up to use it one day at a time?

Teacher: Well, I hope to develop a plan that would allow many of you to use it on the same day. Otherwise, some would have to wait almost a month before getting a chance. You could sign up for shorter times, though, like thirty minutes.

Mary: We could work together on some of the projects.

Teacher: I hadn't thought about that, but I guess you could if it didn't get too noisy.

George: It wouldn't be too noisy if just a few of us used it at once and we talked quietly.

Teacher: Yes, I think that would work. But how would we decide who uses it at a given time?

Sally: The first ones to finish their other work could use it?

Teacher: I don't know about that, Sally. I wouldn't want you all to start racing through your work to be the first to get at the computer. I want you to think about your assignments and do them carefully. Also, I want to make sure that everyone gets a chance.

John: We could just make a list and take turns.

Teacher: Well, maybe we could make two lists, John. One for individual editing time on Mondays, Wednesdays, and Fridays, and one for work on group projects on Tuesdays and Thursdays.

Modeling Social Interactions

You also can use modeling to establish a positive group climate. Model respect for others by treating students pleasantly and by avoiding behavior that would cause anyone to lose face before the group. Treat all students with a respectful manner and tone of voice. This also applies to hall guards, secretaries, custodians, bus drivers, and other school personnel. As much as possible, give directions in the form of requests rather than orders. Use the words *please* and *thank you* regularly.

Ideal group climates feature friendliness and cooperation, but some classes are notable for jealously and destructive competition. Teachers almost always contribute to these problems through direct modeling of sarcasm, scapegoating, and other unprofessional reactions to failure, misbehavior, or minor annoyances. This teaches students to deal with frustration by taking it out on others.

Teachers also can promote ill will by playing favorites and rewarding actions (such as tattling) that pit one student against another. They can create resentments by drawing direct comparisons between students, telling a favored student to write down the names of anyone who misbehaves while they are away, or otherwise placing a student in the position of creating or profiting from a classmate's problems.

Modeling is an ongoing and pervasive component of teachers' classroom functioning. To the extent that you stay aware of your role as a model and regulate your behavior accordingly, you can use modeling as a tool for stimulating desirable imitation and incidental learning. To the extent that you do not, you will miss many opportunities to use modeling as a socialization tool and will stimulate some undesirable incidental learning.

General Management Principles

To establish groundwork for successful classroom management, teachers must (1) earn the respect and affection of students; (2) be consistent and, therefore, credible and dependable; (3) assume responsibility for seeing that their students learn; and (4) value and enjoy learning and expect students to do so, too.

If you have these personal qualities, what steps can you take to establish good classroom management? We begin with general principles of classroom organization, based on the following four assumptions:

1. Students are likely to follow rules that they <u>understand and accept</u>. *(make themselves)*
2. Discipline problems are minimized when students are engaged in meaningful activities geared to their interests and aptitudes.
3. Management should focus on establishing a <u>productive learning environment</u>, <u>rather than control of misbehavior</u>.
4. Your goal is to develop students' inner self-control, not your control over them.

Plan Rules and Procedures in Advance

Effective management begins with planning the kind of learning environment that will support your intended curriculum. Planning attends to both rules and procedures. *Rules* define general expectations or standards for classroom conduct. Useful general rules include "be in your seat and ready to work when the bell rings" and "listen carefully when others speak." Usually, <u>four or five general rules</u>, suited to your grade level and instructional goals, are sufficient. It often is useful to involve students in

4-5 Rules

rule-setting discussions. For example, a music teacher could start by noting, "All of us want a fun and productive atmosphere to allow us to play the best possible music. To do so we have to concentrate. Last year the marching band and I developed four rules. Let's review them and see if these are okay or if we want to make different rules this year."

Procedures are methods for accomplishing daily routines. Evertson (1987) suggested that procedures are needed for the following *activities:* (1) room use (teacher's desk and storage areas, students' desks and storage areas, wastebasket, lavatories, learning centers); (2) transitions in and out of the room; (3) group work (movement to the group setting, expected behavior in and out of the group); and (4) teacher-led instruction and assignments (obtaining help, out-of-seat procedures, talk among students, and what to do after assignments are completed).

Four Activities which need defined Procedure →

Evertson also identified the need for procedures concerning *managing student work:* (1) communicating assignments and work requirements (posting assignments, accepting incomplete or late work, arranging for makeup work and assistance to absentees); (2) monitoring progress on and completion of assignments; (3) feedback (grading procedures that are consistent with the school's policies; what you will do if a student stops doing assignments; how you will communicate with parents); and (4) the grading system (what components it will have, how to organize the grade book, the role of extra credit assignments). The more carefully you think through your preferred rules and procedures, the more prepared you will be to explain them clearly to students and to be consistent in ensuring their implementation.

Establish Clear Rules and Procedures When Needed

Certain aspects of classroom management are part of the daily routine (e.g., use of the toilets and drinking fountains, access to supplies, use of special equipment, behavior during work periods). Be explicit about these and other situations in which procedural routines are required. Explanation is especially important at the beginning of the year and with students in kindergarten or first grade, who are new to school. Some will never have used pencil sharpeners or certain audiovisual, arts and crafts, or computer equipment, so a *demonstration* followed by *opportunity to practice* the use and care of such equipment may be needed. Demonstrations and practice are less necessary with older students, but still important for introducing new responsibilities (such as the use and care of laboratory equipment or how to critique other students' work). Older students also need thorough discussion of rules and procedures, because last year's teacher may have required behavior that differs from what you want this year.

Keep behavioral rules to a minimum and state them clearly with convincing rationales. Present them as means, not ends in themselves. For example, the rationale underlying rules about behavior during work times might stress that students should not disrupt work by classmates (because assignments require careful thinking and concentration). A rule such as "When you finish your assignment, you will remain quiet and not talk to anyone or leave your seats for any reason" would be much more restrictive than necessary. Instead, stress the basic goal of avoiding disturbances to classmates and then list examples of acceptable and unacceptable behavior.

Let Students Assume Responsibility

With proper planning and instruction, even the youngest students can assume many responsibilities. Older students can work independently or in small groups, check their own work, and edit one another's essays. Teachers who unnecessarily do these things themselves lose time that could have been spent teaching and retard students' development of independent responsibility. Often students only need a demonstration lesson or an opportunity to practice the behavior. Time spent giving such explanations and patience in responding to mistakes early in the year pay great dividends later.

Some teachers adopt overly rigid rules on the grounds that they are needed ("If I put out supplementary books, they'll steal them," "If I allow them to work in groups, they'll just copy from one another or waste time"). This attitude avoids the problem rather than solving it. It communicates negative expectations by treating students as if they were infants, and it denies them the chance to develop skills for productively managing their own behavior.

Minimize Disruptions and Delays

Management problems start and spread more easily when students are idle or distracted. Delays frequently result when there is high demand for something that is in short supply, as when the entire class gets supplies from a single container or uses the same computer. Much time can be saved by storing items in several containers and by breaking the class into subgroups or appointing assistants to help instead of lining up the entire class to do something one at a time.

The time needed for distributing supplies can be reduced by having one student from each row or table pass things out. Items should be stored low enough for students to reach and arranged neatly for easy location and replacement. Traffic lanes should be wide enough for students to move freely without bumping into furniture or one another.

In junior high and high school, complicated diagrams, maps, or mathematical computations should be prepared on the chalkboard, an overhead, or a computer before class begins or distributed on handouts rather than constructed during class. Many science experiments and other demonstrations can be partially prepared ahead of time when the preparations themselves do not need to be demonstrated.

When students must wait with nothing to do, four things can happen, and three of them are bad: (1) students may remain interested and attentive; (2) they may become bored or fatigued, losing the ability to concentrate; (3) they may become distracted or start daydreaming; or (4) they may actively misbehave. Therefore, plan room arrangement, equipment storage, preparation of lessons, and transitions between activities to avoid needless delays and confusion.

Plan Independent Activities as Well as Organized Lessons

Disruptions often originate with students who are not working on their assignments or who have finished and have nothing else to do. Therefore, provide worthwhile assignments and have backup plans prepared for times when students finish more quickly than anticipated.

Assignments should be basic parts of the curriculum, providing students with opportunities to practice and apply what they are learning. Plan them as carefully as you plan lessons, make their purposes clear to students when introducing them, and follow up by monitoring progress and providing additional instruction to students who need it. Students must be held accountable for careful work on the assignment if it is to have its desired effects.

Specify what options are available when students finish assignments. If they often finish early, the assignments may be too short or too easy. This may lead to boredom or misbehavior by the more talented students, and it fails to provide struggling students with opportunities to overcome initial failure and develop adaptive problem-solving skills (McCaslin et al., 2006).

[handwritten margin note: tips on independent work →]

To work independently, students must understand what to do and be able to do it with little or no help. Therefore, make sure that they understand what to do before "turning them loose" to work alone or with peers. During independent work times, disruptions are likely if students must wait too long to get help. If everyone seems to need help, the problem is overly difficult or the directions poor. Disruptions also can occur if you become absorbed with individual students to the point of neglecting the rest of the class.

In summary, during independent work times, keep yourself in circulation and available to give immediate help to students who need it. Normally, interactions with individuals should be brief. Provide them with enough guidance to sustain their work, but do not necessarily cover everything they will need to know eventually (you can return after the student does the next set of problems). When many students have the same question or misconception, briefly clarify to the class as a whole. Otherwise, provide private help to those who need it while allowing the rest of the class to work without interruption.

$\mathcal{M}$anagement as Motivation and Problem Prevention

The chapter title refers to *management* rather than to discipline or control. The latter terms have a connotation that we wish to avoid: the idea that managing students is mostly a matter of successfully handling their misbehavior.

Kounin's Study

Jacob Kounin (1970) found that the key to good management is to use techniques that elicit student cooperation and involvement in activities and thus *prevent* problems from occurring. Kounin observed in classrooms to develop information about relationships between teacher behavior and student behavior. Surprisingly, he found that the teachers' methods of responding to discipline problems were unrelated to the frequency and seriousness of such problems in their classes. That is, teachers who had few discipline problems did not differ from those who had many discipline problems on measures of teacher response to student misbehavior.

[handwritten margin note: teacher response to problems was not related to frequency!!! ✗]

The teachers did differ in other ways, however. In particular, the effective managers minimized the frequency of disruptions by keeping students profitably involved in learning activities. They also resolved incidents of minor inattention before they developed into major disruptions. The following were keys to their success.

"Withitness."   Effective managers regularly monitored their classrooms. They positioned themselves so that they could see all students and continuously scanned the room, no matter what else they were doing at the time. They let their students know that they were "with it"—aware of what was happening and likely to detect misbehavior early and accurately. This enabled them to nip problems in the bud before they could escalate. If they found it necessary to stop misbehavior, they focused on the students who started the problem or were most responsible for its escalation. If they were uncertain about who was most responsible, they told the entire group involved to resume working on their assignment (to avoid publicly blaming the wrong student).   ← *Do NOT Blame the wrong student!*

Overlapping.   Effective managers could do more than one thing at a time when necessary. When teaching small groups, they responded to students from outside the group who came to ask questions, but at times and in ways that did not disrupt ongoing group activities. When circulating to check progress on assignments, they met individual needs without disrupting the other students' focus on their work.

Signal Continuity and Momentum.   Effective managers were well prepared and thus able to teach smooth lessons that provided a continuous "signal" to attend to. They seldom confused students with false starts or backtracking to present information that should have been presented earlier. They ignored minor, fleeting inattention but dealt with sustained inattention before it escalated into disruption, using methods that were not themselves disruptive (they moved near inattentive students, used eye contact when possible, etc.). They realized that when teachers deliver extended reprimands or otherwise overreact to minor inattention, they lose the "momentum" of the lesson and break the "signal continuity" that provides focus for student attention.   *← something I need to improve on!*

Group Alerting.   Effective managers frequently used group alerting techniques to maintain or reestablish attention during lessons: looking around the group before calling on someone, keeping students in suspense about who will be called on next by selecting randomly, getting around to everyone frequently, asking for volunteers, throwing out challenges by declaring that the next question is difficult or tricky, and presenting novel or interesting material.

Accountability.   Effective managers sometimes held students accountable for paying attention by requiring them to hold up props, show their answers, or otherwise indicate attention to the lesson; having them respond in unison (while monitoring carefully); asking listeners to comment on peers' responses; circulating and checking performance; and calling on individuals.

Variety and Challenge in Independent Work.   Effective managers provided assignments that were both (1) familiar and easy enough for students to do successfully and yet (2) challenging and varied enough to sustain their motivation. This encouraged students to maintain focus on the assignments even when they were working independently.

Later Studies

Subsequent work by other investigators confirmed that these teacher behaviors are keys to successful classroom management and also showed that they are associated with achievement gains (Brophy & Good, 1986; Gettinger & Kohler, 2006; Teddlie & Stringfield, 1993). The research also showed that classes which seem to run by themselves, with the teacher spending most of the time teaching rather than handling discipline problems, are created by a great deal of preinstruction planning and in-class decision making. Expert managers do not appear to pay much attention to student behavior when they are teaching, but when commenting on videotapes of their classes, they often refer to preventive measures taken to avoid management problems (Emmer & Stough, 2001).

Does not SEEM like discipline is their focus!

Getting the School Year Off to a Good Start

Carolyn Evertson, Ed Emmer, and their colleagues developed detailed information about how teachers handled the first day and the first few weeks of the school year, analyzing the relationships between teacher management and student engagement rates.

Third-Grade Study

Their first study (Emmer, Evertson, & Anderson, 1980) was conducted in twenty-eight third-grade classrooms. It showed that the seemingly automatic functioning of the classrooms of successful managers resulted from thorough preparation and organization at the beginning of the year. On the first day and throughout the first week, these teachers gave special attention to matters of greatest concern to students (information about the teacher and their classmates, review of the daily schedule, procedures for lunch and recess, where to put personal materials, when and where to get a drink). They introduced procedures and routines gradually as needed, so as not to overload students with too much information at one time.

Effective managers not only described what they expected but also modeled correct procedures, took time to answer questions, and, if necessary, arranged for students to practice the procedures and get feedback. Key procedures were formally taught, just as academic content is taught.

Although they focused more on instruction than on "control," effective managers were thorough in following up on their expectations. They reminded students about procedures shortly before they were to carry them out, and they scheduled additional instruction and practice when students did not follow them properly. Consequences were clear and applied consistently. Inappropriate behavior was stopped quickly. Effective managers showed three major clusters of strategies.

Conveying Purposefulness.   Effective managers tried to maximize use of available time for instruction and to see that their students learned the curriculum. Students were held accountable for completing work on time (after being taught to pace themselves by using the clock, if necessary). Regular times were scheduled each day to review independent work. Completed papers were returned promptly, with feedback.

Teaching Appropriate Conduct.   Effective managers were clear about what they expected and what they would not tolerate. They focused on what students should be doing and, if necessary, taught them how to do it. This included not only conduct and housekeeping guidelines, but also learning-related behaviors such as how to read and follow directions for assignments. When students failed to follow procedures properly, they stressed specific corrective feedback rather than criticism or threat of punishment.

Maintaining Attention.   Effective managers continuously monitored students for signs of confusion or inattention and were sensitive to their concerns. Seating was arranged so students could face the point in the room where they most often needed to focus attention. Variations in voice, movement, or pacing were used to refocus attention during lessons. Activities had clear beginnings and endings, with efficient transitions in between.

Effective managers followed up this intensive activity in the early weeks by maintaining their expectations consistently. They continued to give reminders and occasional remedial instruction, and they remained consistent in enforcing their rules.

Junior High Study

A related study of junior high school teachers revealed similar findings, as well as a few differences. Junior high teachers do not need to spend as much time teaching their students how to follow rules and procedures, but they do have to communicate expectations about assignments. Information about what the assignments are and when they are due should be posted, along with any needed instructions about the expected form or quality of the final product. The following behaviors were characteristic of effective junior high managers (Emmer & Gerwels, 2006; Evertson & Emmer, 1982).

Instructing Students in Rules and Procedures.   Effective managers described their rules more completely and installed their procedures more systematically. They were notably more explicit about desired behavior (the dos, not just the don'ts).

Monitoring Compliance with Rules.   They monitored compliance more consistently, intervened to correct inappropriate behavior more consistently, and were more likely to mention the rules or describe desired behavior when giving feedback.

Communicating Information.   They were clearer in presenting information, giving directions, and stating objectives. They broke complex tasks into step-by-step procedures.

Organizing Instruction.   They wasted little time getting organized or accomplishing transitions between activities. They maximized attention and task engagement by maintaining signal continuity and momentum in lessons, overlapping their own activities, and using the other techniques identified by Kounin (1970).

Others who have studied the factors involved in getting off to a good start have reached very similar conclusions. The consensus is that you should be friendly and personable but also businesslike in visibly taking charge and establishing your desired learning environment. Start with simple formats and familiar tasks. Once students begin to follow everyday routines without much special direction, you can begin to phase in more challenging work and more complex formats (small-group activities, special projects, learning centers).

$\mathcal{M}$aintaining an Effective Learning Environment

After getting off to a good start, you can build on it by cueing and reinforcing desired behavior and providing any one-the-spot directions that may be needed.

Use Positive Language to Cue Desired Behavior

Learning is easier and more pleasant when we are shown what *to* do rather than told what *not to* do. Therefore, learn to specify desired behavior in positive terms, as shown in Table 3.1

Negative statements are appropriate at times, such as when a student is doing something that must be stopped immediately (fighting, causing major disruption). Even here, however, your stop message should be followed by statements about desired behavior.

Recognize and Reinforce Desired Behavior

You can reward students' accomplishments not only with grades but also with verbal praise, public recognition, symbolic rewards (stars, happy faces, stickers), special privileges or activity choices, or material rewards (healthy snacks, prizes). Reinforcement provides guidance to learners: Behavior that is rewarded is likely to be repeated, but behavior that is not rewarded is likely to be extinguished (Landrum & Kauffman, 2006). Reinforcement also can develop positive self-concepts, boost motivation, and support a sense of accomplishment.

However, some educational theorists oppose reinforcement even in principle. They urge teachers to build on students' intrinsic motivation to learn, without trying to supplement it through extrinsic reinforcement. Early studies showed that if you begin to reward people for doing what they already were doing for their own reasons, you may decrease their intrinsic motivation to continue the behavior in the future. Furthermore, to the extent that their attention becomes focused on the reward rather than the task itself, their performance tends to deteriorate. They do whatever will garner them the most rewards with the least effort, rather than try to create a high-quality product.

Kohn (1993) drew on such research to argue that the effectiveness of rewards has been exaggerated and to suggest that an emphasis on rewards can make students become less cooperative and more competitive. His views are summarized in the subtitle to his book, which refers to "gold stars, incentive plans, A's, praise, and other bribes."

A great deal of research has been done on the effects of praise and rewards (Sansone & Harackiewicz, 2000). Most of it applies more to student motivation than to classroom management, so it is addressed in detail in Chapter 5. For now, be aware that both the need for and the dangers of rewards have been exaggerated. Decreases in

Table 3.1   Phrasing Directions in Positive Language

Positive Language	Negative Language
Work as quickly as you can on the computer; other students are waiting.	Don't "hog" the computer.
Close the door quietly.	Don't slam the door.
Try to work these out on your own without help.	Don't cheat by copying from your neighbor.
Work quietly.	Don't make so much noise.
Always dispose of used chemicals like this. (demonstration)	That's not how you dispose of chemicals.
Listen to everyone's ideas and respond with arguments that speak to the issues.	I don't want to hear personal remarks and putdowns.
Raise your hand if you think you know the answer.	Don't yell out the answer.
When you finish, put the scissors in the box and bits of paper in the wastebasket.	Don't leave a mess.
These crayons are for you to share—use one color at a time and then put it back so others can use it too.	Stop fighting over those crayons.
Use your own ideas. When you do borrow ideas from the author, be sure to acknowledge them. Even here, try to put them in your own words.	Don't plagiarize.
When you make your class presentation, speak naturally, as you would when talking to a friend.	Don't just read your report to us.
Note the caution statements in the instructions. Be sure to check the things mentioned there before proceeding to the next step.	Take your time when doing this experiment or you'll mess it up.
Be ready to explain your answer—why you think it is correct.	Don't just guess.

performance quality and intrinsic motivation are most likely when reinforcement has the following three characteristics:

1. *High salience.* Large or highly attractive rewards, or rewards presented in ways that call attention to them
2. *Noncontingency.* Rewards are given for mere participation in activities, rather than being contingent on meeting specific performance standards
3. *Unnatural/unusual.* Rewards are artificially tied to behaviors as control devices, rather than being natural outcomes of the behaviors

Reinforcement is most likely to undermine students' intrinsic motivation when it leads them to perceive that their behavior is controlled externally—that they are engaging in an activity only because they must do so in order to earn a reward.

We believe that too much emphasis has been placed on *frequency* of reinforcement and not enough on *quality* issues such as whom to reinforce, under what conditions, and with what kinds of rewards. Attempts to reinforce can be valuable in some circumstances, but ineffectual or even counterproductive in others.

Reinforcement of many student behaviors occurs as a natural consequence of performing the behaviors. For example, attention to lessons and effort on assignments lead to successful performance, which in turn leads to high grades and feelings of satisfaction. Thus, the issue is not whether reinforcement should occur in your classroom, but whether (and if so, how) you should inject additional reinforcement.

Our position is that additional reinforcement is not necessary, although it may be appropriate. It is not necessary because humans can learn by observing models or being instructed. Unlike lower animals, we are not dependent on shaping through reinforcement as our primary learning mechanism. Also, we respond to many motives (self-actualization, cognitive consistency, curiosity) in addition to, and sometimes instead of, the desire for extrinsic reinforcement. Finally, reinforcement from sources other than the teacher (winning an art or music competition, gaining peer acceptance) may be more important than anything the teacher does.

Another complicating factor is individual differences in students' motivational systems. For a given person and situation, certain motives are relevant and others are not, so the success of a reinforcement effort will depend on how well it fits the person's present motives. You will need to monitor your students' responses to consequences intended to be reinforcing, not just assume that they all actually experience these consequences as reinforcing.

Praising Effectively

Praise is usually described as a form of reinforcement, but it does not always have this effect. Sometimes teachers do not even intend their praise to be reinforcing, as when they praise in an attempt to build a social relationship with an alienated student ("I like your new shirt, John"). Even when teachers do intend praise to be reinforcing, students may not perceive it that way. In particular, public praise may be more embarrassing than reinforcing, especially if it calls attention to conformity behavior rather than noteworthy accomplishments ("I like the way that Kate is sitting up straight and ready to listen"). Students generally prefer private, quietly delivered praise to public, loudly delivered praise, and prefer praise for their academic accomplishments to praise for their good conduct (Elwell & Tiberio, 1994; Sharp, 1985).

Praise also has been oversold to teachers. Correlations between teachers' rates of praise and their students' learning gains are too low to be of practical importance (Brophy, 1981). Neither teachers nor students see teacher praise as an important or powerful reinforcer (Ware, 1978). Strategies for eliciting desired behavior in the first place are much more important than praising such behavior after it appears.

To the extent that praise is important, the key to its effectiveness lies in its *quality* rather than its *frequency*. Effective praise calls attention to developments in students' learning progress or skill mastery. It expresses appreciation for efforts or admiration for accomplishments, in ways that call attention to the efforts or accomplishments themselves rather than to their role in pleasing the teacher. This helps students learn to attribute their efforts to their own motivation to learn rather than to external pressures.

Unfortunately, much teacher praise functions less as reinforcement than as an indication of teachers' expectations or attitudes. Brophy and Evertson (1981) found that teachers were credible and spontaneous when praising students they liked, smiling as they spoke and praising genuine accomplishments. They praised disliked students just as often, but usually without accompanying spontaneity and warmth and often with reference to appearance or behavior rather than accomplishments.

Teachers sometimes even praise poor responses as part of a well-intentioned attempt to encourage struggling students, but this can confuse or depress them if they realize they are being treated differently from their classmates. Struggling students need encouragement, but they also need accurate feedback. If they notice that they are frequently praised for minor accomplishments, they may infer that the teacher does not have much confidence in their abilities or potential (Miller & Hom, 1997; Thompson, 1997). Even when praising significant achievements, it is better to focus on the effort and care put into the work, on gains in knowledge or skills, or on the achievement's noteworthy features than to portray the achievement as evidence of the student's intelligence or aptitude.

Praise is most likely to be effective when delivered as spontaneous, genuine reaction to student accomplishments rather than as part of a calculated attempt to manipulate the student. Other guidelines for effective praise are given below and in Table 3.2.

1. Praise simply and directly, in a natural voice, without dramatizing.
2. Praise in straightforward, declarative sentences ("I never thought of that before") instead of gushing ("Wow!") or using rhetorical questions ("Isn't that great!").
3. Specify the accomplishment and recognize any noteworthy effort, care, or perseverance ("Good! You figured it out all by yourself. I like the way you stuck with it without giving up," instead of just "Good!").
4. Call attention to new skills or evidence of progress ("I notice you've learned to use different kinds of metaphors in your compositions. They're more interesting to read now. Keep up the good work").
5. Back verbal praise with nonverbal communication of approval. "That's good" is more rewarding when delivered with a warm smile and a tone that communicates appreciation.
6. Ordinarily, individual students should be praised privately. Public praise will embarrass some students and may even cause them problems with peers. Praising privately shows the student that your praise is genuine and avoids holding the student up as an example to the rest of the class.

Getting and Holding Attention

In this section we suggest techniques for dealing with everyday problems of minor inattention. This is accomplished mostly with "low-profile" techniques that minimize disruptions to ongoing activities.

Table 3.2 Guidelines for Effective Praise

Effective Praise	Ineffective Praise
1. Is delivered contingently	1. Is delivered randomly or unsystematically
2. Specifies the particulars of the accomplishment	2. Is restricted to global positive reactions
3. Shows spontaneity, variety, and other signs of credibility; suggests clear attention to the student's accomplishment	3. Shows a bland uniformity that suggests a conditioned response made with minimal attention
4. Rewards attainment of specified performance criteria (which can include effort criteria, however)	4. Rewards mere participation, without consideration of performance processes or outcomes
5. Provides information to students about their competence or the value of their accomplishments	5. Provides no information at all or only informs students about their status relative to peers
6. Orients students toward better appreciation of their own task-related behavior and thinking about problem solving	6. Orients students toward comparing themselves with others and thinking about competing
7. Uses student's own prior accomplishments as the context for describing present accomplishments	7. Uses the accomplishments of peers as the context for describing student's present accomplishments
8. Is given in recognition of noteworthy effort or success at difficult (for this student) tasks	8. Is given without regard to the effort expended or the meaning of the accomplishment
9. Attributes success to effort and ability, implying that similar success can be expected in the future	9. Attributes success to ability alone or to external factors such as luck or (easy) task difficulty
10. Fosters endogenous attributions (students believe that they expend effort on the task for because they enjoy the task and/or want to develop task-relevant skills)	10. Fosters exogenous attributions (students believe that they expend effort on the task for external reasons—to please the teacher, win a competition or reward, etc.)
11. Focuses students' attention on their own task-relevant behavior	11. Focuses students' attention on the teacher as an external authority figure who is manipulating them
12. Fosters appreciation of, and desirable attributions about, task-relevant behavior after the process is completed	12. Intrudes into the ongoing process, distracting attention from task-relevant behavior

Source: Brophy, J. (1981). Teacher praise: A functional analysis. *Review of Educational Research, 51,* 5–32.

Focus Attention When Beginning Lessons

Establish that you expect each student's full attention to lessons. First, get everyone's attention using a standard signal that tells the class, "We are now ready to begin a lesson."

After giving the signal, pause briefly to allow it to take effect. Then begin briskly, ideally with an overview that provides motivation and a learning set describing what will be done. The pause between giving the signal and beginning the lesson should be brief, just long enough for students to focus their attention. Act quickly if a few students do not respond. If they are looking at you, use expressions or gestures to call for attention. If not, call their names, and if necessary, add a brief focusing statement ("Look here").

Keep Lessons Moving at a Good Pace

Teachers often begin with good attention but lose it by spending too much time on minor points or by causing everyone to wait while students respond repetitively. If only a few students need further review, work with them individually or in a small group.

Monitor Attention during Lessons

Scan the class or group throughout the lesson. Students are more likely to maintain attention if they know that you regularly watch everyone for signs of attention and confusion or difficulty.

Stimulate Attention Periodically

When things become too predictable and repetitive, the mind wanders. You can do several things to help ensure continual attention. One is to vary your facial expressions and gestures. Speak loudly enough for everyone to hear and modulate your tone and volume. Mix information presentation with questions or activities; group responses with individual responses; and reading or factual questions with thought-provoking discussion questions.

You also can stimulate attention directly. For example, you can challenge the class ("Here's tricky question—let's see if you can figure it out."), create suspense ("So, what do you think happened next?"), or call attention to a transition in a way that also stimulates interest ("All right, you seem to know the theory, let's see if you can apply it to a practical problem").

Maintain Accountability

Hold students accountable for attending to lessons continuously (Kounin, 1970). Develop variety and unpredictability in asking questions, so students learn that they may be called on at any time. Occasionally question students again after they have answered an earlier question or ask them to comment about an answer just given by a classmate. Note that these techniques are intended to challenge the class, stimulate interest, and avoid predictability, not to embarrass inattentive students. Ordinarily, you should not say, "Remember, I might call on you at any time, so pay attention." Just use this technique without calling attention to it.

In the early grades, accountability devices are not as important as careful monitoring, because the main problem is helping students to be *able* to follow lessons, not making sure that they *choose* to follow them. In early reading lessons, for example, it may be helpful to have students follow with their finger or a marker, monitoring them regularly to see that they have their place. Here, predictability is probably helpful. Anderson, Evertson, and Brophy (1979) found that teachers who had students read in a predictable order during reading groups got better results than those who called on students randomly. Perhaps the predictable pattern helped students follow the lesson. However, when students become able to keep track without help, and especially if they begin to anticipate what they will be held accountable for and practice it ahead of time, you will need to call on them in less predictable patterns.

Assertive students tend to seek response opportunities and get called on more often than reticent students, so keep track of who has responded and who has not. You can monitor this by tallying response opportunities in a log book (perhaps also keeping track of students' rates of success in handling questions of varying difficulty). Alternatively, you can create a set of cards with your students' names on them and work your way through them (reshuffling after each class) to randomize and equalize participation.

Address questions to the class as a whole and allow time for thinking before calling on a student to respond. When they know they may be called on, students are likely to think about the question and try to form an answer. If you name a student to answer a question before asking it, however, others in the class may turn their attention elsewhere.

Terminate Lessons That Have Gone on Too Long

When lessons continue too long, more of the teacher's time is spent compelling attention and less of the students' time is spent thinking about the material. Teachers usually know this but sometimes pursue lessons anyway because they do not want to get off schedule. However, students do not learn efficiently under these conditions, so the material probably will have to be retaught. Other teachers prolong activities needlessly because they want to give each student a chance to participate individually. This intention is laudable, but when recitation becomes boringly repetitive, it is time to move on.

Independent Work

In this section we discuss some of the special management problems associated with supervision of work on assignments. We focus on elementary reading, although the problems are parallel in other grades and subjects.

Anderson et al. (1985) found that in most classrooms the typical assignment was low-level and repetitive, and directions seldom included statements about what would be learned or how the assignment related to other learning. Explanations were usually procedural (e.g., "Read the sentence and then pick the word that completes it"), with little attention to the cognitive demands of the task. Feedback focused on correctness of answers or neatness of work.

Low achievers often received overly difficult assignments, did poorly on them, and used strategies that allowed them to complete the assignments without understanding what they were supposed to be learning. Their teachers generally emphasized keeping busy and finishing work rather than understanding what was being taught.

Osborn (1984) noted that much of what appears in workbooks is confusing or trivial. Teachers can prevent much wasted time by ensuring that assignments: (1) allow students to work successfully and independently; (2) are interesting and reflect variety in type of assignment and in how it is to be completed; (3) frequently allow students to read for comprehension and pleasure; and (4) relate the content to students' personal lives.

Teachers sometimes want to work in a concentrated, sustained manner with a small group. During these times, the rest of the students will need assignments that they can complete successfully without teacher help. These activities need not be confined to fill-ing blanks, circling, or underlining. Instead, students could be assigned to read and answer questions, write a story or an alternative ending to a story, make journal entries, or engage in other worthwhile literacy tasks. For variety, students could work together on some assignments (two or more students might debate issues in a story or compare endings that they have written independently) (Morrow, Reutzel, & Casey, 2006).

Management of independent work is important at all levels of schooling and in all subjects. Doyle (1984) found that successful managers of junior high English classes established an activity system early in the year and protected it from intrusion or dis-ruption. For the first three weeks, contacts with individual students were brief as the teachers circulated the room and maintained a whole-class perspective. In response to disruptions, they talked about completing the assignment successfully rather than about misbehavior. Less successful managers gave frequent public reprimands that interrupted everyone's work. Observations indicated that if a work system was established effectively by November, the teacher then could spend less time supervising the class and more time with individuals.

Activity System to be able to help individuals

Self-Regulated Management

Students should assume as much responsibility for self-management as they can han-dle. Opportunities for self-evaluation should be provided for academic areas (e.g., com-pare a composition written in September with one written in May and assess their own growth) and social areas (e.g., work collaboratively with peers in increasingly complex ways). In many school situations, a curriculum emphasizing adaptive problem solving and meaningful learning is "sabotaged" by a management system that encourages stu-dent passivity and obedience (McCaslin & Good, 1998).

Students cannot learn self-regulation if the teacher does all of the alerting, ac-countability, and so on. They need to be taught to manage time ("We have fifteen min-utes to finish a task") and procedures ("What is the critical problem? How else might the problem be approached?"). Scaffolding needs to be adjusted to encourage progres-sively more responsibility for self-management.

What constitutes appropriate self-regulation will vary with students' ages and prior experiences and teachers' instructional intentions and expectations. Although younger students need more structuring, support, and guidance, the goal is to help all students become as autonomous and adaptive as possible.

Students should become able to maintain both a focus on learning and the inten-tion to understand and master the material without constant teacher monitoring or en-couragement. They need to transform information and make it their own by integrating current learning with previous learning and their own life experiences.

Encourage your students to develop self-regulation dispositions and skills. For example, teach them how to set goals and to delay gratification (e.g., "I'll do two drafts of the paper before seeking feedback"), as well as to exploit resources appropriately (when and how to get information from teachers, peers, the library, and computers). Help them to develop self-control of learning situations (judge the amount of time it will take to complete an assignment, decide whether it is useful to do something at home or to wait for a study period the next day, etc.) and to set guidelines to organize their time ("I will do at least three problems before class ends so that I can get help if I need it"). Also, help them to develop the capacity for self-assessment.

Students should learn to change themselves, the task, or the environment when it is appropriate to do so. For example, they should recognize affect that promotes passivity (anxiety about how hard the task is, how long it will take, what will happen if they do not complete it), and change their thinking accordingly. They also can change tasks to make them more interesting ("I'll see if I can come up with a general rule that explains the relationships across these problem sets") or change the environment (move away from a noisy friend who is interfering with task completion) (McCaslin et al., 2006).

As students become more sophisticated, they should become adept at allocating their personal resources adaptively, including recognizing when they have reached the point of diminishing returns and should seek new information or a new perspective.

*E*xpanded Conceptions of Teaching and Management

It is self-defeating to try to teach subject matter for understanding while at the same time managing for compliance. Achieving higher-order learning outcomes requires more advanced management approaches, in which the teacher delegates authority to individuals or groups of students rather than trying to personally supervise multiple overlapping activities. If the teacher is trying to create a trusting, cooperative learning environment, the management system must also promote corresponding dispositions, behaviors, and skills.

Building Learning Communities

The management principles presented in this chapter were developed through research done in classrooms that featured teacher presentations and demonstrations, teacher-led discourse, and follow-up assignments. Models of teaching developed more recently tend to emphasize the social construction of knowledge within learning communities (see Chapter 11). The classroom discourse features more interactive discussion, and students are expected to make sense of what they are learning by relating it to their prior knowledge and discussing it with others rather than primarily working alone (Watson & Battistich, 2006).

Managing learning communities still calls for the same basic principles: develop rules and procedures outlining the student role expectations associated with the instructional methods and activities that will be used; communicate these expectations clearly; and to the extent necessary, instruct students in the procedures involved, cue them when these procedures are called for, and follow through by enforcing rules. However, in addition to emphasizing attention to lessons and timely completion of assignments, teachers will need to prepare their students to meet the additional role expectations that the learning communities concept implies.

In whole-class settings, the social construction of knowledge requires not merely listening to the teacher or one's peers, but participating actively in discussion by volunteering comments, citing relevant arguments and evidence to support one's position, and responding to the comments of others in ways that advance the discussion productively. In small-group settings, it requires collaborating with peers to clarify the task or problem involved, generate and assess ideas about ways to approach it, and then implement the negotiated plans.

Students need to listen carefully to one another's contributions and to treat peers with respect, by responding analytically to their substantive content ("I don't think that strategy will work because . . .") and avoiding pejorative comments ("That's a stupid idea!"). The academic disciplines have established forms of discourse that are used in constructing knowledge, such as "I want to argue for/against that hypothesis because . . ." (science), or "My interpretation is that the scene was meant to illustrate the hero's character flaw of . . ." (literature).

These forms of discourse require students to assume greater responsibility for participating actively in lessons and collaborating with peers in small-group learning activities. A broadened approach to classroom management is needed to prepare students for these extended responsibilities. Simply inviting them to generate ideas or self-regulate their learning does not guarantee that important questions will be asked or productive learning activities will occur. It may take considerable time to bring students to the point that the quality of their discourse approaches the ideals embedded in the learning community notion (Morine-Dershimer, 2006).

It is important to adopt management goals that stress internalization and self-regulation of learning, rather than just compliance with external control, for three reasons. First, maintaining control through compliance requires constant monitoring, and if the teacher turns his or her back, students are likely to misbehave. Second, compliance that is not internalized does not transfer from one setting to another or help students develop more generalized self-regulation strategies and dispositions. Third, some learning activities will not be implemented effectively if students function only at a compliance level. For example, effective collaborative learning in small groups is unlikely unless students have been taught how to work together in these settings. Because much work in small groups is unsupervised, the degree to which small groups function effectively will depend on the degree to which teachers succeed in eliciting students' commitment to the goals of the activities and teaching them how to budget their time, work collaboratively, resolve conflicts productively, and so on.

*M*anaging Small-Group Learning

Basic management tasks are similar in large- and small-group settings, but there are special issues to address in small groups (Dunne & Bennett, 1990; Good et al., 1989, 1990; Lotan, 2006; Webb & Palincsar, 1996). Managing several small groups (e.g., seven groups of 4) is more difficult than managing one class of 28 or two groups of 14. You can only interact with a small portion of the class at a time. So, assignments must be appropriate both for learning (task is meaningful and challenging to all students) and for student self-management (groups can handle minor disagreements and know how to get help when needed).

Make group work meaningful by explaining the task and allowing students to discuss its purpose and procedures before moving into small groups. Students may need to role-play or receive instruction in various aspects (what cooperation means, how to handle conflict, helping versus giving answers without explaining, etc.).

Sometimes, one or two students may do all the work or the group may engage in undesirable social behavior, so you will have to hold individuals accountable for accomplishing the group goals (e.g., through class discussion following group work and through later exams). Some groups will finish before others, so they will need to know what to do while they wait for the others to finish. Be sure to socialize students against rushing their work at these times. We will say more about managing small groups in Chapter 6.

SUMMARY

The key to successful classroom management is prevention—teachers do not have to deal with misbehavior that never occurs. Many problems originate when students are confused, crowded together, or forced to wait.

Plan classroom arrangement and equipment storage so that traffic is dispersed and needed items are accessible. Minimize waiting by allowing students to handle most management tasks on their own, by eliminating needless rituals and formalities, and by assigning various jobs to be done simultaneously by different subgroups. Minimize confusion and idleness by preparing appropriate independent work assignments in sufficient quantity and variety and by seeing that students know what to do if they finish or need help.

Specify desired behavior in positive terms, provide instruction and opportunities to practice routines, offer cues or reminders when procedures are to be followed, and monitor students for compliance. Establish clear signals to gain students' attention and alert them when an activity is beginning, provide a brief overview or advance organizer to help them prepare for it, and then keep the activity moving at a brisk pace, avoiding unnecessary delays. If an activity has gone on too long, end it. When it is necessary to hold students accountable for material and to stimulate their continuing attention, avoid predictable questioning patterns that tempt certain students to try to "beat the system." Fade the more directive aspects of management to minimal levels as students acquire the ability to manage their own learning with increasing degrees of autonomy and responsibility.

If you use social constructivist or learning community approaches, adjust your management strategies accordingly. Prepare students to fulfill expanded responsibilities that include constructing knowledge by participating in discourse and collaborating with peers to plan and carry out learning activities.

Consistently applying the strategies presented in this chapter will maximize productive student activity. To be most effective, however, all aspects of good management must occur in combination as a *system*. Attempts to use certain techniques in isolation are unlikely to succeed for long.

SUGGESTED ACTIVITIES AND QUESTIONS

1. Some students might interpret teachers' cues given for accountability purposes as nagging while others see them as helpful hints. Interview three or four different types of students and determine what they think about particular teacher behaviors (Do they like reminders—why? What type?).

   If you do not have access to students, arrange to interview or form a discussion group with three or four classmates to see how you may view the Kounin strategies differently. Are they appropriate in a college setting (e.g., is a predetermined set of dates for quizzes appropriate alerting or needless control?).

[handwritten margin note: students' dif interpretations of teacher strategies]

2. Reread the four vignettes that appear at the start of the chapter. Which of the strategies do you agree with? Why?

3. What routines and procedures will you establish early in the school year?

4. We advise that requests be phrased in a positive language. The examples given in Table 3.1 are primarily elementary-level examples. Write five examples of positive language that would be appropriate at the high school level.

5. Teachers sometimes undermine students' intrinsic motivation by telling them such things as "You've done so well today that I am going to give you a free hour after lunch so you can do the things you really want to do." What guidelines should teachers follow when they summarize learning activities? Apply your ideas to the case study of Ms. Turner in Chapter 1. What would be an effective way to end her lesson? Write out your ending and compare it with those of classmates.

6. Why is it suggested that teachers show variety and unpredictability in asking questions?

7. Specify the minimum set of rules that will be observed in your classroom. Be sure to state them in positive terms. Why are your rules essential for establishing a good learning climate?

8. What preventive steps can teachers take to reduce the number of disruptions they will face?

9. Using the criteria presented for praising effectively, describe how you should respond to these situations: (a) The class as a whole, except for two students, does very well on a test; (b) one of your slowest students struggles but eventually succeeds in doing a relatively easy math problem at the board, in front of the class; (c) one of your alienated underachievers does very well on a test, but you suspect cheating or lucky guessing; (d) Mary and Joe turn in perfect papers again this week, as they have all term long; (e) Randy asks a question that is relevant to the topic and indicates interest and good thinking on his part, although he would have known the answer if he had read the assignment; (f) your lowest reading group finally finishes a reader that the other groups finished weeks ago; (g) dull, methodical Bernie turns in a composition that is trite but neat and error free; (h) creative but erratic Linda turns in a composition that contains exciting content but is written sloppily with many spelling errors.

[handwritten margin note: review praise effectively]

10. In what ways do you expect to manage your classroom just as your K–12 teachers did, and in what ways do you expect to manage it differently?

FORM 3.1. Transitions and Group Management

USE: During organizational and transition periods before, between, and after lessons and organized activities.
PURPOSE: To see if teacher manages these periods efficiently and avoids needless delays and regimentation.
        How does the teacher handle early morning routines, transitions between activities, and cleanup and preparation time?

RECORD ANY INFORMATION RELEVANT TO THE FOLLOWING QUESTIONS:

1. Does the teacher do things that students could do for themselves?

2. Are there delays caused because everyone must line up or wait his or her turn? Can these be reduced with a more efficient procedure?

3. Does the teacher give clear instructions about what to do next before breaking a group or entering a transition? *Students often aren't clear about assignment so they question her during transitions and while she is starting to teach next group.*

4. Does the teacher circulate during transitions, to handle individual needs? Does he or she take care of these before attempting to begin a new activity? *Mostly, problem is poor directions before transition, rather than failure to circulate here.*

5. Does the teacher signal the end of a transition and the beginning of a structured activity properly, and quickly gain everyone's attention? *Good signal but sometimes loses attention by failing to start briskly. Sometimes has 2 or 3 false starts.*

CHECK IF APPLICABLE:

_____ 1. Transitions come too abruptly for students because teacher fails to give advance warning or finish up reminders when needed

_____ 2. The teacher insists on unnecessary rituals or formalisms that cause delays or disruptions (describe)

___✓___ 3. Teacher is often interrupted by individuals with the same problem or request; this could be handled by establishing a general rule or procedure (describe) *See #3 above.*

___✓___ 4. Delays occur because frequently used materials are stored in hard to reach places *Pencil sharpener too close to reading group area, causing frequent distractions.*

_____ 5. Poor traffic patterns result in pushing, bumping, or needless noise

_____ 6. Poor seating patterns screen some students from teacher's view or cause students needless distraction

_____ 7. Delays occur while teacher prepares equipment or illustrations that should have been prepared earlier

FORM 3.2. Classroom Rules and Routines

USE: Whenever sufficient information is available.
PURPOSE: To assess the adequacy of the teacher's system of classroom rules and routines.
Students should be clear about each of the following issues. Check each issue that is handled adequately through classroom rules and routines, and explain the problem when the issue is not handled adequately.

_____ 1. What books and supplies are to be brought to class routinely

_____ 2. Where to sit and store personal belongings

_____ 3. Precisely when class begins and what is expected at that time (in terms of attention to the teacher and advance preparation of materials)

_____ 4. When and for what purposes students may leave their seats

_____ 5. When and for what purposes students may converse with one another

_____ 6. Rules for participation in whole-class or small group lessons (when, if at all, it is allowable to call out responses without first raising one's hand and being recognized)

_____ 7. When it is permissible to approach the teacher with personal concerns and when the teacher should not be interrupted except for emergencies

_____ 8. What to do if you enter the class late or leave it early

_____ 9. Rules regarding use of equipment and learning centers

_____ 10. Procedures for distributing and collecting work or supplies

_____ 11. What forms of student cooperation in working on assignments are allowed or encouraged

_____ 12. Due dates for assignments and penalties for unexcused late, incomplete, or missing work

_____ 13. What will be taken into account in assigning grades

_____ 14. Other (sources of student confusion or managerial difficulty that could be eliminated by clarifying rules or procedures)

NOTES:

Management II: Coping with Problems Effectively

*C*onsistent application of the principles discussed in the previous chapter will minimize problems of inattention and misbehavior. Some such problems will occur, however, and you must be prepared to cope with them. This chapter contains suggestions on how to interpret such problems, accurately identify their causes, and respond effectively. Read the vignettes that follow and consider how you would respond in each situation.

Classroom Vignettes

Elementary School Example

Mr. Brandon is a fifth-grade teacher at Willow Heights Elementary School, located in a well-to-do suburban school district. His students are all from upper-class families, predominantly European Americans but with a 12 percent Asian American representation and a sprinkling of Hispanic Americans and African Americans as well. He has been using small cooperative groups to teach social studies twice a week for thirty minutes.

During small-group time, Mr. Brandon walks the room to monitor the groups' interactions. Today, he overhears Kristin (holding back tears) say, "Carly, that's a cruel thing to say! I am too mature! I've grown up a lot this year!" Carly shrugs and Adam says, "That's right, you have." Then Mark, Carly, and Adam exchange glances, laugh, and say together, "Not!" Now Kristin begins to sniffle. If you were Mr. Brandon, what would you say or do now, if anything? Later?

Middle School Example

Nick Rawlings is an eighth-grader at the middle school in Pattonville, a town of about 8,000 located in an agricultural area. He is sitting in the office awaiting the principal's decision about an out-of-school suspension. The problem started three weeks ago when Nick and five other students created a disturbance during study hall and received a three-day after-school detention. A week after that, a teammate who dislikes Nick shoved him in the locker room after football practice. Nick shoved back, and soon he and Jason Benedict were fighting. The coach reported them (as required by school rules) and the principal gave Nick a three-day in-school suspension.

After this episode, Nick became "fair game." He is not popular, in part because he comes from a poor family. Further, he was retained twice, in the first and third grades, and often is teased because of his family and his poor academic record. One area in which Nick excels is sports. He won the local Punt, Pass, and Kick Contest and represented his school in the state competition. He has been looking forward to playing basketball after the football season ends, but the school has a rule that a student who receives an out-of-school suspension is banned from sports for the rest of the year.

For several consecutive days Nick has been needled relentlessly by team members who dislike him. To his credit, he has refrained from reacting. Today, however, they went too far, and he shoved one of them, knocking him over a bench. According to school rules, the principal should give Nick an out-of-school suspension because this is his third serious infraction.

After Nick tells his side of the story, the principal says, "Nick, there are always reasons why one loses self-control, but there is no acceptable reason. You'll have to live with the consequences. This probably hurts me more than it hurts you, but rules have to be enforced. I have to give you an out-of-school suspension."

Do you agree with the principal's decision? Why or why not?

Junior High School Example

Carolyn Reid is a first-year teacher at Everett, one of three junior highs in a city of about 50,000. The school enrolls a wide array of students from various socioeconomic levels, races, and ethnic backgrounds. Carolyn teaches ninth-grade science. Her third-period class is one of those "fated" classes in which everything that can go wrong does.

Today, there are not enough lab sheets, and while she is rummaging to find more, two lab partners begin the experiment and inadvertently mix the wrong chemicals, causing a fire. Ms. Reid hurriedly puts it out, but in her haste, knocks the Bunsen burner off the table and damages it, so the two students must work with other pairs.

Five minutes later, when the class is finally working on the experiment, Chris Vaughn throws a spitball at Tasha Wood. Tasha watches it land in front of her and smiles to herself. Not satisfied, Chris says in a subdued voice, "Hey, Tasha, look here and give me a smile." Tasha beams, and as she turns to gesture in Chris's direction, she knocks a test tube from her lab table.

How might Carolyn have prevented this situation? What should she do at this point, if anything? Later?

High School Example

Judy Burden teaches an honors English course for seniors at the only high school in Owensboro, a town of about 20,000. She is worried about Allen Thornton, who has been late for her first-period class about half the time and has missed six classes during the first month of school. When Allen is in class, he is cooperative but lethargic. His late arrivals are becoming a joke (and very disruptive). However, he has turned in two acceptable papers. Ms. Burden is meeting with him after class. She confronts him directly: "Allen, I'm concerned about your tardiness and absences. What's going on?" Allen (looking embarrassed) says, "Everything's falling apart this semester! But your class is the only one that I've been late for. Some mornings I just can't get up and get going."

Mrs. Burden: "Why not?" Allen: "I took a job last May at a fast-food chain, and the manager really likes me. In August I was promoted to assistant manager, in charge of the 9 to midnight shift. After midnight, I have to clean up, so I don't get home until 1 A.M. And, if anything goes wrong, like some equipment is dirty or inventories aren't complete, the manager calls me at 6 A.M. to complain or ask questions. I'm trying to get it under control so it won't interfere with my schoolwork, because I really need the job. My family. . . ."

If you were Judy, what would you say or do? Should she talk to Allen's parents? Should consequences be imposed for his excessive absences and tardiness?

$\mathcal{W}$hat Management Problems Do Teachers Face?

Sensational media coverage of a few incidents of school violence has fueled perceptions that schools have become dangerous and drastic measures are needed to make them safe again. In response, legislatures have passed "three strikes" laws and school districts have developed "zero tolerance" policies. However, in recent years, incidents of serious violence have been reported in only about 20 percent of schools and involved only about one student per thousand (National Center for Education Statistics, 2006). Instead of problems with violence or weapons, teachers are much more likely to encounter problems such as attention deficit, hyperactivity, anxiety, depression, substance abuse, or eating disorders.

Meanwhile, laws and policies ostensibly aimed at dangerous students who bring weapons to school often get enforced in ways that go far beyond their intended scope. Beepers, gun-shaped medallions, and nail clippers have been classified as weapons; Midol, asthma medication, and Certs have been classified as drugs; an eleven-year-old was hauled off in a police van for packing a plastic knife in her lunch box to cut chicken; and 2 eight-year-olds were arrested and charged with "making terrorist threats" for wielding a paper gun in class. Largely because of these ill-conceived policies, suspensions and expulsions have risen dramatically in recent years. However, these extreme penalties are levied most frequently on students who are tardy, absent, disrespectful, or noncompliant, not on those who are truly dangerous (Skiba & Rausch, 2006).

Students who do commit criminal acts should be treated accordingly, but it is counterproductive to criminalize minor or one-time misbehavior. Arbitrary expansions of defined grounds for suspension and mindless misapplication of zero tolerance policies are attempts to get rid of irritating or troublesome students, rather than to deal with them effectively. They alienate the suspended students from their schools and make it more difficult for them to succeed academically. This is worrisome, especially because minority students in general and African American males in particular are suspended or otherwise disciplined more frequently and severely than other students, especially for offenses such as "disrespect" that are defined subjectively and thus allow for prejudice and stereotyping (Gay, 2006; Skiba & Rausch, 2006).

Schools need to develop sensible policies concerning weapons and to protect students from bullying and harassment. However, nonviolent students (the vast majority) often present other problems that also deserve attention. In this chapter we offer suggestions for dealing with such problems, beginning with the less serious ones.

Dealing with Minor Inattention and Misbehavior

Techniques for dealing with minor inattention and misbehavior are designed to achieve a single goal: eliminate the problem quickly and with minimal distraction of other students. Use these techniques whenever students are engaged in minor mischief and you want to refocus their attention.

Monitor the Entire Classroom Regularly

Successful classroom managers display "withitness"—they regularly scan the room and nip most problems in the bud. Those who fail to notice developing problems are prone to errors such as failing to intervene until the problem becomes disruptive or spreads to other students, attending to a minor problem while failing to notice a more serious one, or rebuking a student who was drawn into a dispute instead of the one who started it. This makes students more likely to misbehave and also to test teachers by talking back or trying to confuse them. Thus, it is important to monitor the classroom at all times.

Ignore Minor, Fleeting Misbehavior

You should not intervene in every problem, because your intervention may be more disruptive than the problem itself. For example, if a student has dropped a pencil or neglected to put away some equipment, wait until you can address the problem without disrupting ongoing activities. Much minor misbehavior can be ignored, especially when it is fleeting.

Stop Sustained Minor Misbehavior

When minor misbehavior is repeated or intensified, or when it threatens to spread or become disruptive, you will need to stop it. Unless the misbehavior is serious enough to call for investigation (and it seldom is), try to eliminate it quickly and without disrupting the ongoing activity. Use the following techniques to redirect inattentive students.

1. *Eye contact and gesture.* When it can be established, you can cue attention with simple eye contact, perhaps adding head nods or gestures. Eye contact is doubly effective if you monitor regularly. If students know that you continuously scan the room, they will tend to look at you when they misbehave (to see if you are watching). This makes it easier for you to intervene through eye contact.

2. *Touch.* When the students are close by, as in small groups, you can touch them to gain attention. A light tap, perhaps followed by a gesture, delivers the message without need for verbalization. Touching is most useful in the early grades, when much teaching is done in small groups and distraction is a frequent problem. Also, some adolescents resent any touching by teachers.

3. *Physical proximity.* When moving about the room, you often can eliminate minor misbehavior simply by moving close to the offending students. Your presence will motivate them to get busy.

4. *Asking for responses.* During lessons, calling on students for responses compels attention automatically, without requiring mention of the misbehavior. Use this technique with care, however. If you use it too often, students may perceive it as an attempt to "catch" them. Also, your questions must be ones that students can answer. You may need to include reference to discourse that the student did not hear (e.g., "Rachel, Shane says that the villain was motivated by jealousy. What do you think?").

5. *Name dropping.* When giving information rather than asking questions, you can cue the attention of a particular student by inserting his or her name into an instructional statement ("The next step, Rachel, is to . . .").

Dealing with Prolonged or Disruptive Misbehavior

When misbehavior is prolonged, dangerous, or seriously disruptive, you will have to stop it directly. Direct correction is itself disruptive, so use it only when necessary.

Use direct correction when no information is needed—when the disruptive students know what they should be doing and the nature of the misbehavior is obvious (e.g., loud socializing, shooting paper clips, or horseplay). Here, you just need to get the students back on task. For more ambiguous situations in which students may not know what they should be doing or when you are not sure what is going on, you may need to get more information and make some decisions before acting.

Appropriate Direct Correction

There are two effective ways to intervene directly. First, *demand appropriate behavior.* Keep such demands short and direct, naming the students and indicating what they should be doing. Speak firmly, but do not shout or nag. Commands such as "Leon! Get back to your seat and get to work" and "Gail, Laura! Stop talking and pay attention to me" unnecessarily call attention to the misbehavior. Instead, a brief redirection is sufficient: "Leon, finish your work" and "Gail and Laura, look here."

A second direct correction technique is to *remind students of rules and expectations.* If clear rules have been established, you can use brief reminders of these rules to correct misbehavior without sermonizing or embarrassing students unnecessarily. Rule reminders often are the best responses when the class becomes noisy during independent work periods. Rather than naming offenders, just say, "Class, you're getting too loud. Remember, talk only about the assignment, and speak softly." Brief rule reminders are preferable to demanding appropriate behavior because they encourage students to accept responsibility for regulating their own behavior.

Inappropriate Direct Correction

There are several things that you should not do in response to easily interpretable misbehavior. First, *do not ask questions about obvious misbehavior.* If the situation is clear and your goal is simply to return students to productive work, there is no need to conduct an investigation. Also, the questions asked in such situations often are really attacks on the student ("What's the matter with you?" "How many times do I have to tell you to get busy?").

Avoid unnecessary threats and displays of authority. By simply stating how you want students to behave, you communicate the expectation that you will be obeyed. Threats invite power struggles and also indirectly suggest that you are not sure the students will obey.

If students ask why they are being told to do something, give the reasons. If you become defensive and appeal to authority ("You do it because I say so!") you will produce resentment and may trigger an angry outburst. Furthermore, if onlookers believe that you are acting unfairly, your relationship with them will suffer too.

[handwritten: answer "why?"]

Finally, *avoid dwelling on misbehavior (nagging).* In a direct correction situation, there is no reason to describe the present problem in detail or to catalog the student's past misbehavior. Nagging students places you in conflict with them and endangers credibility and respect.

[handwritten: Nagging ⟵]

Teachers sometimes just describe misbehavior instead of changing it. In effect, they tell students that they have given up hope of change ("Carmen, every day I have to speak to you about fooling around instead of doing your work. It's the same again today. How many times to I have to tell you? You never learn."). Instead of ineffectually nagging, the teacher should try to identify the cause of Carmen's misbehavior and develop a solution. Perhaps her assignments are too easy, too difficult, or otherwise inappropriate for her. Perhaps she is "fooling around" with a classmate, so that a conference, and possibly a new seating arrangement, is required. The teacher should discuss it with Carmen and come to an agreement about her future behavior.

[handwritten: find out what causes misbehavior]

Conducting Investigations

When situations are not clear enough to allow you to act, you will need to question one or more students. Your questions should be genuine attempts to get information, addressed primarily to matters of *fact*. Some questions about *intentions* may also be needed to establish what the student was doing and why ("Why did you leave the room?" "Why haven't you turned in your homework?"). However, do not berate students, impugn their motives ("Did you think you could get away with it?"), or raise issues that they cannot answer ("Why didn't you remember to be more careful?").

When questioning to establish the facts in a dispute, talk in private. This avoids putting individuals on the spot in front of the group, where they may be tempted to try to save face with lies or confrontations. When questioning two or more students together, insist that each allow the other to respond without interruption.

When responses conflict, guard against making premature judgments or accusations of lying. Instead, point out the discrepancies and perhaps indicate that you find certain statements hard to believe. This avoids rejecting anyone's statement and leaves the door open for someone to change his or her story.

Make it clear that you expect the truth and back your words with credible actions that cast you as a helper who wants the best for all concerned. There must be no reward for lying and no punishment for telling the truth.

The facts need not always be established in detail. If your goal is to promote long-term development of integrity and self-control, not merely to settle a single incident, it may be useful to leave contradictions unresolved or even to accept a lie or exaggeration without labeling it as such. Such students will respond poorly (conclude that you are picking on them, etc.) if you insist that they are lying when you are unable to prove it. Thus, when confronted with unresolvable discrepancies, remind the students that you try to treat them fairly and honestly and expect them to reciprocate; state that you "just don't know what to think," in view of the contradictions; state that there is no point in further discussion without new information; and restate expectations. Compared with the alternatives (punishing everyone or affixing blame without proof), this procedure promotes progress toward long-run goals by increasing the probability that the students who lied will admit this to themselves and feel remorseful about it.

Conflict Resolution

Most misbehavior can be either prevented or handled on the spot with the techniques described so far. However, students with chronic personality or behavioral problems will require more intensive treatment. Two useful approaches are Gordon's no-lose methods and Jones and Jones' seven-step problem-solving model.

Gordon

Gordon (1974) advocates what he calls the "no-lose" approach to resolving conflicts. It begins with analysis of the degree to which each party "owns" the problem. The teacher owns the problem when the teacher's needs are being frustrated (as when a student persistently disrupts class by clowning). Students own the problem when their needs are frustrated (as when a student is rejected by the peer group). Finally, teachers and students share problem ownership whenever each is frustrating the needs of the other.

Student-Owned Problems.   Gordon believes that student-owned problems call for the teacher to provide sympathy and help, especially in the form of active listening. *Active listening* involves not only inviting students to describe the problem and trying to understand it from their point of view but also reflecting the gist of their statements to show that you have understood them accurately.

Teacher-Owned Problems.   When the teacher owns the problem, Gordon recommends explaining it using "I" messages. *I messages* have three major parts: (1) indicate the specific behavior that leads to the problem ("When I get interrupted . . ."); (2) specify how this behavior affects you (". . . I have to start over and repeat things unnecessarily . . ."); and (3) specify the resulting feelings (". . . and I become frustrated."). Taken together, the three parts link specific student behavior as the cause of a specific effect on you, which in turn produces undesirable feelings in you. The idea is to get the student to recognize both the problem behavior and its effects on you (but without blaming or rejecting the student).

Gordon believes that active listening and I messages will help you and your students to achieve shared rational views of problems and to assume a cooperative, problem-solving attitude. Research by Peterson et al. (1979) showed that I messages reduced disruptive behavior in most students, and other studies have shown mostly positive results (Emmer & Aussiker, 1990).

Shared Problems.   When conflicts are involved (i.e., when problem ownership is shared), Gordon advocates the following six-step *no-lose method* for finding a solution that best satisfies all concerned:

1. Define the problem.
2. Generate possible solutions.
3. Evaluate those solutions.
4. Decide which is best.
5. Determine how to implement the best solution.
6. Assess the effectiveness of this solution after it is implemented. If it is not working satisfactorily for all concerned, begin again and negotiate a new agreement.

Jones and Jones

Based primarily on William Glasser's writings (e.g., Glasser, 1986), Jones and Jones (2001) developed a seven-step model for solving classroom problems.

1. Establish a warm, personal relationship with the student. Problems tend to be smaller and easier to resolve if a positive relationship exists.
2. Ask questions such as "What happened?" to clarify the nature of and reasons for the behavior and encourage the student take personal responsibility.
3. Help the student to make a value judgment by asking questions such as "Is that behavior helping you?" or "Is it helping others?" Students need to see the effects of problem behaviors in the light of their own and others' rights and responsibilities.

ask Questions
← to help
student judge
situation

4. Work out a plan by asking the student what he or she can do differently, as well as what you or other students might be asked to do differently, to solve the problem. At this stage, students who recognize that they need to change their behavior but are unsure about how to do so may need social skills training or other assistance. You also may need to broker agreements by peers to change their behavior (for example, if they have been baiting the student until he or she gets angry and lashes out).

5. Elicit a commitment from the student to follow the plan.

6. After an appropriate time, meet to see if the plan is working.

7. When students do not follow through on their commitments, confront this reality but without either putting down the student or accepting excuses. Reassert expectations and persist in working with the student in the spirit of "Let's analyze why the plan didn't work and develop a new one."

Schoolwide Programs

In recent years, classic approaches to conflict resolution have been incorporated into more general programs that emphasize problem prevention, close teacher–student relationships, and developing learning communities in both the classroom and the school (Elias & Schwab, 2006; McCaslin et al., 2006; Watson & Battistich, 2006). The humanistic philosophy underlying these approaches can be seen in book titles such as *Discipline with Dignity* (Curwin & Mendler, 1988a) and *Teaching with Love and Logic* (Fay & Funk, 1995). It offers a refreshing contrast to the punitive philosophy of rigid three strikes laws and zero tolerance policies.

Freiberg. In the book *Freedom to Learn*, Carl Rogers and H. Jerome Freiberg (1994) offer a model of person-centered classrooms in which students are taught to develop self-discipline by making choices, organizing their time, setting priorities, helping and caring about one another, listening, constructing a social fabric, being peacemakers when others engage in disputes, trusting one another, and learning collaboratively. Creating a person-centered classroom is not a method but a philosophy: Unless teachers believe that their students can be trusted with the responsibilities involved, they won't grant them the freedom they need to make their own choices (and mistakes).

Freiberg (1999) combined classroom management research with person-centered principles to create the Consistency Management and Cooperative Discipline (CMCD) Program. The program involves training school administrators and teachers to develop workable sets of rules, procedures, and behavioral expectations that will be emphasized consistently throughout the school. It incorporates problem prevention strategies as well as emphases on forging positive teacher–student and student–student relationships, identification with the classroom and school, and commitment to learning goals. CMCD improves attendance, classroom and school climate, and student achievement, while reducing disciplinary referrals (Freiberg & LaPointe, 2006).

Comer. James Comer devised the Yale School Development Program as a way to improve the educational experiences of poor minority youth, although the program is applicable in any school (Comer et al., 1999). It seeks to create a school where students feel comfortable, valued, and secure, so they form positive emotional bonds with teachers and a positive attitude toward school. In turn, this facilitates their learning. Three principles underlie the process: (1) schools review their problems in open discussion and a no-fault atmosphere; (2) collaborative working relationships are developed among the principal, teachers, parents, community leaders, and mental and physical health care workers; and (3) all decisions are reached by consensus rather than issued by decree.

Application of the Comer model involves communicating something like the following to a persistently troublesome student: "We know that you are unhappy and that that is part of why you are having trouble in school. We want you in our school, we like you, we know that you can learn and get along, and we want to help you do so. But we cannot tolerate your attacking other students and showing disrespect for your teacher. We know that you don't want to do these things either, so we are going to go a step at a time in helping you make it at school. When you are doing OK at a given step, you can move to the next. You let us know when you think you need more help. When you are not getting along well, we will hold you back. It's up to you. Do you have any ideas about how we can handle this whole thing better? . . ."

Comer model would say " "

This beginning is followed by attempts to ignore minor misbehavior and encourage activities that bring the student positive feedback and success. When the student has a "bad day," it is assumed that something is bothering the student, so he or she is invited to talk about it and is encouraged and helped to reestablish self-control and productive behavior.

"Bad Day" plan

Child Development Project. The Child Development Project integrates research-based principles for developing core social values through a supportive learning community that is centered in the classroom but extends to include the school and the home (through parent involvement activities). Teaching practices include developing warm and supportive relationships with students, helping them to set learning goals and become more self-regulated in their learning, eliciting their ideas regularly, emphasizing prosocial values when discussing behavioral rules and expectations, and frequently allowing students to collaborate in pairs or small groups. The regular curriculum is supplemented with children's literature selections that provide models of and opportunities to discuss what it means to be a principled, caring person. Students are taught to value and care about one another and to resolve conflicts productively. Socialization at the classroom level is extended through schoolwide activities such as cross-age buddies programs and grandparent days, as well as activities in which students engage family members in discussion of topics such as family history. This program has proven effective in improving a broad range of student outcomes (Watson & Battistich, 2006).

Helping Students to Deal with Conflict

Conflict is a normal part of everyday life, because people's agendas do not always coincide. Unless they are taught how to resolve conflicts effectively, students tend to rely on withdrawal or submission, coercive aggression, or trying to get the teacher to force peers to concede. They seldom use integrative negotiation to address the root problem.

David and Roger Johnson (1995) have developed methods for teaching conflict resolution skills designed to help each party (1) achieve his or her goals but also (2) maintain a good working relationship with the opponent in both the short and the long term. Johnson and Johnson (1982) identified the following steps in trying to resolve conflicts of interest:

1. *Confront the opposition* by providing one's view of the conflict and how one feels about it, while asking the opponent to do the same.
2. *Jointly define the conflict* in a way that all concerned can accept. Three guidelines are: (1) describe the behavior that is disliked—do not insult an opponent; (2) define the conflict as a mutual problem to be solved; and (3) define it in the smallest and most precise way possible. Vaguely defined conflicts are inherently difficult to resolve.
3. *Continue communication* of positions and feelings. First understand what the differences are and then attempt to integrate the two positions. The quality of proposed integration and compromises depends on shared understandings of individuals' feelings, perspectives, and needs.
4. *Communicate cooperative intentions.* Communicate that one's motivation is to cooperate in finding a solution, not to win.
5. *Take the opponent's perspective.* Arguing each other's position can help disputants understand the other's perspective and make negotiation easier.
6. *Coordinate motivation to negotiate in good faith.* All participants need to be motivated to seek a successful resolution to the conflict.
7. *Reach an agreement that both parties accept and are committed to implement.* The agreement should specify how individuals will behave differently in the future and how any emerging issues will be resolved.

Teaching basic conflict resolution skills is worthwhile. In addition, you or your school might consider peer mediation programs for students who want to further develop conflict resolution skills and to have the opportunity to practice them in supervised contexts. In these programs, students role-play, react to videotapes, and talk through the advantages and disadvantages of various approaches to conflict resolution (Johnson & Johnson, 2006a; see also the Winter 2004 issue of *Theory Into Practice*).

*P*unishment

Successful classroom managers focus on preventing and solving problems, not punishing misbehavior. This is not surprising, because although punishment can be a powerful tool, its use signifies that a teacher has not been able to cope with a problem. It also communicates lack of confidence in the punished students, indicating that the teacher thinks that their misbehavior is deliberate and they are not trying to improve. Even if accurate, communicating these perceptions can damage students' self-concepts and further reduce their willingness to cooperate.

Teachers who rely heavily on punishment can achieve only limited and temporary success. They may achieve grudging compliance, but at the cost of chronic group tension and conflict. Their students may obey them out of fear when they are present but then become out of control when they are not in the room. Punishment sometimes is necessary, however, and you should use it appropriately when circumstances call for it.

Effective Punishment

Generally, punishment is used only in response to repeated misbehavior. It is a treatment of last resort for students who persist in misbehaving despite continued teacher expressions of concern and assistance. It is a way to exert control over students who will not control themselves. It is not an appropriate response to isolated incidents, even severe ones, if there is no reason to believe that the student will repeat the action. Even with repeated misbehavior, punishment should be minimized when students are trying to improve.

Avoiding punishment

Punishment can control misbehavior, but by itself it will not teach desirable behavior or even reduce the desire to misbehave. When used, it should be employed deliberately as part of a broader response to repeated misbehavior. It should not be applied unthinkingly or vengefully, in response to your own anger.

The effectiveness of a punishment will depend in part on the way you present it to students. Threaten punishment before actually using it, so that students have fair warning. They should see that their own behavior has made punishment necessary.

Tone and manner are important. Avoid dramatizing ("All right, that's the last straw!") or implying a power struggle ("I'll show you who's boss"). Explain the need for punishment in a manner that communicates a combination of concern, puzzlement, and regret over the student's behavior. Your implied message should be, "You have misbehaved continually. I have tried to help with reminders and explanations, but your misbehavior has persisted. I cannot allow this to continue. If it does, I will have to punish you. I don't want to, but I must if you leave me no choice."

Tone + Manner during punishment

v: dont want to

If punishment becomes necessary, it should be related to the offense. If students misuse materials, for example, restrict their use of them for a time. If students continually get into fights during recess, suspend their recess privileges or require them to stay by themselves. Such "response cost" punishments that restrict privileges are preferable to punishments that involve aversives such as severe scolding and physical punishments (Landrum & Kauffman, 2006).

Exclusion from the Group. Place excluded students where they cannot easily attract peer attention, perhaps behind the other students and facing a corner or wall. The idea is to make them feel excluded, psychologically as well as physically.

Whenever possible, tie withdrawal of privileges and exclusion from the group to remedial behavior. Tell students not only why they are being punished, but also what they may do to regain their privileges or rejoin the group ("When you are ready to share with the others without fighting," "When you are ready to pay attention to the lesson"). Giving them a way to redeem themselves will focus their attention on positive behavior and provide an incentive for changing. This is in contrast to "prison sentence" approaches ("You have to stay here for ten minutes." "No recess for three days") that include no explicit improvement demands and make it easy for the student to become

give improvement suggestions as part of punishment

resentful. Even worse are inflexible overreactions ("You'll stay after school for a week, . . . get an F in conduct, . . . have to get special permission to leave your seat from now on") that leave you stuck with either enforcing them or taking them back.

When students indicate that they are ready to behave properly, accept their stated intentions without "grilling" them and then welcome them back into the group. Avoid vague phrases like "Well, we'll see." Instead, instruct them to rejoin the class ("I'm glad to hear that. I hate to have to exclude you from the class. Go back to your seat and get ready for math.").

If excluded students offer only halfhearted pledges to reform, you may wish to hold out for a more credible commitment, especially if there has been a previous history of failure to follow through. Do this with caution, however: It is better to give students the benefit of the doubt than to risk undermining reform efforts. If you do reject a pledge, make your reasons clear. The student must see that you are acting on the basis of observed behavior.

Inappropriate Punishment

Abusive Verbal Attacks. These are never appropriate. Severe personal criticism cannot be justified on the grounds that the student needs it. It has no corrective function and will only cause resentment, both in the victim and in the rest of the class.

Physical Punishment. We do not recommend physical punishment, even where it is legal, for several reasons. First, it places you in the position of attacking students, physically if not personally. This can cause injury and will undermine your chances of dealing with the students effectively in the future.

Although often defended by principals and teachers, physical punishment typically is used counterproductively, mostly by inexperienced or poorly trained personnel who have not learned effective alternatives; used against younger students from lower-class and minority groups, who are unlikely to defend themselves physically or legally; and used for such offenses as tardiness, unfinished homework, or forgotten gym clothing rather than physical aggression or insubordination (Hyman & Wise, 1979). In short, it is used by the ineffective to take out their frustrations on the weak and vulnerable.

Physical punishment is intense and focuses attention on itself rather than on the misbehavior that led to it. Yet, it is over quickly and has an air of finality about it, so it usually fails to induce guilt or acceptance of personal responsibility for misbehavior. Finally, its long-term costs outweigh any short-term benefits. The least controlled, most hostile students usually come from homes where their parents beat them regularly. Violent criminals almost always have home backgrounds in which physical punishment was common (Goldstein, 1999). Physical punishment teaches people to attack others when angry. It does not teach them appropriate behavior, which is the purpose of discipline.

Extra Work. We do not recommend using extra assignments as punishments because this may cause students to view schoolwork as drudgery. Requiring students to copy rules or write compositions about them can be effective, depending on how it is handled. Having them write "I must not disrupt the class" five or ten times might be helpful, but requiring them to write it fifty times calls more attention to the punishment than the rule.

Ask older students to write a composition about how they should behave. This will force them to think about the rationales underlying the rules. Follow up by discussing the composition with the student (punishment is only part of the treatment).

Lowering Academic Grades.   Students who misbehave frequently often are low achievers as well, and lowering their grades as punishment for misbehavior is likely to further alienate them from academic efforts. Except when the punishment is *directly related* and *proportional* to the offense, as when a student who cheats on a test is given a failing grade for that test (and only that test), students should not be punished by having their grades lowered.

Also, avoid consequences such as denial of opportunity to play sports or play in the band as punishments for misbehavior in the classroom. Such punishments are certain to be viewed as unfair and to further alienate the student from school.

Punishment as a Last Resort

We cannot stress too strongly that punishment is a measure of last resort, appropriate only as a way to curb disruptive behavior in students who know what to do but refuse to do it. This does not mean that all nondisruptive problems should be ignored. Chronic withdrawal, daydreaming, or sleepiness can be serous problems, especially if they are related to drug use. However, punishment is not an appropriate response to such behavior. Nor is it helpful for problems such as failure to answer questions or to do assigned work. Students who fail to turn in work should not be punished beyond imposition of standard penalties for late or missing work. More importantly, they should be made to complete the work during free periods or after school (this is not punishment, but insistence that students meet their responsibilities).

For presentation and analysis of an extended vignette illustrating application of the principles discussed to this point in the chapter, see Appendix 4.1.

Choosing Your Role

As students progress through school, their personal and social development affects the role of the teacher and the goals and techniques of classroom management. Brophy and Evertson (1978) identified four developmental stages:

1. *Kindergarten and the early elementary grades.* Here students are socialized into the student role and instructed in basic skills. The emphasis is on teaching them what to do rather than on getting them to comply with familiar rules. Most students are disposed to do what they are told, and likely to feel gratified when they please teachers and upset when they do not. They turn to teachers for directions, encouragement, solace, and personal attention. Teachers spend considerable time teaching them how to carry out basic routines and procedures.

2. *The middle elementary grades.* This stage starts when basic socialization to the student role is completed and continues as long as most students remain adult-oriented and relatively compliant. Students are familiar with most school routines and serious disturbances are not yet common. Creating and maintaining an appropriate learning environment remain central to teaching success, but these tasks consume less time and teachers are able to concentrate on instructing students in the formal curriculum.

3. *The upper elementary or junior high school grades.* As more and more students change their orientation from pleasing teachers to pleasing peers, they begin to resent teachers who act as authority figures. Some become more disturbed and harder to control than they used to be. As a result, classroom management again becomes a prominent part of the teacher's role. Now, however, the primarily focus is motivating students to behave as they know they are supposed to, not showing them what to do, as in the first stage.

4. *The upper high school grades.* As many of the most alienated students drop out of school and the rest become more mature, classrooms once again assume an academic focus. Management requires even less time than it did during the second stage, because students handle most student role responsibilities on their own. Teaching at this level is mostly a matter of instructing students in the formal curriculum, although socialization occurs during informal, out-of-class contacts with individual students.

Consider these developmental aspects of classroom management when thinking about the grade levels at which you want to teach. If you like to provide nurturant socialization as well as instruction, enjoy working with young children, and have the patience and skills needed to socialize them into the student role, you would be especially effective in the primary grades. If you would like to teach in the elementary grades but want to concentrate mostly on instruction, you would be best placed in the middle grades. Grades 7 to 10 would be best if you enjoy or at least are not bothered by "adolescent" behavior and see yourself as a socialization agent and model at least as much as an instructor. The upper high school grades are best if you want to function mostly as a subject-matter specialist.

Teachers as Socialization Agents

At all four levels of schooling, there are problem students who require intensive management and socialization. Many will have social-emotional needs that interfere with their attempts to meet the challenges of schooling. You will have to develop knowledge and strategies for fostering their social-emotional adjustment, as well as enabling them to make satisfactory academic progress. Some teachers are expected to address these needs primarily on their own, especially if they work in an elementary school where they teach the same students all day and have only limited access to social workers or counselors. High school teachers are not expected to assume as much of the student socialization burden, especially with students they see for only one period each day. In fact, at most urban and suburban high schools, dealing with problem students has become more of a school-level function performed by administrators and professional specialists.

In between these two extremes of the elementary teacher–socializer expected to take full charge of the whole child and the secondary subject-matter specialist expected to concentrate on academics, there is a range of teaching situations and associated role expectations. Teachers at middle, junior high, or even high schools may be expected to assume considerable socialization responsibilities if they work within a small team or a "school within a school" arrangement designed to ensure that they get to know their students as individuals. Or, they may be expected to work closely with a school counselor or social worker in seeking to resocialize problem students. On the other hand, if they teach in a large, impersonal, and bureaucratic school, they may be expected only to refer "troublemakers" to the office for "discipline."

Teachers have to decide which problems they are prepared to handle on their own; which require consultation with a school administrator, counselor, psychologist, social worker, or educational specialist; and which require the involvement of community agencies or resources beyond those available at the school. They also need to work with parents, usually to simply share information and perspectives on the problem and develop mutually acceptable plans for addressing it, although in some cases to solicit parent cooperation in arranging for assessment and potential specialized treatment by professionals.

There has been much debate, but little research and certainly no conclusive evidence, about how to handle the most serious behavioral problems: racial and other group tensions; severe withdrawal and refusal to communicate; hostile, antisocial acting out; truancy; drug abuse; refusal to work or obey; vandalism; and severe behavior disorders or criminality. Therapists have not achieved much success in dealing with behavior disorders, and neither they nor correctional institutions have dealt effectively with severe delinquency and criminality. Yet, teachers must cope with such problems while also instructing all students in the curriculum.

Some teachers accept this challenge by addressing the full spectrum of responsibilities with determination to solve whatever problems come along. However, other teachers are philosophically opposed to this level of emphasis on student socialization, are not interested in it, believe that they are temperamentally unsuited to it, or are hesitant to engage in much of it without specialized training. These positions are understandable and, to an extent, justified. Teachers who recognize their limitations and work within them will have more positive effects than those who try to do everything and end up doing nothing very well.

However, there are limits to how much teachers can minimize their roles as authority figures and socializers of students. Research on schoolwide approaches to managing disruptive behavior has shown that administrators and teachers work together in schools that respond effectively to problem students. In contrast, there are more behavior problems in schools where teachers place most discipline issues immediately into the hands of administrators and emphasize control and punishment over helping students to develop more productive behavior (Gottfredson & Gottfredson, 1986; Hawkins, Doueck, & Lishner, 1988; Jones, 1996). Jones argued that teachers should assume responsibility at least for initial efforts at corrective intervention. We also encourage you to take a proactive role in guiding and socializing at least some of your troubled students, especially ones who have no other positive role models.

Difficulties of Socialization

If you do want to socialize students in addition to providing academic instruction, you must be prepared to take other steps:

1. Cultivate personal relationships with students that go far beyond those necessary for purely instructional purposes.
2. Spend time outside of school hours dealing with students and their families without receiving extra financial compensation for your efforts.
3. Deal with complex problems that have developed over a period of years, without benefit of special training as a mental health professional.
4. Perhaps encounter some opposition from school administrators.
5. Perhaps encounter expressions of frustration or resentment from students, their parents, or others involved in the situation.

Teachers typically do not have the luxury of interacting with students in a friendly, noncontrolling therapist's role. Instead, they must find ways to reach disturbed students while still acting as an authority figure and dealing with them on a daily basis. Rewarding experiences occur, but so do frustrations. Some students do not respond despite continued attempts to reach them. Others make initial progress but end up worse than they started. Not all "success cases" respond with overt gratitude. Finally, teachers can work intensively with only so many students at one time, so they must be selective about their "caseloads," holding them to a manageable limit.

Yet, teachers have certain advantages over mental health professionals in helping troubled students. They see their students every day and under a variety of conditions, so they have better information about them than most therapists (who usually must rely on what their clients choose to tell them). Also, teachers are sometimes in a position to take direct action to help students cope with their problems, rather than just coaching them from afar. Even the authority-figure role has its advantages. Teachers can provide consequences (both rewards and punishments) to selected student behavior, and in the process, attempt to resocialize the students' beliefs and attitudes. Finally, teachers' interactions with their students are viewed as normal forms of adult–child contact, so there is no reason for students to feel ashamed or identified as abnormal when their teachers talk with them about their problems.

If you think that you can try to reach students persistently despite frequent frustrations, you probably have a good chance to be a successful socialization agent. Maintaining caring relationships with challenging students does entail "emotional labor," but it also creates opportunities to experience richer satisfactions.

Coping with Serious Adjustment Problems

Most classrooms have students whose serious and continuing problems require individualized treatment beyond that suggested so far. Although different problems require different treatment, certain general considerations apply to all of them.

Do Not Isolate Students or Label Them as Unique Cases.   Labels call undue attention to misbehavior and suggest that more of the same is expected. Behavior problems are harder to eliminate once they become labeled as characteristic of a student.

Stress Desired Behavior.   Stress desired behavior, not the misbehavior the student is showing. Think, talk, and act in a manner consistent with the intention of moving the student toward desired behavior. For example, if property destruction is due to impulsiveness or carelessness, instruct the student about how to handle property carefully. If stealing results from real need (poverty), plan with students ways they can borrow the stolen items or earn the right to keep them. Meanwhile, praise them for progress in acting responsibly or respecting the property rights of others. If students have been stealing to seek attention or express anger, help them recognize this and develop better ways to meet their needs.

Focus on Students' School-Related Behavior.   Seriously disturbed behavior in school is usually part of a larger pattern of disturbance caused by many factors, including some that you can do little or nothing about (parental conflict, inadequate or sadistic parent, poor living conditions). Even so, all students can learn to behave at school. Factors in the home or other out-of-school environments may need to be taken into account, but do not use them as excuses for failing to deal with school problems.

   Generally, you should confine your treatment efforts to school behavior and aspects of the home environment that are closely related to school behavior (such as asking parents to see that students do their homework and get to bed early enough on school nights). Going beyond such expected teacher concerns is risky unless you have both therapeutic expertise and a good relationship with the student and the family.

Build a Personal Relationship with the Student.   Build close relationships with problem students as individuals, both to develop better understanding of their behavior and to earn the respect and affection that will make them want to respond to your change efforts. Take time to talk with them individually, after school or at conferences during school hours. Encourage them to talk about their problems in their own words. Listen carefully and ask questions when you do not understand. Make clear your concern about their welfare (not merely their misbehavior) and your willingness to help them improve.

   Deep-rooted problems will not be solved with one conference. It is sufficient as a first step if both parties communicate honestly and feel that progress has been made. Discussions should continue until mutual understanding is reached and both parties agree to try a particular plan.

   Most of these suggestions reflect the findings of the Classroom Strategy Study, which focused on teachers' reported strategies for coping with students who present chronic personality or behavior problems (Brophy, 1996). Two factors were consistently associated with principals' and observers' ratings of teachers' effectiveness in dealing with difficult students. The first was a *willingness to assume responsibility for solving the problem*. Higher-rated teachers tried to address problems personally, whereas lower-rated teachers often disclaimed responsibility or competence to deal with problems or referred them to the principal. Second, higher-rated teachers emphasized *long-term, solution-oriented approaches to problem solving*, including helping their students to understand and cope with the causes of their misbehavior. In contrast, lower-rated teachers emphasized controlling misbehavior in the immediate situation, often by relying on threat or punishment. The guidelines suggested in the following sections reflect the views of these higher-rated teachers, as well as the findings of other research studies cited.

Showing Off.   Some students continually seek attention by trying to impress or entertain teachers or peers. They can be enjoyable if they have talent for the role and confine it to appropriate times. Often, though, they are exasperating or disruptive. The way to deal with show-offs is to give them the attention and approval they seek, but only for appropriate behavior. Ignore inappropriate behavior, or when it is too disruptive to be ignored, do not call attention to it or make the student feel rejected. Thus, a comment like "We're having our lesson now" is better than "Stop acting silly." Show-offs need constant reassurance that they are liked, and you should try to fill this need. However, their inappropriate behavior should go unrewarded and, as much as possible, unacknowledged.

Unresponsiveness.   Some students lack the self-confidence to participate normally in classroom activities. They do not raise their hands to answer questions and they copy, guess, or leave an item blank rather than ask for help. When they are called on and do not know an answer, they stare at the floor silently or perhaps mumble incoherently. Sometimes this "strategy" is successful, because many teachers become uneasy and give the answer or call on someone else rather than keep such students "on the spot."

Working with shy or inhibited students requires steady and patient pressure for change, applied indirectly and supportively. Attacking the problem by labeling it and urging students to overcome it can backfire by making them more self-conscious and inhibited. Use private talks and special activities or assignments to draw them out, encourage efforts, praise accomplishments, and minimize stress or embarrassment. Ask questions directly rather than preface them with stems such as, "Do you think you could . . . ," which suggest uncertainty and make it easy for students to remain silent. Accompany your questions with appropriate gestures and expressions to communicate that you expect an answer. If you get one, you might say, "Good! Say it louder so everyone can hear." When students appear to be about to answer, but hesitant, help by nodding your head or encouraging verbally, "Say it!" When they do not respond at all, give the answer and then repeat the question or ask the student to repeat the answer. Make it clear to students that they are expected to speak up, give them practice in doing so, and reassure and reward them when they do.

Inhibited students need careful treatment when they do not respond. As long as they appear to be trying to answer the question, wait them out. If they begin to look anxious, intervene by repeating the question or giving a clue. Do not call on another student or allow others to call out the answer.

If necessary, cut off anxiety or resistance before it builds. Students who do not respond to questions requiring a verbal answer can be asked to make nonverbal responses such as shaking their heads or pointing. It is important to get some form of positive response before leaving these students. Do not allow them to "practice" resistance or unresponsiveness.

Tell all of your students to say "I don't know" rather than remain silent when they cannot respond. Many will hesitate to say "I don't know," because previous teachers made comments such as "What do you mean you don't know?" By legitimating "I don't know," you make it possible for students to respond verbally even when they do not know the answer.

These methods can be difficult to apply in large-group situations. Extremely unresponsive students who often do not say anything at all may have to be brought along slowly in individual and small-group situations first. A smaller setting does not necessarily make communication easier, however. Shy students may be encouraged by other students to remain passive during small-group activities (Mulryan, 1992). Getting rid of strong inhibitions or fears takes time, and much progress can be undone by trying to push too far too fast.

Failure to Complete Assignments. Some students do not turn in work because they have not been able to figure out how to do it. This is not a motivational problem; it is a teaching problem that calls for helping students learn what they do not understand. This may seem obvious, but struggling students report that teachers often not only fail to provide this help but also routinely collect seatwork before they can finish it (Weinstein & Middlestadt, 1979).

Show patience and determination with slow students, because they need support and encouragement just to keep trying. Encourage them by pointing out their progress and by making time for remedial teaching with them.

A different problem is presented by students who can do the work but do not finish it or turn it in. The best way to deal with this problem is to stop it early, before it becomes entrenched. From the beginning of the year, be clear about expectations for seatwork and homework. Their purpose and importance should be explained, and the assignments should be collected, checked, and followed up with feedback and, when necessary, remedial work.

Although you may wish to make open-ended assignments (such as identifying problems to do for extra credit or "to see if you can figure them out"), all students should have a clear-cut minimum amount of work for which they are accountable. They should know what to turn in, when it is due, and the consequences for missing the deadline. Also, make it clear that they are expected to finish assignments before they do anything else during independent work times, and monitor to see that they are working productively.

Failure to turn in homework is a more difficult problem, because you cannot monitor and intervene if students are not working properly. You can keep track of whether homework is being turned in, however, and require students who did not complete it to do so during free periods. Those who do not complete the job during free periods should be kept after school. If failure to turn in homework is common, you may need to adjust the nature or difficulty level of the homework or the way it is monitored and corrected.

Attention Deficit and Hyperactivity Problems. Most students have at least occasional problems maintaining concentration on lessons and assignments, but a few show chronic inattentiveness. In the primary grades this typically takes the form of short attention span or distractibility. In later grades it may be manifested more as daydreaming or difficulty in sustaining concentration on work.

Another common problem is behavioral hyperactivity. Certain students show excessive and almost constant movement. They are easily excitable, tend to blurt out answers and comments, are often out of their seats, and even when in their seats are likely to be squirming, jiggling, or bothering other students with noises or movements. Attentional distractibility and behavioral hyperactivity often go together.

Laub and Braswell (1991) collected suggestions from teachers concerning ways to keep distractible students involved in lessons. They recommended seating these students near the teacher and facing the teacher during lessons, as well as creating study carrels or other distraction-reduced environments for them to use when working on assignments. They also recommended standing near these students when presenting lessons or giving instructions, actively involving them by asking them to hold up props or write ideas on the board, using their names or calling on them frequently during lessons, and often using computerized learning, cooperative learning, or other formats that allow for more active participation.

The higher-rated teachers from the Classroom Strategy Study also recommended helping these students learn to monitor and control their attention more successfully. If organization is a problem, you can help distractible students learn to keep track of their things by making schedules, keeping assignment notes and checklists, and periodically taking stock of their accomplishments and reorganizing their folders and work areas.

Despite a diversity of views about the nature and causes of behavioral hyperactivity, research reviews show a great deal of agreement about effective treatment approaches (Barkley, 1998; Bender, 1997; DuPaul & Stoner, 1994; Parker, 2001; Rief, 1993). Three main approaches are commonly recommended: medication, behavioral treatments, and cognitive-behavioral treatments.

The most prevalent therapy, and also the most efficacious and carefully studied, is stimulant *medication*—typically methylphenidate (Ritalin). In about 75 percent of cases, it produces immediate and dramatic reductions in hyperactive behavior and improved performance on tasks requiring concentrated attention. However, two cautions should temper your enthusiasm for using stimulant medication. First, there has been a dramatic increase in the percentages of students diagnosed with attention deficit/hyperactivity disorder (ADHD). This is troublesome, because a great deal of subjective judgment goes into determining whether a student is "hyperactive" or merely more active than most other students but in ways that do not amount to a "disorder" that calls for medical treatment. Many students are unnecessarily being labeled "ADHD" and treated with stimulants that they do not need and that may dispose them toward lifelong drug dependency (Panksepp, 1998). Second, even though stimulant medication reduces hyperactivity, it has only negligible effects on achievement and social behavior (Purdie, Hattie, & Carroll, 2002). Thus, it is only a partial treatment. A comprehensive approach also includes components designed to improve academic skills, motivation to learn, or general intellectual or moral functioning.

Behavioral treatments, particularly contingency contracting and other reinforcement-based methods, are commonly recommended for this purpose. Because hyperactive students often have attention deficits as well, it is important to be clear and specific in stating behavior goals, specifying the contingencies between behaviors and consequences, and reminding them of these contingencies when following through.

Cognitive-behavioral treatments train hyperactive students in skills such as coming to attention and settling into a task, concentrating on task-relevant stimuli, keeping aware of goals and strategies, budgeting time, delaying gratification, and inhibiting inappropriate responses. Early applications of cognitive strategy training with hyperactive students produced mixed results, but the findings have become more promising as effective procedures have been developed and synthesized (Mennuti, Freeman, & Christner, 2006; Miranda & Presentacion, 2000; Robinson et al., 1999). Braswell and Bloomquist (1991) have published a manual for planning and carrying out cognitive-behavioral interventions with hyperactive students.

Popular books and articles on hyperactivity often recommend a fourth treatment: avoiding or limiting exposure to food additives, fluorescent lighting, bright colors, sugars, or other substances described as toxic to children in general or hyperactive children in particular. Unfortunately (because it would be nice to see a complex problem have a simple solution for a change), research does *not* support these ideas.

ideas (not sup. by research)

Several common themes appear in suggestions to teachers about instructing hyperactive students. One is "Don't let these kids turn you off so that you begin to treat them inappropriately." The disruptions caused by hyperactive students can be exasperating, making it difficult for you to be welcoming and supportive with them. Hyperactive students typically report feeling misunderstood and rejected by their teachers and often their classmates, as well as constantly being criticized for doing things they were not even aware of doing (Weiss & Hechtman, 1986).

Don't get so fed up!

A related point is that just because hyperactive students often display normal attention and self-regulation for short periods of time, this does not mean that they can do it all the time "if they really want to." Without blaming them, make these students realize that disruptions take time away from instruction and that hyperactive behavior (especially if aggressive) turns off peers and impedes the formation of friendships. Then reassure them that you and they will work on their problems together.

Higher-rated teachers from the Classroom Strategy Study emphasized the need to increase hyperactive students' awareness of their behavior and its effects on the teacher and their classmates, to impress on them the need to develop better self-control, and to help them do so by giving them cues and reminders, shaping improvements through successive approximations, praising and rewarding such improvements, reducing distractions during work times, and allowing more frequent opportunities to move about (Brophy, 1996).

it is important for them to understand

Defiance.   Most teachers find defiance threatening, even frightening. How can you respond when students vehemently talk back or refuse to do what they are asked to do? To begin with, remain calm so as not to get drawn into a power struggle. The natural tendency of most adults is to get angry and strike back with a show of force to show such students that they "can't get away with it." This may suppress the immediate defiance, but it will probably be harmful in the long run, especially if you lose your temper or publicly humiliate the student.

Pausing a moment before responding to defiance offers two advantages: (1) you gain time to control your temper and think about what to do before acting; and (2) the mood of the defiant student is likely to change from anger or bravado to fear or contrition. When you do act, do so decisively but in a calm and quiet manner. If possible, give an assignment to the class and remove the defiant student for a private conference. If this is not possible or if the defiant student refuses to leave for a conference, state that the matter will be discussed after school. Your tone and manner should communicate serious concern, but not threats. Stating that the matter will be dealt with in a private conference tells the class that you will handle the situation, yet does not humiliate the defiant student or incite further defiance. You can even afford to let the student "have the last word," because the matter will be taken up again later.

Students are unlikely to defy their teachers unless they resent them for some reason. Therefore, be prepared to hear defiant students out. If they claim unfair treatment, entertain the possibility that it is true. Let them say everything they have on their minds *before* responding to the points they raise. This helps you to get the full picture and allows time to think about what you are hearing. If you try to respond to each point as it is raised, the discussion may turn into a series of accusations and rebuttals. Such exchanges usually leave students feeling that their objections have been "answered," but they still are right in claiming unfair treatment.

With some defiant students, it may be important to review your role. Help them understand that you are interested primarily in teaching them, not in ordering them around or playing police officer, but this requires their cooperation. Regardless of the points students raise, express concern for them and a desire to treat them fairly. If you have made mistakes, admit them and promise to change.

Even serious defiance can usually be handled with one or two sessions like these. Although unpleasant, incidents of defiance can be blessings in disguise. They bring out into the open problems that have been brewing for a long time, releasing built-up tensions and leaving the student more receptive to developing a constructive relationship.

Aggression against Peers.   Aggressive students must not be allowed to hurt classmates or damage property. When such behavior appears, demand an end to it immediately. If the student fails to respond, send another student for help and, if necessary and feasible, physically restrain the student who is out of control. Most teachers rarely will be required to intervene in this way, but all should be prepared to do so. Preparation should include training in techniques of restraining students and breaking up fights effectively, as well as clear procedures for handling emergency situations in collaboration with the principal, other teachers, and support staff. Your responsibilities in these situations are first to the safety of yourself and the other students, then to the aggressive student, then to property.

While being restrained, students may respond by straining to get away, making threats, or staging temper tantrums. If so, hold them until they regain self-control. Speak firmly but quietly, assuring them that the problem will be dealt with when they calm down. Reinforce this nonverbally by relaxing your grip as the student tones down resistance.

Do not try to stop a fight by getting between the participants and trying to deal with both at the same time. Instead, restrain one of them, preferably the more belligerent or the one with whom you have less rapport, by pulling him away from his opponent (pull at the belt or waistband, leaving the arms free for self-defense). This will stop the fight, although it may be necessary to order the other participant to stay away. Do a lot of talking at this point, calming the students down and explaining that the matter will be dealt with when they comply. Once they calm down, talk with them individually. Habitually aggressive students must learn that frustration and anger do not justify aggressive behavior. Accept angry feelings that are legitimate or at least understandable, but stress the distinction between feelings and behavior. If angry feelings are not justified, explain in a way that recognizes the reality of the feelings but does not legitimate them ("I know you want to be first, but others do too. So there's no point in getting angry because you have to wait your turn. If you try to be first all the time, everyone will think you are selfish.").

Appeal to the Golden Rule to try to help aggressive students see the consequences of their behavior. Students usually can see that if they dislike and avoid others who bully, cheat, or destroy property, others will dislike and avoid them for the same reasons. Show by example the value of verbalizing feelings and seeking solutions to problems instead of striking out at others. Teach aggressive students that others will know why they are angry only if they tell them and that hitting will only make the others angry too.

Attacks on others for no apparent reason are more serious. Students who do this regularly may require professional treatment. Even so, you can provide assistance in many ways. For example, suppose that a student has developed a self-image as a "tough guy" and actually wants others to fear him. As with any serious problem, deal with the aggressive acting out as it occurs and talk with the student to develop understanding and to explain behavioral expectations. In addition, cope with the problem indirectly, to help both the student and others in the class to see him in a more positive light.

First, avoid labeling the student. Instead, express confidence that he will achieve better self-control and arrange for him to play positive roles toward his classmates. It might be helpful for this student to be used as a tutor to teach academic content or other skills that he may know (tying shoes, operating equipment, arts and crafts, music, or other talents). In reading and role-playing situations, he should be assigned parts that feature kindness, friendship, and helpfulness toward others. He would be ideal for the part of an ogre who everyone feared and disliked until they found out how good he was underneath.

One frequently advocated technique that we do *not* recommend is providing substitute methods for expressing aggression, such as telling the student to hit a punching bag instead of another student. By encourage students to act out hostility against substitute objects, you merely prolong and reinforce immature emotional control. If kept up long enough, this will produce adults who are prone to temper tantrums at the slightest frustration and who spend much of their time building up and then releasing hostile feelings. This sort of person is neither happy nor likeable. Instead of trying to get students to act out all emotions, help them to distinguish between emotions and behavior and between appropriate and inappropriate emotions.

The higher-rated teachers from the Classroom Strategy Study placed firm limits on aggressive students, demanded that they curb their aggressive behavior, and were

REFERENCES
↳
website!

prepared to back their demands with punishment if necessary. However, they also encouraged change by providing these students with instruction in more effective ways of handling frustration and conflicts. For more information about interventions with aggressive students, see Goldstein and Conoley (1997), Hudley and Graham (1993), or Pepler and Rubin (1991). For information about dealing with a broad range of student behavior problems, consult the www.disciplinehelp.com Web site.

Anti-Bullying Programs.   The majority of students experience aggression only rarely if at all, but about 15 percent are involved repeatedly in incidents of bullying, either as bullies or victims (Olweus, 1993). Bullying includes verbal or physical aggression involving teasing, taunting, threatening, hitting, or stealing initiated by one or more students against a victim, as well as intentional exclusion activities that socially isolate the victim. The intimidation occurs repeatedly and amounts to an ongoing pattern of harassment and abuse (Hyman et al., 2006).

Chronic bullies have strong needs for power and control, derive satisfaction from inflicting injury, have little empathy, and often coerce money or other things of value from their victims. Victims tend to be students with low self-esteem who are anxious, insecure, cautious, and unlikely to defend themselves. They often are isolated socially because even peers who sympathize with their plight tend to blame them for their failure to fight back and consider them undesirable as friends.

Teachers and principals tend to underestimate the amount of bullying that occurs in their schools, and often are reluctant to get involved even when they witness it. Students hesitate to report bullying to adults because they find that they are not taken seriously or told to go back to the bully and "work it out," as if the problem were situational conflict rather than ongoing harassment. They think that adult intervention is infrequent and ineffective, and that telling adults will only bring more harassment from bullies.

Such findings have raised consciousness of bullying, and shooting incidents at schools have led to a flurry of anti-bullying education and intervention programs. Many are modeled on that of Olweus (1993), which emphasizes creating a school characterized by warmth, positive interest, and involvement from adults, along with firm limits to unacceptable behavior. Supervision during recess and lunch periods is improved, and everyone is encouraged to monitor for incidents of bullying. When such incidents are observed, nonhostile, nonphysical sanctions are applied consistently.

In classrooms, teachers work with students to develop rules against bullying and engage them in discussion and role-play to teach them how to assist victims and to create a climate where bullying is not tolerated. Students are taught to stand up to bullies, get adult help, and offer support to victims. Other components include cooperative learning activities to reduce social isolation and interventions with individual bullies and victims.

Treatment of bullies begins with consistent administration of consequences for bullying behavior, along with attempts to help bullies acknowledge and take responsibility for their actions, make restitution to victims, and develop empathy. In the short run, bullies need to learn that their behavior is not cost-effective because it is getting them into increasingly serious trouble and isolating them from peers. In the longer run, they need to develop enough empathy for others, Golden Rule morality (do not do things to others that you would not want done to yourself), and prosocial attitudes and behavior to provide a basis for mutually satisfying social relationships.

Intervention with victims begins with establishing anti-bullying behavioral norms and rule enforcement. Follow-up of specific incidents includes taking steps to ensure that victims do not suffer retaliation or further harassment, counseling to help them work through their feelings, and teaching of skills that will help them become better adjusted socially and less likely to be victimized in the future.

Concerns about violence have focused attention on physical attacks, most frequently by boys on other boys. However, there also is reason for vigilance against vicious taunting, social exclusion, rumor spreading, and other forms of bullying practiced more commonly by girls against girls. Resources for anti-bullying education and intervention programs have proliferated in recent years. Useful Web sites can be located by searching under the topic "bullying in school"; useful books include those by Froschl et al. (1998), Hoover and Oliver (1996), Olweus (1993), and Ross (1996).

*A*nalyzing Problem Behavior

Many forms of problem behavior have not been discussed in this chapter—student habits that irritate or disgust teachers, students who bait teachers with provocative remarks, and various signs of child abuse or mental or emotional disorders. When faced with such symptomatic behaviors, you will need to try to find out why the students are behaving as they are, and in the process, develop clues for successful treatment.

Finding Out What Problem Behavior Means

Begin by questioning and observing the students involved. What is the meaning of their problem behavior? Why does the student act this way? Remember, surface misbehavior may simply be a symptom of an underlying problem, and the symptomatic behavior may not be as important as the reasons that are producing it.

If the behavior is an isolated habit, not part of a larger complex of problems, just insist that the student drop it (adding an appropriate rationale). If the objectionable habit is not immoral but merely in violation of school rules, social convention, tact, good taste, or personal preferences, note this distinction. You are justified in forbidding habits that are disruptive or irritating but should not depict them as worse than they really are, so as to make students feel guilty or believe that something is seriously wrong with them.

If the problem behavior is more serious and the student has not given an adequate explanation for it, careful observation is needed. Begin by describing the behavior more precisely. Is it a ritual that is repeated pretty much the same way over and over (masturbating, spitting, nose picking), or is it a more general tendency that is manifested in many different ways (aggression, suspiciousness, sadistic sense of humor)? Is there a recognizable pattern? For example, do students' suspicions center around a belief that others are talking about them behind their backs, or do they think they are being picked on or cheated? If they think others are talking about them, what do they think is being said? If students laugh inappropriately, what makes them laugh? Such information provides clues as to what the behavior means.

Note the conditions under which the behavior occurs. Is it a chronic problem or something that started recently? Does it happen at a particular time or day of the week (when tests are given, for example, or when the student has lost a competition)? Such common elements might point to events that trigger the reaction.

Also, pay attention to what you were doing immediately before the students acted out. Perhaps you triggered the behavior by treating them in ways that they think are unfair. Analyses of this sort place students' problem behaviors in context and may help identify underlying causes. This will move you away from essentially negative, describe-the-problem-but-don't-do-anything-about-it approaches ("How can I get Lynn to stop sulking?") and toward diagnosis and treatment ("How can I help Lynn see that I am not rejecting her personally when I refuse her requests?").

Arranging a Conference

The simplest and often best way to understand students' behavior is to talk to them about it during a private conference. Convey what you have observed, express concern about the behavior, and ask for an explanation. Students usually lack the insight to explain fully why they act as they do, so do not expect them to. Instead, probe for helpful information. If the discussion does produce a breakthrough, fine. If not, something is still accomplished if students learn that you are concerned about them and wish to help.

Conclude conferences in ways that give students a feeling of closure. If the problem behavior has been disruptive, clarify expectations and forge agreements about any special actions to be taken. If the problem requires no special action or if it is not yet clear what action to take, conclude by telling students that you are glad to have had a chance to discuss the problem and are willing to help if they will let you know how.

Bringing in Parents and Other Adults

If students simply refuse to cooperate in seeking acceptable solutions, or if they persistently fail to follow through on their commitments, you may need to involve the parents or seek help from a social worker, counselor, school psychologist, school administrator, or fellow teacher. Discussing the problem with a good resource person, preferably one who is familiar with the situation and has observed in your classroom several times, may yield new insights or suggestions.

Set the stage for effective problem solving with parents by developing collaborative relationships with them right from the beginning of the school year. Family involvement in children's education is associated with better attendance, more positive attitudes toward school, and higher achievement.

When involving parents, the goal is to find solutions for problems, not to assign blame. The parents are likely to be embarrassed about their child's problems and fearful of interacting with you because they believe that the problems are their fault. Whether or not this is true, you will need to focus on problem solving rather than blaming if you want the parents to play a constructive role.

For example, you might begin by saying something like "I'm seeing some concerns with Sarah that I'd like to share with you. I think that if we work together, we can help Sarah deal with these problems successfully." Then, you might describe your observations in a nonjudgmental way and ask the parents if they are seeing similar problems in Sarah's behavior at home.

Sometimes these inquiries will yield information about stress factors (an impending divorce, a death or serous illness in the family, etc.) that help put the child's classroom behavior into perspective (e.g., seeing it as preoccupation with or defense against fears, and indirectly a cry for help). This knowledge would make you better informed and more able to express concern directly in private interactions with the student ("Sarah, I understand that your brother is sick. I wonder if sometimes you think about this instead of working on your assignments").

Merely informing parents about problems is not helpful. If they get the impression that they are expected to "do something," they might just threaten or punish their child and let it go at that. Therefore, make suggestions about how the parents might help their child, and if necessary, try to resocialize their beliefs about effective child rearing. In particular, the need to think of punishment as a last resort and the need for confidence and positive expectations are two principles that many parents violate when their children have problems.

[handwritten margin note: make suggestions to Parents]

If you are calling parents mostly just to get information, make this clear to them, then communicate observations about their child and ask if they can add anything that might increase your understanding. If some plan of action emerges, discuss it with the parents and agree on its details.

If no parental action seems appropriate, bring the conference to some form of closure ("I'm glad we've had a chance to talk about Ramon today. You've given me a better understanding of him. I'll keep working with him in the classroom and let you know about his progress. Meanwhile, if anything comes up that I ought to know, please give me a call."). Parents should emerge from a conference knowing what to tell their child about it and what, if anything, you are requesting them to do. For more detailed information about strategies for creating, maintaining, and improving home–school relationships, see Hoffman (1991), Kauffman et al. (1993), McCaslin and Good (1996), or Weinstein and Mignano (1993).

[handwritten margin note: resources about Parent involvement]

Other Approaches to Classroom Management

Our approach to classroom management is eclectic, stressing principles gathered from many theories. Other approaches stress principles developed within one theory or point of view. Three of the most prominent are assertive discipline, contingency contracting, and cognitive behavior modification.

Assertive Discipline

Assertive discipline was developed by Lee and Marlene Canter (2002) and is promoted through training workshops sponsored by their corporation. It stresses the rights of teachers to define and enforce standards for student behavior that allow them to instruct successfully. These assertive teachers are contrasted with submissive teachers who fail to enforce standards and hostile teachers who do so but in ways that violate the best interests of students. Recommended methods focus on developing specific expectations for student behavior, translating these into a set of rules that specify acceptable and unacceptable behavior, and linking these to a system of rewards and punishments. The most widely used punishment is a penalty system in which the names of misbehaving students are written on the board and check marks are added following their names for repeated offenses. These students are subject to detention or to progressively more serious punishments including notes sent home to parents, time out from the classroom, or referral to the principal.

The Canters have failed to conduct systematic research on the effectiveness of their approach, and the limited research available does not support claims for its effectiveness (Emmer & Aussiker, 1990; Render, Padilla, & Krank, 1989). Also, several critics have voiced philosophical objections. Curwin and Mendler (1988b) characterized assertive discipline as an example of an *obedience model*, in which power-based methods are used to compel students to conform to rules. They consider such obedience models less desirable than *responsibility models*, in which the goal is to develop responsibility for inner self-guidance in students, using methods that emphasize explanations of the rationales for rules and natural consequences of behavior rather than threats and punishment. Similarly, McDaniel (1981) criticized assertive discipline as being "not much more than applied behavior modification and take-charge teacher firmness with rules and consequences" (p. 82). In response to these criticisms, the Canters have added materials on beginning the school year, working with parents, and helping students with homework. Even so, the program retains its primarily behavioral character and thus in our view is less helpful than more eclectically derived programs.

We do see value in several aspects of the assertive discipline approach. In particular, its emphasis on developing and communicating clear expectations for student behavior can be helpful for teachers who lack both confidence and viable strategies for dealing with problem students. However, we believe that the approach places too much emphasis on threat and punishment, so it is less desirable than the approach outlined here, which is based on replicated findings obtained by several research teams working independently.

Contingency Contracting

Teachers can provide reinforcement when students pay attention, do their work, or obey the rules, and can withhold it when they do not. Students can be given a more active role in this process through *contingency contracting*, which involves conferring about possible alternatives and then jointly drawing up a contract that specifies what the student will be expected to do in order to earn contingent rewards. The contract can be purely oral, although it helps to formalize it by having the student write down its details. Contracts might call for students to complete a certain amount of work at a certain level of proficiency, or to improve their classroom behavior in specified ways, in order to earn specified rewards. For example, a level of performance that will require sustained effort (for a particular student) can be required for a grade of A, with lesser requirements for lower grades.

Contracts for behavioral improvement can be developed using the same principles. Conduct that represents the best that can be expected from *this* student at *this* time can be required for maximum reward, with less acceptable levels producing less reward. As students become able to control themselves more successfully, new contracts requiring better behavior can be introduced.

Contingency contracting usually works best when students are presented with a variety of attractive rewards. These "reinforcement menus" might include treats or other material rewards as well as opportunities to spend time in learning centers or other enrichment activities, to go to the library, to play games, or even just to converse with friends. Specified good behavior or acceptable completion of assignments earn so many points, and these points can be "spent" on rewards. The "prices" of the rewards may vary according to their attractiveness and the demand for them. The most popular ones are the most expensive. Occasional changes in menus or prices provide variety and help avoid satiation with particular rewards.

It is harder than it might seem to arrange contingencies so that desired behaviors are reinforced. Sometimes proper contingencies are not established; at other times, the presumed reward does not actually function as a reinforcer. Analyze the behavior modification attempts presented in the following four examples. Are they likely to be successful? Why or why not?

These are all famous psychologists

1. Ms. Bussey has set up a contingency-contracting system. Students who complete assignments get tokens they can spend on rewards. However, the work must be correct. If students come with incomplete or incorrect work, they must return to their desks and finish it correctly.

2. Mr. Skinner gives out goodies every Friday afternoon as a way to motivate students to apply themselves. He sees that everyone gets something but makes sure to give the more desirable items to students who appear to have worked hard during the week. He refers to this as "payday" and says "Good work" to each student when passing out the treats.

Skinner =

3. Ms. Calvin announces that from now on, the student who finishes the afternoon math assignment first will be allowed to dust the erasers.

Calvin =

4. To encourage his students to keep orderly desks, Mr. Caries occasionally (and unpredictably) announces that today students who do a good job of cleaning their desks will get candy. After allowing enough time, he goes around to check and gives candy to those who have neat desks.

Superficially, all four examples are similar: the teacher offers rewards to improve some performance. However, subtle differences make it likely that only Ms. Bussey will succeed. She has attractive rewards available, and students can get them only by turning in complete and correct work. Assuming that all students can do the work assigned to them, the contingencies are such that her rewards will reinforce sustained and careful work on assignments.

Mr. Skinner will not succeed because there is no clear contingency between performance of the behaviors he is trying to reinforce and delivery of the rewards. All students get some kind of reward whether they apply themselves or not, and differences in the attractiveness of the rewards given to individuals depend on his unsystematic perceptions and fallible memory rather than objective evidence of effort. Some students get more than they deserve, and others get less, because Mr. Skinner does not realize how deserving they are. His students will learn that there is no clear contingency between performance and reward, so that few of them will be motivated to work harder by this gimmick, even though they will enjoy the goodies.

Ms. Calvin's scheme is almost certain to fail, for three reasons. First, she should reward effort and accomplishment, not speed. Second, the opportunity to get rewarded exists for only those students who can work fast enough to finish first. Finally, few students will be motivated by the opportunity to dust erasers. Ms. Calvin is offering a weak reinforcer, susceptible to early satiation.

Mr. Caries will also fail. His rewards are contingent on performance of the desired behavior, but their availability is always announced beforehand. Thus, the contingency here is not "Students who have neat desks every day will get rewarded," but "Students who clean their desks whenever Mr. Caries promises rewards will get rewarded." By always announcing the availability of rewards ahead of time, Mr. Caries eliminates their power to reinforce cleanup efforts even when they are not available.

These examples illustrate some of the problems involved in using contingency contracting in schools. The proper contingencies are hard to establish, and satiation with the available rewards is an ongoing problem. When used effectively, however, contingency contracting helps students to see the relationship between their behavior and its consequences. Also, when they draw up the contracts themselves, they are more likely to make meaningful personal commitments because they express them in their own words. Contracts are especially useful for situations in which students know what they are supposed to do and are capable of doing it if they put their minds to it, but currently are not conscientious or motivated enough to do so consistently.

Contracting provides built-in opportunities for teacher–student collaboration in negotiating expectations and rewards. If perfect performance is currently an unreasonable expectation, the negotiation process might yield specifications calling for rewarding a level of improvement that the student views as reasonable and the teacher is willing to accept (at least for now). Contracting also provides opportunities to offer students choices of rewards, thus ensuring that the intended reinforcement is experienced as such.

Cognitive Behavior Modification

Experience with goal setting, self-monitoring, and other cognitive elements of contingency contracting led to the realization that they have important positive effects of their own, independent of the effects of reinforcement. For example, inducing students to set work output goals for themselves can improve performance, especially if the goals are specific and difficult rather than vague or too easy (Rosswork, 1977). Even more powerful is inducing students to monitor and maintain daily records of their own study behavior. If taught properly, students can learn to monitor their behavior more closely and regulate it more effectively (Hughes, 1988).

Self-regulation skills are taught using *cognitive behavior modification* techniques that combine modeling with verbalized self-instructions. Rather than simply telling students what to do, you demonstrate the process—not only by going through the physical motions involved but also by verbalizing the thoughts and other self-talk (self-instructions, self-monitoring, self-reinforcement) that direct the activity.

Meichenbaum and Goodman (1971) originally used this technique with students who made frequent errors on matching tasks because they responded too quickly, settling on the first response choice that looked correct rather than taking time to examine all of the alternatives before selecting the best one. As the models "thought out loud" while demonstrating the task, they made a point of carefully observing each alternative, resisting the temptation to settle on the first one that looked correct, reminding themselves that one can be fooled by small differences in detail that are not noticed at first, and so on. Variations of this approach have been used to teach students to be more creative in problem solving, to help social isolates learn to initiate activities with peers, to help aggressive students control their anger and respond more effectively to frustration, and to help defeated students learn to cope with failure and respond to mistakes with problem-solving efforts rather than resignation.

Cognitive behavior modification approaches have in common the attempt to teach students that they can exert control over their own behavior and handle frustrating situations effectively through rational planning and decision making (Forman, 1993). A simple example is the "turtle" technique of Robin, Schneider, and Dolnick (1976), in which teachers teach aggressive students to assume a turtle position when upset. The students learn to place their heads on their desks, close their eyes, and clench their fists. This gives them an immediate response to use in anger-provoking situations and enables them to inhibit inappropriate behavior and to think about constructive solutions. The turtle position itself is mostly a gimmick; the key is training students to postpone impulsive responding while they gradually relax and consider constructive alternatives.

Douglas et al. (1976) trained hyperactive students to approach seatwork tasks carefully. They used modeling and verbalized self-instruction designed to enable the students to think before acting ("What plans can I try?" "How would it work if I did that?"), to monitor their performances during the task ("What shall I try next?" "Have I got it right so far?"), to check and correct mistakes ("Oh, I made a mistake there—I'll correct it." "Let's see, have I tried everything I can think of?"), and finally, to reinforce themselves ("I've done a pretty good job").

The Think Aloud program of Camp and Bash (1981) is a curriculum designed to teach students to use their cognitive skills to cope with social problems. It teaches them to pose and develop answers to four basic questions: "What is my problem?" "How can I do it?" "Am I using my plan?" and "How did I do?" Think Aloud activities can be used with a class as a whole, although they are probably of most value with impulsive and aggressive students taught in small groups.

Strategy Training.   Other approaches to what is becoming known as strategy training have been developed by theorists working outside of the cognitive behavior modification tradition. Much strategy training involves teaching social skills. Students are given modeling and instruction, then engaged in role-play and other practical application exercises, to teach them better ways of interacting with peers and solving problems. Social skills training programs have been used to teach strategies for initiating and maintaining social conversations, joining ongoing games or group activities, playing or learning cooperatively, and resolving conflicts through negotiation without resorting to aggression. Such training can be effective for improving a wide range of student behaviors (Mennuti et al., 2006; Robinson et al., 1999; Zaragoza, Vaughn, & McIntosh, 1991). For examples of classroom applications, see Cartledge and Milburn (1995), Elias and Clabby (1989), King and Kirshenbaum (1992), Matson and Ollendick (1988), or Walker (1987).

Whenever problem behavior appears because students lack strategies for coping effectively with particular situations, you will need to *teach* them how to handle those situations better—not just *urge* them to do so. The most effective form of strategy teaching is likely to be modeling combined with verbalized self-instructions, because this demonstrates the process directly for students. If you simply provide an explanation, students will have to translate your directions into forms of self-talk that they can use to guide their behavior.

*B*earing the Unbearable

Teachers often must cope with problems that cannot be solved. If enough seriously disturbed students are in the room, you cannot deal with all of them successfully and teach the curriculum too. Something has to give; either the problem has to be reduced or you need help from other professionals. Unfortunately, outside resources adequate to do the job usually are not available, and available resources often are not successful. Genuinely therapeutic treatment is available, but unless the family is able and willing to pay high professional fees, students will likely have to go on waiting lists. They may be treated some months later, but not immediately. Suspending students from school merely deepens their alienation and makes it harder for them to cope when they come back—*if* they come back.

Some problem students may be better off in a transitional or alternative school. At one point, referral of students to alternative programs was associated with extremely low expectations—the student was simply "gotten rid of." Even today, many alternative schools are simply holding operations that segregate the students but do not address their needs effectively. However, some transitional programs are thoughtful and taught by talented adults concerned with helping students to develop emotions, dispositions, and problem-solving capacities for effective functioning (for some positive examples, see Knutson, 1998). Thus, the ethical appropriateness and professional wisdom of referring students to special programs depend on the quality of those programs. In some circumstances, even competent and caring teachers will find some students are better off in a special program than in their classrooms.

It remains true, however, that for many poorly adjusted students, their best prospects for sustained and helpful treatment lie with caring and determined teachers (assisted by other school personnel). For students who are almost old enough to drop out of school or are in danger of being thrown out, this may be their last real chance to head off a lifelong pattern of failure and misery. Consequently, we urge you to "bear the unbearable" as much as you can before giving up on any student.

SUMMARY

Consistent use of the preventive techniques described in Chapter 3 will avert most problems, and the rest can be handled with techniques described in this chapter. Many major disruptions start as minor misbehavior, so monitor your classroom continuously and stop minor problems quickly and nondisruptively.

Much misbehavior can be ignored. When it is fleeting and not disruptive, there is no point in interrupting activities to call attention to it. If misbehavior is prolonged or begins to become disruptive, direct intervention is needed. When students know what they are supposed to be doing and when the nature of their misbehavior is obvious, there is no need to question them. Return them to productive activity as quickly and nondisruptively as possible. When it is not possible to use nondisruptive techniques, call the students' names and tell them what they are supposed to be doing or remind them of the rules. Keep such interventions brief, direct, and focused on desirable behavior. Avoid questions, threats, and nagging.

You will need to question students when misbehavior has been serious or disruptive and you are unclear about the facts. Conduct such investigations privately so students will have less reason to engage in face-saving behavior. Do not make decisions until you have heard everyone out. After gathering the facts, take action aimed at both resolving the present problem and preventing its return. This will mean clarification of expected behavior and perhaps a new rule or agreement. Ordinarily, there will be no need for punishment.

Punishment is a stopgap measure rather than a solution and it involves many undesirable side effects, so use it only as a last resort. Make it clear that the students brought on the punishment through repeated misbehavior, leaving you no other choice. Appropriate forms of punishment include restriction of privileges, exclusion from the group, and assignments that force students to reflect on the rules and their rationales. Punishment should be related to the offense, as brief and mild as possible, and flexible enough to allow students to redeem themselves by correcting their behavior.

A few students with long-standing and severe disturbances will require extraordinary corrective measures. Suggestions for dealing with several common types are given in this chapter. Serious problems require careful observation and diagnosis, followed by individualized treatment. Along with application of the general approach to investigating and developing solutions to problems that is emphasized throughout the chapter, such treatment might involve techniques such as contingency contracting, cognitive behavior modification, or strategy training.

SUGGESTED ACTIVITIES AND QUESTIONS

1. Behavior that one teacher views as a problem may not seem noteworthy to another teacher. Think about the teaching situation you envision yourself in and identify relatively minor behaviors that you would want to eliminate—that you would deal with overtly and publicly. How do your perceptions of minor problems correspond with those of your classmates? Would teachers with more experience react similarly to minor problems? How do you think students would feel about behaviors that you would not tolerate? Would they be more or less lenient than you? Why?

2. Reread the cases presented in Chapter 1. Which of the teachers is the best manager? Why? How could even this teacher have behaved more successfully?

3. Reread the four cases that appear at the beginning of this chapter. Analyze each case and indicate ways in which the situation could be improved.

4. Summarize in seven brief paragraphs the guidelines for dealing with showing off, unresponsiveness, failure to complete assignments, attention deficits, hyperactivity, defiance, and aggression. Practice dealing with these problems in role-playing situations. Specify a hypothetical problem, assign some participants to the student and teacher roles, and allow the rest to observe and provide feedback.

5. Review or construct a list of student behaviors or characteristics that are most likely to embarrass you or to make you anxious. Practice how you will deal with these. For example, if you dislike threats to your authority, list student behaviors likely to anger you and practice how you would respond. Then role-play your response with other participants. For example, how would you respond (if at all) in this situation?

   Teacher: You're right, Frank. What I told you yesterday was incorrect.
   Herb: (*Gleefully bellowing from the back of the room*) You're always wrong! We never know when to believe you.

6. Why do the authors not recommend the use of physical punishment?

7. What steps can you follow to make exclusion from the group effective punishment? In particular, how should you behave when excluding or readmitting students to group activities?

8. A ninth-grade teacher sees Bill Thomas (without apparent provocation) grab Tyrone Johnson's comb and throw it on the floor. Bill and Tyrone begin to push each other. What should the teacher do? Be specific. Write out or role-play the actual words you would use. Would you behave differently if you had not seen what preceded the pushing?

9. Compare how you responded to the vignettes about contingency contracting on page 127 with the responses of a few classmates.

APPENDIX 4.1

APPENDIX 4.1

Analysis of a Problem-Solving Meeting

Many problem-solving principles are exemplified in the following vignette.

Vera Wise is a teacher who is concerned about an increase in the frequency and seriousness of attention-getting behavior over the past few weeks. Increasing numbers of students have been involved, fooling around and calling out remarks instead of working on their assignments. The primary instigators seem to be Bill, Jim, David, and Paul, four boys who sit close together and are part of a clique both in and out of school.

Vera has tried talking individually to each of these boys, as well as to other students, but the problem has worsened. The boys promise to improve their behavior, but they don't. The problem came to a head during the last period this afternoon, when one of the boys (Vera is not sure which) said something obscene and embarrassing to Mary, an attractive girl who is physically well developed. Vera responded by warning the class sharply that this kind of behavior had gone far enough and by telling Bill, Jim, David, and Paul to stay after class to see her about it. Jim started to protest that he hadn't said it, but Vera cut him off with the statement that she wanted to see all four boys and would explain why later. She had decided that this particular incident was not as important as the more general problem, so she would concentrate on changing the behavior of all four boys rather than on trying to find out who made the remark.

At the end of the period, Jim and Paul looked surly, while Bill and David looked sheepish. A few classmates tried to hang around, but Vera made a point of getting rid of them and closing the door before beginning the meeting. The meeting went as follows:

Teacher: As I said in class, the remark made about Mary today was out of line, and it was just the latest in a number of things like that that have been going on recently. I think the time has come to put a stop to it, and I have kept you boys here because you four seem to be responsible for most of it.

The teacher begins by making it clear that she wants to talk about the general issue, not just what happened today, and that she considers all four boys to be responsible. Her behavior throughout the meeting is consistent with this opening statement.

Jim: Like I said before, I didn't do it. Besides, I can't stay because I have to go to practice and coach wants us there five minutes after the bell.

Jim and Paul both try to get off by making excuses. Vera offers to call and "explain," but this offer is refused. Although the offer was genuine in the sense

Paul: Yeah, I didn't do it either and I have to go home and mow the lawn today.

Teacher: Let's get a couple of things straight. First, I'm not especially interested in finding out which one of you embarrassed Mary today. I'm interested in discussing the larger problem of putting an end to this kind of thing. You four are here because you all do it more than anyone else. Furthermore, we're all going to stay here until we settle the problem for good. That includes everyone, Jim. If you like, I will call the coach and explain. Paul, if you want, I will call your home, but you are both going to stay here until we get finished. *(Both Jim and Paul indicate they don't want the teacher to make calls.)*

Jim: Well, David did it, not me. Besides, he does it a lot more than anyone else. When I do it, it's usually because he gets me started. *(David glares but says nothing.)*

Teacher: No good, Jim. David probably does it more, but you are responsible for your own behavior, and you can't use him for an excuse. If you didn't do it yourself a lot, you wouldn't be here now. *(Jim glumly remains silent at this point.)* David, if you did it, I think you should apologize to Mary. She was very embarrassed, and whoever is responsible owes her an apology, but as I said, I don't want to talk about what happened today. I want to talk about what's been going on over the last several weeks, and all four of you have been heavily involved in it.

that she would have followed through if either boy had asked her to, she knew that this was unlikely. Both boys probably knew that they would only compound their troubles if Vera called the coach or a parent. With this response, she cuts off further attempts to escape the meeting and makes it clear that she intends to keep everyone there until she is satisfied. She also makes it specifically clear to Jim again that she is not interested in finding out who insulted Mary but instead is interested in the larger problem.

Now Jim tries to blame it on David. Vera again points out that she is interested in the larger issue and she makes it clear that Jim is both guilty of numerous instances of similar behavior and responsible for his own actions regardless of what other students do. Her suggestion that David apologize is left simply as a suggestion with no attempt to follow up. This is appropriate, because a forced apology in front of the class would only further embarrass Mary and enrage David. The teacher has nothing to lose by suggesting this, and everyone might gain something if David follows through and does apologize to Mary sometime in the future. This statement also is consistent with Vera's later statement that obscenity as such is not as important as respecting other people's rights and feelings. Also, by giving minimal time and attention to the information that David was responsible for today's problem, she again reinforces her

Paul: Well, we won't do it anymore. (*Jim and David immediately nod and say "yes," while Bill nods solemnly.*)

Teacher: Sorry, but that's not good enough, either. I've talked to all of you, more than once. Every time you said that you wouldn't do it again, but you've kept doing it. So I'm afraid I can't take your word on it and let it go at that. We're going to have to discuss this some more and come to some kind of agreement that I can accept.

Paul: Well, what's the big deal anyway? Words that people think are "dirty" don't hurt anybody, and besides, everyone knows what they mean.

Teacher: In the first place, Paul, although it is true that there is nothing really wrong with these words, they are out of place in the classroom. More importantly though, it's not just the words. It's the other things that go with them. For example, today Mary was terribly embarrassed , and no one had the right to do that to her. Also, you are distracting the whole class from their work, and let's not forget that you're supposed to be here to learn, not to goof off. But you're not doing your work. You know that I allow students to talk when they finish their assignments, but you four have been fooling around and making loud remarks instead of working on your assignments and then talking quietly after you finish.

earlier statement that she wants to talk about the larger problem and about all four of the boys.

Under other circumstances, it probably would have been best for Vera to take the boys at their word, perhaps expressing happiness that they have seen the problem and are willing to respond to it in a mature fashion. However, these boys have pledged to change in the past and have not done so, it is appropriate for her to refuse to accept their pledges to change and point out her reasons why. She makes it clear that this discussion is going to continue until a real solution is reached.

Paul now tries to make Vera feel guilty for being unreasonable. She counters nicely by acknowledging that his argument is valid up to a point, but it ignores the larger context that makes it impossible for schools to allow this kind of disruptive behavior. She then makes the even more important point that she is more concerned about students' respect for one another than about one obscenity. The boys are much more likely to feel guilt or shame about having embarrassed Mary than they are about having used obscene language. Finally, Vera adds that the disruptive behavior of these students is interfering with their own work and that of their classmates. This is done in a way that points out implicitly that the teachers' rules are reasonable but these four boys are abusing them.

Jim: Well, I can't help it. I say things without thinking, or else because David or somebody else gets me started. I've tried to stop, but I can't. Besides, it's not natural to try to stop from saying things that pop into your head at times like that.

Teacher: Really! Well, suppose I invited your mother to sit in here for a few days? Do you think you might control yourself then? *(Jim's expression changes from surly self-confidence to confusion and anxiety.)*

Teacher: You don't have to answer the question. You all know the answer; you don't use that kind of language around your mothers, and you don't have any trouble controlling yourself, either. So why don't we drop the lame excuses and start by recognizing that you can and will stop if you make the effort to do so.

Paul: Yeah, but what are we supposed to do then? Sit there and keep our mouths shut?

Teacher: No, I'm not asking you to do anything special. I'm only asking you to follow the rule that applies to everyone in the class: work on your assignment until you finish it. If you have time left over, then you can talk quietly, but without disrupting others.

Paul: But I already said that I would do that.

Teacher: Yes, and I already said that all four of you have failed to keep your word on that. So what are we going to do? I don't want to make this into a big deal. In fact, I think it's silly to have to discuss something like this with students like

At this point, Jim again tries to evade responsibility. In addition to blaming others for "getting him started," he suggests that Vera is asking something unreasonable and unnatural. She wastes no time in dismissing this specious argument, pointing out that self-control is not a problem when the student is sufficiently motivated to show it. Her choice of an example here is particularly apt—students who use obscene language, particularly boys, almost always shrink at the thought of using it in the presence of their own mothers. Vera closes this exchange a little roughly, characterizing what the boys have been saying as "lame excuses." However, this is an accurate description of what has been happening. Also, she stresses personal responsibility for actions. Ultimately, she is not responsible for controlling these boys; they are responsible for controlling themselves.

Paul now takes a new approach, no longer attempting to rationalize the misbehavior but attacking the reasonableness of Vera's request. She counters by again repeating the rule, which is clearly reasonable, and also by making a point of the fact that she is only asking these boys to keep the same rule that applies to everyone else; she is not picking on them or asking them to do anything unusual.

Paul now goes back to repeating his pledge of reform and Vera again points out that he has broken it in the past. She then pulls together a few statements to make the situation clear: the boys have created the problem through their own misbehavior; she doesn't even want to discuss it but they have forced it on her; the problem is serious enough that it is going to be stopped

yourselves, who should know better. But the problem is serious and is getting worse, and I am going to see that it stops before it gets out of hand. If I have to, I'll punish you all severely, but I don't want to do that. I asked you here to lay out the problem and to see if you had any suggestions about how it could be solved. Are there ways I could help by making some changes?

David: Like what kind of changes?

Teacher: Well, I could change your seats and separate you from one another. I could give you extra work or other things to do so that you wouldn't have time to goof off. I could try to arrange to have some of you transferred to other classes. *(These suggestions yield negative reactions, except that Jim agrees to change seats and move away from David.)*

Teacher: Okay, Jim, we'll arrange that. I hope it helps. Are there any other suggestions as to how we can solve this problem? *(Long silence.)*

Paul: All I can think of is what I said before—I won't do it anymore, and this time I mean it. *(The others nod.)*

Teacher: Well, I have to admit that I can't think of anything else other than punishment, and as I said, I don't want that. However, let me warn you right now that if any of you breaks his word this time, I will have to punish you. At the very least, you will have to stay after school for several days, and if there's any repeat of the kind of obscenity that went on today, I

one way or another; she is inviting them to make suggestions and expressing willingness to follow them if they are feasible and have a chance of improving the situation (even though she could act on her own, with no opportunity for discussion).

Vera suggests changes that are unlikely to be acceptable to the boys. <u>This is one way of informing them of possible negative consequences if the problem is not stopped, without actually threatening such consequences.</u> The fact that Jim agrees to change his seat is mildly surprising; it probably results from his own need to try to show that he was serious in his earlier claim that David tends to get him in trouble. In any case, it gives Vera an opportunity to agree with a suggestion, showing good will on her part.

When the boys offer no more suggestions, she changes from refusal to accept pledges of reform to a conditional acceptance. This is the appropriate time to make this switch, because the boys now have ceased their belligerence and rationalization, realizing that they are going to have to change their behavior and begin serious discussion of what might be appropriate in the future.

may have to contact your parents. I mention this because I want you to understand just how serious this problem is, and I want you to know that your word won't be any good in the future if you break it this time.

What about your workbooks? I know that all of you are behind, and that the work you did in the past few weeks contains a lot of sloppy errors because of your fooling around. I want those workbooks brought up to date, the errors corrected, and the books turned in to me for checking shortly. How about Friday? *(Today is Wednesday.)*

Jim: *(Dejectedly.)* I'm way behind, and I have practice again tomorrow and a game Friday night. I'm not sure I can get it in by Friday.

Teacher: All right, what about Monday? That will give you all the rest of the week plus the weekend. *(All nod agreement.)* All right, then, we'll make it Monday.

Remember, I want you not only to catch up but also to review your work over the last three weeks and correct any errors you made because you weren't paying close attention to what you were doing. Work as far as the end of page 128. Okay? *(All agree.)* Is there anything else that any of you wants to add? *(After a brief silence, all shrug or shake their heads negatively.)*

Teacher: Well, there is still the question of what to say in class tomorrow. You four are not the only ones who have been fooling around making remarks. I intend to tell the class

As a hedge against failure to keep the pledge, Vera threatens punishment in the future. However, she does it in a way that does not suggests that she expects to have to use it. Also, the kinds of punishment she mentions help underscore her seriousness about this issue.

In this transition, Vera turns to the problem of incomplete and sloppy workbooks. She requires the students to make this up, but agrees to a delay when a reasonable excuse is given for it. Although this will have a punishing effect in the technical sense, it is not punishment. Vera merely is requiring these boys to do the same things that she requires of other students. The fact that it will cost them extra time and trouble in the next few days is their fault, not hers. This aspect of the discussion also underscores the point made earlier, that failure to do work is one of her concerns, not just hearing obscene words spoken in the classroom.

Finally, in closing the discussion, Vera brings up the question of what is to be said to the class the next day. She makes it clear that she is going to make a statement, but also pledges not to embarrass the four boys

that we discussed the situation and agreed that certain things need to stop, and I intend to remind everyone about the rules. I probably also will stress some of the other things I've pointed out to you, but I don't want to say anything more about our discussion. For your own good, I suggest that you say as little as possible about it yourselves. Perhaps just say that we had a talk and made some agreements.

Also, I would appreciate it if you urged some of your classmates to follow the rules, too, so I don't have to hold sessions like this with anyone else. Anyway, I won't embarrass you or give any details about what we have said and done here, but I think some brief statement needs to be made, because everyone in the class is going to be wondering. Is this plan acceptable? *(All nod agreement.)* Is there anything else? *(All shake their heads negatively.)* Okay, get going, and let's have no more of this.

or divulge any details of this discussion. This again underscores her intention to solve the problem rather than to punish the boys, and reiterates her earlier remarks about avoiding embarrassment of students.

Note, too, that she tries to enlist the help of the boys in this endeavor, suggesting that they minimize discussion about what went on and encourage their classmates to follow the rules. They may or may not do this, and she will make no attempt to check up on them. However, she has nothing to lose with this request, and it emphasizes that the boys share the problem and that they are responsible for solving it.

Note that throughout the discussion Paul and Jim have been vocal and occasionally belligerent. Under other circumstances David might have been, too, but he was guilty of today's incident, so he chose to remain quiet and avoid getting into further trouble. Bill said nothing, except to agree when the group agreed in unison. Perhaps he was embarrassed and remorseful, but it also may be that he regularly responds to such discussions with sullenness and unresponsiveness. If the latter is the case, it is important to make sure that he agrees explicitly to what has transpired, so he cannot claim later that he never consented to it. In this case, Vera judges that Bill has made the same commitment as the other boys, even though he did not speak out for himself.

FORM 4.1. Teacher's Reaction to Inattention and Misbehavior

USE: When the teacher is faced with problems of inattention or misbehavior.
PURPOSE: To see if teacher handles these situations appropriately.
      Code the following information concerning teacher's response to misbehavior or to inattentiveness. Code only when teacher seems to be aware of the problem; do not code minor problems that teacher doesn't even notice.

BEHAVIOR CATEGORIES   CODES

A. TYPE OF SITUATION   A   B   C
  1. Total class, lesson or discussion   1. 3   3   4
  2. Small-group activity—problem in group   2. 3   3   4,6
  3. Small-group activity—problem out of group 3. 1   2   2
  4. Seatwork checking or study period   4. 1   3   4
  5. Other (specify)   5. 4   3   2

B. TYPE OF MISBEHAVIOR   6. ___ ___ ___
  1. Brief, nondisruptive, should be ignored   7. ___ ___ ___
  2. Minor, but extended or repeated. Should   8. ___ ___ ___
     be stopped nondisruptively   9. ___ ___ ___
  3. Disruptive, should be stopped quickly. No 10. ___ ___ ___
     questions needed
  4. Disruptive, questions needed or advisable 11. ___ ___ ___
  5. Other (specify)   12. ___ ___ ___
                                               13. ___ ___ ___
C. TEACHER'S RESPONSE(S)   14. ___ ___ ___
  1. Ignores (deliberately)   15. ___ ___ ___
  2. Nonverbal; uses eye contact, gestures or
     touch, or moves near offender   16. ___ ___ ___
  3. Praises someone else's good behavior   17. ___ ___ ___
  4. Calls offender's name; calls for attention or
     work; gives rule reminder. No overdwelling 18. ___ ___ ___
                                                19. ___ ___ ___
  5. Overdwells on misbehavior, nags   20. ___ ___ ___
  6. Asks rhetorical or meaningless questions
  7. Asks appropriate questions–investigates publicly 21. ___ ___ ___
  8. Investigates privately, now or later   22. ___ ___ ___
  9. Threatens punishment if behavior is repeated 23. ___ ___ ___
 10. Punishes (note type)   24. ___ ___ ___
 11. Other (specify)   25. ___ ___ ___

CHECK IF APPLICABLE

_____ 1. Teacher delays too long before acting, so problems escalate
_____ 2. Teacher identifies wrong student or fails to include all involved
_____ 3. Teacher fails to specify appropriate behavior (when this is not
             clear)
_____ 4. Teacher fails to specify rationale behind demands (when this is
             not clear)
_____ 5. Teacher attributes misbehavior to ill will, evil motives
_____ 6. Teacher describes misbehavior as a typical or unchangeable trait;
             labels student

NOTES:
        # 1, 2, and 4 were all for student # 12 (he seems to be the only
   consistent problem as far as management goes).

FORM 4.2. Teacher's Response to Problem Students

USE: When the class contains one or more students who present chronic, severe problems in personal adjustment[†] or classroom behavior.
PURPOSE: To inventory the teacher's coping strategies.
*   Pick a particular student and check the strategies that the teacher uses for coping with this student.*

A. GENERAL STRATEGIES

_____   1. Control undesirable behavior through demands or threats of punishment

_____   2. Offer incentives or rewards for improved behavior

_____   3. Provide modeling, training, or other instruction designed to teach the student more effective ways of coping (either in general or in particular situations in which problem behavior is frequent for this student)

_____   4. Identify and treat underlying causes believed to be responsible for the student's symptomatic behavior (home pressures, self-concept problems, etc.)

_____   5. Provide counseling designed to increase the student's insight into the problem behavior and its causes or meanings

_____   6. Attempt to change the student's troublesome attitudes or beliefs through logical appeal or persuasion

_____   7. Attempt to provide encouragement, reassurance, or support to the student's self-concept through creating a supportive environment

_____   8. Attempt to develop a close personal relationship with the student

_____   9. Other (describe)

B. SPECIFIC STRATEGIES

_____   1. Minimize conflict by intervening as seldom and as indirectly as possible

_____   2. Use humor or other face-saving or tension reduction techniques when direct intervention is necessary

_____   3. Maintain close physical proximity or monitor the student's behavior closely

_____   4. Use time-out procedures to extinguish disruptive behavior by removing the opportunity for the student to misbehave and be reinforced for it

_____   5. Use time-out procedures to allow the student an opportunity to calm down and reflect after an outburst

_____   6. Use behavior contracts to formalize offers of reward for improved behavior

_____   7. Use modeling or role play procedures to help student learn the self talk that controls adaptive responses to frustrating or threatening situations

_____   8. Adjust work expectations or assignments if these seem inappropriate and appear to be contributing to the problem

(Continued)

FORM 4.2. (Continued)

_____ 9. Adjust seat assignment, group assignment, or other social environment/peer relationship factors

_____ 10. Attempt to develop peer support for the problem student

_____ 11. Attempt to develop peer pressure on the problem student (to stop behaving inappropriately)

_____ 12. Active listening. I statements, or attempts to negotiate no-lose solutions (Gordon's techniques)

_____ 13. Attempt to get the student to recognize problem behavior, accept responsibility, and commit to a plan for improvement (Glasser's techniques)

_____ 14. Contact with family members

_____ 15. Involvement of mental health professionals

_____ 16. Other (describe)

C. ASSESSMENT

Which of these strategies appear to be helpful, and which do not? Which might be more helpful if they were implemented more often, more systematically, or in a different way? Are there strategies that the teacher doesn't use that might be helpful?

CHAPTER 5

Motivation

"You can lead a horse to water, but you can't make it drink." Teachers face the problem summed up in this familiar saying. Appropriate curricula and good teaching are necessary but not sufficient to ensure that students learn. If students minimize their investment of attention and effort, they won't learn much. The degree to which they invest attention and effort depends on their motivation.

Motivation is subjective experience that cannot be observed directly. Instead, it must be inferred from students' self-reports and classroom behavior. For example, Sherry is staring in the direction of the clock. Is she focused on the assignment? If so, is she thinking productively, or might she be upset because she is "lost"? If she is not thinking about the assignment, is this because she has completed it successfully, or might she be bored or preoccupied with some personal matter?

Seemingly similar behavior patterns can result from quite different underlying motivational patterns. For example, McCaslin (1990) interviewed sixth-graders about how they handle the "hard stuff" in mathematics. The following excerpts are from two girls who were persistent and effortful, but quite different in their approach to difficult problems. One tried to solve the problems mostly to get the assignment finished so she could interact with her friends. She made strategic use of fantasies connected with this goal to help her get through the rough spots.

A lot of times I get sick of things so I just want to stop. And I do . . . whenever I'm working and I just get sick of working, I just stop because I can't stand it anymore. I think of things that I like to do. Like in school, I'm going to play with my friends, I think of all the things that are fun that we do, and stuff. But I have to get this done and *right* before I can go to do that.

The other girl was more focused on learning with understanding. Yet, she was less successful in avoiding the frustration and worry that accompanied failure to solve difficult problems easily. Not having developed the ability to use fantasy strategically, she had to distract herself by engaging in alternative activities:

Well, I think I'm going to get them all wrong. And I kind of feel like I have to get up and walk around and think about it. I feel like I have to stop and work on something else for a little bit. I might get up and work on spelling for a minute 'cause that's pretty easy and I don't have to think about it, 'cause spelling I just know the answers and they're right there. I can't think about the math and what I'm going to do. . . . When I get pretty frustrated, I think to myself, "You can't do this," and I start tearing, I start biting my pencil. Then I know I have to get up and do something else. I just get so frustrated with it, I can't think. . . . I start to fiddle with my hands, go like that. I know I have to do something else. 'Cause I really get mad. I don't take a real long (break) time, maybe just 10 minutes. Then I come back to work again. Just to get it out of my mind for a minute.

Students differ dramatically in motivational patterns and related strategies for setting goals, addressing task demands, and making "repairs" when their initial efforts do not succeed. You need to encourage your students to engage in activities with the intention of developing the intended knowledge and skills.

Strategies for Motivating Students

Until motivation began to receive attention from classroom researchers, teachers were forced to rely on advice based on two frequently expressed views that are both incorrect in their extreme forms. The first view is that learning should be fun and that motivation problems appear because the teacher somehow has converted an inherently enjoyable activity into drudgery. We believe that students should find academic activities meaningful and worthwhile, but not fun in the same sense that recreational games are fun. The second view is that school activities are necessarily boring, unrewarding, and even aversive, so that we must rely on extrinsic rewards and punishments.

Recent theory and research have yielded a more balanced and sophisticated approach that includes a rich range of motivational strategies. We summarize this theory and research here, focusing on strategies you can use to motivate your students to learn with understanding. For more information see Brophy (2004), McCombs and Pope (1994), Pintrich and Schunk (2002), and Stipek (2002).

Classroom Vignettes

We begin with two brief vignettes depicting teachers starting instruction on the Declaration of Independence and the U.S. Constitution.

Frank Thomas's Class

Teacher Frank Thomas begins the week this way:

> Read Chapter 17 carefully because it is a key chapter; in fact, questions on it will represent about 50 percent of the next unit test. The Declaration of Independence is a key document, so you should know it "cold." You should also understand the Preamble to the Constitution and be able to discuss it at length. Let's begin by considering the important facts. First, who was the most important person involved in drafting the Declaration of Independence?

Jane Strong's Class

Jane Strong is teaching the same material to similar students. She begins this way:

> Before starting our discussion of important ideas in the Declaration of Independence and the Constitution and their roles in U.S. history, I want to raise four questions to provide some structure. Write these down now. Later, I'll give you time to talk about them in small groups: (1) What is protest? (2) Under what circumstances is it appropriate? (3) Think about the rights and privileges that you have in school and the constraints that apply here. If you were going to write a constitution for our school, what are the three important points you would include? (4) To what extent do you think that your view of a good government for our school is shared by other students?
>
> We need to consider these questions before we begin formal discussion so that you can see the problems of consensus that the Framers of our Constitution faced. To what extent do different individuals see government in the same way? Do they have common expectations for services that facilitate their needs and regulations that inhibit their freedom?
>
> Tomorrow, we are going to draft a constitution for the class. Later, we will consider the Declaration of Independence more formally, organizing our understanding of the document in the following ways: (1) the historical background of its development; (2) the philosophical ideas that influenced its Framers; (3) its continuing effects on life in American society.

Questions

Given these brief glimpses, would you rather have Frank Thomas or Jane Strong as your history teacher? Why? Which teacher's students are likely to be more motivated to learn about the Declaration of Independence and the Constitution? To be more concerned about passing the test and getting a good grade? How might the two classes describe the nature and purposes of learning about history?

Contextual Views of Motivation

Teachers need to consider not only the motives of individual students, but also the motivational potential embedded in classrooms as social settings. Research on motivation has broadened from decontextualized experiments to research in classrooms, from a focus on stable traits to dynamic person-task-social context relationships, and from a focus on cognitive aspects to consider emotions as well (*Elementary School Journal,* 2006; Volet & Jarvela, 2001). These emerging views of motivation fit well with sociocultural views of learning (see Chapter 11).

Sociocultural perspectives on motivation situate the individual within the social contexts in which learning takes place (McCaslin, 2006; Perry, Turner, & Meyer, 2006). For example, discussion of self-regulation often is limited to developments that occur within individuals, but it can be construed as attempts by learners to capitalize on available resources to make learning activities more understandable and doable. McCaslin and Good (1996) have argued that adaptive learning is better characterized as *co-regulated learning* that reflects the social support and emergent interactions with others that enable students to go beyond their current individual interests and limitations.

Thus, there are multiple layers for you to consider in motivating students. Your instruction, feedback, and assignments will influence students' motivation and learning in powerful ways, but so will their opportunities to interact and work collaboratively with peers. In this chapter we focus on the subjective experiences of individuals. Classroom structures that influence students' interactions with one another are explored in detail in Chapter 6, and in Chapter 11 we consider sociocultural theories of learning and motivation that embed these processes within the social contexts of learning communities.

*B*asic Motivational Concepts

Motivational concepts account for the initiation, direction, intensity, and persistence of behavior. *Motives* explain why people do what they do. Motives are distinguished from *goals* (immediate objectives) and *strategies* (methods used to achieve goals and thus to satisfy motives). For example, a person responds to hunger (motive) by going to a restaurant (strategy) to get food (goal). Motives, goals, and strategies are less easily distinguished in analyses of classroom situations that call for intentional learning of cognitive content, because optimal forms of motivation to learn and optimal strategies for accomplishing the learning tend to occur together.

Consider the vignettes presented earlier. If the two classes responded solely to what their teachers emphasized in introducing the Declaration and Constitution, they would develop contrasting motives, goals, and strategies. Frank Thomas's students would be motivated primarily by a desire to do well on the unit test. Given what Frank said about the test, their primary study goal would be to memorize the Declaration, the Preamble to the Constitution, and various facts (names, dates, etc.). Consequently, their study efforts would emphasize rote memorizing strategies.

Jane Strong's students more likely would *want* to learn about the Declaration and Constitution because they found the information interesting and important. Given Jane's introduction, they probably would adopt goals and strategies that involve concentrating on the meanings and implications of the material, placing it in historical context, relating it to personal ideas and experiences, and thinking about its applications to the modern world. This is a much more personalized and meaningful way of processing the information than rote memorization. It involves putting oneself in the place of the Framers and considering the documents as vehicles constructed to accomplish political purposes rather than merely as texts to be learned.

The motives, goals, and strategies that students develop in response to classroom activities depend on both the nature of the activities and how the teacher presents them. If the teacher orients students to focus on grades or other extrinsic rewards, they are likely to adopt goals and strategies that concentrate on meeting requirements that entitle them to acceptable reward levels. They will do what they must to prepare for tests, then forget most of what they learned. It is better when students find learning activities intrinsically rewarding. However, they may not learn what their teacher would like them to learn if the basis for their intrinsic motivation is primarily affective (they enjoy the activity) rather than cognitive (they find it interesting, meaningful, or worthwhile to learn what the activity is designed to teach). Consequently, it is important to *motivate students to learn*—to seek to gain the intended knowledge and skill benefits from learning activities and to set goals and use cognitive strategies that will enable them to do so.

Expectancy X Value Model of Motivation

Many aspects of motivation fit within *expectancy x value theory* (Wigfield & Eccles, 2000). This theory holds that the effort people are willing to expend on a task depends on the product of (1) the degree to which they *expect* to be able to perform the task successfully, and earn whatever rewards this will bring; and (2) the degree to which they *value* those rewards. Effort investment is related to the product rather than the sum of the expectancy and value factors, so people will not willingly engage in the task at all if one factor is missing entirely. We do not invest effort in tasks that do not lead to valued outcomes even if we know that we can perform successfully, nor do we invest in even highly valued tasks if we believe that we cannot succeed on them no matter how hard we try. Thus, you need both to help your students appreciate the value of school activities and make sure that they can complete them successfully if they apply reasonable effort.

The rest of the chapter is organized according to these expectancy x value theory ideas. We begin with basic preconditions, then discuss strategies for establishing and maintaining success *expectations* in students, then describe three sets of strategies for enhancing the *value* that students place on school tasks.

*E*ssential Preconditions for Successful Use of Motivational Strategies

Supportive Environment

To be motivated to learn, students need both ample opportunities to learn and steady encouragement and support. Thus, it is important to organize and manage the classroom as an effective learning community (see Chapters 3 and 4).

Students engage in classroom activities when they perceive their teachers as liking them and responsive to their needs, but become disaffected when they do not perceive such involvement. You can display involvement with your students by learning their names quickly, greeting them warmly each day, getting to know them as individuals, and emphasizing *immediacy* behaviors such as eye contact, smiling, positive gestures, humor, personal examples, and "we"/"our" language (Osterman, 2000; Richmond, 2002).

You can nurture identification with school and motivation to learn by cultivating the development of *caring communities of learners*. Teacher practices such as emphasis on prosocial values, elicitation of student ideas, encouragement of cooperation, display of warmth and supportiveness, and reduced use of extrinsic control methods are related to student behaviors such as engagement and enthusiasm for learning, initiative and self-management of learning activities, and sense of community (Solomon et al., 1997).

Feeling valued, cared for, and supported by others promotes attachment to the group and commitment to its norms and values. Students' sense of membership in a community promotes their attachment and commitment to school, motivation to engage in learning tasks, and valuing of learning. The support, encouragement, identification, and commitment engendered by a caring school community benefits all students, but especially to those who do not get much support outside of school.

Focus on Learning Goals.   A major influence on research on motivation in education in recent years has been achievement goal theory (Ames, 1992; Anderman & Wolters, 2006; Grant & Dweck, 2003). Goal theorists have shown that students who approach a lesson or activity with *learning goals* (also called *task goals* or *mastery goals*) focus on acquiring the knowledge or skills that the activities are designed to develop. In contrast, students with *performance goals* (also called *ego goals*) treat the activity more as a test of their ability to perform than as an opportunity to learn. Their primary concern is preserving their reputations as capable individuals. In striving to meet task demands, they often rely on rereading, memorizing and other surface-level strategies instead of deeper-level knowledge construction strategies.

Goal theorists emphasize managing classrooms in ways that encourage students to adopt learning goals rather than performance goals. Much of what they suggest involves establishing the classroom as a learning community, as described previously. They warn against two particularly counterproductive practices: harsh grading standards that make it unduly difficult to be successful and create preoccupation with grades and grading on a curve, as well as heavy emphasis on public comparisons, and other practices that focus attention on peer comparisons rather than one's own progress. These practices orient students more toward trying to avoid failure than striving for success.

Your students should feel comfortable taking intellectual risks because they know that they will not be embarrassed or criticized if they make a mistake. Your instructional emphasis should be on helping students to achieve mastery rather than on displaying their current abilities to perform, and your evaluation emphasis should be on assessing their progress toward instructional goals rather than on comparing them with one another (Ames, 1992; Patrick et al., 2003; Roeser, Eccles, & Sameroff, 2000; Turner et al., 2002).

Appropriate Level of Challenge or Difficulty

Activities should be at an appropriate level of difficulty. If tasks are so familiar or easy that they constitute nothing but busywork, and especially if they are so difficult that even persistent students cannot handle them, no strategies for inducing motivation are likely to succeed. Tasks are of appropriate difficulty when students are clear enough about what to do and how to do it that they can achieve high levels of success if they persistently employ appropriate strategies.

Meaningful Learning Objectives

Your lessons and activities should teach things that are worth learning. Students are not motivated to learn when engaged in pointless activities such as continuing to practice skills that they already have mastered thoroughly, memorizing lists for no good reason, or copying definitions of terms that are never used. Elementary students should read for information or pleasure in addition to practicing word attack skills, solve problems and apply mathematics in addition to practicing number facts and computations, and write prose or poetry compositions or actual correspondence in addition to practicing spelling and penmanship. Secondary students should learn how and why knowledge was developed in addition to acquiring the knowledge itself and should have opportunities to apply what they are learning to their own lives or to current social, political, or scientific issues.

Moderation and Variation in Strategy Use

Teachers who are recognized as outstanding motivators "flood" their classrooms with motivational elements (Pressley et al., 2003). Even so, motivational strategies can be overused in two respects. First, the need for such strategies varies with the situation. They are essential when content is unfamiliar and its value is not obvious to students, but not when the activity involves things that students are already eager to learn. Second, any particular strategy may lose its effectiveness if used too often or too routinely, so use a variety of motivational strategies.

With these four preconditions in mind, let us consider motivational strategies that you might use with your students.

*M*otivating by Maintaining Success Expectations

Research on *achievement motivation* (Dweck & Elliott, 1983) has established that effort and persistence are greater when people set goals of moderate difficulty (neither too hard nor too easy), seriously commit themselves to pursuing these goals, and concentrate on trying to achieve success rather than on trying to avoid failure. Research on *efficacy perceptions* (Bandura, 1997) has shown that effort and persistence are greater when people view themselves as competent or efficacious—when they believe that they are capable of performing a task successfully and thus earning the rewards that success brings. Research on *causal attributions* for performance suggests that effort and persistence are greater when people attribute their performance to internal and controllable causes rather than to external or uncontrollable causes (Weiner, 1992, 2001).

Encourage your students to develop the following three perceptions and attributional inferences concerning their performance at school:

1. *Sense of efficacy/competence.* Confidence that they have the ability (including the specific strategies needed) to succeed on a task if they invest the necessary effort (Bandura, 1997; Pajares, 1996; Schunk & Zimmerman, 2006)
2. *Attribution to internal, controllable causes.* Tendency to attribute successes to a combination of sufficient ability and reasonable effort; also, tendency to attribute failures to insufficient effort, confusion about what to do, or reliance on inappropriate strategies, but not to lack of ability (Weiner, 1992, 2001; Whitley & Frieze, 1985)
3. *Incremental concept of ability.* Perception of academic ability as potential that is developed incrementally through learning activities rather than as a fixed capacity that limits what they can accomplish (Dweck, 1999)

Program for Success

The simplest way to ensure that students expect success is to enable them to achieve it consistently without much confusion or frustration. However, programming for success does not mean assigning underchallenging busywork.

First, we speak here of *success that leads to gradual mastery of appropriately challenging objectives,* not quick, easy success achieved through "automatic" application of overlearned skills to overly familiar tasks. Pace your students through the curriculum as briskly as they can progress without undue frustration.

Second, keep in mind *your role as the teacher.* Students' levels of success will depend not only on the difficulty of the task itself but also on the degree to which you prepare them through advance instruction and assist their learning efforts through guidance and feedback. A task that would be too difficult for students left to their own devices might be just right when learned with your assistance. Focus your instruction on the *zone of proximal development,* which is the range of knowledge and skills that students are not yet ready to learn on their own but can learn with your help (see Chapter 11).

Programming for success means continually challenging students within their zones of proximal development, yet making it possible for them to meet these challenges by providing sufficient instruction, guidance, and feedback. It may be necessary to provide extra instruction to slower students or give them briefer or easier assignments if they cannot handle the regular ones even with extra help. Nevertheless, you should continue to expect these students to put forth reasonable effort and progress as far as they can. Do not give up on low achievers or allow them to give up on themselves.

Teach Goal Setting, Performance Appraisal, and Self-Reinforcement

Students' reactions to their own performance depend not just on their absolute level of success but also on their perceptions of what this level of performance means.

Goal Setting.   This process begins with *goal setting*. Setting goals and making commitments to trying to reach them increase performance (Bandura, 1997; Locke & Latham, 2002). Goal setting is especially effective when the goals are (1) *proximal* rather than distal (they refer to a task to be attempted here and now rather than in the distant future); (2) *specific* (complete a page of math problems with no more than one error) rather than global (do a good job); and (3) *challenging* (difficult but reachable rather than too easy or too hard). For example, a struggling student faced with twenty mathematics problems of varying difficulty might be asked to make a serious attempt to solve each problem and persist until confident that at least fifteen are solved correctly. In contrast, suggestions such as "Do the best you can," or "Do as many as you can" are too vague to function as specific goals.

> goal: here + now specific challenging #s !

In the case of a long series of activities that ultimately leads to some distal goal, establish proximal goals for each activity and keep students aware of the linkages between successive advances and their eventual achievement of the ultimate goal. Proximal goals usually seem attainable with reasonable effort even to students who doubt their capacities for attaining ultimate goals, and "keeping your eyes on the prize" can help them persist through frustrations (Turner & Schallert, 2001).

> proximal: series of small goals

Goal Commitment.   Goal setting must include *goal commitment*. Students must take the goals seriously and commit themselves to trying to reach them. You may need to negotiate goal setting with some students, or at least stimulate them to think about their performance potential. One way is to list potential goals and ask them to commit themselves to a particular subset. Another is performance contracting, in which students formally commit to a certain level of effort or performance in exchange for specified grades or rewards (Tollefson et al., 1984).

Performance Appraisal.   Finally, students may need help in using *appropriate standards for judging levels of success*. In particular, teach them to compare their work with absolute standards or with their own previous performance rather than with the performance of others (Shih & Alexander, 2000). Your feedback about specific responses must be accurate (errors must be labeled as such if they are to be recognized and corrected), but your more general evaluative comments should provide encouragement. You might note levels of success achieved in meeting established goals or describe accomplishments with reference to what is reasonable to expect rather than to absolute perfection. Help students appreciate their accomplishments to date and imply confidence that ultimate goals will

> label errors but give pos. feedback

be attained (e.g., "You've done a good job establishing your purpose in the first paragraph and structuring each paragraph around a main idea. However, the idea flow across paragraphs is a little choppy. As you revise [or, in your next composition], take time to outline the flow of ideas so that your argument builds step-by-step, and use this outline to sequence your paragraphs. Then you will have a nicely constructed argument"). Notice that this example says nothing directly about the students' abilities or the teacher's confidence that they will be successful. Yet, it implies that the teacher is satisfied with the students' progress, unbothered by the need for some improvements, and expecting to see these improvements emerge as students continue to develop their expertise.

Feedback.   Some students need *specific, detailed feedback* concerning both the strengths and weaknesses of their performance (Butler, 1987; Elawar & Corno, 1985). The feedback should include concepts and language that they can learn to use to describe their performance with precision. This is especially true for compositions, research projects, laboratory experiments, and other complex activities that are evaluated qualitatively. Concerning compositions, for example, you might comment on the relevance, accuracy, and completeness of the content; its organization into a coherent beginning, middle, and end; the style and vocabulary; and so forth.

work on students' ability to accurately evaluate own work.

Zuckerman (1994) found that even first graders can learn to apply individual reference norms and self-evaluation processes when assessing their learning. In this study, students were taught to pay attention to the match between teacher evaluation and self-evaluation. If these two evaluations coincided (regardless of the level of success achieved), the student was praised for accurate self-evaluation. Clear overestimations or underestimations were confronted. Over time, the students became more accurate and evidence-based in assessing their work against objective criteria.

Provide encouragement and helpful feedback whenever students have performed poorly on an important test or assignment. Resilient students will increase their study time and improve their study strategies on their own, but you many need to help others to do so, lest they lower their personal standards or goal commitments (Turner & Schallert, 2001).

Self-Reinforcement.   Students who have been working toward specific proximal goals and who have the concepts and language needed to evaluate their performance accurately can *reinforce themselves* for their progress. Many do this habitually, but others need encouragement to check their work and take credit for their successes. If necessary, compare their current accomplishments with performance samples from earlier times.

PARADOX

One paradoxical feature of student motivation is that self-efficacy perceptions are optimized when they are not at all at issue. That is, learning tends to proceed most smoothly when students are concentrating on doing the task rather than evaluating their performance. Feedback should focus on progress and processes rather than ability or other personal traits (Brophy, 2004; Dweck, 2000; Mueller & Dweck, 1998). This encourages students to develop an *incremental* theory of ability (belief that ability can be increased through effort and learning), rather than an *entity* theory (belief that one's ability is fixed). Students who develop incremental theories are oriented toward learning and tend to respond to failure by making adjustments in their levels of effort or the nature of the strategies they are using.

You will need to reassure some students that they have the ability needed to succeed, if they put forth reasonable effort. However, most of your praise and feedback should focus on the strategies that students are using and the progress they are making, without calling direct attention to either their efforts or their abilities. Emphasis on effort (how hard students had to work in order to succeed) can imply that you believe that their ability is limited (Covington, 1992). Focusing on ability (e.g., "You're really good at this!") conditions students to attribute their successes to high ability, which can set them up for learned helplessness reactions in the future when they encounter failure.

With struggling students, do not emphasize praise of hard work so much as encouragement of persistence and patience. Focus attention on their accomplishments ("Yes, it's hard, but look at what you are doing!"). Portray difficult work not so much as requiring strenuous effort but as challenging them to stay goal oriented and persist in using adaptive learning strategies ("Don't work hard, work smart!"). When giving help, emphasize instrumental help (probing and prompting) rather than gratuitous help (giving answers). Gratuitous help is likely to be perceived as evidence that you believe that the student lacks ability. So are gratuitous praise of minor accomplishments or gratuitous expressions of sympathy, especially if these affective supports are not accompanied by forms of assistance designed to help the student master the task (Graham & Barker, 1990; Henderlong & Lepper, 2002).

Help Students to Recognize Effort-Outcome Linkages

Modeling. Model beliefs about effort-outcome linkages when talking to students about your own learning and when demonstrating tasks by thinking out loud as you work through them. When you encounter frustration or temporary failure, model confidence that you will succeed if you persist and search for a better strategy or for some error in your application of the strategies already tried.

Socialization and Feedback. Stress effort-outcome linkages when giving feedback. Explain that your curriculum goals and instructional practices have been established to make it possible for students to succeed if they apply themselves. When necessary, reassure them that persistence (perhaps augmented by extra help) eventually pays off. Some students may need repeated statements of your confidence in their abilities to do the work or your willingness to accept slow progress so long as they consistently put forth reasonable effort.

Extra socialization is needed with low achievers when you must assign grades according to fixed norms or comparisons with peers rather than according to effort and progress toward individually prescribed goals. You may need to help low achievers take satisfaction in receiving Bs or Cs when such grades represent, for them, significant accomplishment. Express to these students (*and* their parents) your recognition of the accomplishment and appreciation of the effort it represents (Forsterling & Morganstern, 2002).

Portray Effort as Investment Rather Than Risk.   Make students aware that learning may take time and involve confusion or mistakes, but persistence and careful work eventually yields knowledge or skill mastery. This not only represents success on the task involved but also empowers them with knowledge or skills.

Portray Skill Development as Incremental and Domain Specific.   Students need to know that their intellectual abilities are open to improvement rather than fixed and that they possess a great many such abilities rather than just a few. Difficulties in learning usually occur not because students lack ability or do not make an effort but because they lack *experience* with the type of task involved. With patience, persistence, and help from you, they can acquire *domain-specific knowledge and skills* that will enable them to succeed on this task and others like it. Difficulty in learning mathematics need not imply difficulty in learning other subjects, and within mathematics, difficulty in learning to graph coordinates need not mean difficulty in learning to solve differential equations or to understand geometric relationships.

Focus on Mastery.   Stress the quality of students' task engagement and progress toward mastery. Treat errors as learning opportunities, not test failures. Use makeup exams or extra-credit assignments to provide struggling students with opportunities to overcome initial failures through persistent efforts.

Encouraging Effort: An Example

If students appear convinced that they cannot do the work, you will need to pursue a fine line between two extremes. First, repeatedly encourage them and express confidence that they will be able to succeed with continued effort. Do not accept expressions of inability or even legitimize them indirectly through such comments as "Well, at least try." Let them know that they learn the most by doing as much as they can for as long as they can, so they should not seek help at the first sign of difficulty. On the other hand, make it clear that you are available and willing to help if help is really needed (Karabenick & Newman, 2006). Here is how the situation might be handled appropriately.

> **Student:** I can't do number 4.
> **Teacher:** What part don't you understand?
> **Student:** I just can't do it, it's too hard!
> **Teacher:** I know you can do part of it because you've done the first three problems correctly. The fourth one is similar, but just a little more complicated. You start out the same way, but there's one extra step. Review the first three; then see if you can figure out number 4. I'll come back in a few minutes to see how you're doing.

Compare this with the following inappropriate scenario.

> **Student:** I can't do number 4.
> **Teacher:** You can't! Why not?
> **Student:** I just can't do it, it's too hard!

Teacher: Don't say you can't do it—we never say we can't do it. Did you try hard?
Student: Yes, but I can't do it.
Teacher: You did the first three. Maybe if you work a little longer you could do the
      fourth. Why don't you do that and see what happens?

In the first example, the teacher communicated positive expectations and provided a specific suggestion about how to proceed, yet did not give the answer or do the work. Also, in providing feedback about performance on the first three problems, this teacher was more specific in noting that the answers were correct and in attributing this success to the student's knowledge and abilities, thus supporting the students' self-efficacy beliefs. In the second example, the teacher communicated halfhearted and somewhat contradictory expectations, leaving the student with no reason to believe that further effort would succeed. Students need to be socialized to recognize and rely on their own capabilities and to respond to frustration with coping strategies rather than withdrawal or dependency.

Remedial Work with Discouraged Students

Some students become discouraged to the point of "failure syndrome" or "learned helplessness." They tend to give up at the first sign of difficulty and need more intensive and individualized encouragement. A few are bright students who have become accustomed to easy success that they attribute to high ability (rather than to ability plus effort). When they finally encounter challenges they cannot meet with ease, they overreact and conclude that they lack ability for that content or task. Help such students to see that abilities can be developed through persistent learning efforts, and that classroom activities are opportunities to learn, not just to display already developed skills.

You also may encounter a few "committed underachievers" who set low goals and resist "accepting responsibility for their successes" because they do not want to be expected to maintain a high level of performance. Help these students to see that they can attain consistent success with reasonable effort and that their deliberate underachievement is contrary to their long-run best interests (Thompson & Rudolph, 1992).

Most students who need remedial work on their expectations are low achievers of limited ability who have become accustomed to failure. These students may benefit from *mastery learning*: Give them tasks that they should be able to handle, provide individualized tutoring as needed, and allow them to contract for a particular level of performance and to continue to study, practice, and take tests until that level is achieved (see Chapter 7 for more on mastery learning). By virtually guaranteeing success, this approach builds confidence and willingness to commit to challenging goals (Grabe, 1985).

Discouraged students may also benefit from *attribution retraining*, in which they are given modeling, socialization, practice, and feedback designed to teach them to (1) concentrate on the task rather than worry about failure; (2) cope with failure by retracing their steps to find their mistake or by trying another approach rather than giving up; and (3) attribute their failures to insufficient effort, lack of information, or reliance on ineffective strategies rather than to lack of ability.

How to find/fix mistakes

Research on attribution retraining has shown that *success alone is not enough*—even a steady diet of success will not change an established pattern of learned helplessness. In fact, a key to successful attribution retraining is *controlled exposure to failure.* Rather than being exposed only to "success models" who handle tasks with ease, students are exposed to "coping models" who struggle to overcome mistakes before finally succeeding. In the process, the models display constructive responses to mistakes (e.g., by verbalizing continued confidence, attributing failures to remediable causes, and coping by first diagnosing the source of the problem and then correcting the mistake or approaching the problem in a different way). Following exposure to such modeling, students begin to work on the tasks themselves. Conditions are arranged so that they sometimes experience difficulty or failure, but accompanied by coaching that encourages them to respond constructively (Schunk, 1999).

Findings from the Classroom Strategy Study (Brophy, 1996) indicated that higher-rated teachers suggested a combination of support, encouragement, and task assistance to shape gradual improvement in failure syndrome students' work habits. They made it clear to the students that they would not be given work that they could not do, but they were expected to work persistently and turn in assignments done completely and correctly.

Some students suffer from *test anxiety*. They may learn smoothly in informal, pressure-free situations but become anxious and perform below their potential on tests or during situations in which they might be evaluated (e.g., public "solo" performance situations in music or physical education classes). You can minimize such problems by:

- Avoiding time pressures unless they are central to the skill being taught
- Stressing the feedback functions rather than the evaluation or grading functions of tests
- Portraying tests as assessing progress rather than ability
- Where appropriate, telling students that some problems are beyond their present achievement level, so they should not be concerned about failing to solve all of them
- Giving pretests to accustom the students to "failure" and to provide baselines for comparison when posttests are administered later
- Teaching stress management skills and effective test-taking skills and attitudes (See Neveh-Benjamin, 1991; Wigfield & Eccles, 1989; Zeidner, 1998)

Concluding Comments about Success Expectations

The expectancy aspects of motivation depend less on the objective success that students achieve than on how they view their performance: what they see as possible with reasonable effort, whether they define this as success, and whether they attribute it to controllable or uncontrollable factors. The motivation of all students, even the most extreme cases of learned helplessness, is open to reshaping via appropriately challenging demands, persuasion that success can be achieved with reasonable effort, and coaching in coping with initial failure.

Teachers and students need to view academic frustrations and failures realistically and respond to them adaptively. As Rohrkemper and Corno (1988) pointed out, not only is some failure inevitable, but a manageable degree of it is desirable. When students are challenged at optimal levels of difficulty, they make mistakes. The important thing is to arrange learning conditions so that they get useful feedback that will enable them to respond to their mistakes with renewed motivation rather than discouragement.

Inducing Students to Value Learning Activities

The expectancy x value model stresses that student motivation is affected not only by expectations and attributions concerning performance but also by the value that students attach to engaging in the activity. Wigfield and Eccles (2000) suggested that the value side of motivation has four components:

1. *Attainment value.* The importance of attaining success on the task, to affirm our self-concept or fulfill our needs for achievement, power, or prestige
2. *Intrinsic or interest value.* The enjoyment we get from engaging in the task
3. *Utility value.* The role that engaging in the task may play in advancing our career or helping us to reach other larger goals
4. *Cost.* Both direct costs (time and effort that must be committed to the task) and opportunity costs (foregone opportunities pursue other agendas)

Implications for teaching developed from research on the value aspects of motivation typically emphasize either offering incentives for good performance (extrinsic motivation approach) or teaching content and designing activities that students find enjoyable (intrinsic motivation approach). We discuss these two approaches and then turn to a third: stimulating students' motivation to learn.

Strategies for Supplying Extrinsic Motivation

Extrinsic motivation strategies do not attempt to increase the value that students place on the task itself, but instead link task performance to delivery of consequences that students do value.

Reward Good Effort and Performance

The use of rewards has been criticized on the grounds that they undermine students' interest in the activity being rewarded and thus reduce the likelihood that they will engage in that activity on their own initiative in the future. Debate over this claim has produced a great deal of research, summarized in a book (Sansone & Harackiewicz, 2000) and a series of meta-analyses that yielded divergent results.

The research clarified that addressing questions about the appropriate use of rewards requires attention to the nature of the rewards, the ways in which they are introduced and delivered, and the student outcomes under consideration. Rewards can be verbal or tangible, large or small, and salient or nonsalient. They can be given simply for engaging in an activity (engagement-dependent), for completing the activity (completion-dependent), or for not only completing it but also doing so in a way that fulfills some criterion for performance (performance-dependent). The effects of rewards might be considered with respect to immediate task effort or performance, changes in attitudes toward the task (e.g., finding it interesting), or changes in intrinsic motivation to engage in it voluntarily when future opportunities arise.

Using such distinctions, behaviorists Eisenberger and Cameron (1996) concluded that verbal rewards had positive effects on motivation and that tangible rewards only had negative effects when they were given merely for participation, without attention to quality of engagement or level of performance (and even then only when students expected the rewards because they had been announced in advance). They claimed that the harmful effects of rewards had been overstated and advised use of verbal rewards and performance-dependent tangible rewards.

The same authors subsequently published another meta-analysis (Cameron, 2001; Eisenberger, Pierce, & Cameron, 1999) and interpreted the results as showing that the effects of reward on intrinsic motivation are mostly positive or neutral, depending on the nature of the performance requirement. Vague or minimal standards have negative effects because they indicate that the rewarder doesn't care much about the task, but specific, high standards have positive effects because they indicate that the rewarder considers the task important. They concluded that there is no reason for concern about using rewards with low-interest tasks, but that with high-interest tasks it is important to link rewards to accomplishment of specific (preferably high) performance criteria.

Intrinsic motivation theorists criticized the behaviorists' analyses as misleading because they failed to make some important distinctions between situations and included artificial reward procedures that could not be applied in classrooms (e.g., telling participants that they would be rewarded if their performance exceeded that of 80 percent of their peers, but in fact rewarding all who had been assigned to the "reward" group) (Deci, Koestner, & Ryan, 1999b; Lepper, Henderlong, & Gingras, 1999).

In support of their position, Deci, Koestner, and Ryan (1999a, 2001), based on the largest meta-analysis done to date, reported that expected tangible rewards undermine intrinsic motivation, whether those rewards are engagement-contingent, completion-contingent, or even performance-contingent. In fact, the most detrimental type of performance-contingent reward was the one most commonly used in schools, in which the size of the reward depends on the level of one's performance.

Rewards had a strong negative effect on subsequent intrinsic motivation to engage in interesting tasks, but no effect on subsequent intrinsic motivation to engage in uninteresting tasks. Verbal reward (positive feedback) enhanced intrinsic motivation when it was primarily informational but decreased it when it was primarily controlling. The positive effects of verbal rewards were found primarily among college students, whereas the detrimental effects of tangible rewards were noticed primarily with children. These intrinsic motivation theorists concluded that verbal rewards can be used effectively if they are delivered in an informational rather than a controlling manner, and tangible rewards might not be harmful if given occasionally and unexpectedly.

Subsequent attempts to resolve disagreements have failed to do so. A laboratory experiment by Cameron et al. (2005) found that performance-contingent rewards enhanced task interest and subsequent intrinsic motivation to work on the task (finding differences between similar but not identical cartoons), even when rewards were no longer available. However, a more realistic study done with fourth- and fifth-graders found that both completion-dependent and performance-dependent rewards increased performance on mathematics problems during the reward condition, but decreased both performance and intrinsic motivation during a no-rewards follow-up (Oliver & Williams, 2006).

We believe that intrinsic motivation theorists are correct in raising concerns about overuse or inappropriate use of rewards and claiming that in classrooms it is difficult to reward students in ways that (1) take into account their individual learning efforts and progress, and (2) avoid communicating the idea that they engage in activities merely to obtain the rewards rather than to learn what the activities are intended to teach. However, we also believe that behaviorists are correct in claiming that rewards can be used effectively in classrooms, and that the motivational problems facing teachers primarily involve getting students to put forth consistent efforts whether or not they find learning activities enjoyable, not just maintaining intrinsic motivation to engage in activities that they enjoy.

Popular versions of this debate have produced a great deal of overheated rhetoric. Consider corporate-sponsored programs that offer students coupons for pizzas or other rewards in exchange for reading a specific number of books. These programs have been excoriated by Kohn (1993), and reading incentive programs in general have been criticized as violating important principles of motivation theory and literacy engagement (Fawson & Moore, 1999). However, a study of college students who had or had not participated in the "Book It!" reading program when they were elementary students indicated that such participation was not correlated with the college students' interest in reading. Therefore, fears that this program would undermine intrinsic motivation for reading were unfounded. On the other hand, the millions of dollars that the corporation spent implementing (and publicizing!) this program did not increase reading interest (Flora & Flora, 1999).

We conclude that the key to rewarding effectively is to do so in ways that support students' motivation to learn and avoid encouraging them to think that they engage in learning activities only to earn rewards. For example, if students are offered rewards simply for participating in a reading incentive program or are offered significant prizes for reading 100 books, they might begin to view reading as drudgery and expect to be rewarded if they agree to do it. In contrast, more positive effects on motivation might be expected from an approach that rewarded students with public recognition after they: (1) identified a rationale or set of themes for selecting books to be read; (2) wrote a report that illustrated how these themes played out in the books; and (3) presented a brief speech to classmates (followed by questions and answers) about the themes. This approach is similar to other methods that allow students to enjoy public recognition for significant accomplishments (e.g., science fairs where students demonstrate achievements to an interested audience).

In classrooms, rewards are used most appropriately with certain types of tasks. Rewards are more effective for increasing effort than for improving quality of performance, so it is better to use them when there is a clear goal and a clear strategy to follow (arithmetic computation, musical scales, typing, spelling) than when goals are more

[handwritten margin note: when & most rewards are most]

ambiguous or students must discover or invent new strategies rather than merely activate familiar ones. Thus, rewards are better used with routine tasks than with novel ones, with specific intentional learning tasks than with incidental learning or discovery tasks, and with tasks in which speed of performance or quantity of output is of more concern than creativity, artistry, or craftsmanship. Rewards can act as motivators only for those students who believe that they have a good chance to get the rewards if they put forth reasonable effort. To create incentives for the whole class and not just the high achievers, it is necessary to ensure that everyone has reasonable access to the rewards. This may require performance contracting or some other method of individualizing criteria for success. For example, MacIver and Reuman (1993–1994) described an incentives program in which students were rewarded according to their performance on the week's most important quiz, test, project, or assignment. Those who maintained previously established patterns of high performance or improved significantly on less satisfactory performance earned more points than those who slipped or failed to improve.

Portray rewards as verifications of significant achievements. Even when delivering surprise rewards, cast them as expressions of appreciation for your students' efforts and accomplishments, without making too much of the "big surprise." Offer and deliver incentives in ways that encourage students to appreciate their developing knowledge and skills, following the guidelines in Table 3.2.

Call Attention to the Instrumental Value of Academic Activities

[handwritten margin note: useful in life!]

Some knowledge and skills taught in school can be applied in the students' lives. These natural consequences are likely to be more effective for motivating learning efforts than arbitrary extrinsic rewards. When possible, point out that the knowledge or skills being developed enable students to meet their own current needs, provide them with a "ticket" to social advancement, or prepare them for occupational or other success in life. Better yet, cite examples by relating personal experiences or anecdotes about individuals with whom the students can identify (famous people they look up to or former students from the same school).

[handwritten margin note: relate to other people]

Basic literacy and mathematics skills are used daily when shopping, banking, driving, reading product instructions, paying bills, carrying on business correspondence, and planning home maintenance projects or family vacations. Scientific knowledge is useful for everything from coping effectively with minor everyday challenges to making good decisions in emergency situations. Knowledge of history and social studies is useful for social and civic decision making. Knowledge of the information, principles, and skills taught in school prepares people to make well-informed decisions that can save time, trouble, expense, or even lives, and it empowers people by preparing them to recognize and take advantage of the opportunities that society offers. Help your students to see learning activities as creating opportunities and to appreciate that schools are established by society for their benefit.

Competition: A Traditionally Popular but Problematic Extrinsic Incentive

The opportunity to compete can add excitement to classroom activities, whether the competition is for prizes or merely for the satisfaction of winning. Nevertheless, most motivational theorists oppose the use of competition or place heavy qualifications on its applicability as a motivational strategy. There are several good reasons for this.

First, participating in classroom activities already involves risking public failure, and a great deal of competition is already built into the grading system. So why introduce additional competitive elements?

failure "n

Second, competition is even more salient and distracting than rewards. Ames and Ames (1981) found that students working on their own tended to evaluate their progress with reference to their prior performance, appreciating developments in knowledge and skill. In contrast, students working in competitive structures were so focused on winning/losing that they paid little attention to what they were supposed to learn.

distracting

Third, competitions are more coercive than motivational when participation is mandatory. This is especially true when high stakes are attached to the outcomes.

coercive/ mandatory highstakes

Fourth, competition is more appropriate for use with routine practice tasks than with tasks calling for discovery or creativity, and it can be effective only if everyone has a reasonable chance of winning. To ensure this, it may be necessary to use team competition in which the teams are balanced by ability profiles or to use individual competition in which a handicapping system enables each student to compete with his or her own previous performance rather than with classmates.

use handicapping or teams...

Finally, competition creates losers as well as winners, and a loser's psychology tends to develop whenever individuals or teams lose competitions. Individuals may suffer at least temporary embarrassment, and those who lose consistently may suffer more permanent losses in confidence, self-esteem, and enjoyment of school (Epstein & Harackiewicz, 1992; Moriarty et al., 1995). Members of losing teams may devalue one another and scapegoat those whom they hold responsible for the team's loss (Ames, 1984; Johnson & Johnson, 1985).

loosing too often

These considerations should give you pause about introducing competition as a motivational strategy. If you are thinking about doing so, plan to minimize its risks.

Traditionally, competitions have been structured around test scores or other performance measures, but it also is possible to build competitive elements into ordinary instruction by including activities such as argumentative essays, debates, or simulation games (Keller, 1983). In fact, debates or other activities that encourage students to develop conflicting positions rather than seek concurrences can benefit both motivation and learning, although it is important to make sure that the discourse remains constructive and focused on the topic (King & King, 1998).

Concluding Comments about Extrinsic Motivational Strategies

Extrinsic strategies can be effective in certain circumstances, but do not rely on them too heavily. If your students are preoccupied with rewards or competition, they may not pay much attention to what they are supposed to be learning or appreciate its value. The quality of task engagement is higher when students perceive themselves to be engaged for their own reasons rather than in order to please you, obtain a reward, or escape punishment. If students perceive themselves as performing a task solely to obtain a reward, they tend to concentrate on meeting minimum standards rather than on doing a high-quality job. They may write 300-word essays containing exactly 300

preoccupation

words or read only those parts of a text that they need to read in order to answer the questions on an assignment.

Strategies for Capitalizing on Students' Intrinsic Motivation

The intrinsic motivation approach is based on the idea that you should emphasize activities that your students find interesting and enjoyable so that they engage in them willingly. This is an appealing idea, although research on activities that people tend to find intrinsically rewarding suggests that it is difficult to implement in typical classroom settings (Deci & Ryan, 1985; Ryan & Stiller, 1991).

The simplest way to ensure that people value what they are doing is to maximize their free choice and autonomy—let them decide what to do and when and how to do it. However, schools are not recreational settings; students are required to come for instruction in a prescribed curriculum. Most of the time, this requires them to engage in activities that they would not have selected on their own.

Motivation in classrooms also is complicated by the grading system and the public nature of most teacher–student interaction. Anxiety about public embarrassment or low grades is a significant impediment to the learning efforts of many students (Covington, 1992). Even when this is not a problem, students may try to avoid tasks that involve ambiguity (about what will be needed to earn high grades) or risk (due to high difficulty or strict grading standards) and to avoid asking questions or probing deeper into the content because they want to stick with safe, familiar routines (Hughes, Sullivan, & Mosley, 1985). Thus, even if students enjoy particular school activities, their potential for intrinsic motivation may be negated by concerns about embarrassment or failure. Finally, teachers evaluate performance and enforce rules. This sometimes engenders resentment that may interfere with their attempts to motivate students. These considerations underscore the importance of establishing your classroom as a supportive learning community in which you act as an encouraging resource person and de-emphasize your role as an authority figure and evaluator (Bruning & Horn, 2000).

Two main approaches have been advocated for supporting intrinsic motivation in classrooms. The first, based on *self-determination theory,* focuses on teacher–student relationships and emphasizes managing students in ways that help them to feel a sense of autonomy as they engage in learning activities. The second, based on *interest theory,* focuses on the activities themselves and emphasizes keeping students motivated through content they find interesting.

Self-Determination Theory

Self-determination theory began as a theory of intrinsic versus extrinsic motivation (Deci & Ryan, 1985), but has evolved to become a theory of overall well-being in general and autonomous motivation in particular (Vansteenkiste, Lens, & Deci, 2006). It is rooted in the assumption that maintaining a sense of well-being requires satisfying three basic needs: *autonomy* (self-determination in deciding what to do and how to do it), *competence* (developing and exercising skills for controlling the environment), and *relatedness* (affiliation with others).

[handwritten: 3 Basic Needs 1) autonomy 2) competence 3) relatedness]

In other words, people are inherently motivated to feel connected to others within a social milieu, to function effectively in that milieu, and to feel a sense of personal initiative while doing so. Students are likely to experience intrinsic motivation in classrooms that support satisfaction of these autonomy, competence, and relatedness needs. Where such support is lacking, they will feel controlled rather than self-determined, so their motivation will be primarily extrinsic.

Part of the reason that self-determination theorists shifted from a focus on intrinsic versus extrinsic sources of motivation to a focus on perceptions of being autonomous versus controlled in regulating one's behavior was their recognition that in classrooms, students are always under extrinsic pressure to conform to the student role and master the curriculum. They seldom get opportunities to enjoy completely intrinsically motivated activity (doing exactly what they want to do). However, they can feel autonomous (experience self-determination and choice), rather than controlled, if you present activities in ways that enable them to see good reasons for engaging in the activities voluntarily.

[handwritten: good reason to do activity!]

You might suggest that students invest in a learning activity for either extrinsic (earn a reward, avoid punishment) or intrinsic reasons (personal growth, become more healthy and fit). Extrinsic goal framing leads to low-quality engagement featuring rote memorizing and other surface processing strategies. However, intrinsic goal framing leads to high-quality engagement featuring deeper processing.

Interest Theory

Interest implies focused attention to a learning activity that occurs because the student values or enjoys its content or processes. Interesting activities provide learners with opportunities that they find rewarding and want to pursue (Schraw & Lehman, 2001).

Interest theorists distinguish between individual interest and situational interest. *Individual interest* is an enduring disposition to engage with particular content or activities whenever opportunities arise. *Situational interest* is triggered in the moment, emerging in response to something that catches our attention and motivates us to explore it. Situational interest often dissipates quickly, as when we investigate an unexpected sound and discover that it was just the wind blowing something over. However, it can become the basis for more sustained investigation and learning, as when an interesting anecdote about Albert Einstein motivates a reading of his biography, which in turn motivates sustained individual interest in nuclear physics. Interest theorists have studied the attributes of text content and learning activities that make them interesting to most students, as well as ways to establish situational interest in the hope that it can be developed into more permanent individual interest.

Opportunity to Exercise Autonomy and Make Choices

To the extent that doing so is compatible with achieving your curricular goals, you can capitalize on students' intrinsic motivation by providing them with opportunities to exercise autonomy and make choices. You can support autonomy by inviting students to ask questions and suggest ideas for individual learning projects, encouraging them to solve problems in their own ways rather than insisting on a single method, and generally facilitating independent thought and decision making (Reeve & Jang, 2006).

Some teachers regularly offer choices, especially teachers who are more experienced, who are less control oriented, and who have greater confidence in their teaching effectiveness. They report that choice improves affective response by increasing students' interest and personal autonomy. However, they also caution that too much choice can become counterproductive, that some students may take the path of least resistance, and that selection ought to involve attractive alternatives rather than pseudochoices between alternatives that are not valued or are highly unequal (Flowerday & Schraw, 2000). One problematic issue is that some teachers provide more choice opportunities to higher achievers and students who usually choose wisely (Weinstein et al., 2004), but low achievers and less responsible students need choice opportunities as well.

problem: provide choice mostly to high achievers

You can provide choices of assignments or opportunities to exercise autonomy in pursuing alternative ways to meet requirements by allowing students to select topics for book reports, compositions, or research projects, or to select from alternative ways of presenting their work (e.g., a report, a poster, a skit, etc.). When complete autonomy is not feasible, offer a menu of choices or require students to get their choices approved before going ahead with their projects.

Choices are especially feasible when your instructional goals focus on processes (skills) rather than content (knowledge), because many different information sources and instructional materials or media may be useful. Also, if you invite them to do so, your students might be able to suggest additional choices that you would be willing to approve as equivalent alternatives.

Offer choices of topics for research projects or books to read during recreational reading periods. Also, allow students some degree of input and choice regarding assessment (criteria used to evaluate work), social arrangements (seat location, group membership, whether to work alone or with a partner), and various procedural issues (when to complete assignments, the order in which topics will be addressed). Choices are especially important for older students who possess more self-regulation skills and have stronger needs for autonomy and control.

Providing choices usually stimulates intrinsic motivation and sometimes enhances learning (Flowerday & Schraw, 2003). However, too many choices can be counterproductive: Students invited to write essays for extra credit were more likely to write high-quality essays when offered six topics to choose from than when offered thirty (Iyengar & Lepper, 2000). Finally, sometimes choice does not even affect intrinsic motivation, especially if the available choices are all similar to one another or if none is especially appealing (Reeve, Nix, & Hamm, 2003).

Adapting Activities to Students' Interests

Hidi and Baird (1988) found that interest in reading was enhanced when the main ideas in an expository text were elaborated through insertions that featured one of the following motivational principles: (1) character identification (information about people with whom the students could identify, such as those whose inventions or discoveries led to the knowledge under study); (2) novelty (content that was interesting to the students because it was new or unusual); (3) life theme (applications or other connections to things that were important to the students in their lives outside of school); and (4) activity level (content that included reference to intense activities or strong emotions). Subsequent research has shown that text characteristics such as ease of comprehension, novelty, surprise, vividness, intensity, and character identification contribute to situational interest in reading material and that interesting text segments produce superior reading comprehension and recall (Hidi & Harackiewicz, 2000; Wade, Buxton, & Kelly, 1999).

Whenever instructional goals allow, it is helpful to incorporate content that students find interesting or activities they find enjoyable. People, fads, or events that are currently prominent in the news or the youth culture can be worked into everyday lessons as examples of the concepts being learned. For example, a geography teacher sparked interest in studying latitude and longitude by noting that they make it possible to easily find the sunken *Titanic,* even though it lies hundreds of miles out to sea.

Students' interest is sparked when they can ask questions and make comments. Plan lessons and assignments that include opportunities for students to express opinions and make evaluations. For example, after reviewing information about the excesses of the Roman circuses, a history teacher asked his students why they thought such practices had developed and how otherwise cultured people could take pleasure in such cruelty. Students developed insights about issues such as violence in sports and society generally, and the role of peer pressure in escalating aggression once conflict flares up. This same teacher, after describing life in Athens and Sparta, asked students which city they would rather live in and why. Again, this led to a lively discussion that included parallels with modern nations.

Opportunities for Active Response

Students prefer activities that allow them to respond actively—to interact with the teacher or one another, manipulate materials, or do something other than just listen or read. Along with lesson discourse, board work, and assignments, include opportunities to go beyond simple question-and-answer formats in order to do projects, role-play, simulations, computerized learning activities, or educational games. Language arts should include dramatic readings and prose and poetry composition; mathematics should include problem-solving exercises and realistic application opportunities; science should include experiments and other laboratory work; social studies should include debates, research projects, and simulation exercises; and art, music, and physical education should include opportunities to use developing skills in authentic activities, not just to practice the skills in isolation (Perry et al., 2006).

Inclusion of Higher-Level Objectives and Divergent Questions

Even within traditional lesson formats, you can stimulate your students to discuss or debate issues and offer opinions about cause-and-effect relationships. Students need to learn basic facts, concepts, and definitions, but a steady diet of lower-level content soon becomes boring.

Higher-level activities designed to elicit opinions, predictions, suggested courses of action, solutions to problems, or other divergent thinking can be time consuming to implement and difficult to evaluate. Yet they are important, not only for motivational reasons but to ensure that school learning is meaningful and applicable.

The same principles apply to skills instruction. Students need to learn basic skills and often must practice them to the point of smooth, rapid, and "automatic" performance. However, most of this practice should be embedded within application opportunities.

Feedback Features

Students also enjoy tasks that allow them to get immediate feedback that they can use to guide subsequent responses, as in computer games and the pastimes featured in arcades. You can provide such feedback yourself when leading a lesson or circulating during independent work times. When you are less available for immediate response, you still can arrange for students to get feedback by consulting answer keys, following instructions about how to check their work, consulting with an adult volunteer or appointed student helper, or reviewing work in pairs or small groups.

Incorporation of Game Features into Activities

Practice and application activities can be structured to include features typically associated with games or recreational pastimes (Malone & Lepper, 1987). With a bit of imagination, you can transform ordinary assignments into "test-yourself" challenges, puzzles, or brain teasers. Some such activities involve clear goals but require solving problems, avoiding traps, or overcoming obstacles (finding shortcuts for tedious mathematical procedures). Others challenge students to "find the problem" by identifying the goal itself in addition to developing a method for reaching it. Some gamelike activities involve elements of suspense or hidden information that emerge as the activity is completed (puzzles that convey some message or provide the answer to some question once they are filled in). Others involve a degree of randomness or uncertainty (knowledge games that cover a variety of topics at several difficulty levels and are assigned according to card draws or dice rolls). These gamelike features are less distracting from curriculum objectives and more effective in promoting motivation to learn than are competitive games.

Opportunities for Students to Create Finished Products

Workers enjoy jobs that allow them to create products that provide tangible fruits of their labor. Similarly, students are likely to prefer tasks that have their own meaning or integrity over tasks that are mere subparts of some larger entity, and to experience a satisfying sense of accomplishment when they finish such tasks. Ideally, the task will yield a finished product that they can use or display.

Inclusion of Fantasy or Simulation Elements

You can introduce fantasy or imagination elements that engage students' emotions or allow them to experience events vicariously (Moreno & Mayer, 2004). In studying poems or stories, encourage your students to debate the authors' motives in writing the work or to learn about formative experiences in the authors' lives. In studying scientific or mathematical principles, help your students to appreciate the practical problems that needed to be solved or the discoverers' motives that led to development of the knowledge. Alternatively, set up role-play or simulation activities that allow students to identify with real or fictional characters. Elementary teachers can make history come alive by arranging for students to role-play Columbus and his crew debating what to do after thirty days at sea, and secondary teachers can do so by arranging for students to take the roles of the American, British, and Russian leaders meeting at Yalta.

Opportunities for Students to Interact with Peers

Students usually enjoy activities that allow them to interact with peers. You can build peer interaction into whole-class activities such as discussion, debate, role-play, or simulation. Peer-interactive activities are likely to be most effective if (1) they are worthwhile learning experiences and not merely occasions for socializing, and (2) every student has a substantive role to play in carrying out the group's mission (see Chapter 6).

An Example: Project-Based Learning

Blumenfeld et al. (1991) described *project-based learning,* which incorporates many intrinsic motivation principles. *Projects* are relatively long-term, problem-focused units of instruction that integrate concepts from a number of fields of study. Students pursue solutions to authentic problems by asking and refining questions, debating ideas, making predictions, designing plans or experiments, collecting and analyzing data, drawing conclusions, asking new questions, creating products, and communicating their ideas and findings to others.

There are two essential components to projects: (1) a question or problem that drives the activities, and (2) work toward a final product that represents the students' solutions (e.g., a model, report, videotape, or computer program). Motivational elements of project-based learning include: (1) tasks are varied and involve novel elements, (2) problems are authentic and challenging, (3) the work leads to closure in the form of the final product, (4) students exercise choice in deciding what to do and how to do it, and (5) students collaborate with peers in carrying out the work. These motivational elements do not automatically ensure that students will acquire information, generate and test solutions, and evaluate their findings carefully. Projects need to be planned and implemented with attention to the student motivation and knowledge needed to engage in demanding group work (see Chapter 6). For examples of projects developed for the elementary grades, visit www.project-approach.com.

Christ Theo's Temp / HR experiment

web resource

Concluding Comments about Intrinsic Motivational Strategies

When curriculum objectives can be met through a variety of activities, wise teachers will emphasize activities that students find rewarding. However, there are two important limitations on what you can accomplish by doing so. First, opportunities to use intrinsic motivational strategies are limited. You have to teach the whole curriculum, not just the parts that appeal to students. Second, even when learning is enjoyable, it still requires concentration and effort.

Our colloquial language for discussing intrinsic motivation is misleading. We commonly describe certain topics as "intrinsically interesting" and speak of engaging in certain activities "for their own sake." Such language implies that motivation resides in activities rather than in people. In reality, although topics and activities offer exploitable opportunities for motivated action, *people generate their own intrinsic motivation.* We do something not for its sake but for our sake—because it provides enjoyable stimulation or satisfaction. Each of us has a unique motivational system, developed in response to our experiences and to socialization from significant persons in our lives. In the case of motivation to learn, teachers are important "significant persons." Therefore, rather than just responding to your students' existing motivational patterns, think in terms of *shaping* those patterns by encouraging motivation to learn.

Strategies for Stimulating Student Motivation to Learn

By *motivation to learn,* we mean a student's tendency to find learning activities meaningful and worthwhile and to try to get the intended learning benefits from them. In contrast to intrinsic motivation, which is primarily affective, motivation to learn is primarily cognitive. It involves attempts to make sense of an activity and understand the knowledge it develops (Brophy, 2004).

The learning taught in schools is mostly cognitive—abstract concepts and verbally coded information. In order to make good progress, students need to develop and use *generative learning strategies* (Weinstein & Mayer, 1986). That is, they need to process information actively, relate it to their existing knowledge, put it into their own words, make sure that they understand it, and so on. Therefore, motivating students to learn means not only stimulating them to take an interest in and see the value of what they are learning but also providing them with guidance about how to go about learning it.

Model Your Own Motivation to Learn

Model your own curiosity and interests to encourage students to value learning as a rewarding, self-actualizing activity that produces personal satisfaction and enriches one's life. Share your interests in current events and items of general knowledge (especially as they relate to the subject matter being taught). Without belaboring the point, communicate that you regularly read the newspaper ("I read in the paper that . . ."), watch the news ("Last night on the news they showed . . ."), and participate in various educational and cultural pursuits.

By "modeling," we mean more than just calling attention to examples or applications of concepts taught in school. We mean acting as a model by sharing your thinking about such examples or applications, so your students can see how educated people use what they learn in school to understand and respond to everyday experiences in their lives. Without being preachy, relate personal experiences illustrating how literacy knowledge enables you to express yourself effectively in important life situations, how mathematical or scientific knowledge enables you to solve everyday household-engineering or repair problems, or how social studies knowledge helps you to appreciate things you see in your travels or to understand the significance of events in the news.

Teachers' modeling of ways to think about subjects can affect their students' interest in subjects (Long & Hoy, 2006) and self-concepts of ability to learn them (Midgley, Feldlaufer, & Eccles, 1989). Often teachers are unaware of the attitudes they communicate. Consider the following dialogue:

Mrs. Chen: We started out with 18 links and divided them into groups of 3, so how many groups are we going to get?

Jonathan: Six.

Mrs. Chen: Six groups. You're right. We could say 6 groups of 3 make 18, right? Okay, this time, let's say I'm going to take away 1. How many would I have then? . . . Right, 17. I want someone to come up and put these 17 into groups of 2. How many do you end up with?

Lydia: Eight groups plus 1 left over.

Mrs. Chen: Can't you put it in with one of the others? Well, OK, we counted 8 groups of 2, but what else have we got?

Lydia: One left over.

Mrs. Chen: One left over. OK, in math what do we call a leftover?

Lydia: A remainder.

Mrs. Chen: Right. So this problem is a little more interesting—we have a remainder.

While instructing third-graders in division with remainders, this teacher is socializing attitudes as well. She presents the concept of remainders in a way that encourages students to view mathematics with interest and a can-do attitude.

You can model curiosity and interest in learning by responding to students' questions in ways that show that you value the questions. First, acknowledge or praise the question itself: "That's a good question, LaTonya. It does seem strange that the people in Boston threw the tea into the water, doesn't it?" Then, answer the question or refer it to the class: "How about it, class? Why would they throw the tea in the water instead of taking it home?"

If no one is prepared to answer the question, adopt some strategy to address it. You might promise to get the answer, or better yet, invite the student who asked the question to go to the library (or the Internet) to find the answer and then report back to the class. You also can model curiosity in responding to questions for which you do not have ready answers: "I never thought about that before. They must have decided not to steal the tea but throw it into the water instead. How come?"

Communicate Desirable Expectations and Attributions

To the extent that you treat students as if they already are eager learners, they are more likely to become so. Let your students know that you expect them to be curious and to want to learn with understanding. Minimally, avoid suggesting that they will dislike

need students as if they are already motivated -

learning activities or work on them only to get good grades. Preferably, treat them as active, motivated learners who care about their learning and are trying to learn with understanding. One teacher communicated positive expectations by announcing that she intended to make her students into "social scientists." She referred to this idea frequently in comments such as, "Thinking as social scientists, what conclusions might we draw from this information?"

Minimize Performance Anxiety

Engaging in activities with motivation to learn requires willingness to take intellectual risks and make mistakes. Students must be able to concentrate without worrying about whether they can meet performance expectations. Most activities should be structured as learning experiences rather than tests. If they include testlike events (recitation questions, practice exercises), treat these as opportunities to use the material rather than as tests of mastery.

Eventually, you will have to evaluate performance and assign grades. Until that point, stress learning rather than performance evaluation, and encourage students to think in terms of "Let's assess our progress and learn from our mistakes," rather than "Let's see who knows it and who doesn't."

Project Intensity When Appropriate

You can use timing, nonverbal expressions and gestures, and verbal cuing to project intensity and convey that the material is important and deserves close attention. Begin with a direct statement ("I am going to show you how to invert fractions—now pay close attention and make sure that you understand what to do"). Then continue, using public speaking techniques that convey intensity and cue attention: a slow-paced, step-by-step presentation emphasizing key words; unusual voice modulations or exaggerated gestures that focus attention on key terms or procedural steps; and intense scanning of the group to look for signs of understanding or confusion (and to allow anyone with a question to ask it immediately). Everything about your tone and manner should communicate that what is being said is important, so students should give it full attention and ask questions about anything they do not understand.

Reserve intensity for times when you really need to communicate that something is important ("Pay especially close attention"). Likely occasions include introduction of important new terms or definitions, demonstration of procedures, modeling of problem-solving techniques, giving directions for assignments, and attempts to eliminate misconceptions.

Project Enthusiasm for the Curriculum

If you present a topic or assignment with enthusiasm, depicting it as interesting, important, or worthwhile, students are likely to adopt this same attitude (Bettencourt et al., 1983; Newby, 1991). Projecting enthusiasm does not involve pep talks or unnecessary theatrics, but identifying your own reasons for viewing a topic as interesting, meaningful, or important and projecting these reasons to your students. You can use dramatics or forceful salesmanship if you are comfortable with these techniques, but if not, low-key but sincere statements of the value that you place on a topic or activity will be just as effective (Cabello & Terrell, 1994).

how to communicate importance

One history teacher enthusiastically explained that during the Middle Ages, Mediterranean seaports were major trade centers, and places like England were outposts of civilization, but this changed with the discovery of the New World. His presentation included references to maps, reminders about the primary modes of transportation at the time, and characterizations of the attitudes of the people and their knowledge about trade possibilities. His personal interest and detailed knowledge about the topic was projected into an effective presentation that sparked interest and elicited many questions and comments.

Induce Curiosity or Suspense

You can stimulate curiosity or suspense by doing "setups" that make your students want more information about a topic. To prepare them to read about Russia, for example, you could ask if they know how many time zones there are in Russia or how the United States acquired Alaska. Most of them will be surprised to discover that one country encompasses eleven time zones or that the United States purchased Alaska from Russia.

You can encourage your students to generate curiosity by (1) asking them to speculate or make predictions about what they will be learning; (2) raising questions that the learning activity will enable them to answer; and (3) where relevant, showing them that their existing knowledge is not sufficient to enable them to accomplish some valued objective, is inconsistent with the new information, or is currently scattered but can be organized around powerful ideas (Malone & Lepper, 1987).

Some teachers have incorporated techniques for stimulating curiosity within frequently used routines. For example, a mathematics teacher began many classes with an intriguing problem that was written on the board but covered by a rolled-down map. His students learned to anticipate the moment when he would roll it up and "allow" them to see the problem. Another teacher concealed props within a large box that she placed on her desk on days when she was going to do some interesting demonstration. Again, all eyes were on her when she opened that box.

"roll map over math"

Karmos and Karmos (1983) described a mathematics teacher who periodically started a lesson by saying, "Last night I went down to my basement and found. . . ." The first time, he told of a tree that doubled its number of branches each hour, and then used this "discovery" as the basis for posing interesting problems. Other things "found in his basement" included alligators and a diesel train. Whenever this teacher said, "Last night I went down to my basement, . . ." his students knew that they could anticipate some preposterous claim following by some interesting problems.

Last night in my basement...

Make Abstract Content More Personal, Concrete, or Familiar

Definitions, principles, and other abstract information may have little meaning for students unless made more concrete. One way to accomplish this is to illustrate how the content applies to the lives of individuals. We observed a history teacher read aloud a brief selection about Spartacus in order to personalize students' learning about slavery in ancient times. When covering the Crusades, this teacher gave particular emphasis to the Children's Crusade, noting that the children involved were "your age and younger" and that most of them died before the crusade ultimately ended in failure. He also made poignant connections to contemporary Middle Eastern countries in which religion-based zeal has led preadolescents to volunteer to go to war.

You can make abstractions concrete by showing objects or pictures or conducting demonstrations, and relate new content to existing knowledge by using examples or analogies that refer to familiar concepts, objects, or events. A teacher we observed made connections such as (1) the Nile flooding and its effects on Egyptian customs compared to the spring flooding in Michigan and its effects on local customs; (2) the Washington Monument as a modern example of an obelisk; (3) three times the size of the Pontiac Silverdome is an example of the size of the largest Roman circus coliseums; (4) identification of students in the class (or failing that, famous personalities) as descended from the ancient peoples or geographic areas being studied; (5) linking of students' family names to the guilds (Smith, Tanner, Miller, Baker); and (6) explanation of how medieval social and political systems worked by describing the local area as part of the outlying lands surrounding a manor based in Lansing, which in turn would be under the protection of and would pay taxes to the "King of Detroit."

Finally, make sure that your curriculum features gender equity and suitable adaptation to the ethnic and cultural backgrounds of your students. Some may feel excluded and lose interest if they come to believe that a school subject is about "them" rather than "us" (Alton-Lee, Nuthall, & Patrick, 1993; Epstein, 2001). Your treatment of history should include attention to social history, women's roles, and the lives of everyday people, along with political and military events, and should include multiple perspectives on their meanings and implications. Study of literature, biography, and contributions to society and culture should include attention to contributions by women and members of minority groups, especially groups represented in the class.

Induce Dissonance or Cognitive Conflict

When a topic is familiar, students may think they already know all about it and thus may read the material with little attention or thought. You can counter by pointing out unexpected, incongruous, or paradoxical aspects of the content; calling attention to unusual or exotic elements; noting exceptions to general rules; or challenging students to solve the "mystery" that underlies a paradox. Curricula include a great many "strange but true" phenomena, especially in mathematics and science. Calling attention to them can get your students to begin asking themselves, "How can that be?"

Induce Students to Generate Their Own Motivation to Learn

Students can generate self-determined reasons for learning when prompted. You can induce them to generate their own motivation to learn by asking them to think about topics or activities in relation to their own interests and preconceptions.

One way is to use the K-W-L technique (Ogle, 1986). As they are about to begin study of a topic, ask students to relate what they already *know* (or think they know) about the topic and what they *want* to learn about it. During study of the topic, follow up by addressing any misconceptions that emerge and pursuing answers to the questions they raise. As a culmination to the study, ask students to describe what they *learned*.

K-W-L

State Learning Goals and Provide Advance Organizers

Learners retain more when their learning is goal directed and structured around key concepts, so introduce activities by stating learning objectives and providing advance organizers to help students prepare to learn efficiently. Learning objectives and advance organizers also call students' attention to the benefits that they should receive from engaging in a task, so they have motivational benefits as well (Reeve et al., 2002).

Because it is easy to do and takes only a few moments, one might expect teachers to explain activities' purposes and goals routinely. However, in about 100 hours of classroom observation, Brophy et al. (1983) observed only nine activity introductions that included information likely to stimulate motivation to learn. Teachers usually either launched into the activity without any introduction or confined their introduction to explanations of the procedures to be followed. Unfortunately, these findings are typical.

Model Task-Related Thinking and Problem Solving

Show Students What It Means to Approach a Task with Motivation to Learn.   That is, model the beliefs and attitudes that are associated with such motivation (patience, confidence, persistence in seeking solutions through information processing and rational decision making, benefiting from the information supplied by mistakes rather than giving up in frustration, concentrating on the task and how to respond to it rather than worrying about one's limitations).

Induce Metacognitive Awareness of Learning Strategies ?

When motivated to learn, students concentrate their attention, make sure they understand, and integrate new information with existing knowledge. You may need to coach your students in the following cognitive and metacognitive skills for learning and studying effectively (Pressley & Beard El-Dinary, 1993).

Actively Preparing to Learn.   Train your students to learn actively by mobilizing their resources and approaching tasks in thoughtful ways: getting ready to concentrate, previewing tasks by noting their nature and objectives, and developing plans before trying to respond to complex tasks.

Committing Material to Memory.   If material must be memorized, teach techniques for memorizing efficiently: active rehearsal; repeating, copying, or underlining key words; making notes; or using imagery or other mnemonic strategies.

// teach how to memorize

Encoding or Elaborating on the Information Presented.   Usually it is not appropriate (or even possible) to rely on rote memory to retain information verbatim. More typically, students must retain the gist and be able to apply it later. Teach them strategies for identifying and retaining the gist: paraphrasing and summarizing the information to put it into their own words, relating it to what they already know, and assessing their understanding by asking themselves questions.

Organizing and Structuring Content.   Students also need to learn to structure extensive content by dividing it into sequences or clusters. Teach them to note the main ideas of paragraphs, outline the material, use the structuring devices that have been built into it, and take good notes.

Monitoring Comprehension.   In giving instructions for assignments, remind students to remain aware of learning goals, the strategies that they use to pursue them, and the corrective efforts they undertake when the strategies have not been effective. Teach strategies for coping with confusion or mistakes: backing up and rereading, looking up definitions, searching for information that has been missed or misunderstood, retracing steps to see whether the strategy has been applied correctly, and generating possible alternative strategies.

using units, writing clusters

Maintaining Appropriate Affect.   Finally, model and instruct your students in ways to approach learning activities with desirable affect (relaxed but alert and prepared to concentrate, ready to enjoy or at least take satisfaction in engaging in the task) and ways of avoiding undesirable affect (anger, anxiety, etc.)

Concluding Comments: Motivating Students to Learn

Zone of proximal development

Brophy (1999) expanded the concept of zone of proximal development to include the idea that instruction needs to be matched not only to learners' existing knowledge and skills but also to their readiness to appreciate the learning. We cannot expect eager engagement in activities that are so familiar that students have become satiated with them (at least temporarily), or so unfamiliar that students cannot understand or appreciate their potential value. Curricular content and learning activities are well matched to students' current characteristics if they are either already familiar and valued as learning opportunities worth pursuing, or less familiar or valued but nevertheless within their motivational zones of proximal development (so the students can begin to value them if the teacher mediates their learning experiences effectively). The development of such appreciation is more likely to the extent that students perceive some relevance of the learning to their personal agendas.

What we teach in school is primarily cognitive and often abstract, so it often may be difficult for students to see good reasons for learning it or to experience the satisfactions that may be derived from doing so. Students who are ignorant (or misled) about a learning activity such as studying a dramatic play may be unable to generate much appreciation for it because they are unable to see its potential. Those who lack concepts (e.g., foreshadowing, Achilles' heel) and strategies (analyzing plot developments and making predictions based on them, noting clues to characters' personal strengths and flaws) to guide their information processing may not yet be able to experience many of the insights and satisfactions that such study offers. Even those who appreciate the play as a story (rather than merely as "stuff" to be memorized for a test) may not find much personal relevance in it unless they have learned to identify with dramatic characters and think about how they (the students) might act in parallel situations.

In teaching about *King Lear,* for example, you might model the thoughts and feelings involved in savoring the experience and enjoying the aesthetic satisfactions that the play offers (e.g., making connections between its characterization and plot elements and parallel elements in one's own life, putting oneself in the place of Lear and thinking about how one might handle the dilemmas he faced, etc.). In coaching the learning, you might help students to take satisfaction in, develop connections among, or draw implications from the insights they gain as they learn (e.g., by cuing them to think about key aspects of characters' personalities or motives, complimenting them on the insights they develop, or inviting them to speculate about what these insights portend about the outcome of the drama or tell us about what Shakespeare was saying about the human condition).

SUMMARY

The effort that students are likely to invest in a learning activity will depend on how much they value the rewards associated with successfully completing it and the degree to which they expect to be able to succeed and thus reap the rewards. A complete motivational program will attend both to the expectancy aspects and the value aspects of motivation.

Four essential preconditions set the stage for use of recommended motivational strategies: (1) The classroom is a community that supports students' learning efforts; (2) Activities are of appropriate difficulty; (3) Activities lead to worthwhile learning outcomes; and (4) The teacher shows moderation and variation in using motivational strategies.

Four sets of motivational strategies were reviewed. The first set is designed to motivate by maintaining students' success expectations and related perceptions and beliefs. The most basic strategy is programming for success by assigning tasks on which students can succeed if they apply reasonable effort and by instructing them thoroughly so that they know what to do and how to do it. Other strategies include helping students to set appropriate (proximal, specific, challenging) goals, to commit themselves to these goals, to use appropriate standards for appraising their performance, and to reinforce themselves for the successes that they achieve; helping students to recognize the linkages between effort and outcome through modeling, socialization, and feedback; portraying effort as an investment rather than a risk; portraying skill development as incremental and domain specific; focusing on mastery; and doing remedial work with discouraged students.

The other three sets of strategies address the value aspects of student motivation. Extrinsic motivation strategies link task performance to delivery of consequences that students value. They include rewarding good performance, calling attention to the instrumental value of learning activities, and using individual or team competition. If you use rewards or competition, keep in mind potential undesirable side effects (undermining intrinsic motivation, distracting attention from learning goals).

The next set calls for taking advantage of students' existing intrinsic motivation by designing or selecting activities containing elements that students enjoy: opportunities to exercise autonomy and make choices, to respond actively, and to pursue higher-level objectives and divergent questions; tasks that provide immediate feedback; and activities that include gamelike features, allow students to create a finished product, include fantasy or simulation elements, or provide opportunities to interact with peers. Intrinsic motivational strategies increase the likelihood that students will enjoy an activity but do not directly stimulate their motivation to learn what the activity was designed to teach.

To accomplish the latter goal, strategies for stimulating student motivation to learn are needed. Three pervasive features of the classroom learning community support development of motivation to learn as a general trait: modeling the thinking and actions associated with motivation to learn, communicating expectations and attributions implying motivation to learn in your students, and creating a supportive environment for learning. Other strategies are more situation-specific: projecting intensity that communicates the importance of an activity; projecting enthusiasm for the topic; inducing curiosity or suspense; making content more personal, concrete, or familiar; inducing dissonance or cognitive conflict; inducing students to generate their own motivation to learn; stating learning objectives and providing advance organizers; modeling the strategies used when approaching the activity with motivation to learn; and inducing students' metacognitive awareness of their own learning efforts. In effect, motivating students to learn involves adapting modeling, coaching, feedback, and other teaching strategies to address motivational goals as well as more narrow instructional goals.

SUGGESTED ACTIVITIES AND QUESTIONS

1. What does it mean to say that a student "is motivated" or "has no motivation"? What evidence would lead you to make such judgments? How does your answer to these questions compare with those of your peers?

2. Think back to when you were a student similar (in grade level, subject matter, etc.) to the students you plan to teach. What were your favorite learning activities? What were your most valuable learning experiences? Compare your answers with those of peers who plan to teach similar students. What do your answers imply about effective motivational strategies?

3. How does motivation to learn differ from intrinsic motivation to engage in classroom activities?

4. To what extent do you think it necessary or advisable to use extrinsic motivation approaches (rewards, competition)? If you intend to do so, how do you plan to minimize their undesirable side effects?

5. As a person who chose to go into teaching, you probably felt comfortable in classrooms and enjoyed learning activities. Yet, you will teach students who have histories of failure and find schooling to be boring or aversive. How will you cope with such students? With a friend or colleague, role-play your interaction with a student who is alienated to the point of persistent inattention to lessons and failure to complete assignments.

6. Sometimes the toughest part of motivating students is meeting the essential preconditions for developing motivation to learn, especially those calling for worthwhile learning goals and appropriate difficulty levels. What should you do if you find that several activities in the workbooks that come with your adopted curriculum appear to be pointless? Discuss this issue with friends or colleagues.

7. What if certain students cannot handle the same material and move at the same pace as the rest of the class? What might you begin to do differently with these students and how might you explain it to them in ways that would support rather than erode their motivation to learn?

8. Why do the authors make a point of distinguishing between learning and performance when talking about motivating students to learn?

9. The authors note that intrinsic motivation resides in persons rather than in topics or activities, but they talk about emphasizing topics or activities that students find interesting or enjoyable. Explain this seeming contradiction.

10. Similarly, the authors speak of motivation to learn as generated by learners themselves, but suggest that you can stimulate your students to develop it. How can you stimulate development of something that students must develop themselves?

11. Explain the implications of the following statement: We don't do something for its sake, we do it for our sake.

12. How would you respond to unmotivated students who genuinely want to know why they are asked to study Shakespeare's sonnets or the history of ancient Greece?

13. Write a one-page introduction to each of three topics in English, science, or mathematics. What are some elements that you could focus on to create interest, identify application potential, or stimulate curiosity? Is there information that students are likely to find surprising or difficult to believe? Can the content be related to current events or events in the students' lives?

14. Examine students' textbooks in English, science, or mathematics. How satisfactory are their questions and exercises? Find three or four examples that need to be improved, and write out your strategy for improving them or write alternatives that have more motivational (and presumably instructional) value.

15. How can you model curiosity and interest in learning for your students?

FORM 5.1. Attributing Success to Causes

USE: *Whenever teacher makes a comment to explain a student's success.*
PURPOSE: *To see whether the teacher's statements support student confidence and motivation to learn.*
        For each codable instance, code each causal attribution category that applies. How does the teacher explain good performance by students?

CAUSAL ATTRIBUTION CATEGORIES	CODES

1. Effort or perseverance ("You worked hard, stuck to it")

2. Accurate problem representation and solution ("You developed a good plan, followed the right process")

3. Good progress in learning the domain ("You've really learned how to _____")

4. Native intelligence or ability ("You're smart")

5. Compliance ("You listened carefully, did as you were told")

6. Irrelevant attributes ("You're a big boy")

7. Cheating ("You copied." "Did someone tell you the answer?")

8. Other (specify)

NOTES:

1. ___	26. ___		
2. ___	27. ___		
3. ___	28. ___		
4. ___	29. ___		
5. ___	30. ___		
6. ___	31. ___		
7. ___	32. ___		
8. ___	33. ___		
9. ___	34. ___		
10. ___	35. ___		
11. ___	36. ___		
12. ___	37. ___		
13. ___	38. ___		
14. ___	39. ___		
15. ___	40. ___		
16. ___	41. ___		
17. ___	42. ___		
18. ___	43. ___		
19. ___	44. ___		
20. ___	45. ___		
21. ___	46. ___		
22. ___	47. ___		
23. ___	48. ___		
24. ___	49. ___		
25. ___	50. ___		

FORM 5.2. General Motivational Strategies

USE: When the teacher has been observed frequently enough so that reliable information is available.
PURPOSE: To assess the degree to which the teacher's general approach to instruction supports students' self-confidence and motivation to learn.
        How regularly does the teacher follow the motivational guidelines listed below? Rate according to the following scale:

        5 = always
        4 = most of the time
        3 = sometimes
        2 = occasionally
        1 = never

A. ESSENTIAL PRECONDITIONS

_____   1. Maintains a supportive learning environment (classroom atmosphere is businesslike but relaxed, teacher supports and encourages students' learning efforts)
_____   2. Assigns tasks at an appropriate level of difficulty (students can achieve success with reasonable effort)
_____   3. Assigns tasks with meaningful learning objectives (the tasks teach some knowledge or skill that is worth learning)
_____   4. Demonstrates moderation and variation in use of motivational strategies (does not overuse particular strategies to the point that they become counterproductive)

B. MAINTAINING STUDENTS' SUCCESS EXPECTATIONS

_____   1. Programs for success
_____   2. Helps students to develop their skills for goal setting, performance appraisal, and self-reinforcement
_____   3. Helps students to recognize effort-outcome linkages
_____   4. Portrays effort as investment rather than risk
_____   5. Portrays skill development as incremental and domain-specific (rather than as determined by fixed general abilities)
_____   6. Focuses on mastery in monitoring performance and giving feedback (stresses student's continuous progress toward mastery rather than comparisons with other students)
_____   7. If necessary, does remedial motivational work with discouraged students (to help them see that they have ability and can reach goals if they put forth reasonable effort)

C. STIMULATING STUDENTS' MOTIVATION TO LEARN

_____   1. Models own motivation to learn (portrays learning as a self-actualizing activity that produces personal satisfaction and enriches one's life)
_____   2. Communicates desirable expectations and attributions (implying that students see classroom activities as worthwhile and are eager to acquire knowledge and master skills)
_____   3. Minimizes performance anxiety (treats mistakes as understandable and expected; minimizes the threat of tests)

NOTES:

FORM 5.3. Teacher's Response to Students' Questions

USE: *When a student asks the teacher a reasonable question during a discussion or question–answer period.*
PURPOSE: *To see if teacher models commitment to learning and concern for students' interests.*
    Code each category that applies to the teacher's response to a reasonable student question. Do not code if student wasn't really asking a question of if he or she was baiting the teacher.

BEHAVIOR CATEGORIES	CODES

1. Compliments the question ("Good question")

2. Criticizes the question (unjustly) as irrelevant, dumb, out of place, etc.

3. Ignores the question, or brushes it aside quickly without answering it

4. Answers the question or redirects it to the class

5. If no one can answer, teacher arranges to get the answer or assigns a student to do so

6. If no one can answer, teacher leaves it un-answered and moves on

7. Other (specify)

NOTES:

    #7 Explained that question would be
    covered in tomorrow's lesson.

	CODES		
1.	4	26.	___
2.	4	27.	___
3.	1,4	28.	___
4.	4	29.	___
5.	4	30.	___
6.	3	31.	___
7.	4	32.	___
8.	4	33.	___
9.	7	34.	___
10.	4	35.	___
11.	4	36.	___
12.	___	37.	___
13.	___	38.	___
14.	___	39.	___
15.	___	40.	___
16.	___	41.	___
17.	___	42.	___
18.	___	43.	___
19.	___	44.	___
20.	___	45.	___
21.	___	46.	___
22.	___	47.	___
23.	___	48.	___
24.	___	49.	___
25.	___	50.	___

Students' Interactions with One Another

*I*n previous chapters, we have discussed the roles of teachers' expectations, classroom management, and motivational strategies in establishing productive learning environments. Further, it is well established that good teacher–student relationships are an important aspect of classroom life. Teacher actions that are viewed by students as positive and supportive of them are consistently found to correlate with student motivation and achievement (Brophy & Good, 1974; Hamre & Pintra, 2001, 2005; Juvonen, 2006; Murdock, Anderman, & Hodge, 2000; Murdock & Miller, 2003).

In this chapter, we shift focus from the teacher to the students, considering the makeup of the class and how students might interact productively with one another, in terms of achieving both academic and social goals. Good student–student relationships are important conditions if students are to be active and successful learners (Elias & Schwab, 2006; Juvonen, 2006; Johnson & Johnson, 2006b).

Once there was heavy emphasis on excluding "less capable" students from regular classrooms and on assigning the remaining students to more homogeneous groups through tracking at the school level and ability grouping in classrooms. Effective teaching emphasized efficiency in moving students through progressive sequences of instructional objectives, and it was thought that this process would unfold best if students were as similar as possible.

Thinking has changed significantly. Most educators are philosophically opposed to exclusion and homogeneous grouping, arguing that educational approaches should be assessed in terms of efficiency and equity. They argue that heterogeneous classes are as effective as homogeneous classes for accomplishing cognitive outcomes, but are even more effective for accomplishing diversity and social outcomes, such as promoting cultural understandings across racial and ethnic groups (Slavin, 2006).

Students' learning together can be helpful in addressing key curricular goals (as described in Chapter 9) and can allow for students to actively teach one another (along the lines of active teaching we describe in Chapter 10). Social constructivist theories of teaching and learning (described in Chapter 11) expand these arguments by suggesting that increased emphasis on student–student interaction is important for achieving cognitive outcomes as well. In these views, students learn by collaborating with peers in pairs and small groups and by interacting with them during class discussion. Assuming that everyone participates, diversity in students' backgrounds and viewpoints is an asset, not a liability. Thus, heterogeneous classes and groups would be preferable to homogeneous ones. Small-group formats also hold potential for contributing to students' sense of belonging and community, which may enhance commitment to schooling (Juvonen, 2006; Osterman, 2000; Watson & Battistich, 2006).

In this chapter, we discuss the implications of theory and research for issues relating to the composition of the class and to students' interactions with one anther. We begin with the goals of excellence and equity and their implications for student diversity and inclusion. Then we consider tracking and ability grouping. Finally, we address cooperative learning, peer tutoring, and other formats that allow students to learn collaboratively. Later, in Chapter 13, we will discuss student project work in depth. We delay this discussion because many popular forms of student project work involve heavy use of technology (Blumenfeld, Marx, & Harris, 2006; Krajcik, Czerniak, & Berger, 2003; Lambros, 2002; Salavin-Baden, 2003; Stephen, Senn, & Stephen, 2001).

Educational Excellence and Equity

Educational excellence is a continuing concern of the general public. By many criteria, including literacy rates and the percentage of the population who earn high school diplomas and college degrees, education in the United States has been successful both in absolute terms and in comparison with other countries (Berliner & Biddle, 1995; Bracey, 2000; Good & Braden, 2000). Historically, the general public has shown continuing commitment to the public schools and a perception that most of them are adequate, and some outstanding. This said, however, there are problems with education in America, and one concern has been the achievement gap between white and black Americans (Braun et al., 2006; Weinstein, Gregory, & Strambler, 2004). Further, the current high school graduation rate of minority students is unacceptably low.

Acute disenchantment with our schools sets in periodically, either in response to the writings of popular educational critics or as a reaction to events perceived as indications of slippage in the nation's competitive position. For example, the rapid growth of the Chinese economy and the ability of China and India to produce more highly trained engineers than we have in the United States has created new concerns about our public education system. Policy makers have raised even more serious questions about the quality of American education in reports such as *A Nation at Risk* (1983) and even through federal legislation as represented in the No Child Left Behind Act (2001).

When fueled by concern about educational excellence, reforms concentrate on cognitive (particularly achievement test scores) rather than affective or social objectives (McCaslin, 2006; Stipek, 2006), and even here some important achievement areas are neglected (Marx & Harris, 2006). Calls for upgrading schools commonly include recommitment to academic objectives and standards, mandated performance objectives and associated testing programs, increases in course requirements and reductions in course options, more rigorous grading, more challenging curricula, and more homework. Often there are calls for special programs to accommodate the perceived needs of "the best and the brightest": special tracks or courses for gifted elementary students and honors or advanced placement courses for qualifying secondary students.

The "educational excellence" approach identifies school quality with success in maximizing achievement test scores. This is rejected as overly narrow by educators who wish to define school quality at least in part in terms of educational equity: fair and effective treatment of all students regardless of gender, race, ethnicity, socioeconomic status, or handicapping conditions.

Desegregation

Equity concerns were the primary motives behind two of the most widespread school changes during the 1960s and 1970s: desegregation and mainstreaming. Following the Supreme Court's *Brown v. Board of Education* decision in 1954, separate schools for black students were abolished. However, despite notable progress in many school districts, students are still segregated to some extent. In a longitudinal study of performance in one school district, Mickelson (2001) concluded that certain aspects of segregated schooling continue and contribute to maintaining the race gap in academic achievement (because white students have more opportunities to learn). Still, minority students in the district showed better achievement when they received desegregated education. This was especially true for black students.

Whether *Brown v. Board of Education* led to enduring educational improvements is widely debated by policy makers and researchers. The arguments are complex and involve many considerations. An especially informative set of papers describing gains and losses in the past fifty years appears in a special issue of the *American Psychologist* (2004).

Recently, attention has shifted from accomplishing desegregation to addressing the equity issues it introduces: the need for multicultural awareness and fair treatment of different groups, the desire to elicit active participation by all students in classroom activities, and the attempt to get beyond mere tolerance by promoting positive, prosocial interactions among students of different backgrounds.

At the school level, this goal requires minimizing between-class achievement grouping (tracking). In most schools there are substantial correlations among race, socioeconomic status, and achievement, so that creating homogeneous classes in desegregated schools resegregates students and minimizes cross-racial contact.

The degree to which the ultimate goals of desegregation are likely to be accomplished depends on the activities and organizational structures that are used. Within-class grouping tends to resegregate students, and a heavy reliance on traditional whole-class instruction/recitation/seatwork teaching minimizes students' opportunities to interact with their peers. Positive attitudes and frequent cross-race interaction are more likely when teachers frequently use small-group and peer interaction formats, and develop learning environments that encourage project work (Blumenfeld, Marx, & Harris, 2006).

Between-Class Grouping (Tracking)

Between-class grouping involves assigning students to classes that are as homogeneous as possible. Two subtypes are grouping by ability or achievement and grouping by curriculum (Rosenbaum, 1980, 2001). *Grouping by ability or achievement* is more common in elementary and middle schools, where it is often called *homogeneous grouping*. To group 69 third-graders homogeneously, school staff would examine achievement test scores and assign the highest 23 to the top class, the next 23 to the middle class, and the last 23 to the bottom class. There might be some minor variations, such as making the top class a little larger and the bottom class a little smaller. However, the result would be three classes, each much more homogeneous in achievement than if the students had been assigned randomly. Even so, homogeneously grouped classes are usually taught essentially the same curriculum, but with higher-ranking classes taught in greater depth and breadth.

Grouping by curriculum is more frequently used in middle and especially senior high schools. It is commonly called *tracking*. Instead of merely introducing differences in the depth and breadth of instruction in the same curriculum, tracking creates separate curricula for students in the different tracks. College preparatory students take one curriculum, business-secretarial students another, vocational students another, and general education students another. Some ninth-graders take algebra, some prealgebra, some business math, and some general math.

U.S. educators have always been ambivalent about between-class ability grouping (Rosenbaum, 1980). It is a sensible idea in theory because reducing heterogeneity should make it easier for teachers to meet more student needs more consistently. In practice, its effects on achievement are weak and mixed rather than reliably positive, and it appears to have undesirable affective and social effects that conflict with equity goals. Consequently, opposition to tracking has culminated in policy statements by various blue ribbon panels and professional organizations calling for elimination or at least minimization of tracking (Oakes, 2005; Oakes & Lipton, 1992; Oakes & Wells, 2002).

Teachers' attitudes toward tracking tend to vary according to the subject they teach (Dar, 1985; Evans, 1985). Teachers who favor tracking tend to teach subjects such as mathematics or foreign languages in which the content is largely abstract and arranged hierarchically. In contrast, teachers of literature, history, and other humanities and social studies subjects see the least need for tracking, apparently because they can relate their subjects to everyday experience and develop them using commonsense explanations.

Effects on Achievement

In theory, between-class ability grouping should improve achievement and be equally beneficial for both low and high achievers. However, reviews suggest only weak and mixed effects on achievement (Castle, Deniz, & Tortora, 2005; Kulik & Kulik, 1989; Oakes, 2005; Oakes & Wells, 2002; Slavin, 1990, 2006). Research cannot indicate why tracking has not lived up to its theoretical potential, because most investigators have used a black box approach—looking only at outcomes without collecting information about curriculum and instruction in classrooms that might explain conflicting results. If teachers provide essentially the same curriculum and instruction to both tracked and untracked classes, there is little reason to expect either benefits or detriments to student achievement. Such effects can be expected only when teachers differentiate their instruction to different classes. Gamoran (1993) found some Catholic schools where effective teaching occurred in low-track classrooms. These schools (1) did not assign weak or less experienced teachers to lower tracks; (2) communicated high performance expectations to low-track students; (3) focused their curriculum on academics; (4) stressed interactive exchange between teachers and students; and (5) reflected considerable effort on the part of teachers. Studies of tracking do not usually yield such positive findings, possibly because low tracks often become dumping grounds for low achievers instead of mechanisms for meeting their needs more effectively (Castle, Deniz, & Tortora, 2005).

Affective and Social Effects

Critics have identified four types of negative effects that tracking is likely to have on students. First, teachers dislike teaching low-ability classes, spend less time preparing, and schedule less varied, interesting, and challenging activities in them (Oakes, 1985). This is true even in elite schools where most students in low-track classes would be in higher tracks elsewhere (Page, 1991). Unfortunately, the least capable or least experienced teachers are frequently assigned to teach low-track students, especially in low-income schools (Connor et al., 2004).

Compared with their behavior in high-track classes, many teachers in low-track classes are less clear about objectives, introduce content less clearly or completely, make fewer attempts to relate content to students' interests or backgrounds, and are less receptive to students views. Instruction tends to be conceptually simplified and to proceed slowly, with emphasis on rote memory, oral recitation, and low-level worksheets. In contrast, high-track classes study more interesting, complex material, taught at a faster pace and with more enthusiasm.

Second, tracking creates undesirable peer structures in low-track classes. In heterogeneous classes, the brighter and better socially adjusted students tend to assume academic peer leadership, so that most time is spent engaged in academic activities. However, tracking systems place most of these academic peer leaders in upper-track classes, so that lower-track classes can become leaderless aggregations of discouraged students. These students may respond to their low status by refusing to commit themselves seriously to achievement goals and deriding classmates who do (Gamoran & Berends, 1987; Oakes, 2005). Even if teachers approach low-track classes with desirable attitudes and expectations, they may find it difficult to establish effective learning environments if they encounter defeatism or flat-out resistance. Similarly, low-track students who want to accomplish as much as they can may have a difficult time doing so if classmates deride their efforts or if instructional continuity is often disrupted. Experimental data indicate that low achievers assigned to higher groups achieve more than comparable students assigned to lower groups (Mason et al., 1992; Nyberg et al., 1997).

Third, assignment to tracks tends to be permanent: There is little movement from one track to another once initial assignments have been made, and the movement that does occur tends to be downward. The lack of movement from lower to higher tracks is another indication that tracking typically does not lead to adaptive instruction of low achievers. If it did, many of these students would show improved achievement and move up to higher tracks. Thus, initial placement into a low track may categorize a student permanently and close off academic and career advancement options.

Fourth, tracking minimizes contact between students who differ in achievement level, social class, race, or ethnicity (Yonezawa, Wells, & Serna, 2002). Taken together, the data on tracking suggest that it offers little or no advantage as a way to increase student achievement and has some important negative effects on affective and social outcomes. Consequently, we agree with the developing consensus that tracking should be minimized.

If conditions compel homogeneous grouping, we recommend partial arrangements over arrangements that segregate different groups completely. One such compromise is the Joplin plan and its many variations. In the original Joplin plan, students were assigned to heterogeneous classes for most of the day but were regrouped for reading instruction across grades (teachers all taught reading at the same time to make such regrouping possible). For example, a fourth-grade, first-semester reading class might include high-achieving third graders. The class would be taught as a whole or perhaps divided into just two groups, but no more. Students would be assigned strictly according to reading achievement level and would be reassigned when their performance warranted it.

The Joplin plan requires coordinated scheduling and cooperation among teachers, but it simplifies reading instruction by making it possible for each teacher to instruct the entire class as a group or to divide the class into only two subgroups instead of three or more. This simplifies management and increases the time that students receive instruction from the teacher rather than work independently on assignments. Gutiérrez and Slavin (1992) reported that the Joplin plan showed significant positive effects on achievement compared with traditional homogeneous or heterogeneous grouping within grades, although Kulik and Kulik (1989) reported more modest effects.

Consensus is growing around the idea that tracking should be minimized, or delayed as long as possible; and, when used, confined to grouping by curriculum rather than by ability or achievement. Suggestions include postponing tracking by deferring it as late in the grade span as possible; limiting it to subjects in which skill differences are clear detriments to whole-class instruction; using multiple placement criteria to determine track placement; offering students incentives for taking challenging courses; minimizing separate offerings for gifted and special needs students; rotating teachers among track levels; and encouraging students to move up to higher tracks and providing them with extra help when needed. The findings of research by Nyberg et al. (1997) support the latter suggestion. In this study, high school students who scored between the twenty-fifth and sixty-fifth percentile on a standardized achievement test, who formerly would have been assigned to general or vocational tracks, instead were enrolled in college preparatory classes. They did well in these classes and had only half the dropout rate of tracked control students.

However, some controversy remains. Proponents of tracking claim that many of the arguments against it are based more on ideology and theoretical commitments than on empirical findings demonstrating negative effects on students. In addition, advocates of acceleration programs and special courses for gifted students claim that the existing literature supports this particular form of tracking and that additional support would be forthcoming if a broader range of outcome criteria was used to judge its effectiveness (Allan, 1991). Opponents respond that the seeming advantages to tracking suggested by certain studies result from the enriched curriculum enjoyed by high-track students rather than from the homogeneity of their classes. They argue for an enriched curriculum for all students and maintain that there are no advantages but many disadvantages to grouping students homogeneously.

Within-Class Ability Grouping

Ability grouping within classes offers certain advantages over ability grouping between classes. First, only one teacher is involved, so that there is no need for cooperative scheduling. Also, it is easier for you to vary the number and size of groups and to move students from group to group. Whenever you instruct a small group, however, provisions must be made to keep your other students profitably occupied. Consequently, instructional planning and classroom management are considerably more complicated than when you use whole-class methods. The result is that the potential advantages of within-class ability grouping (students receive intensive small-group instruction in content and skills that are closely matched to current achievement) are offset by certain disadvantages (reduction in time taught directly by the teacher, increase in time spent in independent seatwork).

Even in districts that group by achievement at the classroom level, some teachers regroup the students again to further reduce variations in achievement levels. Mason and Good (1993) tested the effects of two models of active teaching on the mathematics learning of over 1,700 fourth-, fifth-, and sixth-grade students drawn from eighty-one classrooms in a district that used regrouping in mathematics. One model was a *structural approach* in which students' diversity was reduced before instruction. Students were divided into two groups on the basis of previous performance, and teachers taught these two groups separately. The *situational approach* involved forming student groups *after* instruction. The teacher initially taught the class as a whole and then provided ad hoc instruction (review, enrichment, etc.) to subsets of students as needed. The situational model proved to be more effective than the structural model. In the situational model, teachers placed more emphasis on development (trying to explore and "connect" mathematical ideas) and on assessing student understanding (encouraging students to explain their thinking). They also found more time to individualize instruction, in part because they spent less time managing groups. Thus, within-class ability grouping may be needed only when student populations are very diverse (Lou et al., 1996).

Remarkably, in view of the long history of reading groups, there have been few studies comparing small-group versus whole-class instruction in beginning reading. A meta-analysis of these studies yielded a near-zero average effect on achievement, suggesting that grouping neither helps nor hurts students' early reading progress (Lou et al., 1996). However, within-class ability grouping for beginning reading is often criticized on logical grounds. First, ability grouping tends to exaggerate preexisting differences in achievement by accelerating the progress of students in the top groups but slowing the progress of students in the bottom groups. Second, high groups seem to benefit not only from faster pacing but from better instruction from the teacher, a more desirable work orientation, and greater attention to the lesson. Third, group membership tends to remain highly stable once groups are formed, so group assignments affect peer contact and friendship patterns in addition to achievement, more so as time goes on. Ability grouping sometimes results in de facto resegregation of students.

Enough problems with within-class ability grouping have been reported to cause educators to question this practice and seek alternatives to it, even educators concerned with beginning reading instruction, where such grouping has been standard practice. The report *Becoming a Nation of Readers* (Anderson et al., 1985), for example, called for reduced emphasis on oral reading in small homogeneous groups and suggested that teachers experiment with alternative settings for reading practice. Some programs have accomplished this through whole-class instruction followed by silent reading and comprehension assignments. As students work on their assignments, the teacher circulates to listen to individuals read orally. Other programs assign students to work in pairs, alternately taking the reader and the listener role. The general trend in recent years has been away from fixed ability groups and toward whole-class instruction and flexible grouping based on current progress and needs (Baumann et al., 2000). It is too early to say whether such alternatives will prove more effective than teaching reading to homogeneous small groups. For a thorough discussion of extant approaches to reading instruction, see a special issue of the *Elementary School Journal* edited by Richard Allington (2006).

We have six suggestions for those considering within-class ability grouping. First, the number and composition of the groups should depend on the variation in achievement and instructional needs among students. If you use within-class grouping to achieve homogeneity among students assigned to the same group, then make sure that such homogeneity is achieved—don't just arbitrarily divide the class into three equal-sized groups. Second, grouping should lead to more effective meeting of instructional needs, not merely to differentiated pacing through the curriculum. Teaching will still have to be individualized within groups, and students who continue to have trouble will need additional instruction. Third, group assignments should be flexible. Assignments should be reviewed regularly with an eye toward disbanding groups that have outlived their usefulness. Fourth, group scheduling and instructional practices should be flexible (a particular group might best meet for forty minutes on one day and twenty minutes the next day). Fifth, because of the potential dangers of labeling effects and because grouping affects peer contacts, teachers should limit the degree to which group membership determines students' other school experiences. Members of the same reading group should not be seated together or otherwise dealt with as a group outside of reading instruction, and if ability grouping is used for mathematics or other subjects, group assignments should be based on achievement in these subjects rather than in reading. Sixth, groups should be organized and taught in ways that provide low achievers with extra instruction. For example, you can assign more students to high groups and fewer students to low groups, thus arranging for more intensive instruction of low achievers within the group setting. Or, you can spend more time teaching to low groups while high groups spend more time working cooperatively or independently.

Planned Heterogeneous Grouping

Small groups do not have to be formed based on student ability, especially if the object is merely to reduce the number of students to be taught together at one time. Beginning reading instruction may be best conducted in small groups when it involves slow-paced oral reading, so even in classrooms composed of students of similar ability, you may want to use small groups for oral reading practice. If so, you do not have to group students by ability. Sometimes it may make more sense to group students randomly, to separate students who tend to become disruptive when assigned to the same group, or to allow friends to work together (Zajac & Hartup, 1997). Elbaum, Schumm, and Vaughn (1997) found that students in grades 3 to 5 preferred mixed-ability groups or pairs for reading over same-ability groups or pairs.

Cooperative Learning

The traditional approach to schooling calls for whole-class lessons followed by independent seatwork. Cooperative learning approaches replace independent seatwork with small groups of students who work on assignments collaboratively. Cooperative learning methods differ according to the task structures and incentive structures that are in effect (Slavin, 1995, 2006).

Small-group learning has become popular because of its potential for engaging students in meaningful learning with authentic tasks in a social setting. Under appropriate conditions, small-group methods can support the social construction of knowledge (i.e., students learning from and with one another). However, small-group instruction varies widely in terms of tasks, group composition, and goals. Small groups can be used for drill, practice, learning facts and concepts, discussion, and problem solving. Even when the purpose of small-group instruction is inquiry or problem solving, good results are not automatic (Blumenfeld, 1992; Blumenfeld, Marx, & Harris, 2006). Educators have much to learn about how to design small-group instruction in order to stimulate comprehension and higher-order thinking (McCaslin & Good, 1996; O'Donnell, 2006; Webb & Palinscar, 1996).

In the rest of this chapter we explore the possible uses and misuses of small groups. You should consider both the potential payoffs and inherent problems associated with small-group instruction. Much more is known about the effects of small-group instruction than about how or why such effects occur, and more is known about its effects on skill and fact acquisition than about how it effects problem solving and conceptual understanding.

Task Structure

The term *task structure* refers to the nature of the task (its goal, the kinds of responses it requires, working conditions, etc.). Task structures may be individual, cooperative, or competitive. *Individual task structures* require students to work alone (except for help from the teacher if necessary). Traditional independent seatwork employs an individual task structure. *Cooperative task structures* require students to collaborate in order to meet task requirements. Assignments that call for students to assist one another in learning or to work together to produce a group product involve cooperative task structures. Finally, *competitive task structures,* such as contests, debates, and various competitive games, require students to compete (either as individuals or as teams) to meet task requirements.

Within groups, members may cooperate in working toward either group or individual goals. When pursuing *group goals,* the members work together to produce a single product that results from the shared labor of the group. For example, the group might paint a mural, assemble a collage, or prepare a skit or report to be presented to the class. When working cooperatively to reach *individual goals,* group members assist one another by discussing how to respond to questions or assignments, checking work, or providing feedback or tutorial assistance. Cooperative work toward individual goals occurs when individual students are responsible for turning in their own assignments but are allowed to consult with one another as they work on those assignments.

Cooperative task structures also differ according to degree of *task specialization.* When there is no task specialization, each member works on the same task. Task specialization occurs when the larger task to be accomplished is divided into several subtasks on which different group members work. For example, one group member might be assigned to do the introduction to a report on a country, another to cover geography and climate, another to cover natural resources and the economy, and so on.

Incentive Structure

Group activities differ in incentive structure. *Incentive structure* (also called *reward structure* or *goal structure*) refers to methods used for motivating students to perform a task. These include the nature of the incentives (e.g., grades, concrete rewards, symbolic rewards) and the rules specifying what must be done to earn them. Like task structures, incentive structures can be individual, cooperative, or competitive. Under *individual incentive structures,* individuals are rewarded if they meet specified performance criteria, regardless of how the rest of the class performs. Under *cooperative incentive structures,* individuals' chances of earning rewards depend not only on their own efforts but also on those of other group members. Here, the teacher rewards groups of students according to the performance that results from their combined efforts. Finally, under *competitive incentive structures,* groups or individuals compete for available rewards. The winners get the most desirable rewards, and the losers get less desirable rewards or no rewards at all. Classes in which grades are assigned according to preset curves involve competitive incentive structures explicitly, and any classes in which grades are assigned at least partly on the basis of comparative performance involve them implicitly.

Cooperative and competitive incentive structures can also be differentiated according to whether they involve group or individual rewards. *Group rewards* are distributed equally to all members of the group. These may involve a single reward to be shared by the group (such as a prize or a treat) or assigning the same reward to each member (if the group's product receives a grade of A, each member receives a grade of A, regardless of that member's contribution to the group product). *Individual rewards* are assigned differentially to individual students depending on effort or performance. For example, students may be encouraged to cooperate with peers in discussing assignments and preparing for a test but are required to take the test individually and are graded accordingly.

Task and incentive structures are independent; a cooperative task structure does not necessarily imply a cooperative incentive structure, and so on. In fact, any incentive structure could be imposed on any task structure, although some such arrangements would be highly artificial and unusual. For example, a teacher could require students to work on assignments alone (e.g., to use an individual task structure) but impose a competitive reward structure by dividing students into teams that never work together but are rewarded partly on the basis of how well team members do as a group on unit tests. Table 6.1 shows the combinations of task and reward structures that are typically used.

[handwritten margin note: Task – Incentive separate, combined in all ways]

Well-Known Cooperative Learning Programs

In this section, we describe some of the best known and widely researched cooperative learning programs.

Learning Together. The Learning Together model was developed by David and Roger Johnson (Johnson & Johnson, 1999, 2006b). Early versions called for students to work cooperatively on assignment sheets in four- or five-member heterogeneous groups. The major interest was in getting students who differed in achievement, gender, race, or ethnicity to work together. The groups handed in a single sheet and were praised as a group for working well together and for their performance on the task.

Experimentation revealed that some variations worked better than others, and eventually the Johnsons identified five elements that should be included in any cooperative learning activity (Johnson & Johnson, 1999):

1. *Positive interdependence.* Students should recognize that they are interdependent with other members of their group in achieving a successful group product. Positive interdependence can be structured through mutual goals (goal interdependence); division of labor (task interdependence); dividing materials, resources, or information among group members (resource interdependence); assigning students unique roles (role interdependence); or giving group rewards (reward interdependence).

2. *Face-to-face interaction among students.* Tasks that call for significant interaction among group members are preferred over tasks that can be accomplished by having group members work on their own.

3. *Individual accountability.* Mechanisms are needed to ensure that each group member has clear objectives for which he or she will be held accountable and receives any needed assessment, feedback, or instructional assistance.

Table 6.1 Possible Combinations of Task and Reward Structures
(All combinations are possible, but some are used more typically than others.)

Task structures	I. Individual*	II. Cooperative**		III. Competitive***	
		a. Individual rewards	b. Group reward	a. Individual rewards	b. Group reward
I. *Individual.* Each student works alone.	Typical	Possible	Possible	Typical	Possible
II. *Cooperative.* Students work together or help one another. **A.** *Group goals.* Individuals cooperate to create a group product. **1.** *Undifferentiated roles* Each student has the same task.	Possible	Possible	Typical	Possible	Typical
2. *Differentiated roles.* Different students perform different tasks.	Possible	Possible	Typical	Possible	Typical
B. *Individual goals.* Individuals help one another to fulfill their respective individual responsibilities. **1.** *Undifferentiated roles.* Each student has the same task.	Typical	Typical	Possible	Typical	Possible
2. *Differentiated roles.* Different students perform different tasks.	Typical	Typical	Possible	Typical	Possible
III. *Competitive.* The task requires students to compete. **A.** *Individual competition.*	Typical	Typical	Possible	Typical	Possible
B. *Team competition.*	Possible	Possible	Typical	Possible	Typical

*Reward depends strictly on one's own performance.
**Reward depends, at least in part, on group performance.
***Reward depends, at least in part, on the outcome of a competition.

4. *Instructing students in appropriate interpersonal and small-group skills.* Students cannot merely be placed together and told to cooperate. They need instruction in skills such as asking and answering questions, ensuring that everyone participates actively and is treated with respect, and assigning tasks and organizing cooperative efforts.

5. *Group processing.* Students must have the time to assess how well the group is performing and to discuss group members' actions that are helpful or unhelpful.

Group Investigation.   Shlomo Sharan and his colleagues (Sharan & Sharan, 1992) developed Group Investigation models in Israel. Group Investigation students form their own two- to six-member groups to work together using cooperative inquiry, group discussion, and cooperative planning and projects. Each group chooses a subtopic from a unit studied by the whole class, breaks this subtopic into individual tasks, and carries out the activities necessary to prepare and present a group report (and is evaluated on the quality of this report).

[handwritten: sounds like edu 201]

Jigsaw.   The Jigsaw approach (Aronson et al., 1978) ensures active individual participation and group cooperation by arranging tasks so that each group member possesses unique information. The group product cannot be completed unless each member does his or her part, just as a jigsaw puzzle cannot be completed unless each piece is included. For example, information needed to compose a biography might be broken into early life, first accomplishments, major setbacks, later life, and world events occurring during the person's lifetime. One member of each group would be given or asked to find the relevant information and assigned responsibility for one section of the biography. Members of different groups who were working on the same section would meet together in "expert groups" to discuss their sections. Then they would return to their regular groups and take turns teaching their group mates about their sections. Since the only way that students can learn about sections other than their own is to listen carefully to their group mates, they are motivated to support and show interest in one another's work. The students then prepare biographies or take quizzes on the material individually.

[handwritten: edu 201 - - - -]

Student Teams-Achievement Divisions (STAD).   Student Teams-Achievement Divisions is a simplification of the Teams-Game-Tournament (TGT) approach (Slavin, 1986). It allows students to learn in heterogeneous groups involving cooperative learning procedures and students are held accountable with a quiz. Quiz scores are translated into team competition points based on how much students have improved their performance over past averages. STAD depersonalizes competition. Rather than compete face-to-face against classmates at tournament tables, students in STAD classrooms try to do their best on quizzes taken individually.

[handwritten: group task / ind. incentive]

Jigsaw II.   Jigsaw II is an adaptation of the original Jigsaw (Slavin, 1980). In the new version, the teacher does not need to provide each student with unique materials. Instead, all students begin by reading a common narrative and then each group member is given a separate topic on which to become an expert. Next, students who have the same topic assignments meet in expert groups to discuss topics and then return to their teams to teach what they have learned to their teammates. Then students take a quiz and their individual scores are summed to compute team scores, and team accomplishments are recognized through a class newsletter.

Slavin and his colleagues have also developed larger programs of curriculum and instruction that include student team learning methods as components. Early efforts included Cooperative Integrated Reading and Composition (CIRC), a language arts program, and Team Assisted Individualization (TAI), a mathematics program. More recent efforts include Success For All, a language arts program, and its extension, Roots and Wings, which includes mathematics, science, and social studies components (Slavin et al., 1996). The student team methods used in all of these programs combine group incentive structures and goals with individual accountability. Slavin believes that this combination of tasks and rewards provides the most effective structure for motivating students not only to pursue their own learning but to encourage and assist their peers' learning within team learning formats (Slavin, 1996).

Brief, Informal Cooperative Learning Structures

As cooperative learning has gained in popularity, teachers have developed additional formats that allow students to work and learn together in pairs or small groups. Many of these are methods for structuring brief, informal periods of cooperative learning that are embedded within larger lessons or activity periods. For example, the teacher might pose a question and then give students time to interact in pairs to discuss how to respond, or might reserve part of the time allocated for work on assignments to give students opportunities to plan how they might approach the assignment before beginning it or to compare and discuss work after they complete it.

In the *Think/Pair Share* method, the teacher poses a question or problem, allows time for students to think by themselves, then has students discuss their ideas with a partner, and finally calls on some of the students to share their (and their partner's) thinking with the whole class. In an alternative version called *Think-Pair-Share,* students first think alone, then share with a partner, then join another pair to interact as a group of four.

In a structure called *Numbered Heads Together*, students are assigned to groups of three or four and given assigned numbers within their group. The teacher poses a problem. Next, students think about this problem individually and then discuss it with their group ("put their heads together"). Next, the teacher calls out a number, and all of the students who have that number stand up. The teacher then calls on one of these students to suggest an answer, and the other students are invited to compare their answers and discuss any discrepancies. This structure is especially useful for review activities or for checking student understanding.

Variations on these structures include elements designed to ensure that each student in the group participates actively. In *Pens in the Middle,* each student places a pen (or pencil) in the center of the group as he or she makes a contribution, and no student can share more ideas until all pens are in the middle. In *Round Robin*, students proceed clockwise around the group, sharing in turn. In *Group Interview,* each student is "interviewed" for a minute or two by other members of the group. More information about these and other informal cooperative learning methods, along with detailed advice about implementing more formal methods, can be found in Baloche (1998) or Kagan (1992). Extended information about creating learning centers can be found in Lawrence, Lawrence, and Samek (2006).

Controlled Conflict and Controversy in Small Groups

David and Roger Johnson and their colleagues developed an interesting variation on small-group cooperative learning methods in which controlled conflict or controversy is introduced into the group. We refer here to intellectual controversy involving conflict of opinion about curricular issues, not physical aggression or other forms of personal conflict (see our discussion of bullying and related issues in Chapter 4). In a review of these issues, Johnson and Johnson (1979, 2006b) found that constructively managed controversy in the classroom promotes a healthy uncertainty about the correctness of one's views, curiosity for more information, and better achievement. Studies conducted since then have supported this interpretation.

Smith, Johnson, and Johnson (1981) and Johnson and Johnson (2006b) studied the learning of sixth-graders about controversial issues such as whether strip mining should be allowed. Students were presented with material offering pro and con views on the issues and directed to study the material either individually or in small groups. Controversy groups were subdivided to represent the two sides and encouraged to debate the issues, but concurrence-seeking groups were directed to study the material together and avoid arguing. The results indicated that the controversy group condition promoted higher achievement, more accurate understanding of both positions on each issue, interest in getting more information, and better attitudes toward classmates and the value of constructive controversy.

Teachers whose subjects lend themselves to controversy and debate (policy issues in social studies and science classes; interpretation issues in humanities and literature courses) should consider including controversy groups among their instructional activities. Students will need to be prepared to participate in controversy constructively by citing relevant arguments and evidence in support of their own position and focusing their attacks on opposing positions but not on the peers who advance those positions (Johnson & Johnson, 2006b; King & King, 1998).

Research on Cooperative Learning Methods

Cooperative versus Traditional Methods

The effects on achievement appear to be related to the use of group rewards based on members' individual performance rather than to the cooperative task structures used (Slavin, 1983, 2006). That is, the student team learning methods that include team rewards (STAD, Jigsaw II) tend to have consistently positive effects on student achievement, whereas the more purely cooperative methods (Learning Together, Group Investigation, and the original Jigsaw) are less likely to produce a significant achievement advantage over traditional techniques (Slavin, 1983, 2006). Perhaps much more "up-front" time is needed to prepare students for the more purely cooperative methods than is needed for simpler peer-tutoring models.

Also, methods that ensure individual group members are accountable to their groupmates produce higher achievement than methods in which it is possible for one or two students to do the work. The most effective methods combine group goals with individual accountability. The findings on task specialization are mixed, probably because its appropriateness varies with subject matter and the instructional objectives pursued. Task specialization seems most useful in social studies and with assignments emphasizing higher-level cognitive skills (Graybeal & Stodolsky, 1985).

motivation →

There is no evidence that group competition offers advantages over other cooperative learning methods so long as arrangements are made to provide group rewards based on the cumulative performance of individual group members. Besides direct group competitions as in Jigsaw II and STAD, good results have been obtained by giving teams certificates for meeting preset standards independently of the performance of other teams and by using task specialization to motivate students to encourage their groupmates. Thus, although the effects of cooperative learning on achievement appear to be primarily motivational, the key is not motivation to win competitions against other teams but motivation to assist one's teammates to meet their individual goals and thus ensure that the team will do well.

Cooperative learning methods that combine group goals and individual accountability consistently achieve gains over traditional instruction methods (Lou, Abrami, & d'Apollonia, 2001; Quin, Johnson, & Johnson, 1995; Slavin, Hurley, & Chamberlain, 2003). Further, there is some evidence to suggest that students of all achievement levels and both genders benefit from cooperative learning (Slavin, 1995) and some evidence that these methods have especially positive value for Hispanic and African American students (Boykin, 1994; Calderón, Hertz-Lazarowitz, & Slavin, 1998).

Effects on outcomes other than achievement are impressive. Cooperative learning arrangements promote friendships and prosocial interaction among students who differ in achievement, gender, race, or ethnicity, and they promote the acceptance of mainstreamed handicapped students by their nonhandicapped classmates.

Group Composition and Processes

3 conclusions

There have been several studies of the effects of group composition and the nature of students' interaction during group meetings, and three main conclusions have emerged from this research.

① explaining

First, whether students master the content depends not only on their entry-level achievement but also on their experiences in the group. Giving explanations to other group members is positively correlated with achievement, even when entry-level ability is controlled. This confirms the findings from peer-tutoring studies (e.g., Graesser & Pearson, 1994) and other research indicating that explaining material to others is an effective learning experience for the explainer as well as the person receiving the explanation. Receiving explanations usually also correlates positively with later achievement scores, indicating that students who know what to ask about and succeed in getting their questions answered are likely to master the material. In contrast, negative correlations with achievement have been noted for asking questions without getting a response or receiving only a direct answer to a question without an explanation of how to arrive at the answer (Nattiv, 1994).

② training

Second, the quality of interaction in small groups can be enhanced through training (Emmer & Gerwels, 2002; Fuchs et al., 1999; Mathes et al., 2003). Compared with those in untrained control groups, students given training in how to interact during small-group activities have been shown to spend more time on task and to go beyond just giving answers by giving more detailed explanations designed to make sure that the listener understands the concept or process.

how to group ③

Third, certain combinations of students seem to work better than others. In mixed groups containing one high achiever, two average achievers, and one low achiever, most of the interaction involved tutoring of the low achiever by the high achiever, with the average achievers remaining relatively passive. Thus, heterogeneous small groups were less effective with average achievers, at least when the students had not been trained in how to interact during small-group activities.

Homogeneous groupings produced mixed results. Groups of average students worked well together, helping one another and interacting actively. However, groups in which the students either were all high achievers or all low achievers did not work well together or interact much about the content. Members of high-achieving groups apparently assumed that no one needed help, and members of low-achieving groups often became frustrated because they were unable to explain material effectively to one another.

Bennett and Cass (1988) studied groups containing either two high achievers and one low achiever (2HL), or two low achievers and one high achiever (2LH). They found that the 2LH groups performed much better than the 2HL groups. When the low-achieving student worked with two high achievers, the low-achieving student was ignored or chose to withdraw from active participation. High achievers performed well in all group settings. Within the context of this study, high-achieving students' performance was not harmed by working with low achievers.

Limitations of Findings on Small-Group Learning

Although research illustrates that students can learn cooperatively under certain conditions, many issues about small-group instruction have not been resolved. Most achievement comparisons have been made in reference to computational skills, simple concepts, and simple application problems. Thus, a relatively narrow range of dependent measures has been explored.

Cooperative learning research has also been questioned on theoretical grounds. For example, many educators question the value of competition if cooperative learning is the goal. Research by Stipek (1986, 2003) and others who have explored intrinsic motivation concepts shows that teachers need to pay careful attention to what happens to students when cooperative behavior is maintained by the use of external incentives over an extended period.

watch out for using ext. incentives!

Researchers have been encouraging more study of group processes in order to determine whether some of the putative goals of small-group instruction are being attained. Bossert (1988–1989) noted that researchers have often failed to verify whether students have even engaged in cooperative interactions, and that when they have observed instructional processes, their results have not always supported theories of cooperative learning.

Mulryan (1989, 1995) studied students' behavior during whole-class and small-group mathematics instruction. She found that students attended better in the small-group than the whole-class context. High achievers attended more than low achievers. Low achievers asked more questions and high achievers did more information giving.

Mulryan argued that the helping roles that emerged in these small groups may not have been useful, especially when the same students played these roles consistently. Such circumstances create a "caste" system that discourages the active involvement of some students, especially low-achieving female students. Without careful teacher structuring and monitoring, the same students who benefit the most from whole-class instruction are also the most likely to learn best in small groups.

During interviews some students indicated that they perceived low achievers as a burden to other members of cooperative groups. Building on Good's (1981) passivity model, Mulryan (1992) identified six types of passive students: the discouraged student, the unrecognized student, the despondent student, the unmotivated student, the bored student, and the intellectual snob. The discouraged students were mainly low achievers who became passive because they perceived the group task as too difficult and thought it better to leave the work to peers who knew more content. The unrecognized students became passive because their initial efforts to participate were ignored. Most were low achievers. Despondent students tended to be passive because they disliked or felt uncomfortable with one or more persons in their group. Bored students did not find the group activities engaging. Intellectual snobs were passive in cooperative work because they thought their peers were less competent and they did not want to constantly explain to them. Social opportunists wanted to talk with peers about social issues and intentional loafers allowed other students to do the work.

Good, McCaslin, and Reys (1992) noted that students' affective reports of satisfaction on questionnaires or in interviews may mask important problems in group functioning. Thus, teachers who use small-group work as a way to engage students in problem solving and higher-order thinking need to develop strategies for monitoring group processes (occasionally tape-recording or sitting in on a group, etc.) in order to assess the quality of the small-group discussions (McCaslin & Good, 1996). For a rich discussion of how to involve students in high-quality discussion in the class and especially in small-group work, see Browne and Keely (2000), Cook and Tashlik (2004), Jacobs, Power, and Loh (2002), and Spiegel (2005).

Potential Advantages and Disadvantages of Cooperative Groups

Some students like small-group work. However, some of this positive attitude may be due to novelty and, in some cases, to misconceptions. For example, Paulus et al. (1993) noted that individuals produce fewer ideas in interactive brainstorming groups than when brainstorming alone, yet often believe that they are more productive in the group. Also, whereas cooperative learning clearly can improve motivation and performance on simple tasks, we do not yet know if it can facilitate and sustain true problem solving and negotiation.

Bossert (1988–1989) contended that four major explanations could account for the success of cooperative methods: (1) reasoning strategies—cooperative groups may stimulate more higher-order thinking; (2) constructive controversy—heterogeneous cooperative groups force the accommodation of the opinions of various members; (3) cognitive processing—cooperative methods increase opportunities for students to rehearse information orally and to integrate it; and (4) peer encouragement and involvement in positive learning interactions increase friendship, acceptance, and cognitive information processing.

There are at least eight additional reasons why cooperative groups may enhance students' achievement and social relations (McCaslin & Good, 1996).

BENGFITS

1. Subject-matter knowledge is increased. The knowledge that the group possesses is almost always greater than the knowledge of any individual.
2. Students value shared learning. It is likely that students will understand mathematics better in small groups because proportionately more group time is spent on conceptual understanding, in comparison to individual time, which tends to be spent on products.
3. Students can regulate their own resources. An individual's work pace can be more flexible in a group setting.
4. Students learn to manage others' resources, coordinate work with others, obtain information from peers, and so on.
5. Students develop appropriate dispositions toward challenging tasks, which are more doable in group settings because of shared expertise.
6. Tasks done in small work groups tend to be more like work done at home (and in many jobs), where everyone pitches in to get a job done.
7. Group members serve as models for one another. Students have the chance to learn important learning-to-learn skills from other students (how to ask questions and how to disagree).
8. Students develop an expanded understanding of self and others and learn to appreciate individual differences (peers are not just "smart" or "dumb"; everyone possesses both weaknesses and strengths). Awareness of variability in aptitude may allow students to be more creative, to view errors as acceptable, and to learn from failure.

Despite these potential benefits, problems develop in some group situations that may prevent or minimize constructive learning. McCaslin and Good (1996) identify several potential problems:

PROBLEMS

1. Students often have misconceptions about academic content and these may be reinforced during small-group interactions.
2. Students shift dependency from teacher to peers.
3. Students value the product more than the process. If group members focus too narrowly on the group product, speed takes precedence over the problem-solving process, and groups pay more attention to product rate than to the process of problem solution.
4. Students value group processes more than the academic product. In some classrooms, attention to "learning to learn with others" may take precedence over subject-matter learning so that much time is spent teaching elaborate and potentially artificial procedures (e.g., for dealing with controversy).
5. Students receive differential attention and status. Some group situations may present little more than an opportunity for high-achieving students to perform for other students. In other groups, high achievers may feel excessive pressure to do the work for the group.

6. Some students will perceive themselves as having little to contribute to their peers. These students may become indebted to other group members.
7. Some students may learn that they do not need to contribute. They may consistently receive feedback suggesting that their skills are not valued.
8. Group accountability may mediate failure-avoiding and success-enhancing behavior. For example, students who have reputations as "know-it-alls" may withhold information so as not to enhance their (unwanted) reputations. Other students may withhold information in an attempt to be fair and to let other students contribute more. Such altruistic behavior may come at the expense of learning.

Conclusions from Research on Cooperative Learning

We recommend cooperative learning methods, although with certain qualifications. First, it is important to view cooperative learning not as a wholesale replacement of traditional whole-class instruction but as an adaptation in which active whole-class instruction is retained but many follow-up activities are accomplished through small-group cooperation rather than through individual seatwork. Peers are not an acceptable substitute for active instruction or coaching by the teacher as the basic method for conveying content to students. Peers can deliver effective explanations about how to respond to specific questions or assignments, but they cannot be expected to have the subject-matter and pedagogical knowledge needed to provide effective advanced organization and structuring of content, systematic development of key concepts, or sophisticated remedial instruction. Nor can students always be expected to tutor one another effectively on tasks that focus on higher-order objectives (Chi, Siler, & Jeong, 2004; O'Donnell, 2006; Ross, 1988), but can be helped to do so (Jacobs, Power, & Loh, 2002; Spiegel, 2005).

Second, cooperative learning approaches may be more feasible and valuable in certain classes than in others. So far, these methods have been used most frequently in (and most of the research supporting them comes from) classes in grades 4 through 9. They may be less relevant or more difficult to implement for teachers working with primary-grade students or upper secondary-school students. Also, methods that emphasize group rewards and individual accountability for one's own effort and performance (STAD, Jigsaw II, TAI) appear to be more appropriate for work in mathematics and other subjects that emphasize individual practice of sequenced skills. Methods that emphasize group discussion and investigation, structured controversy, differentiated roles and responsibilities, or cooperative development of a group product may be more appropriate for social studies and for assignments that focus on application, problem solving, analysis, synthesis, and evaluation.

Third, even students who enjoy learning cooperatively in moderation might tire of it if called upon to do so too often. Fourth, although it may often be important to use methods that involve group rewards and individual accountability, we advise emphasizing cooperation but de-emphasizing competition. Competition is a form of extrinsic motivation that may distract students from basic learning goals unless it is handled carefully. Also, bad feelings that result from losing competitions may undermine the potential of small-group arrangements to improve personal and social outcomes (Ames & Felker, 1979; Johnson & Johnson, 2006b; O' Donnell, 2006).

Fifth, teachers may need to show students how to share, listen, integrate the ideas of others, and handle disagreements. In the early grades, most group assignments probably should be short, highly structured, enjoyable, and unlikely to produce conflict. Students can be moved gradually into longer and more demanding tasks as their skills develop. In the process of discussing tasks and helping one another to learn, students can discover a great deal about how to search efficiently and identify key information, recognize what is given and what is called for in a problem, and formulate problem-solving strategies. However, problem-solving approaches may be problematic, especially if students are not prepared for cooperative work and if student work is not supervised. Problems that call for cognitive flexibility and interpersonal negotiation can generate considerable frustration and anger among students.

If students have had limited experience in cooperative group work, they should be taught needed skills through a series of relatively simple tasks. This allows teachers to emphasize how to work cooperatively and provide feedback about cooperative and social skills. (Bennett & Dunne,1992; Emmer & Gerwels, 2002). It is critical to prepare students both for the social and the cognitive demands of cooperation. Also, some models require the ability to negotiate, compromise, or handle discontinuity and ambiguity.

Finally, teachers who wish to use cooperative learning effectively need to assign tasks and activities that are well suited to it. This often means adapting or substituting for traditional assignments meant for individuals. Good et al. (1989–1990), for example, found that small-group cooperative learning did not work well in many mathematics classes because most assigned tasks involved routine computation practice, an activity that students are accustomed to working on alone and that does not lend itself to cooperative interaction. If students are actually meant to cooperate rather than just compare answers, they need to be assigned problems that admit to a range of formulation and solution strategies that can be discussed and debated, or else be assigned more complicated tasks that must be done in stages requiring cooperative planning and perhaps differentiation of roles for students in the group.

*I*mplementation Guidelines: Cooperative Learning

Johnson et al. (1984; Johnson & Johnson, 2006b) provide some guidelines for planning small-group cooperative learning:

Objectives
1. Specify academic and collaborative skills objectives.

Decisions
2. Decide the size of the group (typically from two to six, depending on the nature of the task, the time available, and the experience of the teacher in using small-group methods).
3. Assign students to groups (preferably by ensuring heterogeneity rather than grouping by ability or allowing students to form their own groups).

4. Arrange the room so that the teacher has access to each group and group members can meet in a circle and sit close enough to each other to communicate effectively without disrupting other groups.
5. Plan instructional materials to promote interdependence (if necessary, give only one copy of the materials to each group or give each group member different materials so as to force task differentiation).
6. Assign roles to ensure interdependence (assign different members complementary and interconnected roles such as summarizer-checker, researcher-runner, recorder, encourager, and observer).
7. Explain the task.
8. Structure positive goal interdependence, peer encouragement, and support for learning (ask the group to produce a single product or use an assessment system in which individuals' rewards are based both on their own scores and on the average for the group as a whole).
9. Structure individual accountability (by using quizzes or randomly selecting group members to explain answers or present the group's conclusions).
10. Structure intergroup cooperation.
11. Explain success criteria.
12. Specify desired behaviors (define cooperative learning operationally by requesting that students take turns, use personal names, listen carefully to one another, encourage everyone to participate, etc.).

Monitoring and Intervening
13. Monitor student behavior (circulate to listen and observe groups in action; note problems in completing assignments or working cooperatively).
14. Provide task assistance.
15. Intervene to teach collaborative skills (where groups are experiencing major problems in collaborating successfully).
16. Provide closure to the lesson.

Evaluation and Processing
17. Evaluate quality and quantity of students' learning.
18. Assess how well each group functions (give feedback about how well the members worked with one another and how they could improve).

Guidelines for small-group work appear deceptively simple. However, some steps may require much time to develop. Also, techniques that may be useful at certain stages (e.g., the assignment of roles) may later become unnecessary or even counterproductive (e.g., interfere with authentic communication when students work as a group). For example, Good et al. (1989–1990) found that role assignment was often artificial and in some cases students spent more time discussing role boundaries than the task. Thus, it may make sense to use roles for a limited time for young students or when cooperative techniques are first being introduced, then discard them and allow students to develop their own communication styles.

A number of valuable sources provide ideas for helping students understand and respond to cooperative learning situations (e.g., Bennett & Dunne, 1992; Cohen, 1994;

Jacobs, Power, & Loh, 2002; Jenkins, 1989; Kagan, 1988; O'Donnell, 2006; Spiegel, 2005). Such sources provide activities that teachers can adapt to their own classrooms. Teachers who are making decisions about group work must understand the long-term reasons why they are using cooperative learning and design activities that help students to work successfully under a specific model. Sometimes activities (even valuable activities) can become ends in themselves and lead to counterproductive behavior, beliefs, and norms.

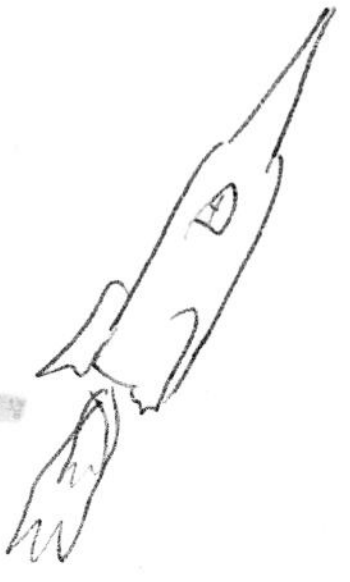

[handwritten margin note: Check out rescources, plan activities, be ready to discard ...]

Cohen (1994) provides a strategy that can be useful in getting students to monitor and to pay attention to group processes. The strategy, amended from Epstein (1972), has been labeled the four-stage rocket. Students are divided into groups and presented with a short discussion task. The teacher observes the groups and notes appropriate and inappropriate discussion techniques, then conducts a whole-class discussion of these observations. Students are told that they will have the opportunity to practice four skills that are necessary if the discussion is to "take off like a rocket": conciseness, listening, reflecting, and everyone contributing. Students practice each skill.

Assuming an appropriate discussion task, such an activity can provide an interesting orientation to small-group work. Conciseness of expression may be a virtue initially, but as they explore open-ended problems, students should be expected to deal with the ambiguities of going beyond the information given and exploring problems. Further, an emphasis on time (only fifteen seconds) may inadvertently suggest to students that *speed* is important. Hence, if you intend to develop a proactive and thoughtful approach to group problem solving, then you must establish these expectations with your students.

Speed is often a primary source of motivation for students, and you will need to work hard to change these dispositions. Further, research has shown that student groups often focus extensively on the procedural aspects of work assignments (Erkens, Prangma, & Jasper, 2005). When students do focus on the task, they often do not reflect on their work or explain their reasoning (Andriessen, 2005; O'Donnell, 2006), and are often not skilled at detecting or correcting logical errors that their peers make (Chi et al., 2004).

Providing Opportunity for Self-Evaluation

Opportunities for self-evaluation are critical if students are to improve their cooperative interactions. Students who have had more or less experience in cooperative settings will need different types of evaluation questions. For example, Figure 6.1 provides a straightforward method for helping young children reflect on group processes. You could have students fill out the sheet individually or in groups. In time, you might allow individuals to explain why they disagree with other group members. Consider the evolutionary nature of questions and activities that encourage students to become more sophisticated participants over time. For example, item 6 in Figure 6.1 might be appropriate when students are beginning to practice group skills, but in time, more mature issues should be addressed.

In evaluating small-group work, consider the needs of individual students and their responsibilities. Samples (1992) argued that one fundamental obligation of teachers is to ensure that the cooperation and autonomy that they attempt to develop in the classroom are authentic. Namely, students have a large voice in defining the task; real problem solving is required (outcomes are not known in advance); a primary source of

Group evaluation

	Always	Sometimes	Never
1. We checked to make sure everyone understood what we did.	_____	_____	_____
2. We answered any questions that were asked.	_____	_____	_____
3. We gave explanations wherever we could.	_____	_____	_____
4. We asked specific questions about what we didn't understand.	_____	_____	_____
5. Anyone who had difficulty got extra practice and help.	_____	_____	_____
6. We paraphrased what others said to be sure we understood.	_____	_____	_____

Group signatures

X _____   X _____

X _____   X _____

Figure 6.1   Evaluation of Group Processes

satisfaction has to come from the experience itself; there are shifts of authority and responsibility within groups; students provide different types of leadership at different times; and the teacher becomes a resource and guide.

Samples noted that consensus and fitting in can be overdetermined and that teachers must foster the integrity of both the "solitary self" and the "social self" in cooperative learning. Some appropriate indicators for assessing authenticity and autonomy include: (1) students are comfortable when they choose to be alone, (2) students occasionally choose to withdraw from a group for temporary exploration, and (3) students respect what they know and what they do not know.

Another example of a self-evaluation or group evaluation form appears in Figure 6.2. This example is from Kagan (1988), who suggested that the first three questions should be addressed frequently and that the other questions on the scale would help students to focus on specific issues from time to time as appropriate.

Mason, Reys, and Good (1990) described three instructional models that could be used for small-group work. Model 1 (Figure 6.3, p. 206) is highly teacher-directed; the lesson begins with a 30- to 40-minute teacher-led active teaching and learning component on a new concept. One 5- to 10-minute student group-work session follows. Model 2 (Figure 6.4, p. 207) employs a recursive pattern in which teacher direction and facilitation components are alternated with student work in groups three or more times. Time allocated for groups is increased to as much as 40 minutes (although this includes some time for teacher assessment, clarification, and new task assignment). In Model 3 (Figure 6.5, p. 208), the teacher's role changes from director to facilitator. Although the teacher fosters an appropriate environment for group

1. What one word would you use to describe how the group was today?

   _____

2. What one word would describe the way you would like the group to be?

   _____

3. Is everyone participating?
   Yes, always _____ Usually _____ Occasionally _____
   Rarely _____ No, never _____

4. Are you (everyone in group) trying to make each other feel good?
   Yes, always _____ Usually _____ Occasionally _____
   Rarely _____ No, never _____

5. Are you trying to help each other feel able to talk and say what you think?
   Yes, always _____ Usually _____ Occasionally _____
   Rarely _____ No, never _____

6. Are you listening to each other?
   Yes, always _____ Usually _____ Occasionally _____
   Rarely _____ No, never _____

7. Are you showing you are listening by nodding at each other?
   Yes, always _____ Usually _____ Occasionally _____
   Rarely _____ No, never _____

8. Are you saying "That's good" to each other when you like something?
   Yes, always _____ Usually _____ Occasionally _____
   Rarely _____ No, never _____

9. Are you asking each other questions?
   Yes, always _____ Usually _____ Occasionally _____
   Rarely _____ No, never _____

10. Are you listening and really trying to answer these questions?
    Yes, always _____ Usually _____ Occasionally _____
    Rarely _____ No, never _____

11. Are you paying attention to each other?
    Yes, always _____ Usually _____ Occasionally _____
    Rarely _____ No, never _____

12. Is any one person talking most of the time?　Yes _____ No _____

13. Is there a way to have a group in which everyone talks equally?
    Yes _____ No _____

Figure 6.2　Evaluation of Group Processes

Source: Dr. Spencer Kagan, Kagan Publishing, www.kaganonline.com. Reprinted with permission from Kagan Publishing.

work by creating interest and outlining pertinent questions, students are the primary orchestrators of learning as they formulate and carry out plans in groups.

In Model 1 students see teacher demonstrations and explanations but also explore and discuss mathematical ideas and problem-solving strategies in both whole-class and small-group settings.

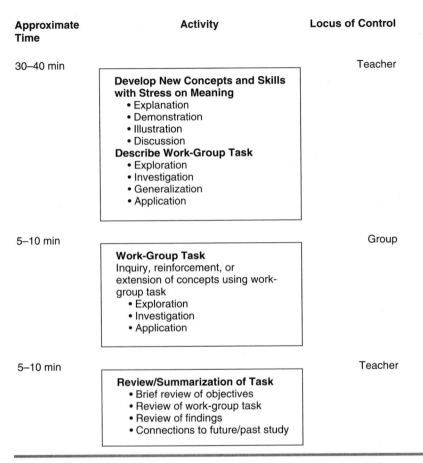

Approximate Time	Activity	Locus of Control
30–40 min		Teacher

Develop New Concepts and Skills with Stress on Meaning
- Explanation
- Demonstration
- Illustration
- Discussion

Describe Work-Group Task
- Exploration
- Investigation
- Generalization
- Application

5–10 min — Group

Work-Group Task
Inquiry, reinforcement, or extension of concepts using work-group task
- Exploration
- Investigation
- Application

5–10 min — Teacher

Review/Summarization of Task
- Brief review of objectives
- Review of work-group task
- Review of findings
- Connections to future/past study

Figure 6.3   A Model of Active Teaching and Active Learning in Mathematics Using Work Groups as an Extension of Teacher Development of a Concept

In Model 2, teachers engage students (through work groups) in a series of connected explorations, each building on the preceding one, and link those explorations with summarization of ideas and stimulation of new ideas. Teachers also model strategies for solving higher-level thinking problems. In Model 3, teachers simply introduce a problem by explaining to students that they have an opportunity to apply previously learned concepts or skills, seek multiple solutions, brainstorm with work-group teammates, and cooperate to develop strategies for solving the problem.

The extent to which Models 1 and 2 are necessary instructional scaffolds prior to Model 3 is an interesting issue that merits additional research. Experience in Model 2 with both frequent peer and teacher interaction may help students to develop mathematical power more effectively than will Model 3, which may place too much responsibility on students too soon. In contrast, Model 3 may be most productive for students who have the capacity for self-evaluation and autonomous mathematical reasoning. It provides students with more control and power over subject-matter knowledge and learning. Fuchs et al. (1998) have argued that occasionally high-achieving students

Approximate Time	Activity	Locus of Control

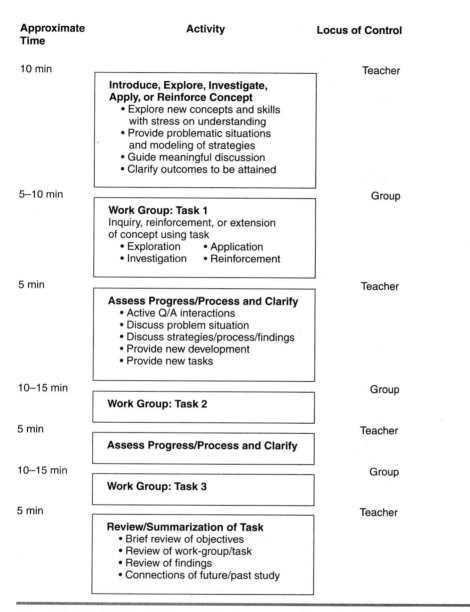

| 10 min | | Teacher |

Introduce, Explore, Investigate, Apply, or Reinforce Concept
- Explore new concepts and skills with stress on understanding
- Provide problematic situations and modeling of strategies
- Guide meaningful discussion
- Clarify outcomes to be attained

| 5–10 min | | Group |

Work Group: Task 1
Inquiry, reinforcement, or extension of concept using task
- Exploration   • Application
- Investigation   • Reinforcement

| 5 min | | Teacher |

Assess Progress/Process and Clarify
- Active Q/A interactions
- Discuss problem situation
- Discuss strategies/process/findings
- Provide new development
- Provide new tasks

| 10–15 min | | Group |

Work Group: Task 2

| 5 min | | Teacher |

Assess Progress/Process and Clarify

| 10–15 min | | Group |

Work Group: Task 3

| 5 min | | Teacher |

Review/Summarization of Task
- Brief review of objectives
- Review of work-group/task
- Review of findings
- Connections of future/past study

Figure 6.4   A Model of Active Teaching and Active Learning in Mathematics Using Groups of Four and Teacher Development in a Recursive Pattern

should have opportunity to work with other high achievers so that collaborative thinking and more sophisticated forms of cognitive conflict and resolution can occur. Model 3 tasks would be good activities for these students. Still, considerable evidence illustrates that children are likely to collaborate and learn more when they are in structured rather than unstructured groups—and this is especially true for younger students (Gillies & Ashman, 1998).

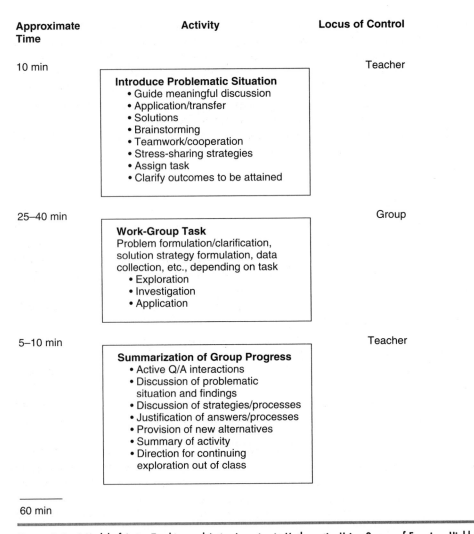

Approximate Time	Activity	Locus of Control
10 min	**Introduce Problematic Situation** • Guide meaningful discussion • Application/transfer • Solutions • Brainstorming • Teamwork/cooperation • Stress-sharing strategies • Assign task • Clarify outcomes to be attained	Teacher
25–40 min	**Work-Group Task** Problem formulation/clarification, solution strategy formulation, data collection, etc., depending on task • Exploration • Investigation • Application	Group
5–10 min	**Summarization of Group Progress** • Active Q/A interactions • Discussion of problematic situation and findings • Discussion of strategies/processes • Justification of answers/processes • Provision of new alternatives • Summary of activity • Direction for continuing exploration out of class	Teacher
60 min		

Figure 6.5   A Model of Active Teaching and Active Learning in Mathematics Using Groups of Four in a Highly Independent Pattern

*A*rranging Tutorial Assistance for Students

Individualized tutoring would be the optimal means of achieving most academic objectives, but classroom management responsibilities severely limit teachers' opportunities to tutor. We recommend that you tutor struggling students as often as you can, both by making time to help them individually during class and by arranging to tutor them outside class if possible. Still, there are limits to what can be accomplished by even the most dedicated teacher.

If teacher aides or adult volunteers are available, tutoring is one important function they can perform. If you structure the tutoring by providing appropriate materials and exercises and by training the tutors in how to fulfill their roles effectively, you can increase the instruction that slower students receive, perhaps enough to make the difference between keeping up with the class or falling increasingly behind (Baker, Gersten, & Keating, 2000). Students can also tutor one another, which is one benefit of student teams and other cooperative learning arrangements. The models that require individual products from students who work in small groups are essentially group tutorial models in which students can receive help as needed.

Cross-Age Tutoring

Cross-age tutoring is commonly used in elementary schools. It generally improves both the attitudes and achievement of students involved (Cohen, Kulik, & Kulik, 1982; Fantuzzo, King, & Heller, 1992; Van Keer, 2004). These desirable outcomes are likely to occur not only for the tutees who receive instruction but also for the tutors who provide it (Rekrut, 1992).

The tutors' achievement gains may also be attributed to improved attitudes or self-concepts rather than to deeper exposure to academic content (because they are tutoring younger students on material several grades below their present status). Tutors often respond very positively to their responsibilities. The role involves serious concern about learning academic content, and it appears to stimulate many tutors to identify more closely with the teacher and to become more concerned about their own learning. Acting as tutors may cause underachievers to take their own work more seriously, or lead antisocial students to become more appreciative of their potential for prosocial interaction with others.

Tutoring should not be overused, however. Students (especially high achievers) should not be asked to do so much of it that they lose opportunities to do challenging or interesting work at their own level. If anything, the potential benefits of the tutor role are greatest for low achievers, who rarely get the opportunity to act as the competent expert giving instruction rather than receiving it. Yet, low achievers often can play this role effectively when tutoring younger students (Bar-Eli & Raviv, 1982).

Tutees also receive many potential benefits. Interactions with tutors are typically friendly and experienced as enjoyable and helpful (Fogarty & Wang, 1982; O'Donnell, 2006) and they provide a change of pace from more typical learning situations. They also provide opportunities for tutees to take a more active role in structuring their learning experiences to meet their needs by asking questions or calling for particular forms of help.

Under some circumstances, students may learn more readily from student tutors than from teachers. In the case of an unresolved personality clash or communication problem between a teacher and a student, for example, the student might not only be more comfortable but also learn more during individualized instruction from an older student. Also, student tutors may use language or examples that are more easily understood than those of the teacher, or may identify learning problems more accurately because they have experienced the same problems recently.

Thomas (1970) showed the value of student tutors in his study of the relative effectiveness of fifth- and sixth-graders versus college students as tutors of second-graders in reading. He found that, in general, elementary school tutors were just as effective as college seniors enrolled in a reading methods course. Although they lacked both the general intellectual development and the specialized knowledge about reading instruction that the college students had, the fifth- and sixth-graders were more comfortable and spontaneous in assuming the role of tutor. Thomas (1970) noted:

> The college-aged tutors seemed to be attempting to coax the tutees into liking them, into enjoying reading materials, and into practicing the reading skills. The elementary-aged tutors, for the most part, were more direct and businesslike. They seemed to accept the fact that the tutees had problems in their schoolwork, and seemed to feel that the tutoring sessions were for teaching those materials in front of them, not for going off in tangents and discussing matters outside the lesson.

In general, though, adults are more effective tutors than children, especially in supplementing nonverbal demonstrations with verbal explanations of related concepts and in helping tutees learn the general principles that specific examples are designed to teach (Ellis & Rogoff, 1982). Fuchs et al. (1994) showed that even after training, the nature of student explanations in tutoring situations tended to be algorithmic, not conceptual. Thus, student tutoring is more likely to be successful when used to provide supervised practice and other follow-up to instruction originally presented by you than when it is expected to stand on its own.

Peer Tutoring by Classmates

You can also allow one classmate to tutor another under specified conditions. When peer tutors have relatively specific roles to play, they can enhance the achievement of other students (Shanahan, 1998; Topping & Ehly, 1998). Mathes, Torgensen, and Allor (2001) have illustrated the success of a tutoring program to improve first-grade reading performance. They attributed the program's success to the efficient use of student and teacher time, the use of critical instructional content generated by the research literature on how to remediate early reading failure, and the relative simplicity of the tutoring routines. Graesser and Pearson (1994) documented the questioning processes that occurred during peer tutoring among college students discussing research methods and seventh-graders discussing algebra. They noted that questions from tutors were only slightly more frequent than teacher questions (in whole-class settings); however, the tutors asked many more questions in the tutorial situation. Student achievement was correlated positively with the *quality* of these questions—but not the *frequency*.

Pearson and Graesser (1999) conceptualized tutoring as a five-step process: (1) A tutor asks a question or provides a problem for the tutee to solve; (2) the tutee answers; (3) the tutor gives feedback; (4) tutor and tutee collaboratively improve the quality of answer; and (5) tutor assesses tutee's understanding of the answer. Steps 4 and 5 are important because these activities cannot be done frequently by teachers working with a whole class. Although these steps appear easy, they are sometimes difficult to implement effectively. For example, in a study of tutoring among college classmates, 80 percent of the questions were asked by the tutors. Hence, tutees were taking little responsibility for asking strategic questions. Further, when they did ask questions, fewer than one-third of the questions focused on areas in which they needed knowledge. Instead, they asked mostly procedural questions. When tutees made errors, tutors gave positive feedback 32 percent of the time and gave negative feedback only 14 percent of the time. When tutees presented vague or incoherent responses, they received positive feedback 40 percent of the time and negative feedback 4 percent of the time. Distressingly, only 2 percent of the 847 examples that tutors generated to help students to learn the material were considered situated or authentic. Finally, rather than engaging tutees in providing their own summary of what they had learned, the tutors typically provided a summary for their tutees. Pearson and Graesser concluded, "Our analyses indicated that the convergence of shared knowledge during the course of tutoring is infinitesimal at best" (p. 74).

Understandably, one weakness of peer tutors is that they are not always prepared to deal with tutees' wrong answers or poor logic (Chi et al., 2004). Thus, you must actively monitor tutoring sessions (occasionally taping or videotaping them) in order to ensure that tutors are helping instructionally and not just simply occupying other students' time. You can only sample a small portion of tutoring segments; however, the return on this effort will be large if you use the information to prepare tutors more effectively.

Peer tutoring must be handled carefully, because it "officially" identifies the tutee as needing help on the material being tutored. Some students may resist this role because they do not believe they need the help (Fogarty & Wang, 1982), because they are afraid of losing face before their peers, or because they believe they know more about the material than the students who are supposed to tutor them (Rosen et al., 1978). Problems of this sort are less likely to occur with cross-age tutoring or with tutoring that occurs within small-group cooperative learning arrangements, although they can occur even here if the same students are always tutored or if the teacher presents the tutoring as remediation rather than as an individualized learning opportunity.

Learning in Dyads

Students can also learn new material together in pairs. Although one member of the pair may have a higher achievement profile, students of unequal ability can work together to explore new problems. For example, Kutnick and Thomas (1990) found that eleven- to twelve-year-old students did better on the cognitively based Science Reasoning Task than did students working individually. These results reflected improvement in both partners' individual performances, not just a simple sharing of abilities.

However, such gains are not automatic. Stacey (1992) explored mathematical problem solving by junior secondary students and found that randomly assigned students working alone did better than did students working as a group (mostly pairs with some triads). During group discussions, students consistently ignored right ideas in favor of simpler but incorrect ideas.

Implementation Guidelines: Peer Tutoring

Peer tutoring or peer learning needs to be monitored to ensure both the value of content and the sensitivity of communication. As in all aspects of classroom life, teachers need to make decisions about when and how to use peer-tutoring and peer-learning dyads. We suggest the following guidelines for teachers considering peer tutoring (for additional suggestions, see Goodlad & Hirst, 1989, or Jenkins & Jenkins, 1987).

Learning Outlook.   Create the mental set that *we learn from one another*. This is more readily achieved when you consistently model and point out to students how you learn from them. Also, stress that the goal is for all students to learn as much as they can and that the true measure of success is how we have improved our own past performance rather than how we compare with others in the class.

Procedural Details.   Decisions need to be made about the following procedural matters:

1. Set aside definite times of the day for tutoring, so students learn that only certain class times are for helping one another.

2. Distribute specific assignments to each tutor each week. For example, "Johnny, this week from 8:00 to 9:00 you will work with Jill and Terry. On Monday you will use flash cards to review the 7, 8, and 9 multiplication tables. Go through each table twice with them and then get individual responses from each. The last time, write down the mistakes that each makes and return the sheet to me. On Tuesday. . . ."

3. Allow a tutor to work with one or two tutees long enough (one or two weeks) so that you can make sequential assignments, and learning exercises are not constantly starting anew. Then switch tutoring assignments to prevent attitudes such as "I'm your teacher" from developing.

4. Do not ask tutors to administer real tests to tutees. One purpose of peer tutoring is to encourage cooperation between students. Asking tutors to quiz their tutees may defeat this purpose.

5. All students should at times be tutors and tutees so they learn that they all can help and can benefit from one another. Slower students given answer keys can help faster ones by listening to their spelling words or administering and scoring math flash card drills.

6. You need not adhere to the tutor model (one student flashes cards, the other responds) but can expand, when appropriate, to small work-team assignments (from two to eight students on a team). Shy students can be assigned to work with friendly extroverts. Students with artistic talents can be paired with bright but unartistic students in teams to gather facts and then represent them graphically. Such combinations allow students to work together and gain interpersonal skills as well as to master content.

7. If students have not participated in peer-tutoring activities before, take your time and be sure that they all understand what to do. The first week, model the behaviors you want. For example, pass out instructions, have all students read them, then tutor one or more in accordance with the directions. Do not just describe what to do; actually do it, modeling the appropriate behaviors. Then, select another two students to model the next set of directions. Then break the group into pairs and go around listening and answering questions. After a few such practice sessions, most students are able to assist others effectively, at least in repetitious drill-like activities.

8. Pairing of best friends is often unwise, for several reasons: Friends tend to drift away from learning exercises; the number of classmates that a given student interacts with is reduced; and, in moments of anger, friends are more likely to become excessively critical or indulge in ridicule.

9. Communicate to parents that all students will both tutor and be tutored by classmates. This is especially important in high-socioeconomic-status areas where some parents may become upset on learning that their child is being tutored by a neighbor's child. Communicate to parents the purpose of the tutor program in a letter or visit and invite the parents to visit at times during the day when tutoring will occur.

SUMMARY

Besides learning through interacting with teachers, students can learn by collaborating with peers in small groups and by interacting with them during classroom discussion. Assuming that everyone participates, diversity in students' backgrounds and points of view should be considered an asset, not a liability.

Under certain conditions and for limited periods of time, it may be useful to accommodate student heterogeneity by grouping students by achievement levels. Some educators advocate between-class ability grouping, which, in theory, should enable teachers to instruct all students more effectively. However, tracking has only weak and mixed effects on achievement, and it creates problems such as negative social labeling effects and removing academic peer leaders from low-ability classes. We recommend that tracking be confined to grouping by curriculum in high school and that grouping by ability or achievement in earlier grades be avoided.

A second strategy for coping with student heterogeneity is within-class ability grouping, especially for beginning reading instruction. If within-class grouping is used, we recommend that it be used to meet particular needs rather than merely to pace students differentially through the same curriculum using the same instructional methods. Group assignments should be flexible and reviewed frequently, and low-group students should get extra and more individualized instruction.

Cooperative learning approaches involve assigning students to small groups for collaborative work on group tasks (members cooperate to produce a single group product) or individual tasks (members help one another complete individual assignments). Successful cooperative learning programs typically feature positive interdependence and face-to-face interaction of group members, individual accountability for mastering assigned material, and instruction of students in how to interact effectively during small-group activities. Incentive structures involving group rewards appear to be responsible for the achievement benefits of cooperative learning (by motivating students within groups to help one another do as well as they can and thus ensure that the group does as well as it can).

The affective benefits of cooperative learning appear to occur either when there is an incentive structure featuring group rewards (even if students work on their own on individual tasks rather than on cooperative tasks) or when the task structure is cooperative and students work together to produce a common product (often under task differentiation conditions calling for each group member to take a unique role or fulfill a unique function). Such cooperative task structures are featured in the Learning Together, Group Investigation, and original Jigsaw methods commonly used in social studies classes or in activities designed to accomplish higher-level cognitive objectives.

Cooperative learning approaches yield significant advantages (in both cognitive and affective outcomes). We recommend that you make at least some use of them as alternatives to traditional independent seatwork. However, most of our knowledge of small groups is based on research in which students worked on relatively simple content. Even when the purpose of small-group instruction is inquiry or problem solving, those results are not automatic (Blumenfeld, 1992). Educators have much to learn about how to design small-group instruction in order to stimulate higher-order thinking and comprehension.

Tutoring by teacher aides or other adult volunteers can be an important supplement to your instruction and a valuable way to provide extra assistance to slower students. So can cross-age tutoring, in which older students tutor younger students. Cross-age tutoring benefits tutors as well as tutees. Peer-tutoring arrangements in which classmates work with one another can also be effective, but careful planning, training, and supervision are necessary so that the program does not become more trouble than it is worth by upsetting parents or engendering resentment among students.

SUGGESTED ACTIVITIES AND QUESTIONS

1. Observe two small groups working on the same topic. In what ways is the group process the same and how does it differ? Is one group more cohesive than another? Why?
2. Interview the observed students. What are their beliefs about the group process? Do students who talked a lot feel differently from those who talked less? Do students who participated less see more talkative students as helpful or bossy?
3. If you plan to use within-class ability grouping, what criteria will you use to assign students to groups initially? When and how will you arrange for regrouping later?
4. What classes (in terms of grade, subject, and student composition) are most and least appropriate for within-class ability grouping? Why?
5. Given your intended (or present) teaching level and your goals, what reasons do you believe are most important for using small-group instruction?
6. What are the relative advantages and disadvantages of cross-age tutoring? Peer tutoring? Which types of students are most or least likely to benefit from peer tutoring? Why?
7. Considering the differences among cooperative learning methods, which would be the most appropriate in your preferred grade level or subject matter? Why?
8. Some research suggests that the quality of questions asked during tutoring exchanges is more related to achievement than the frequency of questions asked. Why would this be?

FORM 6.1. Small-Group Interaction

USE: *Whenever a small group of students is working and the teacher is not a formal part of the group.*
PURPOSE: *To determine how the group spends its time.*
    Make a code every 15 seconds to describe what the group is doing at that moment.

FREQUENCY   TYPE OF CONTACT

————————   1.   Reading (finding information, etc.)

————————   2.   Manipulating equipment

————————   3.   Task discussion: general participation

————————   4.   Task discussion: one or two students dominate

————————   5.   Procedural discussion

————————   6.   Observing

————————   7.   Non-task discussion

————————   8.   Procedural dispute

————————   9.   Substantive (task relevant) disputes

————————   10.   Silence or confusion

FORM 6.2. Individual Participation in Small-Group Interaction

USE: *When a small group is operating and the teacher is not part of the group.*
PURPOSE: *To assess the involvement and participation of individual students during small-group work.*
    Observe the target student for 15 seconds and make a code. Repeat the cycle for the duration of the small-group activity.

FREQUENCY   TYPE OF CONTACT

————————   1.   Reading (finding information, etc.)

————————   2.   Manipulating equipment

————————   3.   Participating in general discussion (talking and listening to others)

————————   4.   Listening to the general discussion

————————   5.   Presenting an idea to group (others are listening to target student)

————————   6.   Talking to individual (an aside: not part of group discussion)

————————   7.   Listening to individual (an aside: not part of group discussion)

————————   8.   Passive (can't tell if student is involved)

————————   9.   Misbehaving

————————   10.   Leaves group

Addressing Heterogeneity in Learning Ability and Achievement Progress

*A*t one time, only the children of the rich received formal education, typically via private tutoring. This is ideal for most educational purposes because the curriculum can be individualized and the tutor can provide sustained personal attention. Unfortunately, private tutoring was (and is) too expensive for most families, so as mass education developed, teachers were called on to work with many students (Kliebard, 2004).

Age became the basis for assigning students to classes, curriculum guidelines were established, and teachers began using commercial textbooks and tests. Certain practices for organizing and managing instruction became well established: the *lock-step curriculum* with its grade-level sequencing, division of the school day into periods for different subjects, and division of subjects into units and lessons; *group pacing,* in which a whole class is moved through the same curriculum at roughly the same pace using largely the same materials and methods; and *whole-class instructional methods,* in which the teacher typically begins a lesson by reviewing prerequisite material, introduces and develops new concepts or skills, then leads a group lesson or supervises a practice or application activity, and then assigns seatwork or homework.

This model periodically becomes the focus of calls for reform. Some critics describe it as unduly teacher dominant, rigidly structured, fostering passive

definitions ⟶

and repetitive learning, or unimaginative and boring. Others acknowledge that it is adequate for average students, but believe that the best students should get enrichment or accelerated pacing, slower students should get extra instruction or more time to master material, and students with special instructional needs should be taught using materials or methods different from those suitable for the majority. Critics commonly call for more variety in curricula and methods, adaptation to individual needs and interests, active involvement of students (through discussions, projects, etc.), and self-regulation of learning.

Despite these criticisms, the traditional model has persisted because it has certain enduring strengths. It works reasonably well for students whose rates of learning and responses to commonly used instructional materials and methods are typical for the grade level. It may even allow teachers to meet more of the needs of more of their students than any other feasible method (Hamre & Pianta, 2005; McCaslin et. al., 2006; NICHHD, 2005). However, it has weaknesses: The majority of students must work without close supervision whenever the teacher works with small groups or individuals, and the teacher cannot get around to each student often enough to provide much individualized instruction.

Many of the biggest challenges you will face, especially as you begin your career, are rooted in the fact that classes usually consist of twenty or more students who present a range of instructional needs and learning interests. Sometimes this range is quite restricted. In these homogeneous classrooms, teachers spend most of their time using whole-class methods to teach all students the same content in the same way. There is some personalization of instruction in response to individual interests, but no significant differentiation of instruction beyond spending extra time with struggling students to help them keep up with the class.

More typically, the classroom composition is heterogeneous enough to require at least some differentiation of instruction to different subgroups or special programming for unique individuals. In Chapters 7 and 8, we consider the kinds of heterogeneity you are likely to encounter and suggest principles for effectively addressing diverse needs. Here in Chapter 7, we focus on differences in students' learning ability and achievement progress. In Chapter 8, we consider differences in gender, socioeconomic and cultural backgrounds, and personal characteristics that may have implications for differentiating or individualizing instruction.

A Heterogeneous Classroom

As you read the following case example, put yourself in the place of the teacher and ask: Would I seek to keep the class together pursuing the same goals via the same curricular content and learning activities? If not, which students might I treat differently from the others? How? Why? What will the rest of the class do at these times? How could I help the students whose knowledge of English is limited? What about the students who go to the resource room during social studies—how could I help them keep up in social studies?

Carolyn Alleman is a sixth-grade teacher at a middle school that draws a diverse population of students from five feeder elementaries. She teaches her homeroom students literacy and social studies, and also supervises them during study periods and other homeroom activities. They leave the room for math and science instruction from other teachers, while Carolyn teaches literacy and social studies to students from other homerooms.

Her homeroom has twenty-six students. These include eight European Americans, eight African Americans, eight Latino students, one Native American, and one Hmong student whose family came to the United States as refugees a few years ago. Six of the Latino students are Mexican Americans. Four have lived in the United States all their lives and are predominantly English speakers; the other two were born in Mexico (one is fully bilingual but the other is a recent immigrant who knows very little English). The other two Latino students are recent immigrants from Guatemala and Nicaragua, respectively. Both are predominantly Spanish-speaking. The Hmong student knows the basics of spoken English, but his vocabulary is quite limited.

The family backgrounds of the students include ten intact families, eight reconstituted or blended families, six single parents, one student being raised by her grandparents, and another who lives in a foster home.

Standardized reading test data are available on twenty-three students (the other three do not yet possess enough English to allow them to be tested validly). Expressed in grade-level equivalent scores, these students averaged 5.5 (fifth grade, fifth month), or slightly below the national norm for sixth-graders. However, their scores ranged from 2.3 to 10.5. Three of the poorest readers leave class for thirty minutes three times a week (during social studies) for small-group instruction in the reading resource room. Three other students leave once or twice a week for work on diagnosed learning disabilities. Finally, two students leave periodically to participate in gifted education.

A bilingual aide comes to the class for one hour each day to work with the students who possess only limited English. For the rest of the day, however, Carolyn is on her own in working with these students.

Finally, one student is legally blind, although she possesses limited vision. An aide is available to work with her for about half of the time, but Carolyn must meet her needs the rest of the time.

Carolyn tries to keep the class together using strategies such as special structuring and tutoring for low achievers, peer buddies to help keep students with limited English or learning disabilities tuned in, cooperative learning groups, and collaboration with special education teachers to ensure that much of the reading done in the resource room focuses on social studies topics being taught in the homeroom.

She leans on her two gifted students and other high achievers to act as tutors or group leaders. However, she tries not to overuse this resource, and she plans special activities for higher achievers at times when she is working to solidify the learning of the slower students before moving on to a new unit.

Carolyn also tries to extend the curriculum into the home by enlisting the involvement of parents in helping low-achieving students keep up. Most of the parents are eagerly responsive, but a few are not, and several others have limited time, limited English, or other constraints on their ability to tutor their children. Even with the latter parents, however, she continues to reach out, maintaining collaborative relationships with them and using a variety of strategies to overcome potential barriers related to time schedules, language and cultural differences, and the parents' own limited educations (see Chapter 8 regarding parent involvement).

The students with whom Carolyn spends the least time are four quiet, average achievers who rarely draw attention to themselves or seek her help. She wants to get to know these students better and keep closer track of their progress, but she rarely gets around to this because of more pressing priorities.

Carolyn keeps a range of textbooks and tradebooks relating to her language arts and social studies curricula on hand (including a few in Spanish), and she augments these with Internet-accessible resources and books obtained from the school library that relate to her current units. She also has four computers. These are used for multiple purposes, so she has to schedule access to them. Working individually, in pairs, or in small groups, her students use the computers to compose and edit poetry and prose for language arts and reports for social studies. Those who need extra work on certain skills get some of it by accessing tutorial programs on the computers (programs that Carolyn feels are worthwhile). She also uses the computers to provide enrichment, primarily in the form of CD-ROM viewing or simulations on social studies topics. She would like to do more of this (set up a computer-based social studies learning center), but she assigns a higher priority to the word-processing and skill-building activities that occupy most computer time. She extends this time by allowing students to use the computers before and between class periods, as well as whenever she is not working with the class as a whole and requiring everyone's attention.

Carolyn follows the principles outlined in Chapters 2 through 6, so she has her students' cooperation and the class functions as a learning community. Still, she struggles to meet everyone's needs. Occasionally, she wistfully thinks about what it might be like to teach a class in which all students were similar. However, such thoughts soon lead to renewed appreciation of the successes she achieves with her challenging class, and this allows her to experience professional satisfactions. As she watches her students progress, she savors her accomplishments.

The classes you teach probably will feature ranges of student diversity not unlike Carolyn's. Consequently, you will need to be prepared to differentiate your instruction to meet special needs.

Toward the Inclusive Classroom

Variation in achievement progress has been commonplace since classrooms began. The names used to describe contrasting students change (e.g., good/poor, brighter/duller, faster/slower, language enriched/deprived), but some students always progress with relative ease while others must struggle to keep up. As intelligence testing became popular, educators began to identify "underachievers" whose grades and achievement test scores were lower than what their IQs predicted. Some of these students were not applying themselves, but others appeared to be working hard yet making slow progress, either in general or in particular subjects. Efforts to understand and address their learning difficulties led to the development of special education as we know it today.

The result has been a proliferation of labels identifying different learning disabilities, diagnostic instruments for assessing them, and prescriptions for addressing them through regular or special education. Some educators accept the validity of these labels and the assessments and treatments associated with them, but others are skeptical. They recognize the reality of specific sensorimotor deficits such as blindness, deafness, or paralysis, but they question the scientific basis for attributing poor school achievement to vaguely described learning disabilities (e.g., difficulties in cognitively integrating sensory input) that cannot be linked to particular malfunctions in the brain or nervous system. Skepticism is especially likely when the warrant for the diagnosis is limited to circular reasoning (e.g., poor progress in reading is attributed to a reading disability, but the only evidence that such a disability exists is the fact that the student is making poor progress in reading).

The proliferation of labels appears to have been counterproductive for both teachers and students. Thirty years ago, if typical teachers were asked about a hyperactive student, they would say something like, "He's a little antsy, but I've been working with him on controlling it. If necessary, I send him on an errand or do something else that allows him to move around and dissipate excess energy." Today, comparable teachers are more likely to say something like, "He's an ADHD kid. He takes Ritalin, but he's still a problem, and I'm not qualified to meet his needs. I think he belongs in a special education room." In a few decades, behavior that once was viewed as a minor deviation from the norm by teachers who felt competent to handle it through minor adjustments in their overall approach, has become viewed as evidence that the student is qualitatively different from "normal" students and needs both medication and removal from the regular classroom.

This might not be so bad if special education labels were more like most medical diagnoses—grounded in scientific understanding of the causes and progress of the disease or disability and leading to prescription of validated treatments for curing them, minimizing their effects, or helping people to cope with them. However, most special education labels are merely symptom descriptions. Affixing one of these labels rarely results in a specific treatment, and even when it does, there usually is little scientific basis for expecting the "prescription" to eliminate the problem. Thus, it is not surprising that research on the progress of students diagnosed with mild learning disabilities usually shows that they do better in regular classrooms than when pulled out for special education in resource rooms (Moore, Gilbreath, & Maiuri, 1998; Salend, 2005).

From Exclusion to Mainstreaming to Inclusion

In Chapter 6, we noted that earlier emphasis on exclusion, tracking, and ability grouping has given way to policies of inclusion. Osgood (2005) summarized the shift as follows:

> Since the beginning of special education, there has existed a continuous dialectic: yes, we should do more to integrate children identified as disabled more effectively in regular education schools and classrooms, but no, we can't do too much, because our teachers don't have the training, our schools don't have the resources, and we don't have the knowledge, strategies, or wherewithal to accommodate more than a certain number of children with certain kinds of disabilities in those settings. Although the dialectic has persisted, the actual conditions have developed to the point where over time, we have been able to include more and more children, with more challenging or severe disabilities, into regular education settings for greater periods of time. From the almost universal segregation of the early 1960s to the extensive integration of exceptional children today under the policy, practice, and legal mandate of inclusion, our regular education classrooms have made definite strides toward being more integrated and more inclusive. (p. 194)

This shift resulted from a buildup of pressure for change in the ways that schools treat students with special needs. A series of court decisions established public education as a universal right rather than a privilege that schools could revoke capriciously.

Also, concern arose about undesirable expectations and labeling effects on students diagnosed as handicapped and about special classes being dumping grounds rather than improved educational settings that provided struggling students with effective treatment. These pressures culminated in passage of Public Law 94-142 (the Education of All Handicapped Children Act) in 1975. This law directed public schools to search out and enroll all handicapped children and to educate them in the *least restrictive environment* in which they could function and still have their special needs met. The idea was to normalize their schooling experience as much as possible. The following continuum of educational environments proceeds from the most to the least restrictive (Salend, 2005):

- Hospital or institution
- Homebound instruction?
- Residential school
- Special day school
- Full-time special education classroom
- Special education classroom with part-time in general education classroom
- General education classroom with resource room assistance
- General education classroom with itinerant specialist assistance
- General education classroom with collaborative teacher assistance
- General education classroom with few or no supportive services

The law called for developing an *individualized educational program* (IEP) for each student who was recommended for special education services. The IEP describes the student's present educational performance, identifies short-term and longer-term goals, and specifies a plan for achieving the goals through a combination of regular classroom teaching and whatever special instruction might be needed.

Periodic reauthorizations of what began as PL 94-142 have changed its name to the Individuals with Disabilities Education Act (IDEA) and extended or clarified regulations specifying the assessment, placement, and instruction of special needs students and the development and implementation of IEPs. Over the years, revisions in both the wording of laws and the language used in the professional literature have shifted emphasis from mainstreaming to inclusion. The *mainstreaming* concept focused on bringing formerly excluded students into regular classrooms and helping them to meet the student role expectations in effect there. The *inclusion* concept is broader, implying that classrooms should be designed and operated as inclusive learning environments flexible enough to meet the needs of all students, whether or not they carry special education labels.

In its strongest form (i.e., all students should be taught in regular classrooms all the time, receiving whatever forms of help they may need to succeed there), the inclusion concept is controversial. Most educators accept it as an ideal, but recognize realistic limits on the degree to which regular classroom teachers can accommodate multiple special needs, even with help from aides or special education teachers. Some educators view full inclusion as ill-conceived, arguing that certain types of students are better served if at least part of their schooling occurs in settings designed especially for them. Those with special interests in attention-deficit, blind, deaf, or gifted students are especially likely to take the latter view.

Since 1975, there have been steady increases in the percentages of students assigned to the various special needs categories. In response to concerns about this, the 2004 IDEA reauthorization called for shifting emphasis from diagnosis and labeling to determining students' instructional needs. For example, instead of moving toward special education labeling whenever students' achievement progress failed to match their potential (as suggested by IQ scores), schools would initially focus on providing these students with intensive, research-based interventions. The students would be diagnosed as learning disabled only if these interventions did not succeed. Subsequent regulations published in 2006 called for providing special help to struggling students at the first sign of trouble, rather than waiting until the third or fourth grade, when many are too far behind to be likely to catch up. For details, see the IDEA home page: www.ed.gov/policy/speced/guid/idea/idea2004.html#news.

Helping Struggling Students to Succeed: A Historical and Research-Based Perspective

Attempts to provide supplemental instruction for low achievers have not been very successful, usually because they paid too much attention to deficits and not enough to making instruction meaningful (Knapp, 1995). Tracking, special education through pull-out instruction, grade retention, and programs for at-risk kindergartners all have tried placing struggling students in homogeneous groups where they could receive more "appropriate" instruction. Ironically, students in these arrangements are likely to receive poorer instruction than if they had remained in regular classrooms (Shepard, 1991).

Grade retention provides a poignant example, due to a remarkable disconnect between research findings and the beliefs of teachers and policy makers. As part of the recent emphasis on standards and testing, many state- and district-level policy makers have been calling for eliminating "social promotion." They believe that unless poorly achieving students face the prospect of being forced to repeat the grade, they will have little incentive to apply themselves to their studies. Most teachers also favor grade retention as a potential option available for occasional use (especially in the early grades). However, teachers tend to view it less as a way to threaten underachievers than as a way to enable students of limited maturity or readiness to "catch up" and begin to achieve more successfully (Tanner & Combs, 1993; Tomchin & Impara, 1992).

These views are understandable if one accepts their premises. However, studies repeatedly show that most students do not catch up when held back; even if they do better at first, they fall behind again in later grades; they are more likely to become alienated from school and eventually drop out, compared to similar students who were promoted; and these findings hold just as much for kindergarten and first-grade students as they do for older students (Brophy, 2006; Jimerson, 2001; Shepard & Smith, 1989). What explains these consistently negative findings? First, part of the rationale for grade retention is based on false premises. Most low achievers do poorly because they are unable to do better, not because they choose to underachieve. Also, there is little evidence that students who achieve poorly in the early grades do so because they lack physical or cognitive maturity, let alone evidence that retention is an effective treatment.

Another problem is that, instead of analyzing low achievers' particular needs and adapting instruction to meet them, grade retention merely requires them to spend another year in the grade (typically under the same conditions that already have proved ineffective with them). They may earn better grades during the repeated year (because they have been through the curriculum already), but they won't show as much academic growth as comparable peers who were promoted. Furthermore, they will have to cope with shame, turmoil, loss of contact with same-age peers, and other social and emotional burdens.

Failing students do not need additional pressures, but additional help, as well as adaptations in curriculum or instruction. Thus, reform efforts that include components such as tutorial reading instruction for poor readers or required participation in assistance programs carried on before or after school hours or during the summer are more likely than retention to be effective (Eisemon, 1997; Fager & Richen, 1999; McCay, 2001; Owings & Kaplan, 2001). The key to success with at-risk students is finding ways to provide them with the amounts and forms of instruction they need in order to master the curriculum.

Pulling students out of regular classes for special "individualized" instruction in resource rooms is frequently mentioned as a strategy for helping students who have difficulty learning. However, there is little evidence that the amount or type of "special" instruction they receive differs from what other students receive. McGill-Franzen and Allington (1990) found that remedial and special education students usually worked alone on tasks involving low-level skills. "Individualized" instruction was often identical for all students in the resource room, even though they had been diagnosed with different "learning disabilities."

In general, the classroom management and instructional approaches that are effective with special students tend to be the same ones that are effective with other students. Within this, students with learning disabilities may need partly individualized curricula and more one-to-one instruction, and students with behavior disorders may need closer supervision (Mastropieri & Scruggs, 2007; Soodak & McCarthy, 2006).

Special needs students are likely to adjust well to regular classrooms if they receive acceptance and support from their teachers and classmates. Teachers' attitudes and expectations are critical. It is important to think of these students as "your own"—as bonafide members of your class, not visitors on loan from the special education teachers. They should participate as fully and equally in your classroom activities as possible and be treated primarily in terms of what they can accomplish (or learn to accomplish with help), not what they cannot do.

Teachers who have not taught in inclusive classrooms often fear that they lack specialized expertise that will enable them to successfully implement inclusion policies. However, when they begin to teach in inclusive settings, they tend to develop positive attitudes toward inclusion principles and confidence in their ability to implement them, especially if they receive inclusion-related training and support. These positive attitudes appear to be well founded. Although results are mixed for students with severe disabilities, those diagnosed with mild disabilities (over 80 percent of all students who carry special education labels) usually do better when left in the regular classroom than when pulled out for special instruction in resource rooms, and their classmates who do not carry special education designations do just as well as before (Mastropieri & Scruggs, 2007; Moore et al., 1998; Salend, 2005). Even so, progress toward inclusion has been slow in about two-thirds of our states. General education teachers still do not feel well prepared to serve students with disabilities, have little time available to collaborate with special education teachers, and make few accommodations for students with special needs (McLeskey & Waldron, 2006).

Given that most special education diagnoses refer to mild rather than severe disabilities, and that what is optimal teaching for these students is mostly the same as what is optimal teaching for other students, the inclusive classroom ideal seems realistic for most teachers. The rest of this chapter will focus on ways that regular classroom teachers can adapt their instruction to address special needs of students with mild learning disabilities. For information about addressing the needs of students with severe disabilities, you should consult special education resources.

*M*astery Learning

One way to adjust traditional whole-class pacing is to allow slower students more time to master your objectives. Traditional teaching allocates fixed learning time for each instructional unit and accepts individual differences in mastery. Mastery learning calls for all learners to master a common set of unit objectives but allows for individual differences in learning time. It assumes that the major difference between learners is the time it takes them to learn, so it provides the slower ones with more time (and usually additional assistance). The original mastery model emphasized individualized tutoring, but it was later adapted for use within the context of group-based instruction (Gentile & Lalley, 2003). Principles of mastery learning have been integrated into diverse instructional methods, including the curriculum reform approach known as Outcome-Based Education (Guskey, 1994).

The heart of mastery learning is the cycle of teaching, testing, reteaching, and retesting. Upon completion of instruction and practice activities, students take formative evaluation tests. Those who achieve preset performance standards (usually, passing at least 80 percent of the items) are certified as having mastered the unit. Certified students then move on to the next unit, or more typically, work on enrichment activities until the entire class is ready to move on. Meanwhile, students who have not met mastery criteria receive additional instruction and practice before their mastery levels are assessed again. Theoretically, these cycles of assessment and reteaching continue until all students reach mastery, but in practice, the class usually moves to the next unit after the second test.

When used as a basic approach for teaching the whole class, mastery learning has been criticized as helping slower students at the expense of faster ones, being too oriented toward basic knowledge and skills, and requiring too much work from teachers. The first concern can be addressed by making sure that the system includes opportunities for faster learners to go beyond basic objectives by engaging in worthwhile enrichment activities (Gentile & Lalley, 2003). The second can be addressed by making sure that the objectives that all students are required to master focus on the most important content—big ideas and generalizable skills (see Chapter 9; Postlethwaite & Haggarty, 1998). The third concern remains a sticking point, however. Teachers often find that whatever benefits they may derive from whole-class models of mastery learning do not justify the greatly increased time and effort required to implement them (Martinez & Martinez, 1999).

Mastery approaches increase (often dramatically) the percentages of students who master basic objectives (Kulik, Kulik, & Bangert-Drowns, 1990). The extra time and instruction they provide to low achievers enable them to master more content than they would otherwise, and to see that they can succeed consistently if they apply reasonable effort. Thus, at least some attempt to implement the mastery learning philosophy appears desirable. A sensible approach may be to identify the most essential learning objectives and see that all students master these, while tolerating more variable performance on other objectives. You can supplement the basic curriculum with meaningful enrichment opportunities that some students work on individually or in groups when you are busy helping other students to catch up.

[handwritten: have advanced activities ready!]

*D*ifferentiated Instruction

Mastery learning adjusts for student differences in time needed to learn, but it uses essentially the same methods to move all students toward the same learning goals. A more complete accommodation is *differentiated instruction,* which introduces variation not only in time to learn but in the methods and materials used to accomplish the learning. The most complete accommodation is *individualized instruction,* which allows students to pursue different achievement goals and to exercise some autonomy in deciding what to learn and how to learn it. Fully individualized instruction is not feasible in most classes, so our discussion of ways to accommodate student diversity focuses on providing differentiated instruction in regular classes.

Teachers can differentiate instruction by adjusting at least four classroom elements: content, process, products, or the learning environment (Tomlinson, 2000). *Content* refers to what students need to learn or how they will get access to the information. Examples of differentiating content include: (1) reading materials at varying readability levels; (2) text passages put on tape; (3) spelling or vocabulary lists at students' readiness levels; (4) ideas presented through both auditory and visual means; (5) reading buddies; and (6) small-group instruction targeted to a special need shared by the students in the group.

[handwritten: adjust 4 elements! 1) content 2) process 3) products 4) environment]

Process refers to the learning activities in which the students engage. Examples of differentiating processes include: (1) tiered activities that engage all students in learning the same concepts or skills, but with different levels of support, challenge, or complexity; (2) interest-based learning centers that allow students to explore topics of special interest to them; (3) developing personal agendas for individual students that include both activities common to the class as a whole and special work that addresses their individual needs; (4) manipulatives or other hands-on supports for students who need them; and (5) providing extra time for struggling students to master basic content while encouraging faster learners to pursue topics in greater depth.

Products are culminating projects that ask students to apply or extend what they have learned. Examples of differentiating products include: (1) allowing options for students to express required learning; (2) rubrics that match or extend students' skill levels; (3) allowing students to work alone or in small groups; and (4) allowing students to create their own assignments (if they contain required elements).

The *learning environment* refers to how the classroom works and feels. Learning environment differentiations include: (1) providing both places to work quietly without distraction and places for students to collaborate; (2) providing materials that reflect a variety of cultures and home backgrounds; (3) developing routines that enable students to get help at times when the teacher cannot help them immediately; and (4) helping students to understand that some of their classmates need to move around, others need quiet, and so on (Tomlinson, 2000).

Other sources of guidelines for differentiating instruction typically mention many of the same strategies identified by Tomlinson. In addition, they suggest strategies such as the following:

- Seating struggling students close by to maximize their involvement and make it easier for you to monitor their understanding and provide help
- Assigning grades at least in part on the basis of how much progress students make, not solely on the level that they attain
- Using highlighting, outlining, graphic organizers, grading rubrics, or study guides to help students recognize big ideas and follow sequences
- Adjusting the levels of complexity of questions, response demands, and follow-up probes to students' current achievement levels
- Helping students prepare for assessments and allowing choice among alternative methods of expressing learning
- Developing self-contained learning activity packages that students can complete at their desks or in learning centers
- Teaching students strategies to use when working independently, such as "use six-inch voices" (to collaborate without making too much noise) or "ask three before me" (to encourage students who need help to attempt to get it from peers before coming to you)

In recommending these forms of differentiated instruction, authors typically caution that teachers should limit their adaptations to those that are truly necessary, assume that the student will be able to understand and respond successfully unless evidence indicates otherwise, minimize the degree to which struggling students are treated differently from their classmates, and normalize their classroom experiences as much as possible (Broderick, Mehta-Parekh, & Reid, 2005; Friend & Bursuck, 2006; George, Lawrence, & Bushnell, 1998; Janney & Snell, 2006; Lawrence, Lawrence, & Samek, 2006; Pierce & Adams, 2004; Sireci, Scarpati, & Li, 2005; Tomlinson, 2001).

The key to differentiating effectively is to make sure that all of your students receive high-quality curriculum and instruction. There is no point to offering multiple ways to learn trivia, or in having one subgroup that mostly does dull drill and another that mostly does fluff. All students need worthwhile activities.

Differentiation via Instructional Materials or Programs

Reformers calling for differentiated instruction have been active in every educational era. At any given time, at least some of their suggestions are adopted by about one-third of elementary teachers, though by less than one-fifth of secondary teachers (Cuban, 1984).

Minimal accommodations! →

Usually these innovations call for shifting responsibility for planning and accomplishing learning from the teacher to the students and for shifting responsibility for communicating content from the teacher to the instructional materials, because it is not possible for one teacher to simultaneously meet the needs of all students (Jackson, 1985).

Innovations typically are popularized by committed advocates (usually without data to back up their claims), thrive briefly, and then wane. Some of their elements may be assimilated into traditional schooling, but the innovations are not retained as complete packages that supplant traditional methods. Typically, this is because reformers make unwarranted assumptions about students' capabilities for independent learning or produce materials or software that are too focused on low-level skills or require too much testing or other managerial complexities.

The increasing availability of computers, coupled with the continuing proliferation of tutoring programs, educational games, and other instructional software, has established computerized instruction as a way for teachers to enrich curricula and respond to student diversity. Computers can help differentiate instruction in two ways. First, tutorial programs can provide some of the assistance that certain students need. Second, especially when multiple computers are available, teachers can spend time with individuals or small groups who need their personal assistance while other class members are engaged in computerized learning activities.

Differentiation has become easier with the development of specialized materials, including many that are augmented with audiovisual components (audiotaped or videotaped instruction, computer software, CD-ROMs) and provide instruction and practice opportunities for students without involving the teacher. Usually an initial assessment determines where students should begin. As they work, they often receive more instruction from the program than from the teacher, who acts mostly as a materials manager and progress monitor. Productive use of these programs requires thoughtful decision making (e.g., supplementing when necessary by adding higher-order questions and application exercises).

Instructional materials and software usually use principles of *programmed instruction* in which students move in small steps from "entry-level" performance toward ultimate objectives. Programs are divided into self-contained modules. Each module reviews prerequisite knowledge or skills, introduces new information, and provides opportunities to practice by answering questions or carrying out tasks. Students receive immediate feedback after they respond, and get extra instruction on material they have not yet mastered.

Information about student achievement using differentiated programs is hard to evaluate because it is confined to scores on criterion-referenced tests that come with the programs. Such data usually show success in meeting the objectives when the program is well implemented. However, Slavin (1984) noted that effective instruction satisfies four conditions: (1) The instruction is high in quality; (2) it is appropriate to the students' levels; (3) students are motivated to work on tasks; and (4) students have adequate time to learn. Slavin argued that differentiated programs have not lived up to expectations because they only address difficulty level. Quality of instruction is reduced because students are not taught directly by the teacher but instead required to learn on their own. They are not adequately motivated because the programs often are boring and seldom offer incentives for moving through the curriculum rapidly. Finally, much classroom time is spent on procedural matters.

Arlin (1982), Carlson (1982), Everhart (1983), and Jones et al. (1985) also high-lighted teachers' difficulties implementing instructional programs and described how students' actual experiences fell far short of what the developers envisioned. Some problems are remediable: Developers can supply more and better materials, offer a more balanced and integrative curriculum rather than just low-level skills, and supply multimedia components that reduce students' need to learn exclusively through reading. However, unless such programs are implemented in very small classes, or with significant help from aides or other adults, teachers will have to rely on other strategies.

Another criticism of such programs is that they are not well suited to teaching higher cognitive processes (thinking, problem solving, creativity) or developing general dispositional states such as interests, attitudes, or values (Jackson, 1985). This is one reason why we recommend that any program requiring students to learn from curriculum materials be used in combination with, rather than instead of, active instruction from the teacher. Active instruction often saves both teachers and students a great deal of time, and teacher presentation underscores the importance of the content and provides opportunities to make it come alive for students. This is especially important for younger students, slower students, and students who come from less advantaged home backgrounds (see Chapter 10).

Even older, brighter students who seem to be progressing well through programmed materials can run into trouble if left on their own too long. Often, they do not even realize the problem. Erlwanger (1975) interviewed bright students who were consistently meeting mastery criteria on unit tests in mathematics. He found that many had developed conceptions that were at least partly incorrect, even though they were turning in correct worksheets and test items. They had invented rules that were useful for solving particular problems but would not work when they had to apply concepts to new situations.

Many teachers have voiced similar concerns about instructional programs: Students "can pass the tests but don't understand the concepts." This is likely to happen if mastery criteria are set too low (70 to 80 percent instead of 90 to 100 percent) or if students continually retake the same test and eventually memorize answers. Even with stiffer mastery criteria and several forms of each test, however, confusion can go undetected unless teachers closely monitor progress and require students to explain concepts in their own words.

Conclusions about Programs for Differentiating Instruction.   It is difficult to generalize about programs for differentiating instruction because there is great variety in these programs. Those that are confined to repetitive drill of low-level skills seem clearly inadequate. So do those that require students to spend a great deal of time handling procedural matters or waiting for attention from the teacher.

No dimension of individual differences has unambiguous implications for instruction (Cronbach, 2002; Good & Stipek, 1983; Perry & Winne, 2001). Some students need extra instruction or learning time, and some need to be retaught in a different way rather than exposed to more of the same instruction.

We do not recommend approaches that require students to spend most of their time working on their own with curriculum materials. We do favor differentiation that accommodates individuals' needs within the group context and achieves an appropriate balance of activities (whole-class instruction, small-group instruction, cooperative learning activities, and individual work). Even within the traditional whole-class approach, you can differentiate instruction to a degree by taking students' interests into account, by asking different kinds of questions or giving varied assignments to different students, by allowing student choice and autonomy when the objectives can be met in different ways, and by using specialized small-group and individualized learning approaches.

Teacher-Mediated Differentiation

Some form of differentiated instruction to groups or individuals may be necessary when classroom composition is extremely heterogeneous. Evertson, Sanford, and Emmer (1981) studied how junior high English teachers adapted instruction in heterogeneous classes compared with the ways they taught more homogeneous classes. The heterogeneous classes had eight- to ten-year spreads in grade-level-equivalent units between low and high achievers.

Observations revealed that all of the heterogeneous classes got off to a bad start because the instructional methods and materials were poorly adapted to students' interests and abilities. Rates of completeness and correctness of assignments were low. These problems continued or deteriorated in some classes. However, after about three weeks, the more effective teachers overcame them to some extent by using the following strategies:

heterogeneity can lead to malfunction BUT

- Special attention and help for lower-ability students
- Limited use of within-class grouping and differentiated materials or assignments
- Limited differential grading based on individualized effort and continuous-progress criteria
- Limited use of peer tutoring
- Frequent monitoring and provision of feedback to all students, coupled with mechanisms to ensure accountability for participating in lessons and completing assignments

Because of these teachers' managerial and instructional skills, not to mention their sheer energy and determination, there was no difference in achievement gain between their heterogeneous and their homogeneous classes. Still, there were limits to what they could accomplish. Meeting the greater range of instructional needs in the heterogeneous classes left them with little time for personalized interactions with students.

Evans (1985) studied what happened when a junior high school switched from tracking to mixed-ability grouping. Some teachers persisted with whole-class methods directed toward high or medium achievers. Most reduced teacher-led class instruction and introduced differentiated assignments, but essentially still taught the heterogeneous groups as whole classes. Lacking the time to teach slower students to the level of mastery, teachers "piloted" them through the curriculum. They often gave answers when students did not supply them, responded to weak answers as if they indicated full understanding, "summarized" answers in ways that elaborated on them considerably, guided students through assignments by simplifying directions and giving feedback that converted cognitive tasks into mere procedural tasks, and allowed students to copy answers without understanding how to arrive at them or why they were correct. Thus, teachers who persisted with whole-class methods in highly heterogeneous classes accepted the appearance of progress from slower students in place of actual progress in mastering the curriculum.

culture of inclusion

Newmann (1992) found that the most important factor contributing to schools' success with students in general and at-risk students in particular was development of a "culture of inclusion" that featured a welcoming attitude toward all students, communication of positive expectations, and support for their learning efforts. Instruction featured thoughtful classroom discourse and work on authentic learning activities.

Responses to diversity combined high academic standards, improving student engagement by making instruction more student-centered, and allowing students more opportunities for autonomy and choice. Traditional classrooms were restructured by connecting students to computers and electronic media, emphasizing cooperative small-group work and individually paced study, and replacing worksheets with projects. However, as they implemented these new techniques, many teachers virtually abandoned complex content. Newman cautioned that the point of adapting instruction is not to build curriculum on students' personal experiences instead of disciplined knowledge, but to show them how disciplined knowledge provides new tools with which to interpret their personal experiences.

Subsequent researchers who also focused on projects and other independent work also found that teacher structuring and scaffolding were essential to enable students to attain intended outcomes. Teachers needed to provide a lot of "front-end support" to lay the groundwork for students to be successful with complex tasks. They needed to be proactive in structuring and scaffolding student learning, using explicitness, task structuring, careful guidance, and questions and feedback to review material and monitor work to make sure that students learned key concepts and skills (Blumenfeld et al., 2006; Mergendoller et al., 2006).

Other studies of response to diversity have yielded more encouraging findings. Rothenberg, McDermott, and Martin (1998) documented the changes that occurred when an urban school eliminated tracking of fourteen- to sixteen-year-old students in some science and social studies classes. Teachers and students in untracked classes began with negative or mixed attitudes, primarily because the teachers taught in the same ways they previously taught tracked classes. As the year progressed, however, the teachers gradually shifted toward more student-centered methods. They did less frontal teaching and spent more time circulating the room to guide small groups as they worked collaboratively. Classroom discourse became more interactive and varied as teachers began to ask more open-ended and higher-order questions, and students began engaging in more extended discussion. Attitudes became much more positive, previously lower-track students showed improved achievement, and previously higher-track students achieved just as highly.

group work in math class

Mevarech and Kramarski (1997) showed comparable results in heterogeneously grouped mathematics classes that featured teacher introduction of new concepts to the whole class followed by problem solving in small heterogeneous groups. In the small groups, students took turns asking and answering questions about the essentials of a problem, potential strategies for solving it, and how it compared to recently solved problems. This approach helped students develop metacognitive awareness of their own mathematical thinking and strategies, and it incorporated diversity as an asset within the groups. Their thoughtful exchanges of ideas resulted in the collaborative construction of knowledge.

Curriculum-Based Measurement

We have noted important weaknesses in some of the strategies developed for helping struggling students. Instructional programs and software designed for self-regulated learning by individual students can provide remedial instruction in their weak areas, but the instruction is of lower quality than active instruction from their teachers. Furthermore, if left alone too long, they may begin to develop misconceptions, even if they are able to pass the curriculum-embedded tests. In mastery learning, if the tests are too short and too focused on memory for isolated bits of information, or if students are repeating the same tests and beginning to memorize answers, students may do well on the tests without having learned the intended understandings or skills.

A more recently developed approach that avoids some of these problems is *curriculum-based measurement,* a method of describing competence and tracking development in basic skills (reading, spelling, mathematics). Instead of measuring content specific to particular instructional modules, curriculum-based measurement focuses on the major skills developed in the yearlong curriculum. Teachers identify the most important of these skills and create about thirty alternate test forms that each sample from the entire year's curriculum. They administer these tests weekly (perhaps more often for students with identified special needs), then graph and analyze the data to track individual progress and identify students who need special help in particular skill areas, and follow through with group or individual instruction targeted to the remediation needs of these particular students.

Use tests to moniter on basic skills

Curriculum-based measurement entails a lot of work in developing and administering tests, analyzing results, and following up with differentiated instruction. However, it produces important benefits that may make it cost-effective for many teachers. First, it focuses on progress in developing the most important skills taught at the grade level (the same skills likely to be emphasized on high-stakes tests). Consequently, it yields information about individual students that is more useful as input to instructional planning than most other test data. Second, it fits well with recent shifts in IDEA regulations calling for targeted interventions with students who are not profiting sufficiently from the regular instructional program. Third, the obtained information helps regular classroom teachers to identify productive ways in which parents might work with struggling students at home and productive ways that they might collaborate with special education teachers to target instruction for students with identified disabilities. Finally, research indicates that using curriculum-based measurement to inform instructional decisions helps teachers to improve the achievement of struggling students (Fuchs, 2004; Fuchs & Fuchs, 2002).

General Principles for Differentiating Instruction

Studies of teachers working with heterogeneous classes suggest certain general principles. First, as the range of student ability increases, whole-class teaching will need to decrease and individual assignments and small-group work will need to increase. However, students can still benefit from exchanging ideas in the large-group setting (speaking before a group, etc.). Furthermore, managerial issues, unit introductions and reviews, demonstration of experiments and use of equipment, and certain other types of information exchange still lend themselves to whole-class presentations.

Matching Assignments to Student Ability

Some students can read well and do so enthusiastically; others have limited skills and interest in reading. To enable such students to work on similar projects, you will need to solve the reading problem. One strategy is to instruct students in independent reading and study skills. Another is to gather materials written at varying levels of difficulty on core topics.

Books are available that differ in detail or vocabulary but allow diverse students to read about the same historical events (the Civil War), famous persons (Booker T. Washington, Marie Curie, César Chávez, Barbara Jordan, Bill Gates), or science topics (global warming, childhood obesity). Furthermore, many stories of literary significance are written with a low vocabulary demand. Students reading at different grade levels could benefit from reading these books, even though you may eventually ask them to respond to the books in different ways.

Memory and Uhlhorn (1991) offered suggestions for using materials written at different ability levels. First, look for easier books that contain brief chapters that end with helpful comprehension questions. Poor readers are unlikely to read for extended periods, at least initially. Follow-up questions should foster processing of main ideas, not just call for miscellaneous facts. Schedule comparable time for all students to work on reading assignments. Even if students realize they are reading at different levels, there will be less social stigma if all are expected to spend the same amount of time completing assignments. Also, outline key concepts that all students are expected to learn, regardless of the difficulty of the texts they use. Finally, use brief study guides presenting open-ended questions to alert students to significant content and help them to prepare for class discussions and unit tests. Write study guide questions using the vocabulary of the text at the lowest level of reading difficulty.

Ciborowski (1992) noted that good and poor readers differ in how they think before, during, and after reading activities (see Table 7.1). You will need to help poor readers develop the skills and strategies that good readers use (e.g., predict what they think they will learn, monitor what they are learning as they read, and compare their conclusions with those of peers). See Friend and Bursuck (2006) for detailed advice on this and other aspects of differentiating instruction to meet special needs.

Preparing Assignments

Prepare assignments with low achievers in mind, even assignments that do not demand a great deal of reading. Make sure that any written directions are clear enough to enable these students to function independently, or you will have to spend a lot of time managing. As students gain independent learning skills, they can be challenged with progressively more complex tasks.

Cooke (1976) suggested three ways to develop individual work cards for students of varying ability who are working on similar historical topics:

Table 7.1 A Comparison of Good and Poor Readers

Good Readers	Poor Readers
Before Reading	
Think about what they already know about a subject	Begin to read without thinking about the topic
Know the purpose for which they read	Do not know why they are reading
Are motivated or interested to begin reading	Lack interest and motivation to begin reading
Have a general sense of how the big ideas will fit together	Have little sense of how the big ideas will fit together
During Reading	
Pay simultaneous attention to words and meaning	Overattend to individual words; miss salience
Read fluently	Read slower and at the same rate of speed
Concentrate well while reading	Have difficulty concentrating, particularly during silent reading
Willing to "risk" encountering difficult words and able to grapple with text ambiguities	Unwilling to "risk"; easily defeated by difficult words and text
Construct efficient strategies to monitor comprehension	Unable to construct efficient strategies to monitor comprehension
Stop to use a "fix-it" strategy when confused	Seldom use a "fix-it" strategy; plod on ahead, eager to finish
Reading skills improve	Reading progress is painfully slow
After Reading	
Understand how the pieces of information fit together	Do not understand how the pieces of information fit together
Able to identify what's salient	May focus on the extraneous, peripheral
Interested in reading more	See reading as distasteful

Source: Adapted from the Orange County Public Schools, Department of Secondary Reading, Orlando, Florida.

1. Develop a core program card for each topic and require all students to complete these activities at their own pace.
2. Develop option cards that provide guidelines for more intensive work, special activities, and so on, and allow students to choose from these.
3. Do not try to develop option cards for each individual (this is unnecessary and impractical) but do produce separate options (or even core cards) for *three or four ability levels.*

Figures 7.1, 7.2, and 7.3 illustrate work cards prepared to enable students at three ability levels to pursue the same historical topic in different ways. Figure 7.1 shows the assignment for slow twelve-year-olds. It focuses on helping students search parts of a passage to find material to make comparatively simple judgments.

Figures 7.2 and 7.3 illustrate assignments for middle- and high-level students. Progressively, instructions are written in less specific terms, students are directed to search more sources, page references are omitted, more deduction is demanded, and supporting evidence for ideas is expected. Students who initially need highly structured assignments like the one depicted in Figure 7.1 eventually will need more assignments like those depicted in Figures 7.2 and 7.3.

Work cards and other forms of *tiered assignments* are among the most popular ways to differentiate instruction across achievement levels, although the lowest achievers may need considerable scaffolding from their teachers to enable them to complete the assignments successfully (Hall, 1997). For guidance and examples of tiered assignments at the secondary level, see Tomlinson and Strickland (2005).

You will have to decide when students of mixed ability can work on the same topic. Perhaps the best strategy in a subject such as history is to identify core understandings that all students can learn and others that more capable students can pursue at more complex and challenging levels. For example, all students might learn about the major causes of the Civil War, but only the more capable students would be assigned research on the details of leadership decisions that shaped them. For more about teaching heterogeneous students, see Evans (1985); Hoover and Patton (1997); Janney and Snell (2004); Kameenui and Carnine (1998); Mastropieri and Scruggs (2007); McNary, Glasgow, and Hicks (2005); or the Special Connections Web site (www.specialconnections.ku.edu).

*I*ndependent Work and Learning Centers

You can use well-chosen independent work and learning center activities to enrich instruction and adapt it to individual differences. One way to create time for working with small groups and individuals is to structure time for students to engage in interesting, creative tasks of their own choosing. Some students, especially high achievers, are indirectly punished (given more of the same work) for finishing their work quickly. Instead, you might provide them with enrichment activities. Students who work slowly are usually denied the opportunity to reflect on what they have done, because they need all of the allotted time just to finish their assignments. As a homework assignment, you might direct them to reread their work and reflect on it.

Older elementary students might develop personal journals in which they write and illustrate stories or record their reactions after they finish assignments. Other possibilities include allowing students to read and review books (e.g., on Native Americans) or to act as resource specialists or tutors for classmates. However, book reports, if overly structured, may do little to encourage reading for enjoyment and interest. Often it is useful for you to discuss the book with the student, including not only the plot but also why the student liked or disliked it. Occasionally, structure long periods of independent work

Roman Britain   Work card 1
HADRIAN'S WALL

    This is a picture of a part of Hadrian's Wall as it is now. You can also see the ruins of the Roman fort at Housesteads.
    Have a copy of *A Soldier on Hadrian's Wall* by D. Taylor on your table.

Things To Do

1. Write down these sentences and fill in the missing words. Pages 14 and 16 of *A Soldier on Hadrian's Wall* will help you.

    a. Hadrian's Wall was built from _____ in the east to _____ in the west. It is _____ miles long.

    b. It was made of _____ .

    c. It measures _____ feet high and _____ feet thick.

    d. In front of the wall was a _____ and behind it was a _____ .

2. Imagine that you are the Roman officer in charge of building the wall. Write a letter to a friend in Rome telling him or her what the various buildings on the wall are and what they are used for. You can find out about these buildings in your book, pp. 16–20.

3. Draw a diagram of one of the buildings in your letter. Label all the parts and sizes of it. If you prefer, make a model of it to scale.

4. Draw and color a picture showing a scene from Hadrian's Wall, perhaps an enemy attack or soldiers marching along it. From the picture on this card, imagine what it must have been like on the wall.

Figure 7.1   An Example of a Work Card for Low-Achieving Students

Roman Britain   Work card 2
                              HADRIAN'S WALL

This is a picture of Hadrian's Wall today.

Read

        A Soldier on Hadrian's Wall by D. Taylor

        Roman Britain by R. Mitchell

        Roman Britain by J. Liversidge, pp. 16–33

        The Romans in Scotland by O. Thomson, Chapter 3

Things To Do

1. Answer these questions as fully as you can:

    a. Why did Hadrian build a wall across Britain?

    b. If you were an enemy of the Romans trying to break through the wall from the north, where do you think its weakest points would be? You will need to find information about the various forts and defenses along the wall.

    c. Another wall was built 20 years later by the Romans in Scotland. Which Emperor built it? Why was it built? How different was it from Hadrian's Wall?

2. Imagine that you are the Roman officer in charge of building Hadrian's Wall. Write a report to the Emperor telling him why you have decided to change the wall from turf to stone and to alter the size.

3. Draw a diagram of a cross-section of the wall, or of a fort, and label it carefully. If you prefer, make a scale model of it.

4. *Either*, as the Roman officer, write an entry for your diary describing an incident on the wall. *Or*, draw and color a picture of the incident. Do both of these if you wish.

Figure 7.2   An Example of a Work Card for Average Students

Roman Britain   Work card 3
HADRIAN'S WALL

Consult the books in the class history library on Roman Britain, in particular *The Roman Frontiers of Britain* by D. R. Wilson; *The Roman Imperial Army of the First and Second Centuries* by G. Webster; *The Romans in Scotland* by O. Thomson; *Handbook to the Roman Wall* by I. A. Richmond.

1. Why did Hadrian build a wall across Britain between the Solway and the Tyne? Why were no other routes suitable?

2. Find a picture of a British hill fort (e.g., Maiden Castle or Hod Hill) and compare it with Housesteads as a fortification. Illustrate your answer.

3. If you were an enemy of the Romans trying to break through the wall from the north, where do you think its weakest points would be? Why?

4. The Emperor Antoninus Pius decided to build a wall in Scotland in about A.D. 142. Imagine and write a conversation between Antoninus and his senior advisor about building the wall in Scotland in which they discuss why Hadrian's Wall is no longer suitable, and in what ways the new wall should be different.

5. *Either* make a scale model *or draw* a picture of part of Hadrian's Wall. Do both if you wish.

Figure 7.3   An Example of a Work Card for High-Achieving Students

for all students and thereby create time for remediation, enrichment, and informal conversations with individuals.

Although companies make filmstrips, tapes, CD-ROMs, and other materials that can be used for independent work, some of the best assignments come from spontaneous events that occur in the classroom. For example, one day during a seventh-grade English class, the principal made one of his frequent PA announcements. At the end of it, Joe Pintozzi said, "Wouldn't it be great if just one day he kept his mouth shut?" After the snickering died down, the teacher, Mr. Thornton, appealed to logic: "But what would happen if he made no announcements?" The class concluded that nothing significant would be lost, because teachers could make announcements. Mr. Thornton then gave the following assignment: "Assume there was no television, radio, or newspaper communication for two weeks. Write a theme on one of the following topics: (1) how your life would be affected, (2) how attendance at sports events would be affected, (3) how someone wanting to buy a house would be affected, (4) how supermarkets could advertise their specials, or (5) think of your own topic and have me approve it."

Your classroom can be arranged to facilitate independent study. Figure 7.4 shows how one teacher arranged her first-grade classroom to allow for both group work and independent activities. This diagram was made as the teacher instructed a reading group. Six students are in a reading group with the teacher, and two are reading at the independent-reading table. This reading center, separated by bookcases from the rest of the room, provides a place where students can read their favorite books in comfort when they finish their work.

Eight students are in the computer center working on individual assignments. Four others are viewing video clips without teacher supervision. The student in charge today runs the machine and calls on others in turn to read the story that accompanies the pictures. When the students finish watching the clips and complete written exercises, they move to another activity at their seats.

When the arrangement shown in Figure 7.4 was recorded, nine students were working independently at their seats and three were at the social studies center. Two of the latter were "buddy reading" stories about the social studies unit that had been printed by classmates, while the third was painting a picture. When the teacher terminated the reading group, all students rotated to a new activity.

Below we present one student's schedule for an entire day. Although a few other students would have the same schedule, there would be many different schedules and the room would be divided to allow for learning centers (see Figure 7.5, p. 240). For example, another student might begin the day in a reading group and end it at the listening post.

Juan's Schedule

8:30–9:15	Math corner
9:15–9:30	Math with his group
9:30–10:00	Reading with his group
10:00–10:15	Morning recess
10:15–10:30	Social studies with entire class
10:30–11:10	Social studies in small-project room
11:15–11:45	Lunch
11:45–12:15	Story center (on alternate day of week, science center)

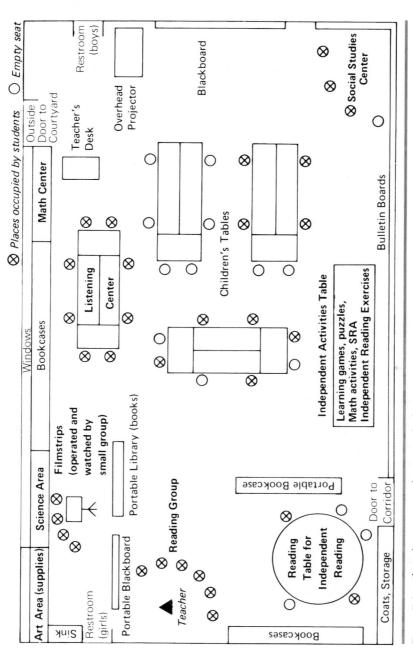

Figure 7.4 Physical Arrangement of a First-Grade Classroom

239

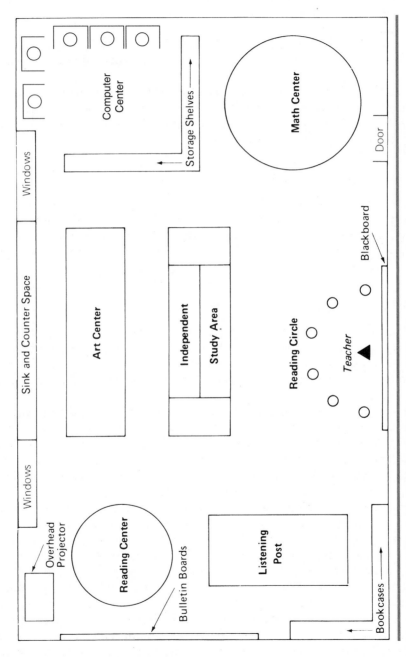

Figure 7.5 A Classroom Divided into Learning Centers

12:15–1:00	Free selection
1:00–1:30	Math instruction with entire class
1:30–2:00	Computer center
2:00–2:15	Recess
2:15–2:30	Listening post (on alternate day or week, writing center)
2:30–3:00	Reading instruction—independent work at the study area

Such scheduling allows students to work at different learning centers or in different project groups; the teacher then has time for instruction of small groups or remedial work with individuals. Although you may prefer not to use centers this heavily, they do add flexibility by increasing variety in assignments.

Self-Regulation of Independent Work

Students need to learn how to use learning centers with minimal teacher guidance. It may be useful to post rules for using equipment and handing in assignments at each center. Young students, for example, might be asked to listen to a story and then respond to questions about it. The questions can be simple, "How many bears were in the story?" or complex, "Listen to the story and then write a new ending to it."

Examples of Elementary Learning Center Assignments

The listening-viewing post is a popular learning place in first- and second-grade classrooms. It is a table equipped with a stack of answer sheets, a can of pencils, six to eight earphones, a tape recorder, and taped stories. The stories may be commercially produced as curriculum tie-ins or recorded by the teacher based on special interests or classroom incidents.

After everyone puts on the earphones, the designated leader starts the tape recorder, stops it at the signal given on the tape, passes out paper and pencils for the questions, starts the tape recorder again, stops it at the end, collects the paper and pencils, and rewinds the tape. After a few drills on procedure, even first-graders are able to function independently at the listening post. Similarly, students can be taught necessary skills for using the computer, video players, and other types of media.

Centers also can be equipped with a variety of photocopied learning sheets, suitable to the ages and aptitudes of learners. For example, in the math corner on April Fool's Day, a second-grade teacher might give students the sheet in Figure 7.6 and ask them to circle all errors that appear in the calendar (or to make their own calendars and see if classmates can find the errors they included).

Many teachers have found special-feature learning centers to be useful. For example, the teacher might write an introduction to a mystery story (three to fifteen pages, varying with reader aptitude). Younger students might be requested to tape-record their own endings to the story; older ones to write their own endings and compare them with those of others. If properly prepared, even young students can provide helpful feedback about peers' writing. At other times, the teacher might pose interesting questions in the special-feature corner: "On one page respond to this question: How would you spend a million dollars? Think! Tell why, as well as what you would buy." "Relate in 200 words

April 2004

Z	M	T	W	T	7	S
	1	2	Ɛ	4	5	6
8	7	9	10	11	21	1Ɛ
14	15	1ʑ	17	18	19	20
12	22	23	24	26	27	28
2ᑫ	30	31				

Figure 7.6   An Independent Worksheet

or fewer how you would feel if you [dropped, caught] the winning pass in a championship football game." "Assume that it is 2035. Describe what you will be doing. How old will you be? What job will you hold?"

Teachers at the same grade level can share ideas for independent learning centers. One might put together several weeks of math work while another makes multiple copies of listening tapes and assignment sheets and a third works on literacy units. Such cooperation enables teachers to produce high-quality units in less time. Once created, units can be used for years with only minor modifications.

A good project for preservice teachers in a college course would be to form work teams (e.g., math, social studies, reading, or science), with each group preparing five to ten projects. In this way, you could swap ideas and learn how to implement learning centers by actually planning and writing sequential units. In addition, you could keep copies of the materials and thus be able to begin teaching with a number of units already prepared. For more suggestions about learning centers, see Lawrence, Lawrence, and Samek (2006).

Independent Work for Secondary Students

Learning centers are most applicable in self-contained elementary classrooms. However, certain secondary subjects are well suited to independent study or group projects.

In addition to allowing students to learn from one another, group projects give secondary teachers time to meet with individuals or to pass from group to group, sharing ideas and talking informally. The guidelines here are similar to those suggested for younger students working in project teams, except that secondary students are able to work without assistance for longer periods. Students may be assigned to one- or two-week projects. Assignments should involve interesting, enjoyable activities that encourage students to think about topics and discuss ideas or solve problems cooperatively.

Topics can be traditional assignments, such as having all groups first do basic research on four candidates seeking the presidential nomination (e.g., summarize their positions on selected issues), then decide how one candidate would respond to a list of questions asked at press conferences in the South, Northeast, Midwest, and West, and then role-play these press conferences.

In such assignments, students (1) begin with a common reading, so they share a base of knowledge that they can use to solve problems; (2) summarize their information and apply it to a particular situation (typically, they are given choices here); (3) present the views of their candidate in a general classroom discussion; and (4) receive feedback from the teacher and classmates.

Most students enjoy working independently to gather information on a problem and use it in simulated situations. Organization is the key. You need to structure the task, identify pertinent resources, and let students know how they will be held accountable. After students have been through the process, you can solicit and use their ideas in creating new tasks. The important elements of group work are that the assignment has a clear focus, each student is held accountable for at least part of the discussion, and tasks are enjoyable and involve authentic learning.

Topics need not always be traditional, content-centered assignments. Attitudes and awareness may be stimulated by combining factual knowledge with students' impressions and values. For example, tenth-graders in a world history class might be divided into four groups. The groups would be presented with summary descriptions of desirable physical and personality characteristics of women in four different countries in the 1850s. One group might then speculate about the cultural factors that led to these notions. Another might respond to questions such as "What were the roles of women in each of these countries and to what extent were women satisfied with these roles?" Later, group discussion could center on the frustrations that led to women's rights movements in the United States and on why some countries allowed women to assume more responsibility than others. When and under what circumstances did women become activists? How did men respond to the emerging independence of women? What is male chauvinism? How has this definition changed across various periods: 1920–1940; 1975–1995? Why do women often make less money than men who do the same job? Can a woman become president? What is women's role in contemporary U.S. life? How will it change from now to 2035?

If you prefer not to devote much time to independent group work, you can still use brief assignments. If you lecture daily or involve the entire class in daily discussion, you will be surprised at how much group assignments can enhance these activities. The basic procedure is as follows: (1) The previous night, assign certain pages to read; (2) at the beginning of the period, divide the class into five small groups, each with two or three different questions to answer; (3) allow ten to fifteen minutes for each group to discuss its answers, look up information, and so forth; (4) bring the class back together and call on an individual to answer one of his or her group's questions. Students from other groups then evaluate the answer and students in the presenting group embellish the answer, defend it with logical argument, and so on.

SUMMARY

Traditional teaching mostly involves working with the whole class as an intact group, with limited individualization at the margins. However, this approach is not sensible in notably heterogeneous classes, especially in the secondary grades. This has led to adaptations such as pull-out instruction, tracking, and grade retention. Unfortunately, those arrangements are more likely to lead to poorer instruction for struggling students than if they had remained in regular classrooms.

We reviewed several ways that you can respond to student differences by introducing a degree of differentiated instruction within the whole-class model and using materials-based, computer-based, or pair and small-group settings to create opportunities for some students to work independently while you interact intensively with the others. Your goal should be to teach low achievers as high a percentage of the regular curriculum as possible, in the same group settings and with the same methods as much as possible.

SUGGESTED ACTIVITIES AND QUESTIONS

1. Visit local schools or classes that purport to implement mastery learning. How do teachers' roles and responsibilities and students' opportunities in these settings compare with those in traditional classrooms? Ask students in both settings about their experiences. Do they think that speed is more important than accuracy? Do they view mistakes differently (e.g., helpful, embarrassing)? What other questions should you ask?

2. Visit a school that uses computers for activities other than drill and practice. Observe at least two students as they work on the computer and try to determine what they are thinking about and attempting to accomplish. If possible, chat with them later to see if your inferences were accurate.

3. Consider your own expectations as a college student. How much structure do you want, and how much freedom, in deciding what courses to take (given your goals)?

4. Pressure on schools to change usually comes from public sources (such as information in newspapers that achievement scores are declining) and from parents. Should students, as consumers, be given more of a say about school procedures and routines?

5. Outline a plan that allows students to spend parts of each day at learning centers. Specify the room arrangement, the nature and location of learning centers, and typical schedules for groups or individuals.

6. To what extent is it reasonable to match content to students' reading level? Consider the subject you are going to teach and assess the extent to which reading materials could be differentiated.

7. As a teacher, how much time would you want to spend in whole-class, individualized, and small-group instruction? Why? Would this vary with particular units? What criteria would you use to decide?

8. What can you do to reduce the potential for social stigma problems when some students are given less demanding assignments than most of their classmates?

FORM 7.1. Student Independence in Individual Work

USE: When students interact with teacher during periods of individual work assignment and/or in open settings.
PURPOSE: To see if individual students or students generally, over time, are becoming more autonomous learners.
    Below is a list of student behaviors that could occur during seatwork assignments. Check each behavior as it happens.

FREQUENCY*   TYPE OF CONTACT

_____   1. After beginning task, student seeks additional instructions
                       about what to do.

_____   2. Student seeks confirmation about being on the right track
                       ("Is this okay?").

_____   3. Student seeks substantive advice from teacher
                       ("Is there another source that could be consulted?").

_____   4. Student seeks evaluative feedback
                       ("What do you think about this conclusion?").

_____   5. Student tells teacher what was done and why
                       (showing, justifying).

_____   6. Student asks teacher what to do next after completing the
                       initial assignment (seeks direction).

*In this particular example, the scale will yield information describing the frequency of different types of contact that occur with the teacher during a given amount of time. However, codes could be entered for individual students or for types of students by assigning them a number (high achievers = 1, middle achievers = 2, and so forth).

FORM 7.2. Learning Centers

USE: In classrooms containing one or more learning centers.
PURPOSE: To describe the content and management of learning center activities.
        Enter a check mark (to indicate presence) or a 0 (to indicate absence) for each of the following questions:

CHECKLIST

_____   1.   Has the center been created with clear curricular objectives in mind (that is, is it designed to ensure that the students learn something rather merely to entertain them)?

_____   2.   Given the curricular goals, are the activities appropriate in difficulty level and otherwise likely to succeed in enabling the students to meet the objectives?

_____   3.   Are the activities interesting or otherwise appealing to the students?

_____   4.   Is there an appropriate amount and variety of materials and tasks (if necessary to accommodate a range of student ability levels)?

_____   5.   Have the students been prepared (via demonstration and practice) in how to use the center?

_____   6.   Has the center been equipped with appropriate furnishings and materials?

_____   7.   Has the design and location of the center taken into account equipment storage and traffic patterns?

_____   8.   Has the teacher posted a schedule or articulated clear guidelines to enable students to know when they can or should use the center?

_____   9.   Are there clear management rules (concerning how many students may use the center at once, who should take charge of the group activities, cleanup and restoration of equipment, etc.)?

_____   10.   Do students know what to do when they get to the center (or can they consult clear guidelines posted at the center when they get there)?

_____   11.   Have provisions been made so that students can get feedback and check their work when they finish center activities?

_____   12.   Do the students know when and how to get help with center activities if they need it?

_____   13.   Is there a clear accountability system for center assignments (students know what they are supposed to do, know when and where to turn in completed work, and know that the work will be checked and followed up)?

_____   14.   Does the center emphasize hands-on activities that allow the students to explore or manipulate (rather than just provide more seatwork but in a different location)?

_____   15.   Have the activities been planned to allow students to work cooperatively or assist one another?

_____   16.   Does the teacher phase new activities into the center as the objectives of earlier activities are met?

COMMENTS:

Affirming the Cultures and Supporting the Achievements of Diverse Students

Melinda Bennett grew up and went to college in Idaho but finds herself teaching in a Southern California school that serves students from diverse racial and ethnic backgrounds. She was apprehensive at first. The layout of the school building, the weekly schedule, and most school routines were reassuringly familiar, but she still felt like a fish out of water. Almost all of her prior social and professional experience had been with people from European American families much like her own.

Melinda had read and heard various things about some of the types of students in her classes, but the information did not help. Students from lower-SES families presumably prefer material rewards to praise or intrinsic rewards. Even if that were true, surely it couldn't mean that she should avoid praising these students' efforts and accomplishments, could it? Students from Latin American countries supposedly are oriented toward cooperative learning. Did that mean that she should try to arrange for them to learn collaboratively most of the time? Shouldn't they also get opportunities to shine as individuals, such as by reading their noteworthy stories or compositions aloud in class or taking a leading role in a play? African American students supposedly are primarily kinesthetic learners and prone to the failure syndrome problems associated with low success expectations. Did this mean that she should keep them involved with hands-on learning activities most of the time and avoid challenging them?

After talking with other teachers, and especially after getting to know her students as individuals, Melinda was relieved to discover that these and other sweeping statements about group differences often are either incorrect or exaggerated, and that even when they are accurate as statistical generalities, they do not apply to many members of the group. She also found that general sociological categories such as social class, race, ethnicity, or minority group membership were not nearly as useful as knowledge about individual students and their families for understanding and suggesting ways to improve their adjustment to schooling. Over time, she integrated her general knowledge with what she learned from personal experience and collegial advice.

There were things to learn. Early on, she overreacted to incidents in the hallways or playground in which what she took to be conflict escalating toward physical aggression between African American boys turned out to be nothing more than ritualized "woofing." She also became disconcerted at first with the ways that some of her students acted when she found it necessary to scold them for misbehavior. Some of her African American students consistently looked down or away instead of maintaining eye contact with her, and some of her Asian students actually smiled. Melinda took these behaviors as signs of disrespect until she learned that, within their respective cultures, these were in fact expected and respectful ways of behaving when being criticized by an adult.

Her students' behavior during lessons was not always what she expected, either. Some of the African American students spoke out of turn on occasion, answering her rhetorical questions or calling out agreement with or comments about something she said. In contrast, some of her Asian students were frustratingly reticent about speaking their minds when she asked for opinions. She later learned that these behaviors reflected discourse participation patterns common in those students' respective cultures.

Melinda also was surprised to find that the parents of some of her Asian students did not respond positively to her initial attempts to involve them in their children's education. She later learned that in most Asian cultures, teachers are viewed as professionals with authority over children's schooling; parents are not supposed to interfere with school processes; and teachers who solicit parent involvement may even be viewed as incompetent. She also found out that many of her East Asian (Chinese, Japanese, Korean) students came from middle-class families who highly valued formal education, but many of her Southeast Asian (Hmong, Laotian, Montagnard) students came from families who had lived in remote rural areas and lacked exposure to any writing system prior to immigration.

Although her initial misconceptions and lack of knowledge about her students' home cultures sometimes created temporary interpersonal tension, Melinda learned to operate effectively in her new environment. Two important traits helped her persist and achieve success. First, she was a *caring* teacher, dedicated to supporting her students' progress as learners and as social beings. Her students, and soon their families, recognized this, so misunderstandings rooted in her lack of knowledge about their home cultures were just minor blips within a larger context of good will and collaboration. Her mistakes would not have been forgotten so easily if she had been perceived as distant or prejudiced. Second, Melinda was a *reflective* professional who learned from her mistakes, sought advice from others, and looked for alternatives when current strategies were not working. This enabled her to make rapid progress in understanding and learning to meet her students' needs, and her openness to input made her school administrators, teaching colleagues, and students and families more willing to help her than they would have been otherwise.

Introduction

The student population in today's schools is the largest in the nation's history. Thanks to an upsurge in immigration in recent decades, it also is the most diverse. In 1972, 78 percent of our students were European Americans, and only 22 percent were minorities (African, Asian, Latin, or Native Americans). By 2004, the latter percentage had risen to 43 percent, and was expected to reach 50 percent within a decade (National Center for Educational Statistics, 2006).

In one sense, this is business as usual. Throughout the nation's history, many of its K–12 students have been immigrants or children of immigrants. Even so, the current student population is unusually diverse. Furthermore, most of the recent immigrants have come from Asia or Latin America, and many face the challenge of learning English while also coping with the other demands of schooling. In 2004, 19 percent of school-age children spoke a language other than English at home, and 5 percent spoke English with difficulty.

In addition to differences in the cultural backgrounds of students from families of diverse national origins, there also are socioeconomic differences that can affect students' readiness and willingness to adapt to the culture of schooling. Schools primarily reflect the knowledge and values of economically and culturally dominant groups in society, so they validate and reinforce the "cultural capital" that students from these advantaged groups bring from home (Nieto, 2004). Cultural capital comes in at least three forms: customs, language, values, and other dispositions of the mind and body; material goods such as pictures, books, and other objects; and educational experiences and qualifications (Bourdieu, 1986). Students from other segments of society, especially students from poor families in general and the urban underclass in particular, often possess little of the kind of cultural capital that would help them to succeed in traditional schools.

Mismatches between school and home cultures can create barriers that make it difficult for many students to feel a sense of belonging in school. In addition, most teachers are middle-class European Americans from suburban or rural backgrounds, increasingly female, and often with little or no knowledge of other languages or cultures. Most also were good students, comfortable in school and successful in meeting traditional student role expectations. Teachers who fit this description will need to adjust their beliefs and approaches to teaching if they are to succeed with students who come from diverse backgrounds.

Actually, all teachers face this problem to some degree. As Nieto (2004) put it,

> Most teachers are sincerely concerned about their students and want very much to provide them with the best education. But, because of their own limited experiences and education, they may know very little about the students they teach. As a result, their beliefs about students of diverse backgrounds may be based on spurious assumptions and stereotypes. These things are true of all teachers, not just White teachers. That is, simply being from a non-White background does not guarantee that teachers will be effective with students of diverse backgrounds or even with students of their own background. (p. xxix)

$\mathcal{T}$oward Culturally Responsive Teaching

There are many views on how schools should handle cultural mismatches. At one extreme are *assimilationists* who want schools to inculcate students in traditional American beliefs and values. At the other extreme are *cultural pluralists* who would encourage students to nurture their racial or ethnic identities and related cultural backgrounds. Assimilationists use the melting pot analogy; cultural pluralists prefer salad bowl or mosaic analogies (Banks, 2006; Gallego, Cole, & LCHC, 2001).

Assimilationists view ethnic identities as inconsistent with modernized societies and believe that strong ethnic attachments are dysfunctional because they promote group over individual rights and separatism over integration. They favor curriculum materials and teaching styles that focus on developing cultural literacy that enables all citizens to participate in a shared civic culture, applying universal competencies to achieve social and economic success (Huntington, 2004; McWhorter, 2000).

Cultural pluralists believe that members of minority groups need strong affiliations with their groups in order to develop valued languages, lifestyles, belief systems, and personal relationships, as well as refuge from the discrimination they might experience in the wider society. They emphasize that the cultures of students of color should not be viewed as disadvantaged, deviant, or deficient, but rather as well ordered and highly structured though different from one another and from the mainstream culture (Smitherman, 1999; Suárez-Orozco & Suárez-Orozco, 2001). They also assert that students of color have certain unique learning characteristics and that curriculum and instruction in schools should be revised to make them more consistent with these characteristics (Boykin, 2000; Gay, 2000; Lee, 2001).

Banks (2006) credits both assimilationists and cultural pluralists with useful ideas, but also notes important flaws in their extreme views. Assimilationists' assumption that learning characteristics are universal rather than partly culture-specific appears questionable, as does their assumption that all students can learn equally well from materials that reflect only the cultural experiences of the majority group. They also tend to talk about mainstream American culture as if it had been fixed by the eighteenth century, when in fact it has been influenced over the years by people from many different cultural backgrounds. Meanwhile, cultural pluralists tend to exaggerate cultural differences, even to the extent of essentializing them (implying that the general characteristics of an ethnic group apply to each individual within it). They also tend to pay insufficient attention to the fact that most members of ethnic groups also participate in the wider culture, and need to be prepared to meet its expectations.

Banks argues for a multicultural position that reflects the concerns of both assimilationists and cultural pluralists, but avoids their extremes. For *multiculturalists,* the primary goal of schooling is to help students learn how to function effectively within their own cultural community, other cultural communities, the national culture, and the global community. Multicultural schools would emphasize equipping all students with basic knowledge and skills and socializing them in core democratic values (such as equality, tolerance, and justice). Beyond this, they would emphasize educating and preparing students to make informed decisions about lifestyles, group commitments, political beliefs, and other cultural choices, rather than inculcating them within a homogeneous worldview. Banks's multicultural stance reflects ideas advanced by others who stress the importance of viewing diversity as a resource rather than a liability and therefore call for culturally responsive teaching.

Culturally responsive teaching involves teaching minority group or immigrant students the same basic curriculum taught to other students (i.e., making sure they master important content and skills), but doing so using forms of communication and social interaction that are familiar to the students and incorporating some of their culture. Gay (2006) reviewed models of culturally responsive teaching put forth by educators working with various ethnic groups including African Americans (Allen & Boykin, 1992; Foster, 1997; Gay, 2000; Ladson-Billings, 2001; Lee, 2001), Native Americans (Lomawaima, 2004; McCarty, 2002); Hispanic Americans (Garcia, 2004; Nieto, 2002), Asian Americans (Pang, Kiang, & Pak, 2004), and Native Hawaiians (Au, 2002). She found six common themes in guidelines for teaching these diverse groups: (1) legitimize their cultures and experiences; (2) include more significant, accurate, and comprehensive information about different cultures and their contributions in all school subjects; (3) use the cultural legacies, traits, experiences, and orientations of diverse students as filters through which to teach them academic knowledge and skills; (4) make learning an active, participatory endeavor in which students are assisted in giving personal meaning to new ideas; (5) build the moral commitment, critical consciousness, and political competence needed to promote social justice and social transformation; and (6) teach the students style-shifting (code-switching) skills so that they can move back and forth between their home and school cultures with ease.

Culturally responsive teaching uses students' out-of-school experiences as resources for grounding understanding and identifying applications of academic concepts and principles. Rather than trying to replace one culture with another, teachers help students to become fully biculturally (or multiculturally) identified and comfortable with both cultures, and able to function competently in each.

A collaborative learning community and warm teacher–student relationships set the stage for culturally responsive teaching. You can act as a cultural mediator and broker for diverse students by caring about their personal well-being as well as their academic progress. You also can build community across racial, cultural, and linguistic differences by inducing students to care for one another and assist one another's learning and by creating an ethos and climate of success in your classroom. Research repeatedly shows that the best teachers combine high expectations for academic achievement with determined efforts to ensure that their students get the instruction and help they need to enable them to meet those expectations.

These successful teachers are "warm demanders" who radiate emotional warmth and personal caring, communicate expectations of reciprocity in both respect and academic engagement among the students and between the students and the teacher, connect with students at personal levels that extend beyond the classroom, and follow up learning demands with facilitative assistance (Kleinfeld, 1975). They combine high expectations and challenging instruction with unequivocal support and personal caring, set clear guidelines for behavior with related skill development, and teach students in the classroom with knowledge of them as human beings in nonschool contexts (Gay, 2006; Hamre & Pianta, 2005).

Learn about Your Students, Their Families, and the Community

Culturally responsive teaching involves becoming familiar with and respecting the knowledge that students bring to school and organizing learning activities so that they are able to use that knowledge. Sleeter (2005) recommends that you walk through the neighborhoods around the school (preferably with a few students) to note what the students see every day that can be connected with the curriculum. What kinds of quantitative reasoning might your students do when they shop with their parents in local stores? What plants, minerals, birds, or animals are they likely to be familiar with (that could be included in science lessons)? Pay attention to what your students notice, talk about, and wonder about.

Talk to parents and school staff who live in the community to find out more about it. In addition to problems and needs, find out about the assets of the community, including the people who live there, and what they want the community to become. Make household visits to familiarize yourself with your students' living circumstances and get information that you might be able to use in the classroom (child's hobbies, parents' occupations, etc.). When working on graphs in mathematics, for example, a teacher in a rural community might have students construct graphs illustrating the frequency with which different crops are grown on the farms at which their parents work (and if relevant, use multiple languages to label them: *flores*/flowers, *la lechuga*/lettuce, etc.). In contrast, a teacher in an urban school might have students construct graphs illustrating the numbers of class members who live on particular streets or in particular neighborhoods, or the numbers of their parents who work in various industries.

Espinosa (2005) recommends talking to family members to gather basic information: who is the student's primary caregiver, who else lives in the home, what language is spoken at home, any special talents or interests that the student may have, the student's primary playmates, the parents' aspirations and expectations for the student, and so on.

Moll (1992) interviewed the families of students enrolled in a bilingual education class to identify resources available in the community that might be capitalized upon at the school, which was located in a primarily Spanish-speaking minority community. He identified the following *funds of knowledge* possessed by members of these households: ranching and farming (horsemanship, animal husbandry, soil and irrigation systems, crop planting, hunting, tracking, dressing game); mining (timbering, minerals, blasting equipment operation and maintenance); economics (business, market values, appraising, renting and selling, loans, labor laws, building codes, consumer knowledge, accounting, sales); household management (budgets, child care, cooking, appliance repairs); material and scientific knowledge (construction, carpentry, roofing, masonry, painting, design and architecture); repairs (airplane, automobile, tractor, house maintenance); contemporary medicine (drugs, first-aid procedures, anatomy, midwifery); folk medicine (herbal knowledge, folk cures); and religion (catechism, baptisms, bible studies, moral knowledge and ethics).

You can capitalize on such funds of knowledge whenever they connect with curriculum content, to personalize lessons for your students and occasionally to integrate parents intellectually into the life of the school. Opportunities for connecting the curriculum to the students' home backgrounds are often missed because instruction stays too close to what is in the textbooks. For example, usually at least some students in a class have parents who are police officers, firefighters, postal workers, and other service workers studied in "community helpers" lessons, but few teachers think to invite these parents to come to the classroom to talk about their jobs.

An important feature of Moll's approach is appreciating the richness of students' homes and communities as sources of cultural capital that are diverse but potentially valuable for grounding their school learning. By incorporating these funds of knowledge into your teaching, you provide your students and their families with powerful evidence that you value them.

Adapt your curricula to feature the cultures represented by your students. Modifications might include a somewhat different selection of content as well as treatment of many more topics as issues open to multiple perspectives rather than as bodies of factual information that admit to only one interpretation. Expose your students to literature or multimedia content sources that feature models who come from their cultural groups, and portray these models not as stereotypes but as nuanced individuals with whom all students can identify. Incorporate living models as well, by arranging for classroom speakers, field trips, or current events discussions that will raise minority students' consciousness of roles and accomplishments to which they might aspire.

Knapp (1995) analyzed how teachers responded to cultural diversity. The most effective ones explicitly accommodated students' cultural heritages by communicating to them that their cultural backgrounds were strengths to be acknowledged and drawn upon in schooling. Here is his description of a bilingual teacher of a combined first- and second-grade class composed of a mixed population of Hispanic-, African-, and European American students:

> Mr. Callio holds high expectations for his students and demands strict accountability for the work assigned to them. He recognizes that his students do not arrive at school with all the skills he would like them to have and plans his instruction accordingly. At the same time, his approach builds in a respect for the strengths and backgrounds of the students in his class. For example, Mr. Callio's classroom is alive with pictures from different parts of the world, showing the different ethnic, racial, and cultural groups represented in his students. One display reads "Yo soy Latin y orgulloso" ("I am Latin and proud of it") in big letters surrounded by pictures of pyramids, indigenous Mesoamericans, and other Latino faces. Another reads "I am African American and proud" and displays pictures of African people, places, and artifacts. Mr. Callio argues that it is imperative to provide positive self-images and role models if a teacher expects students to be driven to succeed. Mr. Callio uses his Spanish extensively in the classroom—and not simply to help those students with limited English proficiency. Rather, he argues that Spanish is an important language to know and encourages his monolingual English speakers to try to learn it. One of the top students in the class, an African-American male, regularly tries to piece together Spanish sentences. (p. 39)

It makes sense for English language learners to value their home language and use it as a learning resource. In addition, in some locales it also makes sense for native English speakers to learn at least the rudiments of a commonly spoken second language (e.g., in some parts of Arizona and Colorado, most classrooms contain many fluent Spanish speakers who could serve as models and resources for helping their teachers and some of their classmates learn Spanish). However, state laws sometimes regulate whether or when languages other than English can be used in the classroom. In some states that mandate English immersion, for example, Mr. Callio's use of Spanish might be illegal.

In addition to incorporating aspects of students' home cultures into class activities, multiculturalists emphasize the importance of affirming those cultures, helping students to become competent in their home languages and cultures, and developing their openness to other cultures. Box 8.1 shows strategies recommended by Garcia (1991) for developing cultural sensitivities in students growing up in today's pluralistic society.

Teaching English Language Learners

Adjustment to school is harder for students who come from homes where a language other than English is spoken, especially students who are just beginning to learn English themselves. American schools have long coped with English language learners, but there is still no broad consensus on the best approach. Assimilationists tend to favor complete English immersion—teach them solely in English all day long until they catch on and begin to succeed with regularity. This usually works to a degree, although not without a year or two of grade repetition. Cultural pluralists tend to favor first-language immersion, in which students learn the rest of the curriculum in their native language while they learn English in their literacy courses, making the switch to full English instruction several years later. Multiculturalists tend to favor various forms of bilingual education, in which the children receive instruction in both languages. Some bilingual programs are designed to transition into English as quickly as possible, others to maintain and support primary language development while also supporting English acquisition, and still others to promote second language development for both English and non-English speakers (Espinosa, 2005).

Along with learning the language itself, English language learners need to learn about communication norms and expectations that may be foreign to them, such as speaking up and actively participating in class rather than just listening and taking notes (or asking questions when confused, which is avoided in some cultures because it implies that the teacher is not competent) (Lee, 2005). The best program for a particular student depends on factors such as age, previous exposure to English, or language support in the home, but the general weight of evidence suggests that the goal should be to help students maintain and build their first language while adding fluency and literacy skills in English, not replacing the home language with English (Au, 2002; CREDE, 2003; Espinosa, 2005; Garcia, 2003). This minimizes culture clash and identity problems for English language learners and supports their progress in mastering the curriculum as a whole.

If your classes include English language learners, it is likely that they will be pulled out several times a week for special English instruction, and a language teacher or paraprofessional who shares their language may come to your class for part of the day to help them understand and respond to their assignments. You can help by welcoming their language and culture. At minimum, learn some of the basic words and phrases (greetings, numbers, happy birthday, and so on), or better yet, have the students teach these

Box 8.1

Strategies for Favorable Intergroup Relations

A Study of Family Life Patterns

This strategy requires that students study each other's families. The study, if handled maturely, should provide insight into the backgrounds and experiences of students from non-traditional families, extended families, and single-parent families. The study should include, but would not be limited to, an analysis of family roles, family livelihood, family problems and concerns, and family recreation patterns.

A Study of Minority and Majority Group Communities. This strategy includes a study of minority and majority group communities. The study would include, but not be limited to, an analysis of organizing generalizations:

1. Communities have similarities and differences.
2. Communities require interlocking relationships, i.e., human interdependence.
3. Community conditions are results of current forces as well as the community's history.

A Study of Intergroup Experiences. This strategy gets at the crux of the intergroup relations approach because all students are taught to analyze objectively the intergroup relations process. The strategy answers this question: What happens when a minority group and a majority group come into contact?

1. Students study in-group/out-group processes, stereotyping, ethnocentrism, elitism, racism, sexism, discrimination.
2. Students study attitudes, values, and beliefs of peers through surveys, personal interviews, and panel discussions.
3. Students study their own attitudes, values, and beliefs as well as their ancestral ties through genealogies, historical lifelines, and "roots" family study.

A Study of Sexism, Gender-Role Stereotyping, and Gender Bias. This strategy emphasizes the idea that each person can develop a unique self-concept and that gender-role attitudes are learned rather than innate characteristics.

1. Students study the sociocultural concepts of self-concept, social roles, gender roles, and gender-role stereotyping.
2. Students study how different societies teach their conception of gender roles through toys, games, and play activities.
3. Students study the autobiographies/biographies of men and women who have defied the gender-role stereotypes of their generation, e.g., Marie Curie, scientist, or Robert Frost, poet.
4. More mature students study existing biological differences between men and women and how they are interpreted differently in different societies. (This refers to the nurture/ nature issue regarding sex differences; students would need to be able to read and evaluate studies conducted by adults for other adults.)

A Study of Social Stratification in Industrial and Nonindustrial Societies. This strategy emphasizes the universal nature of social stratification and the division of labor. By comparing stratification systems in industrial, hunting and gathering, and agricultural societies, students can gain insight into the economic and political reasons for social classes and social roles.

1. Students should study how families "make a living" in a hunting-gathering society, in an agricultural society, and in an industrial society.
2. Students should study the specific characteristics of the stratification systems of industrial societies.

(continued)

Box 8.1

(Continued)

3. Students should study how social classes are like ethnic groups which have distinct values, beliefs, behavioral patterns (customs, traditions, folkways), and dialects.
4. Students should study how social class membership is initially a matter of luck but that in dynamic societies some upward mobility is possible.

A Study of Handicapping Conditions. This strategy requires accurate, timely information at the factual as well as the emotional levels regarding handicapping conditions. The strategy requires a candid examination of handicapping conditions and the social difficulties faced by handicapped individuals.

1. By reading and discussing biographies or autobiographies of handicapped individuals, e.g., Helen Keller or Louis Braille, students can learn about the social and personal impact of handicapping conditions.
2. By researching and group reporting, students can get accurate information about specific handicapping conditions, e.g., Down syndrome, dyslexia, hearing impairment.
3. By role playing and assuming a handicapping condition, students can gain an awareness of the condition's impact on the individual, e.g., ear plugs for hearing impaired or blindfold for visually impaired.
4. By practicing signing, students can learn how specific handicapping conditions require compensatory use of other senses to overcome the specific handicap.

A Study of Racism, Prejudice, Stereotyping in Ethnically and Racially Homogeneous Classrooms. This strategy is intended for classrooms where no visible ethnic or racial mixture of students exists.

1. Students experience in-group/out-group processes vicariously through open-ended stories, role-playing, simulations.
2. Students visit and study ethnic minority community action agencies.
3. Students visit and study schools with high concentrations of ethnic minorities.
4. Resource speakers from ethnic minorities are incorporated into courses of study.

A Study of Intergroup Relations with Emphasis on the Nature of Racism Between In- and Out-Groups. Such a study requires a serious study of the following characteristics of racist and prejudiced thinking.

Emotional Racism. This kind of racism ranges from slight distaste to extreme hate of ethnically and racially different out-groups.

Cognitive Racism. This kind of racism focuses on perceptions of meanings and understandings of what out-group people are like. Whatever the facts may be about the out-group people, the racist person has his or her stereotypes as "facts" about out-group peoples.

Action Racism. This kind of racism is observable; avoidance, discourtesy, exclusion, exploitation, and violence against out-group peoples are evident behaviors of this kind of racism. This is what is considered racial and ethnic discrimination.

Value Racism. This kind of racism focuses on the values a racist person wishes to maintain or preserve. Preservation of racist values ensures material gain; it becomes necessary to maintain racist values to ensure material gain and economic security.

terms to the whole class. Incorporate their home language into classroom activities through song, poetry, dances, rhymes, or counting. Create materials in the home language to represent familiar stories, songs, or poems that will improve early primary-language literacy.

Include simple print materials in the home language in learning centers (see www.bilingualbooks.com or www.leeandlow.com). Label things around the classroom in each of the languages represented in the class (perhaps printing each different language on different-colored paper), and involve parents in home activities that will support their children's development in both languages. The parents may have very limited English, but if you elicit their involvement in a warm and supportive way, they likely will value engaging in school-related activities with their child (in part because the activities provide opportunities for both parents and children to develop their ability to express themselves in English).

Also, modify your own use of English when delivering instruction and providing directions for assignments. To the extent necessary, simplify your language and support it with gestures to help English language learners understand your meanings. Help them adjust to school by installing predictable routines and using standardized phrases for giving instructions.

Frequently allow students who share the same home language to work in pairs or small groups, so they can use the home language as a resource for understanding and addressing questions and assignments. Encourage them to develop and discuss responses in the home language, but then translate into English for communication to you and their classmates.

Obtain dual language dictionaries and other resources that will help you translate back and forth between other languages and English. Use them and other resources (Web sites, school personnel or parents who speak the home language) to develop instructional materials for use and display in the classroom (maps and posters in these languages, visual displays in which key terms are shown in both languages, graphic organizers and other handouts summarizing key information in both languages, translated versions of tests). If students are still in the earlier stages of learning English, arrange to test them in their native language, so that you do not underestimate their abilities or learning progress (Espinosa, 2005; Sanchez & Brisk, 2004). If some speak home languages that are not spoken by anyone at your school, seek out resource persons (possibly including the students' family members) who can help you prepare home-language labels, posters, and tests.

Teaching in Urban Schools

Teaching in urban schools is especially challenging, because these schools usually include more cultural mismatches related to immigrant and minority group status as well as more students whose academic progress is at risk because their home backgrounds equip them with less of the cultural capital that would enable them to succeed easily at school. Some of the challenges of urban schools are systemic and beyond the control of individual teachers: These schools tend to have high concentrations of students living in poverty, higher percentages of single-parent families, lower percentages of credentialed and highly qualified teachers, depersonalized work environments, and aging or limited space and resources (Milner, 2006; Weiner, 2006).

Despite these and other systemic problems, what occurs inside classrooms is still mostly under the control of the teachers, even in large urban schools in high-poverty neighborhoods. Furthermore, what students in these classrooms need is mostly the same mix of components of good teaching that other students need (as outlined in the other chapters in this book), along with some extra determination to connect with them and help them succeed. The same big ideas keep reappearing in research reports and reviews of successful teaching in urban settings: caring teachers and good teacher-student relationships, affirmation of home cultures, high expectations and performance demands coupled with instructional follow-through that enables students to succeed, and a curriculum that features intellectual rigor focused around important knowledge and skills developed through interactive teaching that includes frequent connections to students' life experiences.

Teachers who have been notably successful in urban settings display cultural sensitivity and attention to both excellence and equity goals. They recognize that school knowledge and skills provide cultural capital that their students will need to draw on in building places for themselves in our society, so they make sure that the students succeed academically. In the process, they help their students understand why it is important to succeed academically and recognize that they have the ability to do so if they apply themselves to their studies.

At the same time, they display a welcoming attitude toward the students and their home cultures. They visit homes and get to know family members, inform themselves about the ethnic groups and cultures represented in their classes, adapt curriculum materials and learning activities to connect with their students' lives and cultures, and invite them to bring their personal experiences to bear in participating in lessons and composing writing assignments (Delpit, 1995; Foster, 1997; Gay, 2000; Hale, 2001; Howard, 1999; Irvine, 2003; Ladson-Billings, 1994; Weiner, 2006).

Researchers who have studied teachers who are effective in urban schools, most notably researchers who are themselves African American and have studied teachers who have been successful with African American students, are virtually unanimous in emphasizing certain key ideas to new teachers. First, they make it clear that although fewer barriers to establishing a personal and trusting relationship exist when teacher and student share the same race, ethnicity, or cultural background, the levels of success that teachers achieve in urban settings ultimately depend on how they teach, not their race or ethnicity. European Americans from middle-class suburban or rural backgrounds can learn to succeed in urban settings, city people can learn to succeed in rural settings, and so on.

They add, however, that the important word in this reassuring message is "learn." It isn't just students who can experience cultural mismatches in schools, as the vignette that opened this chapter illustrates. It is crucial for teachers entering new situations to do so with an open mind and willingness to learn—not only from conventional teacher education and professional development sources, but from one's students and their parents, teaching colleagues, and others who may help one to bridge cultural divides (Ballenger, 1999; Ladson-Billings, 2001; Weiner, 2006; Weinstein, Tomlinson-Clarke, & Curran, 2004).

To begin, confront your own prejudices. Many preservice teachers have negative beliefs about and low expectations of success with students of color, even if they have taken coursework in multicultural education (Irvine, 2003). Recall the case studies we asked you to conduct in Chapter 1. Exercises like those can help you to become more aware of your perceptions of different kinds of students.

Negative attitudes and beliefs are often covert or even unconscious, but nevertheless operative. For example, when preservice teachers were asked about their preferences for student teaching placements, most gave socially acceptable responses indicating a high or at least average interest in working in schools with high minority enrollments. However, when informed that their responses would actually affect decisions about their placements, most changed their answers to indicate a preference for working in a suburban school (Terrill & Mark, 2000). Unfortunately, chances are good that, whatever your status characteristics, you possess some attitudes and beliefs about races and ethnic groups that will impede your chances for teaching students from these groups successfully unless you confront them honestly and take whatever steps are needed to change or get past them.

One common but counterproductive strategy for addressing these issues is to try to be "color-blind." Researchers who have studied what makes for success in dealing with students of color typically conclude that it is a mistake for a teacher to say, "I don't see color—I just see individual students." For one thing, this claim is often inaccurate; whether they realize it, many teachers who make this claim are in fact prejudicial and biased in their interactions with minority students. More fundamentally, however, even if it is true that teachers mostly treat all of their students "the same," this will tend to mean treating them as if they all were European Americans from middle-class backgrounds. This stops short of recognizing, affirming, and helping minority students to understand and develop the racial or ethnic aspects of their identities (Irvine, 2003; Milner, 2006).

Profilers of successful teachers in urban schools also agree that the "demander" part of the "warm demander" prototype needs to be emphasized to new teachers. Warmth, sensitivity, caring, and empathy are necessary but not sufficient: Teaching is not very productive if it focuses only on making students feel good in school, experience easy success, and so on. Urban students need warmth and caring combined with determined efforts to teach them empowering knowledge and skills, including direct instruction in the literacy and communication skills needed to succeed in school and in most occupations. The most successful teachers not only encourage but also drive their students to succeed, demanding that they put forth consistent effort and refusing to accept invalid excuses or shoddy work. They often are observed scolding students for not applying themselves, requiring them to correct mistakes or redo assignments, or contacting their parents to enlist their collaboration in making sure that the students take homework seriously.

This kind of follow-through is part of what high expectations and caring are all about. Urban and minority students recognize this, prizing teachers who push them to do their best, but also provide the curriculum and instruction they need to succeed.

Teacher concerns about equity and social justice also need to be translated into empowering curriculum and instruction. Successful teachers in urban settings fill in cultural capital gaps by directly addressing issues related to the culture of power and teaching the rules and strategies that will enable their students to communicate and behave (when necessary) in ways that the dominant culture finds acceptable. These teachers engage in culturally responsive teaching that incorporates and affirms their students' home cultures, but they also make sure that students acquire the cultural capital that will enable them to shift communication styles and in other ways adjust smoothly to situational social expectations.

If your classroom is dominated by just one or two racial or ethnic groups, you may be able to make broad accommodations targeted specifically to those groups (look for books and Web sites that offer guidance about teaching students from those particular backgrounds). But as we noted earlier, systematic accommodations are less feasible in urban classrooms in which a diverse array of cultural backgrounds is represented. Whatever the mix, it remains important for you to break through social-class differences, cultural differences, language differences, and other potential barriers to communication in order to form good relationships with your students and use them to maximize their achievement progress.

Help your students to value diversity, learn from one another, and appreciate different languages and traditions. Treat the cultures they bring to school as assets that provide them with foundations of background knowledge to support their learning efforts and provide you with opportunities to enrich the curriculum for everyone. Think in terms of helping minority students to become fully bicultural rather than in terms of replacing one culture with another. If you are unfamiliar with a culture represented in your class, educate yourself by reading about it, talking with community leaders, visiting homes, and most importantly, talking with students to learn about their past history and future aspirations.

Cultivate Parent Involvement

Parent involvement is a significant component of children's education, correlating with both their achievement and their motivation. Reaching out to parents is especially important when teaching students from minority groups, teaching in urban settings, or teaching in large, bureaucratic schools that create barriers to personal relationships with students. Consider it part of your professional role to invite parents' active participation in their children's education and to build trusting parent–teacher relationships.

As a new teacher, you may not have time to meet with all of your students' parents, but it is important to meet (in their homes) with a range of parents to get a feel for your students' home lives. Also, invite small groups of parents to come to your class to talk about things of general interest. Establish positive and collaborative relationships with parents early in the year, before problems develop and you need to contact some of them to seek help. Talk with parents about ways that they can support your agenda, such as by monitoring their children's television viewing and discussing programs with them, helping them to check out library books, arranging times and places for them to study and do homework, and expressing interest in their schoolwork. Establishing these kinds of high-quality home–school relationships can increase students' attention to homework, short- and long-term achievement goals, school attendance, graduation rates, and educational and professional aspirations (Hong & Ho, 2005).

Beginning teachers consistently report feeling unprepared to work with parents. Be sure to chat with the principal and some of the other teachers at your school to learn about schoolwide efforts to include parents and get advice about how to do so effectively. Communicate clearly to parents that they have important roles to play in their children's school success by encouraging and reinforcing their learning efforts (talking with the children about the value of education, discussing each school day with them, communicating with teachers, coming to school, creating home practices that support schoolwork). Tables 8.1 and 8.2 summarize strategies that schools and teachers can use to reach out to parents and support their productive involvement in their children's schooling.

Personalizing in Response to Individual Differences

In addition to the differences already addressed in this chapter, there are many other group and individual differences that might be used as a basis for differentiating instruction. In fact, it is a professional truism that students are individuals and must be treated as such if we expect to optimize their motivation and learning. As an abstract proposition, this statement is compelling. However, theoretical complexities and practical difficulties arise when we seek to apply it to particular students or situations. We already have commented on the major practical difficulty: One teacher working with twenty or more students has to focus on teaching the group as a whole, and can only differentiate a little around the margins, as time allows.

The theoretical complexities are multiple and deserve thoughtful reflection. A great many claims have been made that teachers need to accommodate this or that dimension of difference among students, but few of these claims are backed by a significant research base establishing that (1) differences on the dimensions are important enough to justify the effort it would take to assess students and provide differentiated curriculum and instruction to different subgroups; (2) the suggestions for differentiating instruction are feasible for implementation in normal classrooms; and (3) if provided, such differentiated treatment would serve the long-run best interests of all of the students involved. To illustrate some of these complexities, we will address two commonly mentioned dimensions of student difference: gender and learning style.

Gender Differences

As children develop in our society, they are exposed to *gender role socialization* suggesting that certain family and social roles, occupations, personal attributes, and ways of dressing and behaving are primarily feminine, while others are primarily masculine. Gender role socialization pervades most children's experiences. It is modeled by the individuals they encounter in their personal lives and in the media, expressed directly in the messages they receive from their parents and peers (and sometimes their teachers), and reinforced through communication of expectations concerning such things as the toys and games they will want to play with, the books they will enjoy reading, or the things that they will want to do in school or in their free time (Bussey & Bandura, 1999;

Table 8.1   Strategies to Increase Schools' Capacities for Inviting Parental Involvement

Create an inviting, welcoming school climate
- Create visual displays in school entry areas and hallways reflective of all families in the school (photos, artifacts, pictures, history); focus on creating a strong sense that "this is *our* school; *we* belong here."
- Attend to the critical role of central factors in the creation of positive school climate: principal leadership; long-term commitment to improving and maintaining positive school climate; creation of trust through mutually respectful, responsive, and communicative teacher–parent relationships
- Develop strong, positive office–staff skills with a consumer orientation; create habitual attitudes of respect toward parents, students, and visitors
- Create multiple comfortable spaces for parents in the school, supportive of parent–teacher conversations and parent networking
- Hire parents or seek parent volunteers who can provide other parents with information on how the school works, translations as needed, advocacy as needed, a friendly presence

Empower teachers for parental involvement; create dynamic, systematic, and consistent school attention to improving family–school relationships:
- Develop routine school practices focused on discussion and development of positive, trusting parent–school relationships; make family–school relationships and interactions a part of the school's daily life and culture, e.g.:
  - Systematically seek parent ideas, perspectives, opinions, questions about school and family roles in student learning
  - Allocate regular faculty meeting time to discuss parental involvement, involvement practices that have been successful in the school, information from other sources on new ideas
  - Develop and maintain an active school file of teacher and parent ideas on what is helpful and effective in inviting parental involvement; raise public awareness of family–school relations in the school; allow development of a school-specific resource bank to support teacher skills and capacities for improved parent–teacher relations
- Develop dynamic in-service programs that support teacher efficacy for involving parents and school capacities for effective partnership with families; programs should:
  - Offer teachers opportunities to collaborate with and learn from colleagues and parents
  - Create opportunities for practice and revision of strategies suggested
  - Enable school development of involvement plans responsive to teacher, family, and community needs

Learn about parents' goals, perspectives on child's learning, family circumstances, culture:
- Offer suggestions for support of child's learning consistent with parents' circumstances
- Focus on developing two-way family–school communication (asking question, listening well to responses)
- Seek parents' perspectives on the child and child's learning; seek parent suggestions and follow through on them
- Adapt current involvement approaches as needed to enhance the fit between invitations and family circumstances; craft new strategies to enhance opportunities for communication

Join with existing parent-teacher-family structures to enhance involvement:
- Use after-school programs to increase family–school communication: include after-school staff in in-house communications, faculty meetings, professional development opportunities

- Use current parent groups (e.g., PTA/PTO) to invite *all* families' participation; work with parent leaders to ensure open access; encourage varied activities of interest to diverse family groups within the school
- In middle and high schools, create advisory structures that allow parents to check in with one adviser for general information on child progress, program planning, etc.
- Seek district and community support for creation of new structures to support family–school interactions and communication (e.g., parent resource room, telephone and e-mail access in classrooms, staff position dedicated to parent–school relationships, school-based family center)

Offer full range of involvement opportunities, including standard approaches (e.g., parent–teacher conferences, student performances) **and new opportunities unique to school and community** (e.g., first-day-of-school celebrations, parent workshops, social/networking events):
- Offer *specific* invitations to specific events and volunteer opportunities at school; schedule activities at times that meet the needs of families with inflexible work schedules
- Advertise involvement opportunities clearly, attractively, repeatedly, using methods targeted to interests and needs of school families

Invite teachers, parents, principal, and staff to student-centered events at school:
- Increase opportunities for informal parent–teacher–staff communications and interactions
- Use these events to seek parent comments and suggestions for involvement
- Use the events as venues for distributing brief, attractively formatted information in appropriate languages on issues in parental involvement (e.g., developmentally appropriate, easy-to-implement suggestions for supporting student learning; information on effects of parental involvement; information on school policies and upcoming events)

Source: Hoover-Dempsey, K., et al. (2005). Why do parents become involved? Research findings and implications. *Elementary School Journal, 106*(2), 105–130. Reprinted by permission of University of Chicago Press.

Martin, Ruble, & Szkrybalo, 2002). To the extent that an activity is gender typed, teachers' and students' attitudes and expectations are likely to be affected.

Attitudes and Beliefs about School Subjects.

Gender typing has been noted in several aspects of schooling. One of these involves subject-matter preferences and related motivational responses. Most studies find that boys value and enjoy mathematics and science more than language arts, but girls show the opposite pattern. These differences extend to preferences within subject areas, as well. In reading, for example, boys are more oriented to nonfiction texts, whereas girls tend to prefer fiction. Within fiction, boys tend to prefer action, adventure, and sports themes, whereas girls tend to prefer plots focusing on romance or personal relationships (Millard, 1997; Wigfield & Eccles, 2002).

Some differences encompass not only preferences or value perceptions but also beliefs about ability and related attributional inferences. Concern is greatest with respect to science and especially mathematics, where several investigators have found that girls believe themselves to possess less domain-specific ability than boys, or that girls are more likely to attribute their successes to luck or other external factors but to attribute their failures to lack of ability (Bornholt, Goodnow, & Cooney, 1994; Guimond & Roussel, 2001; Nosek,

Table 8.2 Strategies to Enhance Parents' Capacities for Effective Involvement

Communicate clearly that *all* parents have an important role to play in children's school success:
- Create explicit, positive school assumptions about the importance of parents' contributions to student success
- Emphasize that all parents, regardless of education level, can support students' school success
- Note that even when student learning tasks surpass parents' knowledge, parents' interest in child's schooling, encouragement, reinforcement for learning, and modeling continue to support student learning and school success
- In all communications (including those below), offer information in multiple formats (e.g., written information that is clear, succinct, in appropriate languages; meeting at school or in community centers; by phone); give clear ideas about where to get more or repeated information

Give parents specific information about *what* they can do to be involved:
- Offer information about what parents do when they are involved, emphasizing the wide range of activities different families employ (e.g., talking about the value of education, discussing the school day, communicating with teachers, coming to school, offering positive reinforcement for learning effort and accomplishment, attending child's school events, creating home practices that support students' schoolwork)
- Listen to parents' ideas about involvement and offer encouragement for those likely to be helpful with the particular child or developmental/grade level
- Give parents suggestions for helping their children targeted to current assignments and learning goals
- Offer time-limited suggestions and learning assignments that require or encourage parent-student interaction; where possible, target suggestions to parents' knowledge, skills, time, and energy
- Draw on published programs of interactive homework (e.g., TIPS) in making homework assignments
- Draw on families' "funds of knowledge" (e.g., Moll, 1992) in creating home learning tasks; create assignments for "homemade homework" that focus on family routines and tasks (Epstein & Van Voorhis, 2001)
- Seek support for parent workshops that offer training and practice in how to help children learn

Give parents specific information about the general *effects* of involvement of student learning:
- Offer information about the behavioral effects of parental involvement (e.g., students spend more time on school tasks, are more attentive in class, pay increased attention to homework and related assignments, do better in school)
- Offer information about the attitudinal effects of parental involvement (e.g., students have more positive attitudes about learning, have a stronger sense of personal ability to learn, are more likely to believe that learning outcomes are related to their effort and work)
- Ask parents for feedback on their perceptions of their involvement activities' influence on their child (e.g., influence on child's behavior, attitudes, learning content, or processes in assignments)

Give parents specific information on *how* their involvement activities influence learning:
- Encouragement supports student motivation for schoolwork
- Communication about the value and importance of education models parents' commitment to schooling
- Positive reinforcement gives information about expected learning behaviors and outcomes

- Creating home practices that support student homework encourages more focused attention to learning tasks

Give parents specific information about curriculum and learning goals:
- Offer information (by grade or course level) on learning goals for a specific period; this enables parents to know what is expected of their children and offers a context for understanding links between learning tasks and learning goals
- Allow time for parent-teacher interactions that clarify learning goals (by phone, in meetings, in conferences); hear parents' concerns, ideas, and goals for children

Offer parents positive feedback on the effects of their involvement:
- Focus on individual parent activities and steps in student progress
- Create multiple opportunities for success (begin with small steps; offer clear notes and comments of thanks for parental help; express clearly that parents' activities are making a difference for the student)

Create and support parent and parent-teacher networks in the school:
- Seek and share information on school, grade-level learning goals
- Share ideas about parent involvement activities that have worked
- Interact in ways that support the development of trust among parents and school staff

Source: Hoover-Dempsey, K., et al. (2005). Why do parents become involved? Research findings and implications. *Elementary School Journal, 106*(2), 105–130. Reprinted by permission of University of Chicago Press.

Banaji, & Greenwald, 2002). In contrast, boys are more likely to credit their successes to high ability but attribute their failures to bad luck, lack of interest, low effort, or other causes that do not imply a lack of ability (Eccles, 1987; Miller, 1986). These differences make girls more vulnerable to learned helplessness and other failure syndrome problems than boys, especially in subjects like mathematics or science about which girls might suspect limitations in their domain-specific abilities.

In any case, it is clear that starting around fifth grade and continuing thereafter, girls' ability beliefs and expectancies for future success in mathematics and science tend to drop below those of boys, even though their grades in these subjects are as good or better than boys' grades. Girls also are more likely to opt out of mathematics and science classes when they begin to get the opportunity to do so, thus cutting themselves off from future career opportunities that require academic preparation in these subjects. These patterns develop as much among brighter girls as other girls.

Boys generally place less value on engaging in academic activities, so the quality of their engagement is more variable. They are more likely than girls to adopt work-avoidant goals or display task resistance. When they adopt learning or performance goals, however, they are likely to focus on achieving mastery or competitive success. In contrast, girls are more likely to focus on putting forth their best efforts and pleasing their teachers (Pomerantz, Altermatt, & Saxon, 2002; Van Hecke & Tracy, 1983). These differences do not always appear, but they show up often enough to be cause for concern because they further contribute to girls' vulnerability to learned helplessness (girls more consistently put forth their best efforts and therefore tend to attribute failures to lack of ability, whereas boys more consistently credit their successes to high ability but explain away their failures).

Interactions with Teachers.   Other studies have focused on gender differences in student behavior and teacher–student interaction patterns (Brophy, 1985). They show that boys are more active and salient in the classroom than girls. Boys have more of almost every kind of interaction that occurs between students and teachers, although the differences are greatest for interactions that boys initiate themselves by calling out answers or by misbehaving and drawing teacher intervention. However, teachers also initiate interactions more frequently with boys, especially to give them procedural instructions, check their progress on assignments, or generally monitor and control their activities.

Along with differences in the quantity of teacher–student interaction, researchers have identified qualitative differences in the ways in which teachers interact with boys versus girls. In particular, words of encouragement or feedback directed to boys tend to focus exclusively on their achievement striving and accomplishments, but some of what is said to girls in parallel situations focuses instead on neatness, following directions, speaking clearly, or showing good manners. Teachers sometimes pay more attention to, ask more thought-provoking questions of, or provide more extensive feedback to boys in mathematics or science classes but to girls in language arts classes.

These trends are observed in varying degrees in almost all classrooms, regardless of whether the teachers are male or female. Sadker and Sadker (1994) suggested that many of them reflect gender differences in styles of participation in social conversation that are pervasive in our society and thus carry over into classrooms: (1) men speak more often and frequently interrupt women; (2) listeners pay more attention to male speakers, even when female speakers use similar styles to make similar points; (3) women participate less actively in conversations but do more passive listening; and (4) women often transform declarative statements into more tentative statements that reduce their ability to influence others ("We could solve this problem using the Pythagorean theorem, couldn't we?"). Brookfield and Preskill (1999) reported similar gender differences during class discussions.

Recommendations.   Gender differences in teacher-student interaction patterns tend to be relatively small in quantity and subtle in quality. Furthermore, most of them reflect gender differences in student behaviors that impact on teachers, rather than consistent teacher tendencies to treat boys and girls differently. Even so, it is wise to remain conscious of gender issues and to monitor your interactions with boys versus girls. This will help you not only to avoid inappropriate gender discrimination but also to take advantage of opportunities to free your students from some of the counterproductive restrictions built into traditional gender role concepts (Hoffmann, 2002).

With regard to subject matter, help your boys to take full advantage of reading and writing opportunities, and in particular, to appreciate poetry and other forms of literature that they might view as feminine. Information about books popular with boys can be found at www.guysread.com. Similarly, help your girls to value and develop their full potential in mathematics and science; for ideas and resources, see http://girlstech. douglass.rutgers.edu. In developing content, use examples and problem contexts that will interest girls as well as boys. Stimulate their interest in and willingness to take courses in these subjects and help them to realize that they can be successful in these subjects if they apply reasonable effort.

Also, where necessary, encourage girls to participate in lessons more actively. Make systematic efforts to observe and get to know each girl as an individual, especially girls who achieve satisfactorily and appear to be well adjusted but rarely initiate contact with you or assert themselves in the classroom. Encourage these girls to speak their minds, call on them to participate if they do not volunteer, assign them to leadership roles for group projects, and take other actions to encourage them to become more assertive. Broaden their perspectives by helping them to realize that the full spectrum of career opportunities is open to them and by using learning experiences such as stories involving females in leadership positions or discussions or assignments focusing on the work of female scientists.

Most teachers have been doing these things in recent years, and along with changes in curriculum materials and pervasive messages about gender equality in the culture generally, they have had a significant effect. Gender gaps in mathematics and science achievement are disappearing rapidly. In fact, gender-related concerns about student motivation and achievement have begun to shift to boys, because recent trends indicate that fewer boys are earning good grades in school, graduating from high school, or attending college (Head, 1999).

$\mathcal{L}$earning Style Differences

Much attention has been focused on the notion of learning styles, especially by people who offer workshops or sell materials purported to help teachers assess their students' learning styles and follow up with differentiated instruction. Learning style inventories address questions such as the following: Are students "verbal learners" who prefer to listen to information or "visual learners" who prefer to read it or see it displayed graphically? Do they prefer to learn alone or with others? Do they prefer to study for frequent short periods or fewer longer periods? Do they like to study in silence, with soothing musical or "white noise" backgrounds, or in potentially distracting environments (next to a playing radio or television)?

Lack of Research Support for Claimed Effects

Critics have noted that the credibility of learning styles enthusiasts is questionable because (1) they tend to make outlandish claims for the effectiveness of the measurement inventories and instructional models they sell; (2) most of the studies purporting to support learning style approaches are too flawed to survive the peer review standards of research journals; (3) most of these studies have been conducted by people with vested interests in positive results who gave instructions to the participants in learning style treatment groups designed to maximize their enthusiasm and positive expectations; and (4) the advice offered by most learning style advocates only emphasizes catering to students' existing preferences, without recognizing that this might not be in their long-run best interests (Curry, 1990; Kavale & Forness, 1990; O'Neil, 1990; Stahl, 1999; Yates, 2000).

Stellwagen (2001) was intrigued by the contrast he noted between enthusiasm for learning styles among many school administrators and teachers compared to the skepticism typically expressed by researchers. He found that some professional journals (e.g., *Educational Leadership*, *NASSP Bulletin*) typically waxed enthusiastic about learning styles, but research journals consistently published reports questioning the value of both the instruments purporting to measure learning styles and the educational programs ostensibly based on them. He expressed concern that learning style categories were being misapplied in ways that led to stereotyping and potentially prejudicial treatment of students.

We also do not see much validity in the claims made by those who urge teachers to assess their students with learning style inventories and follow up with differentiated curriculum and instruction. First, the research bases supporting these urgings tend to be thin to nonexistent. Second, a single teacher working with twenty or more students does not have time to plan and implement much individualized instruction. With respect to student motivation, much more is to be gained by focusing on students' learning goals, values, and expectancies than on the variables emphasized in learning style inventories.

Brain-Based Education and Multiple Intelligences

Similar comments apply to schemes for differentiating instruction according to student profiles developed using supposed measures of cognitive styles, brain hemisphere preferences, or multiple intelligences. Scientifically based examinations of claims about supposedly brain-based education routinely conclude that although exciting knowledge about brain functioning has been accumulating, the research base has not yet progressed to a level that would support recommendations about differentiating instruction. Consequently, claims that particular educational programs are based on brain research simply have no validity (Bergen & Coscia, 2002; Bruer, 1999; Jensen, 2000).

Similarly, although Howard Gardner has updated his multiple intelligences model (Gardner, 1999) and published a book about educational assessments and interventions based on it (Gardner, 1993), scientifically oriented reviewers routinely conclude that there are conceptual problems with his theory (particularly, misapplication of the term *intelligences*), psychometric problems with his measuring instruments (validity not yet demonstrated), a lack of clarity and specificity about what the theory does and does not imply about educational practice, and a lack of systematic research on (let alone clear support for) educational programs supposedly based on this theory (Hunt, 1999; Klein, 2003; Lubinski & Benbow, 1995).

Krechvski & Seidel (2001) offered a useful introduction to the theory of multiple intelligences and its potential applications to education. They suggested that the theory implies the need to individualize students' education as much as possible, teach subjects in more than one way, use project-based learning, and infuse the arts throughout the curriculum. However, they cautioned that the theory should not be taken as a mandate to teach every topic in seven or eight ways. For example, asking students to sing songs about operations learned in a unit on fractions or playing classical music in the background during the lessons are not meaningful uses of music to support mathematics learning. They also cautioned against stereotyping students or overemphasizing celebration of their strengths without paying sufficient attention to their weaknesses.

Conclusions Regarding Learning Styles

Individual difference concepts such as cognitive styles, multiple intelligences, or learning styles can be useful to teachers if adopted only loosely and used primarily as reminders of the value of including a variety of learning activities and formats in the curriculum. However, scientific validity and practical feasibility problems arise if such concepts are emphasized to the extent of seeking to develop individual curricular prescriptions for each student.

We believe that it is worthwhile to learn about your students' preferences and accommodate them by providing opportunities for autonomy and choice whenever doing so will support progress toward learning goals. However, sometimes such accommodation is not feasible or advisable. For example, in order to attain certain learning goals, students must engage in processes that they might prefer to avoid (presentations to the class, debates, cooperative work on a group project). Or, you might have to limit certain students' opportunities to pursue favorite topics or learn in their preferred mode, because if the students spent too much time indulging these preferences, they would fail to develop knowledge or skills needed in school or in life generally. You can accommodate such preferences much of the time, however, and doing so will increase your students' opportunities to experience intrinsic motivation in your classroom.

*A*ccommodating Students' Personal Characteristics

Students who differ in ability and achievement need different assignments to address the same content at varying levels of sophistication. Students also differ, however, in personal and social traits such as energy, assertiveness, sociability, and patience. You may wish to accommodate such differences in students' personalities.

The number of student factors that could be listed for consideration is endless, so there is no point in trying to construct an exhaustive list. However, we can present guidelines for differentiated instruction of a few common student types found in most classrooms. Good and Power (1976) identified the following five types of students, based on characteristics that teachers often emphasize when describing students to researchers.

1. *Successful* students are task oriented, academically successful, and cooperative. They typically participate actively in lessons, turn in complete and correct assignments, and create few if any discipline problems. They tend to like school and to be well liked by both teachers and peers.

2. *Social* students are more person oriented than task oriented. They have the ability to achieve but value socializing with friends more than working on assignments. They tend to have many friends and to be popular with peers but are usually not well liked by teachers because their frequent socializing creates management problems.

3. *Dependent* students frequently look to the teacher for support and encouragement and often ask for additional directions and help. Teachers generally are concerned about the academic progress of these students and do what they can to assist them. Peers may reject dependent students because they tend to be socially immature.

4. *Alienated* students are reluctant learners and potential dropouts. Extremely alienated students reject school and everything it stands for. Some are openly hostile and create disruptions through aggression and defiance. Others withdraw, sitting at the fringes of the classroom and refusing to participate. Teachers tend to reject students who express alienation openly and to be indifferent toward those who express it passively.

5. *Phantom* students seem to fade into the background because they are rarely noticed or heard from. Some are shy, nervous students; others are quiet, independent workers of average ability. They work steadily on assignments but rarely participate actively in group activities because they do not volunteer and are rarely involved in managerial exchanges because they do not create disruptions. If asked to name all of their students from memory, teachers are most likely to forget phantom students.

Good and Power (1976) suggested ways that teachers might differentiate instruction to accommodate students' preferences and needs (see Table 8.3). Although based partly on research, these suggestions are speculative rather than proven guidelines. First, accommodating students' preferences is not the same as meeting their needs. Several studies have shown that allowing students to choose their own learning methods may produce *less* achievement than teaching them in some other way, even if it improves their attitudes toward learning (Clark, 1982; Flowerday & Schraw, 2003). Second, accommodating students' personal characteristics may reinforce these characteristics, including ones that ought to be changed if possible. For example, it would be easy to respond reciprocally to the behavior of phantom, passive-withdrawn, or alienated students by minimizing interaction with them—never calling on them unless they raise their hands or indicate a need for help. This behavior might even maximize the comfort of both the teacher and the students involved. However, it would not enhance these students' achievement.

Table 8.3 offers suggestions for introducing a degree of individualization into your instruction while primarily teaching the class as a group. Some suggestions can be incorporated easily (e.g., interacting more often or more affectively with certain students); others would be more difficult or time-consuming (e.g., preparing different activities for different groups). It may not be possible to vary the activities planned for each day, but each week or unit should provide enough balance to deliver something for everyone.

A single teacher cannot provide optimal curriculum and instruction to all students simultaneously, because different subgroups present conflicting needs and because classroom management considerations take first priority. For example, dependent students (at least until they are taught self-regulation skills and gain the confidence to use them) need close supervision and frequent feedback during independent work. However, wise teachers reserve the first few minutes of seatwork to make sure that students in general and alienated students in particular get started on their assignments. They also learn to keep their interactions with individuals brief so that they can circulate and

Table 8.3 Suggestions for Meeting the Needs of Five Different Types of Students

	Successful	Social	Dependent	Alienated	Phantom
1. Type of information needed from teacher					
a. Substantive explanation of content	Very high	Very high	High	High	High
b. Procedural directions	Low	Low	High	Moderate-high	Moderate-low
c. Socializing, emotional support, humor	Very low	Low-moderate	Moderate	Moderate (establish private rapport)	Low
2. Type of task needed					
a. Reading skills required	High	High	Low	Low	Moderate
b. Task difficulty level	Very high	High	Low-moderate	Low-moderate	Moderate
c. Abstractness level	High	Moderate	Low initially	Low initially	Moderate
d. Cognitive level	High	Moderate	Low initially	Low initially	Moderate
e. Degree of structure (specificity about what to do and how to do it)	Low	Moderate	High	High	Moderate
f. Opportunity to make active, overt responses	Not important	High	High	High	Moderate
g. Opportunity to make choices	Moderate (stress on enrichment)	Moderate (stress on choices to work with others)	Low	Moderate (stress on relevance)	Low
h. Interest value of task to student	Not important	Moderate	Low	High	Low
i. Length of task	Long	Short	Moderate	Moderate	Long
3. Type of response demanded					
a. Written	High	Low	High	Moderate	High
b. Oral	Low	High	Low	Low	Low
c. Physical	Low	Moderate	Moderate	High	Low
4. Individual versus group settings					
a. Individual	High	Low	High	High	High
b. Group	Low	Moderate	Low	Low-moderate	Low
5. Emphasis on competition	High	Moderate	Low initially	Low	Moderate
6. Type of feedback from teacher					
a. Personal praise	Low	Low	Moderate	Moderate (private)	Low
b. Personal criticism	Low	Low	Low	Very low	Low
c. Praise of good work	Low	Moderate	Moderate	Moderate (private)	Low-moderate
d. Criticism of poor work	Moderate	Moderate	Low	Low (but communicate demand)	Low-moderate

Source: Adapted from Good, T., & Power, C. (1976). Designing successful classroom environments for different types of students. *Journal of Curriculum Studies, 8,* 45–60.

be available to students who need immediate help. All students, even the most successful, need monitoring and feedback.

Teachers who develop a workable system for instructing the whole class can then use this system as a base from which to introduce differentiated instruction. It helps if a variety of work settings or assignment formats is available and if the number of students working individually at a given time is limited so that the teacher does not have to provide individualized feedback to the entire class. For example, an elementary-grade teacher might ask dependent, alienated, and social students to work on assignments during the early morning when these students are not involved in reading-group activities. These relatively brief times (typically two 20-minute periods) for individual work could be used profitably by these students (who may react less favorably to longer assignments), especially if the teacher supplies self-checking devices that they can use to monitor their progress. Successful students and phantom students might be engaged in brief small-group projects during these same periods. Later, all students might be engaged in whole-class work in mathematics. In the afternoon, successful students and phantom students could be assigned to individual work while the teacher supervises the small-group work of other students.

However, there is only so much that can be accomplished even by experienced teachers who have developed sophisticated systems for organizing and managing instruction. Consequently, you may want to take the additional step of sharing instructional responsibilities with the students themselves by using cooperative learning approaches or by arranging for students to receive tutorial assistance.

SUMMARY

Minority students and others whose family backgrounds place them at risk for school failure do especially well with teachers who share warm, personal interactions with them but also hold high expectations for their academic progress, require them to perform up to their capabilities, and see that they progress as far and as fast as they are able. These teachers break through social-class differences, cultural differences, language differences, and other potential barriers to communication in order to form good relationships with at-risk students, but they use these relationships to maximize the students' academic progress, not merely to provide friendship or sympathy to them.

At-risk students also do especially well in classrooms that offer inviting social environments. Therefore, help your students to value diversity, learn from one another, and appreciate different languages and traditions. Treat the cultures that they bring to school as foundations of knowledge that can ground their learning efforts and provide you with opportunities to enrich the curriculum for everyone. Think in terms of helping minority students to become fully bicultural rather than in terms of replacing one culture with another. If you are unfamiliar with a culture that is represented in your classroom, educate yourself by reading about it, talking with community leaders, visiting homes, and most importantly, talking with students to learn about their past history and future aspirations.

SUGGESTED ACTIVITIES AND QUESTIONS

1. Multiculturalists call for a blend of assimilationism and cultural pluralism. How do you locate yourself as to what culturally responsive teaching means?

2. Think about your high school teachers. As a group, did they represent a multicultural perspective?

3. Might some aspects of assimilation be more important for some students as a function of their age? Would you teach new immigrants differently in this regard if they were elementary versus secondary students?

4. State laws vary in terms of how much instruction English language learners can receive in any other language. What laws apply in the state in which you expect to teach?

5. The chapter describes how teachers who were not raised in urban areas can come to know more about these settings and the students who live in them. Would this same advice apply to new teachers who grew up in an urban area but now teach in a rural or suburban setting? What special considerations might apply?

6. When you were in middle school, did you prefer to be taught by a same-gender teacher, or did it not matter to you? Did your preferences change in high school? Why or why not?

7. What good is knowledge about group differences in statistical distributions (e.g., girls, on average, have more interest than boys in reading fiction) when there is more variation in reading preferences within girls (and boys) than between girls and boys?

8. How do choices in music listened to, movies seen, and television programs watched vary in your classroom? Do male and female students have similar or different preferences? Do the differences have instructional implications?

9. The chapter identified five types of students (successful, social, dependent, alienated, and phantom). Which types are most likely to benefit from computer-based instruction? The least? Why? Would your answers differ if you interpreted "benefit" to mean learning versus interest?

FORM 8.1. Helping Diverse Students to Feel Comfortable and Achieve
Success at School

*USE: When the teacher has been interviewed and observed frequently enough so that
reliable information is available.*
*PURPOSE: To assess the degree to which the teacher reaches out to students and their
families in order to help the students feel a sense of belonging and to achieve success in
school.*
     *Enter a check mark (✓) for each of the following behaviors that has been or is being
implemented effectively, and a zero (0) for each behavior that was omitted or handled
ineffectively. Then add detailed comments on a separate sheet, emphasizing constructive
suggestions for improvement.*

CHECKLIST

——————   1.   Welcomes and affirms all students' home cultures and experiences

——————   2.   Rather than pretending not to see differences, recognizes and adapts
to them in ways that support all students' personal and academic
development

——————   3.   Seeks to make students bi- or multicultural rather than to suppress
and replace their home cultures

——————   4.   Has made proactive efforts to get to know students' families,
preferably by visiting at least some of their homes

——————   5.   Incorporates references to families' funds of knowledge, occupations,
hobbies, and interests into instruction as examples or applications

——————   6.   Pursues the same basic instructional goals with all students, but in
the process, incorporates aspects of their home cultures and
languages when this supports their learning

——————   7.   Adapts curriculum to connect well with students' prior experiences

——————   8.   Acknowledges and respectfully represents multiple perspectives on
history, social studies, and current events

——————   9.   Teaches about diversity in ways that foster tolerance, empathy, and
appreciation

——————   10.   Wall decorations and available books and videos provide positive role
models and identity support for all of the racial and ethnic groups
represented in the class

——————   11.   Helps students from nondominant cultures to understand the need to
shift vocabulary and communication styles to meet expectations
inherent in dominant culture contexts, and helps them learn how to
do so

——————   12.   Consistently communicates success expectations and effort demands
to all students, but also follows through by providing struggling
students with the instructional support needed to enable them to
meet those expectations

——————   13.   For students with limited English, uses strategies such as providing
special instructions and monitoring or opportunities to collaborate
with same-language peers, to make sure that these students
understand and can succeed on their assignments

——————   14.   Has acquired and makes frequent use of texts and tradebooks, word
cards, and cues, reminders, or checklists written in English language
learners' first languages to help them understand what to do

Teaching Worthwhile Content for Understanding, Appreciation, and Application

*I*n previous chapters we addressed factors involved in setting the stage for productive instruction: teacher expectations, classroom management, student motivation, and cooperative learning environments. We also noted that having to teach twenty or more students forces most teachers to rely on whole-class instructional methods as their basic approach (but modified to adapt to students' individual differences). We now turn to the core topic of instruction itself.

The term *instruction* often appears as part of the longer phrase, curriculum and instruction. Teachers need to make instructional decisions about both content (subject matter) and process (teaching methods). You need to decide what to teach before you think about how to teach it, for two important reasons: (1) You need to make sure that the content you intend to teach is worth teaching; and (2) any given type of content is better suited to some teaching methods than others, so you will need to use methods that are well suited to the content you want to develop. We address issues relating to the content base for teaching here in Chapter 9, then address instructional methods in Chapters 10 and 11.

Consider Laura Hirsch and Rachel Dewey, two prototypical teachers. Both teach literacy and social studies to similar classes in the same middle school. Both are good classroom managers and are well liked by their students, but they approach their subjects quite differently.

Laura Hirsch

In Laura's class, grades are determined by performance on daily assignments and weekly quizzes (40 percent), unit tests (40 percent), and end-of-unit reflection papers (20 percent). Laura prepares her students well for these assignments and tests. First, she asks them to individually review the story in the reader or the social studies chapter section that she assigned as homework the previous night, posing a few questions designed to underscore key ideas. She then elicits students' questions and comments on the reading, encouraging them to respond to one another but providing clarifications and explanations when necessary. Her students know that they should pay careful attention to and take notes on her questions and explanations, because they are likely to appear on the assignments, quizzes, and tests.

Following these text-based lessons, students work individually on seatwork assignments. Laura insists on quiet during these work times, so that everyone can concentrate. The worksheets mostly call for matching, true/false, or fill-in-the-blank responses, but they end with questions asking her students to reflect on what they learned from studying the story or chapter section, then write a paragraph explaining what they view as the most important learning and why. As students work, Laura circulates to help those who need it.

Prior to major quizzes and tests, she schedules review activities. The major assessments include some short-answer essay questions and always end with the question, What have you learned that you most value? If her students pay attention to lessons and work conscientiously on assignments, they should be successful on her tests and well prepared to write their reflection papers.

During literature classes, Laura's questions focus on the details of the stories and how these exemplify the genre (e.g., mystery stories) and techniques (e.g., foreshadowing) under study. Daily assignments and weekly quiz questions focus on defining and recognizing examples of these genres and techniques. Unit tests feature questions such as define foreshadowing, give three examples of foreshadowing in stories read during the unit, and give two reasons why an author might use the foreshadowing technique. They also include at least one question calling for personalized application (e.g., "Choose a plot development that was foreshadowed in one of the stories and tell how it might have been foreshadowed in a different way").

In social studies, Laura's daily assignments and weekly quizzes focus on basic facts about the South American nations under study: each nation's geographical location, climate, major cities and places of interest, historical highlights, primary imports and exports, and so on. Unit tests also include short-answer essay questions calling for students to demonstrate understanding of connections among these facts, such as by showing awareness that much of the economy of Chile reflects the fact that it is a mountainous country in which internal travel is difficult and access to the sea is limited.

At the end of the unit she has students prepare a reflective paper that counts for 20 percent of their grade. She provides three questions and allows them to respond to one of their choice (e.g., Which South American country would you want to live in now? Why? Which one in twenty years? Why?). Sometimes she allows them to write their own questions (subject to her approval).

Rachel Dewey

Rachel emphasizes personalizing the curriculum and engaging students in collaborative learning rather than preparing them for tests. She does give a short test early in each unit to make sure that all of her students can define and give examples of key terms, and sometimes she includes a major test to assess their accomplishment of unit goals. For the most part, however, her students' grades are determined by their work on a variety of learning activities, and her feedback to them emphasizes qualitative critiques and suggestions for improvement.

In literature, Rachel covers fewer stories than Laura but spends more time on each story she decides to include. She begins by having her students read the story individually and then discuss it with a partner. She prepares them for this by introducing the genre and some of its key techniques and by providing questions to guide their analyses. The students read the story individually to enjoy the aesthetic experience. Next, they discuss the story with their partner, focusing on what they liked and didn't like about it and why. Then they work through Rachel's questions to analyze the story with respect to genre techniques. They record their answers and note questions and comments to raise in class. Rachel is usually pleased or at least satisfied with the results of this approach, but sometimes the partners just go through the motions instead of really engaging with the story, or one of them has not read the story.

During the whole-class discussion that follows, Rachel first focuses on the students' aesthetic reactions. She tosses in a few of her own as food for thought (e.g., Would the story be better if it were set in the present instead of the past or if it had a happier ending? What might have happened if the hero had kept his secret instead of telling it to his friend?). When discussion of the aesthetic appreciation aspects of the story has run its course (or if necessary, when time constraints loom), Rachel shifts to genre techniques, starting by eliciting students' answers to her questions and listing these on the board. She then leads a discussion of these issues, making sure to highlight ways that the author used key techniques to construct the story and how they enhanced the story. She wants her students to appreciate what the genre has to offer them as readers and the ways that good applications of genre techniques enhance the power and enjoyment of the stories they read.

Following these class discussions are quiet times during which students write in their journals about their reactions to the story. Rachel supplies questions that they can use to guide their journal writing if they wish. However, she encourages them to write in depth about aspects that they found especially interesting or meaningful, rather than to try to answer each question or confine themselves to the issues raised on the list. She wants them to formulate and record both their aesthetic responses and their developing insights about the genre. As a culmination activity, students compose original examples of the genre (e.g., mystery stories) that will be published in a class anthology. This aspect of her literacy teaching also generally goes well, but sometimes when certain students see that most of their classmates have completed their journal writing, they hurry to finish so they are not perceived as slow writers.

In social studies, rather than give equal time to each South American nation, Rachel overviews the continent as a whole but then focuses on a few nations selected because they exemplify key themes (e.g., Brazil for its rain forest and the cultural and ecological preservation issues it raises; Venezuela for studying the effects of a modern oil industry on a traditional agrarian economy; and Chile as an example of life in a mountain region). For the countries studied in depth, she supplements the text with nonfiction trade books, children's literature, videos, and classroom visits by people who come from or have visited the country. She wants to personalize what her students learn about the country, and especially about the everyday lives and activities of families that include children their age.

Rachel's students also are required to record in their journals their thinking on two questions: (1) What I would and would not like about living in the country, and (2) What I have learned about why things in that country are similar to or different from the way they are in our country. They are encouraged to elaborate about aspects of the country they found particularly interesting or meaningful to learn about. During biweekly meetings with each student, she reads and comments on these journal entries. Rachel is generally satisfied with her decision to reduce breadth of coverage in order to develop big ideas in depth, but she occasionally gets reminded that this decision entails trade-offs (e.g., "Ms. Dewey, why didn't we spend more time on Peru? My friends in Ms. Hirsch's class said that that was their favorite South American country!").

Comparing Laura and Rachel

Would you rather be taught by Laura or Rachel? Why?

If you are like most people, you picked Rachel, citing reasons such as greater enjoyment, more personalized and meaningful learning, and more opportunities to engage in dialogue, collaborate with peers, and apply what you were learning.

Laura is not a bad teacher. In fact, by sticking closely to the text in her curriculum, instruction, and assessment practices, she virtually ensures that her students will achieve success if they invest reasonable effort. However, her curriculum emphasizes broad but shallow coverage of mostly disconnected content. This encourages her students to focus on memorizing material for tests rather than constructing more elaborate and better connected representations that are more likely to be permanent and available for use in life outside of school. In contrast, Rachel covers more limited content but focuses on developing key ideas in depth, personalizes the learning to her students' backgrounds and experiences, and provides opportunities for them to elaborate and connect their learning both through communicating with peers and through personal journal writing.

The two teachers' contrasting instructional methods and activities are rooted in contrasting content bases. Many of the most appealing aspects of Rachel's teaching are time-consuming, but she is able to use them because she has reduced the breadth of her curriculum in order to focus on developing big ideas in depth. In contrast, Laura leans heavily on her textbooks and ends up offering a curriculum that is broader in scope but less coherently structured around big ideas. Rachel's content base supports activities that feature reflection, dialogue, and meaningful applications, whereas Laura's content base leads mostly to fill-in-the-blank exercises and other activities that call for repeating but not using what is learned.

If you share the common preference for Rachel's teaching, be aware that it is an ideal to work toward, not an approach that you can expect to implement successfully right away. For one thing, reducing curricular breadth requires enough knowledge of both subject matter and students to enable you to make good decisions about what content to emphasize and what to reduce or delete. It also requires enough personal confidence and administrative support to enable you to follow through on your decisions in an environment that emphasizes coverage standards and testing.

Also, even as you develop the expertise needed to teach like Rachel, you may find yourself in teaching circumstances that make it more challenging to do so. For example, if you teach in the primary grades or have many students with poorly developed reading skills, you might not be able to use methods that call for students to independently read a story or chapter section, discuss it with a partner, and prepare questions and comments. Similarly, you might have to adjust your approach if you have students who cannot yet write fluently, speak English fluently, or collaborate effectively in pairs or small groups. Whatever instructional methods and activities you use, however, you can at least make sure that what your students learn is focused on big ideas developed with attention to their applications to life outside of school.

Sources of Curriculum

Curriculum debates in all school subjects reflect continuing struggles among supporters of four competing ideas about what should be the primary basis for K–12 education (Kliebard, 2004). The first group believes that schools should equip students with *knowledge that is lasting, important, and fundamental to the human experience.* This group typically looks to the academic disciplines, both as storehouses of important knowledge and as sources of authority about how this knowledge should be organized and taught. The second group believes that *the natural course of child development* should be the basis for curriculum planning. This group keys the content taught at each grade level to the interests and learning needs associated with its corresponding ages and stages. The third group works backward from perceptions of *society's needs,* seeking to design schooling to prepare children to fulfill adult roles in the society. Finally, the fourth group seeks to use schools to *combat social injustice and promote social change.* Consequently, it favors focusing curriculum and instruction around social policy issues.

Most textbook authors (and teachers) see value in all four of these ideas about basic aims and purposes of K–12 schooling, so they create curricula that include each of them, but in varying degrees. Many of the differences among curricula reflect differences in the relative emphasis given to these four curriculum sources.

Other differences appear in the ways that the content is represented and developed. Among the most important of these are (1) the degree to which the content consists of broader but shallower coverage of many topics versus deeper coverage of fewer topics and (2) the degree to which the content is organized into connected networks structured around powerful ideas.

*C*ontent Selection and Representation

Recent research indicates that curricula and instruction tend to emphasize breadth at the expense of depth. Critics routinely complain that textbooks offer seemingly endless parades of disconnected facts rather than coherent networks of connected content structured around powerful ideas. Reports of teaching and learning observed in classrooms suggest a similar picture. Although there are exceptions, most of these descriptions portray teachers as hurriedly attempting to cover too much content and students as attempting to memorize as much as they can. Students spend too much time reading, reciting, filling out worksheets, and taking memory tests, and not enough time engaging in sustained discourse about powerful ideas or applying these ideas in authentic activities.

Disconnected factual information is not very meaningful or memorable. If students lack contexts within which to situate their learning and richly connected networks of ideas to enhance its meaningfulness, they have to rely on rote memorizing instead of more sophisticated learning and application strategies. They remember as much as they can until the test, but then forget most of it afterward. Furthermore, most of what they do remember is inert knowledge that they are not able to apply.

Scholars who have studied this problem are in general agreement about what needs to be done to enable students to construct meaningful knowledge that they can access and use in their lives outside of school. First, there needs to be a retreat from breadth of coverage in order to *allow time to develop the most important content in greater depth.* Second, this important content needs to be *taught as networks of connected knowledge structured around powerful ideas.* Instruction should focus on these important ideas and

(handwritten margin notes:)
1. fund. knowledge
2. child develop—
3. society's needs
4. social change

explain the connections among them as well as the ideas themselves. When this approach is implemented effectively, students may also remember more because facts are tied to something that makes sense.

Note, however, that structuring content around powerful ideas does not mean eliminating opportunities to learn important facts or practice needed skills. In their attempts to address the problem of overemphasizing breadth at the expense of depth, educators sometimes move too far in the opposite direction. For example, the National Council of Teachers of Mathematics (NCTM, 1989) initially published a set of standards and teaching guidelines that was exemplary in many respects but overly optimistic about students' ability to learn and be able to apply key concepts and skills primarily by participating in discussions calling for mathematical reasoning. Complaints from teachers led to a revision that called for more initial presentations and subsequent teacher-led reviews of content, as well as more opportunities to practice and apply skills (NCTM, 2000).

Part of your professional decision making as a teacher will involve finding the right balance between breadth and depth to meet the needs of your particular students. Given today's instructional materials, this often will mean developing powerful ideas in more depth, but sometimes it will mean supplying a broader body of information or providing additional practice or application opportunities. After all, shifting from a mile-wide but inch-deep curriculum to an inch-wide but mile-deep curriculum is not a step forward.

Teaching for Understanding, Appreciation, and Application of Knowledge

A content base that features powerful ideas developed in depth and with emphasis on their connections and applications facilitates approaches to teaching like those used by Rachel Dewey, most notably (1) goals of teaching for understanding and application to life outside of school, (2) content presentations structured around key ideas, (3) questions designed to help students develop and communicate about those ideas, and (4) learning activities that carry students through to the full range of intended outcomes.

These principles are part of a general orientation toward teaching that is emphasized by most contemporary educators: teaching school subjects for understanding, appreciation, and life application. We often will refer to this as *teaching for understanding* for short, but bear in mind that this term implies appreciation and life application as well.

Understanding means that students learn both the individual elements in a network of related content and the connections among them, so that they can explain the content in their own words. True understanding goes beyond the ability to define concepts or supply facts. It involves making connections between new learning and prior knowledge, subsuming the new learning within larger networks of knowledge, and recognizing some of its potential applications (Case, 1997; Newton, 2000; Perkins, 1993). *Appreciation* means that students value what they are learning because they understand that there are good reasons for learning it. *Life application* goals are accomplished to the extent that students retain their learning in a form that makes it readily retrievable and usable when needed in other contexts. Goals of teaching for understanding have implications for both curriculum (teach things that are worth learning and can be applied in life outside of school) and instruction (use methods and activities suited to these goals).

Recently, there has been a confluence of theorizing, research, and publication of guidelines by professional organizations, all focusing on what is involved in teaching for understanding. Analyses of these efforts have identified a set of principles that are common to most if not all of them (Bransford, Brown, & Cocking, 1999). These common elements, which might be considered components in a model or theory describing good subject-matter teaching, are shown in Table 9.1.

Teachers who teach for understanding present information, model skill applications, and structure a great deal of discourse surrounding the content. They use questions to stimulate students to process and reflect on the content, recognize relationships among and implications of its key ideas, think critically about it, and use it in problem-solving, decision making, or other higher-order applications. Some of the questions admit to a range of defensible answers, and some invite discussion or debate (e.g., concerning the relative merits of alternative suggestions for solving problems). The teacher encourages students to explain their answers and to comment on classmates' answers, and also capitalizes on "teachable moments" offered by students' comments or questions (by elaborating on the original instruction, correcting misconceptions, or calling attention to implications that are not yet appreciated).

Table 9.1 Common Elements in Teaching for Understanding

1. The curriculum is designed to equip students with knowledge, skills, values, and dispositions that they will find useful both inside and outside of school.
2. Instructional goals emphasize developing student expertise within an application context and focus on conceptual understanding of knowledge and self-regulated application of skills.
3. The curriculum balances breadth with depth by addressing limited content but developing this content sufficiently to foster conceptual understanding.
4. The content is organized around a limited set of powerful ideas (basic understandings and principles).
5. The teacher's role is not only to present information but also to scaffold and respond to students' learning efforts.
6. The students' role is not only to absorb or copy input but also to actively make sense and construct meaning.
7. Students' prior knowledge about the topic is elicited and used as a starting place for instruction, which builds on accurate prior knowledge and also stimulates conceptual change if necessary.
8. Activities and assignments feature tasks that call for problem solving or critical thinking, not simply memory or reproduction.
9. Higher-order thinking skills are not taught as a separate skills curriculum. Instead, they are developed in the process of teaching subject-matter knowledge within application contexts that call for students to relate what they are learning to their lives outside of school by thinking critically or creatively about it or by using it to solve problems or make decisions.
10. The teacher creates a social environment in the classroom that could be described as a learning community featuring discourse or dialogue designed to promote understanding.

Plans for lessons and activities are guided by the overall curriculum goals (phrased in terms of student capabilities to be developed), and evaluation efforts concentrate on assessing the progress that has been made toward accomplishing these goals. Consequently, activities, assignments, and evaluation methods incorporate a much wider range of tasks than workbooks and tests that focus on recognition and recall of facts and definitions.

It remains important for students to develop fluency in basic facts and skills, such as the number facts and mathematical operations involved in addition, subtraction, multiplication, and division. Being able to access and apply these basics effortlessly and "automatically" enables students to address problems flexibly and solve them efficiently. Teaching for understanding includes providing ample opportunity to learn key facts and skills, but embedding as much of the needed practice as is feasible within the context of applying networks of related knowledge. Thus, most reading skills practice is embedded within lessons involving reading and interpreting extended text, most writing skills practice is embedded within activities calling for authentic writing, and most mathematics skills practice is embedded within problem-solving applications.

Also, skills are taught as strategies adapted to particular purposes and situations, with emphasis on modeling the cognitive and metacognitive components involved and explaining the necessary conditional knowledge of when and why the skills would be used. Thus, students receive instruction in when and how to apply skills, along with opportunities to use them.

Knowledge Networks

Traditional curriculum development assumed that instructional strands are hierarchies of knowledge that you must proceed through linearly. Thus, you introduce a topic by beginning at the lowest (knowledge) level and staying there until a complete base of information has been developed, then move to the comprehension level by helping students begin to translate the information into different terms and probe its connections, then move to the application level, and so on. Movement to higher levels occurs only after mastery of lower levels has been accomplished.

Recent theory and research suggest that most curricular content is not organized in such a hierarchical fashion. Instead, it is better viewed as *knowledge networks* that include facts, concepts, and generalizations, along with related values, dispositions, procedural knowledge (implementation skills), and conditional knowledge (of when and why to apply parts of the network).

An important implication of this concept is that one can enter and begin to learn about a network almost anywhere, not just at the low end of a linear hierarchy. When feasible, this makes it easier to couch learning within an applications context and right from the beginning of instruction. For example, you might begin teaching about a mathematical operation by posing a problem that requires it. Or, you might begin a lesson on climate by asking students to speculate about why it often is wet on one side of a mountain range but dry on the other side.

*T*each Important Content in Depth

Teaching for understanding requires "complete" lessons that are carried through to include higher-order applications of content. What such lessons look like varies with grade level and subject matter, but one common element is limiting breadth of content to allow for in-depth teaching of the content that is included. To teach for understanding, you will need both to (1) limit what you try to teach by focusing on the most important content and omitting or skimming over the rest, and (2) structure what you do teach around important ideas and elaborate it considerably beyond what is in the text.

There is no simple formula to follow when making decisions about how to reduce an overly broad curriculum. Among other things, you will need to take into account your own ideas about the basic purposes of schooling, your school district's and your state's guidelines, and what you know about the subject matter, about available teaching resources and learning activities, and about your students' prior knowledge, topic interest, and learning needs.

Many more things are worth teaching than we have time to teach in school, so breadth of topic coverage must be balanced against depth of development of each topic. This is an enduring dilemma that can only be managed in sensible ways, not a problem that can be solved once and for all. Once you have decided which content to emphasize, however, prepare to represent it as knowledge networks structured around powerful ideas, and to develop those ideas in depth.

*F*ocus on Powerful Ideas

The importance of structuring content around powerful ideas has been recognized at least since Dewey (1902, 1938), who viewed powerful ideas as the basis for connecting subject matter to students' prior knowledge in ways that make their learning experiences transformative. Transformative learning enables us to see some aspect of the world in a new way, such that we find new meaning in it and value the experience (Girod & Wong, 2002). When students explore in depth the concept of biological adaptation, for example, they begin to notice aspects of the appearance and behavior of animals that they did not notice before, and to appreciate the ways in which these observed traits have helped the animals to adapt to their environments (Pugh, 2002). They get more out of trips to the zoo, notice things about their pets that they never appreciated before, and so on.

Transformative

Others who have addressed the classical curricular question of what is most worth teaching have reached similar conclusions. Whether they refer to powerful ideas, key ideas, generative ideas, or simply big ideas (Smith & Girod, 2003), they converge on the conclusion that certain aspects of school subjects have unusually rich potential for application to life outside of school—most notably, powerful ideas developed with focus on their connections and applications.

Powerful ideas have several distinctive characteristics. First, they are fundamental to the subject area in general and the major instructional goals in particular. They tend to

Fundamental

cluster in the midrange between broad topics such as transportation and particular items of information such as the fact that the fuel used in airplanes is not the same as the fuel used in cars. Most are concepts, generalizations, principles, or causal explanations. Examples within transportation include the categories of land, sea, and air transportation; the progression from human-powered to animal-powered to engine-powered transportation; the importance of transporting goods and raw materials (not just people); the role of transportation in fostering economic and cultural exchange; and the development of infrastructure to support a given form of transportation once it gets established (e.g., roads, service stations, traffic control mechanisms).

Powerful ideas are embedded within networks of knowledge and connected to other powerful ideas. Teaching about an object, tool, or action principle, for example, ordinarily would include attention to propositional knowledge (knowledge about what it is, why and how it was developed, etc.), procedural knowledge (how to use it), and conditional knowledge (when and why to use it).

Some aspects of a topic are inherently more generative or transformative than others. Powerful teaching about Iowa, for example, would call attention to its salient historical and geographic features, especially those that help explain its current population makeup and economic emphases (e.g., its soils and climate favor farming in general and certain crops in particular; early settlements and economic enterprises were clustered in the eastern part of the state near the Mississippi River). In contrast, there is little or no application potential in teaching about the state's flag, song, bird, and so on.

Note that you cannot improve parade-of-facts curricula simply by replacing their worksheets with better activities; you must first replace the knowledge component with big ideas that can provide a content base capable of supporting better activities (if you doubt this, try designing worthwhile activities based on information about the states' flags, songs, birds, etc.). Big ideas lend themselves to authentic applications, of which many will be generative and even transformative; trivial facts do not.

Also, note that principles of teaching for understanding apply across the full K–12 grade range. Both the content and the methods used to develop it must be suited to the ages of the students, but the result should be a focus on powerful ideas taught for understanding and application (see Box 9.1).

[handwritten margin note: trivial facts do not lend themselves to meaningful activities.]

Authentic Activities

Learning activities and situations are characterized by affordances and constraints. *Affordances* are exploitable opportunities—the potential for thought and action that activities offer. For example, a discussion affords opportunities for students to engage in dialogue about a topic, whereas an essay assignment affords opportunities to organize their thinking and communicate their ideas in writing. *Constraints* are limitations on the range of thinking and action that activities impose. A teacher might constrain a discussion by requiring that students' contributions be polite and on topic, and might constrain an essay assignment by limiting it to 300 words and requiring that each paragraph begin with a clear topic sentence.

Teaching for Understanding in the Early Grades

Primary-grade students have limited firsthand experience or acquired cultural literacy to bring to bear as they participate in lessons, so teachers in these grades must be especially careful to keep the curriculum connected to their students' prior knowledge. Even so, it is just as important for primary students as for older ones to structure the content around powerful ideas and develop it with emphasis on their meanings and applications to life outside of school. For example, consider the topic of shelter. Primary social studies textbooks emphasize that shelter is a basic human need and then go on to illustrate a great variety of shelter forms (tipis, tropical huts, stilt homes, etc.). However, the texts typically say very little about the reasons why people live in these different kinds of homes and nothing at all about advances in construction technology that have made possible the features of modern housing that most American children take for granted. Students often emerge from these units thinking that people from the past or from other societies have inexplicably chosen to live in primitive or strange forms of housing, without appreciating that local responses to shelter needs usually are well suited to the climate and quite inventive given the available construction knowledge, technology, and materials.

Primary-grade units on shelter and other cultural universals (food, clothing, transportation, communication, occupations, government, etc.) will be much more powerful if taught with emphasis on how practices relating to the cultural universal have evolved over time, how and why they vary across societies today, and what all of this might mean for personal, social, and civic decision making. This will expand students' purviews on the human condition and help them to put their familiar environment and society into historical, geographical, and cultural perspective.

Rather than teach only that shelter is a basic human need and that different forms of shelter exist, instruction might help students to understand and appreciate the reasons for these different forms of shelter. Students could learn that shelter needs are determined in large part by local climate and geographical features, and that most housing is constructed using materials adapted from natural resources that are plentiful in the local area. They could learn that certain forms of housing reflect cultural, economic, or geographic conditions (tipis and tents as easily portable shelters used by nomadic societies, stilt homes as adaptation to periodic flooding, high-rises as adaptation to land scarcity in urban areas). They also could acquire a better appreciation of the fact that inventions, discoveries, and improvements in construction knowledge and materials have enabled many modern people to live in housing that offers better durability, weatherproofing, insulation, and temperature control, with fewer requirements for maintenance and labor (e.g., cutting wood for a fireplace or shoveling coal for a furnace) than what was available to even the richest of their ancestors.

These and related ideas would be taught with appeal to students' sense of imagination and wonder. There might also be emphasis on values and dispositions (e.g., consciousness-raising through age-suitable activities relating to the energy efficiency of homes or the plight of the homeless). Development and application might include a tour of the neighborhood (in which different types of housing are identified and discussed) or an assignment calling for students to take home an energy-efficiency inventory to fill out and discuss with their parents. There might also be reading and discussion of children's literature selections on life in the past (e.g., in log cabins on the frontier) or in other societies or about the homeless in our society today, as well as activities calling for students to plan

continued

Box 9.1

Continued

their ideal homes or simulate the thinking involved in making decisions about where to live given certain location and budgetary constrictions.

Similarly, teaching for understanding about clothing would go well beyond distinguishing among business clothes, work clothes, and play clothes and showing colorful pictures of native costumes around the world. Students would learn big ideas such as clothing is designed and worn for purposes that include protection (from the sun and from insects and work hazards, not just cold or precipitation), modesty, decoration, and communication of personal interests and identities (slogans, team logos); improvements over time have produced clothes that are more durable, water repellant, lightweight and convenient to use; cloth is not a solid like leather or plastic but a fabric woven from thread; thread is spun from raw materials, both natural (wool, cotton) and synthetic; regional differences in clothing patterns reflect differences in climate (which determine the yearly cycle of weather patterns and related clothing needs) and in farming (which produces commonly available plant and animal fabric sources).

Teachers might initiate discussion of some of these ideas by showing pictures of people in business, work, and play settings (or in very warm or very cold climates), asking students to notice and talk about the way the people are dressed, and then scaffolding discussion of why they might be dressed so differently in these different settings. As a lead-in to an explanation about cloth being a fabric woven from thread, the teacher might ask students to examine their own clothing carefully, then invite them to speculate about what it is made of and how it is manufactured. Compared to teachers in higher grades, primary-grade teachers usually will spend relatively more time presenting and developing basic content and relatively less time scaffolding discussion (see Chapter 10), but their curricula should display a similar focus on age-appropriate powerful ideas.

Learning activities should embody affordances and constraints that are well matched to the instructional goals and allow students to learn through engagement in authentic tasks. *Authentic tasks* require using what is being learned for accomplishing the very sorts of life applications that justify the inclusion of this learning in the curriculum in the first place. If it is not possible to engage students in the actual life applications that the curriculum is supposed to prepare them for, you can at least engage them in realistic simulations of these applications. Examples of authentic activities are listed in Table 9.2.

Educators who do not distinguish between school subjects and the academic disciplines that inform them sometimes define authentic tasks narrowly as activities that engage students in doing what disciplinary practitioners do (e.g., conducting inquiry using the forms of discourse and the investigatory tools that characterize the discipline). We view K–12 schooling as broad preparation for life in general, not just as induction into the disciplines. This broader view leads to definitions of authentic activities that emphasize life applications (Brophy, 2001; Wells, 1999). Newmann and associates (1996), for example, specified that authentic activities should afford students opportunities to construct knowledge through disciplined inquiry that has value beyond the classroom. Perkins (1993) suggested that mathematics curricula might place more emphasis on probability and statistics relative to quadratic equations, and that social studies curricula might place more emphasis on the roots of ethnic hatreds relative to the details of the French Revolution. In each example, the recommended content would be applicable to life outside of school for people in general, whereas the other content ordinarily would be applicable only by specialists in the disciplines (in this case, mathematics and history).

← useful outside of school

Table 9.2   Authentic Activities

K–3

Math: Apply basic four functions to problems in saving/budgeting money, sharing/dividing treats

Science: Observe and take notes on plant growth and decomposition, events occurring in the class aquarium

Social Studies: Recreate the school day in a nineteenth-century one-room schoolhouse; implement Mini-Society or other economics simulations calling for students to produce, buy, and sell goods and services

Reading: Listen to and discuss story read by teacher; read good children's literature
Writing: Correspond with pen pals; write thank-you notes to classroom visitors

4–6

Math: Develop specifications for a garden or construction project

Science: Monitor air pollution on each of the four sides of the school building; collect and analyze life forms and residues found in a nearby pond

Social Studies: Plan an extended vacation trip, with maps and itinerary; debate whether the American Revolution was justified

Reading: Read genre fiction, discuss and write reactions; learn and apply content-area reading and study skills

Writing: Write poems and short essays for self-expression; keep journals for recording observations and insights

7–12

Math: Apply probabilities to predicting the relative effectiveness of alternative strategies for addressing a problem or issue; use algebra for solving compound interest problems to inform decisions about loans and investments

Science: Apply scientific principles to household engineering problems (spot removal, appliance troubleshooting); develop projects for science fairs and displays

Social Studies: Debate current policy issues, simulate legislative budget debates (e.g., acting as state legislators representing districts with different agendas)

Reading: Read and discuss youth-themed novels; compare and contrast different authors who work in the same genre or different works by the same author

Writing: Compose short stories, term papers, and other research reports

These examples illustrate that authentic activities involve both curricular elements (focusing on content that has potential applications in life outside of school) and instructional elements (developing this content through activities that afford students opportunities to use what they are learning for authentic purposes). Authentic activities do not occur frequently in classrooms (they are often time-consuming), but when they do, they are associated with a variety of positive outcomes (Avery, 1999; Newmann & Associates, 1996).

time consuming

Additional Criteria for Selecting or Developing Learning Activities

Activities that provide opportunities to develop and apply learning are important components of a well-rounded instructional program. However, some activities are pointless or even counterproductive. Much seatwork is just busywork or is defective in ways that make it unlikely to meet its intended objectives. Frequently, assigned tasks are either too easy or too difficult for most students, poorly coordinated with what is being taught at the time, or likely to confuse or mislead students. Osborn (1984) suggested the following eight guidelines for seatwork and workbook tasks.

1. A sufficient portion of these tasks should be related to current instruction.
2. Another portion should provide systematic and cumulative review.
3. Tasks should reflect the most important (and seatwork-appropriate) aspects of what is being taught.
4. Additional tasks should be available for students who need extra practice.
5. Instructions should be clear and easy to follow; brevity is a virtue.
6. Response modes should feature sustained reading and writing (as opposed to circling, underlining, drawing arrows from one word to another, etc.).
7. Cute, nonfunctional, space- and time-consuming tasks should be avoided.
8. Tasks should be accompanied by brief explanations of purpose.

Brophy and Alleman (1991) suggested the following guidelines for selecting or developing learning activities. First, begin with the unit's *major goals* and consider the kinds of activities that would promote progress toward those goals. With clear goals to provide guidance, you can make good decisions about whether to use activities suggested in the manual that accompanies a textbook and about what other activities may need to be included.

For a specific set of goals, a given activity might be: (1) essential; (2) relevant and useful, but not essential; (3) relevant but less useful than other activities that serve the same functions more effectively; (4) tangentially relevant but not very useful because it does not promote progress toward the goals; or (5) irrelevant or inappropriate to the goals. For example, suppose that an American history course is designed to engender understanding and appreciation of the development of American political values and policies.

With these primary goals, a unit on the American Revolution and the founding of the new nation would emphasize the historical events and political philosophies that shaped the thinking of the writers of the Declaration of Independence and the Constitution. Essential activities would call for research, debate, or critical thinking about the issues that developed between England and the colonies and about the ideals, principles, and compromises that went into the construction of the Constitution. Less essential, but perhaps useful activities might include studying more about the thinking of key framers of the

Constitution or about the various forms of oppression that different colonial groups had experienced. Activities that are similar in form but less useful in content would be studying the lives of Paul Revere or other revolutionary figures who are not known primarily for their contributions to American political values and policies, or studying the details of each of the economic restrictions that England imposed on the colonies. Irrelevant to the goals would be activities that focused on the details of particular battles. To the extent that they are time-consuming (e.g., construction of a diorama depicting the battle of Yorktown), such activities not only fail to deliver goal-relevant benefits but also impose costs by reducing the scope and continuity of the goal-oriented aspects of the unit.

[handwritten: primary criteria relevence feasibility cost-effective]

Activities that are not relevant to some courses might be highly relevant to others. For example, courses in military history would be developed with very different goals than those of the course described above, so activities that developed knowledge of particular battles might be very useful or even essential. Ultimately, the potential pedagogical value of activities must be assessed within the context of the major goals that the curriculum is designed to accomplish.

Other primary criteria include *feasibility* and *cost-effectiveness.* Is the proposed activity feasible given students' prior knowledge and the time, space, and equipment that it will require? Do its expected benefits justify its costs in time and effort?

Activities that do not meet the *primary criteria* of goal appropriateness, feasibility, and cost-effectiveness should not even be considered. In selecting from among activities that do meet these primary criteria, you might consider several *secondary criteria:*

1. Students find the activity interesting or enjoyable.
2. The activity provides opportunities for interaction and reflective discourse, not just solitary seatwork.
3. If the activity involves writing, students will compose prose, not just fill in blanks.
4. If the activity involves discourse, students will engage in critical or creative thinking, articulate and defend problem-solving or decision-making approaches, and so on, not just regurgitate facts and definitions.
5. The activity is targeted for students' zones of proximal development; it is not merely an occasion for exercising overlearned skills.
6. The activity focuses on application of important ideas, not incidental details or interesting but ultimately trivial information.
7. As a set, the activities offer variety and in other ways appeal to student motivation (to the extent that this is consistent with curriculum goals).
8. As a set, the activities include many ties to current events or local and family examples or applications.

Teaching for Understanding: Subject-Specific Examples

To help you envision what is involved in teaching for understanding, we will cite examples drawn from each of the four main subject areas. They all involve the key characteristics of developing powerful ideas in depth and engaging students in authentic applications.

[handwritten: powerful idea + authentic application = understanding]

Literacy

Reading.   Teaching literacy for understanding involves shifting from isolated skills practice to "real" reading and writing. Students spend more time reading extended text and
less time filling out worksheets. They often work cooperatively in pairs or small groups,
reading to one another or discussing texts. Instead of the somewhat artificial stories
found in basal reading series, they mostly read genuine literature written to provide
information or pleasure (children's literature, poetry, biography, nonfictional material
about the physical or social world).

They also are taught strategies for regulating and learning from their reading, such
as noting main ideas, monitoring their comprehension by checking their understanding as they go along, stopping to clear up confusion when necessary, and making predictions about where stories are headed or how they are likely to turn out. Teaching
such strategies for content-area reading and text study can improve learning even
among secondary and college students, by teaching them to recognize and make use of
the structuring elements and other features of well-organized text that can guide efforts
to learn from it (Cook & Mayer, 1988).

Research support is especially strong for teaching readers the following strategies:
summarizing the gist of a passage, emphasizing the main ideas; constructing images to
represent visually what the text is describing verbally; using mnemonic devices to help
remember the meanings of new words; generating story grammar analyses or constructing story maps for narrative passages; generating questions to ask oneself about
the meanings and implications of the text; attempting to answer any questions that have
been included in the text as aids to checking for understanding; and activating relevant
prior knowledge by making predictions about the text and by comparing depicted
events with one's own experiences (Pressley et al., 1989). Low achievers in particular
stand to benefit from instruction in self-regulated reading and study strategies.

A large study of literacy teaching in grades 7–12 indicated that advances in students' abilities to bring to bear higher order thinking in responding to literary texts was
related to their opportunities to participate in discussions intended to develop understanding. In contrast to classrooms in which most discourse was recitation in response
to narrow questions seeking correct answers, the discourse in the most successful classrooms more often featured genuine discussion. More of the teachers' questions were authentic ones that did not have pre-specified answers, and more were "uptake" questions
that incorporated what a previous speaker had said. Questions were designed to draw
out students' opinions and bring multiple perspectives to the analyses of texts, reflecting teacher assumptions that all students had worthwhile opinions to share and that
questions should be used primarily for developing understandings rather than for testing what students already know (Applebee et al., 2003).

Writing.   Goals of teaching writing for understanding and application focus on teaching students to use writing for organizing and communicating their thinking to particular audiences for particular purposes, and teaching skills as strategies for accomplishing
these goals. Thus, composition is taught, not as an impersonal exercise in writing a draft
to conform to the formal requirements of a genre, but as communication and personal
craftsmanship calling for developing and revising an outline, developing and revising

successive drafts for meaning, and then polishing into final form. The emphasis is on the cognitive and metacognitive aspects of developing compositions, not simply on writing mechanics and editing.

Mathematics

Reform documents in mathematics education call for teaching for understanding by emphasizing concepts, not computational operations. Fewer problems are addressed, but more time is taken to analyze and discuss these problems, thus engaging students in mathematical reasoning.

Several studies comparing these newer approaches to more traditional approaches have found that reform methods produced better higher-order mathematical thinking and problem solving, coupled with as good or better lower-order mathematical knowledge and computation skills (Carpenter et al., 1999; Hiebert & Wearne, 1992; Soled, 1990; Staub & Stern, 2002). These findings demonstrate that, within limits at least, gains in understanding, appreciation, and strategic application of skills can be achieved through instruction that emphasizes authentic applications over isolated skills practice, without a corresponding reduction in skills development.

Science

Blumenfeld (1992) drew on case studies of fifth- and sixth-grade science teaching to identify practices that promote student thoughtfulness in learning science. The more successful teachers displayed the characteristics shown in Table 9.3.

A well-known approach to teaching that was originally developed for science education is *conceptual change teaching*. It attempts to help students recognize and correct the scientific misconceptions that frequently distort their learning. Posner et al. (1982) suggested that, to convince students to change their understandings of key concepts, teachers must induce dissatisfaction with their existing concepts and help them to see that the new concepts are intelligible, plausible, and fruitful.

For example, a major point in teaching about photosynthesis is that plants make their own food. Grasping this idea is initially difficult for most students because their experiences include the idea that food is taken in from the outside environment. However, plants do not take in any form of food; they manufacture their own food through the photosynthesis process in which they transform light energy from the sun into chemical potential energy stored as food. The matter that they take in during this process (carbon dioxide, water, and soil minerals) is not food because it is not a source of energy. To understand this, students must go through a process of conceptual change in which they abandon their assumptions based on their own eating experiences and shift to the scientific definition of food as potential energy for metabolism.

Anderson and Roth (1989) developed a conceptual-change teaching approach to accomplish these goals. They begin by asking students to define food and food for plants and to respond to a problem. This provides the teacher with information about the students' conceptions and makes the students more aware of them. Next, students are given explanations about different ways of defining food, including the scientific definition of food as energy-containing matter. Then they are asked to address questions that give

Table 9.3 Teaching for Thoughtfulness in Learning Science

Opportunities

- Topic coverage focuses on a few key ideas developed in depth.
- Learning activities relate to these main ideas, focus on application rather than mere verification, and involve engagement in meaningful problems relating to children's experience or to real events.

Instruction

- Clear presentations highlight main points and critical information, take into account students' prior knowledge, and use examples, analogies, and metaphors.
- Presentations build connections by linking with prior knowledge, making relationships among new ideas evident, focusing on similarities and differences among ideas, and showing their applications.
- Presentations include scaffolding in the form of modeling of learning and of metacognitive and problem-solving strategies.

Press (Use of Questions and Feedback)

- Questions focus attention on main ideas.
- Teacher checks understanding by asking comprehension questions, asking for summarization, asking for application, focusing on content rather than procedures, adding higher-level questions to worksheets, and asking for alternative representations of content.
- Teacher draws out student reasoning by probing, asking for justification or clarification, and elaborating on student responses.
- Teacher uses errors to diagnose and clear up misunderstandings.
- Teacher encourages making of connections by asking about relationships of key ideas to prior knowledge, relationships among new ideas, how an activity's procedures relate to its content, and how the results of the activity illustrate main ideas.

Support

- Teacher helps students to accomplish tasks by breaking down problems, simplifying procedures, modeling procedures, or providing models and examples.
- Teacher promotes independence, self-regulation, and cooperation by encouraging students to work together, providing time for planning, asking about students' individual contributions to group work, and asking students whether they agree or disagree with their group's conclusions.

Source: Adapted from Blumenfeld, P. (1992). The task and the teacher: Enhancing student thoughtfulness in science. In J. Brophy (Ed.), *Advances in research on teaching, Vol. 3: Planning and managing learning tasks and activities* (pp. 81–114). Greenwich, CT: JAI.

them a chance to use this new definition to explain everyday phenomena (Is water food? Juice? Vitamin pills? Can you live on vitamin pills alone? Why or why not?). In subsequent activities, students use the scientific definition of food to analyze experimental observations of plants, note similarities and differences between plants and animals, distinguish materials taken into plants from materials made by the plants during photosynthesis, and distinguish between energy-containing and non-energy-containing materials that people consume. They are frequently asked questions that require them to make predictions and explanations about plants. These and other activities build a network of knowledge that prepares students to see the need for and accomplish the desired changes in their thinking about food, photosynthesis, and related topics.

A meta-analysis of studies of conceptual-change approaches to teaching science indicated that these approaches are generally more effective than traditional approaches that do not explicitly build on prior knowledge and address misconceptions. Even so, certain misconceptions are remarkably persistent even when conceptual-change approaches are used (Guzzetti et al., 1993).

Social Studies

The National Council for the Social Studies (1993) published a vision statement that described powerful social studies teaching as meaningful, integrative, value-based, challenging, and active. Elaboration on these five key features emphasized themes of teaching for understanding. Ideas about good teaching in social studies also have been influenced by the research of Newmann (1990, 1992), with its emphasis on in-depth knowledge of content, skills in processing information, and dispositions toward reflectiveness.

Instruction offers depth on a few related topics, and learning activities encourage students to participate in disciplined inquiry by scrutinizing arguments for logical consistency, distinguishing between relevant and irrelevant information and between factual claims and value judgments, using metaphor and analogy to represent problems and solutions, developing and defending positions by referring to relevant information, and making reasoned decisions. These activities develop a set of dispositions that together constitute *thoughtfulness:* a persistent desire that claims be supported by reasons (and that the reasons themselves be scrutinized), a tendency to be reflective by taking time to think problems through rather than acting impulsively or automatically accepting the views of others, a curiosity to explore new questions, and a flexibility to entertain alternative and original solutions to problems.

Newmann identified six key indicators of thoughtfulness observed in high school social studies classes:

1. Classroom interaction focuses on sustained examination of a few topics rather than superficial coverage of many.
2. Interactions are characterized by substantive coherence and continuity.
3. Students are given sufficient time to think before being required to answer questions.
4. The teacher presses students to clarify or justify their assertions, rather than accepting and reinforcing them indiscriminately.
5. The teacher models the characteristics of a thoughtful person (showing interest in students' ideas and their suggestions for solving problems, modeling problem-solving processes rather than just giving answers, acknowledging the difficulties involved in gaining a clear understanding of problematic topics).
6. Students generate original and unconventional ideas in the course of the interaction.

Thoughtfulness scores based on these indicators distinguished classrooms that featured sustained and thoughtful teacher–student discourse not only from classrooms that featured lecture, recitation, and seatwork but also from classrooms in which teachers emphasized discussion but did not foster much thoughtfulness (because they skipped from topic to topic too quickly or accepted students' contributions uncritically).

Teachers with high thoughtfulness scores also tended to make writing assignments that called for higher order thinking from their students and placed more emphasis on long-range dispositional goals than immediate knowledge and skill goals. They conceded that their students were likely to resist higher-order thinking tasks, but they nevertheless emphasized these tasks in their classrooms. This determination paid off: Students identified their classes as more difficult and challenging, but also as more engaging and interesting. Also, teacher thoughtfulness scores were unrelated to entry levels of student achievement.

Newmann's findings provide cause for optimism because they indicate that thoughtful, in-depth treatment that fosters higher-order thinking about social studies topics is feasible in most classrooms (not just those dominated by high achievers) and that teachers with the determination to do so can overcome students' initial resistance to higher-order thinking activities and even bring the students to the point where they see such activities as more engaging and interesting than lower-order recitation and seatwork. Avery (1999) reported similar findings from a study of high school history teachers.

Conceptual change teaching approaches developed for science education also have applications in social studies. In teaching history, for example, goals often include attempts to broaden students' views of major historical events from traditional Eurocentric views to more nuanced views that take into account multiple perspectives (Roth, 1996). Hynd and Guzzetti (1998) used different texts to teach different groups of high school students about Christopher Columbus. One text presented a traditional view, treating Columbus primarily as a hero; a second text presented a revisionist view, depicting him as a bumbling explorer and a cruel, greedy ruler who decimated peaceful and trusting natives; and the third text presented a more balanced account of his good and bad qualities and refuted common misconceptions about him. The balanced text was more effective than the one-sided texts in changing students' attitudes and reducing their misconceptions.

*K*eep the Goals in Sight

To make good decisions about what to teach and how to teach it, you will need to establish worthwhile goals and keep these goals in sight as you develop and implement your plans. This can be difficult, because as curriculum guidelines get translated into separate strands and then become segmented by grade level and by units within grades and lessons with units, the goals that are supposed to guide the entire process sometimes fade into the background, along with many of the originally recognized connections and intended life applications (Brophy & Alleman, 1993). For example, consider the following four social studies goals.

1. *District-Wide Goal.* Prepare young people to become humane, rational, participating citizens in an increasingly interdependent world.

2. *Program-area goal for social studies, K–12.* Enable students to appreciate that people living in different cultures are likely to hold many common values but also some different values that are rooted in experience and legitimate in terms of their own cultures.

3. *Grade-level goal for social studies, grade 1.* Help students to understand and appreciate that the roles and values of family members may differ according to the structure of the family, its circumstances, and its cultural setting.

4. *Unit-level goal for social studies, grade 1.* Help students to understand that families differ in size and composition.

This last, unit-level goal is phrased in purely descriptive, knowledge-level language, and it is trite for a unit goal even at the first-grade level. It makes no reference to the concepts concerning cultures and roles that are referred to in the higher-level goals, nor to the related values and dispositions (multicultural appreciation and citizen participation). Unless the teacher has a coherent view of the purposes and nature of social education, or unless the manual does an unusually good job of keeping the teacher aware of how particular lessons fit within the big picture, the result is likely to be a version of social studies that is long on isolated practice of facts and skills but short on integration and application of social learning.

In this case, students might learn a few obvious generalities about families (they differ in size and composition, they grow and change, and their members work and play together), but not much about variations in family roles across time and culture, the reasons for these variations, or the lifestyle trade-offs that they offer. This will not do much to advance students' knowledge of the human condition, help them put the familiar into broader perspective, or even stimulate their thinking about family as a concept.

To avoid such problems, you will need to identify the capabilities and dispositions that you want to develop in your students throughout the year as a whole and in each of your instructional units. Then you can examine instructional materials in the light of these goals. Begin by reading the student text (i.e., not the teacher's manual, which contains more guidance and information) to note places where additional structuring or input will be necessary to focus students' learning on important ideas. Then study the manual, assessing its suggested questions, activities, and evaluation devices to determine the degree to which they will help students accomplish your primary goals. You may need to augment the text with additional input (or replace it with something else if necessary), skip pointless questions and activities, and substitute other questions and activities.

[handwritten marginal note: start by reading student text]

Teaching for Understanding in an Era of High-Stakes Testing

Education will always be partly an art, but it also should be partly an applied science in which an established collection of validated procedures is gradually expanded and refined in response to gradual advances in its scientific knowledge base. Unfortunately, education in this country has featured strongly advocated calls for relatively extreme measures, typically based on educational or political ideology rather than reputable research. Some of the "reforms" have been ill-conceived and impractical, but essentially harmless. Others have done more harm than good.

In our view, the ongoing high-stakes testing era has been one of the most counterproductive periods in our educational history. At a time when more and more responsibilities have shifted from the family and other social institutions to the school, politicians have been emphasizing "reforms" that feature unrealistic demands and punitive responses to failures to meet them. Initially in many states, and later at the federal level through the No Child Left Behind (NCLB) legislation, schools have been forced to administer more and more tests, with higher and higher stakes attached to students' scores. Unfortunately, this testing emphasis is being extended to the kindergarten and even the preschool levels, undermining traditional early childhood programs' emphasis on enjoyable experiential learning (Stipek, 2006).

Although they are contrary to the spirit of many educational purposes and goals, high-stakes testing policies would be difficult for informed educators to contest if they were based on solid research or demonstrably successful. They are neither. These policies do little if any good and a lot of harm. It is true that mobilizing to prepare students to take high-stakes tests will raise their test scores, but the raised scores do not mean much when the tests are mostly confined to memory for discrete information or disconnected subskills, and the improved scores mostly reflect specific test preparation rather than improved learning across the curriculum as a whole. In Texas, for example, a focus on preparing students to take the state's achievement test succeeded in raising scores on that test, but the students' scores on national assessments, college entrance exams, and the like remained unchanged (Amrein & Berliner, 2003). In high-stakes testing environments, improved test scores no longer have the meaning they had before the stakes were raised.

The benefits of mobilizing to raise test scores are dubious, but the costs are not. Thomas (2005) documented quite a list of what he called "collateral damage" from high-stakes testing: narrowing of the curriculum, both in the sense of cutting back on teaching other subjects to focus on teaching the tested subjects, and in the sense of focusing instruction in the tested subjects on the material likely to be included in the test, at the expense of a richer coverage; the high costs of implementing testing and its consequences (paying for the tests themselves, test administration and scoring, test preparation materials, follow-up tutoring and other remediation materials and activities, etc., eats up a lot of budget and often leads to reduction or elimination of art and music programs, sports teams, and other nonacademic functions of schooling); both teachers and students get bored and frustrated with the heavy focus on test preparation in lieu of a richer curriculum; lower achieving students face the possibility of being retained in the grade for another year in the short run, which markedly increases the likelihood that they will drop out of school in the long run; and a combination of poor fit between the curriculum and the tests, unrealistic expectations, and punitive policies toward schools and students who fail to meet them creates unnecessary anxiety and frustration for all concerned. Even worse, Nichols and Berliner (2005) have documented hundreds of examples of ways that high-stakes testing has been corrupting the nation's schools, including: administrative and teacher cheating (e.g., by "losing" test data from low achievers), student cheating, excluding low achievers from the testing, and misrepresenting dropout rates.

Most of the reform movements that have come and gone in the past were fads supported by ideological rationales but not kept in place by legal mandates. However, even legal mandates will be reversed when they become political liabilities to their sponsors. Because they are so unrealistic and counterproductive, the NCLB legislation and other mandates sustaining the current high-stakes testing overkill are likely to disappear before long, or at least to be reshaped into something more sensible. Perhaps at that point, the nation will be ready for research-based guidance on curriculum and instruction.

So What Can You Do in the Meantime?

In the meantime, you will have to negotiate some kind of compromise between teaching for understanding and preparing students for high-stakes tests. You cannot ignore curriculum standards, tests, and the pressures associated with them, but there is no need to view them as the complete curriculum or to focus narrowly on test preparation. You can act responsibly to prepare your students for achievement tests, yet embed these efforts within a powerful instructional program.

Case studies reported by Wills (in press) illustrate how some teachers have coped with high-stakes testing pressures. Wills observed in middle-grade classrooms following mandated increases in the instructional time allocated to literacy and mathematics (the focus of the state's high-stakes testing program). The school's principal left it up to individual teachers to decide how they would accommodate this mandate. One teacher eliminated physical education, reasoning that her students had greater needs for rich science and social studies curricula. Most teachers, though, reduced the time allocated to science and social studies to less than half of what it had been before.

Teachers who had been teaching a barren curriculum simply persisted with this approach, except that now they required their students to read and answer questions about textbook chapters at home, so they could spend most class time going over the answers. Meanwhile, teachers who understood the value of thoughtful discourse scrambled to find ways to retain this emphasis while still addressing the full range of prescribed content.

The most successful teacher eliminated or reduced coverage of content she deemed less important, so that her units still included discussions and other activities that asked students to analyze, interpret, or apply their learning to address challenging problems or issues. She made time for this by skipping certain chapters of the textbooks and eliminating the need to work through other chapters by providing her students with succinct summaries of key facts and main ideas. Although she expected her students to read relevant chapters for background and occasionally exposed them to videos or other input sources, her classroom discussions were focused on the material contained in her handouts, which briefly and clearly covered the important information she thought her students needed to know. Her solution was not completely satisfactory, but it did enable her to sustain a focus on big ideas and thoughtful classroom discourse.

SUMMARY

Good teaching features goals of understanding, appreciation, and application. When it is successful, students can explain what they have learned in their own words and connect it to their prior knowledge, appreciate its value because they know that there are good reasons for learning it, and apply it to their lives outside of school. Preparation for such teaching begins with selection of content worth teaching and representation of this content within connected networks structured around powerful ideas. The teaching then focuses on developing these big ideas in depth and with emphasis on their connections and applications. It includes sustained discourse on the meanings and implications of the ideas and authentic activities that provide students with application opportunities.

Planning and implementing such a curriculum require limiting its scope in order to allow time for developing the most important content in depth. Unfortunately, the content found in most K–12 textbooks typically is described as mile-wide but inch-deep, a parade of facts, or trivial pursuit. Furthermore, the recent emphasis on high-stakes testing has created additional pressures toward breadth of coverage (in the subjects included in the testing program). As a result, unless you are willing to teach a barren curriculum focused on test preparation, you will need to take proactive steps to limit the scope of your curriculum and structure your development of the topics that you do cover around powerful ideas and authentic activities. This chapter elaborated issues to consider in making such decisions and emphasized that teaching for understanding is possible even in the current high-stakes testing environment.

SUGGESTED ACTIVITIES AND QUESTIONS

1. Teaching for understanding requires reducing breadth of coverage so as to be able to develop the most important content in greater depth. This creates dilemmas for teachers who are caught between their desire to develop important topics and their felt responsibilities to cover a broader range of content. Focusing on grades at which you teach or intend to teach, interview several teachers about how they respond to this dilemma.

2. Focusing on particular grades and school subjects, interview teachers to determine what they consider to be authentic activities for their students. To what extent do they use similar criteria and identify similar activities? Do they actually use these authentic activities in their teaching, or do they rely more on worksheets and other less authentic assignments? If the latter, why?

3. Examine samples of K–12 textbooks that you use now or likely will use in the future. Do they present networks of connected knowledge structured around powerful ideas, or just parades of disconnected facts? What does this suggest about your use of such texts with students?

4. For each subject that you teach or plan to teach, establish a file of authentic activities that will allow your students to use what they are learning in the process of conducting inquiry, solving problems, or making decisions. Be prepared to use these activities in place of those suggested in the manuals that accompany your curriculum materials, whenever the latter are not worth using.

5. What is the difference between teaching the "main idea" as a concept and teaching about how identifying and focusing on main ideas can be a useful strategy for guiding one's efforts to learn with understanding? What does this imply about your teaching about main ideas, regardless of whether you teach reading to your students?

6. We suggested that there might be limits on the degree to which one could emphasize authentic applications over skills practice without experiencing reductions in skills development. What might these limits be? In the subjects that you teach, are there certain things that simply must be memorized or practiced repeatedly? If so, why?

7. Can you relate the goals and objectives of each of your lessons and activities to larger purposes and goals? Can you see how each lesson or activity contributes to the long-run development of knowledge, skills, values, and dispositions that school subjects ostensibly are designed to develop? Test yourself by selecting a few lessons and activities at random and seeing whether you can explain to others' satisfaction why they are needed in the curriculum. If you have trouble doing this, you may need to think through larger purposes and goals and keep them in mind as you develop your teaching plans.

8. Review and revise (as necessary) the statements you made after reading Chapter 1, when you attempted to identify teaching behaviors and characteristics that are signs of effective teaching. How much has your view of effective teaching changed?

9. Reread the descriptions of the approaches to teaching taken by Laura Hirsch and Rachel Dewey, then write a description of how you intend to teach. How does your approach compare to theirs? What do you conclude from this?

FORM 9.1. Teaching Content for Understanding and Application

USE: When you have detailed information about the curriculum, instruction, and evaluation enacted during a content unit or strand.
PURPOSE: To assess the degree to which the teacher teaches content not just for memory but for understanding and application.
       Enter a check mark for each of the following features that was included effectively in the content unit or strand, and a zero for each feature that was omitted or handled ineffectively. Then add detailed comments on a separate sheet, emphasizing constructive suggestions for improvement.

CHECKLIST

_____   1. *Goals* were expressed in terms of long-term student outcomes (acquisition of knowledge, skills, values, or dispositions to be applied to life outside of school), not just in terms of short-term content mastery.

_____   2. Limited content was taught in sufficient *depth* to allow for development of understanding.

_____   3. The *knowledge* content was represented as *networks* of related information structured around powerful key ideas.

_____   4. In presenting and leading discussions of the content, the teacher helped students to recognize the centrality of key ideas and to use them as bases around which to structure larger content networks.

_____   5. In addition to providing explicit explanations, the teacher asked questions and engaged students in activities that required them to process the information actively, test and if necessary repair their understanding of it, and communicate about it.

_____   6. *Skills* (procedural knowledge) were taught and used in the process of applying information (propositional knowledge) content rather than being taught as a separate curriculum.

_____   7. Most skills practice was embedded within inquiry, problem solving, decision making, or other whole-task application contexts rather than being limited to isolated practice of part skills.

_____   8. If skills needed to be taught, they were taught with emphasis on modeling their strategic use for accomplishing particular purposes, as well as explaining when and why the skills would be used.

_____   9. Content-based *discourse* emphasized sustained and thoughtful discussion featuring critical or creative thinking about key ideas, not just fast-moving recitation over specifics.

_____   10. *Activities and assignments* called for students to integrate or apply key ideas and engage in critical and creative thinking, problem solving, inquiry, decision making, or other higher-order applications, not just to demonstrate recall of facts and definitions.

_____   11. In *assessing* student learning, the teacher focused on understanding and application goals, not just low-level factual memory or skills mastery goals.

Active Teaching

*I*n Chapter 9, we addressed issues related to the *curriculum* part of curriculum and instruction. We now turn to the *instruction* part. Here in Chapter 10 we discuss research relating teacher behavior to student achievement and its implications about the role of the teacher in actively presenting information to students, involving them in interactive discourse, and engaging them in learning activities and assignments. In Chapter 11 we will discuss constructing understandings through social interaction. These ideas imply a need to modify traditional teaching methods so as to create more opportunities for students to construct understandings through productive interactions with the teacher and their classmates. This once again illustrates that teacher decision making, guided by clear goals, is the key to effective instruction.

*I*nstructional Methods as Means to Accomplish Curricular Goals

There are many different approaches to teaching. Joyce, Weil, and Calhoun (2003) described over twenty-five approaches, classified into four types—information processing, social interaction, personal, and behavioral. *Information-processing approaches* organize instruction to present material so that learners can process and retain it most easily. They also attempt to foster students' information-processing skills. *Social approaches* stress the group-living aspects of schooling. Instruction is arranged so that students learn from one another as well as the teacher, who focuses on fostering group relations as well as on instruction. *Personal approaches* draw on humanistic psychology to promote intellectual and emotional development (self-actualization, mental health, creativity). *Behavioral approaches* sequence activities to promote efficient learning and shape behavior through reinforcement. Most of the approaches commonly recommended as methods for teaching subject matter are either information-processing approaches or social approaches.

Specific teaching methods are useful for accomplishing certain purposes in certain situations. No one method is optimal for all purposes in all situations. Using a single method all the time would foolishly treat method as an end in itself rather than as a means of accomplishing one's instructional goals.

A method is most effective when used as part of a coherent instructional program that is *goal oriented*—designed to accomplish clear goals that are phrased in terms of student capabilities to be developed. A goal-oriented program features alignment among the goals themselves and each of the program's components: the content selected for focus; the organization, sequencing, and representation of this content; its elaboration and application during lessons, activities, and assignments; and the methods used to evaluate learning.

Achieving alignment among the elements in an instructional plan requires teacher decision making about goals and methods. Only certain methods are suited to particular goals; other methods are irrelevant or even counterproductive. Given appropriate goals and content, the primary planning task is to identify the combination of methods that is most likely to accomplish the goals. If several methods seem equally appropriate, you might choose on the basis of secondary criteria such as personal preference, student responsiveness, availability of materials, or cost in time and effort.

It may seem obvious that curriculum planning should be goal oriented and feature alignment among its elements, but this ideal model is not often implemented. Teachers typically plan by concentrating on the content and activities, without giving much consideration to goals (Clark & Peterson, 1986). In effect, they leave decisions about goals to the companies who supply their textbooks. This would not be so bad if the texts were clearly goal-oriented and featured alignment among their elements. However, analyses of these texts typically conclude that too many topics are not covered in enough depth; content exposition often lacks coherence; skills are taught separately from knowledge content rather than integrated with it; and, in general, there is little development of key ideas and use of these ideas in ways that help students accomplish major instructional goals (Beck & McKeown, 1988; Brophy, 1992b; Jones, 2000; Squires, 2005).

To achieve coherent programs of curriculum and instruction, you probably will have to elaborate on, eliminate, or even substitute for much of the content in your texts and many of the activities suggested in the manuals. Adjustments also may be needed for reasons other than coherence. For example, the textbook series adopted by an elementary school may align well with the state's mandated goals and assessment test in grades K–4 but not grades 5 and 6. Making good adjustments requires good knowledge of the content as well as familiarity with many instructional methods and awareness of when and why to use them.

Unfortunately, debates about methods are often reduced to false dichotomies (phonics method versus whole-word method, didactic instruction versus discovery learning), as if only two choices were available. Worse, they often imply that there is one best way to teach, when we know that different situations and goals call for different methods.

Research Relating Teacher Behavior to Student Learning

Teachers' decisions about instructional methods need to be informed by research, especially studies of relationships between processes (what the teacher and students do in the classroom) and outcomes (changes in students' knowledge, skills, values, or dispositions). Two forms of process-outcome research are school effects research and teacher effects research.

School Effects Research

School effects research involves correlating process and outcome measures for entire schools. The outcome measures are usually adjusted gain scores on standardized achievement tests. The process measures usually include school-level measures (administrative leadership, school climate) and classroom-level measures (teachers' attitudes and practices). The latter are averaged across teachers to produce a score for the school as a whole. Most school effects studies have focused on basic skills instruction, especially in schools serving socioeconomically disadvantaged populations. Also, most have been correlational rather than experimental, so their findings are subject to multiple interpretations.

Still, it is useful to know that several characteristics are observed consistently in schools that elicit good achievement gains: (1) strong academic leadership that produces consensus on goal priorities and commitment to excellence; (2) a safe, orderly school climate; (3) positive teacher attitudes toward students and expectations regarding their abilities to master the curriculum; (4) an emphasis on instruction (not just on filling time or on nonacademic activities) in using time and assigning tasks to students; (5) careful monitoring of progress toward goals through student testing and staff evaluation programs; (6) strong parent involvement programs; and (7) consistent emphasis on the importance of achievement, including praise and public recognition for students' accomplishments (Cotton, 2000; D'Agostino, 2000; Good & Brophy, 1986; Reynolds et al., 2002; Teddlie & Reynolds, 2000). School improvement programs based on these findings have yielded significant gains in student achievement (Freiberg et al., 1990; Stringfield & Herman, 1996).

These school-level factors may impact what you will be able to achieve at the classroom level. For example, in some schools teachers are encouraged to exchange ideas, which makes it easier for them to learn about new teaching methods. When interviewing for a teaching position, consider school-level factors that might support or hamper your performance.

Teacher Effects Research

Process-outcome research at the classroom level has been done in more grades, in more subjects, and with a broader range of students than school effects research, although it also has concentrated on basic skills instruction. The following are the most widely replicated findings (Brophy & Good, 1986; Chall, 2000; Cotton, 2000; Galton et al., 1999; Gettinger & Stoiber, 1999; Good, 1996; Pellegrini & Blatchford, 2000; Stevens, 1999; Waxman & Walberg, 1991).

Teacher Expectations/Role Definition/Sense of Efficacy.   Teachers who elicit strong achievement gains accept responsibility for teaching their students. They believe that the students are capable of learning and that they (the teachers) are capable of teaching them successfully. If students do not learn something the first time, they teach it again (in a different way, if necessary), and if the regular instructional materials do not do the job, they find or make other ones. In general, they display the qualities recommended in Chapter 2.

Student Opportunity to Learn.   These teachers allocate most of their available time to instruction. Their students spend many more hours each year engaged in academic activities than do students of teachers who are less focused on instructional goals. Furthermore, their mix of learning activities allows their students not just to memorize but to understand key ideas, appreciate their connections, and explore their applications (Blumenfeld, 1992; Taylor et al., 2003).

Classroom Management and Organization.   These teachers organize their classrooms as effective learning environments and use group-management approaches that maximize the time their students spend engaged in lessons and learning activities (see Chapters 3 and 4).

Curriculum Pacing.   These teachers move through the curriculum rapidly but in relatively small steps that minimize student frustration and allow continuous progress.

Active Teaching.   These teachers instruct actively by demonstrating skills, explaining concepts and assignments, conducting participatory activities, and reviewing when necessary. They teach their students rather than expect them to learn mostly on their own by reading texts and working on assignments. However, they do not stress merely facts or skills; they also emphasize understanding and applications. As students' self-regulation skills increase, they are encouraged to assume more responsibility for managing their own learning.

Teaching to Mastery.   Following active instruction on new content, these teachers provide opportunities for students to practice and apply it. They monitor each student's progress and provide feedback and remedial instruction as needed, making sure that the students master key content goals.

A Supportive Learning Environment.   Despite their strong academic focus, these teachers maintain pleasant, friendly classrooms and are perceived as enthusiastic, supportive instructors.

An Example

Table 10.1 shows an active teaching model for fourth-grade mathematics instruction. Its principles were suggested by correlational studies and then tested through experimental studies. Teachers who implemented the model elicited greater achievement gains than control teachers who used methods they had developed on their own. The model calls for teaching mathematics for about forty-five minutes each day, supplemented with homework assignments. New concepts are presented in detail during the development portion of the lesson, and the teacher makes sure that students know

Table 10.1 Summary of Key Instructional Behaviors

Daily Review (first 8 minutes except Mondays)

1. Review the concepts and skills associated with the homework
2. Collect and deal with homework assignments
3. Ask several mental computation exercises

Development (about 20 minutes)

1. Briefly focus on prerequisite skills and concepts
2. Focus on meaning and promoting student understanding by using lively explanations, demonstrations, process explanations, illustrations, and so on
3. Assess student comprehension using
   a. Process/product questions (active interaction)
   b. Controlled practice
4. Repeat and elaborate on the meaning portion as necessary

Seatwork (about 15 minutes)

1. Provide uninterrupted successful practice
2. Momentum—keep the ball rolling—get everyone involved, then sustain involvement
3. Alerting—let students know their work will be checked at the end of the period
4. Accountability—check the students' work

Homework Assignment

1. Assign on a regular basis at the end of each math class except Fridays
2. Should involve about 15 minutes of work to be done at home
3. Should include one or two review problems

Special Reviews

1. Weekly review/maintenance
   a. Conduct during the first 20 minutes each Monday
   b. Focus on skills and concepts covered during the previous week
2. Monthly review/maintenance
   a. Conduct every fourth Monday
   b. Focus on skills and concepts covered since last monthly review

Source: Good, T., & Grouws, D. (1979). The Missouri Mathematics Effectiveness Project: An experimental study in fourth-grade classrooms. *Journal of Educational Psychology, 71,* 821–829.

how to do an assignment (by asking them to demonstrate their knowledge) before releasing them to work on it individually. The assignment is reviewed the next day. The combination of active teaching, opportunity to practice and receive feedback, and frequent testing helps ensure continuous progress (for details, see Good, Grouws, & Ebmeier, 1983).

Instructional models must be adapted to the subject matter, the students, and other contextual factors. For example, Sigurdson and Olson (1992) adapted the fourth-grade model shown in Table 10.1 for use in eighth-grade units on geometry and on fractions, rates, and ratios. The adaptation, which achieved successful results, combined the daily lesson organization features of the active teaching model with some of the curriculum content features associated with efforts to teach mathematics for meaningful understanding (see Chapter 9).

These examples illustrate that although classroom research provides support for instructional principles of varying generality, it cannot identify specific techniques that are ideal for all students and situations. Different learning objectives (mastering well-defined skills versus applying them to problem solving or using them creatively) require different instructional methods. Furthermore, other kinds of objectives (promoting the personal development of individuals or the social development of the group) require still other methods. Finally, at any given time, a given instructional strategy may be better suited to some students than others (Connor, Morrison, & Katch, 2004; Connor, Morrison, & Petrella, 2004). Research can inform you about the relationships between teacher behavior and student outcomes, but you must decide what outcomes you wish to promote and in what order of priority.

The volume of process-outcome studies has slowed in recent years, but this work has continued to document the benefits of active instruction by the teacher (Connor, Morrison, & Katch, 2004; Connor, Morrison, & Petrella, 2004; Kroesbergen, Opdenakker, & VanDamme, 2006; Waxman et al., 1997; Weinert & Helmke, 1995). The rest of this chapter will elaborate the principles involved in accomplishing three basic components of active teaching: presenting information, developing understandings through interactive discourse, and structuring activities and assignments. In the next chapter, we consider methods of assisting students' efforts to construct meaning from these experiences. We have separated our treatment of curricular and instructional issues into three chapters (9–11) for analytic purposes, but bear in mind that planning and teaching about most topics requires integrated application of the principles put forth in each of these chapters.

Presenting Information to Students

Presenting information to the whole class is an efficient way to expose students to content. It allows the teacher to focus the material taught, is easily combined with other methods, and is adjustable to fit the available time, the physical setting, and other situational constraints. Presentation of information is part of the active teaching pattern that is associated with strong achievement gains. Note, however, that most teacher presentations (especially in the early grades) are short ones interspersed with student questions or activities, not extended lectures. In this section, we offer guidelines about when and how to present information to students.

When to Present Information

Despite its continuing popularity, educators have always been ambivalent about information presentation, especially when it is stereotyped as "the lecture method" (Henson, 1996; Johnson & Johnson, 1999; McLeish, 1976). The approach has been criticized for several reasons:

1. Lectures deny students the opportunity to practice social skills.
2. Lectures imply that all students need the same information.
3. Lectures often exceed students' attention spans, so they begin to "tune out."
4. Lectures only convey information; they do not develop skills or dispositions.
5. Students can read facts on their own, so why not use class time for other activities?

These points are well taken. Most of us have known teachers whose lectures were ineffective because they were too frequent and too long. However, these criticisms reflect overuse or inappropriate use of information presentation, not problems inherent in the method itself. If the content is well organized, up to date, and presented appropriately, the method has much to recommend it. Effective presentations provide students with information that would take hours for them to collect on their own, so why force them to search for it when a presentation will allow them to get it quickly and then move on to application or problem solving? The important question is not "Should we present information?" but "When should we present information?" Various authors (Gage & Berliner, 1998; Henson, 1996) have suggested that information presentation is appropriate when:

- The objective is to present information
- The information is not available in a readily accessible source
- The material must be organized in a particular way
- It is necessary to arouse interest in the subject
- It is necessary to introduce a topic before students read about it on their own or to provide instructions about a task
- The information is original or must be integrated from different sources
- The information needs to be summarized or synthesized (following discussion or inquiry)
- Curriculum materials need updating or elaborating
- The teacher wants to present alternative points of view or to clarify issues in preparation for discussion
- The teacher wants to provide supplementary explanations of material that students may have difficulty learning on their own
- The teacher wants to emphasize key concepts in lengthy chapters

These points also are well taken. Good presentations at these times do seem preferable to available alternatives. Also, many of the criticisms can be addressed without abandoning the approach itself. For example, to allow students to learn actively and develop social skills, teachers could give short presentations (perhaps fifteen minutes) to structure problems and provide necessary information, then break the class into small problem-solving groups. Also, interesting, enthusiastic presentations can stimulate interest and raise questions that students will address in follow-up activities.

How to Present Information

Information presentation is an *appropriate* method if used for the purposes outlined above. How *effective* it is will depend on the care and skill with which the material is prepared and delivered. Effective presentations (1) begin with advance organizers or previews that include general principles, outlines, or questions that establish a learning set; (2) briefly describe the objectives and alert students to new or key concepts; (3) present new information with reference to what students already know about the topic, proceeding in small steps sequenced in ways that are easy to follow; (4) elicit student responses regularly to stimulate active learning and ensure that each step is understood before moving to the next; (5) finish with a review of main points, stressing general integrative concepts; and (6) are followed by questions or assignments that require students to encode the material in their own words and apply or extend it to new contexts. Other guidelines include: focus on a few main points rather than attempting to cover too much; supplement the verbal content with appropriate facial expressions and gestures and with visuals or props; and display an outline of the main points or distribute a handout that will help students to follow the structure of the presentation (Bligh, 2000; Chilcoat, 1989; Duffy et al., 1986; Goldin-Meadow, Kim, & Singer, 1999; Roth, 2001).

Adding multimedia elements to presentations is generally a good idea, because students learn better from words and visuals than from words alone. However, it is important not to overload students' information-processing capacities. They learn better when a presentation is pared to its essential elements than when it contains interesting but irrelevant words, pictures, sounds, or music (Mayer, Heiser, & Lonn, 2001; Moreno & Mayer, 2000). PowerPoint and other recent technologies often are misused in these ways (and, as noted in Chapter 13, Powerpoint presentations can encourage students to be nonreflective note takers rather than active listeners).

Two key features of good presentations are the *clarity* of the information and the *enthusiasm* with which it is presented.

Clarity

Clarity is essential if students are to understand concepts and assignments. McCaleb and White (1980) identified five aspects of clarity that observers can attend to in classrooms:

1. *Understanding.* This prerequisite to clarity involves matching the new information to the learners' prior knowledge. Does the teacher
   - Determine students' existing familiarity with the information?
   - Use terms that are unambiguous and within the students' experience?
2. *Structuring.* This involves organizing the material to promote a clear presentation: stating the purpose, reviewing main ideas, and providing transitions between sections. Does the teacher

- Establish the purpose of the lesson?
- Preview the organization of the lesson?
- Provide internal summaries of the lesson or elicit these from students (e.g., "So what have we learned so far?")?

3. *Sequencing*. This involves arranging the information in an order conducive to learning, typically by gradually increasing its difficulty or complexity. Does the teacher order the lesson in a logical way, appropriate to the content and the learners?

4. *Explaining*. When explaining principles and relating them to facts through examples, illustrations, or analogies, does the teacher
   - Define major concepts?
   - Give examples to illustrate these concepts?
   - Use examples that are accurate and concrete as well as abstract?

5. *Presenting*. This refers to volume, pacing, articulation, and other speech mechanics. Does the teacher
   - Articulate words clearly and speak loudly enough?
   - Pace the presentation at rates conducive to understanding?
   - Support the verbal content with appropriate nonverbal communication and visual aids?

Making the Structures Clear. Ausubel's (1963) concept of advance organizers is useful in thinking about how to structure presentations. *Advance organizers* tell students what they will be learning before the instruction begins. For example, a physical education instructor could begin a presentation on hockey penalties as follows: "Today we are going to discuss penalties. We will discuss the differences between minor and major penalties and describe fifteen minor penalties and five major penalties. Then, I will show you twenty slides and ask you to name the penalty illustrated and state whether it is major or minor. Then tomorrow we can use our new skills. We will view a DVD of a real NHL game with the referees' calls edited out, and you will call the penalties."

Advance organizers give students a structure within which they can assimilate the specifics presented by a teacher or text. Without such a structure, the material may seem fragmented, like a list of unrelated sentences. A clear explanation of the nature of the content helps students to focus on the main ideas and order their thoughts effectively. Therefore, begin by letting your students know what they can expect to learn from a presentation and why it is important to know it. Afterward, summarize the main points or ask questions to elicit a summary from students. A clear introduction and strong summary help students remember essential facts and concepts (Luiten, Ames, & Ackerson, 1970; Meichenbaum & Biemiller, 1998; Schuck, 1981).

For extended presentations, periodic *internal summaries* of subparts may be needed in addition to a major summary at the end. Rosenshine (1970) discussed the "rule-example-rule" approach, in which a summary statement is given both before and after a series of examples. He also stressed the importance of "explaining links"—words and phrases such as "because," "in order to," "if . . . then," "therefore," and "consequently" that make explicit the causal linkages between phrases or sentences. These linkages might not be clear without such language. For example, consider the following two sentences:

1. Chicago became the major city in the Midwest and the hub of the nation's railroad system.
2. Because of its central location, Chicago became the hub of the nation's railroad system.

The first example presents relevant facts but does not link them explicitly, as the second example does. If asked, "Why did Chicago become the hub of the railroad system?" most students taught with the second example would respond, "Because of its central location." However, many students taught with the first example would respond "Because it is a big city," or in some other way that indicated failure to appreciate the linkage between a city's geographical location and the role it plays in a nation's transportation system.

Using Clear Language.   In addition to problems with their organizational structure, presentations can lack clarity because of vague or confusing language. Smith and Land (1981) reviewed studies indicating that the effectiveness of presentations is reduced by the presence of vagueness terms and mazes. They identified nine categories of *vagueness terms*:

1. Ambiguous designation (somehow, somewhere, conditions, other)
2. Negated intensifiers (not many, not very)
3. Approximation (about, almost, kind of, pretty much, sort of)
4. "Bluffing" and recovery (actually, and so forth, anyway, as you know, basically, in other words, to make a long story short, you know)
5. Error admission (excuse me, I'm sorry, I guess, I'm not sure)
6. Indeterminate quantification (a bunch, a couple, a few, a lot, a little, some, several)
7. Multiplicity (aspects, kinds of, sort of, type of)
8. Possibility (chances are, could be, maybe, perhaps)
9. Probability (frequently, generally, often, probably, sometimes, usually)

The following example indicates how vagueness terms (italicized) can distract from the intended message.

This mathematics lesson *might* enable you to understand *a little more* about *some things we usually call* number patterns. *Maybe* before we get to *probably* the main idea of the lesson, you should review a *few* prerequisite concepts. *Actually,* the first concept you need to review is positive integers. *As you know,* a positive integer is any whole number greater than zero.

Mazes refer to false starts or halting speech, redundantly spoken words, or tangles of words. The mazes are italicized in the following example:

This mathematics lesson will *enab . . .* will get you to understand *number, uh,* number patterns. Before we get to the *main idea of the,* main idea of the lesson, you need to review *four conc . . .* four prerequisite concepts. A positive *number . . .* integer is any whole *integer, uh,* number greater than zero.

In addition to looking for such problems in teachers' presentations, observers can study the effects of the presentations on students. The students' facial expressions, and especially their questions or responses to the teacher's questions, should indicate that they have acquired the intended understandings. Frequent evidence of student confusion or misunderstanding suggests problems in teacher clarity (see Gliessman et al., 1989, for information about a training program for increasing clarity). Teachers who do not have access to observers can assess the clarity of their presentations by studying students' notes or interviewing students to assess their understandings (see McCaslin & Good, 1996).

Enthusiasm

When teachers are enthusiastic about a subject, students are likely to develop enthusiasm of their own, and ultimately to achieve at higher levels (Patrick, Hisley, & Kempler, 2000; Rosenshine, 1970). Teacher enthusiasm includes at least two major aspects. The first is conveying sincere interest in the subject. This involves modeling, and even shy teachers can demonstrate it (Cabello & Terrell, 1994). The second aspect is dynamic vigor. Enthusiastic teachers are alive in the room; they show surprise, suspense, joy, and other feelings in their voices and they make material interesting by relating it to their experiences and showing that they themselves are interested in it.

Encouraging Student Questions

Students typically ask very few questions during lessons. You can encourage them to do so by using techniques observed in a teacher known for her openness to students' questions. This teacher gave quick answers to some questions (mostly about procedures) and declined to address others because they would divert the discourse from its intended goals. However, she responded more fully to most questions, especially if they addressed an important issue not mentioned previously. If the question was unanswerable in its current form (How much money do they get from taxes?) or based on faulty assumptions (How does the governor pick the capital?), she would rephrase it or ask for clarification before proceeding (both to improve the curricular value of the question and to protect the questioner from embarrassment). She viewed students as well-intentioned learners who ask questions because they want to understand. Realizing that seemingly silly and lower-level questions often have the potential to generate useful discussion, she gave students the benefit of the doubt when she was unsure about their motivation in asking questions. In responding, she focused on the question's possibilities for productive follow-up (Beck, 1998).

Encouraging questions is especially important at the beginning of the term, because some of your students' previous teachers may have discouraged questions or allowed them only at certain times. Warm encouragement of questions shows students that you view them as co-participants and need their questions to help you teach well.

Embedding Information Presentation within Narrative Formats

We have noted that teachers' information presentation, especially in elementary and middle schools, usually does not involve extended and uninterrupted lecturing. Instead, presentation occurs in shorter segments interspersed with questioning of students, inviting their questions or comments, or engaging them in brief activities that allow them to talk about or apply the information presented so far. In these examples, information presentation is embedded within interactive formats.

Another way for teachers to avoid the overly formal kind of lecturing that is not well suited to the learning needs of most students is to embed much of their information presentation within narrative (storytelling) formats. Most young learners do not yet possess a critical mass of cognitive development and domain-specific knowledge to enable them to comprehend and use the disciplinary content structures and associated discourse genres that are used in teaching subjects at relatively abstract and advanced levels. Nor are they able to learn efficiently by reading. Yet, it is just as important for younger students as for older ones to learn from curricula featuring networks of knowledge structured around big ideas. To do this, teachers need to stick to aspects of the content that can be made meaningful to students because they can be connected to their existing knowledge, and especially to their personal experiences.

It also helps if teachers convey this content using text structures and discourse genres with which students already have some familiarity (and preferably, some fluency). One especially useful tool that meets these criteria is the narrative structure, because even the youngest students are already familiar with it through exposure to stories. They are adept at using narrative modes of thinking for describing and remembering things that are important to them. That is, they formulate and remember in story form. The narrative format provides a natural way for them to remember a great many of the details used to fill out the story, organized within the goal-strategy-outcome narrative structure or "story grammar" (Bruner, 1990; Downey & Levstik, 1991; Egan, 1990).

This makes the narrative format a powerful vehicle to use in helping students bridge from the familiar to the less familiar. Children can understand information about the long ago and far away if it is represented as stories of people pursuing goals that they can understand by doing things that they have done themselves. Just as they can understand fictional creatures (e.g., Hobbits) and worlds (e.g., Harry Potter's) conveyed through narrative formats, they can understand stories about the discoveries of scientists or about life in the past or in other cultures. Many aspects of science and social studies are amenable to representation within narrative structures, especially those that involve human actions that occur in steps, stages, or series of events unfolding over time.

A teacher familiar to one of the authors typically uses narrative approaches to establish a common base of knowledge when introducing new science and social studies topics to her primary grade students. She typically begins with stories drawn from her own life, selected not just because they relate to the topic but because they offer opportunities to highlight big ideas or life applications. Then she draws connections to her students' lives (e.g., family emigrations from or vacations taken to countries that will be featured in the lesson, jobs held by family members that connect to products or services to be discussed) or to local examples (farm products, stores, etc.). Having grounded the content in the students' experiences, she then develops a knowledge base structured around big ideas, typically rendered in an informal, storytelling style, often making additional personal or local connections in the process.

Her frequent use of I- and you-language rather than impersonal third-person language gives these narrations a more authentic feel than traditional lecture/explanations, and her frequent references to what "you" might do helps keep students aware of potential life applications. She often uses objects or photos as props, especially if introducing something unfamiliar, and she routinely uses rich imagery and examples to build "word pictures" of what she is describing. She also frequently inserts invented dialogue or mini-dramatizations—fictional but realistic conversations that might have taken place between people living at the time and place under study, or even the thinking (self-talk) that might have been carried out by a single individual (such as an inventor).

Her narratives are engaging as well as informative, but she is careful to keep them focused around big ideas. She does not carry dramatization further than it needs to go (she might don a hat to signify that she is temporarily personifying a character, but she does not use elaborate costumes); she does not use unnecessary props (ordinarily, there is no need to show apples, cars, or other familiar objects, unless she wants to stimulate her students to think about them in unusual ways); and she uses instructional resources only for as long as they are needed and for the purposes for which they were included (e.g., if she wants to show an illustration from a book, she shows and discusses the illustration with reference to the ongoing lesson, but then puts the book aside rather than interrupt the lesson to read the book at this time or to look at other illustrations that are not as relevant). She concludes her initial narrative presentation with a summary review, then shifts from a narrative to a questioning or application mode.

Embedding presentations within this kind of storytelling approach offers several advantages in addition to the ones already mentioned. It removes much of the distance between the teacher as authority figure or expert and the students as learners, shifting the tone from formal lecturing to sharing of inside information about how the world works. It also creates a greater sense of intimacy or "we-ness" between the teacher and students and helps build personal relationships within the learning community. Finally, because it is her own presentation rather than a presentation from a text, it allows the teacher to adapt it to her students' needs and interests, to focus on the big ideas that she views as most important to emphasize (while at the same time omitting a lot of trivial or irrelevant details), and to build connections as she goes (both among the big ideas and between these ideas and her students' prior experiences).

Effective Demonstrations

When learning processes and skills, students need not only verbal explanations but also physical demonstrations. It is important for you to learn to demonstrate effectively, as you may have discovered if you sought out a friend or relative for driving lessons or instructions about how to cook a complicated dish. Professional instructors teach these skills with ease and efficiency, but most other people do not, even if they are able to drive or cook very well.

What's the trick? Expert instructors tailor their demonstrations to learners' needs. They demystify the process not only by showing the physical movements involved but also by verbalizing the thinking that guides these movements. Their explanations emphasize general principles rather than the particular applications that apply to the example at hand. As a result, learners acquire strategies that they can use intelligently and adapt to varying situations, not just fixed routines learned by rote and applied without variation.

Expert instructors break processes down into step-by-step operations. They define each term they introduce and point to each part as they label it. They describe what they are going to do before each step and then talk through the step as they perform it. They give corrections in a patient tone so the learner can concentrate on the task and not worry about looking inept.

The same principles apply to teachers' demonstrations of new academic skills (e.g., word decoding, mathematical problem solving, research and report writing, use of laboratory equipment) and instructions for assignments. A good demonstration proceeds as follows:

1. Focus attention. Be sure that all students are attentive before beginning. If relevant, focus their attention by holding up an object or pointing to where you want them to look.
2. Give a general orientation or overview. Explain what you are going to do, so that students can get mentally set to observe the key steps.
3. If new objects or concepts are introduced, label them. If necessary, have the students repeat the labels. Students cannot follow an explanation if they do not know what some of the words mean.
4. Go through the process step by step. Begin each new step with an explanation of what you are going to do, and then describe your actions as you do them. Think out loud throughout the demonstration.
5. If necessary, perform each action slowly with exaggerated motions.
6. Have a student repeat the demonstration so you can observe and give corrective feedback. If the task is short, have the student do the whole thing and give feedback at the end. If it is longer, break it into parts and have the student first do one part at a time, then combine the parts.
7. In correcting mistakes, do not dwell on the mistake and the reasons for it, but instead redemonstrate the correct steps and have the student try again.

Thinking out loud at each step is crucial, especially when the task is primarily cognitive. While you demonstrate physical procedures such as pouring into a test tube, writing a number on the board, or making an incision, describe how you are filling the test tube to the 20 ml line, carrying two 10 units and adding them to the 10s column, or starting your incision at the breast bone and stopping short of the hip bones. Unless you verbalize the thinking processes that guide what you do and how you do it, some students may learn no more from watching your demonstration than they would from watching a magician perform a baffling trick.

If a demonstration is lengthy, help students follow it by summarizing its subparts and noting the transitions between parts. If continuity is broken by student questions or discussion, reestablish the desired learning set by reminding the students of the overall structure of the presentation and of the place at which it is being resumed.

Developing Understandings through Interactive Discourse

Besides being able to make effective presentations, you will need to learn to plan good sequences of questions that will help your students to develop understanding of content and provide them with opportunities to apply it. Teacher–student discourse occurs in a variety of formats. At one extreme is the *drill* or fast-paced *review* that is designed to test or reinforce students' knowledge of specifics. Here, the emphasis is on obtaining "right answers" and moving at a brisk pace. At the other extreme is *discussion* designed to stimulate students to respond diversely and at high cognitive levels to what they have been learning. Here, the pace is slower and the emphasis is on developing understanding and pursuing implications. Higher-level questions that admit to a range of possible answers are used to engage students in critical or creative thinking. In between reviews and discussions are *question-based content development* activities that vary in pace and cognitive level of question. They include the questioning and response segments that occur between teacher presentation segments, as well as most activities that teachers refer to as "going over the material" or "elaborating on the text."

Educational critics often speak warmly of discussion but criticize drill and even content development as boring, unnecessarily teacher dominated, restricted to low-level objectives, and tending to make students passive and oriented toward producing right answers rather than thinking. Clearly, content should not be developed in ways that create such problems. Many of the problems result from inappropriate use of the method, however, and thus can be minimized or avoided.

Like teacher presentation, content development persists as a common approach to instruction because it has certain legitimate uses and is in some respects well suited to classroom teaching (Farrar, 1986). It allows the teacher to work with the whole class at one time, provides students with opportunities to learn from one another as well as from the teacher, is an efficient way to enable students to practice and receive immediate feedback on their learning of new content, is a convenient way for teachers to check on student understanding before moving on, and is much easier to manage than individualized instruction. Thus, as with information presentation, the operative question is not whether to use question-based content development, but when and how to use it effectively.

Questions as Scaffolds for Learning

The more effective forms of questioning are blended with information presentation within lessons that develop students' understanding of a topic's most important ideas. Questions are asked not only to monitor comprehension but also to stimulate students to think about the content, connect it to their prior knowledge, and begin to explore its applications.

Thus, unless activities are explicitly intended as review or preparation for tests, they ordinarily should not take the form of rapidly paced drills or attempts to elicit "right answers" to miscellaneous factual questions. Instead, such activities should be means for engaging students with the content they are learning. Questions should stimulate students to process that content actively and "make it their own" by rephrasing it in their own words and considering its meanings and implications. Questions should focus on the most important elements and guide students' thinking toward key understandings. The idea is to build an integrated network of knowledge structured around powerful ideas, not to stimulate rote memorizing of miscellaneous information. Questions are devices for teaching, not just for testing.

In the next section, we review advice about questioning techniques offered by various authors. Most of it is based not only on process-outcome research but also on logical analyses of the characteristics of different types of questions and their appropriateness to different instructional goals (Beyer, 1997; Carlsen, 1991; Dantonio & Beisenherz, 2001; Dillon, 1988, 1990; Wilen, 1991).

Cognitive Levels of Questions

Questioning is among the easiest of teacher behaviors to observe and code reliably. Some investigators have used classifications such as fact versus thought questions or convergent versus divergent questions. Others have used categories based on the Taxonomy of Educational Objectives. In its original version (Bloom et al., 1956), the taxonomy identified six cognitive process levels: *Knowledge* questions were classified as low in cognitive demand; *comprehension* and *application* questions as intermediate; and *analysis, synthesis,* and *evaluation* questions as high. A revision of the taxonomy (Anderson & Krathwohl, 2001) also identified six cognitive processes, according to whether the students are asked to (1) remember, (2) understand, (3) apply, (4) analyze, (5) evaluate, or (6) create. Questions calling for students to engage in synthesis to create new understandings are now considered a higher level of response demand than questions that only require students to evaluate what they have read or heard.

So far, research findings based on such classifications have been mixed and relatively uninformative about when and why different kinds of questions should be used. For example, higher-order questions are intended to elicit higher-order responses, but students often respond at a lower cognitive level than the question called for. Also, it is not true that higher-order or complex questions are always better than lower-order or simpler questions, that thought questions are always better than fact questions, or that divergent questions are always better than convergent questions (Dantonio & Beisenherz, 2001).

Varying combinations of lower-order and higher-order questions will be needed, depending on the goals you are pursuing. Certain types of questions are useful for arousing interest in a discussion topic, but other types are needed to stimulate critical thinking about the topic or to see whether students have attained the intended understandings.

You will need to plan *sequences of questions* designed to help students develop connected understandings. Sequences that begin with a higher-level question and then proceed through several lower-level follow-up questions are appropriate for purposes such as asking students to suggest possible applications of an idea and then probing for details about how these applications might work. However, sequences featuring a series of lower-level questions followed by a higher-level question would be appropriate for purposes such as calling students' attention to relevant facts and then stimulating them to integrate these facts and draw a conclusion.

Issues surrounding the cognitive level of questions should take care of themselves if sequences of questions are planned to accomplish worthwhile goals that are integral parts of well-designed units of instruction. However, plans will need to be revised if the questions appear to be random test items or if the questions are all at the knowledge level when the activity is supposed to stimulate students to analyze or synthesize what they have been learning.

Questions to Avoid

Groisser (1964) identified four types of questions that often lead to underproductive responses: (1) yes-no questions, (2) tugging questions, (3) guessing questions, and (4) leading questions.

Yes-No. Yes-no questions typically are asked only as warm-ups for other questions. For example, the teachers asks, "Was Hannibal a clever soldier?" After a student answers, the teacher says, "Why?" or "Explain your reason." Groisser claimed that the initial yes-no questions confuse the lesson focus and waste time, so it is better to ask the real question in the first place.

We see two additional dangers in yes-no questions or other questions that only require a *choice between two alternatives* ("Was it Hamilton or Jefferson?"). First, such questions encourage guessing because students will be right 50 percent of the time, even when they have no idea of the correct answer. If asked such questions frequently, they are apt to try to "read" the teacher for clues about which answer is correct instead of concentrating on the question itself.

Also, choice questions have *low diagnostic power*. Because of the guesswork factor, responses to these questions do not reveal much about students' understandings. Choice questions sometimes are useful for low-achieving or shy students, to provide a warm-up that can help them respond better to more substantive questions that follow. Ordinarily, however, these questions should be avoided.

Tugging. Tugging questions or statements ("What else?" "Yes . . . ?") often follow a halting or incomplete response. They say "Tell me more" but provide no help to the student, so they may be perceived as nagging or bullying.

When students answer correctly but incompletely, you are more likely to elicit an improved response if you ask new, more specific questions. For example, if your initial question was, "Why did the Jamestown settlers live in a fort?" a student might respond, "To protect themselves from the Indians and from animals." If you wanted to focus on the advantages of community living, your next question should cue the student in this direction: "What advantages did they gain from living in a group?"

Guessing. Some questions require students to guess or reason to generate an answer, either because they do not have the facts ("How many business firms have offices on Wall Street?") or because the question has no single correct answer ("If Columbus hadn't discovered America in 1492, what European explorer would have, and when?"). Guessing questions can be useful in capturing students' imagination and involving them in discussions. However, if used inappropriately, they encourage students to guess thoughtlessly rather than think carefully. Guessing questions are useful primarily as parts of larger strategies for helping students to think about what they are learning.

Leading.   Avoid leading questions ("Don't you agree?") and other rhetorical questions ("You want to read about the Pilgrims, don't you?"). *Ask questions only if you really want a response.* Your students should develop the expectation that when you ask a question, something important and interesting is about to happen.

Characteristics of Good Questions

Although the complete definition of a good question depends on context, certain general guidelines can be applied. Groisser (1964) indicated that good questions are (1) clear, (2) purposeful, (3) brief, (4) natural and adapted to the level of the class, (5) sequenced, and (6) thought provoking.

Clear.   Questions should specify the points to which students are to respond. Vague questions can be responded to in many ways (too many), and their ambiguous nature confuses students. For example, Groisser wrote:

> If a teacher of Spanish wished to call attention to the tense of a verb in a sentence on the board and asked, "What do you see here?" the student would not know exactly what was being called for. Better to ask, "What tense is used in this clause?"

Vague questions often result in wasted time as students ask the teacher to clarify the specific attack point. Questions also can be unclear if they are asked as part of an uninterrupted series. Groisser writes of a teacher who,

> in discussing the War of 1812 asks, in one continuous statement, "Why did we go to war? As a merchant, how would you feel? How was our trade hurt by the Napoleonic War?" The teacher is trying to clarify his first question and to focus thinking on an economic cause of the war. In his attempt, he actually confuses.

This teacher should have asked a clear, straightforward question initially ("What was the cause of the War of 1812?"), waited for a response, and then probed for economic causes if the response failed to mention them.

Questions should cue students to respond along specific lines. This does not mean that you cue the answer; it means that you communicate the specific question to which you want the student to respond.

Purposeful.   Purposeful questions help achieve the lesson's intent. Advance planning is helpful here. Such planning should not be too rigid, because it may be worth pursuing an unanticipated teachable moment opened up by a student's question or comment. Still, it is worth remembering that teachers who improvise most of their questions ask many irrelevant and confusing questions that work against achievement of their own goals.

Brief.   Keep your questions brief. Long questions are often unclear or difficult to understand.

Natural. Phrase your questions in natural, simple language (as opposed to pedantic, textbook language) that is adapted to the level of the class. If students do not understand a question, they cannot engage in the kind of thinking that you intend to stimulate.

We do not mean that you should avoid unfamiliar words. Students benefit from learning new words and from exposure to modeling of sophisticated verbal communication. However, take into account your students' vocabularies. When you introduce new words, clarify their meanings and engage students in using the words within application contexts.

Sequenced. If questions are intended as teaching devices and not merely as oral test items, they should be asked in planned sequences, and the answers to each sequence should be integrated with previously discussed material before moving on. Initial questions might lead students to identify or review essential facts. Then, you might ask the students to refine their understandings and apply them to authentic problems ("Now that we have identified the properties of these six types of wood, which would you use to build a canoe?"). Alternatively, you might initiate a problem-solving or decision-making discussion by first posing a question or issue to be addressed, then eliciting suggested resolutions, and then engaging students in critical thinking about the trade-offs that each of the suggested resolutions offers.

The sequence and the meaningfulness of information exchange are critical here, not the cognitive level of each individual question. For example, Table 10.2 shows how a sequence of relatively low-level factual questions can lead students to understand the events that led to the Boston Tea Party and appreciate that those events can be viewed from different perspectives. Key information is tied to the concepts of monopoly and representative taxation, and the questions help students to understand the historical significance of events. For example, "What was the tea worth?"—a simple fact question—will help students to realize that in colonial times tea was quite valuable. The fact that the colonists were willing to dump the tea into the harbor rather than taking it home indicated how outraged they were. Similarly, the question, "Who participated in the Boston Tea Party?" will develop awareness that a wide range of citizens was involved.

In the unreasonable sequence shown in Table 10.3, the fact questions are often trivial and are not used to develop a thoughtful examination of what the Boston Tea Party represented. Questions about the number of ships in the harbor or how the colonists were dressed may allow the teacher to evaluate whether a student has read the book

Table 10.2   A Reasonable Questioning Sequence

1. What was the Boston Tea Party?
2. What events preceded the Boston Tea Party?
3. What is a monopoly?
4. Under what conditions might a monopoly be justified?
5. Do we provide favorable circumstances for certain industries in this country that make it difficult for foreign countries to compete?
6. What did the Boston Tea Party mean to British citizens? To American citizens?
7. Who participated in the Boston Tea Party?
8. How much was the tea worth?

Table 10.3   An Unreasonable Sequence

---

1. What was the Boston Tea Party?
2. How many ships containing tea were in the harbor?
3. How did the colonists dress when they entered the ships to destroy the tea?
4. Define Townshend Duties.
5. Define Coercive Acts.
6. Who was Thomas Hutchinson?
7. On what date did the Boston Tea Party occur?'

---

carefully, but they fail to develop important points. It is usually counterproductive to emphasize such trivial details. The questions evaluating knowledge of the Townshend Duties and Coercive Acts might have been productive if used to place the Boston Tea Party within the context of its antecedents and its subsequent effects, but in this sequence these questions merely test for knowledge of disconnected facts.

Distinctions among the cognitive levels of questions can help you think about the cognitive demands that you place on students, but you need to plan sequences of questions designed to develop purposeful discussion of a topic. A good set of questions is good not merely because it contains a significant percentage of higher-level questions but also because it helps students to think about the topic systematically and emerge with connected understandings.

Thought Provoking.   Good questions are thought provoking. Especially in discussions, questions should arouse strong, thoughtful responses from students, such as, "I never thought of that before," or "I want to find the answer to that question." Discussion should help students to clarify their ideas and to analyze or synthesize what they are learning. Fact questions often are needed to establish relevant information, but subsequent questions should stimulate students to respond thoughtfully to the information and use it rather than just recite it.

Calling on Students to Respond to Questions

Groisser (1964) suggested that questions should be addressed to the whole class, distributed widely, asked conversationally, and sometimes reflected to allow students to respond to classmates' answers. Addressing questions to the class involves first asking the question, then allowing students time to think, and only then calling on someone to respond. This makes everyone responsible for generating an answer. If instead you name a student to respond before asking the question or call on a student immediately after doing so, only the student whom you named is responsible for answering. Other students are less likely to try to answer it for themselves.

There are three special situations in which you might want to call on a student before asking a question: (1) drawing an inattentive student back into the lesson, (2) asking a follow-up question of a student who has just responded, and (3) calling on a shy student who may be "shocked" if called on without warning.

Wait Time.   Students need time to think, but optimal wait time varies with the question and the situation. Rowe (1974a, b) reported findings that at the time seemed remarkable: After asking questions, the teachers she observed waited an average of less than one second before calling on a student to respond. Furthermore, they also waited only about a second for the student to give the answer before supplying it themselves, calling on someone else, rephrasing the question, or giving clues. These teachers minimized the value of their questions by failing to give their students time to think.

time to think please!

Rowe followed up by training teachers to extend their wait times. Surprisingly, most found this difficult to do, and some never succeeded. However, in the classrooms of teachers who extended their wait times to three to five seconds, the following changes occurred:

- Increase in the average length of student responses
- Increase in unsolicited but appropriate student responses
- Decrease in failures to respond
- Increase in speculative responses
- Increase in student-to-student comparisons of data
- Increase in statements that involved drawing inferences from evidence
- Increase in student-initiated questions
- A greater variety of contributions by students

wow!

Longer wait times led to more active participation by a larger percentage of the students, coupled with an increase in the quality of this participation. Subsequent research verified that increasing wait time leads to longer and higher-quality responses and participation by a greater number of students (Rowe, 1986; Swift, Gooding, & Swift, 1988; Tobin, 1983). These changes are most notable among low achievers.

Subsequent research also verified that many teachers are reluctant to extend their wait times because they fear that if they do, they will lose student attention or even control of the class (Kennedy, 2005). This is one of the continuing dilemmas that require teacher decision making and adjustment to immediate situations. Longer wait times are generally preferable because they allow more thinking by more students, but you may have to use shorter wait times when the class is restive or when time is running out and you need to finish the lesson quickly.

The appropriateness of pacing and wait time depends on the objectives of the activity. A fast pace and short wait times are appropriate when reviewing specific facts. However, if your questions are intended to stimulate students to think about material and formulate original responses, you need to allow time for these effects to occur. Students may need several seconds to process complex or involved questions before they can begin to formulate responses to them.

Make it clear to students when you want a slow pace and thoughtful responding. Unless cued, some of them may not realize that they are supposed to formulate an original response rather than search their memories for something taught to them explicitly, and some may think that you are looking for speed rather than quality of response.

Findings on level of question and wait time have informed our suggestions about lesson pacing, teacher expectations, student opportunity to learn, and related topics. We have emphasized that teachers should scaffold students through the curriculum as fast as they are able to progress, but move in steps that are small enough to minimize student frustration and allow continuous progress. We now add other qualifications: In discussing curriculum pacing, we assume a well-rounded curriculum that includes sufficient attention to the full range of cognitive objectives, as well as to skill and disposition objectives. This implies that classroom discourse will frequently take the form of slower-paced discussions of higher-level questions, and not be restricted to fast-paced recitation formats (Cotton, 2000).

Distributing Questions to a Range of Students.   Distribute response opportunities widely rather than allow a few students to answer most of your questions. Students benefit from opportunities to practice oral communication skills, and distributing response opportunities helps keep them attentive and accountable. Also, teachers who interact primarily with a small group of active (and usually high-achieving) students are likely to communicate undesirable expectations and be generally less aware and less effective.

In this regard, make it clear that you expect all students to participate by responding to questions and contributing to discussions. You may need to socialize reticent students to do so and take special steps to scaffold their participation. For example, you might have these students prepare for discussions by writing questions or issues to raise; have them begin by discussing in pairs before shifting to the whole-class format; or include activities designed to prepare students for the next day's lesson as part of the previous day's homework (Wilen, 2004).

[handwritten margin note: Tips to get students participating →]

Feedback about Responses.   Feedback is important both to motivate students and to let them know whether their responses are correct. Yet, teachers often fail to give feedback, especially to low achievers (Brophy & Good, 1974). Sometimes this is appropriate, such as when ideas are being "brainstormed" for later evaluation or the discussion involves exchanges of opinion on questions that do not admit to right and wrong answers. When an answer is either correct or incorrect, however, this information needs to be conveyed.

Unless it is understood that no response indicates correctness, you should give some sort of acknowledgment every time students answer such questions. Feedback need not be long or elaborate, although sometimes it has to be. Often a head nod or short comment like "Right" is all that is needed. Also, you do not always have to provide feedback personally. You can provide access to answer sheets that allow students to assess their own work or arrange for students to provide feedback to one another.

A Conversational Tone.   A common problem with questions to avoid is that they make the teacher appear more interested in quizzing students than in developing understandings (Roby, 1988). This is especially likely to occur when teachers' subject-matter knowledge is weak, so they stick closely to the textbook and ask too many questions that call for students to regurgitate what it says (Cunningham, 1997; Lapadat, 2000). The result is what Carlsen (1997) called an "inquisitorial atmosphere." Questioning students in harsh terms threatens their security and makes it difficult for them to think fluidly. In contrast, questions that present interesting challenges and invite friendly exchanges of views are likely to maximize motivation and yield productive responses.

That is what Groisser (1964) meant when he suggested that questions should be asked conversationally. He also suggested that allowing students to respond to one another is helpful:

Many teachers seize upon the first answer given and react to it at once with a comment or with another answer. . . . It is more desirable, where possible, to ask a question, accept two or three answers, and then proceed. This pattern tends to produce sustaining responses, variety, and enrichment. It encourages volunteering, contributes to group cooperation, and approaches a more realistic social situation.

Such techniques model teacher interest in the exchange of information about a topic (as opposed to pushing for a particular answer) and indicate that there is not always a single correct answer. Also, students are likely to listen more carefully to one another if they are occasionally called on to respond to one another's answers.

Conducting Discussions

Interactive discourse occurs frequently in classrooms, but it seldom takes the form of discussions in which the teacher and students share opinions in order to clarify issues, relate new knowledge to their prior experience, or attempt to answer a question or solve a problem (Alvermann, O'Brien, & Dillon, 1990; Applebee et al., 2003; Tharp & Gallimore, 1988).

Hyman and Whitford (1990) indicated that discussions might be held for at least five worthwhile purposes: (1) *debriefing* discussions that engage students in reflecting on the understandings developed in a shared activity; (2) *problem-solving* discussions focused on attempting to find solutions to problems; (3) *explanation* discussions in which teachers encourage students to describe and analyze a situation in order to develop understanding of why a phenomenon, rule, or policy exists; (4) *prediction* discussions designed to consider probable consequences of an event or action; and (5) *policy* discussions in which students are encouraged to develop and justify stands on public issues.

Wilen (1990) described how a lesson might begin with teacher presentation and content development to establish an initial base of knowledge, then proceed to guided discussion designed to develop understanding, and culminate with reflective discussion in which students synthesize and evaluate information, opinions, and ideas. Compared to question-based content development, *guided discussion* involves more open-ended questions, more responses from several students to the same question, more student-initiated questions and comments, and more probing of initial responses to clarify students' thinking. As the discourse moves toward *reflective discussion*, students engage in more divergent, critical, and creative thinking as they hypothesize solutions, devise plans, predict outcomes, solve problems, judge ideas and actions, and make decisions. Here, you are not so much trying to move the students toward predetermined ends as to engage them in an exchange of views about the meanings and implications of what they have been learning.

To conduct discussions, teachers must adopt a different role from the one they play in developing content, when they act as the primary source of information and the authority figure who determines whether answers are correct. Teachers lead discussions by establishing a focus, setting boundaries, and facilitating interaction, but in other respects they assume a less dominant and less judgmental role. Even if a discussion begins in a question-and-answer format, it should evolve into an exchange of views in which students respond to one another as well as to the teacher and respond to statements as well as to questions.

If ideas are being collected, the teacher should record them (listing them on the board or computer screen) but should not evaluate them. Once the discussion is established, the teacher may wish to participate in it periodically in order to point out connections between ideas, identify similarities or contrasts, request clarification or elaboration, invite students to respond to one another, summarize progress achieved so far, or suggest and test for possible consensus as it develops. However, the teacher does not push the group toward some previously determined conclusion (this would make the activity guided discovery rather than discussion).

The pace of discussions is slow and includes periods of silence that provide opportunities to consider what has been said and formulate responses to it. Dillon (1988, 1990) illustrated that teachers' statements can be just as effective as questions for producing lengthy and insightful responses. Questions even may impede discussions at times, especially if they are perceived as attempts to test students rather than to solicit their ideas. To avoid this problem, Dillon (1979) listed six alternatives to questioning that you can use to sustain discussions.

1. *Declarative statements.* In discussing the effects of war on the domestic economy, you might respond to a student's statement by saying, "When the war broke out, unemployment dropped," rather than by asking "What happens to the unemployment rate in wartime?" The statement provides information that the students have to accommodate and respond to; compared with the question, however, it invites longer and more varied responses.

2. *Declarative restatements.* You can show that you have attended to and understood what students have said by summarizing occasionally. Such summarizing may be useful to the class as a whole, and reflecting students' statements to them may stimulate additional and deeper responding.

3. *Indirect questions.* When a direct question might sound challenging or rejecting, you can make a statement such as, "I wonder what makes you think that" or "I was just thinking about whether that would make any difference." Such indirect questions might stimulate further thinking without generating anxiety.

4. *Imperatives.* Similarly, statements such as, "Tell us more about that" or "Perhaps you could give some examples" are less threatening than direct requests for the same information.

5. *Student questions.* Rather than asking all of the questions yourself, you can encourage students to ask questions in response to statements made by classmates.

6. *Deliberate silence.* Sometimes the best response to a statement is to remain silent for several seconds to allow students to absorb the content and formulate follow-up questions or comments.

In summary, if you expect an activity to involve genuine discussion, make this fact clear to students and alter your own behavior accordingly.

Structuring and Scaffolding Activities and Assignments

There are three main ways that teachers help their students to learn. First, they explain, demonstrate, model, tell stories, or in other ways present information. Second, they interact with students in discourse surrounding the content. Third, they engage students in activities or assignments that provide them with opportunities to practice or apply what they are learning (and in the process, provide coaching, task-simplification strategies, or other forms of scaffolding that may be needed to enable students to complete the activities successfully). Only limited research is available on activities and assignments (Brophy, 1992a), even though students often spend half or more of their time in school working independently (Fisher et al., 1980).

Process-outcome research suggests that independent seatwork is probably overused and is not an adequate substitute either for active teacher instruction or for discussion opportunities. This is especially the case when the seatwork emphasizes time-consuming but low-level tasks. Other research suggests that activities and assignments should be varied and interesting enough to motivate student engagement, new or challenging enough to constitute meaningful learning experiences rather than pointless busywork, and yet easy enough to allow students to achieve high rates of success if they invest reasonable effort.

The effectiveness of assignments is enhanced when teachers explain the work and go over practice examples with students before releasing them to work independently. Once students are released, the work goes more smoothly if teachers circulate to monitor progress and provide help when needed. If the work has been well chosen and explained, most of these "helping" interactions will be brief, and at any given time, most students will be progressing through an assignment rather than waiting for help.

Teachers should monitor performance for completion and accuracy and provide students with timely and specific feedback. When performance is poor, teachers will need to provide not only feedback but reteaching and follow-up assignments designed to ensure that the material is understood.

Structuring and Scaffolding Students' Learning

Teachers who elicit strong achievement gains actively scaffold their students' learning rather than expecting the students to learn primarily from curriculum materials. In a study of mathematics teaching, for example, the more effective teachers' lessons typically followed a three-phase pattern. In the first phase, teachers would demonstrate a new concept or skill and in the process explain, ask many questions, check for understanding, or conduct discussions. The second phase was a "helping" phase in which students gradually made the transition from teacher regulation to self-regulation. During this phase, teachers closely monitored student work and provided help in the form of feedback or additional instruction, or else arranged for the students to work together in pairs or small groups and get feedback or help from their peers. The teachers didn't require students to apply new knowledge independently until they had demonstrated an ability to do so successfully. The third phase of independent work and individual accountability typically made up just a small percentage of lesson time. In contrast to this three-phase pattern, less effective teachers used a two-phase pattern in which they first demonstrated how to do something new while the students watched, then assigned students to spend the rest of the period working problems on their own (Dixon et al., 1998).

Even well-chosen activities need to be effectively presented, monitored, and followed up if they are to have their full impact. This means preparing the students for the activity in advance, providing guidance and feedback during the activity, and structuring post-activity reflection afterward (Brophy & Alleman, 1991).

In introducing activities, stress their purposes in ways that will help students to engage in them with clear ideas about the goals they are trying to accomplish. Talk about purposes and goals may need to be supplemented by statements or questions that call students' attention to relevant background knowledge, modeling of strategies for responding to the task, or scaffolding that will simplify the task for the students (Ferretti, MacArthur, & Dowdy, 2000).

You can scaffold by providing information or help concerning how to complete task requirements. If reading is part of the task, for example, you might summarize the main ideas, remind students about strategies for developing and monitoring their comprehension as they read (paraphrasing, summarizing, taking notes, questioning themselves to check understanding), or provide them with advance organizers that will help them to approach the material in the intended ways. If necessary, provide additional scaffolding in the form of partial outlines or skeletal notes for students to fill in while listening to a presentation or reading an assignment (Kiewra, 1987), study guides that call attention to key ideas and structural elements, or task organizers that help students to keep track of the steps involved and the strategies they are using to complete these steps. For example, if you were discussing careers in a seventh-grade life science class, you might distribute the outline presented in Table 10.4 as a way to help students to take notes effectively.

Once students begin working on activities and assignments, monitor their progress and provide assistance if necessary. Besides keeping these interventions short for the classroom management reasons described in Chapter 3, you ordinarily should provide only minimal forms of help at these times. That is, assuming that students have a general understanding of what to do and how to do it, you should help them past rough spots by providing relatively general and indirect hints or cues. If your assistance is too direct or extensive, you will end up doing tasks for students instead of scaffolding to enable them to do the tasks themselves.

When providing feedback to students working on assignments and when leading subsequent reflection activities, ask questions or make comments that help students to monitor and reflect on their learning (including the strategies they used to process the content or solve problems). Good questions and comments help students to refine their strategies and more systematically regulate their learning (Matsumura et al., 2002).

Instructional elements designed to help students become self-regulated learners are especially important for struggling students. These students usually do not develop effective learning and problem-solving strategies on their own, but they can acquire them through modeling and explicit instruction from their teachers. Poor readers, for example can be taught reading comprehension strategies such as keeping the purpose

Table 10.4   Outline for Student Note Taking on the Topic of Careers in the Biological Sciences

I. Major career fields in the biological sciences
   A. Botanists
   B. Zoologists
   C. Entomologists
   D. Microbiologists
   E. Anatomists
   F. Physiologists
   G. Geneticists
   H. Emerging areas of "synthesis"

II. Employment opportunities
   A. Universities and colleges
   B. Federal government
   C. Private industry
      1. Hospitals
      2. Clinics
      3. Laboratories
      4. Research foundations

III. Working conditions
   A. Qualifications—necessary training
   B. Prospects of employment
   C. Income/fringe benefits
   D. Degree of mobility

IV. References for additional information
   A. History of field
   B. Training program
   C. Career opportunities

of an assignment in mind when reading; activating relevant background knowledge; identifying major points in attending to the outline and flow of content; monitoring understanding by generating and trying to answer questions about the content; or drawing and testing inferences by making interpretations, predictions, and conclusions.

Strategy teaching should include not only demonstrations of and opportunities to apply the strategy but also explanations of its purpose (what it does for the learner) and the occasions on which it would be used (Dembo & Eaton, 2000; Meichenbaum & Biemiller, 1998; Paris & Paris, 2001). Although strategy teaching is widely recommended, it seldom occurs in most classrooms, perhaps because teachers do not know how to do it or are not aware of its importance (Hamman et al., 2000).

The amount of teacher scaffolding needed will depend on students' expertise and the difficulty of the assignment. Novice learners need more scaffolding than more experienced learners, especially in the early stages of learning something difficult. As they gain expertise, they can begin assuming more responsibility for regulating their own learning (Mayer, 2001). In learning to apply science principles, for example, students progress most smoothly if their teachers first provide considerable structuring and scaffolding as they lead them through worked examples (guided practice), but then provide opportunities for them to begin solving problems on their own (independent practice) (Kalyuga et al., 2001).

Most tasks will not have their full effects unless they are followed by *reflection* or *debriefing*. Here, you review the task with the students, provide general feedback about performance, and reinforce the main ideas as they relate to the overall goals. These debriefing and reflection activities should also include opportunities for students to ask follow-up questions, share task-related observations or experiences, compare opinions, or in other ways deepen their appreciation of what they have learned and how it relates to their lives outside of school.

Homework Assignments

Homework refers to assignments that students are supposed to complete during non-school hours. Attitudes toward homework have waxed and waned over the years, and it remains controversial today. Proponents view it as an important extension of in-school opportunities to learn, a vehicle for home–school cooperation in assisting students' learning, and a context within which students can develop independence, time management, responsibility, and other self-regulation skills. Opponents claim that whatever value homework may have is not worth the stress it causes (parent–child conflict, reduced family leisure time, fatigued children). They also suggest that it increases social class differences in achievement by requiring children from families with fewer resources to struggle even more to try to keep up.

For a long time, debates about homework were waged primarily on philosophical grounds. However, recent years have seen the emergence of systematic research on homework (Cooper, 1989; Cooper, Robinson, & Patall, 2006; Corno, 2000; *Educational Psychologist*, 2001; Keith, Diamond-Hallam, & Goldenring-Fine, 2004; Trautwein & Köller, 2003). Guidelines for administrators, teachers, and parents that are informed by this research take a more balanced and analytic view of homework's opportunities and dangers (Cooper, 1994; Cooper, Robinson & Patall, 2006; Hong & Milgram, 2000; Miller & Kelley, 1991; *Theory into Practice*, 2004).

The findings indicate that there is little relationship between the amount of homework and student achievement in the elementary grades, and only modest positive relationships in the secondary grades. Relationships are stronger for the amounts of time that students actually spend doing homework and for their rates of completing the assignments than for the amounts of homework that teachers assign. Failure to complete or turn in homework is a frequent problem.

Elementary teachers are more likely to use homework to review class material and to go over the homework in class. Secondary teachers more often use homework as a way for students to prepare for upcoming classes or to follow up lessons with enrichment or application activities. Struggling students take more time than other students to complete homework activities (if they do complete them), partly because they get less work done at school and therefore have more to complete at home. Many students have negative attitudes toward homework, especially younger students who have not had its purposes explained to them effectively. Negative attitudes are especially likely if the homework typically involves fill-in-the-blank worksheets and other repetitive, low-level tasks.

The same guidelines that apply to assignments done in the classroom also apply to homework assignments, but with the additional constraint that the homework must be realistic in length and difficulty given the students' abilities to work independently. Thus, five to ten minutes per subject might be appropriate for fourth-graders, whereas thirty to sixty minutes might be appropriate for college-bound high school students.

Also, homework performance must be monitored and followed up. Voluntary homework may be of some use to those students who do it conscientiously, but if homework is to have instructional value for the class as a whole, you will need to make sure that it is completed on time and to review it the next day. In addition, some students may need reteaching and follow-up assignments.

Epstein (Epstein, 2001; Epstein & Van Voorhis, 2001) identified ten common reasons why homework is assigned to students. She called these the 10 Ps for *purposes* of homework:

1. *Practice.* To increase speed, mastery, and maintenance of skills
2. *Preparation.* To ensure readiness for the next class; to complete activities and assignments started in class
3. *Participation.* To increase the involvement of each student with the learning task; enjoyment of the fun of learning
4. *Personal development.* To build student responsibility, perseverance, time management, self-confidence, and feeling of accomplishment; also, to develop and recognize students' talents and skills that may not be taught in class; extension and enrichment activities
5. *Peer interactions.* To encourage students to work together on assignments or projects, to motivate and learn from one another
6. *Parent–child relations.* To establish communication between parent and child on the importance of schoolwork and learning; to demonstrate applications of schoolwork to real-life situations and experiences; to promote parental awareness of and support for students' work and progress
7. *Parent–teacher communication.* To enable teachers to inform and involve families in children's curricular activities and enable parents to know what topics are being taught and how their children are progressing
8. *Public relations.* To demonstrate to the public that school is a place of serious work, including homework; also, productive interactions with the public may be designed as student-community homework assignments
9. *Policy.* To fulfill directives from administrators at the district or school levels for prescribed amounts of homework per day or week
10. *Punishment.* To correct problems in conduct or productivity

In our view, the most realistic and important purposes of homework are practice, preparation, personal development, and parent–child relations. Assigning homework for punishment is inappropriate.

Homework assignments are primarily the responsibility of the students themselves to complete, and their length and difficulty should be calibrated accordingly. It is unrealistic to expect parents to play significant instructional roles with respect to these assignments, especially in the secondary grades. Many parents may not have the economic, time, or skill resources needed to do so (Corno, 2000; Grolnick et al., 1997). In the elementary grades, however, there are many opportunities to use home assignments that call for relatively brief forms of parental involvement that do not require special preparation or can be scaffolded by providing simple guidelines for parents to follow.

Especially useful for parent–child relations purposes are assignments calling for students to show or explain their written work or other products to their parents or to interview the parents about their experiences or opinions relating to topics studied in school. Such assignments engage students and their parents in conversations that relate to the curriculum and thus extend the students' learning. Furthermore, both parents and children are likely to enjoy these conversations so their resultant effects should be positive not only for learning but for attitudes toward learning and for strengthened parent–child emotional bonds and dispositions toward extended conversations about school-related topics (Alleman & Brophy, 1998).

SUMMARY

In this chapter we began our consideration of instruction by reviewing research on relationships between teacher behavior and student achievement. Then we addressed three important components of active teaching: presenting information to students, involving them in interactive discourse, and engaging them in learning activities and assignments. In the process, we noted that instructional methods are means, not ends. The appropriateness of such methods depends on the instructional goals, and their effectiveness depends on the quality of their implementation. Research can inform you about the trade-offs that different instructional methods offer, but it cannot tell you what your goal priorities should be.

School effects and teacher effects research have identified factors associated with gains on standardized achievement tests. School effects research points to the importance of strong academic leadership that produces consensus on goal priorities and commitment to instructional excellence, an orderly school climate, positive teacher attitudes and expectations, a focus on instructional use of the available time, careful monitoring of progress toward goals through student testing and staff evaluation programs, strong parent involvement programs, and consistent emphasis on the importance of academic achievement. Teacher effects research indicates the value of teacher role definitions that emphasize positive expectations and a sense of efficacy, time allocation policies that maximize students' opportunities to learn, effective classroom management and organization approaches, pacing that moves students through the curriculum rapidly but in small steps that minimize frustration, active instruction by the teacher (as opposed to expecting students to learn mostly on their own from textbooks and assignments), making sure that students achieve mastery of basic objectives, and maintaining a supportive learning environment.

Lecture/presentation and drill/recitation activities are well suited to the classroom context in certain respects and have their places as parts of a comprehensive approach to instruction. However, you should avoid using these techniques too frequently or in ways that limit the curriculum to rote memorizing of miscellaneous items of information. These techniques are used most effectively in content development segments of lessons in which you help your students to develop networks of knowledge that are built around connected sets of important ideas and learned with their applications in mind.

Information presentation is useful for arousing students' interest in a topic, providing advance organizers and learning sets to help them appreciate the topic's significance and approach it with appropriate learning strategies; bringing together and efficiently communicating important ideas about the topic; and providing information that students will not get from their textbooks. Good presentations are delivered enthusiastically and in clear, well-organized language. Embedding the presentation within a narrative, storytelling structure helps to personalize it and connect it to students' prior knowledge. When instruction focuses on processes or skills, students will need not only verbal explanations but also physical demonstrations. Such demonstrations should focus on the general principles involved and demystify the processes by articulating the thinking that guides observable actions.

Most teacher questioning should scaffold content development or discussion designed to provide opportunities for students to actively think about, respond to, and apply the content being taught. The questions should address a variety of cognitive levels of response and should be clear, brief, natural, and thought provoking. Most of all, they should be selected and sequenced so as to accomplish significant instructional goals. Questions should be addressed to the class as a whole and then followed by sufficient wait time to allow students to process what is being asked and begin to formulate responses to it. Students' responses should receive immediate feedback or other appropriate follow-up.

Discussions do not occur as frequently as they should in most classrooms. They require teachers to switch from the role of information source and authority figure to that of discussion leader who establishes a focus for the discussion and facilitates interaction but does not dominate it unnecessarily. In addition to asking questions, you can stimulate contributions to discussion by making declarative statements or restatements, offering opinions, encouraging students to ask questions or elaborate on their previous statements, or simply remaining silent and waiting for a student to take the initiative.

Learning activities and assignments also are important components of instruction, even though they can be overused, especially when they take the form of silent work on fill-in-the-blank worksheets and other low-level tasks. Activities and assignments are valuable to the extent that they promote progress toward important instructional goals and are feasible and cost-effective given the constraints that apply. The most valuable activities provide opportunities for interaction and reflective discourse rather than just solitary seatwork, and they engage students in thinking critically and creatively about and applying what they are learning, not just regurgitating facts and definitions. To have their full impact, activities and assignments need to be structured sufficiently to enable students to engage in them with awareness of their goals, and student work needs to be monitored and scaffolded sufficiently to ensure that they accomplish those goals satisfactorily. The same principles apply to homework assignments, but with the additional constraint that the assignments must be realistic in length and difficulty given the students' abilities to work independently.

SUGGESTED ACTIVITIES AND QUESTIONS

1. Since research on teaching first began, traditional active teaching has always been found to be used heavily, if not exclusively, in most classrooms, even though educational theorists have been critical of it. Why is this? Can you see ways to (a) avoid overuse of this approach in your own teaching and (b) make sure that you use the approach effectively when you do use it?

2. Give concrete examples of instances when lecturing might be desirable.

3. How can you make your information presentations and skill demonstrations easier for your students to follow and remember?

4. Role-play the process of introducing and ending lessons *enthusiastically* and with *clarity*. Describe the classroom situation (age of students, etc.) so that others may provide you with appropriate feedback.

5. What does it mean to say that questions should be asked not simply to assess student learning but to promote it? How can questions help students to develop important understandings?

6. How should teachers' questioning and feedback strategies in recitations differ from those in discussions?

7. Plan a brief (fifteen-minute) discussion. Write out the sequence of questions you will use to advance the discussion fruitfully, applying the criteria we suggested for effective oral questions. Role-play your discussion if possible.

8. The criteria for effective *oral* questions mostly apply to written questions as well, but there are some exceptions. Try to identify other criteria that are applicable only to written questions. In what important ways do written and oral questions differ?

9. Why should students be allowed to talk freely about opinions that differ from those of the teacher or the book?

10. What is the optimal difficulty level of an assignment?

11. Given your current or intended teaching context (grade level, subject matter, types of students), what kinds of learning activities and assignments will be most needed for enabling your students to meet your instructional goals?

12. What kinds of homework assignments would be appropriate for this teaching context? What would be their purposes?

13. Why does active teaching, in which the teacher presents content to students and structures their subsequent practice and application exercises, generally produce more learning than approaches in which students are encouraged to learn on their own?

14. Why is it impossible to give a precise definition of an *effective teacher*?

15. Interview some first- or second-year teachers and some veteran teachers (with at least eight years in service) concerning their beliefs about classroom discussions. Which group uses more discussion? Why? Are there differences in how they approach the discussion method or in the purposes for which they use it?

16. Think through your experiences with discussion as a student, and discuss them with peers. Can you agree on the trade-offs that the method offers students? In what ways is it a desirable learning method? In what ways is it frustrating or otherwise problematic? What does this imply about when, why, and how to use discussion in your teaching?

FORM 10.1. Teacher Lectures, Presentations, and Demonstrations

USE: When the teacher lectures, presents information, or demonstrates skills to the class.
PURPOSE: To assess the effectiveness of the presentation.
*   Enter a check mark for each of the following features that was included effectively in the presentation, and a 0 for each feature that was omitted or handled ineffectively. Add your comments below, emphasizing constructive suggestions for improvement.*

CHECKLIST

INTRODUCTION

_____ 1. States purpose or objectives
_____ 2. Gives overview or advance organizer
_____ 3. Distributes a study guide or instructs the students concerning how they are expected to respond (what notes to take, etc.)

BODY OF PRESENTATION

_____ 4. Is well prepared; speaks fluently without hesitation or confusion
_____ 5. Projects enthusiasm for the material
_____ 6. Maintains eye contact with the students
_____ 7. Speaks at an appropriate pace (neither too fast nor too slow)
_____ 8. Speaks with appropriate voice modulation (rather than a monotone)
_____ 9. Uses appropriate expressions, movements, and gestures (rather than speaking woodenly)
_____ 10. Content is well structured and sequenced
_____ 11. New terms are clearly defined
_____ 12. Key concepts or terms are emphasized (preferably not only verbally but by holding up or pointing to examples, writing or underlining on the board or overhead projector, etc.)
_____ 13. Includes appropriate analogies or examples that are effective in enabling students to relate the new to the familiar and the abstract to the concrete
_____ 14. Where appropriate, facts are distinguished from opinions
_____ 15. Where appropriate, lengthy presentations are divided into recognizable segments, with clear transitions between segments and minisummaries concluding each segment
_____ 16. When necessary, questions the students following each major segment of a lengthy presentation (rather than waiting until the end)
_____ 17. Monitors student response; is encouraging and responsive regarding student questions and comments on the material

CONCLUSION

_____ 18. Concludes with summary or integration of the presentation
_____ 19. Invites student questions or comments
_____ 20. Follows up on the presentation by making a transition into a recitation activity, a follow-up assignment, or some other activity that will allow the students an opportunity to practice or apply the material

COMMENTS:

FORM 10.2. Questioning Techniques

USE: When teacher is asking class or group questions.
PURPOSE: To see if teacher is following principles for good questioning practices.
For each question, code the following categories:

BEHAVIOR CATEGORIES

A. TYPE OF QUESTION ASKED
    1. Academic: Factual. Seeks specific correct response
    2. Academic: Opinion. Seeks opinion on a complex issue
        where there is no clear-cut response
    3. Nonacademic: Question deals with personal, procedural,
      or disciplinary matters rather than curriculum

B. TYPE OF RESPONSE REQUIRED
    1. Thought question. Student must reason through to a
        conclusion or explain something at length
    2. Fact question. Student must provide fact(s) from memory
    3. Choice question. Requires only a yes-no or either-or
        response

C. SELECTION OF RESPONDENT
    1. Names child before asking question
    2. Calls on volunteer (after asking question)
    3. Calls on nonvolunteer (after asking question)

D. PAUSE (AFTER ASKING QUESTION)
    1. Paused a few seconds before calling on student
    2. Failed to pause before calling on student
    3. Not applicable: teacher named student before asking
        question

E. TONE AND MANNER IN PRESENTING QUESTION
    1. Question presented as challenge or stimulation
    2. Question presented matter-of-factly
    3. Question presented as threat or test

CODES

	A	B	C	D	E
1.	1	2	2	1	2
2.	1	2	2	1	2
3.	1	3	2	1	2
4.	1	2	2	1	2
5.	1	2	2	1	2
6.	1	3	2	1	2
7.	1	2	2	1	2
8.	2	1	2	1	1
9.	1	2	2	1	2
10.	1	2	2	1	2
11.	1	2	2	1	2
12.	1	2	2	1	2
13.	—	—	—	—	—
14.	—	—	—	—	—
15.	—	—	—	—	—
16.	—	—	—	—	—
17.	—	—	—	—	—
18.	—	—	—	—	—
19.	—	—	—	—	—
20.	—	—	—	—	—
21.	—	—	—	—	—
22.	—	—	—	—	—
23.	—	—	—	—	—
24.	—	—	—	—	—
25.	—	—	—	—	—
26.	—	—	—	—	—
27.	—	—	—	—	—
28.	—	—	—	—	—
29.	—	—	—	—	—
30.	—	—	—	—	—
31.	—	—	—	—	—
32.	—	—	—	—	—
33.	—	—	—	—	—
34.	—	—	—	—	—
35.	—	—	—	—	—
36.	—	—	—	—	—
37.	—	—	—	—	—
38.	—	—	—	—	—
39.	—	—	—	—	—
40.	—	—	—	—	—

     Record any information relevant to the following:
Multiple Questions. Tally the number of times the teacher:
1. Repeats or rephrases question before calling on anyone _II_

2. Asks two or more questions at the same time _o_

Sequence. Were questions integrated into an orderly sequence,
or did they seem to be random or unrelated?
   Teacher seemed to be following sequence given in manual
   (led up to next history unit).

Did the students themselves pose questions? *No*

Was there student-student interaction? How much? *None*

When appropriate, did the teacher redirect questions to several
students, or ask students to evaluate their own or others'
responses? *No*

CHAPTER 11

Helping Students to Construct Usable Knowledge

Classroom Vignette

The following is part of the transcript of a fifth-grade literature lesson recorded by Quirk and Cianciolo (1993). The students have read *The Lion, the Witch, and the Wardrobe* prior to this lesson, and now the teacher is asking them to consider the importance of the setting in this story and in fanciful fiction in general. Note her reliance on questioning rather than explanation. As you read, think about how you would assess her method as a way to develop understanding and appreciation of setting as an element of literature. Would you do anything differently? How might you follow up this segment after Martha makes her concluding comment?

Teacher: How important is the setting to this story?
Susie: Very, very.
Teacher: Why?
Susie: Because if the setting was in a different place, they wouldn't have got the wardrobe. And then they wouldn't have gone to Narnia.
Teacher: Okay. Jessica?
Jessica: I think they could have changed the setting a little. They had to make it into a different world, but they didn't have to make it all snow. They could have made it spring and the children always wanted it to be winter.
Teacher: Okay. So they could have changed the seasons very easily. But you said something about it had to be Narnia.

335

Jessica: It didn't have to be Narnia, but it had to be a different world.

Teacher: A different world. Why? That's a very good point, Jessica. Why would it have to be a different world? Darrin?

Darrin: Because it makes you like, interested because you could go through a wardrobe and walk and walk, and then you enter into a new world.

Teacher: Okay, and what do you think, Steve?

Steven: I think it [the setting] is very important, because if you put them [the characters] in a setting like [our town] it wouldn't be exciting. I mean, like in Narnia you have all these monsters and the witch.

Teacher: What does it do to our imagination when we have, as Jessica suggested, another world, or another time, or another place? Barbara?

Barbara: If it's exciting, we want to read more. You can make it the world you want it to be.

Teacher: Absolutely, very good. Jason?

Jason: When it's another world it makes your mind wander and makes you want to get out of everything. But it also makes you think that you're actually in that world. It's kinda boring if it was just in the professor's house or something. But it's more exciting when it's in another world.

Teacher: Why is it okay to have this other world situation in Narnia, but in *The Tales of a Fourth-Grade Nothing,* it is a familiar situation. Judy Blume's books are set in familiar places we can identify like [our town], or whatever. Why is it okay for those books, but I'm hearing some of you say Narnia has to be way out some place. Barbara?

Barbara: Because Judy Blume's telling what could really happen, but here in C. S. Lewis's books it's imagination and imagination has to lead you the way or else you aren't gonna get anywhere.

Teacher: Okay. One last comment. Martha?

Martha: I think that it can be different because of the titles. There wouldn't be a lion, a witch, and a wardrobe in [our town]. It has to be somewhere where anything can happen.

In this lesson, the teacher's goal is to develop understanding of big ideas relating to the role of the setting as a component of fiction. Instead of beginning with an overview presentation, she elicits her students' ideas through questioning. Her questions are open-ended, designed to elicit a range of opinions and ideas, not specific "right" answers. In reacting to each response, she elaborates on the student's idea, connects it to previously expressed ideas or previous lessons, or offers some other substantive feedback beyond (or instead of) indicating whether she views the response as correct. This approach reflects the influence of constructivist views of learning and teaching.

Constructivists believe that students build knowledge through a process of active construction that involves making connections between new information and existing networks of prior knowledge. They emphasize relating new content to the knowledge that students already possess, as well as providing opportunities for students to process and apply the new learning. They believe that before knowledge becomes truly *generative*—usable for interpreting new situations, solving problems, thinking and reasoning, and learning generally—students must elaborate and question what they are told, examine the new content in relation to more familiar content, and build new knowledge structures. Otherwise, the knowledge may remain *inert*—recallable when cued by questions or test items similar to those used in practice exercises, but not applicable when it might be useful in everyday life (O'Connor, 1998; Palincsar, 1998; Steffe & Gale, 1995).

Although the term *constructivist* is relatively new, many constructivist ideas can be traced to John Dewey and Jean Piaget and some go back at least as far as Socrates. Many are embodied in historically significant educational movements such as open education, inquiry learning, and discovery learning, as well as in contemporary movements such as whole-language teaching and portfolio assessment. In fact, the recent (and often unqualified) enthusiasm for constructivism can be seen as the latest round in a repeating cycle in American education, in which popular opinion swings back and forth between teacher-centered and student-centered approaches to instruction. The still more recent emphasis on prescribed curricula, standards, and testing can be seen as the beginnings of a swing back from student-centered toward more teacher-centered approaches to instruction. As a teacher, you will need to find the right balance between teacher- and student-centered instruction, given your grade level, your students, and other aspects of your teaching context.

Current constructivist approaches all involve some subset of the key ideas outlined in the following section (Fosnot, 2005; Phillips, 2000).

*B*asic Constructivist Principles

Constructivist theory and research have focused primarily on learning rather than teaching, but suggest principles for how teachers can support their students' learning. In this section, we consider three basic constructivist principles: (1) learners construct their own unique representations of knowledge; (2) learners make sense of new information by relating it to their prior knowledge; and (3) sometimes new learning results in a restructuring of existing knowledge or a change in the learner's understanding of a key concept.

Knowledge as Constructed

The core idea of constructivism is that *students develop new knowledge through a process of active construction.* They do not merely passively receive or copy input from teachers or textbooks. Instead, they actively mediate it by trying to make sense of it and relate it to what they already know (or think they know) about a topic. This is what we want them to do, because unless students build representations of new learning, "making it their own" by paraphrasing it in their own words and considering its meanings and implications, the learning will be retained only as disconnected and relatively meaningless information. However, each student builds his or her own unique representation of what was communicated, and this may or may not include a complete and accurate reconstruction of the teacher's or textbook's intended meaning. Sometimes what is constructed is incomplete or distorted, even though students may have spent considerable time processing the content.

Even when the basic message is reconstructed as intended, it gets connected to each learner's unique set of prior understandings and interests. As a result, different learners may construct different meanings and implications from the same input. For example, on reading about mountain climbers who overcame potential disasters to achieve their goals successfully, one reader might remember and think about the text primarily as a story about achievement motivation, another as a story about the value of teamwork, another as a story about how shared adventure seals the bond of friendship, and yet another as an illustration of the challenges and special techniques involved in mountain climbing. The students were exposed to the same narrative and their reconstructions all included the same basic story line, but they featured different meanings and potential implications.

The import of such individual differences in students' reconstructions of input from teachers or texts will depend on the instructional goals. If the story was meant to illustrate use of the foreshadowing technique, the teacher would need to make sure that all students noted the elements that exemplified foreshadowing and came to appreciate the ways that they contributed to the story's technical structure and aesthetic pleasures. Beyond this, individual differences in reconstructions (such as relative emphasis on motivation, teamwork, friendship, or climbing techniques) would not matter.

They would matter, however, if the story were intended to inspire students to challenge themselves by setting difficult (but achievable) goals or to help them appreciate the value of a collaborative learning community. The inspirational purpose would call for the teacher to make sure that all students "got the message" about achievement motivation, whereas the collaboration purpose would call for emphasis on friendship and the value of teamwork. The larger point here is that although students may develop quite a range of reconstructions when left to their own devices, teachers can and should scaffold their learning to make sure that all reconstructions include acceptably complete and accurate understandings of the activity's goals and big ideas.

Constructivists emphasize that teachers need to go beyond what they call information *transmission models* (teachers or texts tell, students memorize) and move toward *knowledge construction models* of teaching and learning. These involve structuring reflective discussions of the meanings and implications of content and providing opportunities for students to use the content as they engage in inquiry, problem solving, or decision making. Purely constructivist teaching (starting with questions and sustaining a discussion mode of discourse) is possible in some situations, but more typically the teacher begins by presenting information and developing big ideas using the active teaching techniques described in Chapter 10, then gradually shifts to a more exclusive reliance on discussion. In the process, students use, extend, and even alter the content as they begin to "make it their own."

The Role of Prior Knowledge

Construction of knowledge goes more smoothly when learners can relate new content to their existing knowledge and experience. New content is not first understood in some abstract way and only later related to prior knowledge; instead, it is interpreted from the beginning within contexts supplied by prior knowledge. Networks of prior knowledge that provide contexts for meaningful interpretation of new content are called *schemas* (Anderson, 1984; diSibio, 1982). If new content can be related to existing schemas, activation of these schemas can help learners to develop expectations about the nature of the content, focus on its important elements, and fill in gaps where information is implied rather than stated explicitly. Consider the following paragraph:

When Mary arrived, the woman at the door greeted her and checked her name. A few minutes later, she was escorted to her chair and shown the day's menu. The attendant was helpful but brusque, almost to the point of being rude. Later, she paid the woman at the door and left.

You can interpret and even elaborate this sketchy narrative because you recognize that the events took place in a restaurant: Mary had made a reservation, she was seated by a hostess at a table (not merely in a chair), the "attendant" was a waiter, and the "woman at the door" was a cashier. None of this information was explicit in the text, yet you could infer all of it because you possess a *restaurant schema* that includes such slots as "being seated," "ordering," and "paying the check" (Schank & Abelson, 1977).

Activation of relevant background knowledge facilitates learning of new content, at least if the activated schemas are suited to the instructional goals (Adams, 1990; Bransford, Brown, & Cocking, 1999; Lambert & McCombs, 1998). You can prepare students for story reading by telling them what the story is about and asking questions to activate schemas useful in comprehending it. You also can help students activate relevant prior knowledge by drawing analogies or suggesting examples that link the new content to familiar ideas or experiences, by taking an inventory of what students know (or think they know) about the topic before beginning instruction, or by asking students to make predictions about the content or to suggest solutions to problems based on it. The K-W-L technique described in Chapter 5 is one such way to stimulate relevant prior knowledge when introducing new content.

Knowledge Restructuring and Conceptual Change

When students' existing schemas are not accurate or not well suited to the goals, their activation will interfere with learning. Filtering new content through schemas that are oversimplified, distorted, or otherwise invalid may cause students to develop *misconceptions* instead of the target conceptions. For example, many students believe that the sun obits the earth, because they have "seen" it do so. This belief can cause them to misunderstand what their teacher or textbook is saying about cycles of day and night. They may acquire the accurate understanding that areas of the earth experience daylight at times when they are exposed to the sun, yet continue to believe that cycles of day and night are due to the sun orbiting around the earth instead of vice versa.

Besides adding new elements to an existing cognitive structure, active construction of knowledge may involve changing the structure through processes of *restructuring* and *conceptual change.* Sometimes the needed restructuring is relatively minor and easily accomplished, but at other times students need to undergo more radical restructuring that involves simultaneous changes in large networks of connected knowledge (Carey, 1985; Chinn & Brewer, 1993; Vosniadou & Brewer, 1987).

Radical restructuring can be time-consuming and difficult to accomplish. Mere exposure to correct conceptions may not be enough, because existing misconceptions may cause learners to ignore, distort, or miss the implications of aspects of the new learning that contradict what they "know." It may be necessary to help them first to see the contradictions between what they currently believe and what you are trying to teach, and then to appreciate that the target concepts are more valid, powerful, useful, or in some other way preferable to their existing concepts (see the section on conceptual change teaching in Chapter 9).

Social Constructivist Views of Learning and Teaching

Piaget → individual construction

The basic principles just reviewed were among the first to emerge from constructivist studies of learning and cognition. Influenced heavily by the developmental psychology of Jean Piaget, early studies depicted construction of knowledge as a solitary activity. They focused on an individual learner who develops knowledge through reading texts or through exploration, discovery, and reflection on everyday life experiences.

Classrooms, however, are communities in which most learning takes place within the context of social interaction. Recognizing this, most constructivists have adopted some version of *social constructivism*. In addition to emphasizing that learning is a process of active construction of meaning, social constructivists emphasize that the process works best in social settings in which two or more individuals engage in *sustained discourse* about a topic. Such discussions help participants to advance their learning in several ways. Exposure to new input from others makes them aware of things that they did not know and leads to expansion of their cognitive structures. Exposure to ideas that contradict their own beliefs may cause them to examine those beliefs and perhaps reconstruct them. The need to communicate their ideas to others forces them to articulate those ideas more clearly, which sharpens their conceptions and often leads to recognition of new connections. As a result, cognitive structures become better developed (both more differentiated and better organized).

Social constructivist ideas have been influenced heavily by the writings of the Russian developmental psychologist Lev Vygotsky (1962, 1978). Vygotsky showed that children's thought (cognition) and language (speech) begin as separate functions but become intimately connected during the preschool years as children learn to use language as a mechanism for thinking. Gradually, more and more of their learning is mediated through language, especially learning of cultural knowledge that is not acquired through direct experience with the physical environment. Children initially acquire much of their cultural knowledge through overt speech (conversations with others, especially parents and teachers). Then they elaborate on this knowledge and connect it to other knowledge through inner speech (verbally mediated thinking, or self-talk).

The subjects taught at school are prominent examples of the kinds of cultural knowledge that Vygotsky viewed as socially constructed. He suggested that this learning proceeds most efficiently when children are consistently exposed to *teaching in the zone of proximal development*. The zone of proximal development refers to the range of knowledge and skills that students are not yet ready to learn on their own but could learn with help from teachers. The children already know things that are "below" the zone, or can learn them easily on their own without help. They cannot yet learn things that are "above" the zone, even with help.

The old idea of *readiness* for learning implied that teachers can do little but wait until children become ready to learn something (presumably due to maturation of needed cognitive structures) before trying to teach it to them. In contrast, the idea of teaching within the zone of proximal development assumes that readiness for learning depends much more on accumulated prior knowledge than on maturation of cognitive structures. Therefore, advances in knowledge will be stimulated primarily through the social construction that occurs during sustained discourse, and most rapidly through teaching in the zone of proximal development (Moll, 1990; Newman, Griffin, & Cole, 1989; Rogoff & Wertsch, 1984; Tharp & Gallimore, 1988).

Social constructivists emphasize teaching that features sustained discussion in which participants pursue a topic in depth, exchanging views and negotiating meanings and implications as they explore its ramifications. Along with teacher-structured whole-class discussions, this includes cooperative learning that is constructed as students work in pairs or small groups (King, 1994). Key features of social constructivist approaches to teaching and learning are summarized in Table 11.1. Each feature is contrasted with a parallel feature of the more traditional information transmission approach (as social constructivists view it).

Table 11.1 Teaching and Learning as Transmission of Information versus as Social Construction of Knowledge

Transmission View	Social Construction View
Knowledge as fixed body of information transmitted from teacher or text to students	Knowledge as developing interpretations co-constructed through discussion
Texts and teacher as authoritative sources of expert knowledge to which students defer	Authority for constructed knowledge resides in the arguments and evidence cited in its support by students as well as by texts or teacher; everyone has expertise to contribute
Teacher is responsible for managing students' learning by providing information and leading students through activities and assignments	Teacher and students share responsibility for initiating and guiding learning efforts
Teacher explains, checks for understanding, and judges correctness of students' responses	Teacher acts as discussion leader who poses questions, seeks clarifications, promotes dialogue, helps group recognize areas of consensus and of continuing disagreement
Students memorize or replicate what has been explained or modeled	Students strive to make sense of new input by relating it to their prior knowledge and by collaborating in dialogue with others to co-construct shared understandings
Discourse emphasizes drill and recitation in response to convergent questions; focus is on eliciting correct answers	Discourse emphasizes reflective discussion of networks of connected knowledge; questions are more divergent but designed to develop understanding of the powerful ideas that anchor these networks; focus is on eliciting students' thinking
Activities emphasize replication of models or applications that require following step-by-step algorithms	Activities emphasize application to authentic issues and problems that require higher-order thinking
Students work mostly alone, practicing what has been transmitted to them in order to prepare themselves to compete for rewards by reproducing it on demand	Students collaborate by acting as a learning community that constructs shared understandings through sustained dialogue

Sociocultural Views of Learning and Teaching

All social constructivists emphasize constructing knowledge through social interaction. In addition, many of them hold more specifically *sociocultural views* that build on Vygotsky's ideas about cultural learning in addition to his ideas about teaching in the zone of proximal development.

Sociocultural theorists view learning in classrooms as part of the more general enculturation that takes place as societies equip their new members with needed knowledge and skills. Based on the metaphor of on-the-job training, sociocultural theorists speak of learners as novices undergoing a *cognitive apprenticeship* under the supervision of one or more mentors. Such enculturation occurs within *communities of practice* when mentors impart to novices the knowledge and skills involved in carrying out the community's functions (e.g., as educators, mathematicians, historians, beauticians, carpenters, bakers, etc.).

At first, novices learn through *legitimate peripheral participation*. They already are recognized as legitimate members of the community, but their participation is peripheral because they mostly watch, listen, and carry out beginner-level activities under supervision. As they gain expertise, they progress from peripheral toward more central forms of participation. They begin to function more fully as equals with the mentors who have been teaching them, to assume increasing responsibilities for regulating their own learning, and to act as mentors themselves.

Communities of practice develop specialized vocabulary and forms of discourse that help them to carry out their activities (e.g., analyze a story with reference to concepts such as plot or characterization; analyze a historical account with reference to concepts such as bias or primary versus secondary sources). They also develop specialized tools—not only physical tools but also cognitive tools such as mathematical formulas, musical notation, or any of the processes and skills commonly taught as part of the academic disciplines (Salomon & Perkins, 1998; Wells, 1999). Novices ordinarily acquire specialized discourse and learn to use specialized tools while carrying out the very activities that led the community to invent the specialized discourse and tools in the first place. As they gain expertise, they also begin to use the discourse and tools to generate new knowledge.

Situated Learning

Sociocultural theorists emphasize that naturally occurring learning activities are situated—carried out in particular settings for particular purposes. Knowledge that is developed in these situations typically is invented or designed to accomplish the purposes at hand. Only later does it become aggregated into organized structures such as disciplines or school subjects.

Given that knowledge is adapted to the settings, purposes, and tasks to which it is applied (and for which it was constructed) sociocultural theorists argue that, if we want students to learn and retain knowledge in a form that makes it usable for application, we need to make it possible for them to develop the knowledge in natural settings, using methods and tasks suited to those settings (Lave & Wenger, 1991; Rogoff, 1990; Rogoff,

Turkanis, & Bartlett, 2001). This would require significant adjustments to the traditional curriculum.

Schooling brings people together and thus makes the social construction of knowledge possible, but it tends to teach generic knowledge and skills that have been abstracted and removed from the application settings in which they originated. Too often, this generic learning is forgotten or remains inert—not easily accessible when needed in out-of-school settings. Sociocultural theorists address this problem using models of schooling based on the on-the-job training that occurs as experienced mentors work with novices in apprenticeship situations.

There are limits to the feasibility of shifting significant portions of the school's curriculum to out-of-school settings. However, the notion of situated learning has implications for the design of in-school instruction as well. It implies that we ought to be more conscious of potential applications when we select and plan our teaching of curriculum content, and we should emphasize those applications in developing the content with students.

Scaffolding Students' Learning

Sociocultural ideas about teaching in the zone of proximal development feature the notions of scaffolding and gradual transfer of responsibility for managing learning from the teacher to the student. Instructional *scaffolding* is a general term for the task assistance or simplification strategies that teachers might use to bridge the gap between what students are capable of doing on their own and what they are capable of doing with help. Scaffolds are forms of support that help students progress from their current abilities to the intended goal (Puntambekar & Hübscher, 2005; Rosenshine & Meister, 1992). Like the scaffolds used by house painters, the support provided through scaffolding is temporary, adjustable, and removed when it is no longer needed. Examples of scaffolding include *cognitive modeling* (in which the teacher demonstrates task performance while articulating the thinking that guides it), *prompts* or *cues* that help students when they are temporarily stuck, and *questions* that help them diagnose the reasons for errors and develop repair strategies.

Following Wood, Bruner, and Ross (1976), Rogoff (1990) suggested that appropriately scaffolded instruction includes the following six components:

1. Developing student interest in accomplishing the intended goal of the task
2. Demonstrating an idealized version of the actions to be performed
3. Simplifying the task by reducing the number of steps, so the student can manage certain components and recognize when these are being accomplished successfully
4. Controlling frustration and risk
5. Providing feedback that identifies the critical features of discrepancies between what the student has produced and what is required for an ideal solution
6. Motivating and directing the student's activity sufficiently to maintain continuous pursuit of the goal.

These scaffolding steps are very similar to traditionally formulated principles for demonstrating skills and processes effectively (see Chapter 10). The major difference is the explicit emphasis on transferring responsibility for managing learning from the teacher to the learners (as soon as feasible).

Transferring Responsibility from Teacher to Students

Closely associated with scaffolding is *gradual transfer of responsibility for managing learning.* Early in the process, the teacher assumes most of the responsibility for structuring and managing learning activities and provides a great deal of explanation, modeling, and scaffolding. As students develop expertise, however, they can begin to assume responsibility for regulating their own learning by asking questions and by working on increasingly complex applications with increasing degrees of autonomy. The teacher still provides assistance with challenges that students are not yet ready to handle on their own, but this assistance is gradually reduced in response to increases in student readiness to engage in independent and self-regulated learning. Optimizing the transfer of responsibility requires exercising your professional judgment, informed by knowledge of your students. Transferring too much too soon will frustrate students and disrupt the flow of the lesson, but transferring more slowly than necessary will reduce your efficiency in moving through the curriculum and lead to boredom for at least some of your students.

when to transfer: tricky descision!

Tharp and Gallimore (1988) described a *model of assisted performance* that involves teaching in the zone of proximal development, scaffolding learning through responsive assistance, and transferring responsibility to the learner as expertise develops. Teacher assistance is contingent on and responsive to the learner's level of performance. The emphasis is on patiently allowing learners to handle as much as they can on their own and to learn through their mistakes, except where mistakes might be costly or dangerous.

When necessary, the teacher assists performance through *cognitive structuring*—stating principles or generalizations that pull things together and make for better organized representation of the learning. Cognitive structuring may focus on the content being learned or on the learners' cognitive activities. When focused on the content, cognitive structuring provides explanations (e.g., that the expansion of gases as they are heated occurs because molecular activity increases with temperature). When cognitive structuring focuses on the learners' cognitive activity, it provides reminders of the strategies that students are expected to use (e.g., "So, whenever you come to a new word that you are not sure about, you first look for clues, then put the clues together with what you already know about the word to decide on a meaning, and then check to see if that meaning fits with the rest of the sentence").

Similarly, Collins, Brown, and Newman (1989) described the *cognitive apprenticeship model* of schooling. The model includes four important aspects of traditional apprenticeship: *modeling, scaffolding, fading,* and *coaching.* The master models task performance for the apprentice, provides coaching and other forms of scaffolding as the apprentice practices portions of the task, and then fades these forms of assistance as the apprentice becomes proficient enough to accomplish tasks independently. Cognitive apprenticeship in the classroom includes these same elements, along with additional ones that are needed because of the more abstract content taught there. Modeling includes thinking out loud in order to make the teacher's cognition perceptible to students, and the teacher asking many questions designed to make student cognition perceptible to the teacher as well. Also, by emphasizing authentic tasks and contexts for learning that make sense to the students, teachers attempt to build in some of the task meaningfulness and motivation typical of learning that is situated in the workplace. Finally, to promote transfer, cognitive apprenticeship exposes students to a range of tasks and encourages them to note their common elements and consider their applications to life outside of school.

The concepts of scaffolding and transferring responsibility for managing learning originated in analysis of apprenticeships in which an expert tutors a single novice. However, these concepts also apply to whole-class teaching in which a teacher leads students in discourse or monitoring their work on assignments. Hogan and Pressley (1997) summarized the key elements of the scaffolding model of teaching as shown in Table 11.2.

Inquiry Teaching

Many constructivist approaches to teaching emphasize inquiry methods. Instead of establishing a knowledge base before moving to applications, inquiry methods immediately place students into application or problem-solving contexts, then scaffold their progress as they develop answers to questions or solutions to problems. Most inquiry models are variations on the one introduced by John Dewey (1910), which called for

Table 11.2   A Scaffolding Model of Teaching

1. *Pre-engagement.* Guided by instructional goals and anticipating possible student difficulties, needs, and strategies, the teacher selects an appropriate learning activity.
2. *Establishing a shared goal.* The teacher introduces the activity in ways that help the students see its value and thus adopt the goal of accomplishing its intended outcomes.
3. *Actively diagnosing learners' understandings and needs.* This requires teachers to be familiar with the learning domain involved, including knowledge of students' typical trajectories of progress as they move from novice to more expert status.
4. *Providing tailored assistance.* This might include modeling ideal performance, providing explanations, questioning or leading discussion, or coaching (cuing or prompting) performance.
5. *Maintaining pursuit of the goal.* The teacher may need to support students to help them stay with a difficult or complicated task by requesting clarifications, asking questions, or offering praise and encouragement.
6. *Giving feedback.* This includes both summarizing the progress made so far and indicating what still needs to be accomplished (including making students aware of mistakes and helping them to remedy them).
7. *Controlling for frustration and risk.* This is done at a macro level by establishing a learning community in which mistakes are appreciated as part of the learning process, and at a micro level by giving feedback that helps students to cope with frustration and overcome mistakes as they carry out the activity.
8. Assisting internalization, independence, and generalization to other contexts. This is accomplished by fading assistance as students gain expertise, by engaging them in activities that allow them to generalize what they are learning, and by providing cues, feedback, or other coaching that helps them to develop strategies for addressing problems or to recognize the implications and applications of what they are learning.

Source: Adapted from Hogan, K., & Pressley, M. (1997). Scaffolding scientific competencies within classroom communities of inquiry. In K. Hogan & M. Pressley (Eds.), *Scaffolding student learning: Instructional approaches and issues* (pp. 74–107). Cambridge, MA: Brookline.

engaging students with questions or problems, collecting their ideas about potential solutions, and then scaffolding their investigation of the relative merits of the suggestions and negotiation of agreement on tentative conclusions. In the process, students might engage in various forms of research (Wells, 2001) or work on extended inquiry projects (Singer et al., 2000).

Inquiry methods are popular with social constructivists, especially versions in which pairs or small groups of students work collaboratively to conduct research on aspects of the content that are of special interest to them. The teacher scaffolds by helping each group sharpen the guiding questions, identify and exploit potential information sources, and develop a report of its findings, but students are encouraged to proceed with as much autonomy and self-regulation as they can handle. Usually, the emphasis is more on developing general inquiry skills and dispositions than on developing knowledge of any particular collection of content.

scaffolding for small group inquiry

Inquiry activities vary across subjects, reflecting contrasts in the ways that different disciplines develop knowledge. In mathematics, for example, inquiry often is carried out as whole-class discussions of problems. In other subjects, inquiry is more likely to involve individual or small-group research, in which students consult historical sources and then synthesize an account of a historical event, consult appropriate sources and perhaps generate some new information to address a social science question, or devise and conduct experiments in the sciences. In carrying out these inquiry activities, students learn the discourse genres (stating mathematical conjectures, formulating scientific hypotheses, etc.) and analytic tools (evaluating historical sources, applying statistical tests, using laboratory equipment, etc.) used in the respective disciplines.

Inquiry approaches also are popular with discipline-based subject matter specialists, as can be seen in the contributions to a volume on best practices in teaching each of fourteen school subjects (Brophy, 2001). They fit well both with constructivist views of learning and with ideas about socializing students into the disciplines by engaging them in doing what disciplinary practitioners do (i.e., conducting inquiry on discipline-related questions using the discipline's discourse genres and investigatory tools). Inquiry methods have proven difficult to implement effectively, however, because they demand a great deal of students, who may lack the reading skills, subject-matter knowledge, interest in the research questions, or capacities for self-regulated learning needed to sustain inquiry activities, especially if they will be expected to work on their own for extended periods of time. In practice, extensive structuring and scaffolding often is needed, as when teachers provide students with guides to follow in carrying out and reporting on their inquiry activities.

other Brophy Books about each subject

Challenges

This caution was underscored by Kirschner, Sweller, and Clark (2006), who emphasized that fifty years of research has consistently indicated that minimally guided instruction is less effective than instruction in which the teacher structures and scaffolds students' learning. Guided instruction's advantage over minimally guided instruction begins to recede only when learners have enough prior knowledge to enable them to self-regulate their learning efficiently (i.e., to provide their own "internal guidance"). Kirschner et al. also noted that learning a discipline as a novice is not the same as practicing it as an expert, and cautioned that it probably is a mistake to try to introduce novices to a discipline by engaging them in its processes and procedures without systematically developing a solid base of propositional (content) knowledge.

Subject-Specific Variations on Basic Instructional Models

In the previous section, we noted that the basic model of inquiry teaching takes somewhat different forms in the different subject areas, reflecting differences in the kinds of knowledge generated by the underlying disciplines and the methods they use for doing so. Similar subject-specific variation can be seen in adaptations of the basic models for social constructivist and sociocultural teaching. Each subject has its own unique nature and content, so teachers need to know their subjects thoroughly (including the typical trajectories of progress in these subjects displayed by students at their grade level) in order to make good decisions about content and learning activities. In the following sections, we briefly characterize the ways in which teaching in the main subject areas incorporates constructivist or sociocultural learning principles.

Literacy

Reading.   One well-known constructivist teaching method that was developed originally for literacy instruction is *reciprocal teaching*. Palincsar and Brown (1984) designed reciprocal teaching as a way to teach four comprehension strategies to poor readers: summarizing, questioning, clarifying, and predicting. The teacher does most of the initial modeling and explaining but gradually turns over these responsibilities to the students. Eventually, students take turns acting as the teacher and leading small-group discussions of texts. To begin, the leader notes the title and asks for predictions about the content of the passage. Then the group reads the first segment silently and the leader asks a question about it, summarizes it, and then offers a prediction or asks for clarification if appropriate. If necessary, the adult teacher provides guidance by prompting ("What questions do you think a teacher might ask here?"), instructing ("Remember, a summary is a shortened version; it doesn't include detail"), or modifying the activity ("If you are having a hard time thinking of a question, why don't you summarize first?"). The following dialogue from Palincsar and Brown (1989) illustrates reciprocal teaching as implemented in a first-grade classroom.

> **Teacher:** (*Reading from the text*): The pipefish change their color and movements to blend with their surroundings. For example, pipefish that live among green plants change their color to a shade of green to match the plants.
> **Claire:** (The child leading the discussion): One question that I had about this paragraph is, What is special about the way the pipefish looks?
> **Keith:** (*Clarifying*): Do you mean the way that it is green?
> **Andy:** (*Elaborating*): It's not just that it's green; it's that it's the same color as the plants around it, all around it.
> **Claire:** (*Resuming*): Yes. That's it. My summary is this part tells how the pipefish looks and that it looks like what is around it. My prediction is that this is about its enemies and how it protects itself and who its enemies are.
> **Monty:** They also talked about how the pipefish moves. . . .

Keith: It sways back and forth.

Andy: Along with the other plants.

Teacher: What do we call it when something looks and acts like something else? The way that the walking stick was yesterday? We clarified this word when we talked about the walking stick.

Angel: Mimic.

Teacher: That's right. We said, we would say, that the pipefish mimics the . . .

Several Students: Plants.

Teacher: OK! Let's see if Claire's prediction comes true.

Over time, as students become more familiar with reciprocal teaching activities, the dialogue becomes less routinized and the strategies are used in more flexible ways. The teacher turns over more responsibility for leading and sustaining the dialogue to the students, gradually engaging less in modeling and instruction but more in coaching students' participation in the discussion.

Writing.   Social constructivist approaches to writing instruction involve engaging students in collaborations with their peers. Students might be asked to work together to develop pieces of writing or to act as audiences and constructive critics for one another's writing efforts. In the latter role, students would listen to or read drafts of peers' writings and then ask questions or make suggestions that might help the peers identify possible revisions.

Constructivist approaches to writing also emphasize use of one's own writing for one's own purposes, ranging from simple pleasure to development as a learner. Students may be asked to keep journals to record their daily observations on things of importance to them, as well as to develop their own writing portfolios. A portfolio might include a "personal best," a "most imaginative," a paper from a content area, a paper that shows process and revision, a paper that shows potential for further work, a paper that states and supports an opinion, or a reflective letter that focuses on oneself as a writer. Reflective pieces might address past experiences with writing, the quality of various pieces, the processes that the students used in composing the pieces, their reasons for selecting topics and genres, and their growth as writers across time (Freedman & Daiute, 2001).

Mathematics

Constructivist approaches to teaching mathematics typically call for whole-class lessons in which teachers engage students in generating and discussing potential solutions to problems. The teacher begins by posing a problem and eliciting many different solution suggestions from the students, waiting for and listening to their ideas, encouraging them to elaborate when necessary, conveying an accepting attitude toward their efforts (even if mistaken), and orchestrating discussion of the different ideas within a collaborative problem-solving atmosphere. The problems focus on important mathematical ideas, use multiple representations of the mathematics concepts and procedures involved, can be solved using multiple strategies, and require students to engage in higher level thinking and reasoning.

The teacher seeks to elicit discourse that features mathematical argumentation (about solution suggestions) and collaborative problem solving. Students are encouraged to justify their thinking in terms of the logic and rules of evidence of mathematics (rather than simply deferring to the authority of the teacher or the textbook). Much of the discussion may be conducted in the students' everyday language, although with the teacher reminding them to support their arguments with reference to relevant logic and evidence and eventually helping them to bridge to the more precise and generalizable language of mathematics (Fraivillig, Murphy, & Fuson, 1999; NCTM, 2000; Stein, 2001).

Science

Reform models in science education also emphasize problem-based curricula and social-constructivist approaches to teaching. Students are engaged in doing authentic science by discussing scientific issues, formulating researchable questions relating to those issues, and following through by conducting research—not just in traditional laboratory settings but also in nearby ponds, forests, or other natural environments (National Research Council, 2000).

However, science educators typically emphasize the importance of teacher structuring and scaffolding of these activities, stressing that students are unlikely to acquire the target conceptions if left to explore (and hopefully discover) on their own or engaged in hands-on activities without sufficient attention to minds-on learning. Teachers need to explain key concepts thoroughly, prepare students for experiments by clarifying their goals and key questions, and scaffold their work to make sure that they connect it to big ideas (Klahr & Nigam, 2001; Mayer, 2004; Schauble et al., 1995; Tobin, 1997).

Social Studies

Social studies educators usually emphasize teaching content drawn from history, geography, and the social sciences within the context of preparing students to make personal, social, and civic decisions as citizens of a democracy in an interdependent world. Consequently, they emphasize analysis and discussion of civic issues, particularly by engaging students in thoughtful discourse as described in Chapter 9. The National Council for the Social Studies has published a handbook containing chapters that elaborate the issues analysis approach and illustrate its implementation (Evans & Saxe, 1996).

Constructivist Teaching: Appealing but Difficult

Most educators find portrayals of constructivist teaching attractive, especially when they are contrasted with the transmission stereotype. Certainly the image of a teacher scaffolding co-construction of understandings within a collaborative learning community is more appealing than the image of a teacher lecturing to mostly passive listeners. However, it is important to remember that these are stereotypes: The reality is more complicated.

The Transmission Model as a Straw Person

Self-styled reformers tend to bias their arguments by focusing on the affordances of their favored methods, and on the constraints of the currently dominant methods they would like to supplant. In recent years, constructivists have not only highlighted the potential affordances of constructivist models but also contrasted these models with what they call the transmission model, which they describe primarily with reference to its limitations. The result is something like Table 11.1. This table is useful as a synthesis of constructivists' ideas, but the contrasts it draws between transmission and constructivist methods reflect the constructivists' point of view. After studying the table, one might wonder why anyone would ever engage in transmission teaching.

However, constructivists' typical characterization of transmission teaching is a negatively stereotyped caricature in several respects. First, the very notion of a transmission model of teaching and learning is a straw person developed from a list of ideas that represent polar opposites from constructivist thinking. Few if any educators actually hold this combination of views (certainly not the researchers who developed the sets of findings that we characterized as active teaching in Chapter 10, nor the teachers they studied).

Teacher effects research was an attempt to identify classroom process predictors of achievement gains, not an attempt to validate any particular instructional model. In making decisions about what to measure and in developing interpretations of their findings, the researchers were guided primarily by common sense and the wisdom of practice as synthesized in teacher education texts. To the extent that their work reflected formal theories, these were not behaviorist theories of operant conditioning or transmission models of teaching, but theories stressing the importance of organizing content into coherent, well-structured sequences and making learners aware of this organization of the material, so they could learn it more easily.

None of those researchers viewed knowledge as a fixed body of information, believed that information was somehow transferred automatically from the teacher to the students, or thought that the student role was confined to memorizing or replicating what had been explained or modeled. Nor did they believe that classrooms should be dreary, soulless places in which dominant teachers and passively compliant students played out the same limited roles, day after day. In fact, their findings specifically refuted much of this stereotype, indicating that the teachers who elicited the greatest achievement gains created warm and supportive classroom environments and emphasized interactive discourse over silent seatwork. It was recognized even then that students would construct their own individual understandings of what they were taught, although the knowledge construction process was much less well understood than it is now, and was not given nearly as much emphasis in theories of teaching and learning.

Constructivists sometimes concede all of this but nevertheless argue that the teacher effects research that informed Chapter 10 has limited relevance today because little constructivist teaching was occurring in most of the classrooms observed in those studies. The latter observation is accurate but not as limiting as it might seem at first, because little of the teaching in most of today's classrooms is constructivist teaching. This pattern is likely to continue indefinitely, because approaches to teaching variously called reform models, social constructivist teaching, or sociocultural teaching have proven very difficult to implement in most classroom settings, and thus may have limited practical feasibility despite their theoretical appeal. In contrast, the version of the traditional approach that we have characterized as active teaching is well suited to the affordances and constraints of classrooms (Cuban, 1993).

Constraints on Constructivist Models

Problems with overemphasis on teacher-dominant models such as lecture methods are well known. Sustained lecturing does not promote interaction between prior knowledge and new knowledge or afford the conversations that are needed for students to internalize learning and develop deep understandings. When lectures are implemented poorly or simply used too often, they tend to lead to student boredom and reliance on rote learning methods. However, social constructivist approaches embody their own problems.

Social constructivist approaches require teachers to possess a great deal of subject-matter knowledge, including knowledge about how to teach the subject to students at the grade level; to be able to respond quickly to only partially predictable developments in the discourse; and to structure and scaffold students' learning effectively by providing just the right amount and kinds of help at just the right time. For these and other reasons, social constructivist methods are seldom observed in most classrooms, and when they are, they are often implemented poorly (Airasian & Walsh, 1997; Blumenfeld et al., 1997; Hacker & Tenent, 2002; Myhill & Brackley, 2004; Roelofs & Terwel, 1999; Singer et al., 2000; Weinert & Helmke, 1995; Windschitl, 2002). When teachers engage students in discussions or project learning activities, they often do not introduce these activities with enough emphasis on their goals to allow students to participate in them with a clear idea of their purpose, and they often omit or minimize crucial conclusion and reflection segments needed to bridge between informal learning activities and the more formal representations of knowledge that represent the target outcomes.

Constructivist approaches also require students to participate more actively and take more personal risks in their learning. It may take a great deal of time to get them to the point where they function as a collaborative learning community and interact using the desired discourse genres. Even if they reach this point, limitations in their prior knowledge may prevent them from constructing all of the target understandings.

Heavy reliance on social constructivist discourse models increases the probability that the discourse will stray from the lesson's intended goals and content, and that even when it remains goal relevant, progress toward construction of the intended understandings may be erratic and include frequent verbalization of misconceptions. This can be problematic, because what students carry away from a lesson is heavily dependent on the ideas they hear expressed during the lesson, by either the teacher or their peers. Exposure to misinformation may cause some students to remember a distorted version of the intended learning (Brown, Schilling, & Hockensmith, 1999; Nuthall, 2002). The same can be said of insufficiently structured and scaffolded individual and small-group activities, in which students may spend much of their time confused or exploring blind alleys rather than making good progress in constructing knowledge (Smerdon, Burkam, & Lee, 1999).

The cognitive aspects of co-construction of meaning can become subordinated to students' social agendas, especially when they are operating in small groups away from the supervision of the teacher. Groups may display bickering, exclusion, discounting the contributions of peers, or other departures from the spirit of collaborative learning. Also, students may be exposed not merely to isolated mistaken statements by peers, but to sustained arguments in support of misconceptions. Sometimes, assertive but mistaken peers actually get other group members to regress in their understandings of key concepts (Windschitl, 2002).

An additional concern about constructivist teaching is that it privileges students from advantaged socioeconomic backgrounds who have more of the prior knowledge and other cultural capital needed to function as relatively autonomous and self-regulated learners. Meanwhile, it fails to provide less advantaged students with sufficient access to information and sufficient structuring and scaffolding of their activities to allow them to learn efficiently. Some critics have even characterized an emphasis on constructivist approaches when teaching minority students as the imposition of an inappropriate pedagogy on students who are not part of the dominant culture (Delpit, 1988; Lee, 1999; Richardson, 2003).

An Example: Nuthall's Research

Although sympathetic to social constructivist principles, Graham Nuthall (2002) became pessimistic concerning their feasibility as guides to everyday teaching after studying attempts to implement them in classrooms. He characterized social constructivist teaching as using questions to structure and scaffold problem-oriented discussions and coach students' engagement in activities. Once the students are engaged with a challenging question or problem, the teacher seeks to sustain authentic discussion and debate about significant ideas, using tactics such as asking questions sparingly; listening closely to what students say and responding in ways that connect the discussion so far and position it to move forward; staying with the same topic for several turns and involving more of the students in contributing ideas to it; helping students to clarify their ideas and become more explicit and consistent; making sure that they interact respectfully; and revoicing or reformulating their comments to expand them into more complete statements and emphasize key concepts and causal linkages.

Nuthall noted that social constructivists typically talk as if all students were active participants in classroom discussions, but in fact it is more common for one subset to be highly active and another to remain primarily silent. If unsystematic assessments of learning are based primarily on the statements of the most active participants, they will overestimate the levels of understanding attained by the group as a whole. Also, students' contributions to discussions often make them appear more knowledgeable than they really are (subsequent tests or interviews typically reveal confusion or even misconceptions that were not evident at the time).

Nuthall also noted that effective discussion depends on a base of taken-for-granted knowledge that can be referred to without explanation or elaboration. However, he found that mutually shared knowledge is relatively uncommon unless it relates to an experience that all of the students have shared recently. For example, students typically enter a science or social studies unit knowing almost half of what the teacher intends them to learn from the unit (i.e., they average 40–50 percent on pretests). However, the portion of this prior knowledge that all of the students share in common is only about 10–20 percent at the beginning of the unit, increasing to only about 30–40 percent by the end.

Nuthall found that about 25 percent of what students retain from an instructional unit is acquired via input from peers rather than their teacher; that much of this input is distorted or incorrect; and that these acquired misunderstandings may persist and distort other understandings. His findings imply a need to qualify recommendations of certain teaching tactics favored by social constructivists, especially the popular idea of introducing a lesson or unit by posing a question or problem, inviting students to suggest potential answers or solutions, then listing their responses without questioning them (except to clarify) before initiating evaluative discussion.

There are many advantages to this strategy, cognitive as well as motivational, but it does have the potential for exposing the class to numerous misleading or incorrect ideas. It can be effective for situations in which most of the students' responses are either accurate or reflective of common misconceptions that the teacher wants to elicit and address, but it may be counterproductive if it opens a lot of doors that the teacher would prefer to leave closed. The resulting injection of undesired content will force the teacher to either expand the lesson beyond its intended time and scope (which eliminates something else from the curriculum) or give this content short shrift and run the risk that misconceptions which students received early exposure will stick in their minds instead of the target conceptions emphasized later.

Nuthall also found that, in order to retain a new concept or principle, students needed at least three or four high-quality exposures to it, spaced no more than two days apart. This finding underscores the need for teacher modeling and periodic repetition of big ideas, as well as the fragility of new learning that is not yet firmly established or assimilated. *repetition!*

These and other observations led Nuthall toward two major conclusions about successful implementation of social constructivist teaching. First, such teaching works best when the focus of discussion is on experiences that students have shared with one another (such as carrying out a science experiment or constructing a graphic). In these situations, the referents of their language are mutually accessible, so that shared meaning is not a problem. This is less likely to be true when the discussion focuses on material that has been read or reported about phenomena that students have not mutually experienced.

Second, the aims of social constructivist teaching are more achievable in teacher-led small groups than in the whole-class setting. Small groups make it more likely that all participants will share the same goals, meanings, and understandings, and will participate fully in group processes. They also make it more possible for the teacher to monitor each individual's understandings and intervene as needed.

In summary, despite his enthusiasm for social constructivist theories of learning, Nuthall placed strong qualifications on the feasibility of social constructivist approaches to teaching. Rather than viewing such teaching as the default mode, he conceded that it has its place but only under certain rather restrictive conditions (activities based in shared experiences carried out in small-group settings). Even then, he assumed that there would be much more structuring and scaffolding by the teacher and much less independent student activity than most social constructivists depict.

Situational Differences in the Feasibility of Constructivist Teaching

Some social constructivist educators have written as if their models should be applied universally, without addressing when the model would be used or how it might need to be adjusted to different types of students, subjects, or learning activities. However, constructivist views describe only certain kinds of learning, not *all* learning. Also, the constructivist approaches to teaching need to be assessed on the basis of empirical evidence of their effectiveness, not just their compatibility with constructivist theory. To date, most applications of constructivism have occurred within small pilot studies implemented by professors or small groups of teachers working closely with professors, so it remains to be seen whether these techniques can achieve widespread and powerful implementation in the schools.

Furthermore, most publications on constructivist teaching have been confined to statements of rationale coupled with classroom examples of the principles implemented in practice, without including systematic assessment of outcomes or comparison with other approaches. This makes evaluation of constructivist teaching difficult.

Unfortunately, some constructivists have implied that frontal teaching, skills practice, or independent work on assignments are inappropriate and simply should not occur in classrooms (which instead should focus on whole-class discussions and small-group cooperative learning activities). Others have implied that anything involving discussion or hands-on activity serves worthwhile curricular purposes and will induce students to construct significant understandings. Concerns about such claims have caused more responsible constructivist leaders to criticize much of what has been advocated in the name of constructivism. They have clarified that a complete instructional program will include information presentation as well as constructivist aspects (Sfard, 1998; Staver, 1998; Trent, Artiles, & Englert, 1998; Wells, 1998), and explained that principles for constructivist teaching are much more complex and sophisticated than a simple admonition not to equate teaching with telling (Chazan & Ball, 1999; Cobb, 1994; Driver et al., 1994).

It appears that information presentation is best used for efficiently communicating canonical knowledge (initial instruction establishing a knowledge base) and social constructivist techniques are best used for constructing knowledge networks and developing processes and skills (synthesis and application). In the early grades, this contrast is somewhat muted: Most information presentation occurs during teacher–student interaction segments that also include a lot of teacher questioning. There is little or no extended lecturing, and most opportunities for students to engage in the social construction of knowledge are closely monitored and highly scaffolded by teachers. Later grades more often feature lesson or activity segments that are more exclusively either presentation or social construction of knowledge.

We noted that heavy reliance on social constructivist teaching increases the possibility that the discourse will stray from the lesson's intended goals and content, include frequent verbalization of misconceptions, and make progress toward construction of the intended understandings slower and more erratic. In terms originally introduced by Jacob Kounin (1970) within the context of studying classroom management, it might be said that such lessons have a rough rather than a smooth *flow,* frequently interrupted or sidetracked *momentum,* and a poor *signal* (valid content)-*to-noise* (irrelevant or invalid content) *ratio.*

These dangers become acute when teachers face either of two conditions: (1) young learners with as-yet only partially developed skills for learning through speaking and listening and undeveloped skills for learning through reading and writing, or (2) learners of any age whose prior knowledge is very limited and poorly articulated, so that questions frequently fail to produce responses or elicit irrelevant or invalid statements. An additional challenge in some classrooms is limited fluency in English that prevents many students from efficiently communicating their ideas.

Blending Information Presentation with Social Construction of Knowledge

Attempts to use social constructivist discourse with young children also are complicated by the problem of egocentrism. Primary-grade students often use questions posed by the teacher as occasions for launching stories that they want to tell. These stories may have little or nothing to do with the topic, in which case they distract from the focus of the lesson. In the case of lengthy anecdotes, they derail lesson momentum completely. A teacher familiar to one of the authors minimizes this problem in the learning communities that she establishes by socializing her students to match their comments and questions to the current topic and discourse genre.

She blends information presentation and constructivist teaching in ways that address the limitations of young learners, yet encourage them to personalize their learning and apply it to their lives outside of school. She provides basic information during whole-class instruction early in a lesson or unit, then follows up with small-group or partner activities that allow every student to draw on what he or she knows or has experienced. If necessary, she uses information presentation or demonstration with checking for understanding at the beginning of the segment, then gradually moves to reflective/interactive discussions. Most of her information presentation is communicated using an informal, narrative style that makes it easier to follow and more engaging than the more formal instruction associated with the term *lecture*. It also includes frequent opportunities for students to ask or respond to questions.

Because topic-focused whole-class discussions are difficult to sustain for long with young learners, she frequently scaffolds her students' participation by cueing them to "listen for," "think about," "listen to the story and be ready to share," "listen and decide how you would choose," and so on. If students struggle to respond to her questions, she may help them to express themselves, thus minimizing interruptions and sidetracks. As she scaffolds students' thinking, she often revoices their contributions to articulate big ideas more clearly.

Following (or even in between segments of) whole-class lessons, she frequently will arrange for the students to communicate in small groups ("Talk with your table group to decide what you think was the most important idea") or pairs ("Turn to your partner and share your ideas"). Even these small-group and paired activities, however, may need to be kept short and to be carefully scaffolded if they are to function as worthwhile learning experiences for young learners.

*C*onclusions about Constructivist Teaching

It may be more productive to think about constructivist teaching in its own right rather than in contrast with so-called transmission teaching. Windschitl (2002) noted that the current reform vision of learning has been described as a moderate version of cognitive constructivism nested within a moderate version of social constructivism. Classrooms of teachers seeking to implement this vision would feature eight forms of constructivist activity:

1. Teachers elicit students' ideas and experiences in relation to key topics, then fashion learning situations that help students elaborate on or restructure their current knowledge.
2. Students are given frequent opportunities to engage in complex, meaningful, problem-based activities.
3. Teachers provide students with a variety of information sources as well as the tools (technological and conceptual) needed to mediate learning.
4. Students work collaboratively and are given support to engage in task-oriented dialogue with one another.
5. Teachers make their own thinking processes explicit and encourage students to do the same through dialogue, writing, drawings, or other representations.
6. Students are routinely asked to apply knowledge in diverse and authentic contexts, to explain ideas, interpret texts, predict phenomena, and construct arguments based on evidence, rather than to focus exclusively on the acquisition of predetermined "right" answers.
7. Teachers encourage students' reflective and autonomous thinking in conjunction with the conditions listed above.
8. Teachers employ a variety of assessment strategies to understand how students' ideas are evolving and to give feedback on the processes as well as the products of their thinking.

In addition to these consensus principles that accurately reflect constructivist theorizing, Windschitl (2002) identified pseudoprinciples that reflect common misunderstandings or distortions of constructivist theorizing. These include the notions that direct instruction has no place in the constructivist classroom, that constructivism is nothing more than discovery learning, that students must always be physically or socially active to learn, that there are no rigorous assessment strategies associated with constructivist teaching, and that all ideas, conjectures, and interpretations made by students are equally legitimate. Similarly, Mayer (2004) emphasized that methods of instruction intended to support deep understanding ought to involve cognitive activity rather than behavioral activity, instructional guidance rather than pure discovery, and curricular focus rather than unstructured exploration.

$\mathcal{M}$atching Teaching Methods to Learning Goals

We have noted repeatedly that curriculum and instruction should be goal oriented, with the goals being the intended student outcomes (knowledge, skills, values, and dispositions). The idea is that curriculum content and instructional methods (including learning activities and assessments) need to be aligned with these goals—selected as preferred means for accomplishing the goals and combined into a coherent plan for doing so. Particular methods would be used when teaching focused on the goals for which they were most relevant. Other methods would be used when teaching focused on different goals. At any given time, the methods currently being used would be well matched to the goals currently being pursued.

We also have noted that this seemingly straightforward and logical model is seldom implemented in practice, because teachers' planning typically focuses on the details of implementing lessons and activities, without paying much attention to their goals. Another factor contributing to this problem is that in the literature on instructional methods, arguments often are framed as if the methods were ends in themselves instead of means to accomplish instructional goals. They often imply that the writers' favored methods should be the methods of choice in all instructional situations. This makes no more sense than arguing that a hammer should be the preferred tool for all repair jobs. Like hammers, instructional methods and activities are tools with affordances and constraints that make them well suited to some jobs (i.e., certain learning goals) but not others.

A complete and well-rounded program in any school subject will incorporate a considerable range of curricular and instructional elements and the mixture of these elements will evolve as students proceed through the grades (Weinert & Helmke, 1995). Such programs will not result from application of a few principles rooted in ideology, but they can be constructed on the basis of grounded theory that respects the complexities of classroom teaching and is informed by the accumulated knowledge base produced through educational research.

There is a need for differentiated models of teaching that take into account the different conditions of learning that are presented by different school subjects and (especially) instructional situations. In this regard, many of the currently popular models of teaching and learning require qualification concerning their spheres of application. For example, models that emphasize strategy instruction, situated learning, or modeling, coaching, and scaffolding appear to be well suited to teaching basic literacy and mathematics skills and procedural knowledge in the sciences, social studies, or humanities. However, they are much less well suited to teaching propositional knowledge in the content areas.

Social constructivist and conceptual change models appear to have broader application potential, although with subject-matter differences in how feasible they are and how they are manifested in the classroom. Social constructivist approaches are more feasible for regular use in subjects such as literacy and mathematics that are relatively short on content knowledge but long on processes (procedural knowledge). For subjects like science and social studies that feature a great deal of content (propositional) knowledge, an emphasis on information presentation in the early stages of lessons or units may be required to establish a common knowledge base before moving on to activities that call for processing and applying this knowledge. It is no accident that the most enthusiastic promoters of social constructivist teaching tend to be literacy and mathematics people, whereas the skeptics and qualifiers tend to be science and social studies people (especially those whose research includes formal assessment of students' attainment of target understandings).

For example, it is understandable that teaching models calling for initiating a new topic by engaging students in reasoning about problems are popular among mathematics educators. Such models are most feasible when students are ready to take the next step in moving up a linear trajectory within a hierarchically organized curriculum strand, especially a strand in which relevant propositional knowledge (as opposed to procedural and conditional knowledge) is limited in scope and volume. Such strands are common in mathematics. However, science and especially social studies are much less hierarchical, subsume much broader and deeper domains of propositional knowledge, and much less often afford teaching situations in which students already possess enough prior knowledge about a new topic to allow them to move immediately into addressing topic-relevant problems or issues in an informed way.

Social constructivist and conceptual change models appear most applicable when it is possible to engage students in discussion of topics about which they have a great deal of prior knowledge, especially if this knowledge includes personal life experiences that students can reflect on as a basis for reasoning. They are less applicable when students are getting initial exposure to primarily new propositional knowledge, as when fifth-graders are introduced to chronological treatment of U.S. history. Often it is necessary to first establish a common base of information before attempting to engage students in forms of discourse that implicitly assume understanding of this information. Some social constructivists are being unrealistic, even romantic, in suggesting that teachers should routinely avoid presenting information and instead function only as discussion facilitators.

*P*lanning Your Teaching: Face up to the Complexities

Teaching well is difficult, especially if you aim high by teaching for understanding, appreciation, and application. It requires a good working knowledge of the subject (including its purposes and goals, its most powerful ideas, and the ways in which these ideas are connected and applied), of students (their likely prior knowledge about the subject, including misconceptions, what important knowledge and skills are within their current zones of proximal development), and of pedagogy (how to represent these aspects of the subject to the students and assist them in constructing new understandings). Development of this kind of expertise takes time.

Adapt Teaching to the Situation

The best teaching is adapted to the situation, including the instructional purposes and goals, the students, and the subject matter. For example, the techniques associated with the terms *active teaching, strategy instruction,* and *situated learning* are most relevant when the situation calls for presenting new information, modeling skills, or coaching students as they attempt to implement skills or procedures. In contrast, the techniques associated with terms such as *social constructivism* or *teaching for thoughtfulness* are most relevant when one wishes to develop understanding and appreciation of networks of knowledge through shared construction and negotiation of meanings and implications.

A principle such as *transferring responsibility* for managing learning from the teacher to the students applies to all teaching situations, but figuring out exactly how to apply it (how much modeling, explanation, coaching, and other scaffolding to provide and how quickly to fade this support) takes experience with the content and the students. Even then, some trial and error may be required, because what worked well in the past might not work well with this year's class.

To cope with these complexities and keep your curriculum and instruction well matched to each successive class of students, you will need to be reflective about your practice and prepared to engage in diagnosis and experimentation when your goals are not being met. Most of all, you will need to stay aware of your goals.

$\mathcal{U}$sing Research to Inform Your Teaching

We have emphasized that sound professional decision making is a basic and continuing component of successful teaching. Working within their state and district guidelines, effective teachers determine what curriculum content, instructional methods, learning activities, and assessment approaches are most suited to their classrooms, given the students and subjects they teach.

Achieving clarity about major goals should be the first step in planning, and awareness of those goals should influence subsequent decision making. Arguments about curricular issues (what content is most worth teaching, and why) must be resolved primarily through appeals to basic values rather than through appeals to empirical research, because such arguments concern beliefs about the relative value of different purposes and goals of schooling. Thus, teachers use their values, along with reasoning and critical thinking capacities, to help them make decisions about which content and big ideas deserve the most emphasis or the degree to which instruction should focus on exposure relative to development and application or on knowledge relative to skills.

Research becomes relevant, however, once attention turns to developing plans for teaching particular content at particular grade levels. This is because value-based curricular decisions embody empirically testable assumptions about process-outcome relationships. At least three sets of assumptions are relevant: (1) assumptions about student readiness (that, given their ages and other characteristics, students are ready for the selected content and should be able to achieve the intended learning outcomes if they apply reasonable effort); (2) assumptions about immediate process-outcome relationships (that exposure to the selected content and engagement in the planned activities will enable students to accomplish the learning goals); and (3) assumptions about ultimate generalization and empowerment (that achievement of the learning goals will enable students to apply what they have learned to relevant situations in their lives outside of school, now and in the future). Clarity about goals does not ensure that these hidden assumptions are valid, so there is no guarantee that teachers' decisions and actions undertaken with the intention of accomplishing certain goals will actually succeed in doing so.

The findings of an experiment by Wong (1995) make this painfully obvious. Participants, including experienced inservice teachers as well as preservice teachers, were presented with twelve pairs of "findings" from process-outcome research on teaching. One statement in each pair summarized an actual finding and the other summarized a "finding" that was opposite to the real finding. Sometimes explanations were included along with the summary statements. When participants were asked to state which of each pair was correct, they chose the actual finding only 45 percent of the time. Yet, most considered the statements they selected to be obvious, especially when explanations were provided (in the case of the false findings, these were fictitious explanations). Thus, the participants tended to be quite sure of their beliefs about effective teaching practices, even when they were wrong.

Townsend (1995) reported parallel results from a study very similar to Wong's, and Yates (2005) reported that his teacher education students' ideas about what is obvious and important in teaching effectively were not well matched to the principles emerging from research on teaching. These findings show that you cannot trust your intuitions to lead you to good decisions—you will need to become informed, and stay informed, about relevant research findings.

Nor can you simply look to theory. It is important to have theoretical grounding for your professional practice and to understand why (not just know that) certain practices are preferable to others. However, unless these theoretical explanations have been verified through empirical research, they are simply hypotheses and should be treated as such. Note that seemingly sensible explanations for supposed research findings increased confidence in the findings, even when they were false.

Unfortunately, educational issues often are argued on ideological rather than scientific bases, and policies are undertaken because they conform to a currently popular theory rather than because they have been carefully studied and validated in schools. The result has been an "out with the old, in with the new" approach to educational reform. Instead of a gradual accumulation of knowledge and empirically grounded practice, this leads to cycles that feature swings between extremes. It also leaves teachers confused and cynical about applications of educational theory and research. This is unfortunate, because recent decades have produced a significant body of useful knowledge about teaching, much of which is summarized in this book.

To apply this knowledge base effectively, you will need to resist temptations to look to ideologies or other oversimplifications of the complexities of the profession and instead develop rich repertoires of knowledge and skills that will enable you to make good decisions about the kinds of teaching needed in particular situations. Currently, this means avoiding overreacting to labels such as "transmission models" or "constructivist models" and seeking to develop complete and balanced instructional programs.

A comprehensive approach to teaching encompasses both information presentation and social constructivist techniques (used when suited to the situation), as well as a great many other principles and strategies that are not easily characterized using these labels. Like any other knowledge network, teachers' ideas about their professional practice are likely to be most functional in supporting application if they are structured around basic big ideas. Brophy (1999) suggested the principles shown in Table 11.3 as a short list of big ideas that might anchor effective practice.

Table 11.3 A Short List of Generic Principles for Effective Teaching

1. *A supportive classroom climate.* Students learn best within cohesive and caring learning communities.
2. *Opportunity to learn.* Students learn more when most of the available time is allocated to curriculum-related activities and the classroom management system emphasizes maintaining their engagement in those activities.
3. *Curricular alignment.* All components of the curriculum are aligned to create a comprehensive program for accomplishing instructional purposes and goals.
4. *Establishing learning orientations.* Teachers prepare students for learning by providing an initial structure to clarify intended outcomes and cue desired learning strategies.
5. *Coherent content.* To facilitate meaningful learning and retention, content is explained clearly and developed with an emphasis on its structure and connections.
6. *Thoughtful discourse.* Questions are planned to engage students in sustained discourse structured around powerful ideas.
7. *Practice and application activities.* Students need sufficient opportunities to practice and apply what they are learning, and to receive improvement-oriented feedback.
8. *Scaffolding students' task engagement.* The teacher provides whatever assistance students need to enable them to engage in learning activities productively.
9. *Strategy teaching.* The teacher models and instructs students in learning and self-regulation strategies.
10. *Cooperative learning.* Students often benefit from working in pairs or small groups to construct understandings or help one another master skills.
11. *Goal-oriented assessment.* The teacher uses a variety of formal and informal assessment methods to monitor progress toward learning goals.
12. *Achievement expectations.* The teacher establishes and follows through on appropriate expectations for learning outcomes.

Source: Brophy, J. (1999). *Teaching* (Educational Practices Series No. 1). Geneva: International Bureau of Education.

SUGGESTED ACTIVITIES AND QUESTIONS

1. We discussed several aspects of teaching in this chapter but did not provide a summary synthesizing this information. Show your mastery of the important aspects of the chapter by writing your own summary in a couple of typewritten pages. Compare your summary with those made by classmates and fellow teachers.
2. What are some of the advantages and disadvantages involved when students are asked to summarize material on their own?
3. Most constructivists believe that standardized achievement tests are incomplete or even inappropriate as measures of student learning. To find out what you think about this, obtain samples of standardized achievement tests to study and discuss with peers. What do you see as their strengths and weaknesses as measures of learning outcomes? What does this imply about the strengths and weaknesses of the research reviewed in Chapter 10?
4. Some educators think that there are important differences between active teaching as described in Chapter 10 and helping students to construct usable knowledge as described in

this chapter. Others believe that the former is subsumed within the latter and that the differences are more in underlying philosophy than in what would actually be done in the classroom. Discuss this with peers and see whether you come to agreement on implications for classroom teaching.

5. Learning with understanding is usually described as a process of relating new content to one's existing prior knowledge. But what if students are so unfamiliar with certain content that they possess no readily available schemas within which to assimilate it and very little useful prior knowledge to bring to bear? Is it possible to develop their understanding of such content? If so, can it be done through social constructivist methods or will it be necessary to begin by providing information through texts, teacher explanations, or other input sources? Using a realistic sample from your current or future teaching, plan how you would introduce and develop a topic for which students had little or no prior knowledge.

6. How might you determine your students' zones of proximal development with respect to a particular curriculum unit or topic? What does this imply about forms of preinstructional assessment of student knowledge and thinking that you might incorporate into your teaching?

7. How does ideal scaffolding of students' learning efforts differ from forms of teacher assistance that are less desirable?

8. What are some crucial differences between teachers who rely on discovery learning and teachers who use social constructivist methods to teach for understanding?

9. From a constructivist perspective, why and how might you use technology for certain lessons? What about from an active teaching perspective? Would technology be more crucial or add more value in constructivist teaching or active teaching? Why?

10. You have now completed reading the chapters of this book that describe effective teaching. What important aspects of teacher and student behavior have we neglected? Why do you believe these behaviors are important? What information do you need as a teacher that we have not discussed? Compare your list with others.

FORM 11.1. Social Construction of Knowledge

USE: When a teacher engages students in reflective discussion designed to stimulate construction of knowledge.
PURPOSE: To assess the degree to which the discussion includes features that support social construction of knowledge.

Check each feature that was included in the discussion:
A. POSES A WELL-CHOSEN PROBLEM

___ 1. Problem is appropriate in familiarity, difficulty; Students have enough prior knowledge to allow them to discuss it intelligibly, but they also must engage in reasoning and higher-order thinking
___ 2. Problem is authentic, significant to the students
___ 3. Teacher requires them to predict, explain, develop justified problem-solving or decision-making strategies that call for applying the powerful ideas being developed

B. ELICITS SUGGESTIONS AND RELATED JUSTIFICATIONS

___ 1. Students act as learning community, teacher facilitates
___ 2. Poses problem, calls for ideas about how to approach it
___ 3. Lists suggestions on board or overhead
___ 4. Doesn't judge but calls for clarification, elaboration, justification

C. ELICITS ASSESSMENTS AND DISCUSSION

___ 1. Invites students to critique by offering justified arguments for or against contributed ideas
___ 2. Invites contributors to revise their thinking if they wish
___ 3. Encourages student-student interaction and debate
___ 4. If necessary, scaffolds by breaking question into separate issues or substeps, asking about a neglected aspect, listing what is given or has been agreed upon separately from what still is at issue

D. AS ISSUES GET CLARIFIED, MOVES STUDENTS TOWARD RESOLUTION(S)

___ 1. Tests for consensus when it appears to have developed; if disagreement still exists, asks about unresolved issue(s)
___ 2. If necessary, asks questions to focus attention on unwarranted assumptions, misconceptions, or complications that have not yet been recognized
___ 3. If necessary, temporarily interrupts discussion to allow students time to get more information or interact more intensively in subgroups
___ 4. When consensus is finally achieved, asks questions to help students reformulate what they have discovered about this particular case into more general principles

E. CONSTRUCTS SUMMARY OF MAIN IDEAS AND THEIR CONNECTIONS

___ 1. Invites students to summarize what has been learned
___ 2. If necessary, asks clarification and elaboration questions to make sure that the summary includes all main points and connections between them that need to be emphasized
___ 3. Follows up by having students work individually or in small groups to reconstruct the new knowledge (by writing in journals or composing reports, etc.) and perhaps to apply it to new cases

NOTES:

Assessing Students' Learning

*T*his chapter discusses how teachers can assess student performance accurately and fairly. You will see that students' progress can be measured in various ways, including essay exams, objective exams, portfolios, and rating scales. Each form of assessment has relative strengths and weaknesses, and your choice of assessment must be linked to your instructional goals. Most teachers do not like to assign grades to students, but it is an important task—one that must be done well. Here, we provide detailed information about different ways that you can combine various assessments to provide grades that are both accurate and fair.

*A*ssessing and Grading Student Performance

Tests, papers, and performance exercises are given to assess students' mastery of content. This is not as easy as it appears—just test and grade—because some tests provide poor information about student learning. It will take knowledge and effort for you to develop a good evaluation system.

Professional practice requires that teachers make good decisions about classroom assessment both because testing requires much time and because its effects on students are important (Banks, 2005; Gronlund, 2006). Some teachers spend as much as 50 percent of available time on such activities as quizzes, unit tests, and informal observation (Plake, 1993). Teachers also test frequently. Gullickson (1982) found that 89 percent of elementary school teachers and 99 percent of secondary school teachers relied on testing for evaluation purposes. Most teachers tested at least weekly (95 percent) or biweekly. In a large survey of third through fifth-grade teachers, McMillan, Myran, and Workman (2002) found that the teachers based their grades primarily on performance, effort, and improvement. In this chapter we will discuss how performance, effort, and improvement can be measured and combined to create appropriate grades.

Test Length and Content Coverage

Typically, tests cover only a small portion of the content and objectives taught, so decisions have to be made about what to include. It is important to sample from the full range of content taught and to include enough items to allow reliable measurement. Sometimes this is a straightforward task. In elementary schools, the test likely covers what was taught that week, but even here, tests may leave students guessing about what will be covered. In middle and high school, unit tests and midterm exams require careful planning.

Students will not perceive a test as fair if it emphasizes only a few areas, especially if they thought these were unimportant. An "unfair" fifteen-item test on comparative political systems, for example, might include several questions about evolutionary forces and key individuals who shaped the development of those systems, only a couple of questions about how the systems presently operate, the practical implications of similarities and differences between countries, and no questions about probable future trends.

Table 12.1 shows the percentage of time that eight students of comparable ability spent studying for a test on comparative politics. The student most victimized by the test is Ruth, who spent only 20 percent of her time reviewing historical development,

Table 12.1   Distribution of Test Items, Percentage of Time Spent Studying Three Areas of Comparative Politics, and Student Raw Scores

Test	Historical Development (Percent)	Present Functioning (Percent)	Future Trends (Percent)	Student Scores
	80 (12 Items)	*20 (3 Items)*	*(0 Items)*	
Alice	33	33	33	8
Jane	33	33	33	10
Bill	25	50	25	7
Ted	50	25	25	11
Joan	50	50	0	12
Judy	75	25	0	14
Ruth	20	20	60	7
Tom	33	33	33	10

which turned out to be 80 percent of the exam, and 60 percent of her time studying future trends, a topic not included on the exam.

Table 12.1 also presents the distribution of student scores on the test. Although the distribution is not directly related to the percentage of time spent studying for key parts of the exam, it does correspond closely. In any test situation many factors operate. Bill, for example, may have scored lower than Joan because he was absent during a class discussion that dealt with material needed to answer three of the questions.

Some error of measurement will occur in any test, but a test that unfairly samples content will exacerbate minor problems. The test on comparative politics is not fair. It favors students who guessed correctly about how to prepare for it. As a rule of thumb, test reliability increases with test length, so a thirty-item test is ordinarily more reliable than a fifteen-item test. This assumes that the test equally samples each of the major content areas addressed and that time allocated for test completion is appropriate. Further, it assumes that the test, on average, reflects an appropriate level of difficulty.

Even when a test does sample evenly from all content taught, test items still might favor certain students over others. Sally, for example, might be knowledgeable about baseball, and Ted may not. If some material on the test deals with baseball, Sally may read it more quickly and even remember more of it because she is more familiar with specialized terms, even though she may be no better than Ted in general reading ability. However, if students must read several paragraphs dealing with various topics, these individual differences in knowledge and interest will balance out.

Cognitive Levels of Test Content

Besides sampling from the full range of topics covered, you may wish to sample various levels of understanding of the material. The Taxonomy of Educational Objectives (Bloom et al., 1956) and its revision (Anderson & Krathwohl, 2001) allow you to consider six cognitive demands that test items make on students.

1. *Knowledge.* Remember and recall information. (Who were the first five presidents of the United States? Recite the alphabet. Who wrote Hamlet?)
2. *Comprehension.* Understand the relations between facts or concepts. (Translate a French sentence into English. Predict the probability of rain when given key facts.)
3. *Application.* Use information and procedures that are comprehended. (Given a set of student scores, compute the mean and standard deviation).
4. *Analysis.* Break down an idea into its parts. (Diagram sentences. Identify the setting, plot, and climax of a novel.)
5. *Synthesis.* Rearrange parts to form a new whole. (Write a class play. Watch a film of one's teaching and plan a better strategy.)
6. *Evaluation.* Know the value of methods for given purposes. (Was the play credible, well paced?)

Sampling from each level will yield a balanced view of each student's learning as well. (Some students are good at understanding and remembering discrete facts but have trouble synthesizing them, integrating them with general principles, and applying their knowledge in problem-solving situations; other students have the opposite pattern of strengths and weaknesses). Table 12.2 illustrates a plan for a test that samples both the range of topics taught and a variety of levels of cognitive demand. For simplicity, the six cognitive-level categories from the taxonomy are combined to form two categories. The first (terms, facts, principles) represents the first two levels of the taxonomy (knowledge and comprehension). Table 12.2 also summarizes the teacher's plans for three units. The first unit on weather indicates that the largest percentage of instruction will focus on application of concepts to predict weather. Hence, the exam should emphasize this information.

An outline of goals will help you make instructional decisions (how much time to spend in class, the type of homework to assign) and write appropriate tests. However, do not confuse general knowledge of test expectations with knowledge of specific questions; that is, do not simply teach to the test.

Instructional Objectives

Emphasize key goals during instruction, in constructing tests, and in making suggestions to students about test preparation. In general, instruction is more effective to the extent that teachers have specific plans and communicate clear expectations to students about what they are to learn (Gronlund, 2006). You can communicate effectively by following three steps:

Table 12.2 Three Plans for Classroom Tests with Specification of Content and Cognitive Emphasis

Content	Cognitive Objectives		
	Terms, Facts, Principles	*Applications*	*Total Percentage*
Unit 1: Weather			
A. Atmosphere	20	0	20
B. Air masses and fronts	15	5	20
C. Causes of Precipitation	0	15	15
D. Predicting	0	40	40
E. Control	5	0	5
Unit 2: Weights and Measures			
A. Length	10	0	10
B. Weight/mass	10	0	10
C. Time	10	0	10
D. Standard measures			
1. Metric System	60	0	60
2. GCs	5	0	5
3. KMS	5	0	5
Unit 3: Comparative Politics			
A. Historical development	80	0	80
B. Present function	0	20	20
C. Future Trends	0	0	0

1. *Name the terminal goal.* What will you accept as proof that the learner has achieved your goal? Must the student swim a lap or a mile, design a blueprint, or build a garage?
2. *Specify the conditions under which knowledge will be demonstrated.* Will students write essay questions or deliver a speech; will answers be picked from a list or retrieved from memory; will students evaluate a live debate or analyze written material?
3. *Announce the criteria for acceptable performance.* Fifteen out of twenty correct answers for an A; run a mile in less than eight minutes for a B; write a theme with no grammatical errors to pass the grammar unit review.

Instructional objectives have several advantages and disadvantages.

Advantages of Instructional Objectives

- They increase your awareness of what students should be working on and lead to more optimal planning that includes a wider range of objectives.
- They provide a basis for assessing continuous progress (allowing students to proceed at their own rates) because instruction focuses on specific skills and knowledge.
- Students have a better blueprint for guiding their learning activity; hence, they learn more.

Disadvantages of Instructional Objectives

- They unduly emphasize things that can be measured easily and therefore favor low-level objectives.
- Once established (the teacher invests the time to write objectives and set up a measurement system), the system perpetuates itself; objectives remain the same and spontaneity is reduced.
- A great deal of time is needed to write the objectives.
- They tend to focus on parts of the whole as opposed to more integrative or complete knowledge.

Communicating Expectations to Students

Students need to know what will be emphasized in testing. Table 12.3 shows that students in Ms. James's class should spend most of their time generating ideas; however, they also

Table 12.3 Four Teachers' Criteria for Grading Students' Papers

Teacher	Ideas	Organization	Mechanics	Sentence Structure
Ms. James	70	10	10	10
Ms. Wilson	85	15	0	0
Mr. Adkins	50	10	25	15
Ms. Stanford	50	50	0	0

should polish their language and grammar skills. In contrast, students in Ms. Wilson's class should concentrate on developing major ideas. Mr. Adkins's students know that they should spend about half of the "composition time" on sentence structure, grammar, and so on. Ms. Stanford stresses organization more than the other teachers.

Facts versus Concepts

What does a good test blueprint look like? There is no formula for a good plan. Your plan should clarify instructional goals, assist in planning instruction, and help you to prepare a test that measures intended goals. Sometimes it makes sense to focus only a little on application and emphasize basic facts. Sometimes it makes sense to stress application.

Essay Test Items

There are two basic types of questions you can use on classroom tests: essay and objective. Essay questions, if used correctly, require students to do more than reproduce information. Questions that ask students to predict or to write their own examples are generally better than questions that require students merely to present facts. Consider the five essay questions that follow. Which is the best? Why?

1. What is motivation?
2. Pick four motivational principles, and explain why they are important.
3. Compare and contrast the motivational perspectives as advanced by Weiner and Bandura.
4. Read the attached case study, and analyze it using Deci and Ryan's theories.
5. Read the attached case study, and then select a motivational theory that best explains the problem and what to do about it.

Question 1 provides students an unlimited opportunity for responding, but grading such a question fairly is virtually impossible because some students may give their own definition, whereas others may paraphrase major theorists, and major theorists may disagree about the definition of motivation. Question 2 is not as hard to grade but still leaves much decision making to the student. (Is the principle important to the teacher, the student, or the theorist?)

Question 3 is adequate but probably could be assessed more easily and effectively in the objective test format (because the student is asked to state facts, not process them). Questions 4 and 5 are better essay questions than the first three because they require both thinking and knowledge.

Often teachers write essay questions that only call for factual information. Knowledge and comprehension can be assessed more efficiently and reliably by objective tests. Another common problem is merely telling students to discuss an issue, which forces them to guess what the teacher really wants (What is motivation?).

Some teachers, perhaps because they feel uncomfortable asking so few questions and neglecting so much content, ask too many essay questions and undermine the unique role that an essay question can play. Essay exams are useful to the extent that they provide students with an opportunity to demonstrate their ability to recall, organize, and apply facts and principles. To rush students through five essay questions in fifty minutes is self-defeating.

Asking students to solve problems is an especially good way to use essay questions. For example, "The first paragraph that follows describes the academic problems of Ted Jenkins. The following three paragraphs describe his teacher's attempts to deal with the problems. Compare and contrast the three solutions, giving special consideration to the short-term and long-term effects of the plans on Ted's general dependency, class achievement, and peer status."

Scoring: The Essay Test

Read the two answers that follow in response to the essay question: "Compare the powers and organization of the central government under the Articles of Confederation with the powers and organization of our central government today." What grade should Student A receive? Student B? Which answer is better written? Which conveys more knowledge? More comprehension?

Student A. Our government today has a president, a house of representatives, and a senate. Each state has two senators, but the number of representatives is different for each state. This is because of compromise at the Constitutional Convention. The Articles of Confederation had only a Congress and each state had delegates in it and had one vote. This Congress couldn't do much of anything because all the states had to say it was alright. Back then Congress couldn't make people obey the law and there wasn't no supreme court to make people obey the law. The Articles of Confederation let Congress declare war, make treaties, and borrow money and Congress can do these things today. But Congress then really didn't have power, it had to ask the states for everything. Today Congress can tell the states what to do and tax people to raise money they don't have to ask the states to give them money. Once each state could print its own money if it wanted to but today only the U.S. Mint can make money.

Student B. There is a very unique difference between the Central Government under the Articles of Confederation and the National Government of today. The Confederation could not tax directly where as the National Government can. The government of today has three different bodies—Legislative, Judicial, and Executive branches. The Confederation had only one branch which had limited powers. The confederate government could not tax the states directly or an individual either. The government of today, however, has the power to tax anyone directly and if they don't respond, the government has the right to put this person in jail until they are willing to pay the taxes. The confederation government was not run nearly as efficiently as the government of today. While they could pass laws (providing most of the states voted with them) the confederate government could not enforce these laws, (something which the present day government can and does do) they could only hope and urge the states to enforce the laws.

How hard is it for you to quantify the differences between the two responses? How much better is the response you rate higher? How do you think the grades you assigned compare to those your classmates gave?

Thorndike and Hagen (2004) presented these two answers to graduate students taking a course in tests and measurement. They asked the students to assign a maximum of 25 points to the answers, provided them with a model answer, and stressed that the grades should be based on completeness and accuracy, not grammar or spelling. The papers received a wide variety of scores. Student A's paper received scores ranging from 5 to 25 points, and student B's paper was scored as low as 3 and as high as 25.

These findings indicate that it is important for teachers who use essay tests to develop objective criteria for scoring such tests. Is the paper assigned a 20 or 21 really inferior to the paper assigned a 24 or 25? Be sure that the scores reflect demonstrated student performance, not your biases.

There are two generally acceptable techniques for grading an essay—the point-score method and the sorting method. The *sorting method* is easier to use and, although not as reliable, it can be used fairly. The steps involved are: (1) quickly read all the papers and sort them into piles (A, B, C, pass, fail), placing borderline papers into the higher category with a question mark on them; (2) read the responses again, paying special attention to borderline papers; (3) assign a grade to each paper on the basis of the pile it ends up in.

The *point-score method* calls for (1) a grading key specifying features that should be present in full credit answers (partial credit for each part of the response should be determined in advance); (2) reading all responses to the same question consecutively and assigning earned points to each question as it is read; (3) scoring all responses to the next question; and (4) when all questions have been read, totaling points and assigning a grade.

In general, the point-score method is the best way to grade essay tests because it uses a fixed standard (an answer key) and guards against halo effects that interfere with effective grading. A halo effect refers to the tendency to evaluate on the basis of a global impression rather than according to a specific trait or performance. The sorting method also yields generally reliable scores, however, and teachers who use essay tests often may have to rely on this technique.

Mehrens and Lehmann (1991) recommended that teachers construct model answers to essay questions as they write the questions, not after the test is given. This procedure calls attention to faulty wording, inadequate time allotment, inappropriate difficulty level, and similar problems early enough for teachers to correct them prior to test administration. The strengths of essay tests include their ability to assess student thinking/reasoning, writing, and organizational skills and the fact that they are fairly easy to write. On the other hand, essay tests sample only a small amount of content; are time-consuming to read and grade; and consume much teacher time if helpful information is to be provided to students.

Objective Test Items

Multiple-choice items can measure the same aspects of an educational objective as any other pen-and-paper test, except written expression and originality. Analysis, synthesis, and other levels of cognitive processing can be tested with multiple-choice items, although it is hard to construct such items. The multiple-choice format is the most versatile form of an objective test item. The item has two parts: the stem, which represents the problem;

and three or more response choices, of which one is the correct answer and the others are distracters (plausible alternatives for students who do not know the answer). Consider the following example:

Good and Brophy suggest that test reliability can be enhanced by:

A. Longer tests
B. Informing students about test coverage
C. Giving students extra time to take the test
D. A and B
E. A and C

The primary advantage of the objective test, when properly constructed, is that it provides a relatively unbiased assessment of student performance. The inclusion of partially correct answers reduces the objectivity of the test because judgments have to be made about the degree of correctness, and if answer choices are not plausible, the chances that a student will guess the answer are increased. Often test questions give away answers (the right answer is longer, the stem provides a grammatical clue, and so forth). When test answers can be guessed, the test measures students' ability to take tests rather than their knowledge.

In the time that your students could answer one or two essay questions they could respond to fifty multiple-choice items. Multiple-choice tests allow you to assess much more content than essay tests, and grading responses is much quicker. Despite these qualities, some educators are highly critical of these tests.

Criticisms of Multiple-Choice Testing

Mitchell (1992) contends that overuse of multiple-choice tests has informed students that what counts is memorization and passive recognition of single correct answers. However, she notes that these tests would not be so objectionable if they were part of an evaluation package that included teachers' observations, students' collections of work, essays, and cooperative products.

Mitchell concludes that multiple-choice tests interrupt the teaching and learning process for five reasons:

1. Even at their best, they only ask students to select a response. Students are not required to think.
2. Multiple-choice tests imply that a right or wrong answer is available. Few situations in life have a correct or incorrect answer.
3. The tests rely on memorization and recall of algorithms instead of allowing students to show their understanding of the algorithms.
4. Too often multiple-choice tests include content that is easily assessed rather than important.
5. The tests trivialize teaching and learning.

Multiple-choice exams are overused. However, their *quality*—how the items are written—varies greatly. They are useful for assessing whether students possess sufficient knowledge to inform their thinking and problem solving. For example, knowledge that there was a Republican president for twelve years before Bill Clinton took office is important information if one is attempting to understand how various coalitions in the Democratic Party responded to policy initiatives from the previous Bush administration. Similarly, knowledge that certain chemicals cannot be mixed in the lab may be associated with improved lab safety and may transfer more readily to real-life situations (alcohol and quaaludes cannot be mixed and are often deadly) than platitudes like "just say no." Education has a tendency to move from fad to fad: One current fad is to devalue factual knowledge and objective testing. However, no matter what educators think about the multiple-choice format, mandated state testing guarantees heavy use of this format in most schools. Thus, students need practice on this type of test. Not to give them practice on these items is likely to set them up for failure.

Other Forms of Objective Questions

Three other popular objective test formats are true-false, matching, and brief definition.

In general, *true-false* questions can be constructed much more quickly than multiple-choice items. Unlike multiple-choice questions, the true-false format forces students to choose between two alternatives rather than four or five. Consider the following examples:

Directions: Read each statement and circle whether it is true or false.

- T F   Teacher alerting is an important variable in the Kounin management system.
- T F   According to Good and Brophy, the easiest way to improve a test's reliability is to decrease its length.
- T F   Teachers' managerial success is more dependent on their proactive than their reactive skills.

Students can respond to true-false questions even more quickly than to multiple-choice questions because they are easier to comprehend. True-false questions can be used to good advantage with young children, especially when only a general estimate of student knowledge is necessary. A major limitation of true-false questions is that much content is difficult to express in a true-false form, in part because the truth of a statement may vary with context. Furthermore, students will be correct 50 percent of the time by guessing; hence, the diagnostic power of true-false questions is low.

Short-answer and *completion* items require students to finish a statement from recall rather than recognition. On a multiple-choice test students select (recognize) the best answer from a set of choices. In contrast, in a short-answer format, students provide their own answers. It is considerably more difficult to construct a multiple-choice item that presents four or five carefully written and plausible alternatives than it is to write a stem and to allow students to provide their own answers. However, definition and short-answer items are typically harder to grade than are multiple-choice items.

Directions: Briefly define each term.

A. Alerting

_____

_____

B. Accountability

_____

_____

C. Withitness

_____

_____

D. Stay with action

_____

_____

E. Give up action

_____

_____

Short-answer and completion tests present some of the same scoring problems as essay tests. How would you grade these definitions of alerting?

- Alerting is teacher awareness.
- It is part of the Kounin management system.
- Alerting cannot be used alone.
- Too much alerting makes students dependent.

Obviously, it takes considerably more time to present a question about alerting in a multiple-choice format than to ask students to define alerting. The ease of scoring multiple-choice questions, however, typically compensates for the time needed to construct the items and often yields more reliable scores than those obtained from a completion test.

Alerting is best defined as:

A. Teacher cues students that something will happen.
B. The teacher sees a problem as soon as it happens.
C. The teacher checks a student's work carefully
D. Both A and B
E. Both B and C

Short-answer and completion items are especially useful in math and science courses, where formulas or equations can be requested, and for testing spelling and language, where specific bits of information often are required in order to do more complex problem-solving tasks. In any subject, they are good for testing knowledge of definitions and technical terms (Mehrens & Lehmann, 1991).

Matching exercises require students to link items in one column with corresponding items in another column. These can be very confusing to students unless directions are carefully given as stated below:

Directions: Match the topic in Column A with the name of the researcher associated with that topic in Column B. Write the letter of the researcher associated with the topic on the line next to each number. Each name in column B may be used once, not at all, or more than once.

Column A
_____ **1.** Intelligence tests
_____ **2.** Cognitive development
_____ **3.** Trust vs. mistrust
_____ **4.** Reinforcement
_____ **5.** Modeling
_____ **6.** Formal operations

Column B
A. Freud
B. Skinner
C. Erikson
D. Piaget
E. Kounin
F. Binet
G. None of the above

In this example, students would receive credit for answering F, D, C, B, G, and D for items 1–6, respectively. Matching exercises are useful for testing memory of specific facts: terms, definitions, dates, events, and so on. They are easy to construct and score, as long as each item has just one clearly correct answer. To avoid cuing answers, it is helpful to have more response alternatives (column B in this example) than items (column A) or to include response alternatives that may be used more than once (D in the example).

Conclusions: Types of Test Items

No single type of test or test item is best in all circumstances. Advocates sometimes claim that essay tests are better for measuring higher-level objectives and that objective tests are better for measuring factual recall or other low-level objectives. Things are not that simple, however. Essay tests can be used purely to grade low-level skills (punctuation, capitalization, spelling), with no attention to the creativity of the essay, or they can be used to measure factors such as sentence structure, paragraph structure, or story theme. Similarly, multiple-choice tests can measure learning objectives at almost any level of difficulty or sophistication; they are not restricted to low-level objectives. Still, it is easier to write an essay test to measure higher-order thinking than to write objective tests to accomplish that same purpose.

Other differences between test items are more a matter of teacher or student preference than of necessity. Essay tests, for example, allow students to organize their answers and integrate material. Essay tests are confined to a relatively small portion of the material covered and are time-consuming to grade, and the grading can be highly subjective. Some students with well developed writing skills gain an advantage on these tests (better writing may be seen as more knowledge). Further, the types of evidence that essay tests provide can be measured in other ways (term papers).

Multiple-choice and other objective tests offer advantages such as speed and objectivity of scoring, sampling a much larger number of objectives in the same amount of time, quicker feedback to students, and collecting broader-based data on a wide range of course objectives. Some students, however, have test-taking skills that give them an advantage on this kind of test, independent of content.

Additional Assessment Procedures

Performance Tests

A performance test requires that an individual or a group make a decision, solve a problem, or perform some prescribed behavior like delivering a speech. Some contend that how students use knowledge—not student knowledge as shown on pen-and-paper tests—is the critical variable in determining whether students have mastered material or developed social maturity. Most states use beginning-teacher evaluation assessments in which you will have to demonstrate classroom competency before you become fully certified. State assessments require knowledge (e.g., child development) on pen-and-paper measures as well as an ability to teach as assessed on a performance measure.

Figure 12.1 provides an example of the type of observation systems used to evaluate beginning teachers. In this case, teachers are first asked a few interview questions before the lesson begins, and then an observer using the THOR system assesses teacher performance on several aspects of teaching. (For more information on development of the scale, see Tsang [2003], and see Good et al. [2006] for a description of its use with beginning teachers.)

The advantage of performance measures is that they provide direct evidence that a student can perform a practical skill, or can apply knowledge to solve problems. The disadvantage is that the process of observing the performance of individuals is time-consuming for both students and teachers (or principal and peer teachers). Observation of performance also can increase evaluation anxiety and underestimate capability.

There are many skills that you might want to measure directly: painting a watercolor, keyboarding sixty words a minute, conducting an opinion poll, conducting a counseling interview, giving a speech, and so forth. You can profitably use performance tests or oral presentations as part of your assessment programs. The general procedure you follow is the same as that for construction of classroom tests: (1) identify instructional objectives (content and cognitive skills); (2) plan instructional activities; and (3) assess student learning. A fourth, unique dimension is to help students identify performance criteria and internalize them so that they can progressively assume more responsibility for self-evaluation.

It is important for students to know in advance how their term paper will be graded. Writing comprises various elements and it is useful to determine the emphasis you want to give these elements. The elements include grammar, punctuation, vocabulary, spelling, capitalization, organization, documentation, style and so forth. In contrast, at other times you might emphasize the interpretation and organization of papers rather than structure and grammar. Sometimes you will focus on the quality and accuracy of ideas, logical

Interview **Assessment**

EOS _____ Number of Students in Class: _____

T1: T2: T3:

1. Formal Assessment Criteria and Standards

1	2	3	4	5
The proposed approach to assessment contains no clear criteria or standards.		Assessment criteria and standards have been developed, and are mostly clear to students.		Assessment criteria and standards are clear and have been clearly communicated to students. Clear rubrics have been developed.

T1: T2: T3:

2. Use of Formative Assessment

1	2	3	4	5
Assessment is only used for summative purposes. Teacher has no intent to use assessment to follow-up on students' learning. No formative use of assessments occurs.		Teacher primarily uses assessment for summative purposes rather than as a way to enhance or retain learning. Teacher makes inconsistent attempts to use assessments for formative purposes.		Teacher frequently uses assessments for both formative and summative purposes. Teacher uses assessments as a gauge to enhance and retain student learning over time.

T1: T2: T3:

3. Learning Goals for Students

1	2	3	4	5
Teacher's goals are not clearly defined. Teacher designs lessons without much consideration to broader learning goals or emphasizes trivial learning.		Teacher sets learning goals for students and designs lessons and activities to build all students toward the same goals. Goals are moderately clear.		Teacher sets learning goals for students and designs lessons and activities to build students toward goals. Teacher also provides specialized attention to help students reach learning goals. Goals are clearly defined.

(Continued)

Figure 12.1 The THOR System

Observation   **Assessment**

T1:   T2:   T3:

4. Providing In-Class Feedback and Informal Assessment to Students

1	2	3	4	5	Criteria not all applicable during this lesson
Teacher does not use any means to assess whether students understand the concepts being taught. There is no evidence that any student learning has occurred.		Teacher uses some methods to informally assess student learning. The assessment gives an accurate estimate of student learning and questions are asked of more than just a few students.		Teacher effectively uses in-class assessment or questioning to assess student understanding of material. Assessment is conducted on a large portion of students.	

T1:   T2:   T3:

5. Fairness and Consistency of Formal and/or Informal Assessment

1	2	3	4	5	Criteria not all applicable during this lesson
Assessment methods are rarely used and appear to be prone to inconsistency and subjectivity. Assessments cannot differentiate students who have learned the material from those who have not.		Assessment methods approach fairness and consistency. Assessment methods usually allow students to demonstrate their understanding of the material with some exceptions.		Assessment methods are fair and consistent. Teacher makes students aware of what must be done to demonstrate understanding of the material.	

Observation   **Classroom Management**

                                EOS _____

T1:   T2:   T3:

6. Teacher Interaction with Students

1	2	3	4	5	Criteria not all applicable during this lesson
Teacher demonstrates visible frustration, exasperation, lack of poise or confidence in a way that inhibits learning, or promotes management difficulties.		Teacher is generally poised, confident, and respectful. Teacher rapport with most students is positive with some inconsistencies.		Teacher is confident, respectful and de-monstrates excellent rapport with students. Teacher–student interactions are warm and highly supportive to learning.	

Figure 12.1   Continued

Observation

T1:   T2:   T3:

7. Student Interactions with Other Students

1	2	3	4	5	Criteria not all applicable during this lesson
Student interactions are disrespectful, mean, or ridiculing. Student interactions exhibit a lack of mutual respect.		Student interactions do not inhibit the learning activity, even if the interactions are not directly related to the task.		Student interactions are polite, respectful, and highly supportive of learning. Culture of learning is evident among students.	

T1:   T2:   T3:

8. Management of Instructional Groups and Individuals

1	2	3	4	5	Criteria not all applicable during this lesson
Students not working with the teacher are not productively engaged in learning.		Tasks for work are partially organized, resulting in some off-task behavior when teacher is involved with a group or individuals.		Tasks for work are organized, and students are managed so most students are engaged in learning at all times.	

T1:   T2:   T3:

9. Appropriate Behavior Is Understood and Followed by Students

1	2	3	4	5	Criteria not all applicable during this lesson
Few standards of conduct appear to have been established, or students do not follow standards of appropriate behavior.		Standards of conduct appear to have been established for most situations and most students seem to follow these standards.		Standards of conduct appear to be clear to all students and are consistently followed by students.	

T1:   T2:   T3:

10. Monitors Student Behavior and Provides Feedback

1	2	3	4	5	Criteria not all applicable during this lesson
Student behavior is not monitored, and teacher is unaware of what students are doing, or responses to behavior are disruptive to the lesson.		Teacher is generally aware of student behavior but may miss activities of some students. Responses to behavior are generally appropriate and only slightly disruptive.		Teacher is alert to student behavior. Monitoring is subtle and preventive, or may not be needed. Responses to behavior are appropriate with minimal disruption to class.	

(Continued)

Observation   **Implements Instruction**

EOS _____

T1:   T2:   T3:

11. Instructional Activities Are Congruent with Goals and Lead to Accomplishing Goals

1	2	3	4	5	Criteria not all applicable during this lesson
Students have a difficult time understanding how activities relate to learning goals. Instructional activities do not lead to learning goals that are appropriate for the students.		Students generally see the connection between the lesson and the learning goal. Instructional activities generally lead to accomplishing learning goals.		Students clearly understand the connection between the lesson and the learning goal. Instructional activities are well designed to help all students reach the learning goals.	

T1:   T2:   T3:

12. Giving Directions and Explanations to Students Enhances Student Understanding

1	2	3	4	5	Criteria not all applicable during this lesson
Teacher's directions and/or explanations to an activity are frequently confusing to students, or are clearly too basic for most students.		Teacher's directions and/or explanations to an activity are generally clear and help students understand the content or task.		Teacher's directions and/or explanations to an activity are clearly presented and significantly promote student understanding.	

T1:   T2:   T3:

13. Makes Effective Use of Learning Materials to Achieve Learning Goals

1	2	3	4	5	Criteria not all applicable during this lesson
Teacher communicates the lesson without any use of materials that are appropriate for goals, or materials distract students from learning content.		Teacher complements presentations with use of materials that are appropriate for goals. Materials are somewhat effective in helping students organize and learn content.		Appropriate materials are used and are effective at increasing student understanding of the content as well as improving student engagement.	

Figure 12.1   Continued

Observation:

T1:   T2:   T3:

14. Demonstrating Effective "Bag of Tricks" in Presenting New or Difficult Concepts

1	2	3	4	5	Criteria not all applicable during this lesson
Teacher fails to provide alternative approaches or examples when confronted with students' lack of understanding of new or difficult concepts.		Teacher is somewhat effective at using examples, mental imagery, role modeling, visual representations, etc. to illustrate new or difficult concepts when confronted with student incomprehension.		Teacher is very effective at using examples, mental imagery, role modeling, visual representations, etc. to better illustrate new or difficult concepts when confronted with student incomprehension.	

T1:   T2:   T3:

15. Demonstrates Content Knowledge in Instruction

1	2	3	4	5	Criteria not all applicable during this lesson
Teacher makes content errors, is unable to engage in discussions on the content, or treats the content only very superficially.		Teacher demonstrates generally accurate content knowledge in instruction and in answering student questions when present.		Teacher demonstrates in-depth understanding of the content during instruction and enhances student learning, which may include the use of multiple/alternative techniques.	

T1:   T2:   T3:

16. Student Response to Teacher's Display of Energy and Conviction for the Content Being Taught

1	2	3	4	5	Criteria not all applicable during this lesson
Teacher presents content with little conviction and with little apparent buy-in from students.		Teacher communicates importance of the work with some energy. Teacher is able to draw some students to the content.		Teacher's energy and conviction draws most students to the content.	

(Continued)

Observation:

T1:   T2:   T3:

17. Uses Clear, Accurate, and Expressive Oral Communication

1	2	3	4	5	Criteria not all applicable during this lesson
Teacher's spoken language is inaudible to some students, contains grammar or syntax errors, **or** is unexpressive.		Teacher's spoken language is audible, moderately expressive, and/or grammatically correct.		Teacher's spoken language is clear and very expressive. Use of language and oration enhances understanding and interest.	

T1:   T2:   T3:

18. Quality of Questions

1	2	3	4	5	Criteria not all applicable during this lesson
Teacher's questions are not developmentally appropriate or relevant, **or** teacher fails to ask necessary questions.		Teacher asks questions that are developmentally appropriate and promote instructional intent, which may include basic facts and/or skills.		Most questions are developmentally appropriate and promote thoughtful responses and deeper understanding of content.	

T1:   T2:   T3:

19. Demonstrating Flexibility in Responding to Students' Questions and Interests

1	2	3	4	5	Criteria not all applicable during this lesson
Teacher ignores students' questions or interests, or teacher's response to students leads to major digression from the lesson.		Teacher attempts to accommodate students' questions or interests. The accommodation usually does not decrease the coherence of the lesson.		Teacher successfully accommodates students' questions or interests and enhances learning by using student comments to enhance understanding of the lesson.	

T1:   T2:   T3:

20. Student Engagement and Interest in Lesson

1	2	3	4	5	Criteria not all applicable during this lesson
Majority of students are not engaged actively. Most do not contribute to class discussions, or seem uninterested in the content.		Students are generally engaged in lesson actively. Many are participating in class discussions and all are at least paying attention.		Most students are highly engaged in the lesson. Students display interest in learning the content and actively participate in learning.	

Figure 12.1   Continued

Observation

T1:   T2:   T3:

21. Importance and Value of Content Presented

1	2	3	4	5	Criteria not all applicable during this lesson
Teacher focuses lesson on mostly trivial knowledge, or the lesson does not relate to standards of learning in the content area.		Teacher focuses lesson on generally valuable aspects of the content and standards of learning are generally evident in the lesson.		Teacher focuses lesson on content that represents valuable knowledge that promotes in-depth understanding of the content standards.	

T1:   T2:   T3:

22. Broader View of Content [Code T3 Only]

1	2	3	4	5	Criteria not all applicable during this lesson
The teacher is ineffective at, or does not relate the content of the lesson to course as a whole and/or the potential application of content outside of classroom.		The teacher uses surface characteristics to relate the content of the lesson to the course as a whole and/or practical application.		The teacher effectively connects the content of the lesson, which enables students to see the value and importance of the content as a whole.	

T1:   T2:   T3:

23. Structure of Lesson [Code T3 Only]

1	2	3	4	5	Criteria not all applicable during this lesson
The lesson has no clearly defined structure.		The lesson has a recognizable structure, although it is not uniformly maintained throughout the lesson.		The lesson has a clearly defined structure that enhances learning such as the effective use of a defined beginning, middle, and end of a lesson.	

T1:   T2:   T3:

24. Pacing of Lesson

1	2	3	4	5	Criteria not all applicable during this lesson
The pacing of the lesson is too slow, rushed, or both. Students appear to be bored or confused.		The pacing of the lesson is generally appropriate for the majority of the students. Some students appear to be bored or confused.		The pacing of the lesson is appropriate for students. Most students do not appear to be bored or confused.	

Source: Good, T. L., McCaslin, M., Tsang, H., Zhang, J., Wiely, C.R.H., & Bozack, A. R. (2006, September/October). *Journal of Teacher Education, 57*(4), 410–430. Reprinted by permission.

development of ideas, organization of ideas, style and individuality, and general wording and phrasing. See Figure 12.2 for an example of a rating scale for term papers with this emphasis.

There is much interest in using assignments that allow students to articulate ideas orally and to explain and explore through verbal communication. Sometimes oral evaluations emphasize rather mechanical features of performance that can inhibit performance if they are focused on extensively. For example, a rating developed by Kubiszyn and Borich for analyzing speeches (1984) emphasized enunciation, pronunciation, loudness, word usage, pitch, rate, and gestures. These dimensions have considerable utility in a speech class (see Figure 12.3).

However, if someone used that form for a presentation in a social studies class, it would be silly. This is so because the act of communicating involves many important areas and dimensions that need to be considered if oral presentations are to be more than a verbal multiple-choice test. The extent to which a speaker is genuine, appropriately

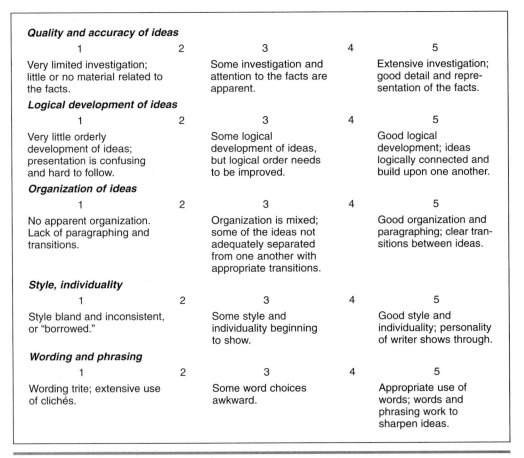

Figure 12.2   Rating Scale for Themes and Term Papers That Emphasize Interpretation and Organization

Source: Educational Testing and Measurement by T. Kubiszyn and G. Borich. Copyright 2007, Wiley & Sons. Reprinted by permission of Wiley & Sons.

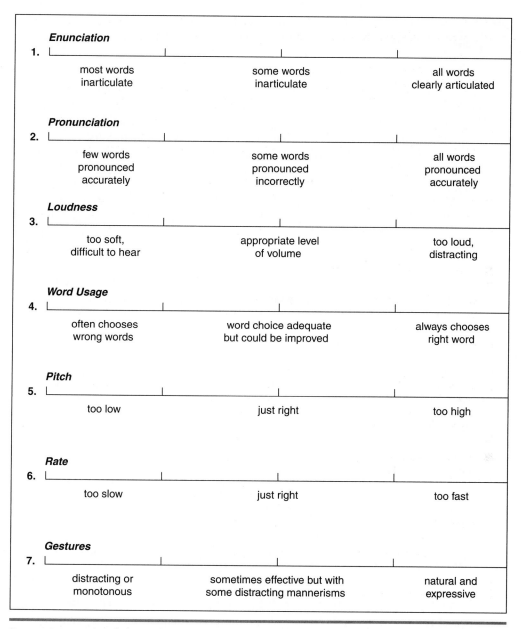

Figure 12.3 Rating Scale for Speaking

Source: Educational Testing and Measurement by T. Kubiszyn and G. Borich. Copyright © 1984, Scott Foresman. Reprinted by permission of HarperCollins College Publishing.

enthusiastic, knowledgeable, and congruent with her or his purpose (informative, entertaining, etc.) is also important. We believe that the key is to develop guidelines that cue students to key major parts of the performance criteria but allow students some latitude in how they perform the task.

Using Rating Scales

Several steps can be taken to improve the reliability of ratings. The first and most important one is to obtain several ratings on different days. All of us vary from day to day and from situation to situation. The more ratings we have the more likely we will be to describe typical, not atypical, behavior. Second, it is important to make a separate rating for each performance element. Teachers must guard against halo effects when they use rating forms. It is easy for a student's previous record of performance to influence the present rating, partly because the identity of the student cannot be masked, as it can be with written papers, and because the rating must be made immediately. Thus, the teacher may not rate students who typically give good speeches as critically as he or she rates other students.

Teachers sometimes use rating scales inappropriately because they divide tasks into too many small steps and fail to obtain a general rating of a project or presentation. Sometimes poor performance on one aspect does not negatively affect total performance (a low score for hand usage may not hurt the speech, whereas poor eye contact may make it totally ineffective). However, teachers should try to include major criteria in the rating form itself. Green (1975) offered the following ten criteria for evaluating a student's oral presentation:

1. Rapport with audience
2. Enthusiastic presentation
3. Effective organization
4. Clarity
5. Correct grammar
6. Good word choice
7. Adequate knowledge of subject
8. Significance of material
9. Stage presence
10. Appropriate gestures

Kubiszyn and Borich (2007) suggest other aspects for rating student presentations:

- Persuasiveness
- Delivery
- Sensitivity to audience
- Overall impression of presentation quality

How can these dimensions be measured? Kubiszyn and Borich (2007) provide one measurement strategy (see Figure 12.4).

Portfolios

A portfolio is an organized set of student work that illustrates student progress over time. It provides an opportunity for students' self-evaluation and self-reflection on their progress. Many types of student work may be included in a portfolio: videotapes, essays,

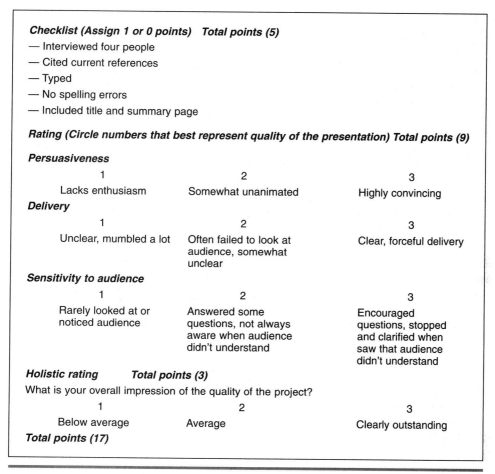

Checklist (Assign 1 or 0 points)   Total points (5)
— Interviewed four people
— Cited current references
— Typed
— No spelling errors
— Included title and summary page

Rating (Circle numbers that best represent quality of the presentation) Total points (9)

Persuasiveness

1	2	3
Lacks enthusiasm	Somewhat unanimated	Highly convincing

Delivery

1	2	3
Unclear, mumbled a lot	Often failed to look at audience, somewhat unclear	Clear, forceful delivery

Sensitivity to audience

1	2	3
Rarely looked at or noticed audience	Answered some questions, not always aware when audience didn't understand	Encouraged questions, stopped and clarified when saw that audience didn't understand

Holistic rating   Total points (3)
What is your overall impression of the quality of the project?

1	2	3
Below average	Average	Clearly outstanding

Total points (17)

Figure 12.4 Combined Scoring Rubric for Current Events Project

Source: Educational Testing and Measurement by T. Kubiszyn and G. Borich. Copyright 2007, Wiley & Sons. Reprinted by permission of Wiley & Sons.

blueprints, reports, photos, results of laboratory experiments, and so on. Moreover, as Jones and Shelton (2006) suggest, portfolios have various purposes and can take various forms. Similarly, Mitchell (1992) notes that portfolios are used for various reasons, including as a teaching tool (e.g., to promote student ownership, to help students and teachers set goals, or to individualize writing instruction), and for the professional development of teachers.

Portfolios are a popular form of authentic assessment. Portfolios allow students to develop a systematic demonstration of their own growth over time (a collection of book reports over the entire year). A portfolio allows students not only to present a copy (electronic or paper) of individual reports but also to reflect on changes over time in writing style, selection of books, and integration of book themes (what do the books as a group say?). One student might reflect on battles of the Civil War and another on the description/analysis of modern opera, and so forth. Another strength of the portfolio is that it allows for individual choice of topic and affords students flexibility in how to organize and present data and arguments. According to Mitchell (1992), a key objective of portfolios is to help students assess their own progress; hence, teachers should frequently ask students questions that encourage thinking (e.g., what have you learned about writing in completing this essay? Why did you select this work to include in your portfolio?).

There is evidence that students are given limited choice in their school work (McCaslin et al., 2006) and some researchers have stressed the importance of giving students more choice (Rathunde & Csikszentmihalyi, 2005). One advantage of portfolios is that they provide a chance for students to choose a topic and to exhibit a commitment to becoming more proficient or knowledgeable over time. Portfolios not only allow choice but choice from a diverse range of potential topics based on personal reflection (What are my strengths? What college will I choose? Which careers interest me?), experience (my growth as a soccer player), and intellectual curiosity (life in China in 1800—competing perspectives).

Except in a few situations (art lab, public speaking class, writing for publication) portfolios are used to supplement assigned papers, formal tests, quizzes, and so forth. This is probably wise because the reliability of grading portfolios is typically very low (see McMillan, 2001). Simply put, one teacher may see a portfolio as a C while another rates it as an A. We suggest that you use the portfolio as one way to bring choice, novelty, and personal expression into the course, but not as your primary source for grading.

If you want to use the portfolio as a key grading source, you will need to take steps to improve the reliability by standardizing grading. As in all aspects of evaluating student performance, teachers need to consider issues of reliability, validity, and grading when using portfolio assessment (Banks, 2005; Gronlund, 2006; Jones & Shelton, 2006; Michelson et al., 2004; Trice, 2000). However, these grading rubrics may place restrictions on student choice in ways that negate the purpose of this learning opportunity—choice and personal expression.

Encouraging Student Performance

Wiggins (1993) argues that teachers need to balance more fairly the needs of the test giver and test takers. He argues that historically most of the burden has been on the test taker and he has proposed an assessment bill of rights for students that includes some of the five following entitlements:

1. Students should be assigned worthwhile assessment tasks that are educative and engaging (i.e., not just memorize lists).
2. Students should be subjected to only minimal secrecy in testing and grading. They should know what constitutes adequate performance standards and what content they are responsible for.
3. There should be clear teacher criteria for grading work and students should be able to see models of excellent work that represents appropriate standards.
4. Students need ample opportunity (most especially time) to produce work that is thoughtful and complete; thus, they need time to self-assess, to redo assignments, and so on.
5. Students should be given opportunities to display and document their achievement. Tests should play to students' strengths, not only to their weaknesses (the traditional way in which many tests operate).

Wiggins (1993) argues that secrecy of testing often gets in the way of challenging students with authentic questions for which they have ample time to reflect, gather information, and assess themselves. Many educators contend that assessments—especially new performance assessments (like portfolios)—should be designed to allow students to show their strengths. Along these lines, Wiggins suggests that criteria should be known in advance by students who are completing a performance assessment. When students do performance assessments, they should not have to guess about how they will be assessed. Knowing in advance how a performance will be graded gives students the opportunity to prepare adequately and to show their strengths.

Obtaining Feedback from Students

After students complete tests or performance assessments, it is useful to occasionally collect information from them regarding their perceptions of the testing procedures and conditions (e.g., did they have sufficient time and resources to do the project?). Figure 12.5 from Wiggins (1993) illustrates a set of questions that a teacher could present to students to get more data about students' perceptions of a particular test.

Please circle the number that best represents your response to each statement (from "strongly agree," 1, to "strongly disagree," 5).

1. This was a fair test of what we learned.   1 2 3 4 5
2. This test was easy, if you studied for it.   1 2 3 4 5
3. This kind of test really makes you think.   1 2 3 4 5
4. This kind of test is new for me.   1 2 3 4 5
5. I did a good job of preparing for this test.   1 2 3 4 5
6. You did a good job of preparing us for the test.   1 2 3 4 5
7. I was unfortunately surprised by the questions you chose.   1 2 3 4 5
8. The directions were clear.   1 2 3 4 5
9. You provided lots of different ways for us to show that we understand what was taught.   1 2 3 4 5
10. There was enough choice in the questions we could select to answer.   1 2 3 4 5
11. Some questions should have been worth more points and/or others worth less.   1 2 3 4 5
12. We were allowed appropriate access to resources (book, notes and so on) during the test.   1 2 3 4 5
13. I expected the grade I got, once I saw the test questions and then later found out the right answers.   1 2 3 4 5
14. There wasn't enough time to do a good job; I know more than I was able to show.   1 2 3 4 5

Figure 12.5 Student Questionnaire on the Test

Source: G. Wiggins (1993). *Assessing Student Performance: Exploring the Purpose and Limits of Testing.* San Francisco: Jossey-Bass. Reprinted by permission of Wiley & Sons.

Implications for Teachers: Classroom Assessment and Test-Taking Skills

Although each teacher and testing situation is unique, we can offer these six general guidelines for assessment:

1. If you consider testing important, it is probably a good idea for you to test frequently over short time spans, so that you can use your test data for reteaching and individualized instruction as well as for grading.

2. Be clear about learning objectives, so as to minimize problems such as lack of content validity.

3. Allow students ample time to finish a test, unless time is a relevant factor.

4. If you intend to test over the entire course content, be sure that your test samples equally from different parts of the course.

5. On the other hand, if you wish to stress certain content, alert students to this so that they can adjust their preparation accordingly. In fact, if you are extremely clear about the objectives, you can give students a number of potential test questions and inform them that the test will be composed of a subset of these questions. This will ensure that the students study all of the material that you consider important.

6. Try to maintain some balance between essay tests (or essay-type assignments) and objective tests, because certain students do notably better on one type of test than the other. A balance between test types is usually preferable to reliance on only one.

Assigning Grades

Most teachers find grading to be among their least favored tasks. However, it is an important tool that must be done well. The hassle of grading can be lessened by proactively developing and communicating your grading plans to students. You are probably familiar with the concept of "grading on the curve." Originally, this method assumed that student mastery of course material would be distributed normally, so grades would also follow a normal distribution: 2 percent A, 14 percent B, 68 percent C, 14 percent D, and 2 percent F. This notion typically does not last long, however, because it involves several faulty assumptions.

First, even if students' efforts are equal, content mastery often does not follow a normal distribution because their aptitudes often do not follow a normal distribution. Second, students' efforts usually are not equal, and many teachers want grades to reflect effort as well as objective achievement. Third, even if both effort and achievement were distributed normally, this in itself would not necessarily mean that grades should be distributed normally. The "ideal" distribution of grades varies with their intended purpose or function: to motivate and reward effort, document progress, measure achievement relative to absolute standards or individualized expectations, or qualify students for advancement or certification, among others.

Teacher-made tests often include questions that seem straightforward to teachers but turn out to be ambiguous to students. Sometimes more than one alternative answer is correct or at least justifiable. Should you credit only the answer you considered to be correct in the first place? Should you credit all answers that are justifiable? Does it make a difference? If your answer to the last question was no, consider the probability that students who receive no credit under one procedure but would have some under another may be outraged, especially if their final grades are affected. Sometimes, due to poor phrasing or typographical omissions, none of the response alternatives is correct. What should you do about these items when you grade the test?

Thinking about these hypothetical situations illustrates some of the complexities involved in grading. It is important to make a distinction between grading and evaluation. Teachers must regularly evaluate both their own behavior and their students' progress if they are to function efficiently, and if the grades ultimately assigned are to be meaningful.

Student progress can be assessed through a variety of evaluation methods besides tests. Students' questions and comments in class, ability to answer questions about content, and performance on special assignments and projects can help a teacher monitor progress. When tests are used, there is no need to return them with letter grades or percentage scores. In addition, or even instead, you can return tests with detailed comments about the strengths and weaknesses of students' efforts, focusing on progress and on ways to improve rather than on how students "did."

Ultimately, though, students will have to take relatively objective tests so that their performances can be compared not only with one another but with the achievement of students in the country at large. External pressures for these test data come from citizens and state educational agencies interested in school quality. Extended pressure for information about student performance on standardized tests was stimulated by the passage of the federal No Child Left Behind law.

Many employers require information about the basic literacy and mathematical skills of prospective employees. Most desirable jobs have educational requirements. Furthermore, employers have become wary of grades because they have seen too many people with high school or college degrees who do not have the skills expected of such graduates. Consequently, in examining transcripts, many employers pay much more attention to scores on standardized tests than to grades. If no such scores are available, they are likely to test prospective employees themselves before offering to hire them. Due to external pressures of this sort, instructors who refuse to grade or who assign very high grades to everyone regardless of performance do not do their students any favors in the long run.

Grading Methods

There are three basic methods you can use when you assign grades. The *individual-standard* method is based on a student's progress in relation to his or her capacity. A bright student must master more material to get an A than a slower student. Such a method demands careful testing at the beginning of the year, and students must be informed of the relative performance levels they need to obtain to get specified grades. The individual-standard method is difficult to implement. If two students score 49 and 60 on a 100-item pretest, for example, how does one set fair standards for what these students must do to earn an A, B, C, or D in the course? Furthermore, most people, including employers and parents, want to know how much students learned or what they can do, not how their performance compares with their ability or potential.

In the *fixed-standard* method, performance levels correspond with different grades on the basis of how students have performed previously. Establishing a standard of performance is difficult for beginning teachers, who may want to obtain tests used by teachers who have taught similar students in order to begin building realistic expectations. The "fixed" standard, however, can vary from teacher to teacher. A 70 on Mr. Marx's algebra exams equals a C; in Ms. Thomas's room it's a D. Still, if you use fixed standards, students know what performance levels correspond to different grades.

Most experienced teachers use a fixed standard to assign grades. (A driver's license exam is a good example of using a fixed standard—to pass the test requires a minimum standard score. In setting the exam, the state has a long history of knowing how past applicants have fared on the test.)

Teachers who know that some parts of a course are more difficult than others may vary their standards from exam to exam: "I know this material is tough, and students in the past have had more trouble on it than any other unit. Thus, on this test, any score above 80 percent will be an A."

Norm-referenced grading compares a student's achievement with the performance of the class rather than a fixed standard of subject-matter mastery. A student's grade depends on how well other students do. If a student scores 90 on an exam, but most other students score above 90, he or she has done poorly. Conversely, if a student scores 70, but most other students score below 70, he or she has done well. This, in practice, is called grading "on the curve."

Implications for Teachers: A Class Grading Example

Consider the record of student performance presented in Table 12.4. Assume that there are thirty students in the class and that each student in the table represents two other students who performed identically. We can see Heather and Jeff earned the most points in the course (90 each) and shared a total class rank of 1.5.

The practical differences in implementing an individual standard, however, are overwhelming, and this method typically creates more misunderstanding and arbitrariness than it resolves. It can be used well to make minor adjustments.

A fixed standard provides a clear basis for assigning grades. It is easy to use, although it may take a great deal of time and thought to establish initial standards. The distribution of grades will vary depending on where the standards are set. Consider the three

Table 12.4 Summary of Student Performance on Five Course Assignments

	Class Presentation (30%)		Assigned Paper (10%)		Exam I (25%)		Exam II (25%)		Homework (10%)			
	Raw	Rank	Raw	Rank	Raw	Rank	Raw	Rank	Raw	Rank	Total	Rank
Heather	27/30	1.0	10	1.5	20/25	5.5	24/25	1	9/10	6.5	90	1.5
James	24/30	8.5	2	8.5	19/25	8.0	12/15	8	9/10	6.5	66	10.0
Jeff	26/30	2.5	10	1.5	24/25	1.0	20/25	4	10/10	2.5	90	1.5
Julia	25/30	5.5	6	5.5	18/25	9.0	18/25	6	10/10	2.5	77	5.0
Pat	25/30	5.5	6	5.5	20/25	5.5	21/25	2	9/10	6.5	81	4.0
Peggy	24/30	8.5	3	7.0	20/25	5.5	14/25	7	8/10	9.5	69	8.0
Sam	23/30	10.0	9	3.0	16/25	10.0	10/25	10	9/10	6.5	67	9.0
Sandra	26/30	2.5	8	4.0	22/25	2.5	20/25	4	10/10	2.5	86	3.0
Skip	23/30	5.5	2	8.5	22/25	2.5	11/25	9	10/10	2.5	70	7.0
Terrill	25/30	5.5	1	10.0	20/25	5.5	20/25	4	8/10	9.5	74	6.0

standards presented below. All would look realistic to teachers and students at the beginning of a course.

Fixed-Standard A	Fixed-Standard B	Fixed-Standard C
A = 94% or above	A = 90% or above	A = 93% or above
B = 85–93%	B = 80–89%	B = 85–92%
C = 75–84%	C = 70–79%	C = 78–84%
D = 60–74%	D = 60–69%	D = 70–77%
F = below 60%	F = below 60%	F = below 70%

If these three standards are applied to the students in Table 12.4, however, different grades will be assigned. In general, standards A and C are higher than B, although standard A is more liberal in the D range than is standard C. Standard B establishes lower cut-off points for the assignment of As, Bs, and Cs than do standards A and C.

Table 12.5 represents the distribution of thirty students. An examination of Table 12.5 and the standards proposed above indicates that no students would have received As if fixed-standards A and C were used in the course. Standard A would have resulted in the assignment of fifteen Ds, whereas in both standards B and C only nine Ds would have been assigned. Furthermore, standard C would have resulted in the assignment of nine Fs, but none would have been assigned using standards A or B. It should be clear that shifting standards by even small percentages can result in different grade distributions.

Table 12.5   Student Scores and the Assignment of Grades Using Three Fixed Standard and Norm-Referenced Comparisons

Student Score	Standard A	Standard B	Standard C	Norm-Referenced Comparisons
90	B	A	B	A
90	B	A	B	A
90	B	A	B	A
90	B	A	B	A
90	B	A	B	A
90	B	A	B	A
86	B	B	B	B
86	B	B	B	B
86	B	B	B	B
81	C	B	C	B
81	C	B	C	B
81	C	B	C	B
77	C	C	D	C
77	C	C	D	C
77	C	C	D	C
74	D	C	D	C
74	D	C	D	C
74	D	C	D	C
70	D	C	D	C–D+?
70	D	C	D	C–D+?
70	D	C	D	C–D+?
69	D	D	F	D
69	D	D	F	D
69	D	D	F	D
67	D	D	F	D
67	D	D	F	D
67	D	D	F	D
66	D	D	F	D
66	D	D	F	D
66	D	D	F	D

As a new teacher, it is hard to determine the appropriate difficulty level of a test. Consider students' scores on their first exam in biology that appear in Table 12.6. If you were using a fixed standard that specified the requirement for earning an A as 92 or above, no student would receive an A. This seems unreasonable unless you have clear evidence that students "blew off" the exam. A better strategy would be for you to look for natural breaks in student scores or for clusters of scores. In this case, students scoring between 86 and 90 would seem to be good candidates for an A.

One could assign grades using norm-referenced standards by inspecting the distribution of scores and allowing *natural breaks* to determine the assignment of letter grades. Whenever there are no explicit standards for judging student performance, as is

Table 12.6   Students' Scores on the First Biology Exam

Student	Score
Alyson	90
Janaé	89
Tom	88
Mike	87
Jessie	86
Ruby	72
Heidi	72
Jay	72
Julian	71
Amanda	70
Andy	65
Aleck	65
Adrienne	64
Roccio	60
Tyler	59
Carrie	58
Sergio	58
Sherif	40
Jose	39
Shawna	39
Josh	30

typically the case in secondary schools, we recommend such norm-referenced comparisons and being fairly liberal in interpreting where natural breaks occur to optimize student effort and motivation.

Recommendations for Grading

Grading should implement your philosophy fairly and clearly. Decisions about grades have to be made on the basis of your particular situation; you may teach in a school that has fixed grading guidelines, or you may have complete freedom to set your own standards. In general, we recommend that grades not be assigned on the basis of individual standards (evaluating performance in terms of ability), except perhaps in a multiage grouping system characterized by continuous assessment. If individual standards are used in grading, they should be applied after the major decisions are made, when the teacher is choosing between two close alternatives (is the grade C− or D+?).

Fixed standards make most sense when teachers have a firm notion of what students can do, so that standards can be based on realistic expectations. In some areas such standards are readily available (the student needs to make at least fifteen out of twenty free throws over three consecutive testings to earn an A), but in other areas it may take some time to establish realistic expectations (to earn an A should a student spell correctly, on average, 90 percent or 95 percent of the assigned vocabulary?).

Teachers who use fixed standards must be careful that a single poor performance does not prevent a student from obtaining a reasonably high mark. If you test frequently, you can do this by allowing students to drop their lowest score. However, allowing students to drop one of only two or three scores can cause as many problems as it solves (consider the situation in which Ted has a 50, 70, 90; and Jim has an 80, 70, and 70). Teachers who are willing to take the extra time necessary to prepare and grade makeup exams can help students continue to make an effort to learn material; that is, teachers can allow students to retake one or two exams instead of dropping their lowest test score.

There is no totally fair way to grade students. Each decision is really a hypothesis about how you can help students perform as well as they can. Individual students are always affected differently by "general" rules. In the example just presented, we can see that Ted will be hurt if one test score is not eliminated; however, if a test score is dropped, Ted will end up with a higher grade than Jim, who has a higher average.

We recommend that beginning teachers use a combination of norm-referenced standards and common sense, unless they are teaching in a nongraded situation or a fixed-standard system (most teachers from fourth grade through high school, however, do assign grades). As teachers gain more experience and have expectations about what students can do, they can shift to fixed standards. It is important to understand though, that when we refer to norms, we do not refer to material norms which guarantee that most students will get a grade of C. We refer to the norm created by the spread of scores in your own classroom. You should look for natural breaks in the distribution of scores to determine grades.

The virtue of the fixed system is that it puts the control of grades in students' hands. If the standards are appropriately fixed, students who work hard can earn good grades. If the standards are too low, however, students are not challenged; if the standards are too high, students will give up.

The major disadvantage to norm-referenced comparisons is that they interpret performance not in terms of some absolute standard (fifteen out of twenty free throws), but in terms of how a student performs in comparison to other students. As a new teacher you sometimes will be surprised by how difficult or easy your test will be for students.

Adjusting Grades

You do not have to rely totally on fixed standards or norm-referenced comparisons. Four possible considerations that you might want to use in making grade adjustments are:

1. Consistency of performance
2. Performance on major course objectives
3. Special-credit work
4. Contract work

If you use any or all of these considerations, however, you should explain to students how they will be used.

After examining the distribution of scores in Table 12.4, we could use consistency of performance as a criterion in borderline cases. For example, Skip, a student with a 70 (see Table 12.4), falls short of the C cutoff. His grade is hurt by his score on the assigned paper and his performance on exam II. However, his performance on exam I is excellent. Here the criterion of consistency does not help us. If his total score was influenced by one low score, we might give him the higher grade, but his performance was inconsistent and is therefore difficult to describe with a single grade.

A second criterion that might help us is the importance of particular objectives. Skip's total course performance is heavily influenced by his performance on a minor task, the assigned paper. If the teacher found the paper difficult to grade or if the assignment was accompanied by consistent student complaints (e.g., not enough time to write), the teacher might assign Skip a higher grade on this basis. But Skip also did poorly on the second exam, and unless the teacher has absolutely no confidence in the grade on the assigned paper, there is no basis for giving Skip a higher mark.

Although the criteria of consistency and importance of objectives may be helpful in making minor adjustments, they sometimes provide no help. For this reason, teachers sometimes allow students to raise their final grades by doing special-credit work or by fulfilling contracts. Assignments that call for mastery and effort are viable ways of assessing student performance and extending teacher flexibility in grading.

Contracting for Specific Grades

Individualized contracts promise specific grades in exchange for specific levels of accomplishment on tasks. For example, an A might require both earning 90 percent on a test and doing a project, a B might call for only earning 90 percent on the test, a C earning 80 percent on the test, and so on. Minimal requirements can be established for those who wish to receive only a passing grade, and progressively more difficult standards can be set for earning higher grades.

In addition to providing students some choice and making a clear connection between effort and assigned grades, contracting allows the teacher to establish requirements that ensure that students master the objectives considered most important or essential to the course. This system works well when all students are capable of achieving the highest grade, although some will require more time and effort to do so than others.

Extensive contracts for grades are usually not feasible in the elementary and middle-school grades, partly because relatively few students have enough experience or the maturity needed to exercise choices appropriately and follow through with independent work. Also, the range of individual differences is often so large that common or standard requirements for everyone in the class may not be practical. Less formalized variations of the same ideas can be developed, however, by making agreements or contracts with individual students, adjusting the requirements so that they are matched appropriately to student abilities and current levels of achievement. Portfolios also offer a way for allowing students choice and extra credit.

Combining Evaluations to Form a Grade

Teachers who use various types of assessment are likely not only to have more diverse information but also more valid information about student performance. However, they must integrate that knowledge to yield a grade that fairly reflects performance across assignments. You may find that some students (perhaps many) take tests better but write less capably and document portfolios less readily than other students. One logical way to solve this problem is to have multiple grades—one for each major evaluation focus in a course.

Unfortunately, for the foreseeable future, most teachers can give only one grade (not four or five) per subject each quarter. Thus, teachers need to be able to combine student performance on diverse activities to create a single grade. Perhaps the most important task is to determine and communicate the weight each measure will contribute to the final grade.

In Table 12.7, the teacher has chosen to use five major assessment areas in one grading period: test A, test B, an area combining five quizzes and ten homework assignments, a theme paper, and a unit portfolio. The teacher has announced to the class that the theme and the portfolio are twice as important as each test and the homework/quiz performance. Thus, the teacher will have to double students' scores in these two areas. The table shows student scores in three formats—raw scores, weighted scores, and weighted scores adjusted for variance. As can be seen in Table 12.7, the highest-scoring student is Jerry, who actually did more poorly in the highest-weighted evaluation areas, even after the scores were weighted (but not after they were weighted for variance).

To represent a student's performance fairly, one has to consider not only the magnitude of the score (e.g., is it higher than most scores?) but the variability or the range of scores (distance from highest to lowest score). For example, students' scores may be close together (all twenty-three students scored above 90 on a 100-point test) or far apart (half a class obtained 100s, one-quarter a score of 50, and one-quarter a score of zero). If teachers are not careful, tests that have more variation (students are spread far apart) will have the most influence on students' final grades—even if such tests are weighted less.

One common mistake is to allow one component (e.g., a quiz, a test) of a grade to influence the final grade too heavily. That is, after engaging in many of the steps described earlier (e.g., specifying to students intended emphasis areas and the weight of various assignments), teachers often fail to implement these criteria when they combine student work to develop a single mark. Given that educators are calling for more varied types of assessment, teachers in today's classrooms must be able to combine marks from different types of assessment to yield a course grade.

Table 12.7   Three Students' Classroom Performance

Student	Test A	Test B	Quiz and Homework	Theme	Portfolio	Total
			Raw Score			
Jan	70	70	60	90	90	380
Jude	80	80	80	80	80	400
Jerry	100	100	90	75	75	440
			Weighted Score			
Jan	70	70	60	90 (2)	90 (2)	560
Jude	80	80	80	80 (2)	80 (2)	560
Jerry	100	100	90	75 (2)	75 (2)	590
			Corrected for Variance and Weighted			
Jan	70	70	60	90 (2) (2)	90 (2) (2)	920
Jude	80	80	80	80 (2) (2)	80 (2) (2)	880
Jerry	100	100	90	75 (2) (2)	75 (2) (2)	890

SUMMARY

Construction of tests requires that you consider a number of issues such as content coverage, test length, item types, weighing, and related matters. Because tests only sample mastery of content taught in a course, it is important to sample from the full range of content and to include enough items to allow reliable measurement. Generally, test reliability increases with test length, so errors of measurement can be reduced by adding items if content coverage and other important qualities are carefully considered.

In addition to content coverage, it is important to consider the levels of understanding involved in test items. The six levels of Bloom's taxonomy provide a convenient reference for planning test items that measure different cognitive levels. Simultaneous examination of content and level permits planning of tests that will adequately cover the instructional objectives of a course. Item type is another critical factor because essay items can be used to assess higher levels in the cognitive domain more easily than objective items. However, it is frequently more difficult to sample a wide range of content with essay questions than with objective items.

Teachers can use various means of assessment other than written tests. Performance tests can capture application of learning. Rating scales provide a basis for directly measuring the quality of performance. Informal assessments, perhaps based on observation supplemented by oral tests, can be used along with more formal assessments like written tests in evaluating student performance.

Developing shared norms about what represents appropriate performance at a particular grade level is an important aspect of classroom measurement. It would seem important that teachers take the opportunity to examine portfolios of other teachers across the district (who teach at the same grade level) to develop appropriate grade level standards. Just as teachers must make decisions about what to include in portfolios—and how much choice students should have in selecting items for inclusion—so, too, must teachers make decisions about the quality of student performance and growth.

The practice of assigning grades according to a normal distribution has become notably less popular in recent years because it fails to take into account the fact that student aptitudes often are not normally distributed in a given classroom. Also, teachers often want grades to reflect effort as well as aptitude because they use them for motivation and reward as well as for documentation of progress.

Grading involves many complexities, but some form of evaluation of student performance is essential. It may involve alternatives such as progress reports or ratings, but the need for accurate and realistic information about progress is essential. When grades are used, teachers can choose the individual standard, which examines a student's progress in relation to capacity; the fixed standard, which uses established criteria; or the norm-referenced system, which compares each student's performance with the performance of the entire class. Each system has advantages and disadvantages, but in most classes, if there are no explicit standards, norm-referenced comparisons seem most practical.

Grading should implement your philosophy as fairly as possible. Because grades may affect motivation and general performance, it is important to examine the implications of all decisions carefully. Grade adjustments can be made on the basis of consistency, performance on major objectives, special-credit work, or contract work. Caution must be used, since grades assigned either too leniently or too restrictively will inhibit motivation and performance.

SUGGESTED ACTIVITIES AND QUESTIONS

1. What would you do if students correctly pointed out to you that your test concentrated on only a quarter of the assigned material, thus benefiting those who studied the tested portion of the material thoroughly and penalizing those who studied all of the material?
2. Some students clearly do better on objective tests than on essay tests, and others do better on essay tests. What implication, if any, does this have for your testing and grading practices?
3. What types of tests do you like and dislike as a student? How might these likes and dislikes affect your behavior as a teacher? Are your biases appropriate for the subject, grade, and types of students that you expect to teach?
4. Considering the grade and subject you expect to teach, how can you evaluate the progress of students who do not read or write English efficiently?
5. The assumption that grading cannot be avoided pervades this chapter. Do you agree with this assumption? If not, what would you propose as a realistic alternative?
6. No matter where you draw the line between grades, some students with the highest marks in a grade range will ask if they can earn extra credit or if you would extend the range down one more point to they can get the grade. How would you respond to these students?
7. Some students, independent of their ability (high- and low-achievement students, male and female students, and so on), develop what is called "fear of success." Among other things, this may include an aversion to high grades, or at least grades that are "too high." Is this "their" problem, or is there something that you as a teacher should try to do about it? If so, what? If you see it as "their" problem, explain your point of view.
8. How should teachers grade highly competent students who consistently do just enough to qualify for a B, even though they could do A-level work with below-average effort? Under what circumstances, if any, might it be appropriate and perhaps helpful to such students to give them less than a B?

CHAPTER *13*

Technology and Classroom Teaching

*I*ntroduction

Technology is an important and exciting part of our everyday lives. Developments in technology are of such wide interest that most newspapers have special sections devoted to new advances in and applications of technology. Technology is also a potential tool for enhancing instruction and learning. Like any tool, (e.g., a paint brush) it can be used for good (a mural) or ill (graffiti). Historically, various technologies (chalk, typewriters, calculators, tape recorders, television, VCRs) have been heralded as ways to revolutionize learning. Yet, there is much evidence that technologies, including computers, have been used poorly in education (Cuban, 2001; Noble, 1997). Further, although much useful advice has been written about how to employ technology effectively, comparatively little research has been done to confirm the utility of this advice (Bolick & Cooper, 2006).

We start with this note of caution because we want to stress that *increased* use of technology in your class is neither good nor bad. The form of instruction (e.g., lecture versus discussion) has never predicted learning because the *quality* (how well the method is used) is much more important (Good, 1996). The same is true of computers and other technology—how it is used is the critical issue. For example, Fuchs and Woessmann (2004) studied the computer use of 174,000 students in thirty-one countries, and concluded that students who used computers several times a week performed less well on achievement tests than peers who used computers less frequently. The goal is to use technology in ways that strengthen classroom learning. If used appropriately to teach content, technology can be quite useful (See Chapter 9 in this text; Ashburn, 2006; Ashburn et al., 2006; Linn, 2006; Wiske, 2006).

Here we describe the implications of technology for teaching. For more technical advice about computers (desktop versus laptop considerations, memory capacities, hardware devices, software applications, interfacing with other technology, warranties, and so forth) see Lever-Duffy, McDonald, and Mitzel (2005) or Bitter and Legacy (2006).

Why Technology Can Be Useful

Advances in technology are potentially beneficial because they allow us to do things quickly. If we want to get a letter from San Antonio to Tucson, today's airmail is superior to the pony express, and even the railroad system. Similarly, writing with a word-processing system is faster and more flexible than earlier rock, chalk, pencil, or typewriter technologies. In addition, e-mail and text messaging are vastly faster than mail. Speed is often a blessing, but it can also be a curse. Sending an inadequate e-mail without sufficient reflection will make any errors more quickly apparent and may result in more work for you.

Computer technology allows us to quantify and reorganize work more quickly. If you are writing a paper that allows a maximum of 1,500 words, your computer gives you a word count with the click of a key. Spreadsheets allow grades to be quickly calculated and recalculated (e.g., what are the effects on grades if I give 5 percent versus 15 percent for extra credit?). It is possible to accurately forecast a class budget for a special project, and reorganize papers and information with a few key strokes.

Advances in computer technology also allow us to do things more precisely or represent them better. For example, yesterday's dentist looking with an unaided eye could detect only the most obvious forms of tooth decay. Today's dentist, aided by technology, can detect decay in its most subtle form at inception. Medical technology has made many types of surgeries less invasive and more successful than even a few years ago. Similarly, today's teacher can represent objects or events in sharp detail (e.g., showing a rocket taking off or using Google Earth to let students see what Yankee Stadium or the Vatican look like). Seeing something more clearly and in better detail is good *if* you are viewing the right thing for an appropriate reason. Just because we *can* is not a compelling reason for using technology, however.

Technology can easily provide access to much useful information and store it for rapid retrieval later. It also can provide access to current, real-time data. As McCrory (2006) notes, Internet access provides current weather conditions around the world, images from the most recent space missions, pictures, and so forth. Such data can enrich student project work (Mergendoller et al., 2006).

In the past, teachers were limited to book illustrations, photos, and copies to present images. Now, you can use DVD and other technology to display events or objects to students in precise and colorful detail. Consider the teaching vignette discussed in Chapter 1. Sally's materials problem (students had to share a map) could have been eliminated had she used computer-generated maps projected on a large LCD screen allowing students to easily see the routes that various trips took. Further, some students might never have seen the violence of a raging sea storm, so showing a video clip for even a few seconds could allow them to understand (and perhaps "feel") the difficulty of an ocean voyage in 1492.

Also, computer technology allows immediate access to a great volume of information. Working alone or with others (perhaps in distant locations), students can obtain information for research or to address problems. Advances in technology have moved the possession of knowledge from the few (monks and the elite) to wide audiences (the printing press—books, newspapers), and now to a high percent of the population (through television and Internet access at home, school, or a library). Information about virtually any issue that arises in class discussion can be accessed almost instantaneously on the Internet. This virtually unlimited access to information can be a valuable learning tool when used appropriately, and it can not only support individual learning but also facilitate cooperative project work (Blumenfeld, Marx, & Harris, 2006; Lajoie & Azevedo, 2006; Linn, 2006).

Of course, there are many worthwhile things that are more difficult to present without technology. For example, students can use a personal digital assistant connected to digital probes to assess the ecological health of a body of water by measuring its temperature, ph level, and oxygen content (McCrory, 2006).

Further, computers can be powerful organizational tools. For example, a personal diary or a project reflection diary provides an important document of self-reflection over time. Today, a student's digitalized diary would allow him or her to analyze personal mood swings or growth in writing ability over time without having to re-read every page. Also, when today's students develop a portfolio of reflections, they can instantaneously correct spelling and grammar errors before handing in the assignment, and can delete extraneous notes and hypotheses or conclusions that they are not willing to share at present.

Technology allows for shared peer learning to occur in real time with other students anywhere in the world. One of the earliest uses of technology in science learning was on a National Geographic Society Web site that allowed students to collect relevant data across the globe (McCrory, 2006). Other science-related Web sites include Kids as Global Scientists (www.onesky.umich.edu/kgs01.html), project GLOBE (www.unc.edu/depts/cmse/programs/GLOBE.html), and Journey North (www.learner.org/jnorth/) where students can participate in watching birds migrate.

Defining Your Teaching Role

We noted that your personal dispositions may make it better for you to teach in an elementary, middle, or high school setting, and that some teachers have more skills and interests in dealing with students' "personal issues" than do others. In the same way, you need to understand your strengths and interests before you choose how to bring technology into your classroom. Some teachers may choose to use it infrequently; others may decide to make it a key component of their instructional approach. Using technology depends in part on your own skill level and degree of motivation to become more technologically savvy.

Other factors may also influence your decisions about technology. For example, if your school has a fully equipped technology center with a highly competent instructor, your use of technology may be limited to those occasions when technology can significantly enhance learning. However, if you teach in a remote rural area, or in an inner-city school in which students have no access to technology at home, you may feel an obligation to help students become literate in technology. Helping students to become computer literate is also a school responsibility. Table 13.1 presents technology standards taken from the National Educational Forum on Technology. It shows that there are many aspects to being technologically literate and these vary from grade to grade. Understandably, some teachers may assume more of these responsibilities than others. These standards are ambitious and map out goals that schools may seek to accomplish over time.

Computer Use in the Classroom

Computer use varies widely. Some teachers use them frequently; others not at all. Interestingly, computers are used in 43 percent of self-contained elementary classrooms, but notably less in secondary subjects such as fine arts, 8 percent; math, 11 percent; social studies, 12 percent; science, 17 percent; and English, 43 percent. By far, the primary use at both levels is for word processing, followed by CD-ROM reference (electronic dictionaries and encyclopedias), skill games, and Internet access (Becker, 2001; Slavin, 2006). "More advanced" software for applications such as multimedia authoring, spreadsheets, databases, simulations, and explorations are not widely used.

These figures may be high estimates of computer use because they are based on survey reports. Two recent studies involving about 1,000 observations of 400 teachers (Good et al., 2006; McCaslin et al., 2006) found virtually no use of technology other than the occasional overhead transparency or listening center equipped with audio-tapes or computerized testing of individual students.

Why do secondary teachers use technology less than elementary teachers even though their students' knowledge and capacity for individual and group project work is more advanced? Probably for three reasons:

1. Secondary school teachers spend less time with students
2. Most high school students possess at least rudimentary technology skills
3. Students' advanced technology skills may threaten some teachers

Teachers of self-contained elementary school classrooms can rotate students across a limited number of computers throughout the day; whereas, most secondary teachers see students only forty-five minutes a day (unless their school practices block scheduling). Many secondary students already have some desktop publishing, word-processing, and Internet access skills. And, some teachers may believe that their limited technology skills (compared to those of their most advanced students) will undermine their content authority ("I know history, but if I try to use technology, it won't look like it!").

Table 13.1   National Educational Technology Standards for Teachers and Students

---

National Educational Standards for Teachers

I.   Technology operations and concepts

Teachers demonstrate a sound understanding of technology operations and concepts.
Teachers:

  A. Demonstrate introductory knowledge, skills, and understanding of concepts related to technology as described in the ISTE National Education Technology Standards for students
  B. Demonstrate continual growth in technology knowledge and skills to stay abreast of current and emerging technologies

II.   Planning and designing learning environments and experiences

Teachers plan and design effective learning environments and experiences supported by technology.
Teachers:

  A. Design developmentally appropriate learning opportunities that apply technology-enhanced instructional strategies to support the diverse needs of the learners
  B. Apply current research on teaching and learning with technology when planning learning environments and experiences
  C. Identify and locate technology resources and evaluate them for accuracy and suitability
  D. Plan for the management of technology resources within the context of learning activities
  E. Plan strategies to manage student learning in a technology-enhanced environment

III.   Teaching, learning, and the curriculum

Teachers implement curriculum plans that include methods and strategies for applying technology to maximize student learning.
Teachers:

  A. Facilitate technology-enhanced plans that address content standards and student technology standards
  B. Use technology to support learner-centered strategies that address the diverse needs of students
  C. Apply technology to develop students' higher-order skills and creativity
  D. Manage student learning activities in a technology enhanced environment

IV.   Assessment and evaluation

Teachers apply technology to facilitate a variety of effective assessment and evaluation strategies.
Teachers:

  A. Apply technology in assessing student learning of subject matter using a variety of assessment techniques
  B. Use technology resources to collect and analyze data, interpret results, and communicate findings to improve instructional practice and maximize student learning
  C. Apply multiple methods of evaluation to determine students' appropriate use of technology resources for learning, communication, and productivity

V.   Productivity and professional practice

Teachers use technology to enhance their productivity and professional practice.
Teachers:

  A. Use technology resources to engage in ongoing professional development and lifelong learning

(continued)

Table 13.1   (Continued)

     B. Continually evaluate and reflect on professional practice to make informed decisions regarding the use of technology in support of student learning

     C. Apply technology to increase productivity

     D. Use technology to communicate and collaborate with peers, parents, and the larger community in order to nurture student learning

VI.   Social, ethical, legal, and human issues

Teachers understand the social, ethical, legal, and human issues surrounding the use of technology in PK–12 schools and apply those principles in practice.

Teachers:

     A. Model and teach legal and ethical practice related to technology use

     B. Apply technology resources to enable and empower learners with diverse backgrounds, characteristics, and abilities

     C. Identify and use technology resources that affirm diversity

     D. Promote safe and healthy use of technology resources

     E. Facilitate equitable access to technology resources for all students

---

National Educational Technology Standards for Students

The technology foundation standards are divided into six broad categories. Standards within each category are to be introduced, reinforced, and mastered by students. These categories provide a framework for linking performance indicators within the Profiles for Technology-Literate Students to the standards. Teachers can use these standards and profiles as guidelines for planning technology-based activities in which students achieve success in learning communication and life skills.

1. Basic operations and concepts
   - Students demonstrate a sound understanding of the nature and operation of technology systems.
   - Students are proficient in the use of technology.
2. Social, ethical, and human issues
   - Students understand the ethical, cultural, and societal issues related to technology.
   - Students practice responsible use of technology systems, information, and software.
   - Students develop positive attitudes toward technology uses that support lifelong learning, collaboration, personal pursuits, and productivity.
3. Technology productivity tools
   - Students use technology tools to enhance learning, increase productivity, and promote creativity.
   - Students use productivity tools to collaborate in constructing technology-enhanced models, prepare publications, and produce other creative works.
4. Technology communication tools
   - Students use telecommunications to collaborate, publish, and interact with peers, experts, and other audiences.
   - Students use a variety of media and formats to communicate information and ideas effectively to multiple audiences.
5. Technology research tool
   - Students use technology to locate, evaluate, and collect information from a variety of sources.

Table 13.1 (Continued)

- Students use technology tools to process data and report results.
- Students evaluate and select new information resources and technological innovations based on the appropriateness for specific tasks.
6. Technology problem-solving and decision-making tools
    - Students use technology resources for solving problems and making informed decisions.
    - Students employ technology in the development of strategies for solving problems in the real world.

Source: Reprinted with permission from *National Educational Technology Standards for Teachers: Preparing Teachers to Use Technology,* © 2002; and *National Educational Technology Standards for Students: Connecting Curriculum and Technology,* © 2000 ISTE (International Society for Technology in Education), iste@iste.org, www.iste.org. All rights reserved. Permission does not constitute an endorsement by ISTE.

Students frequently write letters, reports, stories, essays, and more formal compositions in class. Those who do so using computers often show more willingness to write and to revise, as well as take more pride in their work than peers who write with pen and paper (Cochran-Smith, 1991). Spell-check allows students to focus on content and not the mechanics of writing, and students using computers do not have to worry about poor penmanship or grammar. Computers also allow for almost effortless reorganizing, which requires less time and energy.

The quality of writing also is enhanced by computer use (Kulik, 2003), especially when students have their own computer (Lowther, Ross, & Morrison, 2003). Goldberg, Russell, and Cook (2003) completed a meta-analysis of thirty-five studies and revealed large effect sizes favoring students using computers to write as compared to students who did not. Despite this solid research base, the use of computers for writing has not increased in many classes. Russell and Abrams (2004) surveyed over 4,000 teachers and found that 30 percent had decreased computer use or were forbidden by district policy to use computers in writing activities because the state test (as mandated by NCLB) did not allow for computer writing.

Current use of technology is less prevalent than enthusiasts would like. However, there are good reasons for this. When should you use technology? How do you make these decisions? Cuban (2001) suggests that teachers planning to use technology consider questions like these:

- Can I learn to use the equipment or software quickly? Can my students?
- Does the software add goals that I consider important?
- Will my students find the software fun and motivating?
- How reliable are software, clickers, LCD panels, and so forth?
- Who fixes my learning system if it breaks down?
- Is the time required to learn and use the technology worth the gain in student learning?
- Will computers undermine my instructional authority?
- Have other teachers at my school used the equipment or software?

These are important questions to consider. The more often you can answer these questions favorably, the more likely it is that you will use technology. If an activity is only fun, it could be used occasionally, perhaps for variety, and even then only if one has a large budget for software purchases. The ideal situation is when the software is easy to use and reliable, contains important content or processes, and motivates students to use it. Equipment reliability is a huge issue. If you have limited computer skills and something goes wrong, it can be frustrating and disempowering.

Computer Availability

The availability of computers has grown considerably, yet there still are only 3.8 computers in the typical classroom. The range is wide. Some states average twelve to fifteen computers per classroom, others only one or two (Swanson, 2006). The availability of computers in higher poverty and minority schools has been increasing since 1992 as shown in Figure 13.1, although there are still fewer computers in these schools than in high-SES schools. Also, in high-SES schools, students are likely to have their own laptop computers, which they may or may not be allowed to use in school.

Many students from low-income families do not have computers at home. Figure 13.2 shows the percent of U.S. households that have Internet access as a function of income and location. In homes with incomes of less than $35,000, access to the Internet is only about 20 percent. In homes with incomes exceeding $75,000, 60 percent have Internet access. These differences have implications for teachers in schools with heterogeneous populations. The range in knowledge of technology may cause them to choose technology carefully and to differentiate instruction.

The number of computers available may limit your opportunities to incorporate technology into your instruction. Table 13.2 provides a way of looking at what you can do with fewer or more computers in a self-contained elementary classroom. With one

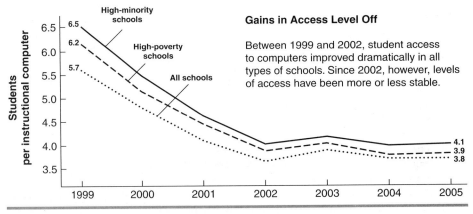

Figure 13.1 Availability of Computers in High-Poverty and Minority Schools

Source: Market Data Retrieval, Public School Technology Surveys 1999–2005. Copyright 2007, Market Data Retrieval. All rights reserved. Reprinted by permission.

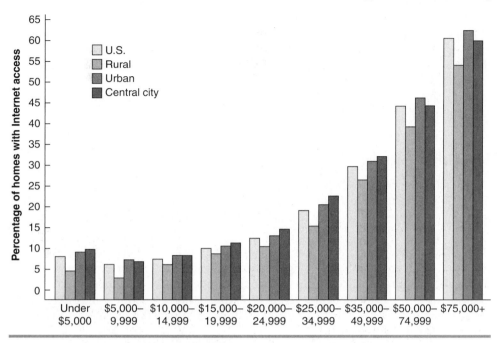

Figure 13.2 Internet Access by Income and Location

Source: From Judy Lever-Duffy et al. *Teaching and Learning with Technology,* second edition. Published by Allyn and Bacon, Boston, MA. Copyright © 2005 by Pearson Education. Reprinted by permission of the publisher.

Table 13.2 Computer Availability Constrains Range of Uses in Self-Contained Elementary Classes

One or Two Computers	Three to Six Computers	Seven to Ten Computers	Fifteen or more Computers
Teacher demonstrations	Teacher demonstrations	Teacher demonstrations	Teacher demonstrations
Student demonstrations	Student demonstrations	Student demonstrations	Student demonstrations
Word processing	Word processing	Word processing	Word processing
Desktop publishing	Desktop publishing	Desktop publishing	Desktop publishing
	Small-group collaborative	Small-group collaborative	Small-group collaborative
		Some individual research	Some individual research
			Complex individual portfolios
			Research papers

or two computers, you are limited to demonstrations (which can still be very valuable) and word processing. You could try to do portfolio work with four to five computers in the class, but the storage and access management issues would demand considerable oversight. Having fewer computers limits instructional opportunities even more sharply in secondary classrooms. And, if your technology skills are limited, multiple computers may not increase your instructional effectiveness.

Some Helpful Technology Tools

Using technology effectively in classrooms requires multiple computers. Other devices like LCD screens and electronic whiteboards make it easier to use technology when teaching the entire class. What technology should you have, other than a computer?

LCD.   Perhaps the best instrument you can possess is a liquid crystal display (LCD) projector. LCDs are rapidly replacing overhead projectors as a more effective means for displaying images and video from a DVD or computer source. LCD large screens allow *all* students to see a video or Internet presentation at the same time. This offers teachers an ideal medium for teaching students how to search the Net if they have not already learned those skills.

LCD screens have the capacity for sharing with a large audience what you have produced yourself or have found elsewhere. Figures 13.3 and 13.4 illustrate how information like the carbon cycle or poetry analysis can be displayed. Countless devices and plans like these can be found on the Internet and displayed when instructionally appropriate.

Whiteboard.   Electronic whiteboards allow students and teachers to create visual displays that others can see. For example, with the use of a whiteboard a student can write an opening paragraph that all can see, read, and react to in order to improve it. A student might solve an equation or a teacher might illustrate an orbit, and so forth. What is displayed on the whiteboard can be saved to a computer file that can be edited (e.g., the class writes, and edits, a play over time). Students who want to review the discussion, or those who were absent, can access the computer file (unlike the old blackboard; once information was erased it was gone forever). However, electronic whiteboards are costly, and unless you use group-generated products frequently, it may be more cost-effective to appoint two or three students to take detailed notes for each lesson.

Handheld Computers.   Personal digital assistant (PDA) computers are increasingly used by teachers and students. PDAs have many advantages. After a class discussion ends, a teacher can quickly summarize a few thoughts and record them, (e.g., which students did not speak, ideas about what to do the next day). Teachers also can connect this recorded information to electronic lesson plans and student files. Students can use PDAs to take notes, list questions they want to ask about later, and access the Internet. The latter capability has downsides—students' Internet choices may not be lesson related, and they might use the technology to chat with friends through text messaging.

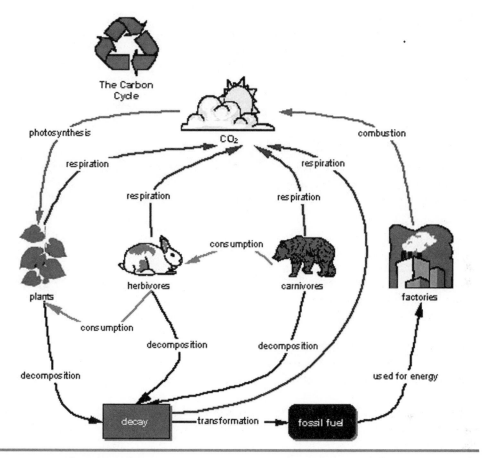

Figure 13.3 The Carbon Cycle

Source: © 2006 Inspiration Software®, Inc. Diagram created in Inspiration® by Inspiration Software, Inc. Used with permission.

Clickers. Clickers (electronic response devices) allow individual students to respond quickly to a teacher's questions (e.g., "Is it okay to proceed or would you like one more example?"). Clickers can also give students a choice in lesson direction without taking any instructional time. For example, a high school history teacher might ask: "Well, I think we have spent enough time on what economic life was like in Germany in the 1300s. Shall we talk now about dress, health, or leisure time activities?"

Clicker feedback can also give students quick information about their content understanding (e.g., the teacher gives an ungraded quiz), and allow students to raise questions when they do not understand. Electronic exchange may be even more useful outside of content knowledge, in areas of values, beliefs, and commitments (e.g., votes on abortion, political beliefs, and so forth). When communicating about controversial

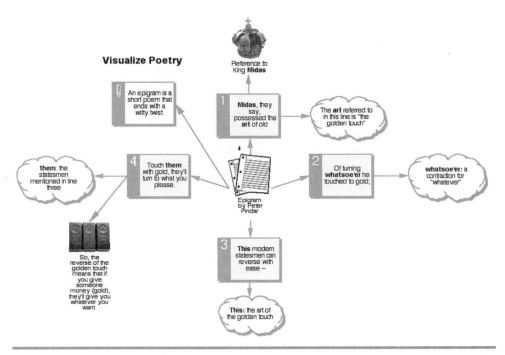

Figure 13.4   Visualization of Poetry Analysis

Source: © 2006 Inspiration Software®, Inc. Diagram created in Inspiration® by Inspiration Software, Inc. Used with permission.

topics (sex education) students may react more candidly than if they do not have to answer publicly.

At times the use of anonymous clicker information may be counterproductive. Students need to develop their abilities to state and defend their ideas publicly. Further, there are times when reflection—not rapid action—is desired. Like any technology, clickers have advantages and undesirable side effects. If overused, they can create a TV game show atmosphere—a *Deal or No Deal* milieu—rather than an educational environment.

Digital Cameras.   Digital cameras allow photographs to be stored on a memory card (like Memory Stick or CompactFlash). They let the photographer see a picture on the display screen immediately after it is taken; this allows you to save good pictures and delete bad ones so that space on the memory card is not wasted. Pictures can be downloaded from the camera to a computer, which then allows them to be used in a variety of formats such as embedding a picture into a report about a class field trip or sending a class photograph home to parents. Students who make PowerPoint presentations can download pictures to make presentations more interesting. However, students may need careful guidance to understand that adequate content presentation (good examples carefully chosen to provide appropriate contrasts) is the goal, not just the glitter of cute but unneeded pictures.

*W*hat Knowledge of Technology Do Students Have?

Much has been written about the millenials—the "net generation" students that you will teach. According to Howe and Strauss (2000), those born after 1982 enjoy group activities, focus on grades and good performance, participate heavily in extracurricular activities, identify with parents, love new technologies, and respect social conventions. On average, they want to achieve and identify with adults' conception of the world more than the baby boomers in the 1960s.

Net generation students are typically described as digitally literate and always "on" or connected. They like to experiment with new things and are socially oriented. They like interactivity, have good visual skills, respond quickly, and have well-developed parallel processing and overlapping abilities. Their new technology is the Web, Instant Messenger (IM), text messaging, and so forth.

Those writing about net generation students are describing the students *on average,* and in comparison to previous generations such as baby boomers who are now contemplating retirement (and whose new technology was the electric typewriter and television), or generation X (whose new technology was video games, computers, and e-mail). If you are a member of the net generation yourself, you know that there is tremendous variation in technological skills and interests among your peers. You may have more video and IM skills than your parents (Shaffer et al., 2005), but some peers are vastly superior to others. For older teachers or those becoming a teacher as a second career, recognize and act on current students' technological capacities and interests.

All teachers must adjust instruction to differences among individual learners. Nichols and Good (2004) report that today's students are active technology users and watch a lot of television, surf the Net, participate in chat rooms, and play lots of video games. However, the instructional implications of this knowledge are difficult to calculate. The fact that today's students consume large amounts of media is apparent, but different youth watch different TV programs and have far-ranging musical tastes. Further, they tend to watch many shows simultaneously and even watch quick summaries of shows so that they are prepared to talk with peers about many shows. "Cliff Notes" have come to the entertainment industry!

Much of this media consumption is done *alone.* Families used to watch TV together, but now parents and children watch different programs in separate rooms. Similarly, young people do not visit one another and share music after school as much as they once did. Instead, they listen to their music alone, perhaps while text messaging a peer across town (Nichols & Good, 2004).

Thus, ironically, many students might often be better served by lectures or brief teacher talks that are devoid of technology such as a PowerPoint presentation. An overabundance of technological tools may diminish students' listening skills and independent thinking abilities. Students enjoy electronic presentations because the information is organized for them, and they especially like them if they are peppered with entertaining video inserts. But such presentations frequently do not require students to meaningfully connect the text to an idea—they simply read what is on the screen or try to write it down verbatim without thinking about the content of the material critically.

As a teacher, you will need to realize that some of your students will need help in listening and learning how to organize information for themselves. Also, today's students may state a preference for social learning, but many spend much of their time at home alone. You will have to teach students the give and take of social learning that occurs when students do projects in groups, including skills to use in cooperative learning (see Chapter 6).

Prensky (2001) notes that some of today's students have short attention spans and prefer to "move on" rather than to reflect on what they have done. Practice is not a preferred activity, and they may have trouble processing written text (with few visuals). Some have difficulty evaluating the worth of different Web sources in part because they do not take enough time to consider the source.

Unless you continue to study technology in a systematic way, it is likely that many of your students will have more advanced technology skills than you do. However, this is true in other areas as well: some of your students will be able to write better essays or sketch better than you can. So, accept the fact that many will know more about new hardware devices and software than you will.

Be receptive to students who can illustrate new applications, and encourage them to share these abilities with you and their peers. The important questions are, "Is the application of technology critical to your content goals?" and "Does technology assist students in acquiring or applying knowledge with more understanding?" If students can identify more powerful ways to use technology for their purposes, so much the better. Your content authority as a teacher does not have to be defined or diminished by your less developed technology skills.

*D*eveloping Your Own Assignments to Personalize Learning

Computers can be used to help students pursue personal interests in interesting ways. For example, a high school psychology teacher might note that students are expressing interest in the National Basketball Association championship series in which, say, the Dallas Mavericks and the Miami Heat are battling for the title. The teacher may ask the students to apply attribution theory (see Chapter 5) to report how newspapers *explain* victories and losses in Dallas and Miami, in Detroit and Phoenix (whose teams almost got in the series) and in two other cities whose teams were never in the playoffs (Atlanta and Portland). Do different newspapers attribute victory to different causes (a lucky call that could have gone either way, some situational factor such as biased referees, or superior talent)? For students with little or no interest in basketball, alternative attribution activities could be organized (e.g., comparing more liberal and more conservative newspapers' coverage of an election).

Teachers can also use technology to increase student engagement and understanding of an activity. In one third-grade classroom that we observed, students had been studying how plays are written—first a title, then a list of characters, and then dialogue and stage directions. To demonstrate their understanding, the students were going to pick a short storybook and turn it into a written play. To make sure students explicitly knew what was expected, the teacher used her computer (hooked to a television monitor so all students could see the screen) and, with a book she had just read to the class, began to demonstrate what she wanted the students to do. She asked prompting questions such as, "What is the title of my play?" "Who are the characters?" and "Should we have a narrator?" Students responded and helped craft the dialogue within the play. As a class they re-read and edited lines. The teacher shifted dialogue around using the Cut and Paste functions on the computer. This activity served several purposes: It provided a model for how students were supposed to complete the activity, it demonstrated the thinking involved in developing a play, and it offered students an opportunity to see that even teachers have to edit and rewrite as part of the writing process. The activity took about thirty minutes and provided students clear understanding of what was expected. Effective use of technology does not have to be frequent, but it must add to the instructional value of the lesson as seen in this example.

Using Software Packages

In addition to the technology units or assignments you create, there are many resources for educational technology. Many professional organizations have abundant samples available for free. Table 13.3 provides Web addresses for some especially useful sites. It is advantageous to check professional Web sites and to consider their recommendations, as the amount of available software is considerable and changes constantly (Lever-Duffy, McDonald, & Mizell, 2005).

Social Studies and Science

Potential uses of technology and computers vary with subject matter. Two subjects that seem to be optimal areas for more use of technology are social studies and science. We begin with a discussion of technology sources in social studies.

Teaching with Artifacts and Historical Source Material

Today's teachers have wide access to a range of documents that can enrich students' history learning. These sources are available on the Internet, often with plans for documents-based lessons (Causey & Armento, 2001). The November/December 2003 issue of *Social Education* was devoted entirely to teaching history with primary sources. The issue provides useful guidance on finding and evaluating sources and how to plan lessons around them. The sources range from old objects found in the home to gravestones in local cemeteries, to reproductions of national documents accessed via the Internet (Brophy & Alleman, 2007).

Teaching ideas and lesson plans devoted to history or social studies teaching can be found on the Internet sites of the journals *Social Education* and *Social Studies and the*

Table 13.3 Web Site Addresses of Technology Resources

American Educational Research Association
http://www.aera.net

Apple Classrooms of Tomorrow
http://www.eworid.com/education/k12/
leadership/acot

Association for Career and Technical
Education
http://www.acteonline.org

Association for Educational
Communications and Technology
http://www.aect.org

Association for Supervision and
Curriculum Development
http://www.ascd.org

Association for the Advancement of
Computing in Education
http://www.aace.org

Center for Children and Technology
http://www2.edc.org/CCT

Computer Learning Foundation
http://www.computerlearning.org

Computer-Using Educators
http://www.cue.org

Consortium for School Networking
http://www.cosn.org

Digital Divide Network
http://www.digitaldiviclenetwork.org

EDUCAUSE
http://www.educause.edu

Global SchoolNet Foundation
http://www.globaischoolnetorg

Intercultural E-Mail Classroom Connections
http://www.teaching.com/iecc

International Council for Educational Media
http://www.aect.org/Affiliates/National/
icem.htm

International Society for Techology
in Education
http://www.iste.org

International Technology Education
Association
http://www.iteawww.org

National Center for Technology Planning
http://www.nctp.com

National Council for Accreditation of
Teacher Education
http://www.ncate.org

National Educational Computing
Conference
http://www.neccsite.org

National School Boards Association
Education Technology Programs
http://wwv.nsba.org/itte

National Telecommunications and
Information Administration
http://www.ntia.doc.gov

Regional Technology in Education
Consortia
http://www.rtec.org

Society for Applied Learning Technology
http://www.salt.org

Society for Information Technology and
Teacher Education
http://www.aace.org/site

Special Education Resource Center (SERC)
http://www.serc.org

TEAMS Distance Learning
http://www.teams.lacoe.edu

Technology in Education
http://www.tie-online.org

U.S. Department of Education, Office of
Educational Technology
http://www.ed.gov/Technology

U.S. Department of Education, Technology
State Contacts
http://www.ed.gov/about/contacts/state/
technology.html

U.S. Distance Learning Association
http://www.usdla.org

www4teachers
http://www.4teachers.org

Source: Judy Lever-Duffy et al. *Teaching and Learning with Technology*, second edition. Published by Allyn and Bacon, Boston, MA. Copyright © 2005 by Pearson Education. Reprinted by permission of the publisher.

Young Learner. For example, Barton (2001) offered guidelines for scaffolding elementary students' analyses of historical photographs. Using as examples several photos of food stores, restaurants, and gas stations taken in the 1940s, Barton explained the value of posing questions about the pictures (e.g., In what year might they have been taken? At what time of day? What are the people doing?), thereby actively involving students in the issue and then discussing the diverse opinions expressed to see if agreement might be reached. If the students have difficulty, the teacher can model pertinent opinions and observations, then cue students' observations by asking questions such as, "Do you think advertising was more important then?" "Why?"

Wyman (1998) described activities built around excerpts from diaries written by children and adolescents whose families migrated west along the Oregon Trail in the middle of the nineteenth century. The excerpts communicate the sights, sounds, and feelings they experienced as they traveled. Wyman suggested three ways in which the excerpts can be incorporated into useful learning activities: (1) identifying and discussing unexpected content; (2) identifying and discussing the implications of reoccurring events such as accidents, lost children, and contact with Indians; and (3) having students imagine that their families were traveling westward along the Oregon Trail and creating their own diaries.

For information about using computers and associated technology for teaching history, see Parham (1994), Schlene (1990), and Seiter (1988). Finally, for information about the History Teaching Alliance, which offers training and resources for history teaching, see Beninati (1991).

Learning Environments and Project-Based Work

Recently, it has become popular to discuss the use of technology in the broader context of learning environments. Essentially, a learning environment approach involves simultaneous attention to the learner (e.g., readiness to learn, background knowledge), the context (individual learning, mixed-ability cooperative group, dyadic tutoring), and task content (memorizing key facts and then applying them, solving mathematical equations and so forth). Learning environments have been designed in various ways and some are well aligned with conceptions of teaching/learning that we discussed in Chapter 10, but others are more connected to conceptions presented in Chapter 11. And, understandably, most involve aspects or a blending of differing conceptions of student learning.

Numerous materials, software, and other technologies have been generated for learning environments of varying scope, content, and academic goals. Blumenfeld, Marx, and Harris (2006) identified a selected list of learning environments (LEs) using four selection criteria. First, LEs have clearly specified subject matter learning goals. Second, LEs have an ambitious scope such that academic material is dealt with breadth or depth in specified ways. Third, LEs have highly developed materials that are based on clear research and theory. Fourth, there is published research to show that LEs have intended impacts. Programs identified by Blumenfeld, Marx, and Harris appear in Table 13.4; most of them deal with science content.

Table 13.4 Selected Learning Environments

Cluster	Learning Environment	Description	Web Site
Discipline-based programs: Mathematics	Cognitive Tutors	Intelligent software environment for high school mathematics classrooms	http://www.carnegielearning.com
	Connected Mathematics Project	Problem-centered middle school mathematics program	http://www.mth.msu.edu/cmp
	Jasper	Video-based mathematics program for middle schools	http://peabody.vanderbilt.edu/projects/funded/jasper/Jasperhome.html
Discipline-based programs: Science	Biology Guided Inquiry Learning Environments (BGuILE)	Technology-infused inquiry for middle school and high school biology	http://www.letussorg/bguile
	GenScope™/BioLogica™	Computer-based genetics program for middle school and high school	http://www.concord.org/biologica
	Guided Inquiry Supporting Multiple Literacies (GIsML)	Guided inquiry science program for elementary students	http://www.soe.umich.edu/gisint
	Kids as Global Scientists/BioKIDS	Technology-based inquiry science program for upper elementary and middle school students	http://www.biokids.umich.edu
	Learning by Design (LBD)	Design-based middle school science program	http://www.cc.gatech.edu/edutech/projects/lbdvievv.html
	Project Based Science (PBS)	Science inquiry curricula focused on everyday experiences for middle school students	http://www.hi-ce.org
	ThinkerTools	Scientific inquiry and modeling software and curricula for middle school science	http://thinkertools.soe.berkeley.edu
	Web-Based Integrated Science Environment (WISE)	Online science inquiry learning environment for grades 5–12	http://wise.Berkeley.edu
	Geographic Data in Education Initiative/World Watcher (GEODE)	Inquiry-based environmental science program for middle school and high school	http://www.worldwatcher.northwestern.edu
Discipline-based programs: Literacy	Literacy Innovation that Speech Technology Enables (LISTEN)	Computerized reading tutor for elementary students	http://www.cs.cmu.edui-listen

Source: Blumenfeld, P., Marx, R. W., & Harris, C. (2006). Learning environments. In W. Damon, R. Lerner, A. Renninger, & I. E. Sigel (Eds.), *Handbook of child psychology (6th ed.), Vol. 4: Child psychology in practice* (pp. 297–342). Hoboken, NJ: Wiley. Reprinted by permission of Wiley & Sons.

Learning environments assume many forms. However, one complex and increasingly popular learning environment is project-based work, especially in science and social studies.

Project-Based Work. In differentiating problems that students can work on collectively, educators commonly define problems as well-structured or ill-structured. Mergendoller et al. (2006) note the characteristics of these two types of problems.

Well-Structured Problems

- All aspects of the problem are given to the learner (e.g., Thirty guests will be at the party. How many twelve-slice pizzas will be needed if each guest eats three slices?)
- Problems require the application of a limited number of standard and well-structured rules or procedures that can be used in predictable ways.
- Solutions have clear linkages (decisions, choices, actions) to address the problem.

Ill-Structured Problems

- Problems possess aspects that are largely unknown.
- Problems have multiple solutions, different ways to solve the problems, or no solution.
- Problems have different criteria for evaluating solutions.
- Problems require learners to make judgments and to express personal opinions.

In Chapter 6, we primarily discussed the use of groups as students interacted around relatively structured problems. In project-based learning, the medium of choice is ill-structured problems that encourage thinking, conflict, adaptation, and other actions. Building on the work of Duch, Groh, and Allen (2001) and Glasgow (1997), Mergendoller et al. (2006) suggest that some additional aspects need to be in place if project-based learning is to work well. These include:

- Projects are sufficiently complex to account for a wide range of ability levels and learning styles.
- Projects are sufficiently complex to require group effort.
- Projects require students to make decisions supported by good arguments and to illustrate their depth of knowledge.
- Projects require students to distinguish necessary information from irrelevant information and to use accurate sources.

Perhaps the largest issue you face in designing project-based work is to stimulate student thinking around motivating and engaging them in driving questions (Blumenfeld et al., 1991; Blumenfeld, Marx, & Harris, 2006). The driving questions that motivate and engage student behavior may be refined or changed as a project develops. Students and teachers can frame driving questions.

Examples of driving questions and the learning units that go with them have been developed by Blumenfeld, Marx, and Harris (2006). Seven of their units are described here:

1. *Air Quality.* The air quality unit focuses on the immediate environment. The driving question they address is, What affects the quality of air in my community?

Students depict their initial representations of air quality through a picture. As the unit progresses, students learn to identify the causes and consequences of common pollutants in their community. They identify the tools scientists use to measure air quality, and develop and present computer models to demonstrate their conceptual understanding of air quality.

2. *Big Things.* In the unit "Big Things," students explore the question, How do machines help me build big things? The unit starts by asking students to identify what they need to know to answer the question. They take a tour of a construction site and discuss the types of machines. Based on this information, students create their own machine design while learning rules about force, motion, levers, planes, and pulleys. The unit wraps up with a discussion of how simple and complex machines are used together to build big things.

3. *Communicable Disease.* This unit asks, How can good friends make you sick? It explores the causes of disease as well as how the human body fights disease from a biological perspective. Topics include discussions of HIV/AIDS and sexually transmitted diseases. As students explore this unit they use concept maps to visually represent relationships and patterns of disease spread, and create a model to represent disease transmission rates when no outward symptoms exist.

4. *Helmet.* This unit asks, Why do I need to wear a helmet when I ride my bike? It focuses on the physics of collision, laws of motion, velocity, stopping time, force, and the relationships among them. Students collect evidence and learn how to read and interpret motion graphs. Using this information and concept maps (they create throughout the unit), students build a helmet that must protect an egg during a fall, and present their results to the class.

5. *New Stuff from Old Stuff.* This unit for seventh-graders asks, How can I make new stuff from old stuff? It explores how to create a new substance from two substances. Specifically, students study chemical reactions and conservation of mass by making soap from fat and sodium hydroxide. Then, they cycle the soap back into fat. The final project asks students to explain why homemade soap is or is not better than commercial soap; alternatively, students can design and test a new soap recipe.

6. *Water.* The water unit has students examine a river in their own community and ask, What is the water like in our river? Students learn about the ecosystem and water quality through river observations, exploring watersheds, analyzing maps, and investigating variables that affect water quality (e.g., fertilizer). They build computer models and revise them throughout the unit as more information is uncovered, and then build and test those models.

7. *What Will Survive?* This unit asks, What will survive in our ecosystem? Students examine two examples of the struggle to survive in natural environments. In the first phase, students use real data collected from scientists to determine the impact of an invasive species on the Great Lakes environment. In the second phase, students use real data collected from scientists to determine the impact of the environmental stress drought has on a species of ground finches in the Galapagos Islands.

*M*anaging Technology Use

All the rules for small-group work that we discussed in Chapter 6 also apply here. Who will take notes? Who will "drive" the computer? Will drivers change within lessons? Several students using a computer together is harder to manage than brainstorming groups in which students all interact, or problem-solving groups in which all students have the problem materials in front of them. Rules need to be taught and internalized by students if the sharing of technology is to be successful.

Proactive planning prevents many problems. If you have only one or two computers, you will need a sign-up system that affords students fair access, and in ways that do not disrupt you or other students. Whether you have four students working on one computer or four students at four different computers, plan the space carefully. Train students about how to use computers and what to do when software fails. If you do not develop contingency plans, your instruction of other students will be interrupted from time to time.

Teachers can facilitate individual students' learning even when they have only a few computers, but it takes planning and monitoring time that could be used in other ways. In Chapter 12 we suggested that portfolios could be used to allow students sometimes to personalize learning; access to computers (if scheduled correctly) allows students to use rich Internet resources as they pursue their interests. To reiterate, managing technology in the classroom involves good application of proactive management that we have discussed in previous chapters. For special issues, such as managing technology laboratories, useful information can be found elsewhere (Bitter & Legacy, 2006; Bolick & Cooper, 2006).

Intellectual Push

A key part of the management system for instruction is to make it clear that the goal of technology usage is to use information wisely—the goal is not simply collection of material. After accessing information, students must learn appropriately from their sources. You will need to determine if students have captured accurate information. Do they understand key ideas? Can they distinguish between knowledge that is widely agreed upon and that which is contested? Students then need to make the information their own as discussed in Chapter 11. After processing the information (e.g., identifying and organizing key ideas), they need to reach and defend conclusions and, in the sense of Bruner (1966), they need to go beyond the information given. When students initiate performance projects (whether using technology or not) they often will benefit from some guidelines and structure. The project-based Web site of the Buck Institute (www.bie.org) has much useful information about enhancing project learning. It suggests that students respond to some of the following points when retrieving information:

- Use information retrieval systems
- Access several information sources
- Actively search for different perspectives
- Ask good questions about information accessed
- Display an overall search strategy (e.g., which sites to visit first and why)

Research has focused on teaching technologies and how software can affect student learning. Little has been written about the teacher's role in using technology to mediate students' learning, and in particular, learning of subject matter (Wallace, 2004). Computers can be a valuable data-gathering source via the Internet. However, do not assume that if it is in cyberspace, it is credible. Cross-referencing is essential. A book by Berson et al. (2004) entitled *Social Studies on the Internet* is a useful and reputable source.

Internet Usage Issues

Students vary in their knowledge of how to use the Internet appropriately and the dangers of Internet use, just as they do in their skills for using technology. Further, just because students use technology skillfully does not mean they have adequate knowledge of ethical aspects of Internet usage.

Perhaps the most critical issue is that Internet users understand that there are possible dangers in participating in chat rooms and other forms of Internet communication. You should convey to students information about danger associated with Internet use, including pornography, kidnapping, false information, identity theft, and so forth. In addition to safety aspects, students need to understand issues of appropriate conduct in Internet use—including copyright laws, privacy, cheating, and related issues. If your school has a computer/technology center, much of the instruction about safety and appropriate usage will likely occur there. Still, your comments as a trusted adult can go a long way in reinforcing or alerting your students to the fact that many dangerous individuals lurk in the background of Internet communication (Bolick & Copper, 2006).

Bitter and Legacy (2006) provide rich advice about social and legal issues involved in technology use, and those wanting detailed information about these issues will find their publication a valuable resource. They provide detailed information and advice about computer fraud, viruses, spam, phishing, e-mail scams, and so on. They have identified a number of useful Web sites including:

- Children's Internet Protection Act: www.ala.org/ala/washoff/WOissues/civilliberties/wascipa/cipatext.pdf
- Digital Millennium Copyright Act: www.asu.edu/counsel/brief/dig.html
- Teacher Act of 2002: www.copyright.gov/legislation/pl107273.pdf#13210
- Child Online and Privacy Acts: www.ftc.gov/bcp/conline/pubs/buspubs/coppa.htm
- Plagiarism: www.plagiarism.org/index.html
- Role-Playing Models: www.vuw.ax.nz/staff/alastair_smith/evaln/ and www.library.jhu.edu/researchhelp/general/evaluating
- Coalition for Equity in Education: www.w3.org/wai; www.cast.org/index.cfm; and www.rit.edu/~easi

SUMMARY

Given the prominent role of technology in society, some readers may be disappointed that we cannot point to a more powerful role for technology in classroom learning. This may change as more classrooms become wireless and when all students have a laptop computer. However, no technology has yet made transformative gains in knowledge acquisition. Technology advances give us access to more information more quickly, but transforming this information into knowledge requires disciplined and thoughtful processing. In its day, the telephone was a powerful technology that made the resources of much of the world a phone call away. But it required that people ask the right questions, listen carefully to the responses obtained, and use the information well. In the end, the Internet and other modern technologies are no different. They greatly enhance our power to see and communicate and to gain complex information quickly, but the information has to be processed and turned into knowledge by the learner.

Technology use in schools is less prevalent than many would recommend, but this is understandable because most classrooms have only a few computers. Secondary teachers' opportunities for using computers are also restricted because they see students for only a short amount of time each day. The biggest use of computers in elementary and secondary classrooms is for word processing. This use of computers for writing is supported by research. Other uses may prove to be desirable, but are not yet supported by research.

Your use of technology in the classroom will depend on your technology skills, your philosophy of teaching, and the technical support you have in the school. The computer offers great potential for quickly retrieving diverse samples of opinion (editorial pages can be obtained from all over the world) and Web-based projects afford unique ways to personalize learning activities. However, in too many cases, computer use is a time filler, not directed toward important instructional goals. Unless it supports progress toward worthwhile goals, quick information access is not a bonus. Computer searches involve strategy, information processing, good thinking, and reflection before knowledge is owned. Teach your students to see technology as a tool, not an end in itself, to help them become better learners, to understand appropriate use of the Internet, and to be aware of legal and social issues.

SUGGESTED ACTIVITIES AND QUESTIONS

1. What was the best technology-based learning experience you had in school? Why was it valuable? Why was technology needed to enhance the lesson?
2. Did your school experience reflect the research findings that computers are used more in elementary than in secondary classes?
3. The authors identify several potential advantages of using technology in the classroom. Can you expand on their list?
4. To what extent, and how, will you use technology in your teaching? Why?
5. Your students will spend much time using technology after school (TV viewing, messaging on their BlackBerries, joining chat rooms, and so forth). Is there anything you can do as a teacher to influence them to use technology productively? Or is this an issue best left to parents? Why do you feel this way?
6. If you are teaching in a low-SES school, how might this restrict your use of technology? What is your role in reducing the digital divide?
7. The authors primarily discuss the use of technology in science and social studies. What other subjects allow for technology? How?

CHAPTER

Growing As a Teacher

*I*n this chapter, we present information that you can use to grow as a teacher. Teachers have common interests, but also different needs; so, in-service programs must be tailored to participants, and teachers must be able to reflect and adapt content to meet their own needs (Dall'Alba & Sandberg, 2006; Glatterhorn, Boschee, & Whitehead, 2006; O'Donnell et al., 2007; Randi & Corno, 1997; Sparks, 2005). Further, you need to consider your own plans for growing as a teacher. As noted in Chapter 1, you need to integrate the theory, research, and concepts presented in this book with your own personality and teaching style and apply them to your classroom.

In this chapter, we start with a description of some common problems that new teachers face. Then we move to a discussion of individual programs for self-growth and informal study groups of volunteer teachers. Then we turn to the staff development that occurs as part of a school or school system's official in-service program. Our attention is focused mainly on ways to enhance teaching during the first few years; however, many ideas are useful even if you have taught for several years. The following vignettes illustrate how colleagues can assist (or hinder) self-evaluation.

An Elementary School Example

Michael Crowe, a first-year teacher at Ridgeway Elementary School, is perplexed. At the end of his first week of teaching, he is worn out and dreads returning to the classroom the following Monday. His class was not out of control, but keeping the students on task kept him fully occupied. He had little time to think about which students he called on or the types of learning opportunities he afforded the class and individual students. He thought about his teacher education program and the advice it had given him, especially the importance of behaving equitably toward all students and focusing class discourse around meaningful ideas. However, he was so consumed with keeping the ship afloat that he had little understanding of where the ship was headed, or why. He wondered if it would always be this way. Should he talk to other teachers about his concerns? Why or why not? What would you do?

A Middle School Example

Janice Taylor is a social studies education major who is student-teaching at Oak Junior High. Oak students come from the same kind of middle-class home that she came from. Still, she is sometimes apprehensive about teaching. She has not been in a middle school for several years, and although she has gained useful information in her college classes, she has never taught. Will students obey her? Can she make them enjoy schoolwork? These doubts increase as the time to start teaching nears. She has observed Ms. Woodward's class for two weeks. In another week she becomes the teacher.

Janice believes Ms. Woodward is a good teacher who treats students fairly and is respected by them. However, Janice is a shy and soft-spoken person who is uncomfortable around loud, assertive people. Consequently, she sometimes gets upset because Ms. Woodward speaks in a booming voice and does not hesitate to give misbehaving students a tongue-lashing or send them out of the room. Her favorite tactic when students are disruptive is to assert loudly, "I'm telling you once and for the last time, listen to your classmates when they talk!" Students typically stop after Ms. Woodward issues "commands."

One week later, when Janice is teaching, she loudly addresses misbehaving students, "I'm telling you once and for the last time, listen to your classmates!" Why did Janice imitate Ms. Woodward's teaching style? How might Janice have taught if she had had a different cooperating teacher?

A High School Example

Jessica Tyler has taught chemistry for fifteen years at Riverside High School, an affluent high school in a western state. She is respected by both colleagues and students. Today she is meeting with Sharon Mendoza, a first-year history teacher. Ms. Tyler believes that peer teacher observation and feedback are useful. The principal encourages teachers to cross subject-matter lines on occasion to help colleagues better understand instructional issues that are not subject-specific (management, clarity, pace, etc.). Today, Jessica observed Ms. Mendoza's third-period class. As they meet to discuss the observation, Ms. Tyler begins the conversation in a direct, business-like way. "Sharon, it was a pleasure to observe in your class. I enjoyed it a lot. It was a good lesson. There are only a few mistakes that I want to talk about."

What do you think about peer observation? Should teachers observe other teachers? Would you like for other teachers to observe you? Would you prefer that the observing teacher teach the same subject as you do? What should happen during a feedback conversation? What do you think of the way Ms. Tyler began the conversation?

*W*hat Do New Teachers Need to Do?

The Interstate New Teacher Assessment and Support Consortium (INTASC) functions as a resource for state agencies and professional organizations for information and standards in certifying teachers (Foster, Walker, & Song, 2007). Extended information about INTASC and its standards can be found at www.ccsso.org/intascst.html. Their ten key principles for teachers are summarized below.

1. Understands the structure of the discipline and tools of inquiry in the discipline she or he teaches, and can make learning knowledge of the discipline meaningful
2. Understands how students learn and develop and can design learning environments that support both the social and intellectual development of students
3. Understands that students learn in different ways and can design lessons for diverse learners
4. Has knowledge of and uses various learning strategies to help students to enhance various performance skills and to encourage good problem solving and critical thinking skills
5. Uses various strategies effectively to help students develop positive skills for collaborative learning in both group an individual learning settings
6. Uses knowledge of effective communication and technology skills to stimulate inquiry and collaboration
7. Is a decision maker and plans instruction on knowledge of students, key curriculum goals, subject matter, and the community
8. Can assess student learning in a variety of ways
9. Is a decision maker who reflects on how her or his teaching impacts students, and actively attempts to continually grow as a professional
10. Develops and uses relations with peers, parents, and community agents to support student learning

This is a considerable list of skills, knowledge, and descriptions to enact. Most teachers will enter the classroom needing to improve and to polish in all of these ten areas, and may have considerable work to do in meeting some standards.

School districts, principals, and experienced teachers also hold expectations for how you should interact and involve students in instructional activities. In Chapter 12, we presented the THOR system as an example of instructional practices expected of beginning teachers in one set of school districts (Tsang, 2003; Good et al., 2006). However, expectations vary considerably, and accordingly you should obtain copies of classroom performance criteria when you accept your job. Most schools allow or even encourage a wide range of teaching styles. Still, most have a set of competencies that they want to see when formal evaluations are conducted. Curriculum mandates are becoming more common, especially in urban districts and in schools where high numbers of students living in poverty are taught (Allington, 2006; McGill-Franzen et al., 2006). The impact of federal policy and most notably state policy vary widely; hence, the degree of imposed curriculum varies from very little to substantial. This is something that you need to consider when deciding on a teaching position. There is considerable literature dealing with how teachers cope with this issue. For example, Valencia et al. (2006) provide a detailed analysis of how beginning teachers dealt with an imposed curriculum. Reading about the experiences of other beginning teachers can be very helpful.

How Do Teachers Spend Their Time?

For over forty years, the National Education Association (NEA) has surveyed teachers about how they use their time. These results consistently suggest that elementary teachers work forty-five to forty-nine hours per week, and secondary teachers forty-six to fifty. Other sources have reached similar conclusions. A Metropolitan Life (2004–2005) study found that most teachers reported working at least forty-six hours in a typical week. However, over one-third reported spending more than fifty-five hours per week. Sometimes teachers are unaware of the time they spend on certain tasks, such as clerical or administrative paperwork. Clearly, teaching demands professional skill and commitment.

How Prepared Are New Teachers?

So what do new teachers worry about most? Historically, new teachers have worried most about issues of classroom management. Veenman (1984) reviewed the problems beginning teachers reported in eighty-three studies. The most widely reported problems were classroom discipline, motivating students, dealing with individual differences among students, assessing students, and communicating with parents. Teachers continue to have concerns about management, but by far their more pressing issues are dealing with parents and individual differences in how students learn (Reynolds, 1995). In a MetLife survey (2004–2005), a nationally representative sample of new teachers reported that their biggest concern was working with parents, especially if they worked in a school serving high numbers of students living in poverty. This concern was notably higher than concern about management and discipline. Thus, new teachers, by their own self-report, have distinct worries about aspects of teaching and do not view themselves as "finished products."

The transition from preservice to in-service teaching can be traumatic as teachers move from the idealistic world of the college classroom into the reality of everyday teaching. New teachers may experience some problems because they have had only general training and are not ready for a specific job. For example, one may student-teach in an inner-city first-grade class but then be assigned to a sixth-grade class in a suburban district. This happens quite frequently (Tsang, 2003).

Further, there are some problems that teachers cannot prepare for in advance. First-year teachers are not only becoming teachers and learning to deal with students, parents, and other adults; they also are assuming new responsibilities (making new friends, paying off loans, etc.). Thus, anxiety and role conflict are common at this time.

Goodson (1992) argued that one of the problems facing beginning teachers is that they typically are asked to implement a curriculum that has been developed by others. In addition to learning to negotiate the school, a new role, and new students, they must simultaneously implement an unfamiliar curriculum and develop a teaching style that fits their context. Bullough (1992) expressed the potential dilemma this way: "At times the two demands are contradictory: the adopted curriculum prohibits establishing a satisfying role; and the desired role makes it difficult to implement the established curriculum" (p. 239). However, other new teachers receive too little structure and must navigate curriculum decisions largely on their own (Esther, 2006). Thus, beginning teachers face myriad situations that yield varying degrees of support and structure.

There are several models for analyzing the development level of teachers (e.g., Hunt & Joyce, 1981; Sprinthall & Thies-Sprinthall, 1983). The first explicit theory describing teacher development was proposed by Fuller (1969). The first stage of teaching is concerned with survival (Will I be liked? Can I control students? Will others think I am a good teacher?). The second stage is concerned with the teaching situation (methods, materials, etc.), and the third stage reflects concern with students (their learning and needs). The early, self-centered concerns are considered less mature than later, more student-centered concerns. However, until you deal with early concerns (Will I survive? Can I refine my teaching skills?), you will have less ability to respond to individual students' needs.

Realistic resources, relevant experience, content knowledge, and good student teaching supervision can help many new teachers to at least move past the survival stage when they enter classrooms. You need to work through a variety of personal (Will anybody listen to me?) and procedural (how to use the computer, how to structure small-group instruction) teaching concerns before you can devote most of your attention to the effects of teaching (i.e., student learning). Understandably, the first few weeks of teaching will be spent developing appropriate routines and management systems. Once the ship is floating on its own, you can turn to self-improvement activities.

Becoming a good teacher involves the acquisition of knowledge, skills, and dispositions that are brought to fruition in the actual practice of teaching in a context. As we have noted, some see teachers as passing through phases from beginner, to teacher, to expert teacher. Dall'Alba and Sandberg (2006) caution that teaching progress is not automatic and that it requires more than accumulating years of teaching experience per se. They argue that experience is a necessary condition for improving practice, but it is not a sufficient condition. They say that professionals must work to understand their practice. We agree with Dall'Alba and Sandberg that to become better you have to learn from your experience through reflection and active decision making. Experience can be a critically important source for improvement, but as Rosenholtz (1989) noted some teachers have the same experience year after year. You become a better teacher through study and work.

Obstacles to Teacher Self-Improvement

Teaching can be, and often is, a rewarding experience and career, but it is also a tough job, especially in the first few years when you develop countless lesson plans for the first time and enact new skills (conducting a parent conference, assigning a student a failing grade, and so forth). One-third of beginning teachers leave within three years and one-half are gone after five years (Alliance for Excellent Education, 2004). Reasons for teacher attrition include low pay and poor working conditions (e.g., poor supervision, too little autonomy). Further, in-service programs that some schools provide err on the side of "pushing" teachers to perform in certain ways rather than allowing them to grow within their own framework of skills and dispositions. This is unfortunate, because there are multiple ways to teach effectively. We will return to this issue later.

Many New Teachers Leave the Field

Teachers leave teaching for various reasons, such as low wages, pregnancy, and to pursue other careers (Kreig, 2006; Provasnik & Dorfman, 2005). They are more likely to leave schools with higher rates of student poverty and higher minority populations (Guin, 2004; Ingersoll, 2004; Provasnik & Dorfman, 2005). Females are more likely to leave than males, as are teachers of math, science, English, and special education (Imazeki, 2005; Ingersoll, 2004; Theobald & Michael, 2001). Also, elementary school teachers are more likely to leave than secondary teachers (Ingersoll, 2004).

Lack of Satisfaction

Burnout is a term that has long been associated with teachers who have had prolonged exposure to stress factors associated with teaching (Maslach, 2003). Its putative causes include exhaustion, depersonalization, lack of recognition, and poor working conditions (Friedman, 2000; Wood & McCarthy, 2002). The pressures of standardized tests reduce teachers' options about what to teach and increase the pressure for their students to do well, which may speed up the process of burning out for some teachers (Nichols & Berliner, 2005).

Another reason why young teachers leave is mismatch between their beliefs about their ability to teach, what they think their first year of teaching will be like, and what they experience. Many expect teaching to be easier than it is, and the resulting shock produces frustration and dissatisfaction. This shock usually does not occur because teacher preparation programs fail to inform preservice teachers about the difficulties. Rather, the problem appears to be a sense of false optimism—it may happen to others but it won't happen to me (Esther, 2006; Weinstein, 1988).

Lack of Teaching Skill

Others have analyzed the problems of beginning teachers. For example, Liston, Whitcomb, and Borko (2006) presented three major arguments about why new teachers have difficulties when they begin to teach:

1. Teacher education programs do not prepare teachers for the specific tasks of teaching.
2. The emotional intensity of the first years of teaching is high.
3. New teachers often find themselves in schools that do not encourage new learning.

The idea that teacher education does not prepare teachers to teach merits comment. At first glance, this is likely to startle some beginning teachers who would have expected their programs to prepare them to teach. Some critics suggest that teacher education is focused too much on theory and too little on how to implement theory. There is also the possibility that teacher education is based on theories that conflict with the theory the employing school or school district endorses.

Darling-Hammond et al. (2005) contend that teachers graduate with a good array of teaching skills, learning theory, a vision of curriculum, and some notion of the purposes of education. However, they do not have the integrative skills (in this text we call these integrative skills action knowledge and decision making) to draw from their foundational knowledge to plan instructional activities adapted to their particular setting. As a result, even those who teach in supportive schools spend much time finding and adapting curriculum materials (Grossman & Thompson, 2004; Kaufmann et al., 2002).

A different problem exists if new teachers possess the "wrong" theory. Liston, Whitcomb, and Borko (2006) noted the distinction between conceptions of reading taught in many teacher education programs and those espoused by other professional groups. They described a study conducted by the National Council on Teacher Quality (NCTQ, 2006) which assessed whether teacher education programs taught the "science of reading," defined as phonemic awareness, phonics, oral fluency, vocabulary, and reading comprehension. The NCTQ report concluded that only 15 percent of seventy-two teacher education programs had courses that included all five components. School districts that adhere to a "science of reading" philosophy will of course be disappointed if teachers do not have the skills or knowledge to implement that philosophy.

According to the 2005 Metlife survey of American teachers, teachers' reasons for leaving were varied. The top five reasons that teachers provided for their departures were:

1. Not finding teaching satisfying
2. Not feeling valued by mentors or principals
3. Poor evaluations
4. Personal issues (e.g., conflict with other teachers)
5. Issues of teaching competency

These teachers reported reasons other than lack of preparation for leaving, including the fact that some simply find teaching unrewarding. Many felt that their preparation programs did not prepare them for these tasks:

• How to work with parents and get them to support their children's learning
• How to work with students of varying abilities and dispositions
• How to get needed resources

However, they also reported that their programs prepared them especially well to:

• Teach subject matter
• Hold students' attention
• Get advice and support from other teachers

Improving as a Teacher

Perhaps the best way to realize a rewarding teaching experience is to focus on how you can improve. If you can see personal progress, current problems and frustrations can be viewed as temporary. Yet, many new teachers are so overwhelmed by problems that they do not take charge of their opportunities. Why is this?

One obstacle to self-improvement stems from how we were socialized. Most of us have seldom taken part in self-evaluation designed not just to uncover weaknesses but to eliminate those weaknesses through constructive plans for improvement. We act this way, in part, because our socialization (especially in school) has not helped us to develop self-evaluation skills. For example, has a teacher ever returned an A paper to you with instructions to reflect on the paper and improve it?

Most of us have had to rewrite papers, but seldom A papers, and rarely have we been asked to rethink and incorporate new ideas of our own. Indeed, schools seldom allowed us time to think about what we were doing. We were too busy finishing assignments to reflect on them. Socialization in schools too often emphasizes and ethos of "do not look back, keep moving forward." Yet you must examine your past and present performances so that you can monitor progress and determine if you are moving forward.

Second, school experiences typically emphasize analytical thinking, not synthesis. Consider the following:

Teacher: Keith, what's wrong with electing members of Congress every two years?

Keith: (*Hesitantly and softly*) Well, ah, I think that they spend too much time trying to be reelected. (The teacher is beaming and nodding, so Keith speaks more confidently and loudly.) Since they face reelection every two years, they always need money. They build their campaign chest primarily with funds from the people who financed their first election, so they owe these people a big debt. It's hard for them to be their own person.

Teacher: Good answer, Keith. Alicia, what did Keith imply when he said, "be their own person"?

Alicia: Well, that the candidates' debts and their continual dependency on special interests who have given money make them cater to these groups. But even if members of Congress are strong, the two-year election procedure is bad because they must continue to run, raise money, and have too little time to do their real job.

Although such discussions are important, they seldom go beyond an analysis that defines the problem. The teacher might point out the desirability of controlling campaign spending and making sources of contributions public knowledge, then challenge students to go beyond common solutions that others suggest. For example, the teacher might suggest to Alicia that senators are elected for six-year terms, but also spend much time running for reelection and make most of their decisions accordingly. Or, the teacher could ask Alicia or other students to suggest ways in which elected representatives could be held accountable: Should they keep weekly logs of how their time is spent, hold regular office hours for the public, or spend a designated number of days in their district or state? Students could be encouraged to debate the value of term limits or to speculate and then to do Internet searches to try to understand the relationship between special interest lobbyists, and campaign finance, and term limits.

Demands are seldom made on students for original, practical suggestions because most of us were socialized in schools that gave us plenty of practice in pinpointing weaknesses, but little experience in solving problems by generating constructive alternatives. As a teacher, you need to change your mind-set from simply analyzing problems to solving them, including problems in your own teaching.

Also, most evaluation we experienced in schools was external and nonconstructive. Evaluative comments told us where we stood, but not how we could improve. This led some of us to avoid evaluation. Because it was associated with the potential for negative consequences, it often evoked the fear that "I'm going to be exposed," not "I'm going to receive useful feedback." Thus, our experiences as students have not required the synthesis of skills we need as teachers to solve problems with new strategies.

Experimenting and Improving

You need to seek feedback to grow, including critical feedback. This starts with your conception of what a "good teacher" is. All teachers have unique strengths and weaknesses. You have to develop a style that allows you to express yourself and teach students in your own way. You may have to experiment with different methods before you find an approach that is right for you. If you try an approach systematically for a reasonable time and it does not work, then discard it and develop techniques that do work. There is no need to teach the way your cooperating teacher did, even though there is evidence to suggest that many beginning teachers are substantially influenced by how their cooperating teachers taught (Calderhead & Robin, 1991; O'Donnell, Reeves, & Smith, 2007).

Even after identifying a satisfying style, successful teachers continue to experiment to find new ways to stimulate student learning. They constantly reflect on their teaching and stay abreast of new research and developments. Given the time demands of teaching, finding time for professional reading and other forms of self-improvement is often difficult, but continued reading is essential if you are to grow professionally.

Teaching Is Difficult

Few teachers excel in all aspects of teaching. All occasionally teach lessons that fail, say the wrong thing to students, and so forth. Although teaching is difficult, one can succeed at it by continuing to strive for improvement. Too often teachers enter classrooms with unrealistically high expectations ("I will capture the interest of every student at every moment, and every lesson I teach will be completely successful"), so that when outcomes do not match expectations, they may become depressed, blame students, or begin to rationalize their behavior rather than to search for new ways to teach (Esther, 2006; Weinstein, 1980). This occurs in part because they do not realize that other teachers also have difficulties.

Like everyone else, teachers tend to talk about successes, not failures. Thus, some teachers, especially new ones, may become anxious and discouraged when they have trouble because they hear primarily the good things that other teachers are doing. They experience feelings of disappointment and ineptness when they do not achieve easy success, yet are reluctant to ask veteran teachers for help because they believe they would be admitting failure (Rosenholtz, 1989). Even when young teachers are assigned mentors, they approach them infrequently (Smylie, 1997).

If you have thoughts like these, dismiss them. Teaching is challenging and exciting work, but it takes time to develop and refine teaching skills. Most experienced teachers are sympathetic to the problems of beginning teachers and are willing to help. However, few of us like to be approached by someone who says, "Tell me what to do." It is better to approach other teachers by telling them you have a teaching problem and would like to exchange ideas and benefit from their experience.

Self-Evaluation

Here we provide you with a way of thinking about your growth as a teacher. For some of you this will be easier than for others because resources, including the provision of mentor teachers, vary widely from school to school.

Starting Self-Evaluation. The first step is to evaluate your current strengths and weaknesses. Reexamine the NTASC standards that were presented at the beginning of the chapter. Then go back through this text and list your behaviors on three pages entitled: (1) Perform Capably, (2) Needs Work, and (3) Not Sure. Take the first list, which represents progress you have made as a teacher, and save it on your computer so you can examine it from time to time and add to it.

You may note that you already ask a variety of factual and higher-order questions and that you ask questions before calling on students. On your list for Needs Work, you may note a tendency not to follow through on warnings or decide that you want to help students to become better self-evaluators. Similarly, you may note that you use no technology resources in class, and you decide you want to add one or two assignments that involve new technology. After thinking about strengths and weaknesses, you will have a working conception of your ability as a teacher and some specific improvements you want to make.

If you have trouble deciding where to start, you might have a teacher whom you respect observe your class and make suggestions. Alternatively, you could listen to or watch a recorded session of your class.

Making Explicit Plans. To improve your teaching, you must be specific—get beyond vague improvement notions that are like halfhearted New Year's resolutions that never get fulfilled. Vague goals such as "I want to teach in diverse ways" are seldom accomplished simply because they do not guide planning. Resolutions are more likely to be fulfilled when they are specific: "I want to increase the time my students spend in small-group and project-based work by 25 percent." Recall that we have been socialized to see problems, but the goal is the constructive search and identification of effective improvement strategies.

Action. After developing goals, choose two or three instructional aspects or beliefs to change or new ones to try. Do not try to change too many things at once, lest you become overwhelmed and discouraged. Address a few issues at a time and monitor your progress. For example, if you try to call on students randomly, you may have to write their names on flash cards and shuffle the stack periodically. Always calling on students who have their hands up is a difficult habit to break.

As you implement a change, assess its effectiveness. After you introduce lessons by telling students why the lessons are important, try to assess whether more students follow the directions or seem interested. Similarly, if you call on students to react to other students' responses, note whether students pay greater attention to discussions.

Individual Self-Study.   Questions that might be useful for self-study include:

- What aspects of teaching do I most enjoy? What does this imply about my beliefs about good teaching?
- What aspects of teaching do I worry about most?
- How do my instructional goals match those of my colleagues?
- Is my curriculum relevant to male and female students and students from various races or ethnic groups?
- Do my low and high achievers indicate that I have equal interest in them?
- Do my questions emphasize understanding or only correct answers?
- How long do I wait for students to respond? Is this figure different for high and low achievers?
- When students work in small groups, do some students do most of the work? Do I really know?
- How do I teach content I am most knowledgeable about, versus content I know least about?
- What percentage of students' days are spent learning new material versus reviewing?
- Do some students who need help rarely seek me out to get it? Which students initiate contact with me and which don't? Why?
- How much time do I spend with individual students each day?
- How much time do I spend in math, social studies, language arts? Do students' achievement gains reflect time spent?
- Are undesirable gender roles or cultural expectations communicated in my class?

Exploring such questions provides information about aspects of your classroom that you might want to change, or identify how you can find out if the change was effective. For example, when I implement peer-tutoring activities, do I have more time to work with individual students?

As we mentioned in Chapter 1, conducting case studies can allow you to explore the ways in which you possibly treat students in different ways without necessarily intending to do so. You may wish to review that material.

Classroom Vignette

Sixth-grade teacher Joe Hernandez's students do less well in math than in other subjects. Joe is puzzled by this. He enjoys teaching math and feels well qualified to do so. Students' attitudes measured earlier in the year were generally positive toward him. However, math drew the most criticism.

Joe decides to obtain anonymous information from students about their problems in math. He is discouraged to find that the information students provide is contradictory and does not lead to suggestions for action. However, one theme is evident in the comments of several students: "I often don't know what I'm supposed to do for my assignment"; "When we start a new unit, I'm always lost"; "I don't understand my work until you explain it the next day."

Subsequently, Joe notices that students seem more aimless when working on math assignments than in other subject. He decides that he does not spend enough time explaining how the work relates to preceding work, modeling how to do problems, and allowing students to generate and discuss examples before they begin work. His plan is to increase his ratio of explanation, modeling, and student verbalization of thinking to the amount of time they do practice work, especially at the beginning of a unit, and to see if this strategy improves students' attitudes and achievement.

Joe's plan is a hypothesis, a good hunch about how to proceed. Such plans must not become "answers" adopted without consideration of their effects on students. Joe might find that some other factor (assignments too long, feedback inadequate) is related more directly to student achievement. By evaluating the effects of his changes in classroom processes on student outcomes, eventually he will find procedures that work for his class. Good decision making requires specific issues and questions, and requires evidence about the effects of classroom change.

You Are Not Alone

You may wish to begin your self-evaluation without feedback from others, and we have provided some considerations for how to do this. Nevertheless, most teachers who want to improve will eventually benefit from discussing their teaching with peers.

If you have access to videotape equipment, arrange to have one or two of your typical lessons videotaped. Do not attempt to construct special units or to review old material. Teach regularly scheduled lessons in your normal fashion. After a couple of weeks, tape new lessons so you can watch for signs of progress in your instruction, decision making, and in student responses.

You can also request release time to work with peers or make arrangements to trade weekly visits with other teachers during free periods. And, you can use student teachers, student observers, or parents on occasion. It usually is best to specify what an observer is to look for, because there is so much to see that he or she may not notice the things you would like to receive feedback about. Observers, of course, can always volunteer additional information (Lewis, Perry, & Murata, 2006).

Curriculum supervisors also can provide relevant feedback. Most supervisors are delighted when teachers make explicit observation requests. However, supervisory visits often are frustrating for the supervisor as well as for the teacher (McDaniel, 1981). Since supervisors may not know the goals of a lesson or how it fits into a unit, it is difficult for them to provide helpful feedback. Armed with a specific request, though, they can provide relevant comments about areas of interest to teachers.

Students can provide useful information anonymously through questionnaires. Expect a variety of comments. Students have unique perspectives, and different students may perceive the same aspect of your teaching as a weakness or strength. However, feedback often includes some comments on which many students agree.

Student feedback is most useful when it is anonymous, and it is usually better to ask for specific reactions. One method is to request three or more statements about both strengths and weaknesses, which encourages students to be specific and to provide a more balanced critique than do global, free-response methods. When you ask students for information it is useful to call their attention to previous changes made in response to student feedback (e.g., "Students last year asked for more reflection time in journal writing, so we now do that for fifteen minutes instead of five"). Conversations are another good way to learn from students. McCaslin and Good (1996) provide detailed advice about useful ways for gaining insights into student perspectives.

Self-Study Groups

In addition to informal observations and feedback, teachers may seek more formal ways to assess and strengthen their teaching. Much of this exchange can focus on observation of teaching practices (Bliss & Reynolds, 2004; Lewis, Perry, & Murata, 2006). Under the right conditions—teachers know what information they want, and peers are sensitive— peer feedback encourages teachers to improve their performance. Moreover, teachers who observe may gain as much as those who are observed (Sparks, 2005).

Self-study groups are especially useful when they allow you to work with teachers who have common problems or self-development goals. Different goals call for different groupings. If the goal is to improve curriculum continuity, teachers in contiguous grades should work together. However, if the goal is to allow elementary and secondary teachers to test their assumptions about what occurs at the other level, then it is important to mix teachers. To promote the exchange of information about teaching style or classroom climate, teachers who teach different subjects and at various grade levels may be needed.

Self-improvement teams may view tapes and provide feedback about one another's teaching, especially aspects that are of special interest to the teacher taped. This procedure contrasts markedly with in-service programs that provide teachers with information on issues that outside consultants discuss. Teachers often view such in-service activities as a waste of time.

Participation in self-study groups should be voluntary, because it involves self-disclosure and honest discussion and evaluation of teaching. Understandably, some teachers may want to assess their own programs and develop their own goals before joining a group. As a beginning teacher, you may want to consider delaying participation in "volunteer" programs if they seem problematic from your point of view.

Three rules should be kept in mind when groups begin. First, group feedback exists to provide you with information to augment self-development. The group provides the perspectives and resources that enable you to develop more specific instructional plans. You should function as a decision maker, setting your own developmental goals. The group functions as a barometer, telling how it views you and suggesting alternative ways to reach *your* goals.

List goals and teaching practices that the group should examine when they view your videotape or observe your classroom. Focus on improving a few areas, and ask the group to restrict its comments to these. After the group has functioned for a few months, the "video teacher of the week" may be ready to ask the group to focus on all dimensions of teaching that were exhibited.

Second, in the group's formative weeks it is important not to overwhelm a teacher with information. Restricting discussion to a few areas will help, as will limiting the number of comments each group member makes. We can profit from only so much information at one time, particularly negative feedback.

In-service groups may benefit from a rule like: Each participant provides a written discussion of two or three strengths and two or three weaknesses. This guideline limits the amount of information you and other teachers receive and focuses attention on a small, manageable list of "points to consider."

Useful feedback focuses on specific ways to improve teaching. Ensuing discussions should include alternative procedures that you and other teachers might use to produce better student outcomes. Thus, you should receive realistic reactions to your performance and information about alternative strategies that might allow you to be more effective.

A third rule is to be honest. Self-study groups lose effectiveness if individuals use either of two participatory styles: Pollyanna and Get-the-Guest. Too many teachers are unwilling to say what they feel about another teacher's behavior, perhaps because they are afraid that frankness will lead others to respond in kind when they are being evaluated. Yet you and other teachers can improve only if you receive honest feedback. Constructive criticism followed by suggestions about how to improve teaching is the best way to augment your self-development. To be sure, teachers should communicate the good things that a teacher does. We all like to know when we have done well, and it is especially important to receive acknowledgment and encouragement for improvement.

Candor is sometimes hard to achieve, even in formal evaluations. As a case in point, Frase and Streshly (1994) reported that some principals provided teachers with inflated evaluations. If peers or principals are to support teacher performance, they must become knowledgeable about aspects of effective teaching, observational analysis, and good clinical skills for interacting with others. Honesty and candor are critical aspects of peer groups (Sparks, 2005).

The other undesirable participant role is the Get-the-Guest carping critic who criticizes excessively and thoughtlessly. Often such behavior is motivated by the need for self-protection, although sometimes such teachers are just insensitive. At any rate, all participants need to deliver criticism tactfully and link it with positive suggestions. Those who cannot temper excessive criticism should not continue in the group.

Develop a Positive Perspective

Given the frequency of teacher burnout and attrition, it is useful to think about your mental health and satisfaction as a teacher. As we discussed in Chapter 2, how we frame problems and what we expect from others may be self-sustaining or fulfilling. Houghton (2001) recommends a strategy of seeing, finding, and using allies in mutually beneficial ways.

- See colleagues as allies
- See students as allies; develop honesty and mutual support
- See parents as allies
- Use professional groups as allies; see issues larger than one's classroom
- Use professional literature as an ally
- See universities and coursework as allies
- See yourself as an ally

We have presented similar ideas since the first edition of *Looking in Classrooms,* however, Houghton's perspective of seeing the environment as full of opportunity (as opposed to problems) and actively seeking allies is a uniquely powerful way to express the issue.

You have limited time to connect with all teachers, but finding a couple of peer teachers to talk to about professional and personal issues helps you to reduce the feeling that you are alone, to have pleasant experiences, and to gain new knowledge. Students can be allies of a different sort if you explain to them the reasons for rules or assignments and build trusting relationships. Seeing students as active learners who have their own ideas and needs (not as people who need to be controlled) frees energy for various constructive endeavors.

Parent–teacher discussions of students' needs and issues can allow both parents and teachers to gain new insights (Walker & Hoover-Dempsey, 2006). Similarly, attending professional meetings allows for new perspectives from peers who teach in different settings and can serve as a source of new ideas as well as reinforcement that some of our enduring problems are problematic for others as well. Visiting other teachers' classrooms can give you useful ideas and it may show that other teachers have problems as well.

$\mathcal{I}$mproving Workplace Conditions for Teaching

Emerging conceptions of supervision are based on recognition of the fact that there is no single approach that is effective for all teachers and all situations (Good, 1996). Various models call for supervisors to understand and use various interpersonal approaches in working with teachers, including directive, collaborative, and nondirective approaches (Glickman, 1990; Joyce, 1981; Joyce & Weil, 1996; Sparks, 2005).

Gordon (1992) discussed several shifts in thinking concerning the supervision of teachers: from control to empowerment, from sameness to diversity, and from occasional supervisor assistance to continuous collegial feedback and support. He noted that the control perspective mandated the forms of teaching that should be in place and include "teacher-proof" curricula and supervisors who consistently tell teachers the "correct" way to teach. More recently, educational leaders have emphasized an empowerment approach that helps teachers to become skilled and reflective decision makers, capable of choosing the form of instruction they will use and suggesting the type of supervisory support they need. Empowerment implies that teachers are involved in collaborative curriculum development and instructional leadership.

There has been increased recognition that workplace conditions must change if teachers are to have time to work with colleagues, engage in collaborative planning activities, and become more involved in making schoolwide decisions. Enhanced opportunity for professional development and teacher leadership can help (1) to enhance democratic functioning in schools, (2) to make better use of teachers' expertise in planning coherent instructional programs, (3) to assist in recruiting capable teachers by making the work more interesting (e.g., more professional autonomy and decision making, etc.), (4) to address the need for instructional and curriculum reform, and (5) to develop a more professional workplace (Hart, 1995; Sparks, 2005). Such collaborative work can also enhance teaching experience by allowing teachers to understand and to learn from their experience, and thus to become a more knowledgeable and effective teacher (Dall'Alba & Sandberg, 2006).

Types of Professional Collaboration

Teacher collaboration is an important part of professional development (Sparks, 2005). Glatthorn (1987) discusses ways in which teachers can collaborate, including professional discussion, curriculum development, peer observation, peer coaching, and action research.

Professional Discussion.   Professional dialogue facilitates reflection about teaching. In groups, teachers can discuss issues of common interest—issues specific to a particular subject (e.g., the teaching of controversy in social science, available software for teaching human physiology) or applicable to all subjects (student motivation, ability grouping, critical thinking). Discussion groups do not have to focus on describing or changing teacher or student behavior; they also can emphasize general professional issues.

There are no systematic data concerning the effects of professional dialogue, but participants' reports about such opportunities are generally positive. Glatthorn (1987) suggests one model based on his experience. Stage one emphasizes external knowledge, or what can be found in the literature about a particular problem (e.g., Do experts agree on the issue—or on strategies for how to respond?). At this stage, participants should not attempt to dispute external knowledge, but rather explore and try to understand it. In the second stage, discussion centers on personal knowledge (What does my experience with the problem suggest? How does our collective sense of the problem compare with what others have said about it?). Through active listening, sharing, and reflection, teachers learn from a healthy tension between personal and external knowledge and from attempting to integrate the two types. The third stage explores future actions (What actions might be taken as a result of increased awareness of the problem and reflection about possible actions?). Depending on the interests of the group, this stage could focus on the needs of individual teachers or on implications for the entire school.

Curriculum Development.   According to Glatthorn (1987; Glatthorn et al., 2006), curriculum development involves cooperative activity in which teachers enhance the district's curriculum guides (e.g., English teachers might create a unit on local or regional dialects). Others have suggested additional ways for teachers to work on curriculum issues. For example, some note that too little attention is given to the processes of science (conducting experiments, making and testing inferences) and too much time is spent on low-level memorization (Blumenfeld, Marx, & Harris, 2006). Their work suggests that it is valuable to study curriculum materials to determine the extent to which the curriculum encourages thinking versus memorization. Teachers might profitably exchange ideas about textbooks, assignments, learning stations, learning kits, computer labs, technology, quizzes, tests, unit reports, and so on. In addition to analyzing materials, teachers can also help one another by developing and sharing materials.

Peer Coaching.   Peer coaching is similar to peer observation but involves some key differences. Peer observation suggests more choice for individual teachers with regard to what will be observed. In contrast, peer coaching is usually based on a staff development theme (often selected by district staff or administrators). Teachers are given theoretical orientation to a model or set of skills, observe it being implemented, and then try to implement it while receiving frequent feedback.

Structure and follow-up appear to be vital to successful staff development efforts. Joyce and Weil (1996) argued that all of the following five elements should be included in good staff development programs:

1. Presentation of theory or description of teaching skills or strategies
2. Modeling or demonstration of teaching skills or strategies
3. Practice in simulated and real classrooms
4. Structured and open-ended feedback about performance
5. Coaching for application—in-classroom, hands-on assistance in transferring new knowledge and skills to the classroom.

Joyce (1981) estimates that fewer than 20 percent of trainees master the skills of a training program if they do not receive feedback about their performance and if they are not coached in how to apply new skills. These conditions often are missing in staff development programs. If coaches are to be helpful, they must be well trained (Danielson & McGreal, 2000; Perkins, 1998).

Action Research.   Action research can be used as a means for pursuing various goals, including increasing teacher reflection, collegial teacher interaction, and teacher status and efficacy; reducing the gap between doing research and implementing its results; and legitimating the professional value of practical classroom concerns. Action research is self-reflective problem solving that can help you improve your performance by direct study. The concept of action research promotes a view of teachers not only as recipients of knowledge but also as professionals who can produce knowledge for themselves and others (Lieberman, 1986; Sparks, 2005).

$\mathcal{S}$ chools as Social Systems

So far we have discussed the effects of professional collaboration and staff development on teachers' development. But school settings also influence teachers' expectations and performance.

Rosenholtz (1989) showed that the social structure of the workplace significantly affects teachers' commitment, leadership, cooperation, and the quality of both teachers' and students' school lives. She analyzed questionnaire data from more than 1,200 teachers concerning social organizational variables within schools (e.g., teacher goal setting, teacher collaboration, etc.). In schools where teachers perceived high goal consensus, they also reported high commitment, and so forth.

In high-consensus schools, only 8 percent of the teachers felt that "there is no time to talk," whereas in moderate- and low-consensus schools 11 and 20 percent of the teachers, respectively, felt this way. Other studies have shown that as many as 45 percent of teachers report no contact with one another during a school day, and another 32 percent report infrequent contact.

Rosenholtz found that only 4 percent of the high-consensus teachers complained about student behavioral problems when they talked with colleagues, but 54 percent discussed curriculum and instruction. In contrast, 28 percent of the teachers in low-consensus schools reported talking about student problems, whereas only 19 percent discussed curriculum and instruction.

When asked, "Where do your new teaching ideas come from?" teachers in "learning-enriched" schools reported a variety of sources: 90 percent reported learning from other teachers, 45 percent from professional conferences, and 72 percent from their own problem solving and creativity. In "learning-impoverished" schools only 32 percent of the teachers reported learning from other teachers, none from professional conferences, and only 4 percent from their own problem solving and creativity.

A key concept in Rosenholtz's theoretical position is uncertainty about how teaching can best be conducted to help students learn. A technical culture is uncertain if outcomes of work are unpredictable. Work in schools reflects an uncertain technical culture because there are few codified means for helping individual students achieve specific goals (e.g., learn problem solving or engage in complex, abstract synthesis). Thus, work in schools is nonroutine and teaching is often fraught with uncertainty.

Organizational uncertainty has consequences. When we are unable to control situations or to make positive things happen, we may question our ability or develop self-protective strategies (refuse to participate, not try) in order to avoid embarrassment. In schools where principals' or teachers' views of their job competence are sufficiently threatened, they may engage in self-defensive tactics to protect their own sense of self-worth.

Although uncertainty is endemic to teaching, it is the social culture in which teaching takes place that determines whether the uncertainty becomes a disability (e.g., teachers develop routine ways to deal with situations that are not routine, deny problems, etc.) or a creative tension (teachers learn to discuss ideas and to collaborate to solve problems and improve teaching). Uncertainty is reduced by two conditions. First, teachers have the opportunity to obtain positive feedback about their abilities from peers and principals in a variety of ways. Second, teachers are provided with occasions to increase their knowledge of teaching and gain more expertise in dealing with more situations. Rosenholtz argues that teachers' commitment to schools and to continued learning is heavily influenced by three workplace conditions: (1) task autonomy—teachers' sense that they can adapt instruction to their own contexts; (2) continuous opportunities for learning that provide them with greater mastery and control of the environment; and (3) "psychic" rewards that ensure their continuous contributions to schools (their opinions are requested, they have the opportunity to interact with peers, they receive needed information when appropriate, etc.). More recent discussions of research on social organization of schools continues to show the robustness of Rosenholtz's insights (Borich, 2007).

The Growing Importance of Staff Development

Today's teachers function in a complex environment of policy, law, regulation, special programs, and professional associations. Modern staff development usually involves groups of teachers working together with specialists, supervisors, administrators, parents, and university personnel. In some districts a large percentage of the discretionary budget is spent on staff development. Yet, planning for staff development in some districts is not always as systematic as it should be. In-service programs are frequently one-time events (a speaker is brought in, but little, if any, follow-up occurs), and too little attention is paid to assessing program effects.

Improving the Entire School

A staff development program should first help teachers to address individual needs. Once these needs are met, teachers can address broader school concerns through cooperative in-service programs. Working collectively to improve is a potent determinant of the value of a staff development program. Little (1981) writes:

> First, the school as a workplace proves extraordinarily powerful. Without denying differences in individuals' skills, interests, commitment, curiosity, or persistence, the prevailing pattern of interactions and interpretations in each building demonstrably creates certain possibilities and sets certain limits. . . . We are led from a focus on professional improvement as an individual enterprise to improvement as particularly an organizational phenomenon. Some schools sustained shared expectations (norms) both for extensive collegial work and for analysis and evaluation of and experimentation with their practices; continuous improvement is a shared undertaking at schools, and these schools are the most adaptable and successful of the schools we have studied. (pp. 9, 10)

Little (1995) notes that in high schools, reform movements and interest in enhancing teacher leadership have presented opportunities for teachers to engage in leadership issues outside of their traditional classroom responsibilities and subject-matter knowledge. Some schools organize along subject lines and place students' and teachers' subject-matter knowledge front and center. Other schools organize in different ways to combat the impersonality and lack of connection that often exist in high schools. For example, teachers and students may be organized in units or house clusters so that teachers teaching different subject matter are working with the same cohort of students. These schools try to focus on schooling more holistically and look at learners as social beings who need to feel connected to their school (Nichols & Good, 2004; Watson & Battistich, 2006).

Staff Development in Effective Schools

How resources are used and how teachers are encouraged to interact with one another help to predict the overall effectiveness of a school (Good & Brophy, 1986; Sparks, 2005). Hence, it is important to consider how best to develop the talents of the teaching staff. Both school and classroom processes must be considered to identify processes and relationships that facilitate or hinder goals at each level. How can schools focus on high-quality instruction at the same time that individual teachers are helping students to develop their talents? How can opportunities for practice, display, and reward of learning accomplishments be improved? How can activities such as school newspapers, journals, and assemblies be used to supplement the efforts of teachers in individual classrooms (Good & Weinstein, 1986)?

The country is addressing a national teacher shortage, and the more schools can do to encourage competent teachers to stay in the field, the better (Alliance for Excellent

Education, 2004). Teachers need new professional information, support, and resources. If staff development can sustain their needs, it can make the field more attractive. Unfortunately, staff development sometimes takes teachers out of the classroom by developing professional skills that are not directly related to and may even interfere with classroom teaching, undermining teacher responsibility for self-evaluation, or seeking to offer routine answers for non-routine problems. As noted in Chapter 11, some schools seem to move from fad to fad rather than develop context-specific solutions that fit their settings.

Teacher–Teacher Communication

Through working with peers teachers can exchange ideas and improve instruction throughout the school. If schools are to affect student outcomes broadly and significantly, teachers must be cognizant of how other teachers in the same school teach.

Lack of teacher–teacher communication can reduce school effectiveness. For example, it is not uncommon to visit schools in which assignments for fifth-graders are less demanding than those for third-graders. Students in lower grades often have more choices of books to read, more freedom to work with other students, and more opportunities to explore creative topics. In some secondary schools, seventh-graders write original essays, but ninth-graders only answer questions about various works of history and English. Such discrepancies not only fail to challenge students to become progressively more independent and self-reliant, but may lower older students' interest in schoolwork. Unfortunately, many teachers do not provide appropriately challenging assignments because they are unaware of what other teachers are doing.

What we advocate is broader than teachers simply sharing information. We refer to a sense of community among teachers who try to develop appropriate, positive expectations for all students and to challenge students by designing tasks based on information obtained in carefully planned and coordinated discussions with other teachers. This is as important for non-subject-matter outcomes as it is for achievement outcomes.

In-Service on School-Level Concerns

There are reasons for schoolwide in-service on issues that affect all teachers. We illustrate one of these possibilities here with discussion of issues embedded in statewide testing that influence all teachers within a school.

The Problem

Until recently, teacher grades and national tests (e.g., Iowa Test of Basic Skills, SAT) were considered sufficient to provide decision makers with data to inform decisions about promotion, honor roll, high school graduation, and college admission. However, state-level administrators increasingly have sought to replace or supplement teachers' professional judgments with state-mandated tests, even to supplant teachers' judgments totally by relying on state tests for high-stakes decisions (e.g., high school graduation). Fortunately, some of these unrealistic expectations for magical increases in student achievement are beginning to recede.

State-developed tests and teacher-made tests (and the grades that teachers assign on the basis of these tests) measure different things. Brennan et al. (2001) compared suburban eighth-grade students' scores on a state-mandated test with grades assigned by their teachers. The grades and test scores correlated only moderately (.50 to .60), which means that some students would be denied promotion to ninth grade if only one criterion was used and cut-off points were sharply defined.

Further, girls' scores in math and science were lower on the state tests than on teacher tests, and African American students did less well on the state math test than on teacher tests. Muller and Schiller (2000) noted that student performance varied by type of student and type of performance measure. They urged policy makers to use multiple measures (including teacher grades), especially when making high-stakes decisions. Similarly, Good, McCaslin, and Legg Burross (see Good & McCaslin, 2005; McCaslin & Good, 2005) found that a state's achievement test would suggest different conclusions than would the Stanford achievement test about student and school progress.

Teachers' judgments about student persistence and ability to apply themselves over time provide important assessment information that cannot be supplied by a one-shot standardized test. Standardized tests can provide useful information, but the critical decision-making information about how to adjust instruction and assess student progress throughout the curriculum comes from teacher-made tests and teachers' informal judgments.

Although policy makers—politicians in particular—stress external testing, many state tests have been hurriedly and poorly prepared, scored, and interpreted (Armor, 2006; Lin, 2000). Thus, state tests often are technically inadequate, even though state policies mandate their use. Also, although state standards usually are touted as "higher" for political reasons, many school districts have higher standards than what is being imposed on them. Thus, different educators in the same state can claim correctly that state standards are either too high or too low. Finally, in some states, the state curriculum and the state test are unevenly aligned or there are mismatches between state and district standards (Blank, Porter, & Smithson, 2001).

Accordingly, school districts face several problems in dealing with state-mandated reform and high-stakes testing programs. First, they must understand the new curriculum and the new test. This can be a huge task because in some cases, state curricula are vague and poorly communicated. For example, Hill (2001) concluded from her study of one school district that the state had provided few details for implementation and inadequate instructional support:

> Imagine, for instance, if the state had provided videotapes of lessons and instructional methods aligned with standards. Or, if it had asked teachers to grapple with fewer sub-objectives but provided more development around each. Or, if it had started with concrete lessons and student work and asked teachers to infer abstract principles from these things. (pp. 313–314)

School District In-Service

If states have not communicated a clear conception of instruction, school districts might assume this role. The state curriculum and test should be carefully examined and different interpretations should be debated and resolved. The principal could be an active facilitator with teachers and the State Department of Education. Teachers could discuss "competing" versions of practice that are consistent with the new model and perhaps prepare appropriate video models and ways of testing reform in their own classrooms (Mason et al., 2005).

After constructing a vision of what the reform entails and the testing that surrounds it, teachers and administrators need to consider if this vision is appropriate in their context. The state-mandated test or curriculum cannot be ignored, but teachers have the professional obligation to analyze state tests and reach professional judgments. In some cases, teachers may determine real differences between the mandated curriculum and what their students need. They may find, for example, that the state test emphasizes memorization and recognition, so they will need to guard against a tendency to narrow the curriculum to drill on lower-level content. In other cases, higher-order problem solving may be demanded prematurely and/or without an adequate orientation to developing key concepts and facts that students need to solve problems.

Concern about the curriculum-narrowing effect of state-mandated tests has been growing among professional educators and associations. Indeed, several professional organizations have prepared joint guidelines to improve on state-mandated tests (American Association of School Administrators, National Association of Elementary School Principals, National Association of Secondary School Principals, National Education Association, and National Middle School Association). Table 14.1 presents nine requirements that these educators feel are necessary for appropriate state standards.

One important in-service activity would be to debate these recommendations and to send school-endorsed recommendations to the State Department of Education. However, even if these recommendations eventually influence some aspects of policy, it will be a long time before extant concerns are resolved. In the short run, teachers need to know that in many cases, there will be sharp discrepancies between state mandates and their own professional judgments about their students' needs, and teachers and schools need to make intelligent compromises between ideal goals and imposed goals.

SUMMARY

The advice and strategies for self-growth we have provided are useful for all teachers. However, the recommendations are especially important for beginning teachers. Unfortunately, too many teachers who experience difficulty deny their problems (at least to others) and fail to avail themselves of help from other teachers and supervisors. New teachers need to use discretion in deciding which teachers to approach for information; some teachers are better sources of information and are more empathic than others, and obviously student teachers and beginning teachers need to exercise tact when they ask for assistance. However, a broader, more pervasive problem is failing to obtain help.

Table 14.1 The Nine Requirements Outlined by Educators for Responsible State Assessment Systems

Requirement 1:   A state's content standards must be prioritized to support effective instruction and assessment.

Requirement 2:   A state's high-priority content standards must be clearly and thoroughly described so that the knowledge and skills on which students need to demonstrate competence are evident.

Requirement 3:   The results of a state's assessment of high-priority content standards should be reported standard-by-standard for each student, school, and district.

Requirement 4:   The state must provide educators with optional classroom assessment procedures that can measure students' progress in attaining content standards not assessed by state tests.

Requirement 5:   A state must monitor the breadth of the curriculum to ensure that instructional attention is given to all content standards and subject areas, including those that are not assessed by state tests.

Requirement 6:   A state must ensure that all students have the opportunity to demonstrate their achievement of state standards; consequently, it must provide well-designed assessments appropriate for a broad range of students, with accommodations and alternate methods of assessment available for students who need them.

Requirement 7:   A state must generally allow test developers a minimum of three years to produce statewide tests that satisfy *Standards for Educational and Psychological Testing* and similar test-quality guidelines.

Requirement 8:   A state must ensure that educators receive professional development focused on how to optimize children's learning based on the results of instructionally supportive assessments.

Requirement 9:   A state should secure evidence that supports the ongoing improvement of its state assessments to ensure those assessments are (a) appropriate for the accountability purposes for which they are used, (b) appropriate for determining whether students have attained state standards, (c) appropriate for enhancing instruction, and (d) not the cause of negative consequences.

Source: The Commission on Instructionally Supportive Assessment (2001, October). *Building tests to support instruction and accountability: A guide for policymakers.* American Association of School Administrators (www.uasa.org), National Association of Elementary School Principals (www.naesp.org), National Association of Secondary School Principals (www.principals.org), National Education Association (www.nea.org), and National Middle School Association (www.nmsa.org).

We encourage you to assess your strengths and weaknesses as a teacher by collecting objective information on your classroom decisions, instructional environment, task selection, and their effects on students. A good way to begin is to consider the concepts and guidelines presented throughout this book, listing those that you believe you use effectively, those that you need to work on or have not tried, and those for which you are uncertain about your performance. The question marks can be reduced by arranging to obtain feedback. You can collect information about some behaviors by keeping records, consulting your students, or arranging to be audio- or videotaped. For many things (e.g., quality of classroom dialogue), it will be necessary for you to arrange to be observed by someone who agrees to visit your classroom and conduct focused observation designed to obtain objective information about the behaviors of interest to you. Your choices of content and what to examine briefly or in depth can be compared in dialogue groups with those of peers.

Observational feedback is also important in providing you with information about the effects of new curriculum plans or teaching techniques that you are trying for the first time. We have offered suggestions for enlisting the help of peer teachers in self-improvement efforts and, in particular, for working with other teachers in cooperative self-help groups. The group approach is likely to be especially valuable, provided that each teacher sets individual priorities and goals, focuses on a few issues at a time, and receives balanced and honest feedback. Self-help programs that follow these guidelines have been popular with teachers and have helped them to increase their awareness of and control over their classroom behavior. We have also argued that at least a part of a school district's in-service program should be organized around the needs of individual teachers and designed to promote professional satisfaction and growth.

SUGGESTED ACTIVITIES AND QUESTIONS

1. Reread the three vignettes presented at the beginning of this chapter. What advice would you have for each teacher?
2. We argue that teachers should take progressively more responsibility for their own in-service education. How realistic is this? What percent of teachers would want to actively participate in in-service activity if it were voluntary?
3. Make a list of all the books and ideas you want to explore. Rank the three things you most want to learn and compare your notes with others'. If you have similar needs and interests, share material and collectively urge the principal to design in-service programs that address these needs.
4. What two concepts or topics do you believe to be the most difficult for you to teach? Arrange to see other teachers present these topics or discuss with other teachers how they teach these concepts.
5. Make a list of your teaching strengths and weaknesses. Make specific plans to improve your two weakest areas.
6. Reread the vignettes in Chapter 1. If these teachers were members of your self-study team, what advice would you offer? Be specific.
7. What is the role of research in defining effective teaching? Can teachers be effective in one school district and not in another? How likely is it that teachers might vary in effectiveness because districts use different criteria for judging effectiveness?

REFERENCES

Adams, M. (1990). *Beginning to read: Thinking and learning about print.* Cambridge, MA: MIT Press.

Adams, R., & Biddle, B. (1970). *Realities of teaching: Explorations with videotape.* New York: Holt.

Airasian, P., & Walsh, M. (1997). Constructivist cautions. *Phi Delta Kappan, 78,* 444–440.

Alhajri, A. (1981). *Effects of seat position on school performance of Kuwaiti students.* Unpublished doctoral dissertation, University of Missouri-Columbia.

Allan, S. (1991). Ability-grouping research reviews: What do they say about grouping and the gifted? *Educational Leadership, 48*(6), 60–65.

Alleman, J., & Brophy, J. (1998). Strategic learning opportunities during after-school hours. *Social Studies and the Young Learner, 62*(3), 10–13.

Allen, B., & Boykin, A. (1992). African-American children and the educational process: Alleviating cultural discontinuity through prescriptive pedagogy. *School Psychology Review, 21*(4), 586–598.

Alliance for Excellent Education. (2004). *Tapping the potential: Retaining and developing high quality new teachers.* Retrieved on May 19, 2006, http://www.all4ed.org/publications/TappingThePotential.pdf

Allington, R. (1991). Children who find learning to read difficult: School responses to diversity. In E. Hiebert (Ed.), *Literacy for a diverse society* (pp. 237–252). New York: Teachers College Press.

Allington, R. (2006). Reading lessons and federal policy making: An overview and introduction to special issue. *Elementary School Journal, 107*(1), 3–13.

Alton-Lee, A., Nuthall, G., & Patrick, J. (1993). Reframing classroom research: A lesson from the private world of children. *Harvard Educational Review, 63,* 50–84.

Alvermann, D., O'Brien, D., & Dillon, D. (1990). What teachers do when they say they're having discussions of content area reading assignments: A qualitative analysis. *Reading Research Quarterly, 25,* 296–322.

American Psychologist. (2004). *Fifty Years On:* Brown v. Board of Education *and American Psychology, 59*(6), 493–556.

Ames, C. (1984). Competitive, cooperative, and individualistic goal structures: A cognitive-motivational analysis. In R. Ames & C. Ames (Eds.), *Research on motivation in education.* Vol. 1: *Student motivation* (pp. 177–208). New York: Academic Press.

Ames, C. (1992). Classrooms: Goals, structures, and student motivation. *Journal of Educational Psychology, 84,* 261–271.

Ames, C., & Ames, R. (1981). Competitive versus individualistic goal structures: The salience of past performance information for causal attributions and affect. *Journal of Educational Psychology, 73,* 411–418.

Ames, C., & Felker, D. (1979). An examination of children's attributions and achievement-related evaluations in competitive, cooperative, and individualistic reward structures. *Journal of Educational Psychology, 71,* 413–420.

Amrein, A., & Berliner, D. (2003). The effects of high-stakes testing on student motivation and learning. *Educational Leadership, 60*(5), 32–38.

Anderman, E., & Wolters, C. (2006). Goals, values, and affect: Influences on student motivation. In P. Alexander & P. Winne (Eds.), *Handbook of Educational Psychology* (pp. 369–389). Mahwah, NJ: Erlbaum.

Anderson, C., & Roth, K. (1989). Teaching for meaningful and self-regulated learning of science. In J. Brophy (Ed.), *Advances in research on teaching.* Vol. 1: *Teaching for meaningful understanding and self-regulated learning* (pp. 265–309). Greenwich, CT: JAI.

Anderson, L. (1989). Implementing instruction programs to promote meaningful, self-regulated learning. In J. Brophy (Ed.), *Advances in research on teaching.* Vol. 1: *Teaching for meaningful understanding and self regulated learning* (pp. 311–343). Greenwich, CT: JAI.

Anderson, L., Brubaker, N., Alleman-Brooks, J., & Duffy, G. (1985). A qualitative study of seatwork in first-grade classrooms. *Elementary School Journal, 86,* 123–140.

Anderson, L., Evertson, C., & Brophy, J. (1979). An experimental study of effective teaching in first-grade reading groups. *Elementary School Journal, 79,* 193–223.

Anderson, L. W., & Krathwohl, D. R. (Eds.). (2001). *A taxonomy for learning and assessing: A revision of Bloom's taxonomy of educational objectives.* New York: Longman.

Anderson, R. (1984). Role of the reader's schema in comprehension, learning, and memory. In R. Anderson, J. Osborn, & R. Tierney (Eds.), *Learning to read in American schools: Basal readers and content texts.* Hillsdale, NJ: Erlbaum.

Anderson, R., Hiebert, E., Scott, J., & Wilkinson (1985). *Becoming a nation of readers: The report of the Commission on Reading.* Washington, DC: National Institute of Education.

Anderson-Levitt, K. M. (2006). Ethnography. In J. Green, G. Camilli, & P. B. Elmore, (Eds.), *Handbook of complementary methods in education research* (pp. 279–295). Mahwah, NJ: Lawrence Erlbaum Associates.

Andriessen, J. (2005). Collaboration in computer conferencing. In A. M. O'Donnell, C. Hmelo-Silver, & G. Krkens (Eds.), *Collaborative Learning, Reasoning, and Technology* (pp. 132–197). Mahwah, NJ: Lawrence Erlbaum Associates.

Applebee, A., Langer, J., Nystrand, M., & Gamoran, A. (2003). Discussion-based approaches to developing understanding: Classroom instruction and student performance in middle and high school English. *American Educational Research Journal, 40,* 685–730.

Arlin, M. (1982). Teacher responses to student time differences in mastery learning. *American Journal of Education 90,* 334–352.

Armor, D. (2006, August). *Can NCLB close achievement gaps?* Teachers College Record. Retrieved August 25, 2006, from http://www.tcrecord.org

Aronson, E., Blaney, N., Stephan, C., Sikes, J., & Snapp, M. (1978). *The jigsaw classroom.* Beverly Hills, CA: Sage.

Ashburn, E. A. (2006). Attributes of meaningful learning using technology (MLT). In E. A. Ashburn & R. E. Floden (Eds.), *Meaningful learning using technology: What educators need to know and do* (pp. 8–25). New York: Teachers College Press.

Ashburn, E. A., Baildon, M., Demico, J., & McNair, S. (2006). Mapping the terrain for meaningful learning using technology in social studies. In E. A. Ashburn & R. E. Floden (Eds.), *Meaningful learning using technology: What educators need to know and do* (pp. 117–140). New York: Teachers College Press.

Ashton, P., & Webb, R. (1986). *Making a difference: Teachers' sense of efficacy and student achievement.* New York: Longman.

Au, K. (2002). Multicultural factors and the effective instruction of students of diverse backgrounds. In A. Farstrup & S. Samuels (Eds.), *What research says about reading instruction* (pp. 392–413). Newark, DE: International Reading Association.

Ausubel, D. (1963). *The psychology of meaningful verbal learning: An introduction to school learning.* New York: Grune & Stratton.

Avery, P. (1999). Authentic assessment and instruction. *Social Education, 65,* 368–373.

Babad, E. (1985). Some correlates of teachers' expectancy bias. *American Educational Research Journal, 22,* 175–183.

Baker, S., Gersten, R., & Keating, T. (2000). When less may be more: A two-year longitudinal evaluation of a volunteer tutoring program requiring minimal training. *Reading Research Quarterly, 35*(4), 494–519.

Ballenger, C. (1999). *Teaching other people's children: Literacy and learning in a bilingual classroom.* New York: Teachers College Press.

Baloche, L. (1998). *The cooperative classroom: Empowering learning.* Upper Saddle River, NJ: Prentice Hall.

Bandura, A. (1997). *Self-efficacy: The exercise of control.* New York: Freeman.

Banks, J. A. (2006). *Cultural diversity and education: Foundations, curriculum, and teaching* (5th ed.). Boston: Allyn and Bacon.

Banks, S. R. (2005). *Classroom assessment: Issues and practices.* San Francisco: Allyn & Bacon.

Bar-Eli, N., & Raviv, A. (1982). Underachievers as tutors. *Journal of Educational Research, 75,* 139–143.

Barkley, R. (1998). *Attention deficit hyperactivity disorder: A handbook for diagnosis and treatment* (2nd ed.). New York: Guilford.

Barton, K. (2001). A picture's worth: Analyzing historical photographs in the elementary grades. *Social Education, 65,* 278–283.

Baumann, J. F., Hoffman, J. V., Duffy-Hester, A. M., & Ro, J. M. (2000). The first R yesterday and today: U.S. elementary reading instruction practices reported by teachers and administrators. *Reading Research Quarterly, 35,* 338–377.

Beck, I., & McKeown, M. (1988). Toward meaningful accounts in history texts for young learners. *Educational Researcher, 17*(6), 31–39.

Beck, T. (1998). Are there any questions? One teacher's view of students and their questions in a fourth-grade classroom. *Teaching and Teacher Education, 14,* 871–886.

Becker, H. J. (2001, April). *How are teachers using computers in instruction?* Paper presented at an annual meeting of the American Educational Research Association, Seattle, WA.

Bender, W. (1997). *Understanding ADHD: A practical guide for teachers and parents.* Upper Saddle River, NJ: Merrill/Prentice Hall.

Beninati, A. (1991). History Teaching Alliance. *OAH Magazine of History, 6*(1), 46.

Bennett, N., & Cass, A. (1988). The effects of group composition on group interactive processes and pupil understanding. *British Educational Research Journal, 15,* 19–32.

Bennett, N., & Dunne, E. (1992). *Managing small groups.* New York: Simon & Schuster.

Bergen, D., & Coscia, J. (2002). *Brain research and childhood education.* Olney, MD: Association for Childhood Education International.

Berliner, D., & Biddle, B. (1995). *The manufactured crisis: Myth, fraud, and the attack on America's public schools.* New York: Addison-Wesley.

Berson, M. J., Cruz, B. C., Duplass, J. A., & Johnson, J. H. (2004). *Social studies on the Internet* (2nd ed.). Upper Saddle River, NJ: Prentice Hall.

Bettencourt, E., Gillett, M., Gall, M., & Hull, R. (1983). Effects of teacher enthusiasm training on student on-task behavior and achievement. *American Educational Research Journal, 20,* 435–450.

Beyer, B. (1997). *Improving student thinking.* Boston: Allyn and Bacon.

Billegas, A., & Lúcas, T. (2002). *Educating culturally responsive teachers: A coherent approach.* Albany: State University of New York Press.

Bitter, G. G., & Legacy, J. M. (2006). *Using technology in the classroom* (brief ed.). Boston: Allyn and Bacon.

Blank, R. K., Porter, A., & Smithson, J. (2001, July). New tools for analyzing teaching, curriculum and standards in mathematics and science. Washington, DC: Council of Chief State School Officers. Retrieved November 27, 2001, from http://publications.ccsso.org/ccsso/publication_detail.cfm?PID=344

Bligh, D. (2000). *What's the use of lectures?* San Francisco: Jossey-Bass.

Bliss, T., & Reynolds, A. (2004). Quality visions and focused imagination. In J. Brophy (Ed.), *Using video in teacher education* (10th Vol. in *The Advances in Research on Teaching Series*). New York: Elsevier Science.

Bloom, B., Englehart, M., Furst, E., Hill, W., & Krathwohl, D. (1956). *Taxonomy of educational objectives: The classification of educational goals. Handbook I: Cognitive domain.* New York: Longmans Green.

Blumenfeld, P. (1992). The task and the teacher: Enhancing student thoughtfulness in science. In J. Brophy (Ed.), *Advances in research on teaching* (vol. 3, pp. 115–160). Greenwich, CT: JAI Press.

Blumenfeld, P., Krajcik, J., Kempler, T., Geier, R., Kam, R., & Gallagher, S. (2006, April). *Opportunity to learn: Teacher instructional practices that account for variation in achievement in project-based science in urban middle schools.* Paper presented at the annual meeting of the American Educational Research Association, San Francisco.

Blumenfeld, P., Marx, R. W., & Harris, C. (2006). Learning environments. In W. Damon, R. Lerner, A. Renninger, & I. E. Sigel (Eds.), *Handbook of child psychology.* (6th ed.) Vol. 4: *Child psychology in practice* (pp. 297–342). Hoboken, NJ: Wiley.

Blumenfeld, P., Marx, R., Patrick, H., Krajcik, J., & Soloway, E. (1997). Teaching for understanding. In B. Biddle, T. Good, & I. Goodson (Eds.), *International handbook of teachers and teaching* (VOL. II, pp. 819–878). Boston: Kluwer.

Blumenfeld, P. C., Soloway, E., Marx, R. W., Krajcik, J. S., Guzdial, M., & Palinscar, A. (1991). Motivating project-based learning: Sustaining the doing, supporting the learning. *Educational Psychologist, 26,* 369–398.

Bolick, C. M., & Cooper, J. M. (2006). Classroom management and technology. In C. M. Evertson & C. S. Weinstein (Eds.), *Handbook of classroom management* (pp. 541–558). Mahwah, NJ: Erlbaum.

Borich, G. (2007). *Effective teaching methods: Research-based practice* (6th ed.). Upper Saddle River, NJ: Pearson.

Bornholt, L., Goodnow, J., & Cooney, G. (1994). Influences of gender stereotypes on adolescents' perceptions of their own achievement. *American Educational Research Journal, 31,* 675–692.

Bossert, S. (1988–1989). Cooperative activities in the classroom. In E. Rothkopf (Ed.), *Review of research in education* (vol. 15, pp. 225–250). Washington, DC: American Educational Research Association.

Bourdieu, P. (1986). The forms of capital. In J. Richardson (Ed.), *Handbook of theory and research for the sociology of education* (pp. 241–258). New York: Greenwood.

Boykin, A. (2000). The talent development model of schooling: Placing students at promise for academic success. *Journal of Education for Students Placed at Risk, 5*(1 and 2), 3–25.

Boykin, A. W. (1994). Harvesting culture and talent: African American children and educational reform. In R. Rossi (Ed.), *Schools and students at risk* (pp. 116–130). New York: Teachers College Press.

Bracey, G. (2000). The TIMSS final year study and report: A critique. *Educational Researcher, 29*(4), 4–10.

Bransford, J., Brown, A., & Cocking, R. (Eds.). (1999). *How people learn: Brain, mind, experience, and school.* Washington, DC: National Academy Press.

Braswell, L., & Bloomquist, M. (1991). *Cognitive-behavioral therapy with ADHD children: Child, family, and school interventions.* New York: Guilford.

Braun, H. I., Wang, A., Jenkins, F., & Weinbaum, E. (2006). The Black-White achievement gap: Do state policies matter? *Education Policy Analysis Archives, 14*(8). Retrieved September 6, 2006, from http://epaa.asu.edu/epaa/v14n8/

Brennan, R., Kim, J., Wenz-Gross, M., & Siterstein, G. (2001). The relative equitability of high-stakes testing versus teacher-assigned grades: Analysis of the Massachusetts Comprehensive Assessment System (MCAS). *Harvard Educational Review, 71*(2), 173–216.

Brenner, M. E. (2006). Interviewing in educational research. In J. Green, G. Camilli, & P. B. Elmore, (Eds.), *Handbook of complementary methods in education research* (pp. 279–295). Mahwah: Erlbaum.

Broderick, A., Mehta-Parekh, H., & Reid, D. K. (2005). Differentiating instruction for disabled students in inclusive classrooms. *Theory Into Practice, 44,* 194–202.

Brookfield, S., & Preskill, S. (1999). *Discussion as a way of teaching: Tools and techniques for democratic classrooms.* San Francisco: Jossey-Bass.

Brophy, J. (1981). Teacher praise: A functional analysis. *Review of Educational Research, 51,* 5–32.

Brophy, J. (1985). Interactions of male and female students with male and female teachers. In L. Wilkinson & C. Marrett (Eds.), *Gender influences in classroom interaction* (pp. 115–142). Orlando, FL: Academic Press.

Brophy, J. (Ed.). (1992a). *Advances in research on teaching.* Vol. 3. *Planning and managing learning tasks and activities.* Greenwich, CT: JAI Press.

Brophy, J. (1992b). The de facto national curriculum in U.S. elementary social studies: Critique of a representative example. *Journal of Curriculum Studies, 24,* 401–447.

Brophy, J. (1996). *Teaching problem students.* New York: Guilford.

Brophy, J. (1999). *Teaching* (Educational Practices Series No. 1). Geneva: International Bureau of Education.

Brophy, J. (Ed.). (2001). *Subject-specific instructional methods and activities.* New York: Elsevier Science.

Brophy, J. (Ed.). (2004). *Using video in teacher education* (10th Vol. in the *Advances in Research on Teaching* series). New York: Elsevier Science.

Brophy, J. (2006). *Grade repetition* (Educational Policy Series No. 6). Paris: International Institute for Educational Planning and International Academy of Education.

Brophy, J., & Alleman, J. (1991). Activities as instructional tools: A framework for analysis and evaluation. *Educational Researcher, 20*(4), 9–23.

Brophy, J., & Alleman, J. (1993). Elementary social studies should be driven by major social education goals. *Social Education, 57,* 27–32.

Brophy, J., & Alleman, J. (2007). *Powerful social studies for elementary students* (2nd ed.). Belmont, CA: Wadsworth.

Brophy, J., & Evertson, C. (1976). *Learning from teaching: A developmental perspective.* Boston: Allyn & Bacon.

Brophy, J., & Evertson, C. (1978). Context variables in teaching. *Educational Psychologist, 12,* 310–316.

Brophy, J., & Evertson, C. (1981). *Student characteristics and teaching.* New York: Longman.

Brophy, J., & Good, T. (1970). Teachers' communication of differential expectations for children's classroom performance: Some behavioral data. *Journal of Educational Psychology, 61,* 365–374.

Brophy, J., & Good, T. (1974). *Teacher-student relationships: Causes and consequences.* New York: Holt, Rinehart & Winston.

Brophy, J., & Good, T. (1986). Teacher behavior and student achievement. In M. Wittrock (Ed.), *Handbook of research on teaching* (3rd. ed., pp. 328–375). New York: Macmillan.

Brophy, J., Rohkemper, M., Rashid, H., & Goldberger, M. (1983). Relationships between teachers' presentations of classroom tasks and students' engagement in those tasks. *Journal of Educational Psychology, 75,* 544–552.

Brouwers, A., & Tomic, W. (2000). A longitudinal study of teacher burnout and perceived self-efficacy in classroom management. *Teaching and Teacher Education, 16,* 239–254.

Brown, A., Schilling, H., & Hockensmith, M. (1999). The negative suggestion effect: Pondering incorrect alternatives may be hazardous to your knowledge. *Journal of Educational Psychology, 91,* 756–764.

Brown, L. (1998). Ethnic stigma as a contextual experience: A possible selves perspective. *Personality and Social Psychology Bulletin, 24,* 163–172.

Browne, M. N., & Keely, S. M. (2000). *Asking the right questions: A guide to critical thinking.* Englewood Cliffs, NJ: Prentice-Hall.

Bruer, J. (1999). In search of . . . brain-based education. *Phi Delta Kappan, 80,* 649–657.

Bruner, J. (1966). *Toward a theory of instruction.* Cambridge, MA: Harvard University Press.

Bruner, J. (1990). *Acts of meaning.* Cambridge, MA: Harvard University Press.

Bruning, R., & Horn, C. (2000). Developing motivation to write. *Educational Psychologist, 35,* 25–37.

Bullough, R., Jr. (1992). Beginning teacher curriculum decision making, personal teaching metaphors, and teacher education. *Teaching and Teacher Education, 8,* 239–252.

Bussey, K., & Bandura, A. (1999). Social cognitive theory of gender development and differentiation. *Psychological Review, 106,* 676–713.

Butler, D. L. (2006). Frames of inquiry in educational psychology: Beyond the quantitative-qualitative divide. *Handbook of Educational Psychology* (2nd ed., pp. 903–927). Mahwah, NJ: Erlbaum.

Butler, R. (1987). Task-involving and ego-involving properties of evaluation: Effects of different feedback conditions on motivational perceptions, interest, and performance. *Journal of Educational Psychology, 79,* 474–482.

Cabello, B., & Terrell, R. (1994). Making students feel like family: How teachers create warm and caring classroom climates. *Journal of Classroom Interaction, 29,* 17–23.

Calderhead, J., & Robson, M. (1991). Images of teaching: Student-teachers' early conceptions of classroom practice. *Teaching and Teacher Education, 7,* 1–8.

Calderón, M., Hertz-Lazarowitz, R., & Slavin, R. E. (1998). Effects of bilingual cooperative integrated reading composition on students making the transition from Spanish to English reading. *Elementary School Journal, 99*(2), 153–165.

Cameron, J., Banko, K., & Pierce, W. (2001). Pervasive negative effects of rewards on intrinsic motivation: The myth continues. *Behavior Analyst, 24,* 1–44.

Cameron, J. (2001). Negative effects of reward on intrinsic motivation—A limited phenomenon. *Review of Educational Research, 71,* 29–42.

Cameron, J., Pierce, D., Banko, K. & Gear, A. (2005). Achievement-based rewards and intrinsic motivation: A test of cognitive mediators. *Journal of Educational Psychology, 97,* 641–655.

Camp, B., & Bash, M. (1981). *Think aloud: Increasing social and cognitive skills—A problem-solving program for children, primary level.* Champaign, IL: Research Press.

Canter, L., & Canter, M. (2002). *Assertive discipline: Positive behavior management for today's classrooms* (3rd ed.). Seal Beach, CA: Canter & Associates.

Carey, S. (1985). *Conceptual change in childhood.* Cambridge, MA: MIT Press.

Carlsen, W. (1991). Questioning in classrooms: A sociolinguistic perspective. *Review of Educational Research, 61,* 157–178.

Carlsen, W. (1991). Subject-matter knowledge and science teaching: A pragmatic perspective. In J. Brophy (Ed.), *Advances in research on teaching* (vol. 2, pp. 115–144). Greenwich. CT: JAI Press.

Carlsen, W. (1997). Never ask a question if you don't know the answer: The tension in teaching between modeling scientific argument and maintaining law and order. *Journal of Classroom Interaction, 27*(2), 14–23.

Carlson, D. (1982). "Updating" individualism and the work ethic: Corporate logic in the classroom. *Curriculum Inquiry, 12*, 125–160.

Carpenter, T., Fennema, E., Franke, M., Empson, S., & Levi, L. (1999). *Children's mathematics: Cognitively guided instruction.* Portsmouth, NH: Heinemann.

Cartledge, G., & Milburn, J. (1995). *Teaching social skills to children and youth: Innovative approaches* (3rd ed.). New York: Pergamon.

Case, R. (1997). Beyond inert facts and concepts: Teaching for understanding. In R. Case & P. Clark (Eds.), *The Canadian anthology of social studies: Issues and strategies for teachers* (pp. 141–152). Vancouver, BC: Simon Fraser University.

Castle, S., Deniz, C. B., & Tortora, M. (2005). Flexible grouping and student learning in a high-needs school. *Education and Urban Society, 37*, 139–150.

Causey, V., & Armento, B. (2001). Strategies for increasing achievement in history. In R. Cole (Ed.), *More strategies for educating everybody's children* (pp. 101–118). Baltimore: Association for Supervision and Curriculum Development.

Chall, J. (2000). *The academic achievement challenge: What really works in the classroom?* New York: Guilford.

Chazan, D., & Ball, D. (1999). Beyond being told not to tell. *For the Learning of Mathematics, 19*(2), 2–10.

Chi, M. T. H., Siler, S. A., & Jeong, H. (2004). Can tutors monitor students' understanding accurately? *Cognition & Instruction, 22*, 363–387.

Chilcoat, G. (1989). Instructional behaviors for clearer presentations in the classroom. *Instructional Science, 18*, 289–314.

Chinn, C., & Brewer, W. (1993). The role of anomalous data in knowledge acquisition: A theoretical framework and implications for science instruction. *Review of Educational Research, 63*, 1–49.

Ciborowski, J. (1992). *Textbooks and the students who can't read them.* New York: Brookline Books.

Clark, C., & Peterson, P. (1986). Teachers' thought processes. In M. C. Wittrock (Ed.), *Handbook of research on teaching* (3rd ed.). New York: Macmillan.

Clark, R. (1982). Antagonism between achievement and enjoyment in ATI studies. *Educational Psychologist, 17*, 92–101.

Cobb, P. (1994). Where is the mind? Constructivist and sociocultural perspectives on mathematical development. *Educational Researcher, 23*(7), 13–20.

Cochran-Smith, M. (1991). Word processing and writing in elementary classrooms: A critical review of related literature. *Review of Educational Research, 61*(1), 107–155.

Cohen, E. (1994). *Designing group work: Strategies for heterogeneous classrooms* (2nd ed.). New York: Teachers College Press.

Cohen, G., Steele, C., & Ross, L. (1999). The mentor's dilemma: Providing critical feedback across the racial divide. *Personality and Social Psychology Bulletin, 25*, 1302–1318.

Cohen, P., Kulik, J., & Kulik, C. (1982). Educational outcomes of tutoring: A meta-analysis of findings. *American Educational Research Journal, 19*, 237–248.

Collins, A., Brown, J., & Newman, S. (1989). Cognitive apprenticeship: Teaching the craft of reading, writing, and mathematics. In L. Resnick (Ed.), *Knowing, learning, and instruction: Essays in honor of Robert Glaser* (pp. 453–494). Hillsdale, NJ: Erlbaum.

Comer, J., Ben-Avie, M., Haynes, N., & Joyner, E. (1999). *Child by child: The Comer process for change in education.* New York: Teachers College Press.

Connor, C., Morrison, F., & Petrella, J. (2004). Effective reading comprehension instruction: Examining child x instruction interactions. *Journal of Educational Psychology, 96,* 682–698.

Connor, C. M., Son, S. H., Hindman, A. H., & Morrison, F. J. (2004). *Teacher qualifications, classroom practices, and family characteristics: Complex effects on first-graders' vocabulary and early reading outcomes.* Ann Arbor: University of Michigan, Department of Psychology.

Cook, A., & Tashlik, P. (2004). *Talk, talk, talk: Discussion based classrooms.* New York: Teachers College Press.

Cook, L., & Mayer, R. (1988). Teaching readers about the structure of scientific text. *Journal of Educational Psychology, 80,* 448–456.

Cooke, B. (1976). Teaching history in mixed-ability groups. In E. Wragg (Ed.), *Teaching in mixed-ability groups.* London: David and Charles Ltd.

Cooper, H. (1989). *Homework.* New York: Longman.

Cooper, H. (1994). *The battle over homework: An administrator's guide to setting sound and effective policies.* Thousand Oaks, CA: Corwin.

Cooper, H., & Good, T. (1983). *Pygmalion grows up: Studies in the expectation communication process.* New York: Longman.

Cooper, H., Robinson, J., & Patall, E. (2006). Does homework improve academic achievement? A synthesis of research, 1987–2003. *Review of Educational Research, 76*(1), 1–62.

Corno, L. (2000). Looking at homework differently. *Elementary School Journal, 100,* 529–548.

Cotton, K. (2000). *The schooling practices that matter most.* Alexandria, VA: Association for Supervision and Curriculum Development.

Covington, M. (1992). *Making the grade: A self-worth perspective on motivation and school reform.* Cambridge: Cambridge University Press.

Craske, M. (1988). Learned helplessness, self-worth motivation and attribution retraining for primary school children. *British Journal of Educational Psychology, 58,* 152–164.

CREDE. (2003). A national study of school effectiveness for language minority students' long-term academic achievement (Research Brief No. 10). Santa Cruz: Center for Research on Education, Diversity and Excellence, University of California.

Croizet, J., Désert, M., Dutrévis, M., & Leyens, J. (2001). Stereotype threat, social class, gender, and academic under-achievement: When our reputation catches up to us and takes over. *Social Psychology of Education, 4,* 295–310.

Cronbach, L. (Ed.). (2002). *Remaking the concept of aptitude: Extending the legacy of Richard E. Snow.* Mahwah, NJ: Erlbaum.

Cuban, L. (1984). *How teachers taught: Constancy and change in American classrooms, 1890–1980.* New York: Longman.

Cuban, L. (1993). *How teachers taught: Constancy and change in American classrooms 1880–1990* (2nd ed.). New York: Teachers College Press.

Cuban, L. (2001). *Oversold and underused: Computers in the classroom.* Cambridge, MA: Harvard University Press.

Cunningham, C. (1997). "Who knows?" The influence of teachers' sociological understanding of science (SUS) on knowledge, authority, and control in the classroom. *Journal of Classroom Interaction, 32,* 24–33.

Curry, L. (1990). A critique of the research on learning styles. *Educational Leadership, 48*(2), 50–56.

Curwin, R., & Mendler, A. (1988a). *Discipline with dignity.* Reston, VA: Association for Supervision and Curriculum Development.

Curwin, R., & Mendler, A. (1988b). Packaged discipline programs: Let the buyer beware. *Educational Leadership, 46*(2), 68–71.

D'Agostino, J. (2000). Instructional and school effects on students' longitudinal reading and mathematics achievements. *School Effectiveness and School Improvement, 11,* 197–235.

Dall'Alba, G., & Sandberg, J. (2006). Unveiling professional development: A critical review. *Review of Educational Research, 76*(3), 383–412.

Danielson, C., & McGreal, T. (2000). *Teacher evaluation: To enhance professional practice.* Princeton, NJ: Educational Testing Service.

Dantonio, M., & Beisenherz, P. (2001). *Learning to question, questioning to learn: Developing effective teacher questioning practices.* Boston: Allyn & Bacon.

Dar, Y. (1985). Teachers' attitudes toward ability grouping: Educational considerations and social organizational influences. *Interchange, 16*(2), 17–38.

Darling-Hammond, L., Banks, J., Zumwalt, K., Gomes, L., Sherin, M., Griesdorn, J., et al. (2005). Educational goals and purposes: Developing a curricular vision for teaching. In L. Darling-Hammond & J. Bransford (Eds.), *Preparing teachers for a changing world: What teachers should learn and be able to do* (pp. 169–200). San Francisco: Jossey-Bass.

Darling-Hammond, L., & Bransford, J. (Eds.). (2005). *Preparing teachers for a changing world: What teachers should learn and be able to do.* San Francisco: Jossey-Bass.

Deci, E., Koestner, R., & Ryan, R. (1999a). A meta-analytic review of experiments examining the effects of extrinsic rewards on intrinsic motivation. *Psychological Bulletin, 125,* 627–668.

Deci, E., Koestner, R., & Ryan, R. (1999b). The undermining effect is a reality after all—Extrinsic rewards, task interest, and self-determination. *Psychological Bulletin, 125,* 692–700.

Deci, E., Koestner, R., & Ryan, R. (2001). Extrinsic rewards and intrinsic motivation in education: Reconsidered once again. *Review of Educational Research, 71,* 1–27.

Deci, E., & Ryan, R. (1985). *Intrinsic motivation and self-determination in human behavior.* New York: Plenum.

Delpit, L. (1988). The silenced dialogue: Power and pedagogy in educating other people's children. *Harvard Educational Review, 56,* 379–385.

Delpit, L. (1995). *Other people's children: Cultural conflict in the classroom.* New York: New Press.

Dembo, M., & Eaton, M. (2000). Self-regulation of academic learning in middle-level schools. *Elementary School Journal, 100*(5), 473–490.

Dewey, J. (1902). *The child and the curriculum.* Chicago: University of Chicago Press.

Dewey, J. (1910). *How we think.* Boston: Heath.

Dewey, J. (1938). *Experience and education.* New York: Collier Books.

Dillon, J. (1979). Alternatives to questioning. *High School Journal, 62,* 217–222.

Dillon, J. (Ed.). (1988). *Questioning and teaching: A manual of practice.* London: Croom Helm.

Dillon, J. (Ed.). (1990). *The practice of questioning.* New York: Routledge.

diSibio, M. (1982). Memory for connected discourse: A constructivist view. *Review of Educational Research, 52,* 149–174.

Dixon, R., Carnine, D., Lee, D., Wallin, J., & Chard, D. (1998). *Review of high quality experimental mathematics research.* Eugene: National Center to Improve the Tools of Educators, University of Oregon.

Douglas, V., Perry, P., Marton, P., & Garson, C. (1976). Assessment of a cognitive training program for hyperactive children. *Journal of Abnormal Child Psychology, 4,* 389–410.

Downey, M., & Levstik, L. (1991). Teaching and learning history. In J. Shaver (Ed.), *Handbook of research on social studies teaching and learning* (pp. 400–410). New York: Macmillan.

Doyle, W. (1984). How order is achieved in classrooms: An interim report. *Journal of Curriculum Studies, 16,* 259–277.

Doyle, W. (2006). Ecological approaches to classroom management. In C. Evertson & C. Weinstein (Eds.), *Handbook of classroom management: Research, practice, and contemporary issues* (pp. 97–126). Mahwah, NJ: Erlbaum.

Doyle, W. (1986). Classroom organization and management. In M. Wittrock (Ed.), *Handbook of research on teaching* (3rd ed., pp. 392–431). New York: Macmillan.

Driver, B., Asoko, H., Leach, J., Mortimer, E., & Scott, P. (1994). Constructing scientific knowledge in the classroom. *Educational Researcher, 23*(7), 5–12.

Duch, B. J., Groh, S. E., & Allen, D. E. (2001). *The power of problem-based learning: A practical "how to" for teaching undergraduate courses in any discipline.* Sterling, VA: Stylus.

Duffy, G., Roehler, L., Meloth, M., & Vavrus, L. (1986). Conceptualizing instructional explanation. *Teaching and Teacher Education, 2,* 197–214.

Duke, N. (2000). For the rich it's richer: Print experiences and environments offered to children in very low and very high socioeconomic status first grade classrooms. *American Educational Research Journal, 37*(2), 441–478.

Dunne, E., & Bennett, N. (1990). *Talking and learning in groups.* London: Macmillan.

DuPaul, G., & Stoner, G. (1994). *ADHD in the schools: Assessment and intervention strategies.* New York: Guilford.

Dweck, C. (1999). *Self-theories: Their role in motivation, personality, and development.* Philadelphia: Taylor & Francis.

Dweck, C. (2000). *Self-theories: Their role in motivation, personality, and development.* Philadelphia: Psychology Press.

Dweck, C., & Elliott, E. (1983). Achievement motivation. In P. Mussen (Ed.), *Handbook of child psychology* (4th ed.), Vol. IV: *Socialization, personality, and social development* (pp. 643–691). New York: Wiley.

Eccles, J. (1987). Gender roles and women's achievement-related decisions. *Psychology of Women Quarterly, 11,* 135–172.

Eder, D. (1981). Ability grouping as a self-fulfilling prophecy: A micro-analysis of teacher-student interaction. *Sociology of Education, 54,* 151–161.

Educational Psychologist. (2001). Special issue on homework (vol. 36, pp. 143–221).

Egan, K. (1990). *Romantic understanding: The development of rationality and imagination, ages 8–15.* New York: Routledge.

Eisemon, T. (1997). *Reducing repetition: Issues and strategies.* Paris: UNESCO (International Institution for Educational Planning).

Eisenberger, R., & Cameron, J. (1996). The detrimental effects of reward: Myth or reality? *American Psychologist, 51,* 1153–1166.

Eisenberger, R., Pierce, W. D., & Cameron, J. (1999). Effects of reward on intrinsic motivation: Negative, neutral, and positive. *Psychological Bulletin, 125,* 677–691.

Elawar, M. C., & Corno, L. (1985). A factorial experiment in teachers' written feedback on student homework: Changing teacher behavior a little rather than a lot. *Journal of Educational Psychology, 77,* 162–173.

Elbaum, B., Schumm, J., & Vaughn, S. (1997). Urban middle-elementary students' perceptions of grouping formats for reading instruction. *Elementary School Journal, 97,* 475–500.

Elementary School Journal. (2006). Special issue on reading research and policy. Guest Editor: Richard Allington.

Elias, M., & Clabby, J. (1989). *Social decision-making skills: A curriculum guide for the elementary grades.* Rockville, MD: Aspen.

Elias, M., & Schwab, Y. (2006). From compliance to responsibility: Social and emotional learning and classroom management. In C. Evertson & C. Weinstein (Eds.), *Handbook of classroom management: Research, practice, and contemporary issues* (pp. 309–342). Mahwah, NJ: Erlbaum.

Ellis, S., & Rogoff, B. (1982). The strategies and efficacy of child versus adult teachers. *Child Development, 53,* 730–735.

Elwell, W., & Tiberio, J. (1994). Teacher praise. *Journal of Instructional Psychology, 21,* 322–328.

Emmer, E. (1971). *Classroom observation scales.* Austin: Research and Development Center for Teacher Education, University of Texas.

Emmer, E., & Aussiker, A. (1990). School and classroom discipline programs: How well do they work? In O. C. Moles (Ed.), *Student discipline strategies: Research and practice* (pp. 129–166). Albany: State University of New York Press.

Emmer, E., Evertson, C., & Anderson, L. (1980). Effective classroom management at the beginning of the school year. *Elementary School Journal, 80,* 219–231.

Emmer, E. T., & Gerwels, M. C. (2002). Cooperative learning in elementary classrooms: Teaching practices and lesson characteristics. *The Elementary School Journal, 103*(1), 75–91.

Emmer, E., & Gerwels, M. C. (2006). Classroom management in middle and high school classrooms. In C. Evertson & C. Weinstein (Eds.), *Handbook of classroom management: Research, practice, and contemporary issues* (pp. 407–437). Mahwah, NJ: Erlbaum.

Emmer, E., & Millett, G. (1970). *Improving teaching through experimentation: A laboratory approach.* Englewood Cliffs, NJ: Prentice-Hall.

Emmer, E., & Stough, L. (2001). Classroom management: A critical part of educational psychology, with implications for teacher education. *Educational Psychologist, 36,* 103–112.

Epstein, C. (1972). *Affective subjects in the classroom: Exploring race, sex and drugs.* Scranton, PA: Intext Educational Publishers.

Epstein, J. (2001). *School, family, and community partnerships: Preparing educators and improving schools.* Boulder, CO: Westview.

Epstein, J., & Harackiewicz, J. (1992). Winning is not enough: The effects of competition and achievement orientation on intrinsic interest. *Personality and Social Psychology Bulletin, 18,* 128–138.

Epstein, J., & Van Voorhis, F. (2001). More than minutes: Teachers' roles in designing homework. *Educational Psychologist, 36,* 181–194.

Erickson, F. (1986). Qualitative methods in research on teaching. In M. Wittrock (Ed.), *Handbook of research on teaching* (3rd ed., pp. 119–161). New York: Macmillan.

Erickson, F. (2006). Definition and analysis of data from videotape: Some research procedures and their rationales. In J. Green, G. Camilli, & P. B. Elmore (Eds.), *Handbook of complementary methods in education research* (pp. 279–295). Mahwah, NJ: Erlbaum.

Erkens, G., Prangsma, M., & Jasper, J. (2005). Planning and coordinating activities in collaborative learning. In A. M. O'Donnell, C. Hmelo-Silver, & G. Erkens (Eds.), *Collaborative learning, reasoning, and technology* (pp. 233–263). Mahwah, NJ: Erlbaum.

Erlwanger, S. (1975). Case studies of children's conceptions of mathematics (Pt. I). *Journal of Children's Mathematical Behavior, 1,* 157–283.

Espinosa, L. (2005). Curriculum and assessment considerations for young children from culturally, linguistically, and economically diverse backgrounds. *Psychology in the Schools, 42,* 837–853.

Esther, T. (2006). *Predicted beliefs about teaching: The missing link between teacher preparation and beginning performance.* Unpublished master's thesis, University of Arizona, Tucson.

Evans, J. (1985). *Teaching in transition: The challenge of mixed ability grouping.* Philadelphia: Open University Press.

Evans, R., & Saxe, D. (Eds.). (1996). *Handbook on teaching social issues.* Washington, DC: National Council for the Social Studies.

Everhart, R. B. (1983). *Reading, writing, and resistance: Adolescence and labor in a junior high school.* Boston: Routledge and Kegan Paul.

Evertson, C. (1982). Differences in instructional activities in higher- and lower-achieving junior high English and math classes. *Elementary School Journal, 82,* 329–350.

Evertson, C. (1987). Managing classrooms: A framework for teachers. In D. Berliner & B. Rosenshine (Eds.), *Talks to teachers* (pp. 54–75). New York: Random House.

Evertson, C., & Emmer, E. (1982). Preventive classroom management. In D. Duke (Ed.), *Helping teachers manage classrooms*. Alexandria, VA: Association for Supervision and Curriculum Development.

Everston, C., & Green, J. (1986). Observation as inquiry and method. In M. C. Wittrock (Ed.), *Handbook of research on teaching* (3rd ed., pp. 162–213). New York: Macmillan.

Evertson, C., Sanford, J., & Emmer, E. (1981). Effects of class heterogeneity in junior high school. *American Educational Research Journal, 18,* 219–232.

Evertson, C., & Weinstein, C. (Eds.). (2006). *Handbook of classroom management: Research, practice, and contemporary issues.* Mahwah, NJ: Erlbaum.

Fager, J., & Richen, R. (1999). *When students don't succeed: Shedding light on grade retention* (ERIC Report No. ED 431 865). Portland, OR: Northwest Regional Educational Laboratory.

Fallona, C., & Richardson, V. (2006). Classroom management as a moral activity. In C. Evertson & C. Weinstein (Eds.), *Handbook of classroom management: Research, practice, and contemporary issues* (pp. 1041–1062). Mahwah, NJ: Erlbaum.

Fantuzzo, J. W., King, J. A., & Heller, L. R. (1992). Effects of reciprocal peer tutoring on mathematics and school adjustment: A component analysis. *Journal of Educational Psychology, 84,* 33–39.

Farrar, M. (1986). Teacher questions: The complexity of the cognitively simple. *Instructional Science, 15,* 89–107.

Fawson, P., & Moore, S. (1999). Reading incentive programs: Beliefs and practices. *Reading Psychology, 20,* 325–340.

Fay, J., & Funk, D. (1995). *Teaching with love and logic.* Golden, CO: Love and Logic Press.

Feiman-Nemser, S. (1983). Learning to teach. In L. Shulman & G. Sykes (Eds.), *Handbook of teaching policy* (pp. 150–170). New York: Longman.

Fenstermacher, G. (1983). How should implications of research on teaching be used? *Elementary School Journal, 83,* 496–499.

Ferretti, R., MacArthur, C., & Dowdy, N. (2000). The effects of an elaborated goal on the persuasive writing of students with learning disabilities and their normally achieving peers. *Journal of Educational Psychology, 92,* 694–702.

Fisher, C., Berliner, D., Filby, N., Marliave, R., Cahen, L., & Dishaw, M. (1980). Teaching behaviors, academic learning time, student achievement: An overview. In C. Denham & A. Lieberman (Eds.), *Time to learn* (pp. 7–32). Washington, DC: National Institute of Education.

Flora, S., & Flora, D. (1999). Effects of extrinsic reinforcement for reading during childhood on reported reading habits of college students. *Psychological Record, 49,* 3–14.

Flowerday, T., & Schraw, G. (2000). Teacher beliefs about instructional choice: A phenomenological study. *Journal of Educational Psychology, 92,* 634–645.

Flowerday, T., & Schraw, G. (2003). The effect of choice on cognitive and affective engagement. *Journal of Educational Research, 96,* 207–215.

Fogarty, J., & Wang, M. (1982). An investigation of the cross-age peer tutoring process: Some implications for instructional design and motivation. *Elementary School Journal, 82,* 451–469.

Forman, S. (1993). *Coping skills interventions for children and adolescents.* San Francisco: Jossey-Bass.

Forsterling, F., & Morgenstern, M. (2002). Accuracy of self-assessment and task performance: Does it pay to know the truth? *Journal of Educational Psychology, 94,* 576–585.

Fosnot, C. (Ed.). (2005). *Constructivism: Theory, perspectives, and practice* (2nd ed.). New York: Teachers College Press.

Foster, B. R., Walker, M. L., & Song, K. H. (2007). *A beginning teaching portfolio handbook: Documenting and reflecting on your professional growth and abilities.* Upper Saddle River: NJ: Pearson Prentice Hall.

Foster, M. (1997). *Black teachers on teaching.* New York: New Press.

Fraivillig, J., Murphy, L., & Fuson, K. (1999). Advancing children's mathematical thinking in everyday mathematics classrooms. *Journal for Research in Mathematics Education, 30,* 148–170.

Frase, L., & Streshly, W. (1994). Lack of accuracy. feedback. and commitment in teacher evaluation. *Journal of Personnel Evaluation in Education, 1,* 47–57.

Freedman, S., & Daiute, C. (2001). Instructional methods and learning activities in teaching writing. In J. Brophy (Ed.), *Subject-specific instructional methods and activities* (pp. 83–110). New York: Elsevier Science.

Freeman, D., & Porter, A. (1989). Do textbooks dictate the content of mathematics instruction in elementary schools? *American Educational Research Journal, 26,* 403–421.

Freiberg, H., Prokosch, N., Treister, E., & Stein, T. (1990). Turning around five at-risk elementary schools. *School Effectiveness and School Improvement, 1,* 5–25.

Freiberg, H. J. (1999). Consistency management and cooperative discipline. In H. J. Freiberg (Ed.), *Beyond behaviorism: Changing the classroom management paradigm* (pp. 75–97). Boston: Allyn and Bacon.

Freiberg, H. J., & Lapointe, J. (2006). Research-based programs for preventing and solving discipline problems. In C. Evertson & C. Weinstein (Eds.), *Handbook of classroom management: Research, practice, and contemporary issues* (pp. 735–786). Mahwah, NJ: Erlbaum.

Friedman, I. (2006). Classroom management and teacher stress and burn-out. In C. Evertson & C. Weinstein (Eds.), *Handbook of classroom management: Research, practice, and contemporary issues* (pp. 925–944). Mahwah, NJ: Erlbaum.

Friedman, I. A. (2000). Burnout in teachers: Shattered dreams of impeccable professional performance. *In Session: Psychotherapy in Practice, 56*(5), 595–606.

Friend, M., & Bursuck, W. (2006). *Including students with special needs* (4th ed.). Boston: Pearson.

Froschl, M., Sprung, B., Mullin-Rindler, N., Stein, N., & Gropper, N. (1998). *Quit it! A teacher's guide on teasing and bullying for use with students in Grades K–3.* Wellesley, MA: Wellesley Center for Research on Women.

Fuchs, L. (2004). The past, present, and future of curriculum-based research. *School of Psychology Review, 33,* 188–192.

Fuchs, L., & Fuchs, D. (2002). Curriculum-based measurement: Describing competence, enhancing outcomes, evaluating treatment effects, and identifying treatment nonresponders. *Peabody Journal of Education, 77*(2), 64–84.

Fuchs, L., Fuchs, D., Bentz, J., Phillips, N., & Hamlett, C. (1994). The nature of student interactions during peer tutoring with and without practice, training, and experience. *American Educational Research Journal, 31,* 75–103.

Fuchs, L., Fuchs, D., Hamlett, C., & Karns, K. (1998). High-achieving students' interactions and performance on complex mathematical task as a function of homogeneous and heterogeneous pairings. *American Educational Research Journal, 35*(2), 227–267.

Fuchs, L. S., Fuchs, D., Kazden, S., & Allen, S. (1999). Effects of peer-assisted learning strategies in reading with and without training in elaborated help giving. *The Elementary School Journal, 99*(3), 201–221.

Fuchs, T., & Woessmann, L. (2004). *Computers and student learning: Bivariate and multivariate evidence on the availability and use of computers at home and at school* (CESifo working paper 1321). Retrieved July 18, 2006, from www.SSRN.com

Fuller, F. (1969). Concerns of teachers: A developmental conceptualization. *American Educational Research Journal, 6,* 207–226.

Gage, N., & Berliner, D. (1998). *Educational psychology* (6th ed.). Boston: Houghton Mifflin.

Gallego, M., Cole, M., & Laboratory of Comparative Human Cognition. (2001). Classroom cultures and cultures in the classroom. In V. Richardson (Ed.), *Handbook of research on teaching* (4th ed., pp. 951–997). Washington, DC: American Educational Research Association.

Galton, M., Hargreaves, L., Comber, C., & Wall, D. (1999). *Inside the primary classroom: 20 years on.* London: Routledge.

Gamoran, A. (1993). Alternative uses of ability grouping in secondary schools: Can we bring high-quality instruction to low-ability classes? *American Journal of Education, 102,* 1–22.

Gamoran, A., & Berends, M. (1987). The effects of stratification in secondary schools: Synthesis of survey and ethnographic research. *Review of Educational Research, 57,* 415–435.

Garcia, E. (2003). *Student cultural diversity: Understanding and meeting the challenge.* Boston: Houghton Mifflin.

Garcia, E. (2004). Educating Mexican American students: Past treatment and recent developments in theory, research, policy, and practice. In J. A. Banks & C. A. M. Banks (Eds.), *Handbook of research on multicultural education* (2nd ed., pp. 491–514). San Francisco: Jossey-Bass.

Gardner, H. (1993). *Multiple intelligences: The theory in practice.* New York: Basic Books.

Gardner, H. (1999). *Intelligence reframed: Multiple intelligences in the 21st century.* New York: Basic Books.

Gay, G. (2000). *Culturally responsive teaching: Theory, research, and practice.* New York: Teachers College Press.

Gay, G. (2006). Connections between classroom management and culturally responsive teaching. In C. Evertson & C. Weinstein (Eds.), *Handbook of classroom management: Research, practice, and contemporary issues* (pp. 343–370). Mahwah, NJ: Erlbaum.

Gentile, J. R., & Lalley, J. (2003). *Standards and mastery learning: Aligning teaching and assessment so all children can learn.* Thousand Oaks, CA: Corwin.

George, P., Lawrence, G., & Bushnell, D. (1998). *Handbook for middle school teaching* (2nd ed.). New York: Longman.

Gettinger, M., & Kohler, K. (2006). Process-outcome approaches to classroom management and effective teaching. In C. Evertson & C. Weinstein (Eds.), *Handbook of classroom management: Research, practice, and contemporary issues* (pp. 73–96). Mahwah, NJ: Erlbaum.

Gettinger, M., & Stoiber, K. (1999). Excellence in teaching: Review of instructional and environmental variables. In C. Reynolds & T. Gutkin (Eds.), *Handbook of school psychology* (3rd ed., pp. 933–958). New York: Wiley.

Gillies, R., & Ashman, A. (1998). Behavior and interactions of children in cooperative groups in lower and middle elementary grades. *Journal of Educational Psychology, 90*(4), 746–747.

Girod, M., & Wong, D. (2002). An aesthetic (Deweyan) perspective on science: Case studies of three fourth-graders. *Elementary School Journal, 102,* 199–224.

Glasgow, N. A. (1997). *New curriculum for new times: A guide to student-centered, problem-based learning.* Thousand Oaks, CA: Corwin Press.

Glasser, W. (1986). *Control theory in the classroom.* New York: Harper & Row.

Glatthorn, A. (1987). Cooperative professional development: Peer-centered options for teacher growth. *Educational Leadership, 44,* 31–35.

Glatthorn, A. A., Boschee, F., & Whitehead, B. M. (2006). *Curriculum leadership: Development and Implementation.* Thousand Oaks: Sage.

Glickman, C. (1990). *Supervision of instruction* (2nd ed.). Boston: Allyn and Bacon.

Gliessman, D., Pugh, R., Brown, L., Archer, A., & Snyder, S. (1989). Applying a research-based model to teacher skill training. *Journal of Educational Research, 83,* 69–81.

Goldberg, A., Russell, M., & Cook, A. (2003). The effect of computers on student writing: A meta-analysis of studies from 1992–2002. *Journal of Technology, Learning, and Assessment, 2*(1), 1–51. Available from www.jtla.org

Goldenberg, C. (1992). The limits of expectations: A case for case knowledge about teacher expectancy effects. *American Educational Research Journal, 29,* 517–544.

Goldin-Meadow, S., Kim, S., & Singer, M. (1999). What the teacher's hands tell the student's mind about math. *Journal of Educational Psychology, 91,* 720–730.

Goldstein, A. (1999). Aggression reduction strategies: Effective and ineffective. *School Psychology Quarterly, 14,* 40–58.

Goldstein, A., & Conoley, J. (Eds.). (1997). *School violence intervention: A practical handbook.* New York: Guilford.

Good, T. (1981). Teacher expectations and student perceptions: A decade of research. *Educational Leadership, 38,* 415–423.

Good, T. (1996). Teacher effectiveness and teacher evaluation. In J. Sikula, T. Buttery, & E. Guyton (Eds.), *Handbook of research on teacher education* (2nd ed., pp. 617–665). New York: Macmillan.

Good, T., & Braden, J. (2000). *The great school debate: Choice, vouchers, and charters.* Mahwah, NJ: Erlbaum.

Good, T., & Brophy, J. (1972). Behavioral expression of teacher attitudes. *Journal of Educational Psychology, 63,* 617–624.

Good, T., & Brophy, J. (1986). School effects. In M. C. Wittrock (Ed.), *Handbook of research on teaching* (3rd ed., 570–602). New York: Macmillan.

Good, T., Grouws, D., & Ebmeier, H. (1983). *Active mathematics teaching.* New York: Longman.

Good, T., & Marshall, S. (1984). Do students learn more in heterogeneous or homogeneous achievement groups? In P. Peterson, L. Cherry-Wilkinson, & M. Hallinan (Eds.), *The social context of instruction: Group organization and group processes.* Orlando, FL: Academic Press.

Good, T., McCaslin, M., & Reys, B. (1992). Investigating work groups to promote problem solving in mathematics. In J. Brophy (Ed.), *Advances in research on teaching* (vol. 3, pp. 115–160). Greenwich, CT: JAI Press.

Good, T., McCaslin, M., Tsang, H., Zhang, J., Wiley, C. R. H., Bozack, A. R., & Hester, W. (2006). How well do first year teachers teach: Does type of preparation make a difference? *Journal of Teacher Education, 57*(4), 1–21, 410–430.

Good, T., & Nichols, S. (2001, Spring). Expectancy effects in the classroom: A special focus on improving the reading performance of minority students in first-grade classrooms. *Educational Psychologist, 36*(2), 113–126.

Good, T., & Power, C. (1976). Designing successful classroom environments for different types of students. *Journal of Curriculum Studies, 8,* 1–16.

Good, T., Reys, B., Grouws, D., & Mulryan, C. (1989–1990). Using work groups in mathematics instruction. *Educational Leadership, 47,* 56–62.

Good, T., & Stipek, D. (1983). Individual differences in the classroom: A psychological perspective. In G. Fenstermacher & J. Goodlad (Eds.), *Individual differences and the common curriculum* (82nd yearbook of the National Society for the Study of Education, Part I, pp. 9–43). Chicago: University of Chicago Press.

Good, T. L., & McCaslin, M. (2005). *Theoretical analysis and implemention: A study of comprehensive school reform programs in Arizona 2000–2005,* Vol. 1: *School contexts and CSR leadership.* U.S. Offices of Educational Research and Improvement. Grant No. R306S000033.

Good, T. L., & Weinstein, R. (1986). Teacher expectations: A framework for exploring classrooms. In K. Zumwalt (Ed.), *Improving teaching* (pp. 63–86). Alexandria, VA: Association for Supervision and Curriculum Development.

Goodlad, S., & Hirst, B. (1989). *Peer tutoring: A guide to learning by teaching.* New York: Nichols.

Goodson, I. (1992). Studying teachers' lives: Problems and possibilities. In I. Goodson (Ed.), *Studying teachers' lives* (pp. 234–249). New York: Teachers College Press.

Goodson, I. (1997). The life and work of teachers. In B. Biddle, T. Good, & I. Goodson (Eds.), *International handbook of teachers and teaching* (vol. 1, pp. 135–152). The Netherlands: Kluwer Academic Publishers.

Goodwin, A. L. (1997). Historical and contemporary perspectives on multicultural teacher education: Past lessons, new directions. In J. King, E. Hallins, & W. Hayman (Eds.), *Preparing teachers for cultural diversity* (pp. 5–22). New York: Teachers College Press.

Goodwin, A. L. (2001, April). *The case of one child: Making the shift from personal knowledge to informed practice.* Paper presented at the annual meeting of the American Educational Research Association, Seattle, WA.

Gordon, S. (1992). Paradigms, transitions, and the new supervision. *Journal of Curriculum and Supervision, 8*(11), 62–76.

Gordon, T. (1974). *T.E.T. Teacher effectiveness training.* New York: McKay.

Gottfredson, G., & Gottfredson, D. (1986). *Victimization in six hundred schools: An analysis of the roots of disorder.* New York: Plenum.

Grabe, M. (1985). Attributions in a mastery instructional system: Is an emphasis on effort harmful? *Contemporary Educational Psychology, 10,* 113–126.

Graesser, A., & Pearson, N. (1994). Question asking during tutoring. *American Educational Research Journal, 31,* 104–137.

Graham, S., & Barker, G. (1990). The down side of help: An attributional-developmental analysis of helping behavior as a low-ability cue. *Journal of Educational Psychology, 82,* 7–14.

Grant, H., & Dweck, C. (2003). Clarifying achievement goals and their impact. *Journal of Personality and Social Psychology, 85,* 541–553.

Graybeal, S. S., & Stodolsky, S. S. (1985). Peer work groups in elementary schools. *American Journal of Education, 93,* 409–428.

Green, J., Camilli, G., & Elmore, P. B. (2006). *Handbook of complementary methods in education research.* Mahwah, NJ: Erlbaum.

Green, M. (1975). *Teacher made tests* (2nd ed.). New York: Harper & Row.

Groisser, P. (1964). *How to use the fine art of questioning.* New York: Teachers' Practical Press.

Grolnick, W., Benjet, C., Kurowski, C., & Apostoleris, N. (1997). Predictors of parent involvement in children's schooling. *Journal of Educational Psychology, 89,* 538–540.

Gronlund, N. (2006). *Assessment of student achievement* (8th ed.). San Francisco: Allyn and Bacon.

Grossman, P., & Thompson, C. (2004). District policy and beginning teachers: A lens on teacher learning. *Educational Evaluation and Policy Analysis, 26,* 281–301.

Guimond, S., & Roussel, L. (2001). Bragging about one's school grades: Gender stereotyping and students' perceptions of their abilities in science, mathematics, and language. *Social Psychology of Education, 4,* 275–293.

Guin, K. (2004). Chronic teacher turnover in urban elementary schools. *Education Policy Analysis Archives, 12,* 42.

Gullickson, A. (1982). *The practice of testing in elementary and secondary schools.* Unpublished paper, University of South Dakota. (ERIC document Reproduction Service No. ED 229 391).

Guskey, T. (1994). Defining the differences between Outcome-Based Education and Mastery Learning. *School Administrator, 51*(8), 34–37.

Gutiérrez, R., & Slavin, R. E. (1992). Achievement effects of the nongraded elementary school: A best evidence synthesis. *Review of Educational Research, 62*(4), 333–376.

Guzzetti, B., Snyder, T., Glass, G., & Gamas, W. (1993). Promoting conceptual change in science: A comparative meta-analysis of instructional interventions from reading education and science education. *Reading Research Quarterly, 28,* 117–155.

Hacker, D., & Tenent, A. (2002). Implementing reciprocal teaching in the classroom: Overcoming obstacles and making modifications. *Journal of Educational Psychology, 94,* 699–718.

Hale, J. (2001). *Learning while black: Creating educational excellence for African-American children.* Baltimore: Johns Hopkins University Press.

Hall, S. (1997). The problem with differentiation. *School Science Review, 78,* 95–98.

Hamman, D., Berthelot, J., Saia, J., & Crowley, E. (2000). Teachers' coaching of learning and its relation to students' strategic learning. *Journal of Educational Psychology, 92,* 342–348.

Hamre, B., & Pianta, R. (2005). Can instructional and emotional support in the first-grade classroom make a difference for children at risk of school failure? *Child Development, 76,* 949–967.

Hamre, B. K., & Pianta, R. C. (2001). Early teacher-child relationships and the trajectory of children's school outcomes through eighth grade. *Child Development, 72,* 625–638.

Hart, A. (1995). Reconceiving school leadership: Emergent views. *Elementary School Journal, 96,* 9–28.

Hawkins, D., Doueck, H., & Lishner, D. (1988). Changing teaching practices in mainstream classrooms to improve bonding and behavior of low achievers. *American Educational Research Journal, 25,* 31–50.

Head, J. (1999). *Understanding the boys: Issues of behaviour and achievement.* London: Falmer.

Henderlong, J., & Lepper, M. (2002). The effects of praise on children's intrinsic motivation: A review and synthesis. *Psychological Bulletin, 128,* 774–795.

Henson, K. (1996). *Methods and strategies for teaching in secondary and middle schools* (3rd ed.). New York: Longman.

Hidi, S., & Baird, W. (1988). Strategies for increasing text-based interest and students' recall of expository texts. *Reading Research Quarterly, 23,* 465–483.

Hidi, S., & Harackiewicz, J. (2000). Motivating the academically unmotivated: A critical issue for the 21st century. *Review of Educational Research, 70,* 151–179.

Hiebert, J., & Wearne, D. (1992). Links between teaching and learning place value with understanding in first grade. *Journal for Research in Mathematics Education, 23,* 98–122.

Hill, H. (2001). Policy is not enough: Language and the interpretation of state standards. *American Educational Research Journal, 38*(2), 289–318.

Hoffman, S. (Ed.). (1991). Educational partnerships: Home and school community. *Elementary School Journal, 91*(3). Special issue.

Hoffmann, L. (2002). Promoting girls' interest and achievement in physics classes for beginners. *Learning and Instruction, 12,* 447–465.

Hogan, K., & Pressley, M. (1997). *Scaffolding student learning: Instructional approaches and issues.* Cambridge, MA: Brookline Books.

Hong, E., & Milgram, R. (2000). *Homework: Motivation and learning preference.* Westport, CT: Bergin & Garvey.

Hong, S., & Ho, H. (2005). Direct and indirect longitudinal effects of parent involvement on student achievement: Second-order latent growth modeling across ethnic groups. *Journal of Educational Psychology, 97,* 32–42.

Hoover, J., & Oliver, R. (1996). *The bullying prevention handbook: A guide for principals, teachers, and counselors.* Bloomington, IN: National Education Service.

Hoover, J., & Patton, J. (1997). *Curriculum adaptations for students with learning and behavior problems: Principles and practices* (2nd ed.). Austin, TX: Pro-Ed.

Hoover-Dempsey, K., Walker, J., Sandler, H., Whetsel, D., Green, C., Wilkins, A., & Closson, K. (2005). Why do parents become involved? Research findings and implications. *Elementary School Journal, 106*(2), 105–130.

Horn, R. (2001). Shooting classroom video. *Phi Delta Kappan, 83*(2), 107–108.

Houghton, P. (2001). Finding allies: Sustaining teachers' health and well-being. *Phi Delta Kappan, 82*(9), 706–711.

Howard, G. (1999). *We can't teach what we don't know: White teachers, multiracial schools*. New York: Teachers College Press.

Howe, N., & Strauss, W. (2000). *Millennials rising: The next great generation*. New York: Vintage Books.

Hoy, A., & Weinstein, C. (2006). Student and teacher perspectives on classroom management. In C. Evertson & C. Weinstein (Eds.), *Handbook of classroom management: Research, practice, and contemporary issues* (pp. 181–219). Mahwah, NJ: Erlbaum.

Hudley, C., & Graham, S. (1993). An attributional intervention to reduce peer-directed aggression among African-American boys. *Child Development, 64,* 124–138.

Hughes, B., Sullivan, H., & Mosley, M. (1985). External evaluation, task difficulty, and continuing motivation. *Journal of Educational Research, 78,* 210–215.

Hughes, J. (1988). *Cognitive behavior therapy with children in schools*. Elmsford, NY: Pergamon.

Hunt, D., & Joyce, B. (1981). Teacher trainee personality and initial teaching style. In B. Joyce, C. Brown, & L. Peck (Eds.), *Flexibility in teaching*. New York: Longman.

Hunt, E. (1999). Multiple views of multiple intelligence. *Contemporary Psychology, 46,* 5–7.

Huntington, S. (2004). *Who are we? The challenges to America's national identity*. New York: Simon & Schuster.

Hyman, I., Kay, B., Tabori, A., Weber, M., Mahon, M., & Cohen, I. (2006). Bullying: Theory, research, and interventions. In C. Evertson & C. Weinstein (Eds.), *Handbook of classroom management: Research, practice, and contemporary issues* (pp. 855–884). Mahwah, NJ: Erlbaum.

Hyman, I., & Wise, J. (Eds.). (1979). *Corporal punishment in American education: Readings in history, practice and alternatives*. Philadelphia: Temple University Press.

Hyman, R., & Whitford, E. (1990). Strategic discussion for content area teaching. In W. Wilen (Ed.), *Teaching and learning through discussion: The theory, research and practice of the discussion method* (pp. 127–146). Springfield, IL: Charles C. Thomas.

Hynd, C., & Guzzetti, B. (1998). When knowledge contradicts intuition: Conceptual change. In C. Hynd (Ed.), *Learning from text across conceptual domains* (pp. 139–163). Mahwah, NJ: Erlbaum.

Imazeki, J. (2005). Teacher salaries and teacher attrition. *Economics of Education Review, 24,* 431–449.

Ingersoll, R. M. (2004). Four myths about America's teacher quality problem. *The Yearbook of the National Society of the Study of Education, 1,* 1–33.

Irvine, J. (2003). *Educating teachers for diversity: Seeing with a cultural eye*. New York: Teachers College Press.

Isenbarger, L., & Zembylas, M. (2006). The emotional labor of caring in teaching. *Teaching and Teacher Education, 22,* 120–134.

Iyengar, S., & Lepper, M. (2000). When choice is demotivating: Can one desire too much of a good thing? *Journal of Personality and Social Psychology, 79,* 995–1006.

Jackson, P. (1968). *Life in Classrooms*. New York: Holt, Rinehart and Winston.

Jackson, P., Boostrom, R., & Hansen, D. (1995). *The moral life of schools*. San Francisco: Jossey-Bass.

Jackson, P. W. (1985). Private lessons in public schools: Remarks on the limits of adaptive instruction. In M. C. Wang & H. J. Walberg (Eds.), *Adapting instruction to individual differences* (pp. 66–81). Berkeley, CA: McCutchan.

Jacobs, G. M., Power, M. A., & Loh, W. I. (2002). *Teacher sourcebook for cooperative learning: Practical techniques, basic principles, and frequently asked questions*. Thousand Oaks, CA: Corwin Press.

Janney, R., & Snell, M. (2004). *Teacher's guides to inclusive practices: Modifying schoolwork* (2nd ed.). Baltimore: Brookes.

Janney, R., & Snell, M. (2006). Modifying schoolwork in inclusive classrooms. *Theory Into Practice, 45,* 215–223.

Jenkins, J., & Jenkins, L. (1987). Making peer tutoring work. *Educational Leadership, 44*(6), 64–68.

Jenkins, L. (1989). *Making small groups work.* Oxford: Penguin Educational.

Jensen, E. (2000). Brain-based learning: A reality check. *Educational Leadership, 57*(7), 76–80.

Jimerson, S. (2001). Meta-analysis of grade retention research: Implications for practice in the 21st century. *School Psychology Review, 30,* 420–437.

Johns, M., Schmader, T., & Martens, A. (2005). Knowing is half the battle: Teaching stereotype threat as a means of improving women's math performance. *Psychological Science, 16,* 175–179.

Johnson, D., & Johnson, R. (1979). Conflict in the classroom: Controversy and learning. *Review of Educational Research, 49,* 51–70.

Johnson, D., & Johnson, F. (1982). *Joining together: Group theory and group skills* (2nd ed.). Englewood Cliffs, NJ: Prentice-Hall.

Johnson, D., & Johnson, R. (1985). Motivational processes in cooperative, competitive, and individualistic learning situations. In C. Ames & R. Ames (Eds.), *Research on motivation in education.* Vol. 2: *The classroom milieu* (pp. 249–286). Orlando, FL: Academic Press.

Johnson, D., & Johnson, R. (1995). *Teaching students to be peacemakers* (3rd ed.). Edina, MN: Interaction.

Johnson, D., & Johnson, R. (1999). *Learning together and alone: Cooperative, competitive, and individualistic learning* (5th ed.). Boston: Allyn and Bacon.

Johnson, D., & Johnson, R. (2006a). Conflict resolution, peer mediation, and peacemaking. In C. Evertson & C. Weinstein (Eds.), *Handbook of classroom management: Research, practice, and contemporary issues* (pp. 803–832). Mahwah, NJ: Erlbaum.

Johnson, D. W., & Johnson, R. (2006b). *Joining together: Group theory and group skills* (9th ed.). Englewood Cliffs, NJ: Prentice-Hall.

Johnson, D., Johnson, R., Holubec, E. J., & Roy, P. (1984). *Circles of learning: Cooperation in the classroom.* Alexandria, VA: Association for Supervision and Curriculum Development.

Jones, B. F., Friedman, L. B., Tinzmann, M., & Cox, B. E. (1985). Guidelines for instruction-enriched mastery learning to improve comprehension. In D. Levine (Ed.), *Improving student achievement through mastery learning programs* (pp. 91–154). San Francisco: Jossey-Bass.

Jones, E. (1990). *Interpersonal perception.* New York: Freeman.

Jones, M., & Shelton, M. (2006). *Developing your portfolio: Enhancing for the early childhood student or professor.* New York: Routledge.

Jones, R. (2000). Textbook troubles. *American School Board Journal, 187*(12), 18–21.

Jones, V. (1996). Classroom management. In J. Sikula, T. Buttery, & E. Guyton (Eds.), *Handbook of research on teacher education* (2nd ed.). New York: Macmillan.

Jones, V., & Jones, L. (2001). *Comprehensive classroom management: Creating communities of support and solving problems* (6th ed.). Boston: Allyn and Bacon.

Joyce, B. (1981). A memorandum for the future. In B. Dillon-Peterson (Ed.), *Staff development/organization development.* Alexandria, VA: Association for Supervision and Curriculum Development.

Joyce, B., & Weil, M. (1996). *Models of teaching* (5th ed.). Boston: Allyn and Bacon.

Joyce, B., & Weil, M. (2000). *Models of teaching* (6th ed.). Boston: Allyn and Bacon.

Joyce, B., Weil, M., & Calhoun, E. (2003). *Models of teaching* (7th ed.). Boston: Allyn and Bacon.

Jussim, L., & Harber, K. (2005). Teacher expectations and self-fulfilling prophecies: Knowns and unknowns, resolved and unresolved controversies. *Personality and Social Psychology Review, 9,* 131–155.

Juvonen, J. (2006). Sense of belonging, social bonds, and school functioning. In P. A. Alexander & P. H. Winne (Eds.), *Handbook of Educational Psychology* (2nd ed.) (pp. 655–674). Mahwah, NJ: Erlbaum.

Kagan, S. (1988). *Cooperative learning: Resources for teachers.* Riverside: University of California.

Kagan, S. (1992). *Cooperative learning* (8th ed.). San Juan Capistrano, CA: Kagan Cooperative Learning.

Kalyuga, S., Chandler, P., Tuovinen, J., & Sweller, J. (2001). When problem solving is superior to studying worked examples. *Journal of Educational Psychology, 93,* 579–588.

Kameenui, E., & Carnine, D. (1998). *Effective teaching strategies that accommodate diverse learners.* Upper Saddle River, NJ: Merrill.

Karabenick, S., & Newman, R. (Eds.). (2006). *Help seeking in academic settings: Goals, groups, and contexts.* Mahwah, NJ: Erlbaum.

Karmos, J., & Karmos, A. (1983). A closer look at classroom boredom. *Action in Teacher Education, 5,* 49–55.

Kauffman, D., Johnson, S. M., Kardos, S. M., Liu, E., & Peske, H. G. (2002). Lost at sea: New teachers' experiences with curriculum and assessment. *Teachers College Record, 104*(2), 273–300.

Kauffman, J., Hallahan, D., Mostert, M., Trent, S., & Nuttycombe, D. (1993). *Managing classroom behavior: A reflective case approach.* Boston: Allyn and Bacon.

Kaufman, J., & Rosenbaum, J. (1992). The education and employment of low-income black youth in white suburbs. *Journal of Education and Policy Analysis, 14,* 229–240.

Kavale, K., & Forness, S. (1990). Substance over style: A rejoinder to Dunn's animadversions. *Exceptional Children, 56,* 357–361.

Keith, T., Diamond-Hallam, C., & Goldenring-Fine, J. (2004). Longitudinal effects of in-school and out-of-school homework on high school grades. *School Psychology Quarterly, 19*(3), 187–211.

Keller, J. (1983). Motivational design of instruction. In C. Reigeluth (Ed.), *Instructional-design theories and models: An overview of their current status* (pp. 383–434). Hillsdale, NJ: Erlbaum.

Kennedy, M. (2005). *Inside teaching: How classroom life undermines reform.* Cambridge, MA: Harvard University Press.

Kiewra, K. (1987). Notetaking and review: The research and its implications. *Instructional Science, 16,* 233–249.

King, A. (1994). Guiding knowledge construction in the classroom: Effects of teaching children how to question and how to explain. *American Educational Research Journal, 31,* 338–368.

King, C., & Kirschenbaum, D. (1992). *Helping young children develop social skills: The social growth program.* Pacific Grove, CA: Brooks-Cole.

King, R., & King, J. (1998). Is group decision making in the classroom constructive or destructive? *Social Education, 62,* 101–104.

Kirschner, P., Sweller, J., & Clark, R. (2006). Why minimal guidance during instruction does not work: An analysis of the failure of constructivist, discovery, problem-based, experiential, and inquiry-based teaching. *Educational Psychologist, 41*(2), 75–86.

Klahr, D., & Nigam, M. (2004). The equivalence of learning paths in early science instruction: Effects of direct instruction and discovery learning. *Psychological Science, 15,* 661–667.

Klein, P. (2003). Rethinking the multiplicity of cognitive resources and curricular representations: Alternatives to "learning styles" and "multiple intelligences." *Journal of Curriculum Studies, 35,* 45–81.

Kleinfeld, J. (1975). Effective teachers of Eskimo and Indian students. *School Review, 83*(2), 301–344.

Kliebard, H. (2004). *The struggle for the American curriculum, 1893–1958* (3rd ed.). New York: Routledge.

Knapp, M. (1995). *Teaching for meaning in high-poverty classrooms.* New York: Teachers College Press.

Knutson, J. (1998). A second chance: Alternative high schools take different approaches. *Educational Horizons, 76,* 199–202.

Kohn, A. (1993). *Punished by rewards.* Boston: Houghton Mifflin.

Kounin, J. (1970). *Discipline and group management in classrooms.* New York: Holt, Rinehart & Winston.

Krajcik, J., Czerniak, C. M., & Berger, C. F. (2003). *Teaching children science: A project-based approach.* New York: McGraw-Hill.

Krechevsky, M., & Seidel, S. (2001). Minds at work: Applying multiple intelligences in the classroom. In J. Collins & D. Cook (Eds.), *Understanding learning: Influences and outcomes* (pp. 44–59). London: Paul Chapman.

Krieg, J. M. (2006). Teacher quality and attrition. *Economics of Education Review, 25,* 13–27.

Kubiszyn, T., & Borich, G. (1984). *Educational testing and measurement.* New York: Scott Foresman.

Kubiszyn, T., & Borich, G. (2007). *Educational testing and measurement: Classroom application and practice* (8th ed.). Hoboken, NJ: Wiley.

Kulik, C., Kulik, J., & Bangert-Drowns, R. (1990). Effectiveness of mastery learning programs: A meta-analysis. *Review of Educational Research, 60,* 265–299.

Kulik, J., & Kulik, C. (1989). Meta-analysis in education. *International Journal of Educational Research, 13,* 221–340.

Kulik, J. A. (2003). *Effects of using instrumental technology in elementary and secondary schools: What controlled evaluation studies say* (SRI Project Number P10446.0001). Arlington, VA: SRI International.

Kutnick, P., & Thomas, M. (1990). Dyadic pairings for the enhancement of cognitive development in the school curriculum: Some preliminary results on science tasks. *British Educational Research Journal, 16,* 399–406.

Ladson-Billings, G. (1994). *The dreamkeepers: Successful teachers of African American children.* San Francisco: Jossey-Bass.

Ladson-Billings, G. (2001). *Crossing over to Canaan: The journey of new teachers in diverse classrooms.* San Francisco: Jossey-Bass.

Lajoie, S. P., & Azevedo, R. (2006). Teaching and learning in technology-rich environments. In P. A. Alexander & P. H. Winne (Eds.), *Handbook of educational psychology* (2nd ed., pp. 803–820). Mahwah, NJ: Erlbaum.

Lambert, N., & McCombs, B. (1998). *How students learn: Reforming schools through learner-centered education.* Washington, DC: American Psychological Association.

Lambros, A. (2002). *Problem-based learning in K–12 classrooms: A teacher's guide to implementation.* Thousand Oaks, CA: Corwin Press.

Landrum, T., & Kauffman, J. (2006). Behavioral approaches to classroom management. In C. Evertson & C. Weinstein (Eds.), *Handbook of classroom management: Research, practice, and contemporary issues* (pp. 41–71). Mahwah, NJ: Erlbaum.

Lapadat, J. (2000). Construction of science knowledge: Scaffolding conceptual change through discourse. *Journal of Classroom Interaction, 35,* 1–14.

Laub, L., & Braswell, L. (1991). Appendix C: Suggestions for classroom teachers of ADHD elementary students. In L. Braswell & M. Bloomquist (Eds.), *Cognitive behavioral therapy with ADHD children: Child, family, and school interventions* (pp. 349–354). New York: Guilford.

Lave, J., & Wenger, E. (1991). *Situated learning: Legitimate peripheral participation.* Cambridge: Cambridge University Press.

Lawrence, C. M., Lawrence, G., & Samek, L. S. (2006). *Organizing classrooms for small-group instruction: Learning for mastery.* Lanham, MD: Rowman & Littlefield Education.

Lee, C. (2001). Is October Brown Chinese? A cultural modeling activity system for under-achieving students. *American Educational Research Journal, 38,* 97–142.

Lee, O. (1999). Science knowledge, worldviews, and information sources in social and cultural contexts: Making sense after a natural disaster. *American Educational Research Journal, 36,* 187–220.

Lee, O. (2005). Science education with English language learners: Synthesis and research agenda. *Review of Educational Research, 75,* 491–530.

Leinhardt, G., Putnam, R., Stein, M., & Baxter, J. (1991). Where subject knowledge matters. In J. Brophy (Ed.), *Advances in research teaching* (Vol. 2, pp. 87–113). Greenwich, CT: JAI Press.

Lepper, M., Henderlong, J., & Gingras, (1999). Understanding the effects of extrinsic rewards on intrinsic motivation—Uses and abuses of meta-analysis. *Psychological Bulletin, 125,* 669–676.

Lever-Duffy, J., McDonald, J. B., & Mizell, A. P. (2005). *Teaching and learning with technology* (2nd ed.). Boston: Allyn and Bacon.

Lewis, C., Perry, R., & Murata, A. (2006). How should research contribute to instructional improvement? The case of lesson study. *Educational Researcher, 35*(3), 3–14.

Lewis, R. (2006). Classroom discipline in Australia. In C. Evertson & C. Weinstein (Eds.), *Handbook of classroom management: Research, practice, and contemporary issues* (pp. 1193–1214). Mahwah, NJ: Erlbaum.

Lieberman, A. (1986). Collaborative research: Working with, not working on. *Educational Leadership, 43,* 28–33.

Linn, M. C. (2006). WISE teachers: Using technology and inquiry for science instruction. In E. A. Ashburn & R. E. Floden (Eds.), *Meaningful learning using technology: What educators need to know and do* (pp. 45–69). New York: Teachers College Press.

Linn, R. L. (2000). Assessments and accountability. *Educational Researcher, 29*(20), 4–15.

Liston, D., Whitcomb, J., & Borko, H. (2006). Too little or too much: Teacher preparation and the first years of teaching. *Journal of Teacher Education, 57*(4), 351–358.

Little, J. (1981). *School success and staff development in urban desegregated schools: A summary of recently completed research.* Paper presented at the annual meeting of the American Educational Research Association, Los Angeles.

Little, J. (1995). Contested ground: The basis of teacher leadership in two restructuring high schools. *Elementary School Journal, 96,* 47–64.

Locke, E., & Latham, G. (2002). Building a practically useful theory of goal setting and task motivation: A 35-year odyssey. *American Psychologist, 57,* 705–717.

Lomawaima, K. (2004). Educating Native Americans. In J. A. Banks & C. A. M. Banks (Eds.), *Handbook of research on multicultural education* (2nd ed., pp. 441–461). San Francisco: Jossey-Bass.

Long, J., & Hoy, A. (2006). Interested instructors: A composite portrait of individual differences and effectiveness. *Teaching and Teacher Education, 22,* 303–314.

Lotan, R. (2006). Managing group work in the heterogeneous classroom. In C. Evertson & C. Weinstein (Eds.), *Handbook of classroom management: Research, practice, and contemporary issues* (pp. 525–540). Mahwah, NJ: Erlbaum.

Lou, Y., Abrami, P. C., & D'Apollonia, S. (2001). Small group and individual learning with technology: A meta-analysis. *Review of Educational Research, 65,* 283–318.

Lou, Y., Abrami, P. C., Spence, J. C., Poulsen, C., Chambers, B., & D'Apollonia, S. (1996). Within-class grouping: A meta-analysis. *Review of Educational Research, 66*(4), 423–458.

Lowther, D., Ross, S., & Morrison, G. (2003). *When each one has one: The influences on teaching strategies and student achievement of using laptops in the classroom.* Paper presented at the annual meeting of the American Educational Research Association, Seattle, WA.

Lubinski, D., & Benbow, C. (1995). An opportunity for empiricism. *Contemporary Psychology, 40,* 935–938.

Luiten, J., Ames, W., & Ackerson, G. (1970). A meta-analysis of the effects of advance organizers on learning and retention. *American Educational Research Journal, 17,* 211–218.

MacIver, D., & Reuman, D. (1993/94). Giving their best: Grading and recognition practices that motivate students to work hard. *American Educator, 17*(4), 24–31.

Maeroff, G. (1991). Assessing alternative assessment. *Phi Delta Kappa, 73,* 273–281.

Malone, T., & Lepper, M. (1987). Making learning fun: A taxonomy of intrinsic motivation for learning. In R. Snow & M. Farr (Eds.), *Aptitude, learning, and instruction: III. Conative and affective process analysis* (pp. 223–253). Hillsdale, NJ: Erlbaum.

Martin, C., Ruble, D., & Szkrybalo, J. (2002). Cognitive theories of early gender development. *Psychological Bulletin, 128,* 903–933.

Martinez, J., & Martinez, N. (1999). Teacher effectiveness and learning for mastery. *Journal of Educational Research, 92,* 279–285.

Marx, R. W., & Harris, C. J. (2006). No child left behind and science education: Opportunities, challenges, and risks. *The Elementary School Journal, 106,* 467–477.

Marzano, R., & Marzano, J. (2003). The key to classroom management. *Educational Leadership, 61*(1), 6–13.

Maslach, C. (2003). Job burnout: New directions in research and intervention. *Current Directions in Psychological Science, 12*(5), 189–192.

Mason, B., Mason, D. A., Mendez, M., Nelson, G., & Orwig, R. (2005). Effects of top-down and bottom-up elementary school standards reform in an underperforming California district. *The Elementary School Journal, 105,* 353–376.

Mason, D., & Good, T. (1993). Effects of two-group and whole-class teaching on regrouped elementary students' mathematics achievement. *American Educational Research Journal, 30,* 328–360.

Mason, D., Reys, B., & Good, T. (1990). *Three models of active teaching and learning in mathematics using work groups* (Technical Report No. 492). Columbia: University of Missouri, Center for Research in Social Behavior.

Mason, D., Schroeter, D., Combs, R., & Washington, K. (1992). Assigning average-achieving eighth-graders to advanced mathematics classes in an urban junior high. *The Elementary School Journal, 92,* 587–599.

Mastropieri, M., & Scruggs, T. (2007). *The inclusive classroom: Strategies for effective instruction* (3rd ed.). Upper Saddle River, NJ: Pearson Education.

Mathes, P. G., Torgensen, J. K., & Allor, J. (2001). The effects of peer-assisted literacy strategies for first-grade readers with and without additional computer-assisted instruction and phonological awareness. *American Educational Research Journal, 38*(2), 371–410.

Mathes, P. G., Torgensen, J. K., Clancy-Menchetti, J., Santi, K., Nicholas, K., Robinson, C., & Grek, M. (2003). A comparison of teacher-directed versus peer-assisted instruction to struggling first-grade readers. *The Elementary School Journal, 103,* 461–479.

Matson, J., & Ollendick, T. (1988). *Enhancing children's social skills: Assessment and training.* Oxford: Pergamon.

Matsumura, L., Patthey-Chavez, G., Valdés, R., & Garnier, H. (2002). Teacher feedback, writing assignment quality, and third-grade students' revision in lower- and higher-achieving urban schools. *The Elementary School Journal, 103,* 3–25.

Mayer, R. (2001). *Multimedia learning.* New York: Cambridge University Press.

Mayer, R. (2004). Should there be a three-strike rule against pure discovery learning? The case for guided methods of instruction. *American Psychologist, 59,* 14–19.

Mayer, R., Heiser, J., & Lonn, S. (2001). Cognitive constraints on multimedia learning: When presenting more material results in less understanding. *Journal of Educational Psychology, 93,* 187–198.

McCaleb, J., & White, J. (1980). Critical dimensions in evaluating teacher clarity. *Journal of Classroom Interaction, 15,* 27–30.

McCarty, T. L. (2002). *A place to be Navajo: Rough Rock and the struggle for self-determination in indigenous schooling.* Mahwah, NJ: Erlbaum.

McCaslin, M. (1990). Motivated literacy. In J. Zutell & S. McCormick (Eds.). *Literacy theory and research: Analyses for multiple paradigms* (39th Yearbook, pp. 35–50). Rochester, NV: National Reading Conference, Inc.

McCaslin, M. (2006). Student motivational dynamics in the era of school reform. *The Elementary School Journal, 106,* 479–409.

McCaslin, M., Bozack, A., Napoleon, L., Thomas, A., Vasquez, V., Wayman, V., & Zhang, J. (2006). Self-regulated learning and classroom management: Theory, research, and considerations for classroom practice. In C. Evertson & C. Weinstein (Eds.), *Handbook of classroom management: Research, practice, and contemporary issues* (pp. 223–252). Mahwah, NJ: Erlbaum.

McCaslin, M., & Good, T. (1996). *Listening in classrooms.* New York: HarperCollins.

McCaslin, M., & Good, T. (1998). Moving beyond the conception of management as sheer compliance: Helping students to develop goal coordination strategies. *Educational Horizons, 76*(4), 169–176.

McCaslin, M., & Good, T. L. (2005). *Theoretical Analysis and Implemention: A Study of Comprehensive School Reform Programs in Arizona 2000–2005,* Vol. 2: *Classroom practices and student motivational dynamics.* U.S. Offices of Educational Research and Improvement. Grant No. R306S000033.

McCaslin, M., Good, T., Nichols, S., Zhang, J., Wiley, C., Bozack, A., Burross, H., & Cuizon-Garcia, R. (2006). Comprehensive school reform: An observational study of teaching in grades 3 through 5. *The Elementary School Journal, 6,* 313–331.

McCaslin, M., & Murdock, T. (1991). The emergent interaction of home and school in the development of students' adaptive learning. In M. Maehr & P. Pintrich (Eds.), *Advances in motivation and achievement* (Vol. 7, pp. 213–260). Greenwich, CT: JAI Press.

McCay, E. (Ed.). (2001). *Moving beyond retention and social promotion.* Bloomington, IN: Phi Delta Kappa International.

McCombs, B., & Pope, J. (1994). *Motivating hard to reach students.* Washington, DC: American Psychological Association.

McCrory, R. S. (2006). Technology and teaching: A new kind of knowledge. In E. A. Ashburn & R. E. Floden (Eds.), *Meaningful learning using technology: What educators need to know and do* (pp. 141–160). New York: Teachers College Press.

McDaniel, T. (1981). The supervisor's lot: Dilemmas by the dozen. *Educational Leadership, 38,* 518–520.

McGill-Franzen, A., & Allington, R. (1990). Comprehension and coherence: Neglected elements of literacy instruction in remedial and resource room services. *Journal of Reading, Writing, and Learning Disability, 6,* 149–180.

McGill-Franzen, A., Zmach, C., Solic, K., & Zeig, J. L. (2006). Curriculum materials for elementary reading: Shackles and scaffolds for beginning teachers. *The Elementary School Journal, 107,* 67–91.

McLeish, J. (1976). Lecture method. In N. Gage (Ed.), *The psychology of teaching methods;* 75th Yearbook of the National Society for the Study of Education Part I, pp. 252–301. Chicago: University of Chicago Press.

McLeskey, J., & Waldron, N. (2006). Comprehensive school reform and inclusive schools. *Theory into Practice, 45,* 269–278.

McMillan, J. H. (2001). *Classroom assessment: Principle and practice for effective instruction* (2nd ed.). Boston: Allyn and Bacon.

McMillan, J. H., Myran, S., & Workman, D. (2002). Elementary teachers' classroom assessment and grading practices. *Journal of Educational Research, 95*(4), 203–213.

McNary, S. J., Glasgow, N. A., & Hicks, C. D. (2005). *What successful teachers do in inclusive class-rooms.* Thousand Oaks, CA: Corwin Press.

McWhorter, J. (2000). *Losing the race.* New York: Free Press.

Mehan, H. (1997). Tracking untracking: The consequences of placing low-track students in high-track classes. In P. Hall (Ed.), *Race, ethnicity, and multiculturalism: Policy and practice* (pp. 115–150). New York: Garland.

Mehrens, W., & Lehmann, I. (1991). *Measurement and evaluation in education and psychology* (4th ed.). Fort Worth, TX: Holt, Rinehart & Winston.

Meichenbaum, D., & Biemiller, A. (1998). *Nurturing independent learners: Helping students take charge of their learning.* Cambridge, MA: Brookline.

Meichenbaum, D., & Goodman, J. (1971). Training impulsive children to talk to themselves. *Journal of Abnormal Psychology, 77,* 115–126.

Memory, D., & Uhlhorn, K. (1991). Multiple textbooks at different readability levels in the science classroom. *School Science and Mathematics, 91,* 64–72.

Mennuti, R., Freeman, A., & Christner, R. (Eds.). (2006). *Cognitive behavioral interventions in educational settings: A handbook for practice.* New York: Routledge.

Mergendoller, J. R., Markham, T., Ravitz, J., & Larmer, J. (2006). Pervasive management of project-based learning: Teachers as guides and facilitators. In C. M. Evertson & C. S. Weinstein (Eds.), *Handbook of classroom management* (pp. 583–615). Mahwah, NJ: Erlbaum.

Metlife Survey of American Teachers. (2004–2005). Retrieved September 22, 2006, from http://www.metlife.com/WPSAssets/16176418591118756128V1FATS_2004.pdf

Mevarech, Z., & Kramarski, B. (1997). IMPROVE: A multidimensional method for teaching mathematics in heterogeneous classrooms. *American Educational Research Journal, 34,* 365–394.

Michelson, E., Mandell, A., & Contributors. (2004). *Portfolio development and the assessment of prior learning: Perspectives, models, and practices.* Sterling, VA: Stylus.

Mickelson, R. (2001, Summer). Subverting Swann: First- and second-generation segregation in the Charlotte-Mecklenburg schools. *American Educational Research Journal, 38*(2), 215–252.

Midgley, C., Feldlaufer, H., & Eccles, J. (1989). Change in teacher efficacy and student self- and task-related beliefs in mathematics during the transition to junior high school. *Journal of Educational Psychology, 81,* 247–258.

Miles, M., & Huberman, M. (1994). *Qualitative data analysis* (2nd ed.). Thousand Oaks, CA: Sage.

Millard, E. (1997). *Differently literate: Boys, girls and the schooling of literacy.* London: Falmer.

Miller, A. (1986). Performance impairment after failure: Mechanism and sex differences. *Journal of Educational Psychology, 78,* 486–491.

Miller, A., & Hom, H. (1997). Conceptions of ability and the interpretation of praise, blame, and material rewards. *Journal of Experimental Education, 65,* 163–177.

Miller, D., & Kelley, M. (1991). Interventions for improving homework performance: A critical review. *School Psychology Quarterly, 6,* 174–185.

Milner, H. R. (2006). Classroom management in urban classrooms. In C. Evertson & C. Weinstein (Eds.), *Handbook of classroom management: Research, practice, and contemporary issues* (pp. 491–522). Mahwah, NJ: Erlbaum.

Miranda, A., & Presentacion, M. (2000). Efficacy of cognitive-behavioral therapy in the treatment of children with ADHD, with and without aggressiveness. *Psychology in the Schools, 37,* 169–182.

Mitchell, R. (1992). *Testing for learning.* New York: Free Press.

Moll, L. (Ed.). (1990). *Vygotsky and education: Instructional implications and applications of socio-historical psychology.* Cambridge: Cambridge University Press.

Moll, L. (1992). Bilingual classroom studies and community analysis. *Educational Research, 21,* 20–24.

Moore, C., Gilbreath, D., & Maiuri, F. (1998). *Educating students with disabilities in general education classrooms: A summary of the research* (Report No. ED 419 329). Washington, DC: Office of Special Education and Rehabilitative Services.

Moreno, R., & Mayer, R. (2000). A coherence effect in multimedia learning: The case for minimizing irrelevant sounds in the design of multimedia instructional messages. *Journal of Educational Psychology, 92,* 117–125.

Moreno, R., & Mayer, R. (2004). Personalized messages that promote science learning in virtual environments. *Journal of Educational Psychology, 96,* 165–173.

Moriarty, B., Douglas, G., Punch, K., & Hattie, J. (1995). The importance of self-efficacy as a mediating variable between learning environments and achievement. *British Journal of Educational Psychology, 65,* 73–84.

Morine-Dershimer, G. (2006). Classroom management and classroom discourse. In C. Evertson & C. Weinstein (Eds.), *Handbook of classroom management: Research, practice, and contemporary issues* (pp. 127–156). Mahwah, NJ: Erlbaum.

Morrow, L., Reutzel, D. R., & Casey, H. (2006). Organization and management of language arts teaching: Classroom environments, grouping practices, and exemplary instruction. In C. Evertson & C. Weinstein (Eds.), *Handbook of classroom management: Research, practice, and contemporary issues* (pp. 559–581). Mahwah, NJ: Erlbaum.

Mueller, C., & Dweck, C. (1998). Praise for intelligence can undermine children's motivation and performance. *Journal of Personality and Social Psychology, 75,* 33–52.

Muller, C., & Schiller, K. (2000, April). Leveling the playing field? Students' educational attainment on states' performance testing. *Sociology of Education, 73,* 196–218.

Mulryan, C. (1989). *A study of intermediate-grade students' involvement and participation in cooperative small groups in mathematics.* Unpublished doctoral dissertation, University of Missouri-Columbia.

Mulryan, C. (1992). Student passivity during cooperative small groups in mathematics. *Journal of Educational Research, 85,* 261–273.

Mulryan, C. (1995). Fifth and sixth graders' involvement and participation in cooperative small groups in mathematics. *The Elementary School Journal, 95,* 297–310.

Murdock, T. B., Anderman, L. H., & Hodge, S. A. (2000). Middle grades predictors of high school motivation and behavior. *Journal of Adolescent Research, 15,* 327–351.

Murdock, T. B., & Miller, A. (2003). Teachers as sources of middle school students' motivational identity: Variable-centered and person-centered analytic approaches. *The Elementary School Journal, 103,* 383–399.

Myhill, D., & Brackley, M. (2004). Making connections: Teachers' use of children's prior knowledge in whole class discourse. *British Journal of Educational Studies, 52,* 263–375.

National Center for Educational Statistics. (2006). *The condition of education 2006* (NCES Report 2006-072). Washington, DC: US Department of Education.

National Center for Education Statistics. (2006). *Indicators of school crime and safety: 2005* (NCES 2006-001). Washington, DC: U.S. Department of Education.

National Commission on Excellence in Education. (1983). *A Nation at Risk: The Imperative for Educational Reform.* Washington, DC: U.S. Department of Education.

National Council for the Social Studies. (1993). A vision of powerful teaching and learning in the social studies: Building social understanding and civic efficacy. *Social Education, 57,* 213–223.

National Council of Teachers of Mathematics. (1989). *Curriculum and evaluation standards for school mathematics.* Reston, VA: NCTM.

National Council of Teachers of Mathematics. (2000). *Principles and standards for school mathematics.* Reston, VA: NCTM.

National Council on Teacher Quality. (2006). *What education schools aren't teaching about reading and what elementary teachers aren't learning.* Retrieved May 20, 2006, from http://www.nichd.nih.gov/ publications/nrp/smallbook.htm

National Institute of Child Health and Human Development (NICHHD)—Early Childhood Research Network. (2005). A day in third grade: A large-scale study of classroom quality and teacher and student behavior. *The Elementary School Journal, 105,* 305–323.

National Research Council. (2000). *Inquiry and the national science education standards: A guide for teaching and learning.* Washington, DC: National Academy Press.

Nattiv, A. (1994). Helping behaviors and math achievement gain of students using cooperative learning. *The Elementary School Journal, 94,* 285–298.

Naveh-Benjamin, M. (1991). A comparison of training programs intended for different types of test-anxious students: Further support for an information-processing model. *Journal of Educational Psychology, 83,* 134–139.

Neito, S. (2004). *Affirming diversity: The sociopolitical context of multicultural education* (4th ed.). Boston: Allyn and Bacon.

Newby, T. (1991). Classroom motivation: Strategies of first-year teachers. *Journal of Educational Psychology, 83,* 195–200.

Newman, D., Griffin, P., & Cole, M. (1989). *The construction zone: Working for cognitive change in school.* Cambridge: Cambridge University Press.

Newmann, F. (1990). Qualities of thoughtful social studies classes: An empirical profile. *Journal of Curriculum Studies, 22,* 253–275.

Newmann, F. (Ed.). (1992). *Student engagement and achievement in American secondary schools.* New York: Teachers College Press.

Newmann, F., & Associates. (1996). *Authentic achievement: Restructuring schools for intellectual quality.* San Francisco: Jossey-Bass.

Newton, D. (2000). *Teaching for understanding: What it is and how to do it.* London: Routledge Falmer.

Nichols, S. (in press). High-stakes testing: Does it increase achievement? *Journal of Applied School Psychology.*

Nichols, S. L., & Berliner, D. C. (2005). *The inevitable corruption of indicators and educators through high-stakes testing* (EPSL-0503-101-EPRU). Tempe, AZ: Education Policy Research Unit Educational Policy Studies Laboratory, Arizona State University. Retrieved May 26, 2005, from http://www.asu.edu/educ/epsl/EPRU/documents/EPSL-0503-101-EPRU.pdf

Nichols, S. L., & Good, T. L. (2004). *America's teenagers-myths and realities: Media images, schooling and the social costs of careless indifference.* Mahwah, NJ: Erlbaum.

Nieto, S. (2002). *Language, culture, and teaching: Critical perspectives for a new century.* Mahwah, NJ: Erlbaum.

Nieto, S. (2004). *Affirming diversity: The sociopolitical context of multicultural education* (4th ed.). Boston: Pearson.

No Child Left Behind Act of 2001, Pub. L. No. 107-110, 115 Stat. 1425 (2002).

Noble, D. D. (1997). A bill of goods: The early marketing of computer-based education and its implications for the present moment. In B. J. Biddle, T. L. Good, & I. F. Goodson (Eds.), *International handbook of teachers and teaching* (vol. 1, pp. 1321–1285). Dordrecht: Kluwer Academic Publishers.

Nosek, B., Banaji, M., & Greenwald, A. (2002). Math = male, me = female, therefore math ≠ me. *Journal of Personality and Social Psychology, 83,* 44–59.

Nuthall, G. (2002). Social constructivist teaching and the shaping of students' knowledge and thinking. In J. Brophy (Ed.), *Social constructivist teaching: Affordances and constraints* (pp. 43–79). New York: Elsevier.

Nyberg, K., McMillin, J., O'Neill-Rood, M., & Florence, J. (1997). Ethnic differences in academic retracking: A four-year longitudinal study. *Journal of Educational Research, 91,* 33–41.

Oakes, J. (1985). *Keeping track: How schools structure inequality.* New Haven: Yale University Press.

Oakes, J. (2005). *Keeping track: How schools structure inequality* (2nd ed.). New Haven, CT: University Press.

Oakes, J., & Lipton, M. (1992). Detracking schools: Early lessons from the field. *Phi Delta Kappan, 73,* 448–454.

Oakes, J., Quartz, K., Gong, J., Guiton, G., & Lipton, M. (1993). Creating middle schools: Technical, normative, and political considerations. *The Elementary School Journal, 93,* 461–480.

Oakes, J., & Wells, A. S. (2002). Detracking for high student achievement. In L. Abbeduto (Ed.), *Taking sides: Clashing views and controversial issues in educational psychology* (2nd ed., pp. 26–30). Guilford, CT: McGraw-Hill Duskin.

O'Connor, M. (1998). Can we trace the "efficacy of social constructivism"? In P. D. Pearson & A. Iran-Nejad (Eds.), *Review of research in education* (vol. 23, pp. 25–71). Washington, DC: American Educational Research Association.

O'Donnell, A. (2006). The role of peers and group learning. In P. A. Alexander & P. H. Winne (Eds.), *Handbook of Educational Psychology* (2nd ed., pp. 781–802). Mahwah, NJ: Erlbaum.

O'Donnell, A., Reeve, J., & Smith, J. (2007). *Educational Psychology: Reflection for action.* Hoboken, NJ: Wiley.

Ogle, D. (1986). K-W-L: A teaching model that develops active reading of expository text. *Reading Teacher, 39,* 564–570.

Oliver, R., & Williams, R. (2006). Performance patterns of high, medium, and low performers during and following a reward versus non-reward contingency phase. *School Psychology Quarterly, 21,* 119–147.

Olweus, D. (1993). *Bullying at school: What we know and what we can do.* Cambridge, MA: Blackwell.

O'Neil, J. (1990). Making sense of style. *Educational Leadership, 48*(2), 4–9.

Opdenakker, M., & Van Damme, J. (2006). Teacher characteristics and teaching styles as effectiveness enhancing factors of classroom practice. *Teaching and Teacher Education, 22,* 1–21.

Osborn, J. (1984). Workbooks that accompany basal reading programs. In G. Duffy, L. Roehler, & J. Mason (Eds.), *Comprehension instruction: Perspectives and suggestions* (pp. 163–186). New York: Longman.

Osgood, R. (2005). *The history of inclusion in the United States.* Washington, DC: Gallaudet University Press.

Osterman, K. F. (2000). Students' need for belonging in the school community. *Review of Educational Research, 70*(3), 323–368.

Owings, W., & Kaplan, L. (2001). *Alternatives to retention and social promotion.* Bloomington, IN: Phi Delta Kappa International.

Page, R. N. (1991). *Lower-track classrooms: A curricular and cultural perspective.* New York: Teachers College Press.

Pajares, F. (1996). Self-efficacy beliefs in academic settings. *Review of Educational Research, 66,* 543–578.

Palardy, J. (1969). What teachers believe-what children achieve. *The Elementary School Journal, 69,* 370–374.

Palincsar, A. (1998). Social constructivist perspectives on teaching and learning. *Annual Review of Psychology, 49,* 345–375.

Palincsar, A., & Brown, A. (1984). Reciprocal teaching of comprehension-fostering and comprehension-monitoring activities. *Cognition and Instruction, 1,* 117–175.

Palincsar, A., & Brown, A. (1989). Classroom dialogues to promote self-regulated comprehension. In J. Brophy (Ed.), *Advances in research on teaching.* Vol. 1: *Teaching for meaningful understanding and self-regulated learning* (pp. 35–71). Greenwich, CT: JAI.

Pang, V., Kiang, P., & Pak, Y. (2004). Asian Pacific American students. In J. A. Banks & C. A. M. Banks (Eds.), *Handbook of research on multicultural education* (2nd ed., pp. 542–563). San Francisco: Jossey-Bass.

Panksepp, J. (1998). Attention deficit hyperactivity disorders, psychostimulants, and intolerance of childhood playfulness: A tragedy in the making? *Current Directions in Psychological Science, 7,* 91–98.

Parham, C. (1994). Ten views of the past: Software that brings history to life. *Technology and Learning, 14*(6), 36–39, 42–45.

Paris, S., & Paris, A. (2001). Classroom applications of research on self-regulated learning. *Educational Psychologist, 36,* 89–101.

Parker, H. (2001). *Problem solver guide for students with ADHD: Ready-to-use interventions for elementary and secondary students with attention deficit hyperactivity disorder.* Plantation, FL: Specialty Press.

Patrick, B., Hisley, J., & Kempler, T. (2000). "What's everybody so excited about?": The effects of teacher enthusiasm on student intrinsic motivation and vitality. *Journal of Experimental Education, 68,* 217–236.

Patrick, H., Turner, J. C., Meyer, D. K., & Midgley, C. (2003). How teachers establish psychological environments during the first days of school: Associations with avoidance in mathematics. *Teachers College Record, 105,* 1521–1558.

Paulus, P., Dzindolet, M., Poletes, G., & Camacho, L. (1993). Perception of performance in group brainstorming: The illusion of group productivity. *Personality and Social Psychology Bulletin, 9,* 78–89.

Pearson, N., & Graesser, G. (1999). Evolution of discourse during cross-age tutoring. In A. O'Donnell, & A. King (Eds.), *Cognitive perspectives on peer learning* (pp. 69–86). Mahwah, NJ: Erlbaum.

Pelligrini, A., & Blatchford, P. (2000). *The child at school: Interactions with peers and teachers.* New York: Oxford University Press.

Pepler, D., & Rubin, K. (Eds.). (1991). *The development and treatment of childhood aggression.* Hillsdale, NJ: Erlbaum.

Perkins, D. (1993). Teaching for understanding. *American Educator, 17*(3), 8, 28–35.

Perkins, S. (1998). On becoming a peer coach: Practices, identities, and beliefs of inexperienced coaches. *Journal of Curriculum and Supervision, 13,* 235–254.

Perry, K., & Weinstein, R. (1998). The social context of early schooling in children's social adjustment. *Educational Psychologist, 33*(4), 177–194.

Perry, N., Turner, J., & Meyer, D. (2006). Classrooms as contexts for motivating learning. In P. Alexander & P. Winne (Eds.), *Handbook of Educational Psychology* (2nd ed., pp. 327–348). Mahwah, NJ: Erlbaum.

Perry, N., & Winne, P. (2001). Individual differences and diversity in 20th century classrooms. In L. Corno (Ed.), *Education across the century: The centennial volume* (100th Yearbook of the National Society for the Study of Education, Part I; pp. 100–139). Chicago, IL: University of Chicago Press.

Peterson, R., Loveless, S., Knapp, T., Loveless, B., Basta, S., & Anderson, S. (1979). The effects of teacher use of I-messages on student disruptive and study behavior. *Psychological Record, 29,* 187–199.

Phillips, D. (Ed.). (2000). *Constructivism in education: Opinions and second opinions on controversial issues* (99th Yearbook of the National Society for the Study of Education, Part I). Chicago: University of Chicago Press.

Pianta, R. (2006). Classroom management and relationships between children and teachers: Implications for research and practice. In C. Evertson & C. Weinstein (Eds.), *Handbook of classroom management: Research, practice, and contemporary issues* (pp. 685–710). Mahwah, NJ: Erlbaum.

Pierce, R., & Adams, C. (2004). Tiered lessons. *Gifted Child Today, 27,* 58–66.

Pintrich, P., & Schunk, D. (2002). *Motivation in education: Theory, research and application* (2nd ed.). Englewood Cliffs, NJ: Prentice-Hall.

Plake, D. (1993). Teacher assessment literacy: Teachers' competencies in the educational assessment of students. *Mid-Western Educational Researcher, 6,* 21–27.

Pomerantz, E., Altermatt, E., & Saxon, J. (2002). Making the grade but feeling distressed: Gender differences in academic performance and internal distress. *Journal of Educational Psychology, 94,* 396–404.

Posner, G. (1985). *Field Experience: A guide to reflective teaching.* New York: Longman.

Posner, G., Strike, K., Hewson, K., & Gertzog, W. (1982). Accommodation of a scientific conception: Toward a theory of conceptual change. *Science Education, 66,* 211–228.

Postlethwaite, K., & Haggarty, H. (1998). Towards effective and transferable learning in secondary school: The development of an approach based on mastery learning. *British Educational Research Journal, 24,* 333–353.

Prawat, R. (1989). Promoting access to knowledge, strategy, and disposition in students. A research synthesis. *Review of Educational Research, 59,* 1–41.

Prensky, M. (2001). *Digital game-based learning.* New York: McGraw-Hill.

Pressley, M., & Beard El-Dinary, P. (Guest editors). (1993). Special issue on strategies instruction. *Elementary School Journal, 94,* 105–284.

Pressley, M., Dolezal, S., Raphael, L., Mohan, L., Roehrig, A., & Bogner, K. (2003). *Motivating primary grade students.* New York: Guilford.

Pressley, M., Johnson, C., Symons, S., McGoldrick, J., & Kurita, J. (1989). Strategies that improve children's memory and comprehension of text. *The Elementary School Journal, 90,* 3–32.

Provasnik, S., & Dorfman, S. (2005). *Mobility in the Teacher Workforce* (NCES 2005-114). U.S. Department of Education, National Center for Education Statistics. Washington, DC: U.S. Government Printing Office.

Pugh, K. (2002). Teaching for transformative experiences in science: An investigation of the effectiveness of two instructional elements. *Teachers College Record, 104,* 1101–1137.

Puntambekar, S., & Hübscher, R. (2005). Tools for scaffolding students in a complex learning environment: What have we gained and what have we missed? *Educational Psychologist, 40,* 2–12.

Purdie, N., Hattie, J., & Carroll, A. (2002). A review of the research on interventions for Attention Deficit Hyperactivity Disorder: What works best? *Review of Educational Research, 72,* 61–99.

Quin, Z., Johnson, D. W., & Johnson, R. T. (1995). Cooperative versus competitive efforts and problem solving. *Review of Educational Research, 65,* 129–143.

Quirk, B., & Cianciolo, P. (1993). *The study of literature in a fifth-grade classroom: One teacher's perspective* (Elementary Subjects Center Report No. 83). East Lansing: Michigan State University, Institute for Research on Teaching, Center for the Learning and Teaching of Elementary Subjects.

Randi, J., & Corno, L. (1997). Teachers as innovators. In B. Biddle, T. Good, & I. Goodson (Eds.), *International handbook of teachers and teaching* (vol. 1, pp. 1163–1121). Dordrecht, The Netherlands: Kluwer.

Rathunde, K., & Csikszentmihalyi, M. (2005). The social context of middle school: Teachers, friends, and activities in Montessori and traditional school environments. *The Elementary School Journal, 106*(1), 59–80.

Raudenbush, S. (1984). Magnitude of teacher expectancy effects on pupil IQ as a function of the credibility of expectancy induction: A synthesis of findings from 18 experiments. *Journal of Educational Psychology, 76,* 85–97.

Reeve, J., & Jang, H. (2006). What teachers say and do to support students' autonomy during a learning activity. *Journal of Educational Psychology, 98,* 209–218.

Reeve, J., Jang, H., Hardre, P., & Omura, M. (2002). Providing a rationale in an autonomy-supportive way as a strategy to motivate others during an uninteresting activity. *Motivation and Emotion, 26,* 183–207.

Reeve, J., Nix, G., & Hamm, D. (2003). Testing models of the experience of self-determination in intrinsic motivation and the conundrum of choice. *Journal of Educational Psychology, 95,* 375–392.

Rekrut, M. D. (1992, April). *Teaching to learn: Cross-age tutoring to enhance strategy acquisition.* Paper presented at the annual meeting of the American Educational Research Association, San Francisco, CA.

Render, G., Padilla, J., & Krank, H. (1989). What research really shows about assertive discipline. *Educational Leadership, 47*(7), 72–75.

Reynolds, A. (1995). The knowledge base for beginning teachers: Education professionals? Expectations versus research findings on learning to teach. *The Elementary School Journal, 95,* 199–221.

Reynolds, D., Creemers, B., Stringfield, S., & Schaffer, G. (2002). Creating world class schools: What have we learned? In D. Reynolds, B. Creemers, S. Stringfield, & G. Schaffer (Eds.), *World class schools: International perspectives on school effectiveness* (pp. 276–293). New York: Routledge Falmer.

Richardson, V. (2003). Constructivist pedagogy. *Teachers College Record, 105,* 1623–1640.

Richmond, V. (2002). Teacher nonverbal immediacy: Uses and outcomes. In J. Chesebro & J. McCroskey (Eds.), *Communication for teachers* (pp. 65–82). Boston: Allyn and Bacon.

Rief, S. (1993). *How to reach and teach ADD/ADHD children: Practical techniques, strategies, and interventions for helping children with attention problems and hyperactivity.* West Nyack, NY: Center for Applied Research in Education.

Rimm-Kaufman, S., & Sawyer, B. (2004). Primary-grade teachers' self-efficacy beliefs, attitudes toward teaching, and discipline and teaching practice priorities in relation to the responsive classroom approach. *Elementary School Journal, 104,* 321–341.

Robin, A., Schneider, M., & Dolnick, M. (1976). The turtle technique: An extended case study of self-control in the classroom. *Psychology in the Schools, 13,* 449–453.

Robinson, T., Smith, S., Miller, M., & Brownell, M. (1999). Cognitive behavior modification of hyperactivity-impulsivity and aggression: A meta-analysis of school-based studies. *Journal of Educational Psychology, 91,* 195–203.

Roby, T. (1988). Models of discussion. In J. Dillon (Ed.), *Questioning and discussion: A multidisciplinary study* (pp. 163–191). Norwood, NJ: Ablex.

Roelofs, E., & Terwel, J. (1999). Constructivism and authentic pedagogy: State of the art and recent development in the Dutch national curriculum in secondary education. *Journal of Curriculum Studies, 31,* 201–227.

Roeser, R., Eccles, J., & Sameroff, A. (2000). School as a context of early adolescents' academic social-emotional development: A summary of research findings. *The Elementary School Journal, 100,* 443–471.

Roeser, R. W. (2002). Bringing a "whole adolescent" perspective to secondary teacher education: A case study of the use of an adolescent case study. *Teaching Education, 13,* 155–178.

Rogers, C., & Freiberg, H. J. (1994). *Freedom to learn* (3rd ed.). New York: Merrill.

Rogoff, B. (1990). *Apprenticeship in thinking: Cognitive development in social context.* New York: Oxford University Press.

Rogoff, B., Turkanis, C., & Bartlett, L. (2001). *Learning together: Children and adults in a school community.* New York: Oxford University Press.

Rogoff, B., & Wertsch, J. (Eds.). (1984). *Children's learning in the "zone of proximal development."* San Francisco: Jossey-Bass.

Rohrkemper, M. (1981). *Classroom perspectives study: An investigation of differential perceptions of classroom events.* Unpublished doctoral dissertation, Michigan State University.

Rohrkemper, M. (1985). The influence of teacher socialization style on students' social cognitions and reported interpersonal classroom behavior. *The Elementary School Journal, 85,* 245–275.

Rohrkemper, M., & Corno, L. (1988). Success and failure on classroom tasks: Adaptive learning and classroom teaching. *The Elementary School Journal, 88,* 299–312.

Rohrkemper, M., & Corno, L. (1998). Success and failure in classroom tasks: Adaptive learning and classroom teaching. *The Elementary School Journal, 100*(5), 409–442.

Rosen, S., Powell, E., Schubot, D., & Rollins, P. (1978). Competence and tutorial role as status variables affecting peer-tutoring outcomes in public school settings. *Journal of Educational Psychology, 70,* 602–612.

Rosenbaum, J. E. (1980). Social implications of educational grouping. In D. C. Berliner (Ed.), *Review of research in education* (Vol. 8). Itasca, IL: Peacock.

Rosenbaum, J. E. (2001). *Beyond college for all: Career paths for the forgotten.* New York: Russell Sage Foundation.

Rosenholtz, S. (1989). *Teachers' workplace: The social organization of schools.* New York: Longman.

Rosenshine, B. (1970). Enthusiastic teaching: A research review. *School Review, 78,* 499–514.

Rosenshine, B., & Meister, C. (1992). The use of scaffolds for teaching higher-level cognitive strategies. *Educational Leadership, 49*(7), 26–33.

Rosenthal, R., & Jacobson, L. (1968). *Pygmalion in the classroom: Teacher expectation and pupils' intellectual development.* New York: Holt, Rinehart, & Winston.

Ross, D. (1996). *Childhood bullying and teasing: What school personnel, other professionals, and parents can do.* Alexandria, VA: American Counseling Association.

Ross, J. (1988). Improving social-environment studies problem solving through cooperative learning. *American Educational Research Journal, 25,* 573–591.

Ross, J. (1998). The antecedents and consequences of teacher efficacy. In J. Brophy (Ed.), *Advances in research on teaching.* Vol. 7: *Expectations in the classroom* (pp. 49–73). Greenwich, CT: JAI Press.

Ross, S., Smith, L., Lohr, L., & McNelis, M. (1994). Math and reading instruction in tracked first-grade classes. *The Elementary School Journal, 95,* 105–120.

Rosswork, S. (1977). Goal-setting: The effects of an academic task with varying magnitudes of incentive. *Journal of Educational Psychology, 69,* 710–715.

Roth, K. (1996). Making learners and concepts central: A conceptual change approach to learner-centered, fifth-grade American history planning and teaching. In J. Brophy (Ed.), *Advances in research on teaching.* Vol. 6: *Teaching and learning history* (pp. 115–182). Greenwich, CT: JAI.

Roth, W. (2001). Gestures: Their role in teaching and learning. *Review of Educational Research, 71,* 365–392.

Rothenberg, J., McDermott, P., & Martin, G. (1998). Changes in pedagogy: A qualitative result of teaching heterogeneous classes. *Teaching and Teacher Education, 14,* 633–642.

Rothstein, R. (2000). Toward a composite index of school performance. *The Elementary School Journal, 100*(5), 409–442.

Rowe, M. (1974a). Science, silence, and sanctions. *Science and Children, 6,* 11–13.

Rowe, M. (1974b). Wait time and rewards as instructional variables, their influence on language, logic, and fate control: Part I—Wait time. *Journal of Research in Science Teaching, 11,* 81–94.

Rowe, M. (1986). Wait time: Slowing down may be a way of speeding up! *Journal of Teacher Education 37,* 43–50.

Russell, M., & Abrams, L. (2004). Instructional uses of computer for writing: The effects of state testing programs. *Teachers College Record, 106*(6), 1332–1357. Retrieved May 23, 2006, from www.tcrecord.org

Ryan, R., & Stiller, J. (1991). The social contexts of internalization: Parent and teacher influences on autonomy, motivation and learning. In P. Pintrich & M. Maehr (Eds.), *Advances in motivation and achievement* (vol. 7, pp. 115–149). Greenwich, CT: JAI Press.

Sadker, M., & Sadker, D. (1994). *Failing at fairness: How America's schools cheat girls.* New York: Scribner.

Salavin-Baden, M. (2003). *Facilitating problem-based learning.* Philadelphia: Open University Press.

Salend, S. (2005). *Creating inclusive classrooms: Effective and reflective practices for all students* (5th ed.). Columbus, OH: Pearson Education.

Salomon, G., & Perkins, D. (1998). Individual and social aspects of learning. In P. D. Pearson & A. Iran-Nejad (Eds.), *Review of research in education* (Vol. 23, pp. 1–24). Washington, DC: American Educational Research Association.

Samples, R. (1992). Using learning modalities to celebrate intelligence. *Educational Leadership, 50,* 62–66.

Sanchez, M., & Brisk, M. (2004). Teachers' assessment practices and understandings in a bilingual program. *NABE Journal of Research and Practice, 2,* 193–208.

Sands, M., & Kerry, T. (Eds.). (1982). *Mixed ability teaching.* London: Croom Helm.

Sansone, C., & Harackiewicz, J. (Eds.). (2000). *Intrinsic and extrinsic motivation: The search for optimal motivation and performance.* San Diego: Academic Press.

Schank, R., & Abelson, R. (1977). *Scripts, plans, goals, and understanding.* Hillsdale, NJ: Erlbaum.

Schauble, L., Glaser, R., Duschl, R., Schultze, S., & John, J. (1995). Students' understanding of the objectives and procedures of experimentation in the science classroom. *Journal of the Learning Sciences, 4,* 131–166.

Schlene, V. (1990). Computers in the social studies classroom: An ERIC/ChESS sample. *History Microcomputer Review, 6*(2), 45–47.

Schmidt, W., & Buchmann, M. (1983). Six teachers' beliefs and attitudes and their curriculum time allocations. *The Elementary School Journal, 93,* 35–98.

Schraw, G., & Lehman, S. (2001). Situational interest: A review of the literature and directions for future research. *Educational Psychology Review, 13,* 23–52.

Schuck, R. (1981). The impact of set induction on student achievement and retention. *Journal of Educational Research, 74,* 227–232.

Schunk, D. (1999). Social-self interaction and achievement behavior. *Educational Psychologist, 34,* 219–227.

Schunk, D., & Zimmerman, B. (2006). Competence and control beliefs: Distinguishing the means and ends. In P. Alexander & P. Winne (Eds.), *Handbook of educational psychology* (2nd ed., pp. 349–367). Mahwah, NJ: Erlbaum.

Seiter, D. (1988). Resources for teaching with computers in history. *History Microcomputer Review, 4*(2), 37–38.

Sfard, A. (1998). On two metaphors for learning and the dangers of choosing just one. *Educational Researcher, 27*(2), 4–13.

Shaffer, D. W., Squire, K. R., Halverson, R., & Gee, J. P. (2005, October). Video games and future learning. *Phi Delta Kappan,* 105–111.

Shanahan, T. (1998). On the effectiveness and limitations of tutoring in reading. *Review of Research in Education, 23,* 217–234.

Sharan, Y., & Sharan, S. (1992). *Expanding cooperative learning through group investigation.* New York: Teachers College Press.

Sharp, P. (1985). Behavior modification in the secondary school: A survey of students' attitudes to rewards and praise. *Behavioral Approaches with Children, 9,* 109–112.

Shepard, L. (1991). Negative policies for dealing with diversity: When does assessment and diagnosis turn into sorting and segregation? In E. Hiebert (Ed.), *Literacy for a diverse society: Perspectives, practices, and policies* (pp. 279–298). New York: Teachers College Press.

Shepard, L., & Smith, M. (1989). *Flunking grades: Research and policies on retention.* London: Falmer.

Sherin, M. (2004). New perspectives on the role of videos in teacher education. In J. Brophy (Ed.), *Using video teacher in education* (10th vol. in *The Advances in Research on Teaching series*). New York: Elsevier Science.

Shih, S., & Alexander, J. (2000). Interacting effects of goal setting and self- or other-referenced feedback on children's development of self-efficacy and cognitive skill within the Taiwanese classroom. *Journal of Educational Psychology, 92,* 536–543.

Sigurdson, S., & Olson, A. (1992). Teaching mathematics with meaning. *Journal of Mathematical Behavior, 11,* 37–57.

Singer, J., Marx, R., Krajcik, J., & Chambers, J. (2000). Conducting extended inquiry projects: Curriculum materials for science education reform. *Educational Psychologist, 35,* 165–178.

Sireci, S., Scarpati, S., & Li, S. (2005). Test accommodations for students with disabilities: An analysis of the interaction hypothesis. *Review of Educational Research, 75,* 457–490.

Skiba, R., & Rausch, K. (2006). Zero tolerance, suspension, and expulsion: Questions of equity and effectiveness. In C. Evertson & C. Weinstein (Eds.), *Handbook of classroom management: Research, practice, and contemporary issues* (pp. 1063–1089). Mahwah, NJ: Erlbaum.

Slavin, R. (1983). *Cooperative learning.* New York: Longman.

Slavin, R. (1986). *Using Student Team Learning* (3rd ed.). Baltimore: Johns Hopkins University, Center for Research on Elementary and Middle Schools.

Slavin, R. (1996). Research on cooperative learning and achievement: What we know, what we need to know. *Contemporary Educational Psychology, 21,* 43–69.

Slavin, R., Madden, N., Dolan, L., & Wasik, B. (1996). *Every child, every school: Success for all.* Thousand Oaks, CA: Corwin.

Slavin, R. E. (1980). *Using Student Team Learning* (Rev. ed.). Baltimore: Johns Hopkins University, Center for Social Organization of Schools.

Slavin, R. E. (1984). Component building: A strategy for research-based instructional improvement. *The Elementary School Journal, 84,* 255–269.

Slavin, R. E. (1990). Ability grouping and student achievement in secondary schools. *Review of Educational Research, 60,* 417–499.

Slavin, R. E. (1995). *Cooperative learning: Theory, research, and practice* (2nd ed.). Boston: Allyn and Bacon.

Slavin, R. E. (2006). *Educational psychology: Theory and practice* (8th ed). Boston: Allyn and Bacon.

Slavin, R. E., Hurley, E. A., & Chamberlain, A. (2003). Cooperative learning and achievement: Research and theory. In N. J. Smelser & P. B. Baltes (Eds.), *International Encyclopedia of the Social and Behavioral Sciences* (pp. 2756–2761). Oxford: Pergamon.

Sleeter, C. (2005). *Un-standardizing the curriculum: Multicultural teaching in the standards-based classroom.* New York: Teachers College Press.

Smerdon, B., Burkam, D., & Lee, V. (1999). Access to constructivist and didactic teaching: Who gets it? Where is it practiced? *Teachers College Record, 101,* 5–34.

Smith, E., & Anderson, C. (1984). *The Planning and Teaching Intermediate Science study: Final report.* East Lansing: Institute for Research on Teaching, Michigan State University.

Smith, J., & Girod, M. (2003). John Dewey and psychologizing the subject-matter: Big ideas, ambitious teaching, and teacher education. *Teaching and Teacher Education, 19,* 295–307.

Smith, K., Johnson, D., & Johnson, R. (1981). Can conflict be constructive? Controversy versus concurrence seeking in learning groups. *Journal of Educational Psychology, 73,* 651–663.

Smith, L., & Land, M. (1981). Low-inference verbal behaviors related to teacher clarity. *Journal of Classroom Interaction, 17,* 37–42.

Smith, N. I. (1980). Meta-analysis of research on teacher expectation. *Evaluation in Education, 4,* 53–55.

Smitherman, G. (1999). *Talkin that talk: Language, culture, and education in African America.* New York: Routledge.

Smylie, M. (1997). Research on teacher leadership: Assessing the state of the art. In B. Biddle, T. Good, & I. Goodson (Eds.), *International handbook of teachers and teaching* (vol. 1, pp. 521–592). Dordrecht, The Netherlands: Kluwer.

Soled, S. (1990). Teaching processes to improve both higher and lower mental process achievement. *Teaching and Teacher Education, 6,* 255–265.

Solomon, D., Battistich, V., Kim, D., & Watson, M. (1997). Teacher practices associated with students' sense of the classroom as a community. *Social Psychology of Education, 1,* 235–267.

Soodak, L., & McCarthy, M. (2006). Classroom management in inclusive settings. In C. Evertson & C. Weinstein (Eds.), *Handbook of classroom management: Research, practice, and contemporary issues* (pp. 461–489). Mahwah, NJ: Erlbaum.

Sparks, D. (2005). *Leading for results: Transforming, teaching, learning, and relationships in schools.* Thousand Oaks: Corwin Press.

Spiegel, D. L. (2005). *Classroom discussion: Strategies for enhancing all students, building higher-level thinking skills, and strengthening reading and writing across the curriculum.* New York: Scholastic Teaching Resources.

Spradley, J. (1979). *The ethnographic interview.* New York: Holt.

Sprinthall, N., & Thies-Sprinthall, L. (1983). The teacher as an adult learner: A cognitive-developmental view. In G. A. Griffin (Ed.), *Staff development* (82nd yearbook of the National Society for the Study of Education). Chicago: University of Chicago Press.

Squires, D. (2005). *Aligning and balancing the standards-based curriculum.* Thousand Oaks, CA: Corwin Press.

Stacey, K. (1992). Mathematical problem solving in groups: Are two heads better than one? *Journal of Mathematical Behavior, 11,* 261–275.

Stahl, S. (1999). Different strokes for different folks? A critique of learning styles. *American Educator, 23*(3), 27–31.

Staub, F., & Stern, E. (2002). The nature of teachers' pedagogical content beliefs matters for students' achievement gains: Quasi-experimental evidence from elementary mathematics. *Journal of Educational Psychology, 94,* 344–355.

Staver, J. (1998). Constructivism: Sound theory for explicating the practice of science and science teaching. *Journal of Research in Science Teaching, 35,* 501–520.

Steele, C. (1992). Race and the schooling of Black Americans. *The Atlantic, 269,* 68–78.

Steele, C. (1997). A threat in the air: How stereotypes shape intellectual identity and performance. *American Psychologist, 52,* 613–629.

Steele, C., & Aronson, J. (1995). Stereotype threat and the intellectual test performance of African Americans. *Journal of Personality and Social Psychology, 69,* 797–811.

Steele, C., Spencer, S., & Aronson, J. (2002). Contending with group image: The psychology of stereotype and social identity threat. In M. Zanna (Ed.), *Advances in experimental social psychology* (vol. 34, pp. 379–440). San Diego: Academic Press.

Steffe, L., & Gale, J. (Eds.). (1995). *Constructivism in education.* Hillsdale, NJ: Erlbaum.

Stein, M. (2001). Teaching and learning mathematics: How instruction can foster the knowing and understanding of number. In J. Brophy (Ed.), *Subject-specific instructional methods and activities* (pp. 111–144). New York: Elsevier Science.

Stellwagen, J. (2001). A challenge to the learning style advocates. *Clearinghouse, 74,* 265–268.

Stephien, W. J., Senn, P. R., & Stephien, W. C. (2001). *The Internet and problem-based learning: Developing solutions through the Web.* Tucson: Zephyr Press.

Stevens, R. (Ed.). (1999). *Teaching in American schools.* Upper Saddle River, NJ: Merrill.

Stipek, D. (1986). Children's motivation to learn. In T. Tomlinson & H. Walberg (Eds.), *Academic work and educational excellence* (pp. 197–221). Berkeley, CA: McCutchan.

Stipek, D. (2002). *Motivation to learn: Integrating theory and practice* (4th ed.). Boston: Allyn and Bacon.

Stipek, D. (2006). No child left behind comes to preschool. *Elementary School Journal, 106*(5), 455–465.

Stringfield, S., & Herman, R. (1996). Assessment of the state of school effectiveness research in the United States of America. *School Effectiveness and School Improvement, 7,* 159–180.

Suárez-Orosco, C., & Suárez-Orosco, M. (2001). *Children of immigration.* Cambridge, MA: Harvard University Press.

Swanson, C. (2006, May 4). Tracking U.S. Trends. *Education Week,* 50–56.

Swift, J., Gooding, C., & Swift, P. (1988). Questions and wait time. In J. Dillon (Ed.), *Questioning and discussion: A multidisciplinary study* (pp. 192–212). Norwood, NJ: Ablex.

Tanner, C., & Combs, F. (1993) Student retention policy: The gap between research and practice. *Journal of Research in Childhood Education, 8,* 69–75.

Taylor, B., Pearson, P., Peterson, D., & Rodriguez, M. (2003). Reading growth in high-poverty classrooms: The influence of teacher practices that encourage cognitive engagement in literacy learning. *Elementary School Journal, 104,* 3–28.

Teddlie, C., & Reynolds, D. (Eds.). (2000). *The international handbook of school effectiveness research.* New York: Falmer.

Teddlie, C., & Stringfield, S. (1993). *Schools make a difference: Lessons learned from a 10-year study of school effects.* New York: Teachers College Press.

Terrill, M., & Mark, D. (2000). Preservice teachers' expectations for schools with children of color and second-language learners. *Journal of Teacher Education, 51,* 149–155.

Tharp, R., & Gallimore, R. (1988). *Rousing minds to life: Teaching, learning, and schooling in social context.* Cambridge: Cambridge University Press.

Theobald, N. D., & Michael, R. S. (2001). *Teacher turnover in the Midwest: Who stays, leaves, and moves? Policy issues.* Washington, DC: North Central Education Laboratory.

Theory Into Practice. (2004). Special issue on homework. *43,* 171–241.

Thomas, J. (1970). *Tutoring strategies and effectiveness: A comparison of elementary age tutors and college tutors.* Unpublished doctoral dissertation. University of Texas.

Thomas, R. M. (2005). *High-stakes testing: Coping with collateral damage.* Mahwah, NJ: Erlbaum.

Thompson, C., & Rudolph, L. (1992). *Counseling children* (3rd ed.). Pacific Grove, CA: Brooks/Cole.

Thompson, T. (1997). Do we need to train teachers how to administer praise? Self-worth theory says we do. *Learning and Instruction, 7,* 49–63.

Thorndike, R., & Hagen, E. (2004). *Measurement and evaluation in psychology and education* (7th ed.). New York: Prentice Hall.

Tobin, K. (1983). The influence of wait-time on classroom learning. *European Journal of Science Education, 5*(1), 35–48.

Tobin, T. (1997). The teaching and learning of elementary science. In G. Phye (Ed.), *Handbook of academic learning: Construction of knowledge* (pp. 369–403). San Diego: Academic Press.

Tollefson, N., Tracy, D., Johnsen, E., Farmer, W., & Buenning, M. (1984). Goal setting and personal responsibility for LD adolescents. *Psychology in the Schools, 21,* 224–233.

Tomchin, E., & Impara, J. (1992). Unraveling teachers' beliefs about grade retention. *American Educational Research Journal, 29,* 199–223.

Tomlinson, C. (2000). *Differentiation of instruction in the elementary grades* (ERIC Digest). Champaign, IL: ERIC Clearinghouse on Elementary and Early Childhood Education (Publication #ED443572).

Tomlinson, C. (2001). *How to differentiate instruction in mixed-ability classrooms* (2nd ed.). Alexandria, VA: Association for Supervision and Curriculum Development.

Tomlinson, C., & Strickland, C. (2005). *Differentiation in practice: A resource guide for differentiating curriculum, grades 9–12.* Alexandria, VA: Association for Supervision and Curriculum Development.

Topping, K., & Ehly, S. (1998). *Peer-assisted learning.* Mahwah, NJ: Erlbaum.

Torff, B., & Sessions, D. (2005). Principals' perceptions of the causes of teacher ineffectiveness. *Journal of Educational Psychology, 97,* 530–537.

Townsend, M. (1995). Effects of accuracy and plausibility in predicting results of research on teaching. *British Journal of Educational Psychology, 65,* 359–365.

Trautwein, U., & Köller, O. (2003). The relationship between homework and achievement—Still much of a mystery. *Educational Psychology Review, 15,* 118–145.

Trent, S., Artiles, A., & Englert, C. (1998). From deficit thinking to social constructivism: A review of theory, research, and practice in special education. In P. D. Pearson & A. Iran-Nejad (Eds.), *Review of research in education* (vol. 3, pp. 277–307). Washington, DC: American Educational Research Association.

Trice, A. D. (2000). *A handbook of classroom assessment.* New York: Longman.

Tsang, H. Y. (2003). *Using standardized performance observations and interviews to assess the impact of teacher education.* Unpublished doctorial dissertation, University of Arizona.

Turner, J., Midgley, C., Meyer, D., Gheen, M., Anderman, E., Kang, Y., & Patrick, H. (2002). The classroom environment and students' reports of avoidance strategies in mathematics: A multimethod study. *Journal of Educational Psychology, 94,* 88–106.

Turner, J., & Schallert, D. (2001). Expectancy-value relationships of shame reactions and shame resiliency. *Journal of Educational Psychology, 93,* 320–329.

Valencia, S. W., Place, N. A., Martin, S. D., & Grossman, P. L. (2006). The confluence of two policy mandates: Core reading programs and third-grade retention in Florida. *The Elementary School Journal, 107,* 93–120.

Van Hecke, M., & Tracy, R. (1983). Sex differences in children's responses to achievement and approval. *Child Study Journal, 13,* 165–173.

Van Keer, H. (2004). Fostering reading comprehension in fifth grade by explicit instruction in reading strategies and peer tutoring. *British Journal of Educational Psychology, 74,* 37–70.

Vansteenkiste, M., Lens, W., & Deci, E. (2006). Intrinsic versus extrinsic goal contents in self-determination theory: Another look at the quality of academic motivation. *Educational Psychologist, 41,* 19–31.

Veenman, S. (1984). Perceived problems of beginning teachers. *Review of Educational Research, 54,* 143–178.

Volet, S., & Jarvela, S. (Eds.). (2001). *Motivation in learning contexts: Theoretical advances and methodological implications.* Oxford, UK: Pergamon.

Vosniadou, S., & Brewer, W. (1987). Theories of knowledge restructuring in development. *Review of Educational Research, 57,* 51–67.

Vygotsky, L. (1962). *Thought and language.* Cambridge, MA: MIT Press.

Vygotsky, L. (1978). *Mind in society: The development of higher psychological processes* (M. Cole, V. John-Steiner, S. Scribner, & E. Souberman, Eds.). Cambridge: Harvard University Press.

Wade, S., Buxton, W., & Kelly, M. (1999). Using think-alouds to examine reader-text interest. *Reading Research Quarterly, 34,* 195–216.

Walker, J. M. T., & Hoover-Dempsey, K. V. (2006). Why research on parental involvement is important to classroom management. In C. M. Evertson & C. S. Weinstein (Eds.), *Handbook of Classroom Management: Research, Practice, and Contemporary Issues* (pp. 665–684). Mahwah, NJ: Erlbaum.

Walker, H. (1987). *The ACCESS program (Adolescent curriculum for communication and effective school skills).* Austin, TX: Pro-Ed.

Wallace, R. (2004). A framework for understanding teaching with the Internet. *American Educational Research Journal, 41,* 447–488.

Wanlass, Y. (2000). Broadening the concept of learning and school competence. *The Elementary School Journal, 100,* 513–528.

Ware, B. (1978). What rewards do students want? *Phi Delta Kappan, 59,* 355–356.

Watson, M., & Battistich, V. (2006). Building and sustaining caring communities. In C. Evertson & C. Weinstein (Eds.), *Handbook of classroom management: Research, practice, and contemporary issues* (pp. 253–279). Mahwah, NJ: Erlbaum.

Waxman, H., Huang, S., Anderson, L., & Weinstein, T. (1997). Classroom process differences in inner-city elementary schools. *Journal of Educational Research, 91,* 49–59.

Waxman, H., & Walberg, H. (Eds.). (1991). *Effective teaching: Current research.* Berkeley, CA: McCutchan.

Webb, N., & Palincsar, A. (1996). Group processes in the classroom. In D. Berliner & R. Calfee (Eds.), *Handbook of educational psychology* (pp. 841–876). New York: Macmillan.

Webb, N. M. (1982). Student interaction and learning in small groups. *Review of Educational Research, 52,* 421–445.

Weiner, B. (1992). *Human motivation: Metaphors, theories and research.* Newbury Park, CA: Sage.

Weiner, B. (2001). Intrapersonal and interpersonal theories of motivation from an attribution perspective. In F. Salili, C. Chiu, & Y. Hong (Eds.), *Student motivation: The culture and context of learning* (pp. 17–30). New York: Kluwer Academic/Plenum.

Weiner, L. (2006). *Urban teaching: The essentials.* New York: Teachers College Press.

Weinert, F., & Helmke, A. (1995). Learning from wise Mother Nature or Big Brother Instructor: The wrong choice as seen from an educational perspective. *Educational Psychologist, 30,* 135–142.

Weinstein, C., & Mayer, R. (1986). The teaching of learning strategies. In M. Wittrock (Ed.), *Handbook of research on teaching* (3rd ed., pp. 315–327). New York: Macmillan.

Weinstein, C., & Mignano, A., Jr. (1993). *Elementary classroom management: Lessons from research and practice.* New York: McGraw-Hill.

Weinstein, C., Tomlinson-Clark, S., & Curran, M. (2004). Toward a conception of culturally responsive classroom management. *Journal of Teacher Education, 55,* 25–38.

Weinstein, C. S. (1988). Preservice teachers' expectations about the first year of teaching. *Teaching and Teacher Education, 4,* 31–41.

Weinstein, N. D. (1980). Unrealistic optimism about future life events. *Journal of Personality and Social Psychology, 39,* 806–820.

Weinstein, R. (1976). Reading group membership in first grade: Teacher behaviors and pupil experience over time. *Journal of Educational Psychology, 68,* 103–116.

Weinstein, R., Gregory, A., & Strambler, M. J. (2004). Intractable self-fulfilling prophecies: Fifty years after *Brown v. Board of Education. American Psychologist, 59*(6), 511–520.

Weinstein, R., & Middlestadt, S. (1979). Student perceptions of teacher interactions with male high and low achievers. *Journal of Educational Psychology, 71,* 421–431.

Weinstein, R., Soule, C., Collins, F., Cone, J., & Mehorn, S. K. (1991). Expectations and high school change: Teacher-researcher collaboration to prevent school failure. *American Journal of Community Psychology, 9,* 333–364.

Weinstein, R. S., & McKown, C. (1998). Expectancy effects in "context": Listening to the voices of students and teachers. In J. Brophy (Ed.), *Advances in research on teaching: Expectations in the classroom* (pp. 215–242). Greenwich. CT: JAI Press.

Weiss, G., & Hechtman, L. (1986). *Hyperactive children grow up: Empirical findings and theoretical considerations.* New York: Guilford.

Wells, G. (1998). Some questions about direct instruction: Why? To whom? How? And when? *Language Arts, 76,* 27–35.

Wells, G. (1999). *Dialogic inquiry: Towards a sociocultural practice and theory of education.* New York: Cambridge University Press.

Wells, G. (2001). The case for dialogic inquiry. In G. Wells (Ed.), *Action, talk, and text: Learning and teaching through inquiry* (pp. 171–194). New York: Teachers College Press.

Whitley, B., & Frieze, I. (1985). Children's causal attributions for success and failure in achievement settings: A meta-analysis. *Journal of Educational Psychology, 77,* 608–616.

Wigfield, A., & Eccles, J. (1989). Test anxiety in elementary and secondary school students. *Educational Psychologist, 24,* 159–183.

Wigfield, A., & Eccles, J. (2000). Expectancy-value theory of achievement motivation. *Contemporary Educational Psychology, 25,* 68–81.

Wigfield, A., & Eccles, J. (2002). The development of competence beliefs, expectancies for success, and achievement values from childhood through adolescence. In A. Wigfield & J. Eccles (Eds.), *Development of achievement motivation* (pp. 91–121). San Diego: Academic Press.

Wiggins, G. (1993). *Assessing student performance: Exploring the purpose and limits of testing.* San Francisco: Jossey-Bass.

Wilen, W. (1990). Forms and phases of discussion. In W. Wilen (Ed.), *Teaching and learning through discussion: The theory, research and practice of the discussion method* (pp. 3–24). Springfield, IL: Charles C. Thomas.

Wilen, W. (1991). *What research has to say to the teacher: Questioning techniques for teachers* (3rd ed.). Washington, DC: National Education Association.

Wilen, W. (2004). Encouraging reticent students' participation in classroom discussions. *Social Education, 68,* 51–56.

Wills, J. (in press). Putting the squeeze on social studies: Managing teaching dilemmas in subject areas excluded from state testing. *Teachers College Record.*

Windschitl, M. (2002). Framing constructivism in practice as the negotiation of dilemmas: An analysis of the conceptual, pedagogical, cultural, and political challenges facing teachers. *Review of Educational Research, 72,* 131–175.

Wiske, M. S. (2006). Teaching for meaningful learning with new technologies. In E. A. Ashburn & R. E. Floden (Eds.), *Meaningful learning using technology: What educators need to know and do* (pp. 26–44). New York: Teachers College Press.

Wong, L. (1995). Research on teaching: Process-product research findings and the feeling of obviousness. *Journal of Educational Psychology, 87,* 504–511.

Wood, D., Bruner, J., & Ross, G. (1976). The role of tutoring in problem solving. *Journal of Child Psychology and Psychiatry, 17,* 89–100.

Wood, T., & McCarthy, C. (2002). *Understanding and preventing teacher burnout* (Report No. EDO-SP-2002-3). Washington, DC: ERIC Clearinghouse on Teaching and Teacher Education, American Association of Colleges for Teacher Education.

Wragg, E. (Ed.). (1976). *Teaching in mixed ability groups.* London: David and Charles Limited.

Wyman, R. (1998). Using children's diaries to teach the Oregon Trail. *Social Studies and the Young Learner, 10*(3), M3–M5.

Yates, G. (2000). Applying learning style research in the classroom: Some cautions and the way ahead. In R. Riding & R. Rayner (Eds.), *International perspectives on individual differences.* Vol. 1: *Cognitive styles* (pp. 347–364). Stamford, CT: Ablex.

Yates, G. (2005). "How obvious": Personal reflections on the database of educational psychology and effective teaching research. *Educational Psychology, 25,* 681–700.

Yin, R. K. (2006). Case study methods. In J. Green, G. Camilli, & P. B. Elmore, (Eds.), *Handbook of complementary methods in education research* (pp. 279–295). Mahwah, NJ: Erlbaum.

Yonezawa, S., Wells, A. S., & Serna, I. (2002). Choosing tracks: "Freedom of choice" in detracking schools. *American Educational Research Journal, 39*(1), 37–67.

Zajac, R., & Hartup, W. (1997). Friends as coworkers: Research review and classroom implications. *The Elementary School Journal, 98,* 3–13.

Zaragoza, N., Vaughn, S., & McIntosh, R. (1991). Social skills interventions and children with behavior problems: A review. *Behavioral Disorders, 16,* 260–275.

Zeidner, M. (1995). Adaptive coping with test situations: A review of the literature. *Educational Psychologist, 30,* 123–133.

Zeidner, M. (1998). *Test anxiety: The state of the art.* New York: Plenum.

Zuckerman, G. (1994). A pilot study of a ten-day course in cooperative learning for beginning Russian first graders. *The Elementary School Journal, 94,* 405–420.

NAME INDEX

SUBJECT INDEX